NEW DISCOVERY
ENCYCLOPEDIA

Assistant Editor
Jacqui Bailey

Editorial

Jennifer Justice   Angela Wilkinson
Yvonne Messenger   Isabelle Paton

Contributors

David Lambert   Keith Lye
David Heidenstam   Keith Wicks
Catherine Dell   Andrew Kershaw
Markie Robson-Scott   Stefanie Harwood
Christopher Maynard   Christine King

Published in 1990 by Rainbow Books, Elsley House,
24–30 Great Titchfield Street, London W1P 7AD
Originally published in 1979 as *Knowledge Encyclopedia*.
Revised editions published in 1981 and 1988.

© Grisewood & Dempsey Ltd 1979, 1981, 1988

ISBN 1 871745 02 0

Printed and bound by Printer Portuguesa
in Portugal.

NEW DISCOVERY ENCYCLOPEDIA

Editor
John Paton

RAINBOW
·BOOKS·

PREFACE

IN compiling this New Discovery Encyclopedia, the editorial team had one overriding aim: it must be a work for all members of the family. To this end, we have kept three questions constantly in mind in our choice of entries and in the general plan of the book: *Is an entry likely to be looked up?* The inclusion of obscure and too technical material would make the encyclopedia difficult to read. *Is the text really understandable by someone who knows little or nothing about the subject?* This editorial test for style was simple,

but, we hope, effective. *Is the information required by the reader easy to find?* The alphabetic arrangement was imperative, and to add to the usefulness of the encyclopedia it was decided to divide the information on certain subjects into two tiers. At the end of many articles in the main text there is a hollow triangle ◁. It points to additional textual material on the subject, inside the grey line on that or the adjacent page. This additional text contains facts and figures or other information ancillary to the main definition of the

NEW DISCOVERY ENCYCLOPEDIA

subject. Measurements throughout the encyclopedia are are in both metric and Imperial form.

The illustrations form an integral and important part of this book. Photographs, drawings, diagrams and maps have been chosen both to supplement the text and give additional visual insight into many of the subjects.

The numerous cross-references are of the utmost importance. They are printed in SMALL CAPITALS and their use will ensure that the reader is guided to the maximum amount of information on any topic. An item which does not appear alphabetically in the main body of the book will often be found in the index. And the index will also guide the reader to the facts and figures contained in the Appendix.

We hope that the New Discovery Encyclopedia will prove to be a most useful source of essential information and enjoyment.

The Editor

A

◀ Aborigine natives of New Guinea. The distant ancestors of these people were among the first to colonize the island of New Guinea, which until about 8000 years ago was joined to Australia. The New Guinea natives have many similar physical characteristics to the Australian aborigine. Both belong to the Australoid race.

AARDVARK Large, grey-skinned burrowing animal from Africa which feeds mainly on TERMITES. It is about 2 metres (6 ft) in length and has a long narrow snout. The aardvark (Dutch for 'earth pig') digs a deep burrow and hides there until dark, when it comes out, attacks a termite nest and licks up the swarming insects with its long sticky tongue.

ABACUS A simple kind of calculating machine, used for thousands of years in many different parts of the world. It consists of a wooden frame with several wires running across it. Strung on the wires are beads, or counters. The abacus is still widely used in China.

ABORIGINES The earliest known inhabitants of a country. Nowadays the word is applied particularly to the native people of AUSTRALIA. The Australian aborigines probably came from south-east Asia about 40,000 years ago. When white men first came to Australia in 1788 there were about 300,000 of them, spread all over the continent. The early

▲ The Australian aborigines were nomads, moving from place to place in search of food. They now control their own land in some areas.

settlers treated the aborigines very badly, driving them from their land and killing many of them. Others died of starvation and disease. From the mid-1800s efforts were made to protect them, and reserves were set aside for their use.

Today the aborigines have rights as Australian citizens, with opportunities for education and employment. Their numbers are increasing.

ABRAHAM According to Biblical tradition, the father of the Jewish people (c.1900 BC), specially blessed by God. The Book of Genesis tells many stories of Abraham.

◀ The aardvark is a very timid animal. If caught away from its burrow it digs a hole for itself at astonishing speed with its very powerful claws.

ABRASIVES Substances used for grinding, smoothing or polishing the surfaces of other materials. A hard abrasive called carborundum (silicon carbide) is used in grinding-wheels for shaping metals. Jewellers use much softer abrasives, such as ferric oxide, for polishing gold and silver.

ABSTRACT ART A 20th-century style of painting and sculpture. Abstract works of ART are not realistic, like a photograph, but are made up of forms and colours that the artist chooses and arranges in a certain way. Famous abstract artists include Pablo PICASSO, Henry MOORE and Jackson Pollock.

ABYSS A deep or bottomless place, usually used to refer to the deepest parts of the oceans, below 2000 metres (6500 ft). No light penetrates these waters and the pressure is many times greater than it is at the surface. Many strange fishes inhabit abyssal waters. Some have huge eyes; some have none at all. Others have special light-producing organs which make them glow in the dark. Many fishes have huge jaws and teeth with which to seize prey; others lure them with 'fishing-rod' projections on their heads.   ▷

ACACIA See WATTLE.

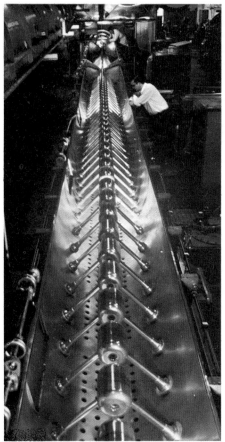

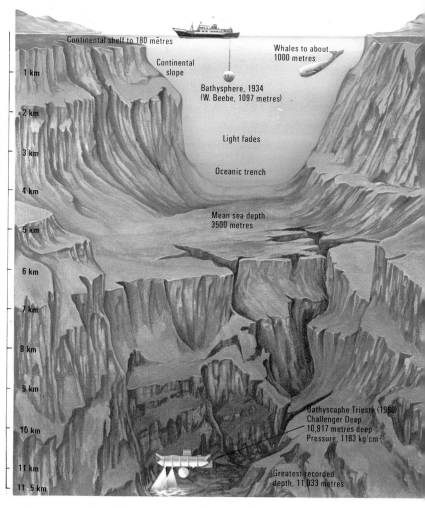

Continental shelf to 180 metres

Whales to about 1000 metres

Continental slope

1 km

Bathysphere, 1934 (W. Beebe, 1097 metres)

2 km

Light fades

3 km

Oceanic trench

4 km

Mean sea depth 3500 metres

5 km

6 km

7 km

8 km

9 km

10 km

Bathyscaphe Trieste (1960) Challenger Deep 10,917 metres deep Pressure, 1183 kg/cm²

11 km

Greatest recorded depth, 11,033 metres

11.5 km

▲ Huge cracks in the floor of the ocean abyss may be 11 km (nearly 7 miles) deep.

◀ In the linear accelerator, beams of particles pass through the holes in the centre of the tubes. The particles are speeded up by powerful electric fields until they hit the target atoms and break them apart.

ACCELERATION In everyday life, we use the term acceleration to describe an increase in speed. However, to a scientist, acceleration means much more than this. The scientist defines acceleration as the rate of change of VELOCITY, and this term involves *direction* as well as speed. Therefore, when a body moving at constant speed changes direction, a scientist would say that the body accelerates in the new direction. For example, if you are walking due north and then turn left, you have accelerated in a westerly direction. You have also undergone deceleration (a loss of acceleration) in a northerly direction.

ACCELERATORS, PARTICLE Scientists working in nuclear physics use machines

ABYSS The greatest ocean depth so far discovered is the Challenger Deep in the Marianas Trench in the western Pacific Ocean. It is 11,033 m (nearly 7 miles) deep. The US bathyscaphe *Trieste* went down to a depth of 10,912 m (35,802 ft) in this area in 1960, taking nearly five hours to reach the bottom.

A heavy weight dropped into the sea over the Challenger Deep would take an hour to reach the bottom.

Vast areas of the deep ocean floor are covered by what is called Red Clay – it covers an area of more than 130 million sq km (50 million sq miles). But this clay accumulates so slowly that some sharks' teeth lying on its surface are from species that have been extinct for thousands of years.

ACIDS Some animals and plants use acids to defend themselves. When a bee or ant stings you, it injects acid beneath your skin. Nettle leaves are covered with fine hairs which prick the skin and inject acid. Rhubarb leaves contain poisonous oxalic acid.

The hydrochloric acid in our stomach is so strong that it can eat through iron. But it does not harm us because a film of mucus lines the walls of our stomach and protects it from the acid. If the acid does get to the stomach wall and starts to eat it away, we have an 'ulcer'.

Sulphuric acid is the most important industrial chemical. Much of it is used in the making of fertilizers and in the steel industry. Car batteries are filled with dilute sulphuric acid.

▲ A synchrotron is used to increase the speed of charged particles. A beam of particles is fed from a linear accelerator into the synchrotron, a circular tube surrounded by powerful magnets. The particles travel round the tube many times, getting faster and faster. The magnets hold the beam in the tube until it is released to strike the target.

called particle accelerators to study the structure of ATOMS. The tiny particles from which atoms are made are accelerated to extremely high speeds and then directed towards a target. Atoms in the target may be split up by the fast-moving particles. For this reason, accelerators are sometimes called *atom smashers*. But this description is misleading, for the particles sometimes join with the target atoms to form new, larger atoms. During acceleration, the particles travel along a straight or spiral tube that may be up to 3 km (2 miles) long. (See NUCLEAR ENERGY)

ACCOUNTING The way in which businesses record, present and analyze their financial affairs. It is usually carried out by specially trained accountants.

ACHILLES A legendary Greek warrior,

hero of the Trojan Wars in HOMER's *Iliad*. According to later legends, Achilles died when an arrow hit his only weak part, his heel. (See TROY)

ACIDS The characteristic sour taste of vinegar and lemon juice is caused by the presence of chemical substances called acids. These weak, dilute acids do us no harm. Some acids are, in fact, essential to life. The digestive juice in the stomach contains acid that enables us to digest (break down) proteins in our food. From these proteins are formed various AMINO ACIDS, without which we could not live. The body uses them to build up other types of protein. Some acids, such as concentrated HYDROCHLORIC, NITRIC or SULPHURIC, are corrosive, poisonous liquids that quickly burn our skin or clothes. Acids turn blue litmus red.

ACNE A condition affecting the fatty glands in the skin, causing blackheads and inflamed eruptions on the face. Acne is caused by glandular changes and is very common during adolescence between the ages of 14 and 20. Frequent washing can help.

ACOUSTICS The study of SOUND is called acoustics. A classroom is said to have poor acoustics if the teacher's voice sounds so boomy that you cannot make out what is being said. Acoustic engineers specialize in sound *insulation* and *treatment*. Insulation to prevent unwanted sounds entering a room also stops sounds in the room getting out. Both features are important in a recording

◄ The ruins of the theatre at Delphi, built in the 4th century BC. These early theatres had excellent acoustics. The audience sat on stone seats which were built up around the stage, forming a bowl shape. The voices of the actors on the stage below could be clearly heard, even by people sitting high up at the back.

Act

studio. Unwanted sounds from outside would spoil the recordings. And the ear-splitting noise of a pop group at full blast might upset the neighbours if the sound could escape from the studio. Double walls, suspended ceilings and floors mounted on springy material are all used to increase sound insulation. For, by eliminating rigid connections between the inside and outside of the studio, sound transmission is greatly reduced. Suitable acoustics are obtained in a room by treatment with materials and devices chosen for the way they absorb or reflect sound.

ACTING The art of portraying a character in the theatre, on television or in films. Even children's imaginary games such as 'Cowboys-and-Indians' are a form of acting. In the same way a professional actor uses his imagination, though the actions and words are provided by the playwright. The good actor must be able to take the part of a beggar or a king with equal ease. He or she must learn how to move about on stage and to speak clearly. Actors must also be able to use make-up and to look comfortable in even the most elaborate costumes. ▷

ACT OF UNION The result of a treaty between England and Scotland that merged the two countries into the United Kingdom of Great Britain (1707).

ACUPUNCTURE An ancient type of medical treatment in which thin needles are used to puncture various parts of the body. Developed by the Chinese about 5000 years ago, it is still in use today. It is often used in the treatment of such things as headache, asthma and arthritis.

ADAM, ROBERT Scottish architect (1728–1792), the most famous of four brothers, whose work influenced the style of building, furniture and decoration throughout the late 18th century. Adam based many of his designs on those of ancient Greece and Rome, which he much admired.

ADAPTATION Process by which animals and plants adjust to their environment. Adaptation usually occurs over a long period of time – perhaps thousands of years – and is part of the EVOLUTION of a particular species: fishes grew gills to breathe underwater and owls developed big saucer eyes to see in the dark. Climate and feeding are major causes of adaptation. Cacti survive in hot desert lands because their stems are modified for water storage, and giraffes developed a long neck to help them eat tree-top foliage. Adaptation is a continuing process: many insects, for instance, have built up resistance to pesticides and are no longer killed by the chemicals. ▷

▲ *Two very different acting styles: Mime, by Marcel Marceau, who performs without using words; and a scene from a No play, Japanese theatre which has not changed for 300 years.*

ADDER A poisonous snake, usually marked with a zigzag band edged with dark spots. Found in Europe, its bite is painful but not often fatal. The adder is the only poisonous snake in Britain.

ADELAIDE The capital of South Australia, Adelaide has a population of 969,000 including its suburbs. It stands on the Torrens River near the Gulf of St Vincent. A major port and a leading trading and manufacturing centre, it was founded in 1836 as a settlement for free immigrants.

ADHESIVES Glues, gums, cements and other substances used to bond together two surfaces are known as adhesives. For centuries, man has used adhesives obtained from

▶ *This giant saguaro cactus grows in the deserts of America. It has adapted to survive the heat and drought by storing the water it needs in its large stems.*

ACTING Throughout history actors have been looked at in many different ways. In ancient Greece they enjoyed honours and privileges. In ancient Rome they were banished from the city. And in Britain, until recently, they were regarded as rogues and vagabonds.

ADAPTATION Some desert plants have adapted to long periods of drought by putting down very long roots – up to 30 m (100 ft) long in some species, such as the mesquite. These roots reach down to water supplies deep underground.

Flowers and insects have adapted side by side for the last 150 million years or more. Some flowers and insects have become so well adapted that a flower can be pollinated only by one kind of insect. Certain orchids, for example, have flowers that closely resemble female insects. Male insects of the correct species try to mate with the flowers, and in so doing they pick up pollen. The pollen is then transferred to the next flower.

ADHESIVES The world of tomorrow may be one without screws and nails. A few drops of a plastic adhesive will be enough to weld any surfaces together in a permanent bond. Houses and cars may be held together entirely by new synthetic glues.

For any adhesive to make a really strong bond, the surfaces to be stuck together must be absolutely clean and free from damp or grease. The amount of grease in a single fingerprint can be enough to ruin a joint.

animal and vegetable sources. Fish glue, for example, is extracted from fish heads and bones by boiling. And gum arabic is obtained from several types of acacia tree. The gum flows naturally from the bark and a high yield is ensured by making cuts in it. In recent years, great advances have been made in the production of synthetic adhesives. Epoxy adhesives, for example, are so strong that they can be used instead of rivets to join parts of aircraft bodies. ◁

ADJECTIVE In grammar, a word used to modify, or describe, a noun. An adjective may follow the verb (The water is *cold*), or it may directly precede the noun (The *cold* water). Most adjectives can be 'compared' (*cold*, *colder*, *coldest*). ▷

ADOLESCENCE The period of life when a person moves from childhood to adulthood. It usually starts at the beginning of puberty, at age 12 or 13, when the sex organs become capable of functioning. At this time boys' voices break, girls' breasts fill out, and pubic hair grows on both girls and boys. Adolescence is for many children a time of physical and emotional upheaval, as they move from being totally dependent on their parents to becoming independent, mature adults. Sometimes the adolescent's eagerness to experiment with 'adult' things such as drink, sex and drugs causes conflict between him and his parents, school or community.

ADONIS In Greek mythology, a young man famous for his beauty and loved by the goddess Aphrodite (VENUS). ▷

ADRENAL GLANDS Paired glands that lie above the kidneys in mammals. The inner part of the adrenal glands, the *medulla*, produces the HORMONE adrenalin, which causes increased heart activity and higher blood pressure in moments of stress. The outer portion,

▲ *The adhesive powers of epoxy resin are almost legendary. The weight of this ten-ton tanker is being supported by two pieces of metal (marked by the box) which have been glued together.*

or *adrenal cortex*, produces important STEROIDS, including CORTISONE. These steroids help to control the body's sugar and salt balances.

ADRIATIC SEA An arm of the MEDITERRANEAN SEA, between Italy, Yugoslavia and Albania. Covering 155,400 sq km (60,000 sq miles), it is a major tourist area.

ADVERB In grammar, a word used chiefly to modify, or describe, a verb. Most adverbs in English have the ending *-ly* (He ran *quickly*). Some are identical to related adjectives (He worked *hard*).

ADJECTIVE Position in a sentence is an important test of whether a word is an adjective. Try fitting a word into both spaces in a sentence such as: 'The . . . . dog is very . . . . . An adjective like 'black' will fit easily into both spaces.

Some adjectives become other parts of speech when they are pronounced differently. For example, the adjective 'separate', as in 'separate rooms', is pronounced differently from the verb 'separate', as in 'separate the tall from the short'.

ADONIS According to the Greek legend, Adonis was loved by both Aphrodite and Persephone. Persephone kidnapped him and refused to give him up, so Aphrodite appealed to Zeus, king of the gods. Zeus decreed that Adonis must spend half of each year with Aphrodite and the other half with Persephone.
  Adonis was killed by a wild boar while out hunting, and, as Aphrodite knelt over his body, anemones sprang from the ground where her tears fell.

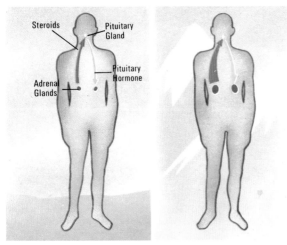

◀ *The adrenal glands help the body to adjust to dangerous conditions, such as extreme cold. If our bodies get too cold we die, so we need more sugar and use up more steroids in our blood to keep warm. The pituitary gland releases a hormone which causes the adrenal glands to produce extra steroids. These steroids release more sugar, which gives us the energy to keep warm.*

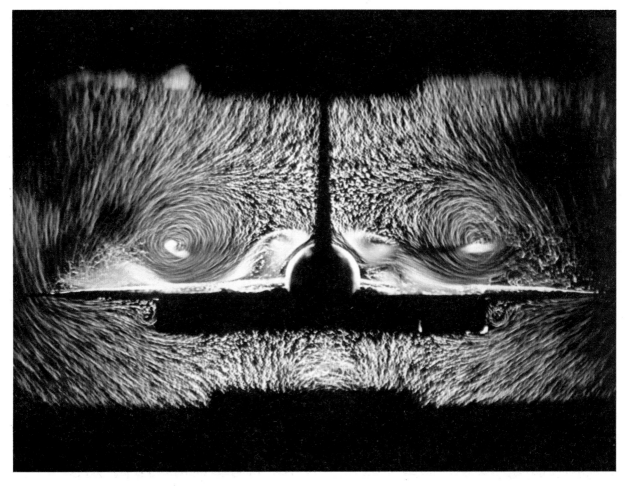

AERODYNAMICS The wind tunnel is the most widely used tool for research in aerodynamics.

Strangely enough, there were wind tunnels before there were aircraft. In 1871, J. Browning and F. Wenham built an apparatus in which a steam-driven fan blew air over a model mounted in a tunnel, almost exactly what happens in a modern wind tunnel. But today's tunnels are much more complicated. They can generate air speeds of up to 30,000 km/h (18,641 mph) and can simulate different kinds of atmospheric conditions.

The shape that gives least air resistance to a body moving at a speed less than the speed of sound is that of a falling drop of water. It is blunt and rounded at the forward end, and pointed at the tail.

ADVERTISING The business of promoting and selling products, services or ideas. Playbills were an early form of poster advertising, and the first newspapers carried notices and advertisements for servants, goods and lost articles. Today advertising is big business – throughout the world about £10,000 million is spent every year, about two-thirds of this in the United States. Advertising makes use of all the major media, including newspapers, magazines, television, radio, direct mail and outdoor billboards.

AERODYNAMICS The study of air moving around solid objects. In some cases, the air is flowing around a stationary structure, such as a bridge or building. In other cases, the object is a vehicle, such as a car or plane, moving through air. An important aspect of aerodynamics is streamlining. This involves shaping an object so that air flows smoothly around it with little turbulence. Streamlining is particularly important with high-speed vehicles. Resistance to their passage through the air is reduced by careful design. And it is the aerodynamic design of the wings that enables an AIRCRAFT to fly. ◁

▲ *A model of a plane is put into a wind tunnel to test the aerodynamics of its wings. The wind tunnel tests show how the air will flow around the aircraft when it is travelling at different speeds. The wings have been designed to move through the air as smoothly as possible. By carrying out these tests, the designers can study the amount of resistance to the air the wings will create.*

▼ *Car designers test the aerodynamics of a new car by placing a model inside a wind tunnel. By studying the flow of air around the car it can be streamlined to improve its performance at high speeds.*

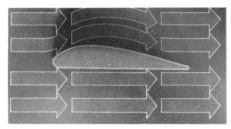

AERONAUTICS An aircraft flies because of the *lift* generated by the movement of the wings through the air. The wing of an aircraft has a special shape called an *aerofoil* (above). It is flat at the bottom and curved at the top. When air passes over the top surface it has to travel faster than the air beneath the wing, because it has further to go. This means that the air pressure above the wing is less than the pressure below it. The suction produced in this way lifts the wing, and the higher the speed, the greater the lift. The lift is increased by angling the wing slightly upward.

There are four forces which act on an aircraft. The first is lift, and to produce lift the wings must move through the air at a high enough speed. So the aircraft needs a second force, *thrust,* to push it forward. This thrust comes from either a propeller or a jet.

As thrust drives the aircraft forward another force, *drag,* tries to hold it back. Drag is caused by the resistance of the air. The fourth force acting on an aircraft in flight is its weight. The aircraft would fall to the ground were it not for the lift produced by the wings.

In the air, the pilot must be able to control the aircraft. He must make it climb, turn and descend. He must be able to correct pitch (up-and-down movement of the nose and tail), roll (dipping of the wings to one side or the other), and yaw (slewing from side to side).

An aircraft's tail works like the tail feathers of an arrow. The horizontal tail surfaces help to reduce the up-and-down pitching movement, and the vertical fin helps reduce tail-wagging yaw. The slant of the wings up and away from the body helps counteract roll. This is called the *dihedral angle.*

The pilot needs instruments to help him fly the plane. The most important instruments are an altimeter to tell him his height; an air-

▶ *A pilot has two main controls to steer an aircraft: the rudder bar and the control column. Two foot pedals are connected to the rudder bar which moves the rudder (a flap on the tailplane) from side to side. As it moves, the airflow pushes against it and this turns the aircraft. The control column is joined to the elevators (flaps on the tail) and the ailerons (flaps on the back edge of the wings). The pilot uses the elevators to control the height of the plane. By moving the ailerons the pilot can roll the aircraft to left or right.*

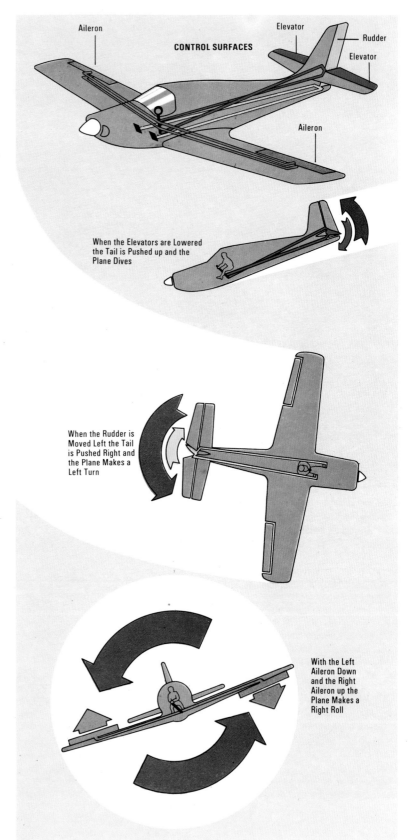

CONTROL SURFACES

Aileron

Elevator

Rudder

Elevator

Aileron

When the Elevators are Lowered the Tail is Pushed up and the Plane Dives

When the Rudder is Moved Left the Tail is Pushed Right and the Plane Makes a Left Turn

With the Left Aileron Down and the Right Aileron up the Plane Makes a Right Roll

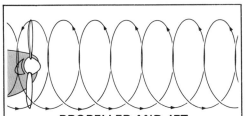

PROPELLER AND JET

Above, the corkscrew path traced by the tip of a propeller as it turns and moves forward. The faster it turns, the greater the force of thrust.

A jet engine (below) sucks air in, compresses it, and ignites it with fuel in the combustion chamber. The exhaust gases escape out of the tailpipe at very high speed and the aircraft is thrust forward.

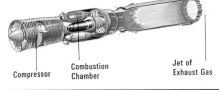

Compressor | Combustion Chamber | Jet of Exhaust Gas

Spoilers

Ailerons

Flaps

▶ The back edge of an airliner wing as it lands. The flaps are rolled out and down to increase lift (by adding extra wing area and increasing the curve of the wing) and drag. The extra lift is needed to keep the plane airborne at a low speed, while the drag helps to slow the plane down. During take-off the flaps are only partly rolled out and are not dropped down. Large aircraft have flaps on the front (leading) edge of the wings too. The spoilers are raised at the moment of touchdown to kill (spoil) the lift and increase drag still more.

◀ A European Airbus taking off from the runway. The aircraft must accelerate very rapidly along the runway so that it can take off in as short a distance as possible.

AERONAUTICS People used to think that birds lift themselves bodily into the air and stay there simply by flapping their wings. In fact, a bird's wings do something far more complicated. They perform two quite different functions. One is to give forward thrust, achieved by a sort of sculling motion with the wing tips. The other is to give lift, which is achieved by the shape of the wings.

speed indicator to show his speed through the air; a compass to show direction; a vertical speed indicator to show how fast the aircraft is climbing or dropping; and an attitude director which shows whether the craft is flying straight and level. It is impossible to judge this without instruments except when flying very near the ground. (See AERODYNAMICS; AIRCRAFT) ◁

AEROSOL An aerosol is a gas which has solid or liquid particles in it. Natural aerosols include CLOUDS, mist, smoke and FOG. Paints, polishes, insecticides and many other products are now packaged in aerosol cans. Pressing a button on the can releases the contents as a fine spray.

AESCHYLUS A Greek poet (525–456 BC),

regarded as the founder of the Greek drama. Only seven of 90 plays survive, of which the masterpiece is the trilogy *Oresteia*. He also wrote *The Persians, Seven against Thebes*, and *Prometheus*.

AESCULAPIUS A mythical Greek physician, he was thought to be the son of Apollo, and to have been killed by Zeus for restoring the dead to life. He later became the god of medicine and is represented bearing a serpent-entwined staff.

AESOP Traditionally, a writer of ancient Greece (c.600 BC), author of hundreds of fables, though his existence is doubted. Aesop's fables include famous tales such as *The Tortoise and the Hare* and *The Goose that laid the Golden Egg*.

AFGHANISTAN A republic in south-western ASIA, Afghanistan has 17,672,000 people (1984 est.) and an area of 647,497 sq km (250,000 sq miles). The capital is Kabul. The country is largely mountainous and most people are Moslem farmers or nomadic herdsmen.

AFRICA The second largest continent after Asia. About two-thirds of Africa is in the tropics and the continent is mostly hot. Dense rain forests cover low-lying areas around the equator. But high tablelands inland are cooler and forests give way to grassland, while high peaks near the equator are snow-capped. Away from the equator, the rainfall diminishes and SAVANNA (grassland with scattered trees) covers vast areas. In the north, the savanna merges into dry scrub and finally into the great SAHARA, the world's largest and hottest desert. The chief deserts in the south are the Kalahari and the Namib. North Africa and the far south-west of South Africa have hot, dry summers and mild, moist winters. The forests, uplands and the savanna are rich in wildlife.

The people of North Africa are mainly Moslem ARABS or BERBERS. In central and southern Africa, most people are Black Africans. Some Black Africans are Christians or Moslems, but some follow traditional beliefs. The Black Africans are divided into about 1000 ethnic and language groups, ranging from the tiny PYGMY to the tall Dinka and Nuer, who reach a height of 2.1 metres (7 ft). There are major European minorities in southern Africa (South Africa and Zimbabwe), and Asians live in some parts of southern and central Africa. Africa is thinly-populated. But the population is growing rapidly by about 3.01 per cent a year.

▲ The changing face of Africa: These students at Ibadan university in Nigeria represent a new generation of Africans and a growing movement away from the villages towards a more industrial society.

About three-quarters of all Africans are farmers, more than in any other continent. Farming techniques are often primitive and droughts occur, causing famine. Africa has many valuable minerals, including gold (South Africa), diamonds (South Africa, Zaire), copper (Zaire, Zambia) and iron ore (West Africa). Africa has little coal, but Nigeria, Libya and Algeria are oil producers. Africa is the least industrialized continent and most people are poor. The only truly industrialized nation is South Africa.

Africa was the home of one of the greatest early civilizations, ancient EGYPT. However, little is known about the early history of Black Africa. In 1497 a Portuguese, Vasco da GAMA (c.1469–1524), became the first European to sail round Africa to India. For the next 300 years, Africa was a source of slaves, many millions of whom were transported to the Americas. In the 1800s, European explorers opened up the interior of Africa. They helped
▷

◀ Present day Africa is still largely agricultural and many of its people follow a way of life that has remained unchanged for hundreds of years. In this African market, traders still sell their grain in the traditional manner.

AFRICA: FACTS AND FIGURES

Area: 30,319,000 sq km (11,706,000 sq miles).

Population: 537,000,000 (1984 est.).

Longest river: Nile, 6670 km (4145 miles) long.

Greatest waterfall: Victoria Falls on the Zambesi river, 102 m 335 ft) high, and more than 1600 m (1 mile) wide.

Largest lake: Victoria, the second largest freshwater lake in the world, 69,452 sq km (26,815 sq miles).

Population density: 18 per sq km (47 per sq mile). About 90 per cent of the people live in the country, only 10 per cent in towns. Nigeria has more people than any other African nation, 80,555,000.

Highest mountain: Kilimanjaro, 5895 m (19,341 ft) in northern Tanzania. Although Kilimanjaro is almost on the equator, its peak is covered with snow all the year round.

There are still between 100,000 and 200,000 pygmies in Africa. The adults are only about 1.5 m (5 ft) tall and they live mainly in the tropical rain forests of the Zaire basin.

The great Sahara desert covers 8,400,000 sq km (3,200,000 sq miles) of northern Africa. This desert was once rich grassland. Prehistoric paintings found on rock walls at Tassili in south Algeria show men hunting lions, elephants and antelope.

It comes as a surprise to most people to learn that Africa is almost as wide from east to west as it is long from north to south. From north to south it measures 7080 km (4400 miles) and from east to west 6035 km (3750 miles).

The lowest point in Africa is the Qattara Depression in Egypt. It is 132 m (436 ft) below sea level.

ATLANTIC OCEAN

Tangier
Algiers
Tunis
Rabat Fés
Constantine
Casablanca
TUNISIA
MEDITERRANEAN SEA
Marrakech
Sfax
MOROCCO
Benghazi
ATLAS MOUNTAINS
Tripoli
Alexandria
Cairo
CANARY IS.
Suez
ALGERIA
LIBYA
Las Palmas
EGYPT
Nile
SAHARA DESERT
Aswan
MAURITANIA
MALI
NIGER
Dongola
Nouakchott
Timbuktu
Agadez
SUDAN
Senegal
CHAD
Khartoum
Dakar
SENEGAL
Bamako
L. Chad
Banjul
GAMBIA
Niamey
Djibouti
GUINEA
BURKINA
Kano
N'Djamena
ETHIOPIA
BISSAU
Bissau
FASO
Ouagadougou
Addis Ababa
GUINEA
Niger
NIGERIA
ETHIOPIAN
Conakry
SIERRA
CENTRAL AFRICAN
HIGHLANDS
Freetown
LEONE
CÔTE
GHANA
Ibadan
EMPIRE
SOMALI REPUBLIC
Monrovia
D'IVOIRE
TOGO
Lagos
BENIN
Mogadishu
LIBERIA
Accra
Lomé
CAMEROON
Bangui
UGANDA
KENYA
Abidjan
Porto-Novo
Malabo
Yaoundé
Kampala
Nairobi
M.
SAO TOME
EQUATORIAL
Kenya
& PRINCIPE
GUINEA
Libreville
L. Victoria
RWANDA
Mombasa
GABON
CONGO
CONGO BASIN
Bujumbura
Kigali
M.
Zaire
BURUNDI
Kilimanjaro
Zanzibar
Brazzaville
Kinshasa
Tabora
Dar es Salaam
Cabinda
ZAIRE
TANZANIA
INDIAN OCEAN
L. Tanganyika
L. Malawi
Luanda
COMORO IS.
ATLANTIC OCEAN
ANGOLA
Huambo
ZAMBIA
Lilongwe
MALAWI
MOZAMBIQUE
Antananarivo
Benguela
Lusaka
Zambezi
NAMIBIA
Harare
MADAGASCAR
Beira
ZIMBABWE
Windhoek
Limpopo
NAMIB DESERT
BOTSWANA
Walvis Bay
KALAHARI
Gaborone
Maputo
DESERT
Pretoria
Mbabane
Johannesburg
SWAZILAND
Orange
Maseru
DRAKENSBERG
Durban
SOUTH
LESOTHO
AFRICA
East London
Cape Town
DRAKENSBERG
Port Elizabeth

■ Capital Cities

0   500   1000 miles

0   500   1000   1500 Kilometres

to stamp out the slave trade, but, by the late 1800s, European powers had colonized most of Africa. European governments ruled until the 1950s. However, between the 1950s and the 1970s, nearly all of Africa's 57 nations (including the islands) became independent.

AFRIKAANS One of the two official languages (with English) of the Republic of SOUTH AFRICA. Afrikaans comes from Dutch, the language of the early white settlers, and is spoken by about 65 per cent of the white population. *Veld* and *trek* are familiar Afrikaans words.

AGAMEMNON According to Greek legend, the king of Mycenae who led the Greeks in the Trojan War. Stories about him are told in HOMER's *Iliad* and AESCHYLUS' *Oresteia*.

AGATE A semi-precious stone, a kind of chalcedony. Agate is marked by bands of colour and takes a high polish. Different types include moss agate and eye agate.

AGEING Most animals, including man, have a fixed life span – that is, a particular age when they are likely to die. Although some individuals may be lucky or stronger and so live longer than others, most have about the same length of life.

In countries with plenty of food and good medical services, people generally live to between 70 and 80 years. Women live a little longer than men. In Britain, about one out of every 1000 babies will live to be 100. Some live even longer than that, but no one knows the highest age ever reached by man. ▷

AGINCOURT, BATTLE OF One of the most famous battles of the HUNDRED YEARS' WAR. On October 25, 1415 an English army led by HENRY V defeated the French. The heavily armoured French knights fell under a hail of arrows from the longbows of the English archers.

AGRICULTURE The cultivation of the soil to produce food or useful materials such as cotton, rubber, wood, medicine and dyes. It also includes the raising of animals for food (meat, milk, eggs, butter) or for materials (wool, fur, skins).

The earliest men were hunters and food gatherers. FARMING came later, some time during the Neolithic Period (9000–7000 BC). The earliest centre of agriculture was MESOPOTAMIA, the fertile belt between the rivers Tigris

◄ *Some parts of the body begin to age almost from birth, but it is only after adolescence that real ageing occurs. Slowly, over the years, the body becomes less efficient and less adaptable. The fibres in the skin become less elastic and the skin wrinkles. Sight, hearing, touch, taste and smell all become steadily less sensitive and the body becomes weaker and less resistant to disease. But although we can see the ageing process and the changes that take place, no one as yet knows exactly why it happens.*

AGEING A year-old baby has all the brain cells (neurons) it will ever have. Every day after that it will lose some of those cells, and they will never be replaced. It is thought that this is why old people lose some of their mental efficiency – what we call senility. They have lost too many of their brain nerve cells.

Women live longer than men. A baby boy born today can expect to live to about 67, a girl to 74. When a boy is 20, he can expect to live to 70; a girl of 20 can expect to live to 76.

Despite many claims of people having lived to a very great age, there is still no verified record of anyone living to see his or her 114th birthday. The greatest human lifespan of which we can be sure is that of Mrs D. Filkins of New York, USA. She died only 150 days short of her 114th birthday. No one in Britain has lived beyond the age of 112.

AGRICULTURE Machinery has completely changed the farmer's way of life. Before 1830, cutting an acre of wheat by hand took about 40 hours. Now a large combine harvester can cut and thresh the same area in just seven minutes.

The world's population is increasing at the rate of about two percent each year, and may well double in 35 years. At present, food production is increasing at about the same rate as population. But it is increasing more rapidly in the developed countries than in the less developed countries. If people are not to starve, greater efforts must be made to increase agricultural production in Africa and south-east Asia.

Man has bred sheep, pigs, cattle, and poultry for thousands of years. Hens now lay at least 250 eggs each year, which is 15 times more than wild hens lay. Cows now produce more than 4500 litres (1000 gallons) of milk each year, which is about 20 times more than a wild cow produces.

AIR When air is compressed and reduced to a temperature of about −200°C it becomes a colourless liquid. When the temperature of liquid air is allowed to rise slowly it is possible to obtain in their pure state each of the gases present in air.

and Euphrates. Farming spread from there to Egypt and later to Europe. Today agriculture is the world's biggest industry.

To feed the rapidly increasing population on our planet agriculture has been forced to become more productive. Progress in science and technology has helped to make modern farming more efficient. New, hardier and more productive strains of crops such as wheat have been developed by scientists, and animals have been specially bred to produce more meat. The horse and plough have been replaced by the tractor and other machines which sow, tend and harvest crops faster and more efficiently than ever before.   ◁

AIR The colourless mixture of gases that makes up the ATMOSPHERE surrounding the Earth. Gravity pulls the air towards the Earth and prevents it escaping into outer space. Ignoring water, solid particles and AIR POLLUTION, the air consists mainly of nitrogen (78 per cent by volume) and oxygen (21 per cent). The remaining one per cent is mostly argon, although minute quantities of other gases are also present. These include CARBON DIOXIDE, neon, helium, methane, krypton, nitrous oxide, HYDROGEN, ozone and xenon. OXYGEN is the gas that we must breathe to stay alive. Green plants use carbon dioxide in a process microbes, and debris from meteoroids and satellites that have burnt up on entering the atmosphere. The amount of water vapour in the air varies considerably from place to place. Hot air can hold much more water vapour

than cold air (see HUMIDITY). BAROMETERS measure air pressure in order to predict changes in the weather.

AIRCRAFT The problems of human flight have always interested man. In the Middle Ages people believed that witches were able to fly through the air, but the first man to think about flight from a technical point of view was LEONARDO DA VINCI. His notebooks contain many sketches showing designs for flying machines.

The first real pioneer in the study of heavier-than-air flight was Sir George Cayley. He made several successful model gliders in about 1800 and discovered the chief conditions of stability in aircraft.

In 1891 the German Otto Lilienthal built full-sized gliders in which he made more than 2000 flights before he killed himself in a crash in 1896.

In America, two brothers, Orville and Wilbur WRIGHT from Dayton, Ohio, were also flying gliders. Then, in 1903 they went to Kitty Hawk in North Carolina, with a biplane powered by a 4-cylinder petrol engine which they had built themselves. In this aircraft, the *Flyer*, Orville made the first powered, sustained, and controlled flight in history. The

▼ Tractors are the most adaptable and labour-saving agricultural machines. With appropriate trailers they can be used for ploughing, cultivating, harvesting, planting, as well as for general transport of farm animals, crops, and animal feed.

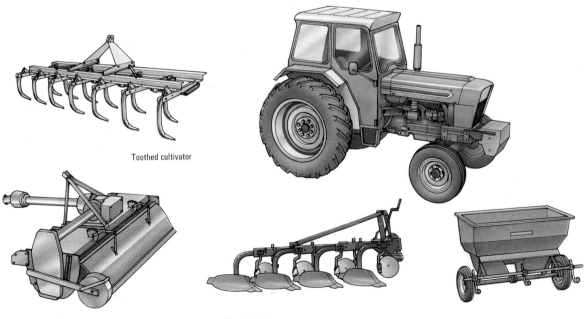

Toothed cultivator

Tiller and Roller

Metal plough

Automatic potato planter

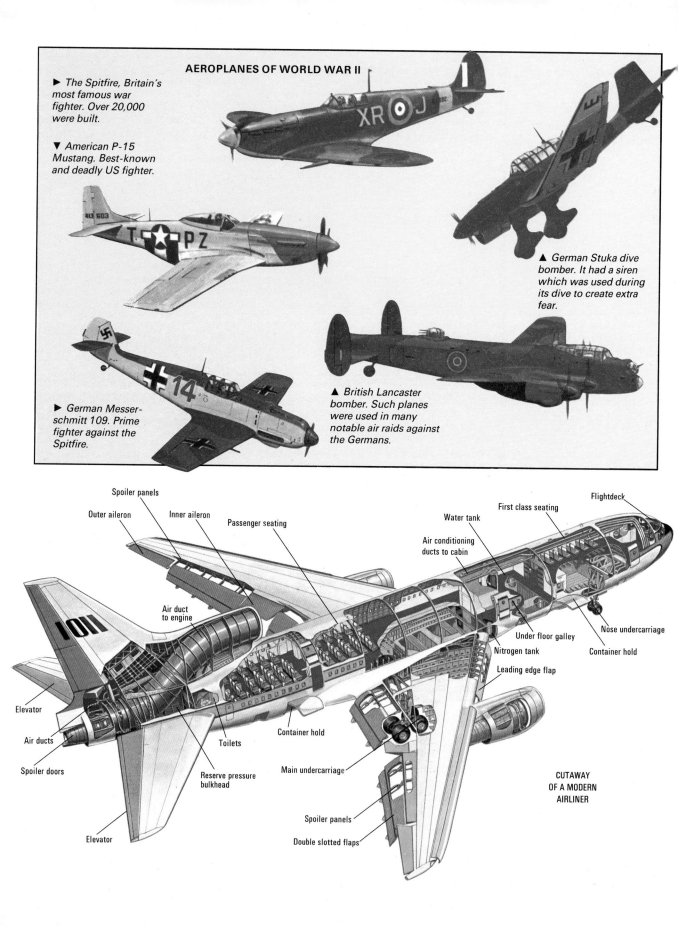

AEROPLANES OF WORLD WAR II

► The Spitfire, Britain's most famous war fighter. Over 20,000 were built.

▼ American P-15 Mustang. Best-known and deadly US fighter.

▲ German Stuka dive bomber. It had a siren which was used during its dive to create extra fear.

► German Messerschmitt 109. Prime fighter against the Spitfire.

▲ British Lancaster bomber. Such planes were used in many notable air raids against the Germans.

Spoiler panels

Outer aileron

Inner aileron

Passenger seating

Water tank

Air conditioning ducts to cabin

First class seating

Flightdeck

Air duct to engine

Under floor galley

Nitrogen tank

Nose undercarriage

Container hold

Leading edge flap

Elevator

Air ducts

Spoiler doors

Toilets

Container hold

Main undercarriage

Reserve pressure bulkhead

Elevator

Spoiler panels

Double slotted flaps

CUTAWAY OF A MODERN AIRLINER

AIRCRAFT The Wright brothers made four flights that first day at Kitty Hawk on December 17, 1903. Although the first, and most famous, flight lasted only 12 seconds, the fourth lasted 59 seconds and took the aircraft over 260 m (852 ft).

The heaviest aircraft to fly was the Boeing E.4A, a transport version of the 747. It weighed about 386 tonnes and cost $117 million.

The first person to be killed in an air crash was Lt. T. E. Selfridge of the US Army Signal Corps. In 1908 he was taken on a demonstration flight by Orville Wright at Fort Myer, Virginia. The plane crashed, killing Selfridge.

The first man to fly an aircraft in Australia was Colin Defries. He flew a Wright biplane for over 1½ km (1 mile) at Sydney on December 9, 1909. The first flight in an Australian aircraft was by John Duigan of Victoria on July 16, 1910.

The fastest aircraft ever to have flown is the American Space Shuttle. It first flew piggyback on a Boeing 747 in 1977. In 1981 it was blasted off on its first solo flight. It operates as a spacecraft at about 28,000 km/h (17,600 mph). Its landing speed is about 360km/h (220 mph).

The first successful rocket fighter aircraft, the German Me-16 *Komet*, was flying in 1944. It achieved a speed of over 800 km/h (500 mph), with a very high rate of climb, but its fuel was exhausted in about 10 minutes of powered flight.

In 1919, the Italian designer Gianni Caproni built his Model 60. The huge machine had nine wings and eight 400-horsepower engines, designed to lift the 14-tonne aircraft and 100 passengers. After two trial flights over Lake Maggiore the plane broke up and never flew again.

flight lasted some 12 seconds and covered a distance of 37 metres (127 ft).

In 1906 the Brazilian Alberto Santos-Dumont made the first powered flight in Europe in an aircraft named *14-bis*, a biplane which flew tail-first.

Three years later, in 1909, Louis BLÉRIOT was the first man to fly across the English Channel, in his type *XI* monoplane. The flight took 36½ minutes.

By 1912 the nations of Europe were beginning to think about the ways in which aircraft could be used by the military. At the start of World War I in 1914 aircraft were used for reconnaissance and photographic work, but soon there were 'fighters' and 'bombers' and the aircraft industries in Europe and America grew rapidly.

After the war, in 1919, the Atlantic was crossed non-stop for the first time, from Newfoundland to Ireland, by the British airmen John William Alcock and Arthur Whitten Brown in a twin-engined Vickers *Vimy* biplane.

At this time the seaplane came into its own in civil aviation because it appeared to offer greater safety for flights over the sea. Then came the flying-boats. The British Short *Calcutta* flew on the Empire routes. The German Dornier company built several successful flying-boats, followed by the American Boeing *Clipper* four-engine long-range monoplanes.

Between the wars there were many notable flights. In 1924 two US Army Douglas biplanes made the first round-the-world flight. In 1926 Alan Cobham flew a *D.H.50* to India, Australia and South Africa, establish-

◁

▲ Top: Louis Blériot taking off near Calais, France, on the first flight ever across the English Channel.

▲ In the cockpit of the Concorde. The flight engineer keeps a watchful eye on his instruments.

◀ Engineers examine an aircraft engine. Gamma rays from a radioisotope (left) pass through the engine intake and imprint an image on pieces of film wrapped around the outside (shown being placed in position). The pictures show up any faults in the engine.

◄ *Inside an airport control tower. Radar and other aids keep the air traffic control in touch with all aircraft in flight in their area. The control panel shows the position of all the aircraft on the runways.*

ing the Empire air routes. In the same year Lt-Commander Richard Byrd of the US flew over the North Pole. (Later, in 1929, he flew over the South Pole.) The year 1927 saw the first solo flight across the Atlantic from New York to Paris by Charles LINDBERGH in his monoplane *Spirit of St Louis*.

During World War II from 1938 to 1945 aviation progress speeded up enormously. Famous fighter aircraft such as the *Hurricane* and *Spitfire* came into service in time to beat the German Air Force in the Battle of Britain. The Americans built the Boeing *Flying Fortress* day-bomber and then the B-29 *Superfortress* which could carry a bomb load of 9000 kg (20,000 lb). Germany produced the famous ME 109 fighter and, in 1944, the ME 262 Messerschmitt jet-fighter came into service.

After the war the US aircraft industry began building aircraft for most of the world's airlines – *DC-6s*, *Constellations*, *Stratocruisers*. Then Britain produced the first successful jet airliner – the *Comet*. In 1958 the American four-engined jets, the Douglas *DC-8* and the Boeing 707 came into service.

The start of the 70s saw a move towards aircraft that either had the advantage of great speed, such as the Anglo-French *Concorde*, or enormous capacity, like the Boeing 747 jumbo-jet, capable of carrying 400 passengers at around 1000 kph (600 mph). (See AERODYNAMICS; AERONAUTICS)

AIR POLLUTION The contamination of the air by substances, usually man-made, that are dangerous to life or property. Most pollution is caused by the burning of fuels such as coal and oil. Chemical industries and cement works produce dangerous fumes and dust. Many countries have passed Clean Air acts to control air pollution. ▷

AIRPORT The modern airport is really a

small town. There are passenger buildings, immigration, customs and health buildings, restaurants, bars, shops, mail handling areas, airline offices, freight offices, car parks, press offices and many other services needed for efficient aircraft handling.

The most important part of an airport is its runways. With planes weighing 350 tonnes and landing speeds of 300 kph (180 mph) concrete is used to withstand the wear of aircraft taking off and landing. The length of runways has increased greatly since the arrival of the big jets. Most major airports have at least one runway over 3 km (2 miles) long.

The nerve centre of the airport is the control tower. Here complex electronic equipment is used to control the arrival and despatch of hundreds of aircraft every day. Automatic landing systems are used to guide in planes in the worst weather. ▷

AIRSHIP An airship is a lighter-than-air craft that is powered and can be steered by its pilot. Airships are sometimes called 'dirigibles' from a French word meaning to 'steer'.

The first airship was flown by the French engineer Henri Giffard in 1852. It was 44 metres (144 ft) long and was propelled by a 3 horsepower steam engine. But the most famous name in airship history is that of the German Count Ferdinand von Zeppelin (1838–1917). He built his first airship in 1900 and this provided the pattern for over a hundred other Zeppelins that flew thousands of miles in peace and war.

After World War I the British *R34* was the first to cross the Atlantic Ocean, in 1919. Roald Amundsen flew over the North Pole in 1926. The British *R101* crashed into a hill in France in 1930. The great Zeppelin *Hindenburg* was destroyed by fire in New Jersey in 1937. She had been inflated with highly explosive HYDROGEN gas. HELIUM gas does not have quite as much lift as hydrogen but is safer

ALBANIA: FACTS AND FIGURES
Highest mountain: Mount Korabi, 2750 m (9020 ft).
Longest rivers: Drini, 280 km (174 miles); Semani 253 km (157 miles).
Currency: Lek.

ALBATROSS The narrow wings of the wandering albatross are longer than those of any other bird. Wing spreads of 3.5 m (11½ ft) have been recorded. In the past these large birds were sometimes killed by sailors, who used salt pork as bait. But a superstition grew up that it was bad luck to kill an albatross, and Samuel Taylor Coleridge tells of this in his poem 'Rime of the Ancient Mariner'.

because it does not burn.

Interest in airships died out during World War II. The only real advantage of the airship over the aeroplane was its ability to carry heavy loads. Its disadvantages were its slow speed, unmanoeuvrability and vulnerability to the weather. Some people think that the airship may still come into its own. ◁

ALBANIA A small, mountainous communist republic in south-eastern EUROPE. Its population is 2,901,000 (1984 est.) and the area is 28,748 sq km (11,100 sq miles). The capital is Tirana. Most people are farmers. Cereals, grapes, mulberry leaves and olives are grown. ◁

ALBATROSS Large, long-winged seabird found mainly in the southern hemisphere. Albatrosses spend most of their time in the air except during the breeding season when they nest in colonies on remote Pacific islands. ◁

ALBINO Person or animal with no PIGMENT (colouring) in the skin, hair and eyes. Albino

▲ This albino squirrel has no pigment to give it any colouring. Albinism is hereditary, passed on from the parents, and appears only when the animal lacks the genes which produce the 'plans' for pigment.

people have pale milky skin, white hair and pink eyes – where blood shows through the IRIS. Albino animals include white mice and white rabbits.

ALCHEMY A forerunner of the science of CHEMISTRY. It centred around attempts to change ordinary metals into gold and the search for the 'Philosopher's Stone' which it was thought would have the power to carry out this change. Alchemy was practised as early as 100 BC in Alexandria in Egypt. It was popular in Europe during the Middle Ages, and became closely associated with ASTROLOGY.

ALCOHOLS A group of chemical compounds all containing the hydroxyl (OH) group in their formula. Alcoholic drinks contain ethyl alcohol (ethanol), which has the formula C_2H_5OH. Methyl alcohol (methanol), formula CH_3OH, is also known as wood spirit. It is the poison present in methylated spirit.

◀ The study of alchemy was a strange mixture of magic and science and most alchemists were very secretive, using many mystical signs and symbols to guard their findings. This painting shows the German alchemist Hennig Brand in his laboratory. Brand discovered the element phosphorus in 1669.

▲ Head ot Alexander the Great, a brilliant leader who took command of the Greek armies at the age of 22.

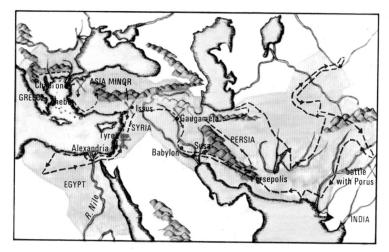

▲ The route Alexander followed into Asia. In ten years he had conquered the greatest empire the world had seen.

ALEXANDER THE GREAT King of Macedon in ancient GREECE and one of the greatest generals of all time (356–323 BC). Through a series of conquests he created an empire that stretched from Greece to India. He died in Babylon at the age of 33 and was buried in Alexandria, named after him. ▷

ALFRED THE GREAT King of Wessex (849–899) who saved England from conquest by the Danes. A wise ruler in peacetime, he organized the army, built an excellent navy and encouraged learning among his people.

ALGEBRA A branch of mathematics in which general symbols are used to represent various quantities. For example, the algebraic formula for the area of a circle is: $a = \pi r^2$. In this formula, a represents area and r is the radius of the circle. π is the Greek letter *pi*, a constant equal to approximately 22/7.

ALGERIA A North African republic, independent since 1962, Algeria has 21,052,000 people (1984 est.) and an area of 2,381,741 sq km (919,595 sq miles). The capital is Algiers. Most of its Moslem ARAB and BERBER people are farmers, but oil is the most valuable product. ▷

ALICE SPRINGS A town in Northern Territory, Australia, it is the commercial centre of central Australia and it is a popular tourist resort. It has about 5000 people.

ALKALIS The group of chemical compounds called alkalis includes the household chemical caustic soda (sodium hydroxide). Any metal hydroxide soluble in water is known as an alkali. The solution formed turns red litmus paper blue. Solutions of strong alkalis feel soapy and may burn the skin.

ALLAH An Arabic word meaning 'the God'. According to the Moslem religion Allah is the one true God, and MOHAMMED, the founder of ISLAM, was the prophet of Allah.

ALLERGY A condition caused by the sensitivity of the body to certain substances, including bacteria, pollen, dusts, moulds, foods and drugs. The reaction often takes the form of hay fever, asthma, rashes or intestinal upsets, and may be mild, severe, or occasionally fatal. ▷

ALLIGATOR Type of crocodilian found only in two parts of the world: the Yangtze River valley in China and the south-eastern United States. Alligators can be distinguished from crocodiles by their teeth: when the mouth is shut, the crocodile has both rows of teeth exposed, but the alligator only shows its top teeth.

ALLOY A mixture or compound of two or more metals. Alloys have metallic properties, though they do not conduct heat and electri-

▼ The American alligator was hunted almost to extinction because of the popularity of its skin for making leather goods.

ALEXANDER THE GREAT As a boy, Alexander was strong and fearless. He is said to have tamed the wild horse Bucephalus, a horse that no one else dared to ride. This famous horse carried Alexander on his campaigns as far as India, where it died. There Alexander built a city called Bucephala on the Hydaspes river in memory of his great horse.

ALGERIA: FACTS AND FIGURES
Highest mountain: Mount Tahat, 2918 m (9571 ft).
Longest river: Chéliff, 692 km (430 miles).
Official language: Arabic, but French widely spoken.
Currency: Dinar.
Religion: Moslem.

ALLERGY Allergies such as hay fever, asthma and eczema often run in families. If both parents have an allergy, no matter which one, their children have about a 70 per cent chance of developing one too.

Skin tests can often help in identifying allergies. The doctor injects small quantities of some of the most common substances that cause allergies in separate areas beneath the skin. If the patient is allergic to one of the substances, the skin becomes red and swollen in the appropriate area.

▲ *A ski resort in the Swiss Alps. The Alps stretch in a broad arc for over 1000 km (620 miles) across southern Europe, from France into Yugoslavia.*

ALLOY Sometimes an alloy behaves quite differently from any of the metals in it. This is what makes alloys so useful. Tin is a soft metal; so is copper. But a mixture of copper and tin – bronze – is a very hard alloy. It is so hard it can be used to make machine tools. Bronze was probably the first alloy discovered by man. Early men used it for making spearheads and swords.

ALMOND An almond tree with white blossoms produces bitter almonds, one with pink blossoms produces sweet almonds. Bitter almonds are used for the manufacture of prussic acid and flavourings. The blossom of the almond tree contains the deadly poison prussic acid.

ALUMINIUM For a long time aluminium was so difficult to extract from its ores, it was a precious metal. Napoleon III had a set of aluminium cutlery made, and an aluminium rattle for his infant son.

AMAZON RIVER The rubber tree is native to the Amazon basin. The Indians of that area used to dip their feet in the liquid latex from the rubber tree. When this hardened, they had a pair of rubber boots which protected their feet and ankles.

AMBER The ancient Greeks called amber *'elektron'*. It is from this that we get our words 'electricity' and 'electron'. When amber is rubbed with a dry cloth it will attract small pieces of paper. It has become charged with static electricity.

AMBERGRIS Ambergris is often found floating in the sea, having been regurgitated by a sperm whale. Usually the pieces weigh only a few grams, but in 1912 a huge lump weighing over 450 kg (1000 lb) was found in a whale's intestine. It was bought for over £20,000.

city as well as pure metals. Alloying two metals often improves the properties of either metal alone: for example, brass, an alloy of copper and zinc, is much harder and stronger than either. ◁

ALMOND Tree cultivated in southern countries for its edible nuts (almonds); further north it is grown for ornament. The almond's delicate pink blossom – appearing before its leaves – is a welcome sign of spring. ◁

ALPHABET A set of written signs or symbols called 'letters' that can be combined to represent spoken words. The word 'alphabet' comes from the first two letters of the Greek alphabet – *alpha* and *beta*.

The earliest forms of WRITING included the cuneiform characters of MESOPOTAMIA and the HIEROGLYPHS of ancient Egypt. It is thought that later alphabets, including the PHOENICIAN, Greek and Latin alphabets, may have developed from these. Our alphabet is closest to the Latin alphabet. Other modern alphabets include the Cyrillic alphabet (used in Russia), the Greek and Hebrew alphabets.

ALPHA PARTICLE The nucleus of a helium ATOM is called an alpha particle. It consists of two protons and two neutrons and is positively charged. Many radioactive substances emit alpha rays – that is, streams of alpha particles (see RADIOACTIVITY).

ALPS This great mountain range, in south-central EUROPE, extends from France, through Switzerland and southern Germany, into Austria and Yugoslavia. The highest peak, Mont Blanc in France, is 4810 metres (15,781 ft) above sea level. There are road and rail tunnels and numerous passes.

ALUMINIUM Of all the metals present in the Earth's crust, aluminium is the most

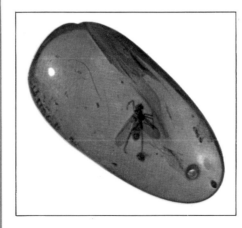

▲ *A piece of polished amber containing the body of an insect, preserved almost intact.*

common. It is found mainly in an ore called bauxite. Aluminium is a good conductor of heat and electricity. The metal is white in colour and about one-third as heavy as iron. ◁

AMAZON RIVER The world's second longest river, the Amazon flows 6437 km (4000 miles) from Peru through Brazil to the Atlantic Ocean. In the 1540s a Spanish explorer saw female Indian warriors on its banks and so the river was named after the Amazons of Greek legends. ◁

AMBER Fossilized resin from prehistoric trees which, carved and polished, is used to make jewellery. Some specimens contain insects trapped millions of years ago. ◁

AMBERGRIS A valuable greasy substance found in the intestine of the sperm whale and used since ancient times to make perfumes. ◁

AMERICA The world's longest land mass, America extends north-south about 15,300 km (9500 miles). It contains NORTH AMERICA, CENTRAL AMERICA and SOUTH AMERICA.

During the great Age of Exploration, Christopher COLUMBUS (1451–1506) was the first European to reach America when, in 1492, he sighted San Salvador in the BAHAMAS. On his third expedition (1498–1500), he sighted South America. In 1497 an Italian, John Cabot (1450–1498), sailing on behalf of Britain, reached Newfoundland and Nova Scotia in North America. However, at that time, the explorers believed that they had

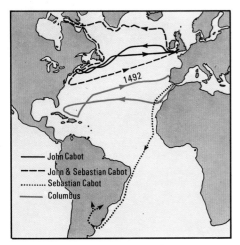

◀ The routes to America taken by Columbus and John Cabot. Cabot was accompanied by his son, Sebastian, who later voyaged to South America.

John Cabot
John & Sebastian Cabot
Sebastian Cabot
Columbus

reached Asia, which explains why the original inhabitants of America were called Indians. Later in the 1500s people realized that a new continent had been discovered. It was named America after the forename of Amerigo Vespucci (1451–1512), an Italian merchant who had explored South America and the West Indies between 1497 and 1503.

The highest peak in America is Mt Aconcagua in Argentina, South America, in the ANDES range. It is 6960 metres (22,835 ft) above sea level. South America also contains America's longest river, the AMAZON.

AMERICAN INDIANS The first Indians to reach North America may have crossed from Asia to Alaska on a land bridge over 20,000 years ago. They spread throughout the continent, grouped into different tribes. In the eastern woodlands lived the Iroquois and Algonquin tribes, who farmed and hunted small game. The Sioux, Comanche and Blackfoot tribes lived off the herds of bison on the Great Plains. The Navajos, Hopis and Apaches hunted and herded sheep in the southwest. With the arrival of the white man the Indians were gradually killed or moved onto special Indian reservations. Today, their descendants are working to restore their rights and keep their culture alive.   ▷

AMETHYST A purple variety of QUARTZ, long used as a semi-precious gem. It is often found in crystallized crusts lining the cavities of rocks.

AMINO ACIDS Essential organic acids which link to form PROTEINS in living tissue. As many as 21 different amino acids may be included in a protein molecule. Man cannot produce all the amino acids he needs. Eight of them have to be obtained from foods and are broken down during DIGESTION. They are then regrouped to form new proteins.

AMMONITE The name of the fossil shell of an extinct type of coiled MOLLUSC. Ammonites were common during the Mesozoic Era, 225 to 65 million years ago.

AMOEBA A one-celled animal that moves about by changing its body shape and 'eats' by wrapping itself round food particles. Amoebas reproduce by fission (splitting in two). (See CELL)

AMPERE The SI UNIT of electric current. It is defined as the intensity of a current that produces a force of 2×10^{-7} newtons per metre between two thin, straight, conductors of infinite length when flowing through them. Amperes are represented by the symbol A. (see ELECTRICITY AND MAGNETISM)   ▷

AMPHIBIANS Animals that live both on land and in water. Most amphibians have moist thin skins and spend their adult life on land but return to the water to breed. Their

▼ An Indian chief before the arrival of the Pilgrim Fathers. European colonists gradually caused the displacement of Indian tribes, pushing them further to the west, and into reservations.

AMERICAN INDIAN In 1980 there were about 1.4 million Indians living in North America. Almost all now live on special reservations. Arizona has over 160,000 American Indians from 13 different tribes — more than any other US state.

The North American Indian had only one domestic animal until the arrival of the Europeans. It was the dog.

AMPERE The unit of flow of an electric current was named the ampere in honour of André Ampère (1775–1836). His breakthrough in mathematical principles led to the invention of the telegraph amongst other equipment.

AMPHIBIANS There are about 3,000 species, divided into three orders, the *Anura* or *Salientia* (frogs and toads), the *Caudata* (newts and salamanders), and the *Gymnophiona* or Apoda (small, worm-like creatures with no limbs).

Amphibians have an unusual method of breathing. They can breathe through their skin as long as it is kept moist. So the skin of an amphibian must be kept moist all the time. Despite this, some frogs and toads live in deserts. They manage to survive by retiring to moist burrows during the heat of the day.

ANACONDA Although the anaconda is the largest snake in the world, it is not the longest. Pythons are longer but not as thick and heavy. Anacondas are capable of eating enormous meals. One 8-metre (26 ft) snake was found to contain a caiman (alligator) nearly 2 metres (7 ft) long. But they do not have to eat very often. After consuming a large meal, an anaconda can go for up to a year without eating.

young, called tadpoles, are fish-like and breathe with gills; gradually, they change into air-breathing creatures. Two main groups of amphibians exist today: the jumping, tail-less FROGS and toads; and the tailed NEWTS and SALAMANDERS. ◁

AMSTERDAM Capital of the NETHERLANDS, Amsterdam has 994,000 people. This graceful city is intersected by tree-lined canals. It is a port and manufacturing centre.

ANACONDA Largest living snake. Anacondas, up to 11 metres (36 ft) long, are greyish-brown with black spots; they live in the swamps and rivers of the northern forests of South America and feed off birds, mammals and fish. ◁

ANAESTHESIA A word that means the absence of sensation, or pain. It is used in medicine to prevent pain during SURGERY and other treatments. Anaesthesia can be brought about by the inhalation of gas, or by an injection into a vein or the spine.

ANDERSEN, HANS CHRISTIAN A Danish writer (1805–1875), author of a famous collection of fairy tales, including *The Wild Swans*.

ANDES MOUNTAINS This lofty mountain range extends down the western side of SOUTH AMERICA. The highest peak, Aconcagua, is in Argentina, near the Chile border. It is 6960 metres (22,835 ft) above sea level. The Andes contains active volcanoes and earthquakes are common.

Wood anemone

ANEMONE Pale fragile spring flower growing wild in the woodlands of Europe and Asia. Anemones – also called wind-flowers – take their name from *anemos*, the Greek word for wind. Cultivated varieties, with stronger colours, are popular garden flowers.

ANGLE Where two lines or planes intersect, the space between them is called an angle. It is a measure of the amount of turning required to bring one line or plane into contact with the other one. Angles are usually measured in degrees. One complete turn is 360° (360 degrees). Angles less than 90° are termed

▼ *These 17th century gabled houses line one of Amsterdam's many canals. They belonged to merchants who became wealthy as the Dutch exploited the rich East Indies spice trade.*

▲ *Top (left to right): Some Honeypot ants are fed with honeydew and 'store' the food in their bodies. Harvester ants store seeds inside their nests for the winter. Leafcutter ants make a compost from leaves to grow fungus. They use the fungus as food. Some ants keep aphids (small insects) on tree roots. The aphids suck the honeydew from the plant and the ants 'milk' the aphids. Below: the life cycle of an ant begins when the queen lays her eggs. Worker ants carry the eggs to a nursery where they stay for several days until they hatch as* larvae. *The growing larvae are fed by more worker ants. In the pupal chamber the larvae spin cocoons, in which they turn into* pupae. *The pupae are carried to the hatching chamber where the young ants emerge from the cocoons. The old cocoons are taken away and stored in a refuse chamber.*

acute; 90° is a *right angle;* and angles between 90° and 180° are called *obtuse. Reflex* angles are those between 180° and 360°.

ANGLO-SAXONS The name given to the German tribes that settled in Britain between AD 400 and 600. By the 7th century they had formed several kingdoms, including Mercia, Northumbria and Wessex. The early Anglo-Saxons were soon converted to CHRISTIANITY and contributed much to the field of art, especially in church ARCHITECTURE (see NORMAN ARCHITECTURE) and ILLUMINATED MANUSCRIPTS. Anglo-Saxon rule came to an end in 1066 with the NORMAN invasion.

ANGOLA A republic in west-central AFRICA, Angola became independent in 1975. It has 8,540,000 people and covers 1,246,700 sq km (481,354 sq miles). The capital is Luanda. ▷

ANIMALS All living things are divided into two groups, animals and plants. Although, under the microscope, animals and plants have a similar structure – they are both made up of CELLS – there are certain basic characteristics which distinguish the two. The most important distinction is feeding. Animals and plants feed in very different ways. Plants – if they are green – are food creators: through PHOTOSYNTHESIS they are able to make their own food. Animals are food consumers: they cannot create food; they must have it ready-made and so feed on plants or on other animals that have themselves eaten plants. Another important difference is growth. Animal growth is limited: most animals develop to a certain size and shape and then stop growing. In contrast, plant growth is unlimited: plants often just keep on growing. There are other differences which apply to most – but not all – animals and plants. Movement is one. Animals are generally free to move and plants are not. Senses are another. Most animals are able to see, hear, smell, touch and taste. All but the simplest animals have a skeleton, muscles, some sort of blood system and special organs for breathing, digesting, excreting (getting rid of waste matter) and reproducing. Today there are about 1,300,000 known animal species on the Earth ranging from the microscopic one-celled speck of jelly called AMOEBA to the most developed of all MAMMALS, man. The world's animals belong to one of three large groups: the PROTOZOA – one-celled animals; the INVERTEBRATES – animals without backbones; and the VERTEBRATES – animals with backbones. ▷

Ant

ANT Many ants like to feed on honeydew, a sweet substance secreted by greenfly and other aphids. Some, like the meadow ant, keep aphids underground in their nests, and 'milk' them like cows. In summer, the aphids are kept out of doors on nearby plants.

Some species of ants have come to rely so much on slave ants that they will starve to death when surrounded by abundant food if the slaves are removed.

The largest ant in the world is believed to be the bull ant of Queensland, Australia. The workers have been measured at a length of 38 mm (1½ inches).

ANT Ants, distinguished from other INSECTS by their narrow waists, live in all but the coldest parts of the world. There are about 7,000 species and nearly all are social insects: they live in colonies which may contain as few as a dozen ants or as many as 200,000. The colony consists of a mated female – the queen, a number of males and many sterile wingless females – workers – who find food, build the nest, often underground, and care for the young. In many species, workers have stings as a defence; others squirt acid at their enemies. Ants get food in three ways: some species hunt small insects; others collect seeds, nectar and honeydew – the sticky liquid given out by greenfly; while some S. American ants actually produce their own food by growing FUNGI on beds of chewed leaves in their nests.

◁

ANTARCTICA An icy continent around the South Pole, Antarctica has an area of 13,209,000 sq km (5,100,000 sq miles). It has no permanent population, but scientists and whalers spend periods there. The first certain landing on Antarctica took place in 1831. But it was not until December 14, 1911 that the Norwegian Roald Amundsen (1872–1928) became the first man to reach the South Pole. Most of Antarctica is blanketed by ice, up to

4270 metres (14,000 ft) thick. In places, high peaks jut through the ice and some coastal strips are ice-free.

ANT-EATER Toothless animal living in the tropical forests and swamps of South and Central America. The ant-eater is active only at night when it attacks the nests of ANTS and TERMITES, using a long curved claw. It then picks up the insects with its long sticky tongue.

ANTELOPE Swift graceful animal found chiefly in Africa. Antelopes live off grass and leaves and range in size from the Eland, 2 metres (6 ft) tall, to the tiny Pigmy antelope, only 30 cm (1 ft) high. GAZELLES and GNUS are two well-known kinds of antelope.

ANTHROPOLOGY A word that means the scientific study of man. There are two main divisions – physical anthropology and cultural anthropology. Physical anthropology is the study of the origins and EVOLUTION of man; cultural anthropology is the study of man's activities, including social organization and the development of civilization.

Charles DARWIN first established the idea that man was descended from an ape-like animal ancestor. The search began to find this 'missing link' in man's history. As a result of a number of important discoveries, we now know that a relative of man's earliest 'human' ancestor was *Australopithecus*, an ape-like creature with remarkably human teeth that walked in an upright posture. Between this creature (5–2 million years ago) and modern man there are Java Man (500,000 years), *Pithecanthropus*, or Peking Man (360,000 years), NEANDERTHAL MAN (100,000 years) and CRO-MAGNON MAN (c. 20,000 years ago).

ANTIBIOTICS Chemical substances that are used to destroy the micro-organisms, or germs, that cause disease. The first and most famous antibiotic was PENICILLIN, discovered by Alexander FLEMING in 1928.

ANTIBODY A substance produced by the body to fight invading VIRUSES. Vaccination uses this reaction to create immunity to disease. Antibodies can also cause allergic reactions. (See VACCINE; ALLERGY)

ANTICYCLONE A circular wind system surrounding a stable mass of high pressure air, often creating clear, calm weather.

◄ Anthropologists study the present day culture and way of life of primitive people such as this hunting party of South American Indians. The life style of these Indians has changed very little over centuries, and through them we can form ideas about how the first races of men may have lived.

ANTIFREEZE A substance used to lower the FREEZING point of water. In winter, motorists add antifreeze to the water in their cars. This makes the water remain liquid well below 0° C (32° F). A common antifreeze is *ethylene glycol*.

ANTIQUES Almost any object, often furniture, that is old and for which there is a market. Expensive antiques are sought by collectors because they are fashionable or rare; but many more common and ordinary articles are also sold as antiques.

ANTISEPTIC An antiseptic is a substance that stops the growth of micro-organisms, such as FUNGI and BACTERIA, that cause disease. A British surgeon called Joseph LISTER introduced antiseptics to SURGERY in the 1860s. He applied a dressing soaked in carbolic acid to a patient's wounded leg. The acid prevented the wound from becoming infected, and it healed rapidly. Many antiseptics are now used in surgery.

APE Man's nearest living relative. Some 70 million years ago, a group of MAMMALS called primates appeared on the Earth. In time, the first primates evolved into MONKEYS and apes; by about 12 million years ago, there were five kinds of ape. One of these apes, called *Ramapithecus*, was the ancestor of man; the other four were the ancestors of today's apes: the CHIMPANZEE, GORILLA, ORANG-UTAN and GIBBON. Apes are very similar to man but there are some differences: their feet are made to

► The largest member of the ape family is the gorilla. A male gorilla can grow up to 1.8 metres (6 ft) tall and weigh up to 200 kg (450 lb).

grasp as well as walk, whereas human feet cannot grasp. Because they live partly in trees, their legs are shorter and their arms longer than man's. And, although the ape has a larger brain than any other animal except man, it is still only half the size of the human brain. ▷

APHID Tiny soft-bodied insect. Aphids breed very quickly and are among the worst insect pests. They do great harm to plants by feeding off the sap and by carrying VIRUSES from one plant to another. ▷

APOLLO In Greek mythology, the most important god after ZEUS. Young and handsome, he was the Greek ideal of youth.

APOSTLES The twelve disciples, or followers, of Jesus, who were entrusted by him with teaching and administering the new Christian faith. (See BIBLE; JESUS CHRIST)

APPENDIX A small, narrow tube attached to the large INTESTINE and closed at one end. When inflamed, it causes the disease known as appendicitis, and often has to be removed.

APPLE The world's favourite fruit grows in most temperate countries. Apples are round and juicy, red to green in colour and are either sweet (eating apples) or sour (cooking apples). There are over 1000 varieties of apple. Ac-

▲ A bronze head of Apollo. He was the god of light, music, poetry, prophecy and healing.

APE All 11 species of anthropoid ape live in the tropical regions of Africa and the Far East. The only great ape to be found outside Africa is the orang-utan, which lives a solitary life in the lowland forests of Borneo and Sumatra. Orang-utans are becoming increasingly rare. Fewer than 5,000 are estimated to remain in the wild.

APHID There are about 8,000 known species of aphids. About 160 different plant viruses, two-thirds of all those known, are transmitted by these insects.

APPLE The apple belongs to the rose family, *Rosaceae*, genus Malus. The fruit is really a pome and bears from 2 to 5 seeds.

The popular Granny Smith apple was named after Maria Smith who emigrated to Australia in 1839. By grafting seedlings in her garden, she produced a strain of apple that was superior to any other in Australia, and before long, Granny Smiths were being grown by the million.

AQUEDUCT Many aqueducts were built before the time of the Romans. About 530 BC the Greek engineer Eupalinus dug a water supply tunnel over 800 metres (900 yds) long through the middle of a hill in Samos. He drove the tunnel from both ends and the tunnelers met in the middle with an error of only a metre.

Between 312 BC and AD 226 the Romans built 11 aqueducts to supply their city with water. The most famous was the Marcia, completed in 140 BC. It was 92 km (57 miles) long. Later, two other aqueducts were built on top of it. The Marcia aqueduct was built of stone blocks.

ARCHAEOLOGY Early this century, people keenly sought man's early ancestors. In 1908, Charles Dawson found bits of human skull at Piltdown in Sussex, England. Experts from the British Museum thought the bits to be 500,000 years old – they had discovered the missing link between apes and man. But much later, tests proved Piltdown Man to have a modern ape's jaw and a human braincase only a few thousand years old. The Piltdown bones had been carefully faked. Archaeological frauds are often carried out for money. Before World War I, the Riccardi family of Italy forged huge statues of ancient Etruscan warriors. They were bought by the New York Metropolitan Museum of Art and their forgery only came to light years later.

In 1803 Lord Elgin brought to England a large part of the great Parthenon frieze from the Acropolis in Athens. Before Lord Elgin removed the frieze it had already been damaged by the effects of a Venetian shell exploding a powder magazine in the Parthenon in 1687. It is possible that Lord Elgin's action in removing the frieze saved it from further damage during the Greek war of independence. The frieze, usually called the Elgin Marbles, is in the British Museum, London.

cording to the Bible, the apple was the forbidden fruit eaten by Adam and Eve in the Garden of Eden. ◁

AQUALUNG A device that allows divers to breathe under water, often called *scuba* (Self-Contained Underwater Breathing Apparatus). It supplies breathing gas from gas bottles worn by the diver.

AQUARIUM A glass tank in which aquatic animals and plants are kept alive, either for research purposes or purely for decoration. Today public aquaria contain larger animals such as dolphins and whales.

AQUEDUCT A man-made channel or pipe for carrying water, often a bridge across a valley. The most famous aqueducts were built by the Romans. ◁

ARABS The Arabs are people who speak Arabic, and who share a common tradition and culture. Many of them are Moslems. They live in a broad belt of land stretching across North Africa and including much of southwestern Asia.

Arabic is a Semitic language, which originated in Arabia. In the AD 600s, Moslem armies, inspired by the teachings of the Prophet MOHAMMED, spread north, east and west, converting people to ISLAM and building a great empire (see CRUSADES). From the 1200s, the Moslem empire was replaced largely by Turkish rule. In the 1800s and 1900s, the Arabs worked for independence from foreign rule and they also strove for unity among their people. The Arabs opposed the creation of the state of ISRAEL and several Arab nations joined together to fight the Israelis in 1948, 1956, 1967 and 1973.

The Arab world, much of which is desert, was once extremely poor. However, several Arab nations, including ALGERIA, BAHRAIN, IRAQ, LIBYA, SAUDI ARABIA and the UNITED ARAB EMIRATES, have recently become major oil producers. Revenue from oil sales is being spent on developing these nations and on assistance to other Arab countries.

ARCH A curved structure of stones that can support a load, used to cover an opening, such as a doorway, gateway, or the ceiling of a church. Roman and Norman arches were round; Gothic arches were pointed. (See ARCHITECTURE; GOTHIC ARCHITECTURE; NORMAN ARCHITECTURE)

ARCHAEOLOGY The scientific study of man's history through the material remains and monuments of the past. These may include artifacts (things people have made with their hands), houses, temples, graves or fortifications. Even a garbage pit can help to

A typical archaeological 'dig'. Uncovering ancient remains is very slow and painstaking work. After the top layer of soil has been removed each following layer has to be cleared by hand so as not to damage any 'finds'.

▲ *When this cup was found it was so badly corroded it was impossible to see what it was.*

▲ *The cup was sent to the British Museum. There it was photographed by X-ray. The photographs showed that beneath the dirt and rust it was beautifully engraved. The cup was carefully cleaned and restored to its original state (below). It was found to be 3500 years old and was named the Bull Cup of Cyprus.*

reveal how people lived. Archaeologists study all these things, from the most impressive monuments to the humblest pin, in an attempt to piece together the puzzle of the past.

Modern archaeology began during the RE-NAISSANCE, when there was a revival of interest in the culture of ancient GREECE and ROME. It became fashionable to collect ancient works of art. Often the sites from which these works were taken were carelessly destroyed in the rush to cart off plunder. But by the early 19th century a more scholarly approach began to develop. Archaeologists uncovered sites methodically, noting all they found and where they found it. Gradually many exciting and important archaeological discoveries were made, including the remains of ancient TROY (1871); the early Greek civilization at MY-CENAE (1876); the MINOAN civilization at Knossos, in Crete (1899); the Sumerian city of Ur in MESOPOTAMIA (1922); and the tomb of the

Why should a hollow vessel float in water? Why should a block of wood float but a piece of lead sink? The answer lies in the density of the objects and of water. *Archimedes Principle* says that when any object is placed in a liquid, it experiences an upthrust equal to the weight of liquid displaced. As an object sinks into the liquid, it displaces more and more liquid, and there may come a point when the upthrust is equal to the weight of the object. The object floats. Wood floats on water because it is less dense.

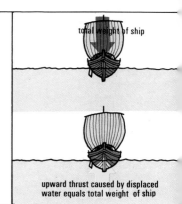

total weight of ship

upward thrust caused by displaced water equals total weight of ship

pharaoh TUTANKHAMEN in Egypt (1922).

Today, science helps the archaeologist in his work. RADIOCARBON DATING and *dendro-chronology* (dating by tree-rings) help to establish when particular objects were made. Aerial photography helps archaeologists to locate sites that are not visible from the ground. Photos often show crop shadows or patterns in the earth that indicate where old ditches were dug or buildings once stood. Infrared and X-ray photography can show up designs under the rotted surface of a bronze bowl. Archaeology has even gone under water: with modern diving equipment, archaeologists can explore sunken wrecks and other long-lost remains of the past. ◁

ARCHAEOPTERYX A prehistoric bird that lived during the Jurassic Period (200 to 135 million years ago). About the size of a large crow, it had jaws with teeth, like a lizard, and feathers on its back and wings.

ARCHERY The sport or art of shooting with a BOW AND ARROW. Archery was once important in both hunting and warfare; today it is chiefly used in sport. Its use as a weapon died out after gunpowder was brought to Europe in the 1400s. ▷

ARCHIMEDES A Greek mathematician (287–212 BC), formulator of the famous principle named after him and inventor of the Archimedean screw. ▷

ARCHITECTURE A word used to describe the art and science of designing buildings. It comes from two Greek words meaning 'chief builder'. The Roman architect Vitruvius, who lived 2000 years ago, said that architects should combine usefulness, strength and beauty in their work. Today that is still a good description of the aims of architecture.

◄ *Top: The architects of ancient Egypt built this pyramid in about 2950 BC. Below: An example of Renaissance architecture, which copied ancient Greek and Roman styles.*

ARCHERY In flight shooting, the archer tries only for distance, very heavy bows being used. For standing flight shooting the record is 1065 m (1165 yds), set up by the American Don Brown in 1977. In free-style flight shooting the archer lies on his back with the bow strapped to his feet. Both hands are thus free to draw the bow. The record in this class of shooting is 1854 m (1 mile 268 yds), set up by H. Drake of the USA in 1971.

ARCHIMEDES There is a story that Archimedes, single-handed, destroyed the Roman fleet which was attacking Syracuse. He set up a battery of mirrors and directed the Sun's rays at the ships' sails, setting them on fire. He is also said to have held a Roman armada at bay for several years with engines of war that hurled great rocks at the enemy ships.

Archimedes died in Syracuse as it was being sacked by the Romans in 212 BC. The story is told that he was stabbed to death by a Roman soldier whom he scolded for interrupting him while he was thinking about some mathematical problem.

ARCTIC The pack ice at the North Pole is only 5 m (16 ft) thick.

The largest city in the Arctic is Murmansk, famous as the port to which Allied aid to Russia was delivered during World War II. It has a population of about 300,000.

The average depth of the Arctic Ocean is 1280 m (4200 ft); its greatest depth is 5333 m (17,500 ft).

The Arctic is much milder than the Antarctic. The South Pole is a desolate place, frozen solid to great depths all the year round. The North Pole temperatures are moderated by the sea just under the pack ice. The coldest spot in the Arctic is nowhere near the North Pole; it lies hundreds of miles south in Siberia.

The Egyptians designed and built great temples and PYRAMIDS of stone. Over their doorways they used huge crosspieces of wood to support the weight of the stones above. But the ancient Babylonians and Assyrians used bricks for building, as wood and stone were scarce. They were first to develop the ARCH, for the crosspieces could not be made of brick.

The ancient Greeks created some of the world's finest architecture in about the 600s BC. Their temples and other public buildings had graceful COLUMNS and were decorated with beautiful sculpture. The Romans copied and developed Greek architecture. They also made great use of arches and designed their houses with baths and central heating.

After the fall of the Roman Empire in the AD 400s, architecture developed mainly in the BYZANTINE EMPIRE. Early Christian churches had vaults and domes. Moslem architecture which developed after the AD 600s, used domes, wide, pointed arches, and tall towers, called minarets.

In western Europe a heavy style of architecture called ROMANESQUE developed, but by 1200 the lighter, graceful Gothic style had appeared. Gothic cathedrals had tall, slender pillars; high, vaulted roofs; and beautiful stained glass windows. During the RENAISSANCE, Italian architects borrowed ideas from ancient GREECE and ROME, and by the 1600s architecture was much freer and more decorated, in a style called BAROQUE.

In Britain and America buildings were

▲ *In 1818 an early Arctic explorer, John Ross, set out to search for the Northwest Passage. During the voyage Ross, an Englishman, had his first meeting with Eskimos.*

never quite so elaborate as on the Continent, and a style called Georgian, after the 18th-century British kings, became popular. During the 1800s many earlier styles were revived and often mixed together, sometimes with unfortunate results. Later, new building materials such as iron and steel made many changes in structure possible, including the modern skyscraper, built on a steel frame. Skyscrapers made the maximum use of small sites in crowded cities. (See ASSYRIA; BABYLONIA; GOTHIC ARCHITECTURE; NORMAN ARCHITECTURE)

ARCTIC The Arctic is a cold region around the North Pole. It includes the Arctic Ocean, many islands and the northern parts of EUROPE, ASIA and NORTH AMERICA.

The Arctic is sometimes defined as the area north of the Arctic Circle (latitude $66\frac{1}{2}°$ N). But some scholars describe it as the region north of the tree line, the northern limit for the growth of trees. This treeless zone is called the TUNDRA. In winter, temperatures plummet down to $-34°$ C $(-30°$ F). The Arctic Ocean freezes over and the land is blanketed by snow. In spring, temperatures rise and the snow and ice start to melt. Summer temperatures reach about $7°$ C $(45°$ F) and plants, such as grasses, mosses and low shrubs, grow. These plants attract migrating animals, such as caribou and reindeer. The largest group of people in the Arctic are the ESKIMOS of the Canadian Arctic and GREENLAND.

The Arctic Ocean covers about 14,090,000 sq km (5,440,000 sq miles). Early explorers faced tremendous difficulties and their ships were often trapped or even crushed in the sea ice. The North Pole was first reached in 1909 by the American Robert E. Peary (1856–1920). ◁

ARGENTINA A republic in SOUTH AMERICA, Argentina has an area of 2.776.889 sq km (1,072,163 sq miles) and 30,097,000 people (1984 est.). The capital is Buenos Aires. Argentina's wealth comes from its vast pampas (plains) which provide rich farmland and pasture. It is a major producer of beef, wheat, millet, sorghum and wool. ▷

ARISTOTLE A Greek philosopher (384–322 BC), student of PLATO and the inventor of logic. His writings covered many areas, including nature, politics and metaphysics. (See BOTANY)

ARITHMETIC The branch of mathematics concerned with counting and calculating, using numbers. The four basic operations in arithmetic are addition, subtraction, multiplication and division.

ARKWRIGHT, RICHARD An English inventor (1732–1792), best known for developing a spinning frame which made factory-produced cotton cloth possible.

ARMADA A Spanish word that means 'armed force', generally used to refer to the huge Spanish fleet that attempted to invade England in 1588. The heavy, slow, Spanish galleons fell prey to the swifter and better armed English ships, and the crippled fleet was driven back to Spain. (See DRAKE, SIR FRANCIS; ELIZABETH I) ▷

ARMADILLO The only armoured MAMMAL. Armadillos, found mostly in South America, are protected by a shield of bony scales; they are small animals, under 1 metre (3 ft) long, and live mainly on insects, particularly ants.
▷

ARMENIA People who speak Armenian live between the Black and Caspian seas in IRAN, TURKEY and the Armenian Soviet Socialist Republic in RUSSIA. Many Armenians have longed for a nation of their own and an independent Armenian Republic did exist, briefly, between 1918 and 1920.

ARMOUR Coverings to protect the body from injury in battle have been worn since the

▲ *In the Middle Ages battles were fought in heavy armour, like this 14th century helmet.*

BRONZE AGE (2500 BC). Armour reached the peak of its development during the MIDDLE AGES. Beginning with a suit of mail (linked rings of iron), more and more plate armour was added until the soldier and his horse were almost entirely encased in metal. Armour helped protect the knight in direct combat, but with the invention of gunpowder and changes in the tactics of warfare such heavy armour was gradually abandoned. ▷

ARMY The first armies appeared as early as 2500 BC when the Egyptians organized militia to repel barbarian attacks. The Greeks developed armies of foot soldiers, or INFANTRY,

▼ *In modern armies, soldiers, such as these American troops in Vietnam, are equipped to fight in any part of the world.*

ARMADA The Spanish Armada totalled about 130 ships. In this number were 20 powerful galleons, 4 galleasses, some 40 armed merchantmen, and other supply ships. The fleet was manned by over 7,000 seamen, and the ships carried about 19,000 soldiers. There were 2,000 cannon and enough food for at least six months.

ARMADILLO The armadillo's shell is arranged in a series of flexible bands. The number of bands ranges from three to twelve, according to the species.

The nine-banded armadillo is unique in that it always gives birth to identical quadruplets. They result from the division of one ovum, something which very rarely happens in other mammals. The four babies are, of course, always of the same sex and exactly alike.

The smallest of the 21 species of armadillo is the fairy armadillo of Bolivia and Argentina. It is about 150 mm (6 inches) long, and bright pink in colour. The face is totally covered with long white hairs.

In some regions, armadillos are hunted for food. The common armadillo is sometimes called the 'poor man's pig' because its flesh tastes like pork.

ARMOUR Some armour was immensely heavy. That worn by Charles V of Spain, together with his horse's armour, weighed no less than 100 kg (220 lb). It is preserved in the Royal Armoury in Madrid.

◄ *The history of art is almost as old as the history of man himself. This African cave painting dates from the late Stone Age.*

ART The most valuable painting in the world is thought to be the *'Mona Lisa'* by Leonardo da Vinci, which hangs in the Louvre in Paris. It measures 77 x 53 cm (30½ x 21 inches), and it is said that Francis I of France once had it hanging in his bathroom.

organized into *phalanxes*, tighly formed ranks of spearmen. The Roman army was based on the Greek, but developed into a more efficient force which conquered and held the vast Roman empire. It was based on the legion, a highly manoeuvrable unit of CAVALRY and heavy and light infantry. Today's armies had their beginnings in the 17th century when tactical groupings emerged.

ART Since earliest times men have created visual images. Beautiful sculptures and fres-

◄ *The history of art is almost as old as the history of man himself. This African cave painting dates from the late Stone Age.*

coes from ancient EGYPT, GREECE and ROME still survive. Christianity greatly influenced the development of western art after the fall of Rome; during the MIDDLE AGES painters depicted religious scenes, often in a stiff, unrealistic style. With the RENAISSANCE there came a new flowering of art. Such painters as LEONARDO DA VINCI and MICHELANGELO exercised a new-found freedom, making their subjects more life-like. In northern Europe Dutch painters like REMBRANDT depicted everyday scenes.

In the 1700s and early 1800s many artists based their work on Greek and Roman art. Later painting became more realistic and natural, but by the 1870s a new style, called IMPRESSIONISM, was developing. Impressionist artists such as MONET and RENOIR painted with little dabs of colour, producing soft, almost misty outlines.

Painting in the 20th century became even freer, and included the ABSTRACT ART movement and its offshoot, CUBISM. (See BAROQUE ART; BYZANTINE ART; FINE ARTS; FRESCO; MINIATURE PAINTING; MOSAIC; MOSLEM ART; POP ART; ROMANESQUE ART; SCULPTURE; SURREALISM; WATER COLOUR) ◁

ARTERIES The vessels that carry BLOOD from the HEART to the tissues and organs of the body. The most important and largest artery is the *aorta*, which leaves the left ventricle of the heart and runs down the body near the spine. From the aorta various branches supply different parts of the body: the *carotid* artery goes to the head and neck; the *renal* to the kidneys; the *celiac* to the stomach and liver; the *pulmonary* to the lungs.

ARTHRITIS A group of diseases, chronic and acute, that cause inflammation and stiffening of the joints. The most common are rheumatoid arthritis and osteoarthritis.

ARTHUR, KING A legendary British king, probably a chieftain who led a force against the invading SAXONS in about AD 500. A vast body of legends and tales grew up about him, making him the most famous figure in medieval literature.

ASBESTOS A name given to several fibrous materials. The most important of these is *calcium magnesium silicate*. Asbestos is used mainly for its flame-proofing and heat-insulation properties.

◄ Le Repas *(The Meal)*, by the 19th century French artist Paul Gauguin. Gauguin belonged to the Post-Impressionist school of painting.

35

ASIA The largest continent, Asia covers an area greater than that of North, Central and South America combined. Asia also has more people than any other continent. CHINA and INDIA alone contain more than one-third of the world's people. However, the average population density in Asia is less than that of Europe. This is because vast areas are too cold, dry or mountainous to support more than a few people. But such places as the GANGES-Brahmaputra delta, the river valleys of China and the island of JAVA are among the most thickly-populated places in the world.

A continent of contrasts, Asia stretches from the ARCTIC tundra in the north to the hot equatorial lands of INDONESIA. It contains some of the world's driest lands, including hot deserts in the south-west and cold deserts in the north-eastern interior. However, Cherrapunji, in north-west Indonesia, holds the world rainfall record. In one year (1860–1), 2646 cm (1042 in) of rain fell. Asia also has the world's highest mountain range, the HIMALAYAS, and the lowest depression on land, the DEAD SEA shoreline.

Members of the three great families of man are found in Asia. Caucasoids live in the south-west and also in the northern parts of the Indian sub-continent. Mongoloids, including the Chinese and Japanese, occupy most of eastern Asia. And a few Negroids are found in the south-east and in the PHILIPPINES. Asia was the home of all the world's great religions. BUDDHISM, CHRISTIANITY, HINDUISM, ISLAM, JUDAISM and Shintoism began in Asia.

Two-thirds of Asia's people are farmers. Many are extremely poor and droughts and floods often cause famines. The chief food crops are rice and wheat. Many crops are grown for export. They include citrus fruits, cotton, jute, rubber, spices, tea and tobacco. The only truly industrialized nation is JAPAN, now the third largest trading nation in the world, after the USA and West Germany. However, some other nations, such as China, are industrializing quickly.

Asia gave birth to many great early civilizations. They include those of MESOPOTAMIA, BABYLON, ASSYRIA, China and the Indus valley. European influence began in the 1500s and, by the late 1800s, most of southern and south-eastern Asia was ruled by European powers. However, after World War II, when Japan occupied many parts of Asia, most colonies in Asia became independent. Another event of great importance occurred in 1949, when the Chinese communists took complete control of mainland China. In 1975 communist governments also took over in VIETNAM, LAOS and KAMPUCHEA.

ASPHALT A sticky black mixture of minerals containing bitumen. Asphalt is obtained from natural deposits and also as a petroleum byproduct. It is used mainly for surfacing roads and for waterproofing. ▷

ASS Small (1.2 metres – 4 ft high) horse-like animal. There are two known species of wild ass – the sandy-red Asiatic ass and the grey African ass – but few survive. The domestic DONKEY is descended from a type of African ass. ▷

ASSASSINATION A word used to refer to the murder of a public figure. It comes from the Assassins of Persia, a 12th-century sect that believed it was their sacred duty to kill their enemies.

ASSEMBLY LINE In manufacturing, a method of production whereby the product, such as a car, moves through different stages of assembly until it emerges complete at the other end. Each worker repeats a particular job on every car.

ASSYRIA An ancient Mesopotamian empire that flourished from about 1300 BC to 612 BC. At its height Assyria ruled a huge area from Persia in the east to Egypt in the west. The Assyrians, whose culture was based on that of Babylonia, built their empire with the help of one of the most efficient and ferocious armies of the ancient world. They used chariots, light and heavy infantry, bowmen and slingers, and were masters of siege warfare. The Assyrians were also skilful administrators, governing even the most distant provinces through a hierarchy of officials with the king at the head. The power of Assyria was finally ended when

▼ This Assyrian relief carving on stone, shows a group of Assyrian soldiers besieging a city. In the centre of the carving is a battering ram. The Assyrians were masters of the techniques of warfare, they introduced the use of body armour and were the first to develop a cavalry.

its capital city, Nineveh, was captured by a combined force of Medes, Babylonians and Scythians in 612 BC. (See BABYLONIA; MESOPOTAMIA)

ASTEROIDS Minor PLANETS, most of which orbit the Sun in a belt between Mars and Jupiter. More than 2000 asteroids are known to exist. The majority have diameters of less than 160 km (100 miles). ▷

ASTHMA A respiratory disease that causes spasms of the bronchial tubes, wheezing, coughing, and difficulty in breathing. In most cases asthma is caused by ALLERGY to dust, pollens or certain foods.

ASTIGMATISM A common eye defect in which the lens cannot focus sharply, causing the sufferer to have blurred vision. (See CORNEA)

ASTROLOGY The study of the heavenly bodies in order to predict the future. As a part of many primitive religions, astrology grew out of the belief that the movements of the Sun, Moon and PLANETS somehow affected the movement of life on Earth. (See ASTRONOMY)

ASTRONAUTICS The science of space travel. Included in astronautics are: the design and construction of spacecraft and launching ROCKETS; the selection and training of personnel; the control and tracking of spacecraft; telecommunications; and combatting the physical and mental problems experienced by astronauts.

Spacemen are called *astronauts* in the United States and *cosmonauts* in the Soviet Union. The first astronauts were the pilots of high-flying, rocket-propelled aircraft that reached the fringes of space. These pilots seemed to suffer no ill effects during their brief periods of space travel. But many experiments had to be carried out before man could be sent on long missions into the unknown. How would the human body stand up to the punishing forces encountered during blast-off of a space rocket? And how would it then react to long periods of weightlessness in space? How difficult would it be to eat and drink in an environment where there is no 'up' or 'down'? And what other hazards would man have to cope with in space? All these questions had to be answered. Also, many technical problems had to be solved in order to provide reliable spacecraft.

By the early 1960s, the Russians and Americans had both made considerable advances in space technology. Manned SATELLITES were made to orbit the Earth. And the duration of spaceflights was steadily increased. By the end of the decade, the Americans had achieved

ASPHALT In some places asphalt is found on the surface of the Earth in what are called asphalt lakes. One in Venezuela covers 400 ha (1000 acres) to a depth of about a metre.

A large proportion of the world's roads are surfaced with asphalt. It is usually mixed with sand and powdered limestone, heated and poured onto a concrete roadbed. Then it is smoothed and rolled.

ASS The male ass, called a jack or jackass, is mated with a mare to produce a mule. The she-ass or jennet is mated with a stallion to produce a hinney. Mules and hinneys cannot breed.

ASTEROIDS The largest known asteroid is Ceres – it was also the first to be discovered, in 1801. Its diameter is 1003 km (623 miles); its distance from the Sun is 414 million km (257 million miles); and the length of its year is 4.6 of our years.

Other large asteroids are Pallas (diameter 608 km, 378 miles), Vesta (538 km, 334 miles), Hygeia (450 km, 279-miles), and Euphrosyne (370 km, 230 miles).

ASTRONAUTICS The first man--made object in space was the Russian satellite *Sputnik I,* launched on October 4, 1957. The first man in space was the Russian Yuri Gagarin, on April 12, 1961. The only woman in space was Valentina Tereshkova in 1963. The first Moon landing was made by the un-manned Russian *Lunik 2* on September 14, 1959. The first man on the Moon was Neil Armstrong, when he stepped off the lunar module of *Apollo 11* on July 20, 1969.

The oldest astronaut so far to have entered space is Karl G. Henize. He was 58 when he took part in the *Challenger* Space Shuttle Mission in July 1985.

There are 11 main engines on a huge Saturn 5 rocket. Five of these are on the first stage, each one consuming 3 tonnes of fuel a second. With all the fuel loaded for blast-off, the entire rocket weighs some 3000 tonnes. It has about two million working parts.

their ambition of landing men on the Moon (see SPACE EXPLORATION).

Because of the high mental and physical stress that astronauts undergo, the selection of personnel is a lengthy business. In the United States, *pilot* astronauts are chosen from experienced pilots with at least a bachelor's degree in science or engineering. *Scientific* astronauts are chosen from personnel with a doctor's degree or equivalent experience in engineering, science or medicine. All would-be astronauts are given numerous medical tests to check their mental stability and physical fitness. After these tests and extensive interviews, a small proportion of applicants are selected for training as astronauts.

Trainees attend lectures and demonstrations covering a wide range of subjects. For, once in space, they must be able to cope with all kinds of problems. Electrical or mechanical failures might occur in the spacecraft. Or a fellow astronaut might become ill

▲ These astronauts are training to operate under conditions of weightlessness. In order to carry out this training the astronauts are put into an aircraft which dives from a high altitude, at the same speed as a person would fall at if he jumped out without a parachute. During the dive, the aircraft and everything in it is at zero gravity and is weightless. Here, the astronauts are practising drinking liquids during weightlessness.

and need urgent medical attention. Astronauts also need to understand such subjects as meteorology, astronomy, space flight and navigation, geology, telecommunications and computer theory.

In addition to theoretical work, astronauts are given extensive practical training. On the ground, computer-controlled machines simulate most spaceflight conditions. Experience of weightlessness is given in diving aircraft. And, just in case a returning spacecraft should land off-target, astronauts are given survival training. They are taught how to conserve food and water and live in almost any conditions until help arrives. For, without the right preparation, man can perish just as easily on Earth as in the depths of space. ◁

ASTRONOMY Man's first scientific observations were concerned with astronomy – the study of the SUN, MOON, STARS, PLANETS and other heavenly bodies. An interest in such things was important to early man. For the rising and setting of the Sun determined his working day. In summer, he noticed that daylight hours were longer than in winter. And the Sun rose much higher in the sky. At night, other regular changes in the heavens were observed. The positions of stars changed throughout the year. And the Moon went through a series of changes every 29½ days. We now refer to these changes in the Moon's appearance as its *phases*. The phases of the Moon provided early man with a convenient way of dividing up the year. Hence, in Babylonian calendars, alternate months had 29 and 30 days. So the end of each month was marked by the completion of the Moon's phases.

Early CALENDARS proved to be inaccurate. Stars expected to become visible at certain times failed to appear. And the seasons gradually became out of step with the months. So, from time to time, the calendar was corrected to make it correspond with astronomical observations. We correct our modern calendar every leap year by adding an extra day.

The development of the calendar enabled early astronomers to forecast the appearance

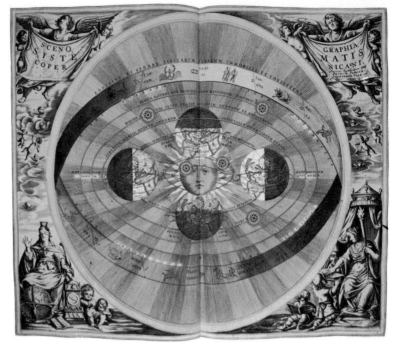

▲ *An early astronomical chart showing the Earth moving around the Sun. For centuries people thought the Earth was the centre of the universe.*

of COMETS and the dates of ECLIPSES. It was simply a matter of looking at past records to see how often these events occurred. But the ability of astronomers to predict future events was generally regarded as something of a miracle. So people who were worried about their own future tended to turn to astronomers for advice. This led to the development of ASTROLOGY, which is supposed to show how the heavenly bodies affect our personal lives. Also, because man had no scientific explanation for his astronomical observations, he used myths and legends instead. As a result, astronomy remained a confused mixture of fact and fiction for thousands of years.

Around 600 BC, the Greeks started to adopt a much more scientific approach to astronomy. They sought logical reasons for their observations, and made detailed records. In the 300s BC, ARISTOTLE deduced that the Earth was curved. And, about a century later, Aristarchus of Samos reasoned that the planets revolve around the Sun. However, most people preferred the idea of an Earth-centred UNIVERSE, and this theory remained popular for many centuries.

Then, in the 1540s, a Pole called Nicolaus ▷

◄ *Modern astronomers use powerful telescopes, like this 100-cm (40-in) refracting telescope at the Yerkes Observatory in Chicago.*

ASTRONOMY One question that astronomers have not, so far, been able to answer is whether there is life elsewhere in the universe. But when we think about the vast distances to other worlds, this is not very surprising. If the Sun were the size of a football, the nearest star – Alpha Centauri – would be about 13,000 km (8000 miles) away. This shows how alone in space we are. But it now seems almost certain that there must be intelligent life somewhere other than on Earth. In our galaxy alone – the Milky Way – there may be 1,000 million planets on which people something like ourselves could develop. And our galaxy is only one among millions of other galaxies in the universe. Scientists believe that somewhere among this inconceivably large number of planets there must be living creatures not too different from us. But getting in touch with them over the vast distances and time involved will not be easy.

The galaxy Andromeda is the Milky Way's nearest neighbour, yet when we see it in the sky we are looking at light that began to travel towards us before the first true men appeared on Earth.

Aurorae

Meteors

Noctilucent clouds

Ozone layer

Tropopause

◄ The outer part of the atmosphere is the exosphere, which gradually merges into space. It begins over 500 km (310 miles) above the Earth.

◄ The ionosphere is between 80 and 500 km (50 – 310 miles) above the Earth. There is very little oxygen. Disturbances in the ionosphere, caused by streams of particles from the Sun, form glowing lights called aurorae. The temperature rises with height from −80°C at 80 km to about 1200°C at 500 km. Artificial satellites orbit the Earth in the ionosphere.

◄ The stratosphere lies between the tropopause and about 80 km (50 miles) above the Earth. The temperature is constant at about −55°C at the lower levels, but rises to about 10°C at about 50 km (30 miles). Then it falls again to about −80°C at 80 km. The rise in temperature is probably caused by the layer of ozone which filters out some of the ultraviolet radiation from the Sun. This radiation would be fatal to life on Earth if it were to reach the surface. The noctilucent (luminous) clouds in the stratosphere probably consist of meteoric dust. Jet aircraft often fly in the lower stratosphere.

◄ The lowest level of the atmosphere, the troposphere extends to about 18 km (11 miles) over the equator, 10–11 km (6–7 miles) over the middle latitudes and 8 km (5 miles) over the poles. The troposphere contains most of the mass of the atmosphere, including moisture and other particles. The troposphere is separated from the stratosphere by the tropopause, where the temperature becomes stable at about −55°C.

COPERNICUS revived the idea that the Sun was at the centre of our planetary system. Gradually, others accepted the truth. Another major advance occurred in 1608, when Hans Lippershey invented the TELESCOPE. This important new tool enabled astronomers to make many interesting discoveries, notably new planets in our SOLAR SYSTEM. But the ninth planet, Pluto, was not discovered until 1930. The following year saw the start of a new chapter in astronomy when Karl Jansky detected radio waves coming from outer space. This led to the important technique known as RADIO ASTRONOMY. Discoveries made using radio telescopes include the strange objects known as QUASARS and PULSARS. (See PLANETARIUM)

ATHENS The capital of GREECE, Athens achieved its greatest brilliance in the 400s BC, when it was the capital and cultural centre of Attica. The ancient city was built around a hill called the Acropolis, an ancient fortress and religious centre. The Acropolis, which is 60 metres (200 ft) above the city, contains the ruins of superb temples, including the PARTHENON (built between 447 and 438 BC). It is an outstanding tourist attraction, along with the National Archaeological Museum. Athens is now a busy city with 3,027,000 people. About 2,000,000 tourists visit it every year.

ATHLETICS A term that includes a whole range of different sporting competitions: cross-country and track running, relay running, jumping (including long, high and triple jumps and pole vaulting), hurdling, throwing (including javelin, discus, shot putt and hammer throw), and tug of war.

Athletic events formed part of the OLYMPIC GAMES in ancient Greece, founded in 776 BC. Some athletics were practised during the Middle Ages, but real interest was not revived until the 19th century. Sports at schools and universities became popular, and the Olympic Games themselves were revived in 1896. In 1912 the International Amateur Athletic Federation was founded, and today almost every country practising athletics is a member.

ATLANTIC OCEAN The second largest ocean, the Atlantic covers 81,662,000 sq km (31,530,000 sq miles). It contains a massive underwater mid-oceanic ridge. New crustal rock is being added along this ridge and so the ocean is widening by a centimetre or so per year.

ATMOSPHERE The Earth's atmosphere can be divided into four distinct bands. Most of the AIR is concentrated in a relatively small band called the *troposphere*. This extends from sea level to about 8 km (5 miles) in polar regions. Over the equator, the troposphere extends to a height of about 18 km (11 miles). Above the troposphere is the *stratosphere*, the junction between the two being called the *tropopause*. Jet aircraft often fly in the lower stratosphere to avoid weather disturbances at lower altitudes. From the top of the stratosphere, 80 km (50 miles) up, to a height of

Electron

Proton

Neutron

▲ *The nucleus of an atom is made up of even tinier particles called protons and neutrons. A carbon atom has six electrons orbiting a nucleus of six protons and six neutrons.*

▲ *Everything around us is made up of groups of tiny atoms, but they are so small we cannot see them. An atom consists of a central nucleus surrounded by electrons. If the nucleus were the size of a lift button, then the whole atom would be the size of a skyscraper.*

◄ *Early charts of the atomic weights of elements and models of atoms, used by the chemist John Dalton in his lectures.*

500 km (300 miles) is the IONOSPHERE. It contains charged particles produced by ionization. Above the ionosphere is the *exosphere*. This is the fringe of the atmosphere and the start of outer space.   ▷

ATOLL A circular CORAL reef surrounding a body of water, or lagoon. Atolls are found in tropical seas, especially in the Pacific and Indian oceans. They are thought to be formed by coral growth around now-submerged volcanoes.

ATOM All substances are made up of particles called atoms. These are so tiny that a line of 50,000,000 atoms, side by side, would be only one centimetre (0.4 in) long. Atoms themselves are made up of even tinier particles called *electrons*, *protons*, and *neutrons*. Protons and neutrons are found at the centre of atoms and form the part called the nucleus. Electrons orbit the nucleus, rather like planets orbiting the Sun. Protons have a positive electric charge, electrons have a negative charge, and neutrons have no charge. Normally, an atom has an equal number of protons and electrons. Their equal, but opposite charges cancel out, so that the atom has no overall charge.

The simplest type of atom is that of HYDROGEN. A single electron orbits a nucleus containing just one proton. Atoms of other ELEMENTS contain more electrons and protons. They also have neutrons in the nucleus.

The *atomic number* of an element is the number of protons in each of its atoms. Every element has a different atomic number, ranging from 1 for hydrogen to 105 for hahnium. Altering the number of protons in an atom

ATMOSPHERE If the Earth were the size of an apple, all our atmosphere, the oceans, and the Earth's crust beneath our feet, which is about 50 km (30 miles) thick, added together, would be as thick as the skin of the apple.

In an area the size of the United States alone there falls on the land every year more than 4 million tonnes of table salt, 2½ million tonnes of sodium sulphate, and 36 million tonnes of calcium compounds – all in rain water.

ATOM About the year 400 BC the ancient Greek philosopher Democritus gave the atom its name. It comes from the Greek *atomos*, meaning 'uncuttable'. Democritus believed that if you cut anything in half, and then cut it in half again, and again, and again, you must reach a point when tiny particles are reached which simply could not be cut any smaller. These particles were atoms. Until about 1890, scientists still thought of atoms as being tiny 'uncuttable' solid particles. Then the electron was discovered, and, after a while, it was found that the atom, far from being a solid ball, was mostly empty space.

If a piece of uranium 25 mm (1 inch) across was blown up until it was as big as the Earth, a single atom in the piece of uranium would be only 25 mm across. The nucleus of the atom would be so small that a powerful microscope would be needed to see it at all.

Ninety per cent of all the atoms in the universe are hydrogen and 9 per cent are helium. All the other elements together make up only one per cent of all atoms.

ATOMIC BOMB The first atomic bomb took five years to produce before it was exploded on top of a steel tower near Alamogordo, New Mexico, in July, 1945. It weighed about 4 tonnes, and some 500,000 people were involved in its making.

ATOMIC ENERGY Scientists in many countries are trying to harness the power of the hydrogen bomb so that we can all have plenty of cheap energy. The process is called thermonuclear fusion and it involves making hydrogen atoms rush together so that they release enormous amounts of energy. But hydrogen atoms do not fuse together easily. The temperature for such fusion to take place must be about 100 million degrees centigrade, and this enormously high temperature must be maintained for at least a second.

would change its identity – that is change it into an atom of a different element. Transformations like this can be carried out using machines called nuclear ACCELERATORS.

Altering the number of neutrons in an atom does not change its identity. It is still an atom of the same element, and has the same chemical properties. Atoms of the same element, but containing different numbers of neutrons, are called ISOTOPES.

Most of the mass of an atom is contained in its neutrons and protons. The mass of these particles is almost equal. An electron has only 1/1836 times the mass of a proton. The *mass number* of an atom is simply the sum of its neutrons and protons. It is used mainly to identify different isotopes of the same element. For example, one chlorine isotope has 18 neutrons and 17 protons in the nucleus. Another chlorine isotope has 20 neutrons and 17 protons. Where necessary, these two forms can be distinguished by writing the mass numbers with the chemical symbols thus: Cl–35 and Cl–37, or Cl^{35} and Cl^{37}. (See ATOMIC BOMB; ATOMIC ENERGY; NUCLEAR ENERGY) ◁

ATOMIC BOMB The atomic bomb derives its explosive power from a process called nuclear fission (splitting). Certain types of URANIUM or PLUTONIUM atoms are made to undergo rapid fission in a CHAIN REACTION. In a fraction of a second, a vast amount of energy is produced, mainly in the form of heat. The resultant explosion can have the same destructive power as tens of thousands of tonnes of TNT. The blast destroys buildings and other structures. The heat causes fires over a large area. And other RADIATION causes death or sickness. Radioactive debris may fall to the

ground years after the explosion. (See ATOM; ATOMIC ENERGY; FUSION; NUCLEAR ENERGY; RADIOACTIVITY) ◁

ATOMIC ENERGY Energy released by the nuclei of ATOMS when matter is destroyed. Atomic energy is also called NUCLEAR ENERGY. It is produced in ATOMIC BOMBS, HYDROGEN BOMBS and nuclear reactors. By destroying only a tiny amount of matter, a vast amount of energy is produced.

To scientists in the 1800s, it seemed that MASS and energy could not be destroyed or created (see CONSERVATION LAWS). But, early this century, the German physicist Albert EINSTEIN showed that these theories had to be changed. Mass and energy, he said, were different forms of the same thing. So, if it ever became possible to destroy mass, energy would be produced in its place. According to Einstein's mass-energy equation, $E = mc^2$, where E is energy, m is mass and c is the speed of light. Because c is so large – about 300 million metres per second (980 million feet per second) – multiplying m by c^2 gives an extremely high value for E, even when m is quite small. This is why such a large amount of energy is produced by nuclear reactions.

Many years went by before Einstein's theory was proved. For no one had discovered how to destroy mass. But this became possible in the 1930s. At that time, scientists were investigating atomic structure by bombarding atoms of various elements with fast-moving particles. It was found that uranium–235 atoms could be split up by bombarding them with neutrons. In this fission (splitting) process, heat was produced and mass lost – exactly as Einstein had said. Also, the bombarding neutrons removed more neutrons from the uranium. The Italian scientist Enrico Fermi realized what this implied. If a few neutrons could release more neutrons from the uranium, perhaps these, in turn, could be used to cause further fission reactions. And perhaps, in this way, a whole chain of reactions could be built up to produce vast amounts of heat. This dream was realized in 1942. In Chicago, Fermi became the first person to produce a controlled CHAIN REACTION to release atomic energy. This nuclear reaction was a major advance in the new science of nuclear physics.

With World War II in progress, and with the threat that the Nazis were developing nuclear weapons, the US Government started its own project to develop an atomic bomb.

◀ *The explosion of an atomic bomb creates a huge mushroom-shaped radioactive cloud. This shape has become a symbol of the destructive power of the atom. The force of an atomic explosion is caused when all the energy in the atoms is released in a fraction of a second.*

Auc

Instead of having a controlled nuclear reaction, the fission process had to operate extremely quickly. This would cause a sudden, high energy release, with devastating consequences. In July 1945, the United States tested their first atomic bomb. And, just one month later, they used the new weapon against Japan. This brought a rapid end to the war. By 1952, the United States had developed an even more powerful nuclear weapon – the hydrogen bomb. This depends on a process called nuclear FUSION, in which atoms join together with a release of energy. Fortunately, although many countries now have the hydrogen bomb, it has never been used against another nation. Scientists are trying to find out how to control fusion reactions to produce energy for peaceful purposes.   ◁

AUCKLAND The largest city in NEW ZEALAND, Auckland with its suburbs has a population of 864,000 (1984 est.). This attractive, modern city on North Island is a major port and a leading manufacturing centre.

AURORA A display of coloured light in the night sky. Aurorae are seen in polar regions. They occur when charged particles from the Sun enter the ATMOSPHERE and collide with gas molecules in the IONOSPHERE.

AUSTEN, JANE A well-known English author (1775–1817), popular for her portrayal of the life and customs of her time. Her novels include *Pride and Prejudice* and *Sense and Sensibility.*

AUSTRALASIA Consisting of AUSTRALIA, NEW ZEALAND, Papua NEW GUINEA and various PACIFIC islands, Australasia (also Oceania) has an area of 8510 sq km (3285 sq miles) and 24,000,000 people (1984 est.). The original inhabitants include Australian ABORIGINES; Melanesians, such as the people of

Papua New Guinea; Micronesians; and Polynesians, such as the MAORIS. Most Australians and New Zealanders are now of European descent.

AUSTRALIA The largest country in Oceania, Australia is sometimes regarded as a continent in itself. There are three main land regions. The mineral-rich Western Plateau is a dry tableland with some mountain ranges. The Central Plains are flat and mostly dry. Water for livestock comes from artesian wells which tap water-bearing rocks beneath the surface. The Eastern Highlands run from Cape York in the north to VICTORIA and TASMANIA in the south. The mostly narrow eastern coastlands are Australia's most densely-populated region. Northern Australia is warm all the year round. The south has warm summers, but winters are cooler. About two-thirds of Australia is too dry for farming.

Australia is thinly-populated. About 90 per cent of the people live in urban areas and the four largest cities, SYDNEY, MELBOURNE, BRISBANE and ADELAIDE, contain over half of Australia's people. Many Australians are descendants of British immigrants but, since 1945, many immigrants from other parts of Europe have arrived. The first Australians were probably the Tasmanian Aborigines, who died out in 1876. The Australian ABORIGINES now number about 100,000.

The economy was first based on farming. Wool, beef and dairy products are still important items. Only two per cent of the land is under crops, but yields are high and crops are varied. Manufacturing and mining now dominate the economy. Australia is one of the world's chief mineral producers. Bauxite, iron ore and lead are leading exports.

In the early 1600s, the Dutch explored the north and west coasts and, in 1642, Abel TASMAN (1603–59) discovered Tasmania. But

AUSTRALIA: FACTS AND FIGURES
Area: 7,686,849 sq km (2,967,909 sq miles).
Population: 16,200,000 (1987 est.)
Capital: Canberra.
Highest peak: Mt Kosciuski, 2230 m (7316 ft), in the Australian Alps, New South Wales.
Longest river: Darling, 2739 km (1702 miles) long.

STATES
Australian Capital Terr: pop. 230,800; capital, Canberra.
New South Wales: Pop. 5,437,000; capital, Sydney.
Northern Territory: Pop. 126,300, capital, Darwin.
Queensland: Pop. 2,505,000; capital, Brisbane.
South Australia: Pop. 1,353,000; capital, Adelaide.
Tasmania: Pop. 440,000; capital, Hobart.
Victoria: Pop. 4,076,000; capital, Melbourne.
Western Australia: Pop. 1,383,000; capital, Perth.

▼ Right to left: Past the eastern Pacific coast of Australia, the land rises to form the Great Dividing Range. Rain falling on the highlands collects beneath the dry central plains. To the west the land is desert.

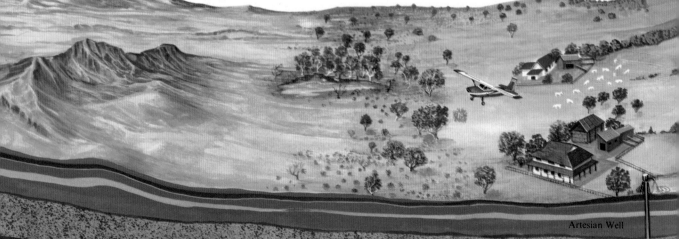

Artesian Well

A colony of European wild rabbits was released in Australia in the 1850s as a source of food and skins. These rabbits multiplied and spread so quickly that they became a serious threat to the country's sheep- and cattle-grazing lands. It was not until after World War II that the introduction of the virus disease myxomatosis almost completely wiped out Australia's rabbit population. But eventually some rabbits developed an immunity to the disease and new, more powerful, kinds of myxomatosis virus had to be developed. The use of these and poisoned baits are now keeping the rabbits in check.

AUSTRIA: FACTS AND FIGURES
Highest point: Grossglockner 3798 m (12,462 ft).
Principal rivers: Danube and Inn.
Language: German.
Religion: Roman Catholic.
Currency: Schilling.

AZORES: FACTS AND FIGURES
Area: 2390 sq km (922 sq miles).
Highest point: Pico, 2320 m (7612 ft), on Pico Island. The Azores are about 640 km (400 miles) long, and are only about 2092 km (1300 miles) from Cape Grace, Newfoundland.

the Dutch lost interest and it was the Briton Captain James COOK (1728–79) who first explored the fertile east coast in 1770. In 1788 Britain set up a convict settlement on the site of Sydney and, in 1793, the first free settlers arrived (see BRITISH EMPIRE). In 1901 Australia became an independent Commonwealth. Ties with Britain were strong. But, recently, Australia has diversified its trade and established strong links with the USA and nations in Asia. ◁

AUSTRIA A federal republic in south-central EUROPE. Austria has 7,552,000 people (1979 est.) and an area of 83,849 sq km (32,374 sq miles). The capital is VIENNA, a historic city which is the chief industrial centre. Austria is a land-locked, mountainous nation. Alpine mountain ranges cover about three-quarters of the country. The lowest land is in the north, where the DANUBE valley is the most important farming region. Austria is sandwiched between East and West Europe. But it has remained neutral and does not belong to any military alliances. ◁

AUTOMATION Originally, production by self-operating machines that reduced the need for human operators. Today automation is applied to such widely differing things as piloting aircraft, controlling traffic, and updating bank balances.

AYERS ROCK The world's largest rock, in central Australia. It is about 9 km (6 miles) around its base and 335 metres (1100 ft) high.

AZORES Nine Portuguese islands, 1200 km (750 miles) west of PORTUGAL in the Atlantic. The Azores gained partial autonomy in 1976. Population: 290,000. Capital: Ponta Delgada. ◁

▲ The massive Ayers Rock stands alone in the flat central plains of Australia.

AZTECS A tribe of Mexican Indians who lived in what is now Mexico City (then Tenochtitlán) at the time of the Spanish conquest (1520). (See CORTÉS, HERNANDO; CONQUISTADORS). The Aztecs then ruled an empire that covered a huge area in southern MEXICO. Though they had neither the wheel nor beasts of burden such as the horse, their civilization was quite advanced. They developed a solar calendar of 18 20-day months plus 5 'empty days', forming the 365-day year. Aztec life centred around religion. They had many gods and believed in 13 heavens and 9 underworlds. Carvings of the plumed serpent-god, Quetzalcoatl, decorated many of their walls and temples. Aztec ceremonial dress was richly adorned with gold, silver and exotic feathers. The Aztecs built great pyramids with broad stairways leading to the temple-shrine at the top. There many humans were sacrificed during their religious rites, usually by having their heart cut out.

Water-bearing Rock

B

BABOON A large MONKEY of Africa and Arabia with a muzzle like that of a dog. Baboons live in bands of ten to over a hundred animals and are fast runners on all fours because their front and hind legs are about the same length. They live chiefly on fruit, insects and roots, but the herds, especially the males, can be fierce fighters, and have been known to attack a lion. The ancient Egyptians worshipped the baboon as a sacred animal.

BABY The newborn human baby is quite helpless compared to the young of other animals. It depends on others for everything it needs to keep it alive – food, protection and warmth. The average newborn baby is 51 cm (20 in) long and weighs between 2.5 and 3.5 kg (6 and 8 lb). By the end of the first year a healthy child usually triples its birth weight.

Doctors agree that breast milk is the ideal food for a baby; the baby is usually fed for the first time 12 to 24 hours after it is born.

During the first few weeks a baby will respond to sounds and light, but it cannot recognize voices for several weeks. It can recognize faces some time after 4 months. Infants may speak a few words towards the end of the first year, can sit up at about 6 or 7 months, crawl at 10 months and take their first few steps at about 12 months.

In the year 1900, about a quarter of all babies born in Western European countries died before they were a year old. Now only about 3 per cent of babies die during that first year. (See REPRODUCTION)

BABYLON AND BABYLONIA Babylon was an ancient city, capital of Babylonia, a region that occupied the fertile area between the rivers Euphrates and Tigris in what is now called IRAQ. The most famous Babylonian king was Hammurabi (1711–1669 BC). He drew up a code of law for his people which covered an enormous range of subjects, including the legal rights of women and children. Hammurabi was a scholar and poet and built up an enormous library.

Babylonian records were written in cuneiform writing on soft clay tablets. Cuneiform takes its name from the wedge-shaped marks made by the reed stilus (pen) on the clay.

After Hammurabi's death various tribes sacked and conquered Babylon. In 626 BC a new empire had been established in Babylonia. This Chaldean empire reached its peak under Nebuchadnezzar (606–562 BC) who built magnificent temples, palaces and the Hanging Gardens of Babylon, one of the Seven Wonders of the ancient world. By 540

▼ *The most ferocious-looking member of the baboon family is the male mandrill. The vivid colours on its face and fur act as a warning signal to other animals.*

46

▲ Badgers are peaceful animals, although they can be fierce fighters when threatened. They are also among the most playful of all animals. Often the whole family will come out for evening games.

BACON Francis Bacon was one of the first people to experiment with refrigeration. In 1626 he tried to preserve the flesh of a chicken by stuffing the (dead) bird with snow. Unfortunately he caught a chill during the experiment and died from it soon afterwards.

BADEN-POWELL During the Boer War, Baden-Powell defended the town of Mafeking for 217 days when it was besieged by South African (Boer) guerillas. The relief of Mafeking in May, 1900, made 'B-P' into a British national hero overnight. In 1908 he chose the motto of the South African Constabulary – 'Be Prepared' – as that of his new Boy Scout movement.

BC the whole of Babylonia was ruled by Cyrus the Great, King of Persia. (See ARCHITECTURE; ASTRONOMY)

BACH J. S. Johann Sebastian Bach (1685–1750), one of the greatest composers of all time, was born in Eisenach, Germany, to a family of musicians. His composing life can be divided into three parts. The first began in 1708 when he was appointed organist at the court of Weimar. There he composed much of his great organ music. The second period was spent at the court of Cöthen (1717–23) where he composed most of his orchestral music, including the Brandenburg concertos. In the third period from 1723 he composed most of his choral masterpieces, the *Passions* and the great *B Minor Mass*.

BACON, FRANCIS English philosopher and statesman (1561–1626). Bacon thought that scientists should study things as they really are in nature. Then they should try to work out what caused something to be as it is. This is how modern scientists work. ◁

BACON, ROGER Early English scientist (c. 1214–c. 1294). He taught that it is better to see for yourself than accept without question what other people tell you. He made a powerful magnifying glass and showed how glasses can be used to help people with weak sight. He foretold that ships would be driven by engines and that machines would fly.

BACTERIA Tiny one-celled organisms which belong to the lowest division of the plant kingdom. They can be seen only with a powerful microscope. Bacteria reproduce by dividing their single CELL into two identical parts. Some bacteria cause diseases, but many others are helpful to man. They are found almost everywhere – in the air, in the soil and in the depths of the ocean.

When an animal or plant dies, bacteria consume the dead matter and eventually return it to the soil. Bacteria also purify sewage and make cheese and yogurt. But others turn meat rotten, sour milk and make butter rancid.

Parasitic bacteria cause many diseases of man, including tuberculosis, diphtheria, pneumonia, typhoid and various kinds of BLOOD poisoning. These harmful bacteria are what we call germs, and they can be controlled by antibiotics such as PENICILLIN and by VACCINES. (See ANTISEPTICS; BOTANY)

BADEN-POWELL, ROBERT Founder of the BOY SCOUT movement in 1908, Baden-Powell (1857–1941), with his sister Agnes, also started the Girl Guides in 1910. ◁

BADGER A short-legged burrowing animal about 1 metre (3 ft) long. Its coat looks grey from a distance, but the hairs are actually black and white. The most striking feature is

Bad

the black and white striped head. Badgers are carnivorous creatures but they also eat a variety of plant food. They excavate large burrows (setts) which they leave only at night.

▷

BADMINTON A tennis-like game played with light rackets and a feathered shuttlecock across a high net within a rectangular court. It comes from an ancient game called 'battledore and shuttlecock' which was brought to England from India in about 1870. The name comes from Badminton, Gloucestershire, the home of the Duke of Beaufort who laid down the rules for the game in 1877.

BAGHDAD The capital of IRAQ, Baghdad has 3,800,000 people. This Moslem city an important route centre in ancient times. The modern city was founded in AD 762.

BAGPIPE One of the oldest musical instruments in the world, the bagpipe consists of two or more reeded pipes and a leather bag that is inflated with air breathed into it by the player or from bellows. The bagpipe dates from as early as 1000 BC. Today it is most often associated with Scottish music.

BAHAMAS An island group in the ATLANTIC OCEAN off the south-eastern USA. Independent since 1973, the Bahamas attract tourists because of the warm winter climate and fine beaches ▷

BAHRAIN An island and independent state in the Persian Gulf whose wealth is based on oil discovered in the desert in 1932. ▷

BAIKAL, LAKE The world's deepest freshwater lake. It is in central SIBERIA, USSR, and is fed by 300 streams. The maximum depth is 1741 metres (5712 ft) and it is 627 km (390 miles) long.

BAKING POWDER A white powder used to make cakes and scones light and spongy. It contains sodium bicarbonate (baking soda) and an acid – usually tartaric acid – which act together to make the dough rise when liquid is added.

BALANCE A device that weighs things. Balances used in laboratories include the single-pan and two-pan chemical balance. In the two-pan balance a pan is suspended at each end of the bar. A pointer, attached to the centre of the bar, swings across a scale as the bar moves up and down. The substance to be weighed is placed in one pan and weights are added to the other pan until the pointer remains motionless at zero. Some balances are enclosed in glass cases to protect them from draughts and moisture.

▲ *Europeans, particularly from the colder, northern countries, flock to the Balearic islands in summer to enjoy the beautiful Mediterranean weather and many fine beaches.*

BALBOA, VASCO NUÑEZ DE Spanish explorer and CONQUISTADOR (1475–1517) who was the first European to see the Pacific Ocean.

BALEARIC ISLANDS An archipelago and Spanish province in the MEDITERRANEAN. The four large islands are Majorca, Minorca, Ibiza and Formentera. The islands are popular tourist resorts. The capital is Palma, on Majorca. Area: 5014 sq km (1936 sq miles); population: 655,910 ▷

BALKANS This mainly mountainous region consists of ALBANIA, BULGARIA, GREECE, European TURKEY and most of YUGOSLAVIA. Politically, it was an unstable region in the late 1800s and early 1900s, because it contains a great variety of peoples, languages and religions.

BALLET The most important form of stage dancing today is ballet. Early ballets were performed as part of court entertainments in the 16th century in Italy and France. During the 1600s ballet developed quickly in France under Louis XIV, who encouraged the ballet and founded a dancing school in Paris. Women dancers did not appear on stage until 1681, although the ladies of Louis' court appeared in court ballets before that. Modern ballet really began during the late 1700s with the French ballet master Jean Georges Noverre, who made ballet a five-act DANCE drama.

BALLET British ballet has become world famous, largely through the efforts of Marie Rambert and Ninette de Valois. Marie Rambert established the Ballet Rambert; Ninette de Valois became head of the Vic-Wells Ballet in 1933, with Alicia Markova as its leading dancer. The Vic-Wells Ballet moved from Sadler's Wells to Covent Garden and later became the Royal Ballet, with Frederick Ashton as its chief choreographer and artistic director. Margot Fonteyn made her début at Sadler's Wells in 1935 when she was 16 years of age.

THE BALLET

arabesque Position in which dancer stands on one leg with arms extended, body bent forward from hips, while other leg is stretched out backwards.

ballerina Female ballet dancer.

barre Exercise bar fixed to classroom wall at hip level; dancers grasp it when exercising.

battement Beating movement made by raising and lowering leg, sideways, backwards, or forwards.

corps de ballet Main group of ballet dancers, as distinct from soloists.

entrechat Leap in which dancer rapidly strikes heels together in air.

fouetté Turn in which dancer whips free leg round.

glissade Gliding movement.

jeté Leap from one foot to another.

pas Any dance step.

pas de deux Dance for two.

pas seule Solo dance.

pirouette Movement in which dancer spins completely round on one foot.

positions Five positions of feet on which ballet is based (see illustrations).

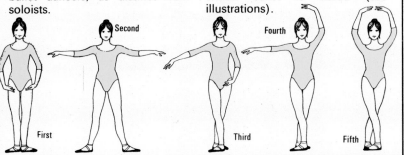

First, Second, Third, Fourth, Fifth

▲ *A ballet class at an English Royal Ballet Company school. Dancers have to practise daily to keep their bodies in top condition.*

The romantic period of ballet followed (1830–1870), during which such famous ballets as *Les Sylphides*, *Giselle* and *Coppelia* were written.

France was the main home of the ballet until the late 1800s, when the Russian ballet became supreme. The Russian impresario Sergei Diaghilev introduced the Russian ballet to other parts of Europe in the early 1900s. Since his death (1929) great national ballet companies have grown up in many countries.

Ballet dancers today must begin their training by the time they are 10 years old. They must practise hard for the whole of their careers. After they stop dancing, many become teachers or choreographers (dance arrangers). ◁

BALLISTICS The science dealing with the propulsion and flight path of projectiles, such as rockets, bullets and shells. *Interior* ballistics is concerned with propulsion techniques. *Exterior* ballistics deals with flight paths, or trajectories. The shape of a bullet's trajectory resembles a PARABOLA.

BALLOONS The first lighter-than-air craft to carry man through the air was the hot-air balloon built by Joseph and Etienne Montgolfier, which carried its pilot, Pilâtre de Rozier, to a height of 25 metres (84 ft) for four minutes on October 15, 1783. The first hydrogen balloon, built by the French physicist J. A. C. Charles, made a 43-km (27-mile) journey in December of the same year. In 1785 the American Dr Jeffries and the French pioneer Jean-Pierre Blanchard successfully crossed the English Channel by balloon.

Ballooning gained popularity during the 19th century, when balloons were used by showmen, scientists interested in weather research, and as military observation posts. Today ballooning is a popular sport as well as an important tool for scientific research. Balloons equipped with sophisticated instruments (*radio-sondes*) investigate conditions in the upper atmosphere and send the information back to scientists on Earth. ▷

BAMBOO Giant GRASS (30 metres – 100 ft high) growing in tropical lands, especially in south-east Asia. Bamboos have many uses: their shoots are eaten as vegetables and their hollow woody stems are used for building houses, constructing tools and furniture and for making paper. ▷

BANANA A soft pulpy fruit with a thick skin which turns yellow when ripe. They grow in bunches from tall plants, and are cultivated in most tropical countries. The banana is rich in CARBOHYDRATES.

BANDICOOT A rat-like MARSUPIAL of New Guinea and Australia. Bandicoots are nocturnal insectivores, and range in size from 9 cm to 60 cm (3.5 in to 23.5 in) in length. ▷

▲ *One of the first flights in a hot-air balloon, over the palace at Versailles in 1783.*

▼ *Below left: A modern hot-air balloon. These balloons carry cylinders of gas to provide the heat to make the balloon rise.*

▼ *Bandicoots use their claws and snout to dig up their food of roots and insects from the forest floor. They live in nests built from sticks and grass.*

BALLOONS Although the first manned flight took place in October 1783, earlier in that same year the Montgolfier brothers launched a trial balloon. In it were a duck, a sheep and a hen. The balloon made a successful flight; when the hot air in the balloon cooled, it floated gently down to earth, the gondola smashed open, and the three animals stepped out, unharmed.

In order to stay aloft during the first ever airborne crossing of the English Channel in 1785, Jean-Pierre Blanchard and Dr. John Jeffries were forced to undress and throw all but their underwear overboard.

On May 21, 1972, a toy balloon was released at Atherton, California. It finally came to rest 20 days later at Pietermaritzburg, South Africa.

BAMBOO Some species of bamboo grow at a rate of over 90 cms (35 inches) a day. One species can grow to a height of 36 m (118 ft), with a stem nearly one metre round.

BANDICOOT This Australasian marsupial was named after an Indian rat (as big as a cat and very destructive), which it resembles.

BANGLADESH: FACTS AND FIGURES
Main rivers: Ganges, Brahmaputra, and Meghna.
Highest point: The Chittagong Hills rise to a height of 1230 m (4034 ft).
Currency: Taka.
Official language: Bengali.
Religion: Moslem, with Buddhist, Hindu and Christian minorities.
Climate: Tropical, with heavy rains from June to September.

BANKS The world's first banknotes were issued in China about AD 1170, at a time when copper was scarce and not enough coins could be minted. In Europe, the first paper money was issued by the Bank of Sweden in 1661. The Bank of England's first – handwritten – notes were circulated in 1694.

The biggest bank vault in the world is in the Chase Manhattan Building, New York City. It weighs 1,000 tonnes and has doors weighing about 45 tonnes that can be easily closed with one finger.

BARBADOS The Portuguese named this island Los Barbados ('bearded') because of the abundance of bearded (or moss-hung) fig trees. Nowadays, Barbados is the most densely populated of the West Indian islands, with 576 people per sq km. The majority of Barbadians are descendants of slaves brought from Africa to work the island's plantations, on which the chief exports of sugar, molasses and rum depend. The tiny coral island is only 34 km (21 miles) long and 23 km (14 miles) wide.

BANGLADESH Formerly the eastern part of PAKISTAN, Bangladesh became an independent republic in 1971, after a war. It has 96,730,000 people and an area of 143,998 sq km (55,598 sq miles). The capital of this flat, wet nation is Dacca. Most people are farmers, but there is much poverty. ◁

BANJO A stringed instrument related to the guitar, introduced into America by slaves from West Africa and associated with black 'minstrel' music and jazz.

BANKS Businesses that specialize in handling MONEY. Many types of financial institution are called banks, including commercial banks, central banks (such as the Bank of England), and merchant banks. Commercial banks, the most common, accept deposits and loan money to individuals, businesses, and even government. ◁

BANTU A group of people living in central and southern AFRICA who all speak one of the Bantu languages. There are about 70 million Bantus of many different tribes, and hundreds of Bantu languages, including Swahili and ZULU.

BAPTISTS A Christian denomination (founded 1609) which believes that baptism should be actively sought by the believer. The method of baptism is usually total immersion.

BARBADOS An island in the WEST INDIES. Part of the British Commonwealth, it became independent in 1966. Population: 252,000; capital: Bridgetown. ◁

BARBITURATES Organic chemical com-

▼ There are about 1000 known species of barnacle. The young swim about freely, but the adult attaches itself to an underwater surface, such as the side of a whale or fish, a rock, or even the bottom of a ship.

pounds that are salts of barbituric acid. Many barbiturates are powerful drugs used for their hypnotic, sedative or anaesthetic properties. Short-acting barbiturates are effective for three to six hours, intermediate-acting types for six to ten hours, and long-acting types for eight to twenty-four hours.

BARIUM An extremely reactive silver-white metal used in many ALLOYS. The compound barium sulphate blocks X-RAYS. It is given to patients before X-ray examination to show up the digestive tract.

BARK Outer covering of a TREE trunk or branch. Each year the protective layer of CORK surrounding the trunk dies off and a new cork layer forms just inside the old. The dead layer is the bark. As the years go by, the bark thickens with the addition of further dead layers. Many barks are used for tanning and dyeing and in making medicines.

BARLEY Hardy CEREAL distinguished by its beard – long whiskers growing from the end of the grain sheath. Barley is cultivated mainly for animal feeding but the best grain is used to make malt for brewing beer.

BARNACLE CRUSTACEAN existing in millions along the coast. The barnacle lives inside a shell and is attached by its head to an underwater object such as a rock or ship's hull. It puts out feathery legs which comb the water for food.

BAROMETER Instrument for measuring atmospheric pressure, usually in connection with WEATHER FORECASTING. The *aneroid* barometer contains an evacuated metal capsule

▼ An aneroid barometer

Partially Evacuated Drum

with flexible sides. Any change in the surrounding air pressure causes the sides to move. This movement is magnified mechanically and used to deflect a needle across a scale calibrated to show atmospheric pressure. In the mercury barometer, the height of a mercury column varies with atmospheric pressure.

BAROQUE ART The term applied to the grand and richly ornamented style of art prevalent in Europe during the 17th and early 18th centuries. The paintings of such artists as Caravaggio in Italy, RUBENS in Antwerp, and VELASQUEZ in Spain made use of the contrast of light and dark, large and imposing figures, rich colour and a naturalistic style to create dramatic works filled with movement and emotion. Religious works glorified the mysticism of the saints and the agonies of the martyrs. Baroque art was closely linked with the magnificent scale of the ARCHITECTURE of the period.

BASEBALL A game, originating in America, that is played with a ball and bat by two teams of nine players each, on a diamond-shaped plot, the sides of the diamond being 27.4 metres (90 ft). The pitching distance is 18.4 metres (60 ft 6 in). ▷

BASKETBALL A game in which two teams of five players each attempt to score points by throwing a ball through one of two metal rings suspended above each end of a rectangular court. The court measures 26 × 14 metres (85 × 46 ft), the baskets 3 metres (10 ft) high, and 45.7 cm (18 in) in diameter.

BASQUES A people who live in the PYRENEES in south-west France and in SPAIN in areas bordering the Bay of Biscay. They are the purest descendants of the original prehistoric people of Europe. Their language is unlike French or Spanish. Many Basques would like a country of their own.

BASSOON A bass wind instrument, one of the double-reed family. It dates from Renaissance times, and has great technical flexibility.

BASS STRAIT The strait that separates TASMANIA from mainland AUSTRALIA. An important shipping route, its width varies from 130 km to 250 km (80 miles to 155 miles).

BAT The only true flying mammal. Bats are mouse-like with large, leathery wings. They usually spend the day asleep, hanging upside down by their feet, then come out at night for food. Some types of bat eat insects, others feed off fruit. Fruit-eating bats see well in the dark, but the insect-eaters have poor vision so,

▲ The vampire bat feeds on the blood of mammals, such as cattle and large birds.

instead of relying on their eyes, they emit a stream of high-pitched sounds and find their way – and their food – by echo location. ▷

BATHYSCAPHE An underwater vessel invented by the Swiss physicist Auguste Piccard for exploring the ocean depths. Designed as the underwater counterpart of a balloon or airship, it descended over 9 km (6 miles) in 1953. ▷

BATTERY An arrangement of cells for producing an electric current. Usually, the current is generated by chemical action. *Primary* cells are useless when they have run down. But *secondary* cells can be recharged and used again and again. This is because the chemical reactions that take place in secondary cells are reversible. In the recharging process, a current from another source is passed through the cells. This restores the chemicals to their

▼ The US Navy bathyscaphe Trieste. *In 1960 Trieste descended to the world's deepest part of the ocean bed, a depth of 10,912 metres (35,802 ft). The descent took 4¾ hours.*

BASEBALL Although baseball is regarded as America's national game, it is not only played in the US. It is a major spectator sport in Japan and Latin America, has strong support in several European countries and is also played in Australia.

Alexander J. Cartright drew up the basis for the game's rules in 1845. The following year, his team (the New York Knickerbockers) played the first game under his rules. They went down 23-1 to the New York Baseball Club in a 4-innings game.

BAT With their acute hearing, bats can detect sound waves vibrating at a frequency of 50,000 vibrations a second. This means that the waves are very high pitched. The human ear can only detect up to about 20,000 vibrations a second.

Copper Disc

Salt Impregnated Cloth

Zinc Disc

▲ The voltaic pile was the first battery. It was invented by Alessandro Volta. He found that a layer of salt-impregnated cloth, sandwiched between layers of zinc and copper, produced an electric current.

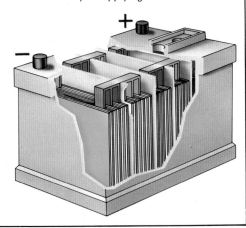

▼ Most car batteries consist of six lead-acid cells connected in series. Each cell gives about 2 volts, so the whole battery gives about 12 volts. Unlike a simple cell, the lead-acid battery can be recharged when it runs down. To do this, a current is sent through it in the opposite direction to the flow that occurs when the battery is supplying a current.

BATHYSCAPHE *Trieste*, the US Navy's steel bathyscaphe, descended to a record 10,912 m (35,802 ft) in 1960. There was a danger that the vessel would collapse if it went any deeper, as by then the pressure had built up to more than 1 tonne per square centimetre. All-glass bathyscaphes are now being developed which will be able to go even deeper underwater.

BAYEAUX TAPESTRY No one is certain exactly when this tapestry was made. However, most scholars agree that it was within memory of the Norman Conquest, perhaps around the year 1080. At one point on the tapestry the 'caption' says that the illustration shows the death of King Harold of England. The scene is of one soldier with an arrow in his eye and another being cut down by a mounted French knight. The English have long preferred to think of the former victim as the King and the latter as one of his bodyguards. However, a French history written in 1068 clearly states that the English King was cut down by four horsemen, and not killed with an arrow in his eye.

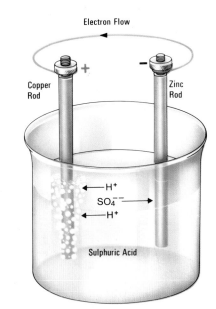

Electron Flow

Copper Rod

Zinc Rod

H^+
SO_4^{--}
H^+

Sulphuric Acid

▲ A simple cell consists of two electrodes, in this case a copper rod and a zinc rod, immersed in an electrolyte of weak sulphuric acid. The chemicals in the acid are split up into charged particles – hydrogen ions (H) which are positive and sulphate ions (SO_4) which are negative. Positive zinc ions go into the electrolyte from the zinc electrode, leaving the electrode with too many electrons – it is negative. These excess electrons flow round the wire to the copper rod, which becomes negative and attracts the positive hydrogen ions. These form bubbles of hydrogen gas on the copper electrode.

original state. The reactions that take place in primary cells cannot be reversed in this way.

In its simplest form, a cell consists of two different electrical CONDUCTORS in a chemical solution called the electrolyte. The chemicals in the solution are split up into charged particles called IONS. Negative ions have an excess of electrons (negative charges), and positive ions have a deficiency of electrons. In the cell, negative ions go to one electrode and positive ions go to the other one. As a result, one electrode acquires a negative charge and the other becomes positively charged. When a wire or other conductor is connected between the electrodes, a current of electrons flows through it from the negative to the positive electrode. (See ELECTRICITY AND MAGNETISM; ELECTROLYSIS)

BATTLESHIP A large, heavily armoured naval ship with batteries of guns. The first ironclad warship was launched in 1860; in 1906 the most famous battleship, Britain's HMS *Dreadnought*, appeared. After World War II the battleship was retired in favour of faster, more manoeuvrable craft. (See SHIPS)

BAYEAUX TAPESTRY Nearly 70 metres (230 ft) long, the Bayeaux TAPESTRY was made in the 11th century. It tells the story of the invasion of England by WILLIAM THE CONQUEROR. ◁

BEAN Plant with long pods containing kidney-shaped seeds (beans). Beans are grown as a vegetable for man and a fodder crop for cattle. The main varieties are broad beans, runner beans – with edible pods – and kidney beans; a type of kidney bean – the navy bean – is used for baked beans. (See SOYBEAN)

BEAR Heavily-built animal with strong limbs, thick fur but small eyes and ears; although carnivorous, it also eats a lot of fruit and vegetables. Bears live in many parts of the world. The most common species is the Brown

▼ The huge Kodiak bear of North America was once worshipped as a god by some American Indian tribes.

▲ The Beatles at the peak of their influence on popular music in 1967.

bear, found in North America, eastern Europe and the Himalayas. Two kinds of American brown bear, the Alaskan Kodiak and the Grizzly are huge: they can reach 3 metres (10 ft) in length and weigh over 750 kg (1650 lbs). The creamy Polar bear is adapted to life in the Arctic: hair on the soles of its feet provides insulation and a sure grip on the ice; also, its front paws are part-webbed to help it swim. Various Black bears live in North America and Asia; they are smaller and often good tree-climbers. The only bear in South America is the Spectacled bear, so named because of white rings round its eyes.

BEARINGS Devices used in machines and vehicles to support turning shafts. Bearings

▼ A beaver's lodge. If the water is too shallow for a lodge the beavers build a dam. Their living chamber is above the water level and is reached through underwater tunnels.

are designed to allow rotation with a minimum of FRICTION. This increases efficiency by reducing energy losses. Ball and roller bearings are the most common types. Both provide rolling action between the shaft and the housing on which it is mounted.

BEATLES, THE British rock group which greatly influenced the popular music of the 1960s. Its members were John Lennon, Paul McCartney, George Harrison and Ringo Starr (Richard Starkey). ▷

BEAVER Amphibious animal found in northern Europe and North America. Weighing up to 40 kg (88 lb) and about 1 metre (40 in) long, beavers are the world's second largest rodent. They are skilled engineers: with their sharp teeth they cut down trees to build dams

BEATLES The Beatles are the most successful popular music group ever, in terms of recorded sales. By 1985 some 1000 million records, tapes and CDs of their music had been sold, even though the group disbanded in 1970.

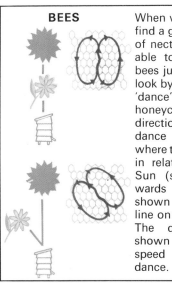

BEES When worker bees find a good source of nectar, they are able to tell other bees just where to look by means of a 'dance' on the honeycombs. The direction of the dance shows where the source is in relation to the Sun (straight towards the Sun is shown by a verticle line on the comb). The distance is shown by the speed of the dance.

Most bees are solitary, but some species are social: they live in colonies and each insect works for the good of the whole community. A bee colony is ruled by the queen who does nothing but lay eggs. Most of the other bees – as many as 60,000 – are infertile females called 'workers' whose job is to build and clean the nest, collect food, make honey and look after the young. There are also some males – 'drones' – whose only task is to mate with the queen. Two common social species are the large, hairy bumble bee and the smaller honey bee, often kept in hives.

BEETHOVEN, LUDWIG VAN German composer and musician (1770–1827) who wrote some of the world's greatest music, particularly for symphony orchestra. He wrote nine symphonies, six concertos, plus numerous works for chamber ensemble and solo piano. ◁

BEETLE The INSECT world is divided into some thirty groups or 'orders'; the largest group consists of beetles. There are over 250,000 species of beetle in the world. Like most other insects they have three body segments, three pairs of legs, two pairs of wings and a pair of antennae – for feeling and smelling. Unlike other insects, the first pair of wings is hard and is not used to fly but to protect the second pair. Beetles have strong biting jaws and, although they do not hurt man, some kinds are harmful in other ways; the black and yellow Colorado beetle ruins entire potato crops while the Death Watch beetle destroys old buildings by attacking the timber. But other species, such as LADYBIRDS, help man by eating insect pests. Some beetles are land animals but others are aquatic. Their life cycle is like the BUTTERFLY'S: egg, larva, chrysalis, adult. ◁

BEIJING formerly spelled Peking, is the capital of China. It has a population of 9,330,000. The Imperial City in the centre of Beijing was once open only to the emperor and his family. It is now a vast museum.

BEETHOVEN Following in his father's (and grandfather's) footsteps, young Ludwig became a musician at an early age. He had a piece of piano music published when he was 12 years old, and gave his first public performance soon afterwards. In 1792, he went to Vienna to study under Haydn, but in 1801 he began to lose his hearing. By 1820, Beethoven was stone deaf, but he had managed to complete his 9th (and final) symphony. In the last years of his life however, he composed another five quartets – hearing the music only in his mind.

BEETLE The world's largest beetle is the Goliath beetle which weighs up to 96 g (3.4 oz) and may measure up to 12 cm (4¾ in) in length.

across streams; then, in the pond created by the dam, they construct their house or 'lodge' using branches and mud.

BECKET, THOMAS À An English churchman, Chancellor and Archbishop of Canterbury. St Thomas à Becket (1118–1170) quarrelled with HENRY II and was murdered in Canterbury Cathedral.

BEDOUIN ARAB people belonging to nomadic tribes, each tribe ruled by a sheik. The Bedouins live in Iraq, Jordan, Saudi Arabia and North Africa.

BEE Winged insect belonging to the same group as ants and wasps. Bees live on POLLEN and nectar which they collect from flowers; while doing this, they cause pollination – vital for the growth of seeds and fruit. In this way, bees are useful to man. They are also useful for their HONEY which they make from the nectar.

▼ The Hercules beetle lives in the rain forests of South America. It is one of the world's largest beetles.

▼ The elm bark beetle tunnels under the bark of elm trees. It spreads the fungus which causes Dutch elm disease, a disease which has killed huge numbers of elm trees in Europe and North America.

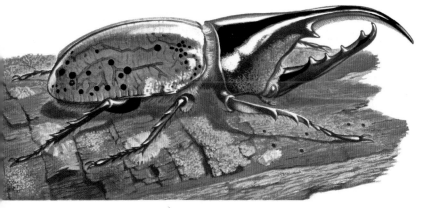

◀ Antwerp, Belgium's chief seaport, has many graceful buildings such as these in the main square.

▶ Alexander Graham Bell, making the first call on the New York to Chicago telephone line in 1892.

▼ After World War II, West Berlin was divided into three sectors, under the control of the US, Britain and France; although in fact it is governed by West Germany. Severely bombed during the war, West Berlin has made an amazing economic recovery. Today, it is one of the leading industrial centres of western Europe.

BELGIUM A European monarchy, Belgium has 9,884,000 people (1985 est.) and an area of 30,513 sq km (11,781 sq miles). The capital is Brussels. Belgium is a rich industrial nation. Flemish is spoken in the north; French in the south; and German in the south-east. ▷

BELL The name for a wide variety of vessel-shaped percussion instruments made of metal. The sound is produced when the vessel is struck by a hammer, or clapper. Bells are as old as civilization, dating from Assyrian times (3000 years ago) or earlier. For centuries most bells were made of bronze. In Europe bell-making was revived about the 8th century and from the 14th century on there were many master bellmakers who cast bells, or groups of bells with varying tones (called *carillons*), for churches. ▷

BELL, ALEXANDER GRAHAM Scottish-American inventor who perfected the TELE-PHONE (1847–1922). The first public demonstration of the telephone was given in 1876. In 1878 he founded the (American) Bell Telephone Company.

BELLBIRD The name given to three species of bird: the crested bellbird (*Oreoica gutteralis*) and the bell minor (*Manorina melanophrys*) of Australia, and *Anthornis melanura* of New Zealand.

BELLINI, GIOVANNI A leading painter of the Italian RENAISSANCE (c. 1430–1516), one of a famous family of artists. Bellini painted many fine religious works. TITIAN was one of his pupils.

BENZ, KARL German engineer and automobile pioneer (1844–1929) who produced the first petrol-powered MOTOR CAR in 1885.

BERBERS The original inhabitants of North AFRICA who are Caucasoid racially and Moslem by religion. Berber tribes include the Riffs, the Kabyles of Algeria, and the nomadic Tuaregs of the Sahara.

BERLIN A divided city in GERMANY. East Berlin (population 1,098,000) is the capital of the German Democratic Republic (East Germany). West Berlin (population 1,985,000) is part of the Federal Republic of Germany (West Germany), although it is completely enclosed by East Germany.

▶ Designed by Karl Benz in 1893, this 2¾ horsepower Benz 'Velo' was the first motor car to be produced in quantity.

BELGIUM: FACTS AND FIGURES
Highest point: Botrange, 694 m (2277 ft).
Longest river: Schelde-Meuse, 925 km (575 miles) long.
Official languages: Dutch (Flemish), French, German.
Currency: Belgian franc.
Religion: Roman Catholic.

BELL There are many old European superstitions connected with church bells. Their ringing was believed to purify the air and disperse plague; to drive away a dead person's ghost at a funeral; to halt storms and lightning. In the Middle Ages, new church bells were given gifts and specially consecrated. Afterwards, everyone celebrated.

BERMUDA This is just one of a group of about 300 islands, known as the Bermudas. The group was discovered in 1515 by a Spaniard, Juan Bermudez. The first inhabitants were British colonists under Sir George Somers, who were shipwrecked there *en route* for North America in 1609.

BIBLE The word 'bible' comes from the name of an ancient town in the Lebanon called Byblos, which is just north of modern Beirut. Long ago, this was one of the chief markets and export centres in the Mediterranean area for papyrus – a paper-like material made from reeds, on which early books were written. Byblos was thriving by 2500 BC, and archaeologists believe that the first alphabet was probably developed there around 1500 BC.

BERLIOZ, LOUIS HECTOR French composer of the Romantic movement (1803–1869) who wrote works on a vast scale for orchestra.

BERMUDA A British colony in the North ATLANTIC, Bermuda has 79 000 people. The main industry is tourism. Area: 53 sq km (20 sq miles); capital: Hamilton. ◁

BERNINI, GIOVANNI BAROQUE sculptor (1598–1680), famed for carvings full of movement and amazing detail, such as his figure of *David* and those of *Apollo and Daphne*.

BESSEMER PROCESS A STEEL-making process developed in 1856 by British inventor Sir Henry Bessemer (1813–98). The process consists simply of blasting air through molten pig iron to remove impurities. Measured quantities of carbon and other substances are then added to produce the particular type of steel required.

BETA PARTICLES Electrons or POSITRONS emitted by the nuclei of radioactive ATOMS. Streams of beta particles are known as beta rays. Beta particles are created when a neutron changes into a proton, or vice versa.

BETHLEHEM The birthplace of Jesus, today it is a town about five miles south of Jerusalem. (See JESUS CHRIST)

BIBLE The collective name for the sacred scriptures of the Christian religion. The Bible is divided into two main parts: the Old Testament, which contains the history of the Jewish religion; and the New Testament, which deals with the life and work of Christ and the Apostles. The earliest versions of the Old Testament probably date from about 1000 BC; the New Testament was put together in the first two centuries AD. (See APOSTLES; CHRISTIANITY; JESUS CHRIST; JUDAISM) ◁

BICYCLE A lightweight, two-wheeled vehicle driven by power supplied by the rider's leg muscles. The first bicycle was built by a Frenchman, De Sivrac, in about 1790. In 1816 a German, Baron Karl Von Drais, built an improved model called a *draisine*. The early bicycles were propelled by the rider pushing his feet against the ground. Later, pedals were added. The famous penny farthing bicycle had pedals attached to its huge front wheel. By the end of the 1880s, bicycles resembling today's models appeared, with two wheels of equal size; rubber tyres filled with air; ball bearings; gears; and sprung saddles. (See BRAKES)

BILLIARDS An indoor game played with three balls and a long cue, on a rectangular table covered in green baize. Scoring is by pocketing the object or cue ball, or by cannons. (See SNOOKER)

BINARY STARS Pairs of stars that rotate about their common centre of gravity. Gravitational attraction keeps the two stars together (see GRAVITY). About one-third of the star-like objects in the sky are actually binaries. Their separate stars can sometimes be seen through a telescope.

BICYCLES

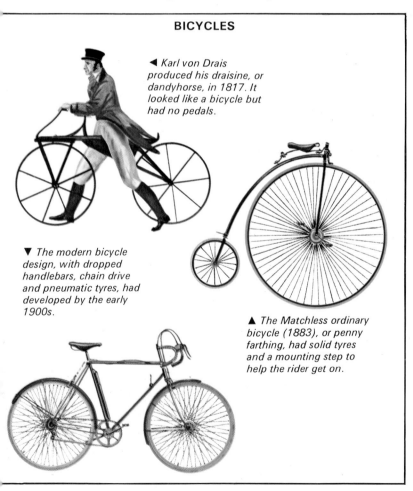

◀ Karl von Drais produced his draisine, or dandyhorse, in 1817. It looked like a bicycle but had no pedals.

▼ The modern bicycle design, with dropped handlebars, chain drive and pneumatic tyres, had developed by the early 1900s.

▲ The Matchless ordinary bicycle (1883), or penny farthing, had solid tyres and a mounting step to help the rider get on.

▼ In a typical binary star system, one star is bigger than the other. They both orbit around a point called the barycentre.

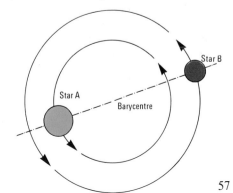

Star A

Star B

Barycentre

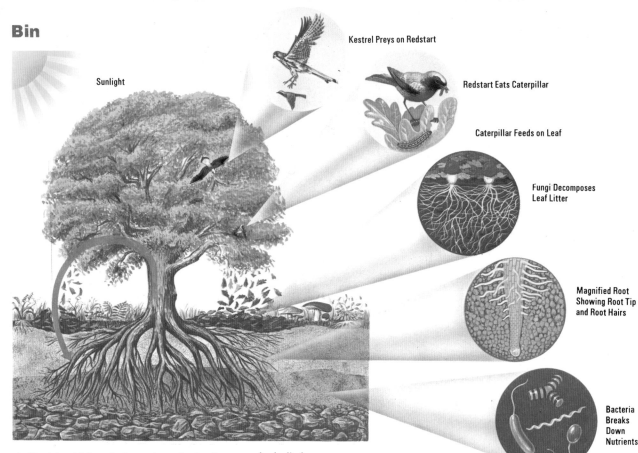

Sunlight

Kestrel Preys on Redstart

Redstart Eats Caterpillar

Caterpillar Feeds on Leaf

Fungi Decomposes
Leaf Litter

Magnified Root
Showing Root Tip
and Root Hairs

Bacteria
Breaks
Down
Nutrients

▲ *Studying biology helps us to understand how all living things relate to each other and to their environment. Plants turn sunlight into energy and it is passed on to animals when they eat the plants. When animals die they decompose (break down into particles) and mix with soil. The energy in the particles, or nutrients, is then re-used by plants. In the diagram above, the roots of the oak tree absorb the nutrients in the soil and re-cycle them. The blue arrow shows how dead leaves from the tree are broken down by fungi and bacteria. The nutrients from the leaves pass into the soil and are absorbed again by the hairs on the roots of the tree. The nutrients give the tree energy to grow new leaves. The caterpillar uses the leaves as food to provide its own energy. This energy then passes on to the redstart bird when it eats the caterpillar. In turn, the redstart is eaten by the kestrel. When the kestrel dies it will return energy to the soil and the cycle will start all over again.*

BINOCULARS Twin optical instruments for use with both eyes. Opera glasses and prismatic binoculars are all forms of binocular TELESCOPES. Binocular MICROSCOPES have twin eyepieces but use only one objective lens.

BIOCHEMISTRY The science which describes the structure and function of living things through the study of their CHEMISTRY. Biochemistry is also used to study the composition, structure and action of foods, drugs, poisons and intoxicants such as beer and other alcoholic beverages.

Some of the earliest biochemical studies of the human body were carried out by Joseph Priestley (1733–1804) and Antoine LAVOISIER (1743–1794), who showed that RESPIRATION is a process of combustion whereby inhaled oxygen is used to 'burn' food into energy. Today biochemists have been able to isolate, identify and often artificially create many of the important chemical substances of the body, such as HORMONES and VITAMINS. Biochemists have also 'designed' new drugs, and their work has been applied to the invention of the artificial kidney and other such life-saving machines. One important branch of biochemistry sprang out of the discovery of antibiotics, used to fight disease. (See BIOLOGY) ▷

BIOLOGICAL CLOCKS Almost all living things have certain natural rhythms which regulate feeding, MIGRATION and other behaviour. When these rhythms appear to be used by a creature to measure the passage of time, they are called biological clocks. They include such things as the opening and closing of flowers, the ability of bees to learn when certain flowers are open, and the skills of navigation shown by migrating birds. ▷

BIOLOGY The science of life. The purpose of biology is to answer the question: What is life? When biologists study a certain plant or animal their aim is not to find out more about

BIOCHEMISTRY A revolutionary step forward in the treatment of disease occured in 1928, when it was discovered – quite by accident – that drugs (later called antibiotics) which were the product of living organisms could be used to combat bacteria. A Scottish scientist, Sir Alexander Fleming, had been growing a bacteria at his laboratory in Paddington, London. He found that the spores of a fungus which blew in through an open window were destroying the bacteria. The fungus was identified as *Penicillium notatum,* and its active ingredient – the antibiotic penicillin – was eventually purified and isolated in 1940 by Sir Howard Florey and Ernst Chain. Since then, many other life-saving antibiotics have been discovered by the world's biochemists.

BIOLOGICAL CLOCKS The bean aphid is so perfectly adapted to natural time that it can either produce live young or lay eggs according to the length of the day and the season of the year. If daylight lasts more than 14 hours 55 minutes, live young are born, to take advantage of the extra warmth; but if the day is shorter, eggs are laid to wait for the next sunrise before hatching.

BIRD The huge, flightless moas of New Zealand were the largest birds that ever lived. Some species stood up to 4 m (13 ft) tall, and they relied for survival on their fast running speed and enormous strength. It is known that moas were still alive around AD1000, when the first Polynesian (Maori) settlers reached New Zealand. However, they died out – or were killed off – soon after, and they are only known to the modern world from their remains which have been found preserved in marshes.

An egg laid by an ostrich – the largest living bird – measures as much as 17 cm x 13 cm (7 in x 5 in), with roughly the same volume as 25 hens' eggs. In contrast, the bee hummingbird – which is the smallest living bird – lays an egg little more than 8 mm ($\frac{1}{3}$ in) in length.

that particular species; it is to find out more about life: how life works, how CELLS function, how organisms (living things) exist, etc. Like any other major science, biology is divided into specialized branches. Some of the most important branches are *taxonomy* – describing plants and animals and arranging them in a logical system; *biogeography* – dividing the world into zones according to its animal and plant life; ECOLOGY – discovering the relationships between living things themselves and between living things and their environment; *anatomy* – studying the structure of organisms, how they are made up; *embryology* – studying the development of organisms, how, for instance, a tiny seed grows into a great tree; *histology* – examining cells as part of an organism; *cytology* – studying the cell itself; and genetics, the science of inheritance – how, for example, a characteristic such as eye colour, is passed down from one generation to another. As well as trying to work out what life is, modern biologists are seeking answers to two other big questions: How did life begin? Does life exist on other planets? (See BIOCHEMISTRY; GENE)

BIONICS – Science that uses living systems as models for new technology. In bionics, biologists and engineers work together: they study the structure and function of certain plants or animals to find new ideas for machines. Developments include a ship's propeller modelled on the tail of a fish and a ground-speed indicator for planes based on the design of a honey bee's eye.

BIRD VERTEBRATE animal with feathers and front limbs adapted as wings. There are about 9000 species of birds in the world today; they are all shapes, sizes and colours and have many different habits. Although all birds have wings, not all birds can fly. For example, the world's largest bird, the OSTRICH, cannot fly, but it can run very fast, faster than an antelope. The PENGUIN too is flightless, it uses its wings as paddles for swimming. But basically birds are flying creatures and their bodies are specially adapted for flight. Their skeletons are particularly strong yet very light. The tiny HUMMINGBIRD, for instance, which can fly 800 km (500 miles) non-stop, weighs less than 30 g (one oz).

Flying uses a great deal of energy and so birds spend much of their time eating. They eat all kinds of food: VULTURES live off carrion, SWALLOWS feed on insects, OWLS eat small animals, PUFFINS have a diet of fish, Honeycreepers drink nectar and PIGEONS peck at grain and seeds. As birds have no teeth, they catch and, if necessary, cut food with their beaks. There are many different types of beak, each suited to a certain diet. The flesh-eating EAGLE, has a powerful hooked beak for tearing its victim apart, while the KINGFISHER uses its sharp-edged beak to seize slippery fish. To help them find food, birds have exceptionally good eyesight and hearing – but little sense of smell. A Blackbird can hear a worm wriggling under the ground and a Kestrel, poised high in the sky, can see a tiny mouse scuttling through the grass below.

Birds are the only feathered members of the animal kingdom. They have two sorts of feathers; those all over their body, called contour feathers, keep them warm and dry; the large flight feathers in the wings and tail, help them fly. Both types of feather are regularly renewed by *moulting*, a process in which the old feathers are dropped and replaced by new ones. Feathers are often brightly coloured. The Canary has brilliant yellow plumage, the FLAMINGO, pink and the Central American Quetzal, is bright green and crimson.

Birds generally lay their eggs in nests. Nests vary greatly from species to species. Some simply use a cliff ledge or hollow in the earth, others build complex structures. The Emperor Penguin makes no nest at all, but carries its egg in a fold of skin at the front of the body; in complete contrast, Tailor Birds stitch leaves together with cobweb and fibres to form a pouch, lined with soft grass. The number of eggs laid also varies, some species lay only one egg a year, others fifteen or more.

Many birds migrate; that is, they spend the breeding season in one country but fly to a warmer country for the winter. The Arctic Tern is one of the greatest travellers; it breeds in the Arctic then escapes the northern hemisphere's winter by flying 20,000 km (12,427 miles) south to spend the southern hemisphere's summer in Antarctica. (See MIGRATION) ◁

WING SHAPES

An eagle's broad wings give it enough lift to soar high in the air on rising air currents.

A swift has narrow, pointed wings that help it to fly at speed and yet twist and turn with great ease.

An albatross's long, narrow wings allow it to glide effortlessly over the sea for days on end.

A duck's short, wide, powerful wings give it plenty of lift.

Bir

BIRTH CONTROL A term used to refer to any means by which human beings prevent or postpone the birth of children, by using drugs or mechanical devices for preventing conception, or by sterilization.

BISON Huge ox-like animal weighing up to a tonne or more (1016 kg). Bisons have short horns and long, shaggy hair on the head, neck, shoulders and forelegs; most bisons live in North America but there are a few in eastern Europe.

BLACK HOLES In ASTRONOMY, areas of space in which the pull of gravity is so strong that nothing can escape, not even light. They are believed to form when giant STARS collapse at the end of their lives. Giant black holes may exist at the centres of GALAXIES, providing the power source for objects such as QUASARS. ▷

BLACK SWAN A bird native to Australia, the black swan (*Cygnus atratus*) has black plumage and a red bill. It has been adopted as the emblem of Western Australia.

BLAST FURNACE A furnace for producing IRON from iron ore (iron oxide). A mixture of iron ore, limestone and coke is loaded into the top of the furnace tower. Hot air from a blast stove is fed in near the bottom. This makes the coke burn at a high temperature. In the resulting chemical reactions, the iron ore is reduced to iron. This is removed in molten form from the bottom of the furnace. Impurities from the ore combine with the limestone to form a slag. This floats on top of the molten iron.

BLASTING The technique of using EX-PLOSIVES to break up or disperse large volumes of earth or rock. Blasting is used widely in quarrying, mining, engineering, and agriculture, and in some military operations.

BLÉRIOT, LOUIS French aviator (1872–1936), the first man to fly across the Channel by plane. Blériot made the flight on July 25, 1909, taking off from Calais in France and landing near Dover, England in a monoplane he had designed and built. (See AIRCRAFT)

BLINDNESS A disability where useful vision is lacking, either through total or partial absence of sight. Blindness may be present at birth or acquired later in life through accident or disease.

BLOOD A fluid (plasma), containing several types of CELLS, that flows all round the body through the blood vessels. Pumped by the HEART, the blood carries nourishment to different parts of the body and carries away

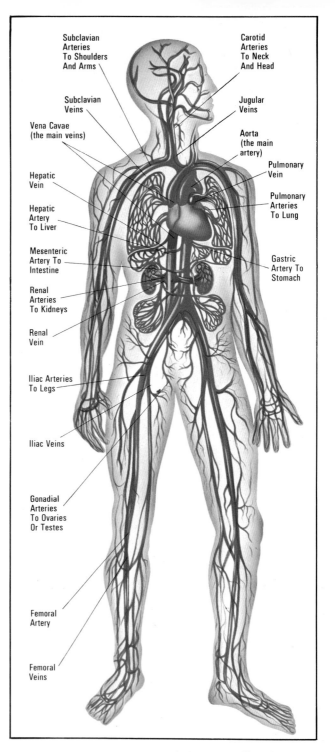

▲ *A simplified diagram of the circulatory system. The arteries (shown in red) carry blood full of oxygen from the heart to the organs and limbs. Then the veins (shown in blue) carry the blood back to the heart to collect more oxygen.*

waste products.

The human body has about 6 litres (10 pints) of blood, though the amount varies greatly. About 60 per cent of blood is plasma; the rest consists of red and white cells and

BLACK HOLES If a star ten times bigger than our Sun collapsed (or imploded), it would be compressed into a black hole less than 65 km (40 miles) across.

BLOOD The eggs laid by the common garden snail – about 30 a year – contain a chemical that is used to determine blood groups.

This chemical is normally extracted from human blood, but five donors are needed to yield as much as is contained in one pinhead-sized snail's egg.

BOA The boa constrictor is not dangerous to humans, and can safely be kept as a pet. However, if two boas are kept together in a cage, cannibalism may occur. For instance, if prey is seized by both snakes – one at each end – in swallowing it they move towards each other. When their two snouts touch, the larger snake will devour the smaller one.

BOBSLEDDING Both two-person boblet and four-person bobsleigh events are contested in the Olympic Games, the results being based on four descents of the course. Speeds of up to 160 km/h (100 mph) have been known, and although the machines are equipped with brakes they are only to be used in emergencies because of the damage they cause to the track.

BONAPARTE The famous French prophet Nostradamus, who was born in 1503, predicted the rise of Napoleon Bonaparte and accurately described many of his achievements and also his eventual downfall. He foresaw the French emperor as an evil force, and referred to him as 'the first Antichrist'.

platelets. The red cells, or corpuscles, contain *haemoglobin*, which gives blood its red colour. They carry oxygen from the LUNGS to the tissues of the body. The white corpuscles act primarily as fighters of disease by destroying BACTERIA that enter the body. The platelets play an important part in the clotting of blood.

Every person may be classified into blood groups A, B, AB, or O. They may also be grouped according to whether or not their blood contains the rhesus factor. (See ARTERIES; RHESUS FACTOR; VEINS) ◁

BLUE BABY A baby suffering from HEART defects, in which blood containing carbon dioxide mixes with oxygenated blood to give the baby's skin a bluish tinge.

BOA A large tropical snake sometimes reaching 9 metres (30 ft) in length. Boas kill their prey by squeezing it to death. The best known of the *Boidae* family is the boa constrictor. ◁

BOATS AND BOATING A boat is often defined as a small craft adapted for travel on water, propelled by paddles, oars, sails or some form of engine. The first boats were probably floating logs; later hollowed-out CANOES, rafts and boats of skin, and eventually wooden planks were developed. Modern boat hulls are often made of fibreglass. Today boating is a popular sport. Pleasure boats include speedboats, motorcruisers, SAILING boats, skiffs, punts and dinghies.

BOBSLEDDING A fast and dangerous winter sport in which steel bobsleds are raced on a specially constructed ice run. It is an Olympics sport. ◁

BOER WAR The conflict between Great Britain and the Boer, or Afrikaner, states of the Transvaal and the Orange Free State over control of southern Africa (1899–1902). (See SOUTH AFRICA)

BOILING POINT The temperature at which a liquid boils and changes to gas. The boiling point of any liquid varies with the surrounding pressure. Unless otherwise stated, boiling points are given for conditions of standard atmospheric pressure (760 mm of mercury).

BOLEYN, ANNE The second of the six wives of HENRY VIII of England (c. 1507–1536), and mother of ELIZABETH I.

BOLIVIA A republic in west-central SOUTH AMERICA, Bolivia has 6,730,000 people (1985 est.) and an area of 1,098,581 sq km (424,164 sq miles). The legal capital is Sucre, but the seat of government is at La Paz. Bolivia is the poorest nation in South America.

BONAPARTE, NAPOLEON French Emperor and military leader (1769–1821) whose conquests made France the most powerful nation in Europe until his downfall in 1815.

Born in Corsica, the son of a lawyer, Napoleon distinguished himself as a soldier in the years following the FRENCH REVOLUTION. In 1799 he became First Consul of France, and in 1804 he was crowned Emperor. His territorial ambitions gradually brought many countries under French control. A disastrous retreat from Russia in 1812 contributed to his downfall. He was finally defeated at WATERLOO, in Belgium, on June 18, 1815. He died in exile on the island of St Helena six years later. ◁

BOND, CHEMICAL The linkage between two ATOMS in a MOLECULE. An *ionic*, or *electrovalent* bond consists of an attraction between atoms with opposite electric charges. Atoms joined by a *covalent* bond share two electrons, one provided by each atom. In a *coordinate*, or *dative* bond, one atom provides both the shared electrons. A *hydrogen* bond joins covalently bonded hydrogen atoms to another atom. Atoms may be linked by more than one bond (see VALENCE).

BONE The main supporting tissue in VERTEBRATES. The human SKELETON has 206 bones which support the body, protect many delicate tissues and organs, and enable the body to move by acting as levers controlled by MUSCLE action. Bones are made up of organic material and inorganic substances such as CALCIUM. They are subject to many diseases, including rickets, a softening of bone tissue caused by lack of Vitamin D.

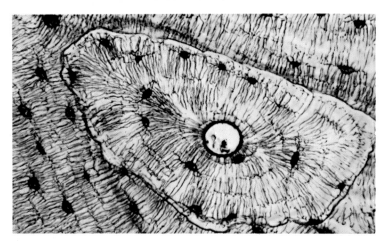

◀ *A piece of the outer layer of a bone, seen through a microscope. This outer layer is the hard, heavy part of the bone. The dark spots are living bone cells, which take in minerals from tiny blood vessels that flow through the bone and build new bone tissue.*

BOOKS AND BOOKBINDING The history of books goes back to 3000 BC when books were written on rolls of PAPYRUS in Egypt. By the period of the Roman Empire both papyrus and PARCHMENT (made from sheepskin) were used as writing materials. After the fall of Rome the making of books was kept alive in the monasteries of Europe. Beautiful hand-written books with elaborate and richly coloured decorations appeared (see ILLUMINATED MANUSCRIPTS). PAPER was introduced into Europe by the Moors, though it had originated in China. But the greatest revolution in PRINTING was the invention of movable type by Johann GUTENBERG, who printed his famous *Bible* between 1452 and 1456. Today, book production is highly automated – huge four-colour presses can produce thousands of copies of a book in an hour. Bookbinding is the process by which printed sheets are made into the completed book. Though hand bookbinding is still a fine art, most books today are bound by machine.

BOOMERANG A throwing-stick used as a hunting weapon by the ABORIGINES of Australia, specially shaped so that it returns to its thrower if it fails to hit its target.

BORNEO The world's third largest island, Borneo has an area of 746,543 sq km

▼ *A page from Gutenberg's 15th century Bible, one of the first books to be printed.*

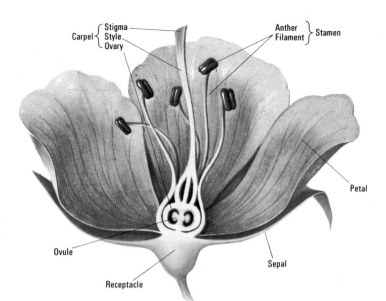

▲ *By studying botany we learn all about the different parts of a plant and what they do. The diagram above shows the main parts of a typical flower. The green sepals cover and protect the flower when it is a bud and later help to support the soft petals. Petals are usually brightly coloured and attract insects to the flower to help it pollinate. Inside the sepals and the petals are the reproductive organs, the stamens (male) and the carpels (female). The tip of the stamen, the anther, produces pollen, and pollen grains from the anther are carried to the tip of the carpel, the stigma. Then the pollen grain forms a tube which grows down through the style and ovary so that the reproductive cells in the pollen can fertilize the female egg in the ovule. When the egg has been fertilized the flower dies and the egg develops into a seed.*

(288,242 sq miles). About three-quarters of the island, called Kalimantan, is in INDONESIA. Most of the rest, Sarawak and Sabah, is in MALAYSIA, with the small Brunei Sultanate on the north coast. ▷

BOSTON TEA PARTY A protest against British taxation when the people of Boston, USA, dressed as Indians, dumped British tea into Boston harbour (December 16, 1773). (See REVOLUTIONARY WAR, AMERICAN)

BOSWELL, JAMES Scottish author (1740–1795), whose *Life of Samuel Johnson* is one of the most famous biographies in the English language.

BOTANY The study of PLANTS. Plants are important to man. They provide him with food and with many other useful products such as wood, fibres (e.g. cotton, jute), rubber, drugs and dyes. Because man is so dependent on plants, he has studied them for a long time. The first botanists lived in ancient Greece over 2000 years ago. One of the most famous was

BORNEO The world's largest flower is produced by the plant *Rafflesia arnoldii*, which is commonly found in the forests of Borneo. The flower may measure more than one metre (3 ft) across, and its petals are 2 cm (¾ in) thick. With their powerful scent of rotting meat, these blooms often weigh as much as 6.8 kg (15 lb) apiece.

BOTANY In 1768, Captain James Cook's first landfall in Australia was at a place he orginally named Stingray Bay. However, he later changed the name to Botany Bay, in honour of the remarkable plant collections made in the area by Sir Joseph Banks, a famous naturalist who had volunteered to accompany Cook on the *Endeavour*. Nowadays, Botany Bay is surrounded by the airport and suburbs of Sydney.

BOTSWANA: FACTS AND FIGURES Botswana is surrounded by South Africa, Namibia, Rhodesia and Zambia. It lies more than 480 km (300 miles) from either the Atlantic or Indian oceans.
Principal rivers: Shashi, Okavango, and Chobe.
Official religion: Christian.
Language: English.
Currency: Pula.

THE MAIN PARTS OF A PLANT

Flower: The part of a flowering plant concerned with reproduction. Most flowers have both male and female organs. The male part produces pollen which pollinates the female part (usually of another flower) – and leads to the production of a seed – from which a new plant grows.

Leaf: A plant's leaves are its food-making factories, containing chlorophyll, which uses sunlight to make food from carbon dioxide in the air and water in the soil. The veins carry water up from the roots and transport food made in the leaves to the rest of the plant.

Stem: This supports the leaves and flowers. It contains tubes to carry water and food around the plant, and it stores food.

Roots: These anchor the plant to the ground, absorb water and mineral salts from the soil, and in some cases (for example, the carrot) store food. The root cap protects the root as it forces its way down in the soil in search of water, the root hairs actually absorb the water.

Terminal bud
Flower
Axillary bud
Lamina (leaf blade)
Branch
Petiole (leaf stalk)
Node
Stem
Primary root
Secondary root

the philosopher ARISTOTLE who had a large garden in Athens where his students learnt about plants first hand. Today, botany is a very advanced science and is divided into many specialized branches. Some branches are concerned with certain plant groups: for example, *mycology* is the study of FUNGI while *bacteriology* deals with BACTERIA. Other branches concentrate on various aspects of plant life: plant *taxonomy*, for instance, covers the naming and CLASSIFICATION of plants and plant *morphology* is the science dealing with what plants look like – their form and structure. Another division of botany is concerned with the economic importance of plants; this section includes sciences such as forestry, and horticulture which studies the cultivation of vegetables, fruit and garden flowers. ◁

BOTSWANA Republic of southern AFRICA, formerly called Bechuanaland. Part of the British Commonwealth, it became independent in 1966. Population 1,046,000; capital: Gaborone. ◁

BOTTICELLI, SANDRO Italian painter of the RENAISSANCE (c. 1444–1510), known for such delicately drawn female figures as those in *La Primavera* and *The Birth of Venus*.

BOW AND ARROW One of the earliest weapons invented by man, the bow and arrow was in use in Egypt over 4000 years ago. During the Middle Ages the crossbow and longbow were popular, but were eventually replaced by firearms. (See ARCHERY)

BOWER BIRDS Eighteen species of the family *Ptilonorhynchidae*, native to Australia and New Guinea. The males build stick bowers, often decorated with flowers, shells, and small bones, with which to attract the females.

BOWLING An indoor game in which a 10–16 lb (about 4.5 to 7 kg) ball is rolled along a wooden alley in an attempt to knock down ten bottle-shaped wooden pins.

BOWLS An outdoor game played on a flat lawn, or green, across which balls (bowls) of about 12.5 cm (5 in) in diameter are rolled. The object is to roll them as close as possible to a small white ball called the jack.

BOXING The sport or art of self defence by use of the fists. Boxing as a sport was part of the ancient Greek Olympics in 688 BC. Today it is still a popular sport, following formal rules set out by the Marquis of Queensberry in the 1860s.

BOYLE, ROBERT Irish chemist and physicist (1627–1691), often called the 'father of modern chemistry', who formulated Boyle's Law on the properties of gases. (See CHEMISTRY)

BOY SCOUTS An organization for boys founded in Britain by Robert BADEN-POWELL (1908). Today it is an international body with more than 8 million members in 100 countries.

BRADMAN, SIR DONALD One of the greatest of all Australian cricket batsmen (1908–   ). He scored over 300 runs on two occasions and recorded six double centuries in Test matches alone.

BRAHMS, JOHANNES German composer (1833–1897) of choral, orchestral, chamber and piano music, and nearly 200 songs.

BRAILLE The touch system of reading and writing for the blind, invented by Louis Braille (1809–1852). The letters of the Braille alphabet are represented by raised dots.

BRAIN The central and most complicated part of the NERVOUS SYSTEM. It controls all bodily processes and is where all thinking takes place. The brain receives messages along nerves from all parts of the body and sends signals to muscles and glands to take any necessary action.

The brain consists of the *cortex*, or *cerebrum* (the largest part), the *cerebellum*, the *midbrain*, the *pons* and the *medulla oblongata*, which connects it with the spinal cord. The brain is also divided into various lobes, or sections. The frontal lobes control movements of the body – the left half controls the right half of the body, and vice versa. These lobes also have important speech, intellectual and emotional functions. The *parietal* lobes receive nerve messages from all parts of the body via the spinal cord. Hearing is centered in the parietal and *temporal* lobes. The *occipital* lobes are responsible for sight.

BRAKES Devices for slowing or stopping movement of machines or vehicles. On a bicycle, hard brake blocks press against the wheel rims when the brake levers are pressed. FRICTION between the rims and the blocks resists the motion, thus slowing the bicycle.

BRANDY An alcoholic drink distilled from wine, originally, from around the town of Cognac in France, but today produced in many parts of the world.

BRASS An ALLOY of zinc and copper, sometimes with small amounts of other metals. The proportions of zinc and copper are varied to produce particular properties. Brass with a high zinc content is hard and brittle. Admiralty brass, used on ships, contains 70 per cent

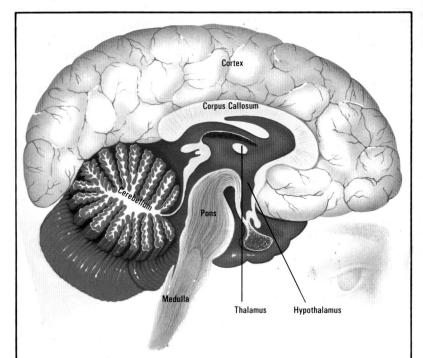

▲ The main parts of the brain: The cortex *(see below) makes up 80 per cent of the brain. The* pons *links the cortex with the* cerebellum *which controls balance and co-ordinates movement. The* medulla, *connecting the pons and the spinal cord, helps to control heart and breathing rates, and digestion. The* thalamus *receives and sorts out information signals from the body before sending them on to the cortex. It is also the part of the brain where pain is felt. The* hypothalamus *regulates the body temperature. The* corpus callosum *connects the right and left parts of the cortex.*

▼ The cortex is divided into a right and left hemisphere. Each hemisphere is made up of four lobes which control different functions of the body. Scientists have worked out which functions are controlled by which area, but we cannot be sure of the exact functions of different parts of the cortex because all the lobes are interconnected.

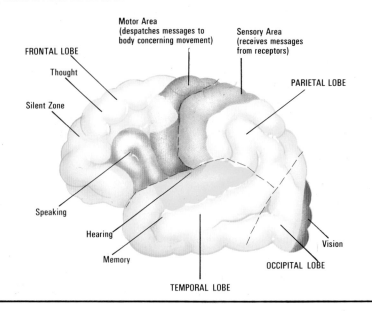

BREAD A food usually made of wheat (or maize, oat, barley, rye) flour, baked with yeast to make it rise. It is one of man's oldest and most important foods, dating back to at least 2000 BC.

BREEDING Developing a special kind of animal or plant by the careful selection of parents. There are two methods of breeding. One consists of crossing two different kinds to produce a totally new kind called a *hybrid*, the other is to choose two exceptional parents of the same kind to produce the best possible offspring. Breeding is essential in agriculture: crops are developed to suit particular climates, resist certain diseases and give high yields; livestock is bred to produce better meat, more milk, etc. (See REPRODUCTION)

BRICKS AND BRICKLAYING The oldest man-made building material (see ARCHITECTURE), bricks are moulded blocks of heat-hardened clay. Today most bricks are machine-made. Good bricklaying is highly skilled work. Often ornamental designs are worked into brick walls.

BRIDGE A structure that will support traffic over a river, valley, road or other obstacle. It may be made of such materials as wood, brick, concrete, iron, steel or aluminium. Different types of bridge include girder, trestle, cantilever, arch, suspension and movable bridges. Suspension bridges are the lightest of all and can cover wider spans than any other.

BRIDGE, GAME OF A popular card game related to whist. Contract bridge is today the most widely played form of bridge.

BRISBANE The capital of QUEENSLAND, Australia, Brisbane has 1,138,000 people. It is a major seaport and a trading and manufacturing centre. Brisbane was a convict settlement between 1824 and 1839. Free settlers arrived in 1842 and Brisbane became the capital of Queensland in 1859.

BRITISH EMPIRE The name given to the areas of the world ruled by Britain between the 16th and 20th centuries. It was the largest of the European colonial empires and extended to every continent. The Empire was held together by the British Navy, then the most powerful naval force in the world. It reached its peak in the 19th century under Queen

BRITISH EMPIRE Queen Victoria's Diamond Jubilee, held in June 1897, is generally regarded as the high-point of the British Empire. At that time the Empire covered more than 26,400,000 sq km (10,200,000 sq miles) – over a quarter of the Earth's surface; and had a population of more than 387,400,000 people.

copper and 29 per cent zinc. One per cent of tin is added to increase CORROSION resistance.

BRAZIL The largest country in SOUTH AMERICA, the republic of Brazil has an area of 8,511,965 sq km (3,286,488 sq miles) and 132,580,000 people (1984 est.). The capital is Brasilia (pop. 1,177,000), but the largest cities are São Paulo (pop. 8,493,000) and Rio de Janeiro (pop. 5,091,000). The vast forested AMAZON basin is under-developed, but there are healthy uplands in the centre and south and the south-east coast is thickly-populated. Brazil leads the world in producing bananas and coffee. Beef, cocoa, cotton, maize, sugar-cane and tobacco are also important.

▲ *Grenadier Guards on parade in front of Buckingham Palace in London.*

VICTORIA and dissolved most rapidly after World War II, when most British colonies became independent. The Empire contained four principal types of possession: the dominions, which were settled permanently by Europeans and later became self-governing; the colonies, in which British officials ruled non-British populations; the Indian Empire, the greatest and grandest part of the British Empire; and the British-protected territories which were controlled by Britain to a greater or lesser degree. (See AUSTRALIA; CANADA; INDIA; NEW ZEALAND; SOUTH AFRICA) ◁

BRITISH ISLES The British Isles contain two large nations, the United Kingdom of Great Britain and Northern Ireland (comprising ENGLAND, Northern IRELAND, SCOTLAND and WALES) and the Republic of Ireland, and two small British dependencies, the Isle of Man and the Channel Islands. Separated from mainland Europe by the NORTH SEA, the Strait of Dover and the ENGLISH CHANNEL, the British Isles have a combined population of over 60 million.

Despite their northerly position, the British Isles have a mostly mild and moist climate, because the prevailing south-west winds are warmed by the offshore North Atlantic Drift, an ocean current which originates in the CARIBBEAN SEA. The weather is changeable, partly because of the depressions, or 'lows', which come from the Atlantic Ocean.

The highest peak is Ben Nevis in Scotland, at 1343 metres (4406 ft) above sea level. The

longest river is the Shannon in the Republic of Ireland. It is 386 km (240 miles) long. The United Kingdom of Great Britain and Northern Ireland is a leading trading and manufacturing nation. Farming is the chief industry in the Republic of Ireland. ▷

BRITTEN, BENJAMIN British composer (1913–1976) with an international reputation, particularly in the field of opera and choral music (*A Ceremony of Carols, Peter Grimes*).

BROADCASTING The transmission to the public, through TELEVISION and RADIO, of sound and vision by radio waves. Radio broadcasting in Britain began in 1922; the BBC was set up in 1927. VHF (Very High Frequency) broadcasting was set up in 1955. Television transmission in Britain began in 1932 and the first colour TV was introduced in 1966. TV was not introduced in the USA until 1939, but by 1967, 94 per cent of American homes had TV sets.

BROKEN HILL City in western NEW SOUTH WALES, Australia, about 420 km (260 miles) north-east of Adelaide. It is a mining centre for the silver-lead-zinc deposits discovered there in 1875. Two dams supply water to the city, which lies in an arid region. Population: 28,810.

BRONTË SISTERS Three British sisters (Charlotte 1816–1855; Emily 1818–1848; and Anne 1820–1849) who during their short lives wrote several classics of ENGLISH LITERATURE, including *Jane Eyre* (Charlotte Brontë) and *Wuthering Heights* (Emily Brontë). ▷

BRONTOSAURUS More properly called *Apatosaurus*, a giant sauropod DINOSAUR about 25 metres (80 ft) long.

BRONZE This term usually refers to an ALLOY of copper and tin. Other substances may be present too. For example, phosphor bronze contains a small proportion of phosphorus. Gun metal is bronze containing added zinc. Silicon bronze and aluminium bronze contain no tin. ▷

BRONZE AGE The name given to a period of prehistory when tools, ornaments and weapons were mostly made of bronze, an alloy of copper and tin. Bronze Age dates vary enormously in different parts of the world, but the earliest centre was in MESOPOTAMIA (3000 BC). Bronze Age culture is usually associated with the first true civilizations and the development of cities.

BUCCANEERS The name given to the pirates who plundered Spanish ships and colonies in America during the 17th and 18th

BRITISH ISLES Around 40,000 years ago, the first migrants moving into Britain simply walked across from the continent of Europe. Even after the sea separated Europe and Britain 9,000 years ago, Stone Age people could still travel back and forth quite easily, as the Channel was shallow and fordable.

BRONTË The Brontë family lived in the parsonage at Haworth, a moorland village in west Yorkshire, England. Their home is now a museum and library, and both Charlotte and Emily are buried in the nearby village churchyard.

BRONZE The commonest bronze is that used for coins. A typical composition would be 97% copper, 0.5% tin, and 2.5% zinc. The so-called Admiralty gunmetal contains 88% copper, 10% tin, and 2% zinc. Phosphor bronzes usually contain less than 0.5% phosphorus, with about 6% tin. Aluminium bronzes contain no tin at all, but up to about 12% aluminium. Silicon bronzes also contain no tin.

BUG The dried, pulverized bodies of the bug *Dactylopius coccus* – found in Peru and Mexico – are used to make cochineal, which is a brilliant crimson dye used in confectionery, medicines and cosmetics. The sticky resin exuded by another variety, *Laccifer lacca*, is made into shellac, which is used in varnishes, wax, linoleum, inks and insulation materials.

BULGARIA: FACTS AND FIGURES
Principal rivers: Danube and Maritsa.
Highest Mountain: Musala Peak, 2740 m (8987 ft).
Language: Bulgarian.
Currency: Lev.
Religion: Bulgarian Church, a branch of the Eastern Orthodox Church. The government discourages religions.
During the 19th century, when Bulgaria was part of the Ottoman Empire, Turkish troops massacred thousands of Bulgarian nationalists. In 1878, Russian forces moved in to rescue their 'brother Slavs', and the two countries have maintained close links ever since.

centuries. The name comes from the French *boucanier*, 'hunter of wild oxen'.

BUCKINGHAM PALACE The London residence of the British royal family, at the west end of St James's Park, originally built as Buckingham House in 1703–5.

BUD New-growing part of a plant. Buds appear at the tip of the stem and on its side in the *axils* – angles made by last year's leaves. During the winter, buds are protected by special leaves then, in spring, they grow into flowers or leaves. Often, some side buds are kept in reserve: they only open if the main bud at the tip is damaged. (See BULB)

BUDDHA (SIDDHARTHA GAUTAMA) The founder of the religion of BUDDHISM (c. 563 BC–483 BC). He taught his new faith throughout northern India for 40 years; by the time he died Buddhism was well established.

BUDDHISM The religion and philosophy founded in India by Gautama BUDDHA in the 6th century BC. The goal of Buddhists is to reach a state of perfect peace, called *Nirvana*, which is achieved by the practice of humility, self-control, non-violence, and generosity.

▼ *Buddhists monks stand before the shrine of a reclining Buddha. In Buddhism it is important to actively practice the teachings, rather than to just believe in them.*

Buddhists do not worship a particular god or gods. From India Buddhism spread to China and the rest of the Far East. Today, one estimate places the number of Buddhists in the world at 220 million.

BUDGET A kind of account, which records money coming in against money spent. In Britain the national account has been called a budget since 1733.

BUFFALO Heavily-built wild CATTLE, found mainly in India and southern Africa. Most kinds of buffalo are black-haired with big horns and, as they like being near water, they often live in swamps. The Indian buffalo has long been domesticated: it is used as a work animal and also provides milk and meat.

BUG Any INSECT that lives by piercing tissues and sucking out the juices; some feed on animals or other insects, others attack plants. Most bugs have wings and live on land but some are wingless and some are aquatic.   ◁

BUILDING CONSTRUCTION The art of designing, planning and erecting structures with walls, floors and roofs for use as homes, offices, schools, hospitals, places of worship, factories and so on.

BULB Underground food store at the stem base of certain plants such as tulips and onions. A bulb consists of swollen, fleshy leaves called scales surrounding one or more buds. The scales are full of food – usually starch – which they supply to the BUD as it develops. When the scales have given all their food to the growing shoot they wither but new scales – next year's bulb – form inside them.

BULGARIA A communist republic in south-eastern EUROPE, Bulgaria has 9,293,000 people (1986 est.) and an area of 110,912 sq km (42,823 sq miles). The capital is Sofia. Farming, mining and manufacturing are all important, as is tourism on the Black Sea coast.   ◁

BULLDOZER A machine mounted on a tractor used for excavating land, clearing undergrowth and other obstacles by pushing the unwanted material away with a broad horizontal blade.

BULLET A spherical or conical missile of lead used as ammunition in FIREARMS of small calibre such as rifles, pistols, machine guns and revolvers.

BULLFIGHTING An art and sport popular in Spain in which the bullfighter shows his mastery over a bull in a series of formal movements, usually climaxed by the killing of the bull with a sword.

Bun

BUNSEN BURNER A gas burner widely used to produce heat in laboratory experiments. It is named after its German inventor, Robert Bunsen.

BUOY A floating wood or metal structure used at sea as a navigational marker or for mooring a boat or small ship.

BURKE AND WILLS Two of Australia's most famous explorers, Robert O'Hara Burke (1821–1861) and William John Wills (1834–1861) crossed the continent from south to north in 1860–1861.

BURMA A republic in south-eastern ASIA, Burma has 37,614,000 people (1984 est.) and an area of 676,552 sq km (261,218 sq miles). The capital is Rangoon. Farming is the chief industry and the Irrawaddy and Sittang river valleys are the most important regions. ▷

BURNS, ROBERT Scottish poet (1759–1796) famous for many popular poems and songs written in the Scottish dialect.

BUSHBABY A small African mammal which lives in trees. Nocturnal, it sleeps by day and is active at night. It has large eyes and a bushy tail and can leap up to 4.6 metres (15 ft) from branch to branch.

BUSHMEN A primitive negroid race living in southwest AFRICA (Namibia) and Botswana. Short in stature, the bushmen are primarily hunters, using poison-tipped arrows, spears and knives. ▷

BUTTER A food made from the fats contained in MILK. The cream from milk is pasteurized, cooled and then ripened by adding a BACTERIA 'starter'. Finally it is churned into butter and stored at freezing point until marketed.

▲ Some moths have antennae that poke out from their heads like palm fronds or feathers. Each antenna has about 40,000 nerve cells, that are sensitive to touch and smell.

BUTTERFLIES AND MOTHS Butterflies and moths make up the *Lepidoptera* (scaly wings) group of INSECTS. The group is a large one: there are about 10,000 butterfly species and 100,000 moth species in the world. All Lepidoptera have wings covered with tiny overlapping scales and feed using a *proboscis* – a tube for sucking out nectar from flowers and over-ripe fruit. Butterflies and moths have a four-stage life history: egg, CATERPILLAR, chrysalis and adult. During the chrysalis stage, which lasts from ten days to five years or more according to species, the caterpillar body is broken down and rebuilt into an adult insect; the adult's life is usually very short. There are two main differences between butterflies and moths: firstly, butterflies have clubbed antennae or feelers, those of moths are not clubbed; secondly, when resting, butterflies hold their wings vertically over their backs, but moths fold their wings down. Also, it is often true – but not always – that butterflies have brilliant colours and fly by day, whereas moths are dull-coloured and night-flying. ▷

BYZANTINE ART The style of art and decoration that flourished under the rulers of the Eastern Roman Empire, from about AD 330 to 1500. Byzantine art was influenced by

◀ These primitive bushmen still hunt wild animals for their food.

BUSHMEN There is a legend that the bushmen of the Kalahari Desert know the location of a secret oasis where enormous quantities of huge diamonds lie scattered on the ground. One story describes how these people once captured a white soldier who had become separated from his unit on a desert patrol. He was taken to the oasis, but then escaped and later raised money for an expedition. Several weeks later he was found dead in the desert with a bushman's arrow piercing his heart. A map showing the route to the oasis, and several rough diamonds, were found in his pockets. However, no one has ever been able to read the map successfully, so the secret of the oasis has ever since remained with the bushmen.

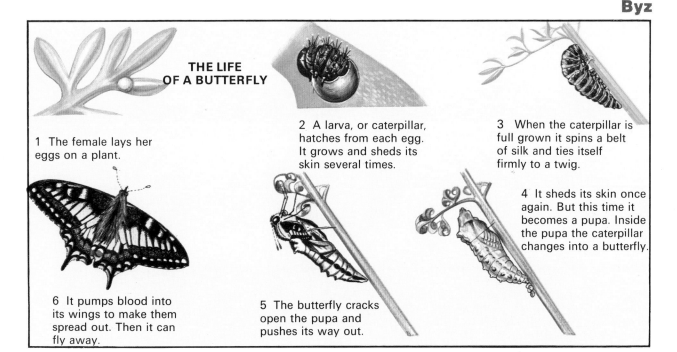

THE LIFE OF A BUTTERFLY

1 The female lays her eggs on a plant.

2 A larva, or caterpillar, hatches from each egg. It grows and sheds its skin several times.

3 When the caterpillar is full grown it spins a belt of silk and ties itself firmly to a twig.

4 It sheds its skin once again. But this time it becomes a pupa. Inside the pupa the caterpillar changes into a butterfly.

5 The butterfly cracks open the pupa and pushes its way out.

6 It pumps blood into its wings to make them spread out. Then it can fly away.

BUTTERFLIES AND MOTHS The Solomon Islands in the South Pacific are home to both the largest and rarest butterflies in the world. Females of the giant bird-wing *Troides victoriae* can weigh over 5 g (0.18 oz), and have a wingspan exceeding 30 cm (12 in).

Greek, Roman and Oriental art, though it developed a distinct character of its own. Elaborate MOSAICS were the most striking feature of Byzantine art – richly coloured mosaic scenes for the walls and domes of Byzantine churches such as those of San Vitale, Ravenna, Italy, are famous. The subjects were generally formally arranged and human figures were stylized – that is, they were flat, two-dimensional and often rigidly unrealistic. Byzantine artists also created much in the field of the decorative arts, producing richly decorated ENAMELS, textiles, jewellery and woven silks. (See COSTUME)

The architecture of the Byzantine Empire, like its European contemporary, Romanesque architecture, developed from Roman architecture, and is known for large, domed churches. Perhaps the most famous of these is Hagia Sophia (AD 532–537) in Istanbul (once the city of Byzantium, capital of the Empire), now a mosque. Another remarkable Byzantine building is St Mark's in Venice, rebuilt in the 11th century. (See BYZANTINE EMPIRE)

BYZANTINE EMPIRE The eastern Roman Empire, founded when the Roman Empire was divided in AD 285. After the fall of ROME (AD 476) the eastern half of the empire grew as the western half declined. The Byzantine Empire, with its capital Byzantium (later called Constantinople and now Istanbul), grew rapidly in size and wealth and developed a civilization that had a lasting effect on European history. The Empire lasted for over a thousand years, falling in 1453 when Constantinople was captured by the Turks. One of the most famous rulers of the Byzantine Empire was the Emperor Justinian (482–565), who codified Roman law in the *Corpus juris civilis* (553), which became the foundation for most European law. Byzantine civilization reached a high standard and made many outstanding contributions to the fields of art and ARCHITECTURE. (See BYZANTINE ART)

◀ *Byzantine Art is famous for its richly coloured mosaics, made from glass and marble. This mosaic, from the church of Sant' Apollinare Nuovo in Italy, shows the Three Wise Men bringing gifts to the infant Christ.*

C

CABBAGE Popular vegetable grown for its heart of tight, unopened leaves which is used for cooking and in salads and pickles. Most cabbage varieties have green leaves but some have white or red leaves.

CABINET In the British government, a group of ministers, headed by the Prime Minister, who form the central body of political power. (See GREAT BRITAIN)

CACTUS A spiny plant which grows in very dry, desert regions, mainly native to North and South America. Cacti absorb water during the rains and store it in their swollen stems or leaves. There are several hundred different varieties. (See ADAPTATION)

CAESAR, JULIUS Roman general and statesman (c. 100–44 BC) who rose to be sole leader of ROME. His dictatorship put Rome on the path from republic to empire. Caesar's great power made him many enemies, and he was assassinated as the result of a republican conspiracy in 44 BC.

CAIRO The capital of EGYPT, Cairo has 11,500,000 people (1985 est.), including its suburbs. It was founded in about AD 649. Its many mosques and museums and the nearby PYRAMIDS attract many visitors.

◄ *The leaves on the golden barrel cactus are reduced to a mass of sharp spines. These spines help the cactus to save water by giving off less water vapour.*

▼ *Left to right: The prickly pear with large swollen stems;* Lithops *and* Stapelia *both store water in their thick stems and leaves; a barrel cactus with part cutaway, showing water-storing tissue.*

CALCUTTA The Black Hole of Calcutta was an infamous dungeon in Fort William, the 18th-century British fort. In 1756 the Newab of Bengal took the fort and threw 146 British prisoners into this small airless room. Only 23 of the prisoners survived.

CALIFORNIA: FACTS AND FIGURES
California was admitted to the Union in 1850 as the 31st state. It is known as the Golden State because of its gold production.
Highest point: Mount Whitney, 4418 m (14494 ft) in the Sierra Nevada, the second highest mountain in the United States.
Lowest point: Death Valley, 86 m (282 ft) below sea level.
The California gold rush of 1849 caused a great increase in the population

CALIGULA This unstable Roman emperor, who had a reputation for odd and unpredictable acts, is best remembered for having his horse elected a Consul (chief magistrate) of Rome. He was assassinated by one of his guards.

▲ Gaius Julius Caesar was one of the greatest rulers of ancient Rome. But his popularity with the people and the growth of his power created enemies for him in the senate. Some senators were afraid that Caesar might try to make himself a king. They hatched a plot to murder him and he was stabbed to death on March 15, 44 BC.

CALCIUM A white, highly reactive metal obtained from the compound calcium chloride. Calcium compounds have many uses in industry. Quicklime (calcium oxide) is used as a fertilizer and for making mortar and glass.

CALCULATING MACHINES See COMPUTERS.

CALCULUS A branch of mathematics dealing with changing quantities. In *differential* calculus, rates of change are calculated. Speed, for example, is found by working out the rate at which the distance from a given point changes with time. And acceleration is the rate at which VELOCITY changes. The reverse process – the calculation of a quantity from its rate of change is called *integral* calculus.

CALCUTTA A port on the Bay of Bengal, Calcutta has 9,194,000 people, including its suburbs, and is INDIA's largest city. Main exports include jute, hides, oil and grain. ◁

CALENDAR A means of organizing time into useful units such as years, months, etc. Lunar calendars (based on the phases of the Moon) were developed in Egypt as early as 3000 BC. The modern calendar is based on the Gregorian Calendar, established by Pope Gregory XIII in 1582. (See ASTRONOMY; AZTECS)

CALIFORNIA California, in the southwestern UNITED STATES of America, is the USA's third largest state, but the most populous, with over 26,300,000 people. Its capital is Sacramento, but the chief cities are LOS ANGELES and SAN FRANCISCO. This scenic state is one of the most prosperous in the USA. ◁

CALIGULA, GAIUS JULIUS Third emperor of Rome, notorious for his savagely cruel reign (AD 12–41; emperor from AD 37). ◁

CALLIGRAPHY The art of WRITING beautiful scripts by hand. Calligraphy has been a study since the RENAISSANCE and has followed different styles and fashions in each century. It has lost its practical importance since the invention of the typewriter, though it is still one of the minor arts.

◄ The 'Calendar Round' was invented by the Aztecs of Mexico in the 6th century BC. The Aztecs adapted the calendar from the Mayas. It was based on a 52-year cycle. Each year of the cycle was divided into 365 days, or 18 months of 20 days each. The left-over period was a time of five 'unlucky days'. The signs of the 20 days of the month can be seen in this carved stone calendar, in the inner circle of rectangles.

CALVIN In 1533, the local authorities in Paris forced John Calvin to leave the city because of his religious ideas. He fled to the city-state of Geneva in Switzerland which, under his influence, became a hothouse of Protestant ideas. These ideas spread quickly, and Calvin's teachings bred the Huguenots in France, the English and American Puritans and the Dutch Reformed Church, as well as the Presbyterians in Scotland.

CANADA: FACTS AND FIGURES
Area: 9,976,170 sq km (3,851, 820 sq miles).
Population: 25,150,000 (1984 est.).
Capital: Ottawa, in Ontario.
Highest peak: Mt Logan, 6050 m (19,850 ft) above sea level, in Yukon Territory.
Longest river: Mackenzie, 4241 km (2635 miles) long.

▲ Top: A plaice can change the colour of its upper side to camouflage it on the seabed.

▲ The rhinoceros viper's brilliant colour patterns help to camouflage it by breaking up the outline of its shape against the shadowy green foliage.

CALORIE A unit of heat measurement in the CGS (centimetre-gram-second) system. One calorie is the amount of heat required to raise the temperature of one gram of water by one degree Celcius. One calorie is equal to 4.1855 JOULES. The Calorie (spelt with a capital) is a unit used in the calculation of food and fuel energy. It is equal to 1000 calories.

CALVIN, JOHN French religious writer and Protestant reformer (1509–1564) whose teachings form the basis of Scottish Presbyterianism. (See REFORMATION) ◁

CALYPSO is a kind of song with a strong rhythm which developed in the West Indian island of Trinidad. It originated in the work songs of African slaves. Calypso singers often make up the words of a song as they go.

CAMBODIA See Kampuchea.

◀ The Arabian camel has been domesticated since ancient times. The camel's ability to survive in hot, dry conditions makes it a valuable work animal in desert regions.

CAMEL Valuable desert animal. There are two species: the Arabian (one-humped) camel and the Bactrian (two-humped) camel. Both are suited to desert life. They eat almost anything, need little water and, when food is scarce they live off the fat stored in their humps. Camels are kept for transport; they also provide milk, meat, hair and skin. An Arabian breed, the dromedary, is a good riding animal.

CAMEO An engraving in relief on a stone such as onyx, sardonyx and rock crystal. Popular as JEWELLERY and decoration since the 4th century BC.

CAMOUFLAGE The disguising of a creature (protective coloration, etc.) or an object (military installation) to make it look like something else, or to conceal it altogether.

CAMPING An activity involving temporary living out of doors. A permanent way of life for primitive or nomadic peoples, camping in Western society is a form of recreation. Campers sleep in basic accommodation (tents or lean-to's). Organized campsites with more elaborate facilities are also popular today.

▲ Portraits were often popular subjects for cameos. This cameo is called the 'Gemma Augusta'. It shows the portrait of the first Roman emperor Caesar Augustus, and was carved in the 1st century BC. The diadem of gold and gems was added in the Middle Ages.

CANADA The world's second largest country after the USSR, Canada contains vast tracts of cold wilderness and most people live within 320 km (200 miles) of the southern border with the USA. Canada's first inhabitants, the AMERICAN INDIANS, came to North America from Asia about 20,000 years

Can

PROVINCES AND TERRITORIES OF CANADA

Province or Territory	Area (sq km)	Population (1986 est.)	Capital
1. Alberta	661,187	2,389,500	Edmonton
2. British Columbia	948,599	2,905,900	Victoria
3. Manitoba	650,089	1,078,600	Winnipeg
4. New Brunswick	73,437	721,100	Fredericton
5. Newfoundland	404,518	580,200	St John's
6. Northwest Terr.	3,379,693	50,900	Yellowknife
7. Nova Scotia	55,491	883,800	Halifax
8. Ontario	1,068,586	9,181,900	Toronto
9. Prince Edward Is.	5,657	128,100	Charlottetown
10. Quebec	1,540,685	6,627,200	Quebec
11. Saskatchewan	651,902	1,021,000	Regina
12. Yukon Territory	536,326	22,900	Whitehorse

ago. Later arrivals were the ESKIMOS. But the largest groups today are descendants of British immigrants (45 per cent of the population), French immigrants (29 per cent) and German immigrants (6 per cent). English and French are the official languages and Quebec province is especially French in culture. In the 1970s Quebec's provincial government announced that a vote would be held to discover whether its people wanted to break away from Canada and set up their own independent French-speaking nation.

Farming, fishing and forestry are important industries and Canada is one of the world's leading mining nations. It leads in asbestos, nickel and zinc production and many other minerals are mined. But manufacturing is now the most valuable industry. The chief manufacturing region is in the St Lawrence River valley and around the GREAT LAKES.

The Dominion of Canada was set up by Britain in 1867 and it became a sovereign state in the Commonwealth in 1931. (See BRITISH EMPIRE; NORTH AMERICA) ◁

CANAL Man-made channel for carrying water. Canals include waterways for the movement of ships and barges, irrigation canals, and outlets from reservoirs. Before the railways, canals were the most important means of transporting heavy and bulky goods. Between 1760 and 1830 over 7564 km (4700 miles) of canal were cut in England alone. Ship canals connect two oceans or seas and have greatly shortened distances at sea. Other canals connect important inland cities with the sea. (See PANAMA CANAL; SUEZ CANAL)

CANARY ISLANDS These 13 volcanic Spanish Islands are in the Atlantic Ocean off north-west Africa. Farming and tourism are the chief industries. Population: 1,368,000.

CANBERRA The capital of the Commonwealth of Australia, Canberra lies in southeast Australia on land acquired in 1911 from New South Wales. The city was designed by Walter Burley Griffin, a Chicago architect. Most of its construction was delayed by economic depression and World War II until after 1945. Population: 256,000. ▷

CANCER A general term for all types of malignant growths or TUMOURS. Cancer may attack almost any part of the body, including the blood (see LEUKAEMIA), and it occurs in animals as well as man. Cancerous tissue grows rapidly and invades or destroys adjacent tissue, often spreading (*metastasizing*) to other parts of the body by way of the blood or lymph system. The most common type of cancer is skin cancer.

The cause of cancer is still not known, though it is probable that many factors contribute to the development of malignant growth. The best 'cure' is early detection, when cancer may often be successfully treated by surgery, drugs or radiation.

CANDLE A source of light made from WAX surrounding a wick of flax or cotton. Important from ancient times until the invention of

CANBERRA The word 'canberra' means 'meeting place' in the Aboriginal language. The general location of the city was chosen after nine years of argument and controversy between the states of Victoria and New South Wales, and the Australian national government.

CANNING Nicolas Appert, a French confectioner, is known as the 'father of canning'. He first sealed food in glass jars and then boiled them. This process won him a French government award, and he established the world's first cannery in 1812. Shortly afterwards, Bryon Donkin – a partner in John Hall's Dartford Iron Works – adapted Appert's idea and opened the first British cannery at Bermondsey in London. The cans were made of iron, coated with tin, and were opened by using a chisel and a hammer.

▶ *Banff National Park, high in the Canadian Rockies, is a popular holiday resort. The spectacular mountain scenery attracts thousands of hunters, hikers, climbers and skiers to western Canada every year.*

CANOE Canoeing was pioneered as a sport in 1865, by a British barrister called John Macgregor. The Canoe Club came into being on July 26 of the following year.

On April 25 1936, Geoffrey W. Pope and Sheldon P. Taylor set off from New York City to make the longest canoe journey in history. They finally arrived at Nome, Alaska on August 11, 1937, having travelled a distance of 11,531 km (7,165 miles) along the river systems of America.

CAPE YORK PENINSULA Important rock paintings have been discovered here in recent years. A commercial pilot discovered over 100 galleries from the air, and these have been followed up on the ground.

oil and electric lamps, candles today are used largely for decorative and religious purposes.

CANE The hollow, jointed stem of large reeds and grasses, such as BAMBOO and sugar cane, used to make walking sticks and cane furniture.

CANNING The preserving of FOOD in hermetically sealed tins, or cans, which are then sterilized with their contents by subjecting them to high heat. Canning was first developed commercially in the early 19th century, when there was a need to preserve food to be carried to armies in the field. At first the containers were glass, sealed with wired cork stoppers; later the tin 'canister' (can) was developed. Today canning is speeded up by the use of many automatic processes ·for washing, sorting, grading, peeling and coring the raw product, and for filling and sealing the cans. ◁

CANOE A small craft that is pointed at both ends, propelled by a paddle. The earliest canoe was a hollowed-out log. The modern canoe, which may be of wood, fibre-glass, aluminium, or canvas, has its origins with the North American Indians, who built canoes of birchbark stitched over a wooden frame. Today the most popular craft used in canoeing is the KAYAK, often wrongly called a canoe. (See BOATS and BOATING) ◁

CAPE YORK PENINSULA A 725-km (450-mile) long peninsula that forms the north-eastern part of QUEENSLAND, Australia. ◁

CAPILLARY TUBE A tube, usually glass, of extremely small diameter. Water will rise up a capillary tube if one end is placed below the surface. This effect is caused by an attraction between glass and water molecules.

CAPITAL In architecture, a term used to describe the top of a COLUMN, often elaborately decorated. Types of capital include Doric, Ionic and Corinthian.

CARAT A term used as a measure of weight for precious stones such as DIAMONDS. One carat is equal to 200 milligrams. Carat is also used as a measure of the purity of GOLD. Most gold is a mixture of gold and ALLOY. One carat is 1/24th pure gold, therefore 9 carat gold is 9 parts pure gold mixed with 15 parts alloy.

CARBOHYDRATE An organic substance made up of CARBON (C), HYDROGEN (H) and OXYGEN (O). Carbohydrates include SUGAR, STARCH and CELLULOSE, and are found in many types of food. They are vital to the human body because they provide energy. The body converts carbohydrates into a simple sugar called GLUCOSE. The glucose is then carried in the blood to muscles and other tissues, where it is burned (oxidized) to provide energy. Important carbohydrate foods in our diet include sugar, bread and potatoes.

CARBON A non-metallic element present in all living organisms. Carbon occurs naturally as soot, charcoal, graphite and diamond. These allotropes – physically different forms – all have the same chemical properties. Soot and charcoal are known as amorphous carbon. This means that they have no definite shape or form. Amorphous carbon consists of tiny fragments of graphite crystals. Graphite is soft because its atoms are joined together by weak BONDS. The strong bonds between the carbon atoms of diamond make it the hardest substance known to man. There are more compounds of carbon than of all the other elements put together. The study of carbon compounds forms the branch of CHEMISTRY described as *organic*. (See CARBON CYCLE; ELEMENTS)

CARBON CYCLE A series of reactions in which CARBON is continuously circulated between living organisms and their surroundings. In a process called PHOTOSYNTHESIS, plants use CARBON DIOXIDE gas from the air to make various other carbon compounds. Energy from sunlight is absorbed during this process. Animals eat the plants, or else eat other animals that have eaten plants. The carbon compounds in this food are broken down in the animals' bodies. As a result, energy is released and carbon dioxide produced. In this way, animals obtain the energy necessary for life processes. The carbon dioxide is returned to the air when the animals breathe out (see RESPIRATION), thus completing the cycle. Carbon dioxide is also released when dead organisms decay and when certain fuels are burnt.

Doric | Ionic | Corinthian

There were three main styles of Greek capital, the Doric, Ionian and Corinthian styles. The Doric style was severe and simple; the Ionic order was carved and scrolled. The Corinthian style, popular from the 5th century BC onwards, was elaborately decorated with scrolls and acanthus leaves.

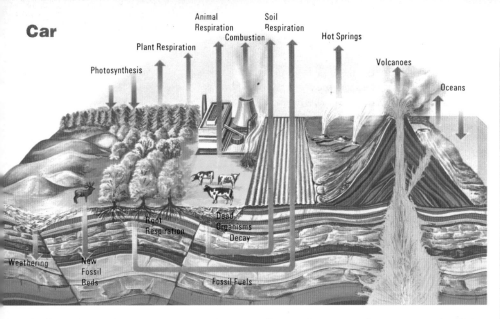

Photosynthesis · Plant Respiration · Animal Respiration · Combustion · Soil Respiration · Hot Springs · Volcanoes · Oceans · Weathering · New Fossil Beds · Root Respiration · Dead Organisms Decay · Fossil Fuels

▲ *The carbon cycle circulates carbon and oxygen between the atmosphere, the soil, and living organisms. Carbon dioxide is absorbed by plants and they return oxygen to the air. Animals take in the carbon when they eat plants, and then, when they breathe, they take in oxygen and release carbon dioxide. Plants and animals acting together thus keep the amounts of carbon dioxide and oxygen more or less constant. Plants, especially their roots, also give off carbon dioxide during respiration, and the decay of dead organisms releases more of the gas. Burning plant materials uses up oxygen and gives out carbon dioxide.*

CARBON DIOXIDE A heavy, colourless gas with the chemical formula CO_2. It is present in the atmosphere and used in PHOTOSYNTHESIS, part of the CARBON CYCLE. Carbon dioxide is the fizz in fizzy drinks. Solid carbon dioxide is called dry ice.

CARBON MONOXIDE A colourless, odourless, poisonous gas with the chemical formula CO. It is present in the exhaust gases of motor cars. Carbon monoxide is also produced when fuel is burnt with insufficient oxygen.

CARBURETTOR The part of an INTERNAL COMBUSTION ENGINE that mixes the fuel (usually petrol) and air in the correct proportions before the vapour is sucked into the cylinders.

CARIBBEAN SEA Part of the ATLANTIC OCEAN, the Caribbean Sea lies between the West Indies and Central and South America. It has an area of about 2,590,000 sq km (1,000,000 sq miles). The sea became notorious in the 1500s and 1600s because of the activities of pirates.

CARIBOU Wild REINDEER of North America. Caribou, generally greyish-brown,

live on the TUNDRA in summer eating lichen and mosses but move south to the forests in winter. Unusually for deer, both the male and female have antlers.

CARICATURE A drawing of a person that exaggerates certain characteristics, both physical and personal, to create a humorous effect. Caricatures are often used to criticize public figures.

CARNIVORE Flesh-eating animal or plant. Many creatures feed on the flesh of other animals. They range from FOXES and OWLS to LIONS and SHARKS; even LADYBIRDS are carnivores: they eat insects. Carnivorous creatures catch their food in different ways: the CHEETAH chases its prey; the SPIDER sets a trap with its web; the COBRA attacks with poison... Carnivorous plants eat insects. Their leaves are designed to trap insects which are then digested with special juices; the sundew, for example, uses sticky leaves to capture its victims. (See VENUS' FLYTRAP)

CARPENTRY The craft of construction in wood, of such things as buildings, roof frames, staircases, floors, fencing, doors, windows and shop fronts. Finer carpentry, such as furniture-building, is often called cabinet-making. Carpenters today have a number of power tools, such as drills and saws, to help them shape wood, and machines to make a variety of wooden joints.

CARPETS Heavy floor coverings of woven or knotted material. The making of carpets originated in the Middle East, in Turkey,

▶ *The barn owl is a carnivore, and is well adapted for hunting its prey at night. With its large eyes and efficient ears, it can see and hear small mammals from a great distance.*

Persia and Egypt. Today the best carpets still come from this area, as well as from India and China. Carpets are classified according to their method of production: hand-knotted, plush, tufted, and non-woven. ▷

CARRIAGE A form of wheeled transport for carrying passengers. The carriage became popular on the Continent in the 1300s; later it was introduced into England. A carriage was distinguished from a COACH by the fact that the roof was not a part of the body framework.

CARROT Plant grown for its large, orange-red root which is used as a vegetable. Carrots, full of vitamins A and C, are generally cooked but can also be eaten raw.

CARTHAGE A great Phoenician trading centre founded in the 700s BC on the north coast of Africa near present-day Tunis. Carthage dominated the western Mediterranean in the 600s BC, but eventually clashed with the growing power of Rome. The three PUNIC WARS were fought between Rome and Carthage, resulting in the final destruction of Carthage in 146 BC. (See PHOENICIA)

CARTOON A drawing that makes its own point, often humorous, and is often accompanied by a caption. The word cartoon also refers to a film made up of a number of drawings to provide animation. Perhaps the most famous cartoon animator was Walt DISNEY, who revolutionized the cartoon film technique. His cartoon characters Mickey Mouse and Donald Duck became popular all over the world. ▷

CASH REGISTER A machine, or till, that records and adds together the amount of money put into it. Today cash registers are

▲ *Young members of the cat family love to stalk and pounce on a moving object. When this cheetah cub grows up it will face far more dangerous prey than its mother's tail.*

complicated devices that can perform other useful functions such as recording information for stocktaking.

CASPIAN SEA The world's largest inland body of water. The salty Caspian Sea has an area of 371,800 sq km (143,550 sq miles) in the southern USSR and in Iran. ▷

CASSOWARY A large, flightless bird of New Guinea and Australia, related to the OSTRICH, EMU and rhea. It may stand over 1.5 metres (5 ft) tall and can run at speeds up to 48 km (30 miles) an hour.

CASTE A strict social class system, determined by birth, that until recently controlled the organization of society in INDIA. Members of different classes could not mingle, and the caste-less 'untouchables' had no social standing at all.

CASTING A manufacturing process for making replicas of solid objects in metal. Molten metal is poured into a mould made from the original object or model. On cooling, the metal solidifies to form the replica.

CAT A member of the family of furry flesh-eating MAMMALS that includes the LION, TIGER, JAGUAR, LEOPARD, CHEETAH and COUGAR. All cats have lithe, agile bodies, strong cutting teeth, and sharp claws which are particularly useful for climbing. Cats are built to resist

◄ *The lightweight two-wheeled carriage was a popular form of private transport. This elegant Chinese carriage would have marked its owner as a man of importance.*

CARPET The world's first mechanical carpet sweeper was invented as a cure for headaches. An American china shop owner called Mr. Bissell felt sure that his headaches were caused by the dusty straw in which his china was packed. To eliminate the dust, he invented the carpet sweeper. Although his headaches continued, his carpet sweeper – which was marketed in the late 19th century – became an instant commercial success.

CARTOON A full-sized design for a painting or tapestry is also called a cartoon. The design is transferred to the final surface by pricking, indenting or tracing.

CASPIAN SEA Much of the world's finest caviar comes from the sturgeon fisheries on the Caspian Sea.

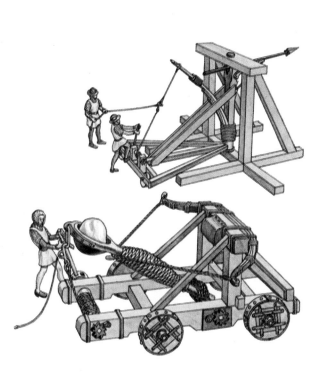

CATERPILLAR The caterpillar of the elephant hawk moth uses a subtle disguise to ward off predators. When threatened, it takes on the appearance of a (miniature) pit viper by retracting its legs and rolling on its back to reveal a pair of false 'eyes'. Its 'deadly snake' appearance scares off most predators.

injury because of the structure of their limbs and through a keen sense of balance. The animal's rough, rasp-like tongue helps it to scrape meat from bones and clean its fur properly. Cats are basically nocturnal creatures, their eyes are adapted to see in dim light and their whiskers help them to feel their way in the dark. When hunting at night, they rely on sound as their hearing is very acute. Cats were probably first domesticated by the ancient Egyptians from wild African and European species. Most ordinary domestic cats are short-haired and many of them are tabby – brownish or grey with dark stripes. Other standard cat colours are ginger, tortoise-shell and black – often with white markings. There are many domestic breeds. Some of the best-known are the fast-running, tail-less Manx cat; the Russian blue, remarkable for its striking blue coat and vivid green eyes; the white long-haired Persian; and the fawn, blue-eyed Siamese, descended from the sacred temple cat of Thailand. ◁

CATACOMBS Underground cemeteries containing passageways and crypts for the burial of the dead. The most famous catacombs are those in Rome, used by the early Christians, with over 800 km (500 miles) of passages.

CATAMARAN A twin-hulled dinghy for sailing or racing, originally developed by primitive peoples for its stability in surf. Today it is a popular leisure craft.

▲ *Left: Two types of medieval catapult. The top one fired a heavy bolt, often tipped with some flammable material. The bottom picture shows a giant crossbow, the beam of which was winched back to propel a large stone with terrific force. Right: The* trebuchet *was a variation on the catapult. The great arm was winched down and when released, the counterweight made it fly upright to hurl its missile.*

CATAPULT An ancient war machine used for hurling rocks, heavy arrows or fire bombs. Catapults were used by the Greeks and Romans, and were the chief siege weapon until the development of cannon. A modern development of the catapult is the device used on aircraft carriers to launch planes.

CATERPILLAR Common name for the LARVA of BUTTERFLIES, MOTHS and sawflies. Caterpillars have long, thin bodies, several pairs of legs and strong biting jaws which work sideways. A caterpillar's main function is to grow bigger so it spends its time feeding – mostly on leaves. Caterpillars live about a month before they change into a chrysalis, the next stage in the insect's life history. ◁

CATHEDRAL The main church of a diocese, in which a bishop or archbishop has his *cathedra* (Latin for 'chair'). Many large towns and cities of Europe have magnificent cathedrals built during the MIDDLE AGES, beautifully decorated with elaborate stonework and richly coloured STAINED GLASS. Famous cathedrals include Chartres and Reims in France; Canterbury and York in Britain; and Cologne in West Germany. St Peter's in Rome is really not a cathedral but a *basilica*, because it is not the official seat of the Pope, who is also the Bishop of Rome. English cathedrals are characterized by cloisters and by two separate places of worship inside, the choir and the nave.

CATHODE-RAY TUBE An evacuated glass tube in which cathode rays (streams of ELEC-TRONS) are produced. The tubes are used for displaying images in TELEVISION sets, OSCIL-LOSCOPES and RADAR equipment. A narrow beam of electrons produced at one end of the tube strikes a screen at the other end. The screen is coated with chemicals called *phosphors*. These glow when struck by the electrons. By suitably deflecting the beam, it is made to trace out an image on the screen.

CATTLE Large heavily-built grass-eating MAMMALS. Wild cattle are all horned and include the BISON, BUFFALO and YAK. Domestic cattle are descended from the *auroch*, a wild species that once lived in Europe but is now extinct. Cattle were first domesticated some 6000 years ago, since then they have become indispensable to man and are kept all over the world for their meat and milk, and other products including leather, glue and soap. Cattle eat about 68 kg (150 lb) of grass a day and digest it in an odd way. Their stomachs have four parts: the grass is swallowed whole and stored in the first part; next, it goes into the second part to be softened and turned into balls called cuds; the cuds are sent to the mouth for chewing, then go back to the third part and are finally digested in the fourth. ▷

CAVALRY Originally, the part of an ARMY that fought on horseback. The Assyrians and Persians used cavalry as early as 800 BC. Cavalry units were a part of armies right up until World War II.

CAVE A naturally-formed underground chamber, usually connected with the Earth's surface and formed by mechanical (sea waves) or chemical (water on limestone) EROSION. ▷

CAVIAR The eggs, or roe, of certain species of fish, especially the STURGEON, prized as a delicacy.

CEDAR A tall coniferous tree belonging to the PINE family. It has spiny leaves and cones and is best known for its very hard, sweet-smelling wood.

CELL Unit of living matter. All living things – plants and animals – are made up of tiny units called cells. Each cell consists of a jelly-

▲ *One of a hoard of five gold Celtic torcs, found at Ipswich on the east coast of England. Torcs were made by early Celtic smiths and were worn around the neck.*

like mass called PROTOPLASM surrounded by a very thin membrane or skin. At the centre of the cell is its 'brain' or nucleus, made of a special type of protoplasm; the nucleus controls the cell's activity. Most animals and plants have millions of cells but the simplest forms of life have only one cell: one-celled animals are called PROTOZOA and one-celled plants, protista. In a complicated being like man there are many different cells – skin cells, bone cells, blood cells, etc – each with its own function; but in very simple beings, all the functions of life are carried out by every cell.

CELL, ELECTRIC See BATTERY

CELLULOSE The CELL walls of all plants are made up almost entirely of cellulose. It makes up more than 95 per cent of the FIBRES of such plants as cotton and flax and about one half of wood fibre. ▷

CELTS Warlike barbarian people from south-eastern Germany who occupied much of northern Europe, including Britain, during the five centuries before Christ. They sacked Rome in 390 BC and travelled as far east as Galatia in Asia Minor. The Celts were grouped into tribal kingdoms. They followed a religion steeped in magic and ritual, and practised human sacrifice. Celtic craftsmen made beautiful metal shields and ornaments decorated with handsome geometric designs. The Celtic language formed the basis of Welsh and GAELIC. After the Roman occupation of Britain, the Celtic way of life survived only in Ireland, Scotland, Wales and Cornwall.

CEMENT An important building material used to make mortar and concrete. Mortar is a mixture of cement powder, sand and water, sometimes with added lime. It is used for binding bricks together. CONCRETE contains cement, sand, water and gravel or chippings.

CENSUS An official count of the population of a country, taken at regular periods. The first census was taken by the ancient Romans for tax purposes.

CATTLE Aurochs, a wild ox which once roamed the forests of Europe, became extinct in the Middle Ages. However, two zoologists, Lutz and Heinz Heck – using their knowledge of heredity – put evolution into reverse to bring back the aurochs by crossing strains and mating cattle with auroch characteristics.

When the first calves were born, they selected the most suitable to mate, and so on, until finally – ten years after they began their researches – an auroch calf was born. This spurred the Hecks on, and now there is a herd of aurochs in Berlin zoo.

CAVE The world's largest cave at Carlsbad in New Mexico, USA, is about 1300 m (4260 ft) long by over 200 m (660 ft) wide and 100 m (330 ft) high.

CELLULOSE The human body's digestive system can cope with most things we eat. But it cannot break down cellulose. Any plant cellulose that we eat travels through us undigested.

It is the cellulose in wood that makes it indispensable as a fuel and a construction material. Wood's cellulose is also used to make paper. The cellulose in cotton and linen makes them man's most important textile materials.

Cell membrane
A thin wall holding the cell together and controlling what the cell takes in (such as oxygen, nutrients and essential chemicals) and what it allows out (waste products, such as carbon dioxide and chemicals needed elsewhere in the body).

Endoplasmic Recticulum
A network of interconnected channels within which protein (and some carbohydrates) are manufactured. The proteins are made in the tiny bodies on the sides.

Mitochondria
The cell's power stations, they contain enzymes which trigger the conversion of nutrients into energy. There may be as many as 800 in one cell.

Cytoplasm
This fills the space between the cell membrane and the nucleus. Mostly water, it is a jelly-like substance in which the organelles are suspended. Protoplasm refers to everything inside the cell.

Lysosomes
Bean-shaped bodies containing enzymes which can break down bacteria and also any damaged organelles within the cell. They thus act as the cell's internal scavengers.

Golgi Bodies
Flat, bag-like channels which appear to store chemicals and proteins, in readiness for despatch from the cell.

Centrioles
A group of cylindrical bodies which are involved in cell division. They occur in pairs in a structure called the centrosome.

Nucleus
The cell's brain. It contains the chromosomes, fine threads of DNA which carry the genes. These control the exact make-up of the cell, and the chemical processes that take place within it. They determine every characteristic that a human possesses.

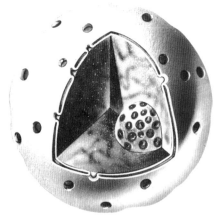

▲ A cutaway drawing of a typical cell (about 10,000 times larger than life) and some of its organelles, the specialized structures suspended in the cytoplasm.

Cen

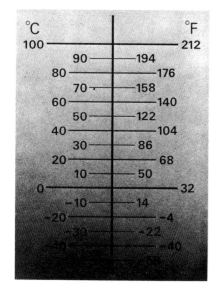

▲ A comparison of the Centigrade and Fahrenheit temperature scales. To convert a Centigrade temperature to Fahrenheit, multiply by 9/5ths and add 32. To convert Fahrenheit to Centigrade, subtract 32 and multiply by 5/9ths.

CENTAUR In Greek mythology, a creature with the torso, arms and head of a man and a horse's body. They were wild, lawless and often savage beings.

CENTIGRADE SCALE A measuring scale divided into 100 degrees. The term usually refers to the Celcius temperature scale. On this scale, 0° is the temperature at which water freezes, and 100° is the temperature at which it boils.

CENTIPEDE Small animal with a long thin body made of segments, each segment having a pair of legs. Centipedes live in damp places – under logs and stones – and feed on insects and other small creatures. Although 'centipede' means '100 feet', some centipedes have only 30 feet, others over 300. ▷

CENTRAL AMERICA This region forms a land bridge between North and South America. It consists of the independent republics of COSTA RICA, EL SALVADOR, GUATEMALA, HONDURAS, NICARAGUA and PANAMA, together with the country of BELIZE, a former British colony. The Panama Canal runs through Panama. The region has an area of 521,415 sq km (201,319 sq miles) and a population of about 25,200,000 (1984 est.). Most people in this rugged, tropical area are poor farmers of Spanish, American Indian or mixed origin. There are some Blacks. Bananas, coffee, cotton and sugar are exported.

CENTRIFUGAL FORCE An outward force produced by a body rotating in a circle. The centrifugal force balances the *centripetal* force, which keeps the object in its circular path.

CERAMICS A term covering all items that are made of clay mixed with water and baked hard. Ceramics include PORCELAIN and POTTERY of all kinds, and are nearly as old as man himself – the clay pot was one of the first manmade objects. (See TERRA-COTTA)

CEREAL Edible cultivated GRASS. Cereals form the main food of most of the world's population. They also feed important meat-producing animals such as cattle, sheep and pigs. The main cereals are WHEAT, BARLEY, RYE and OATS – grown in temperate zones; and RICE, maize and MILLET – grown in countries with hot summers.

CEZANNE, PAUL French painter of the Post-Impressionist period (1839–1906), whose sense of form and colour revolutionized painting of the early 20th century and influenced modern ABSTRACT ART.

CHAD A republic of north central AFRICA. Once a French colony, now a member of the French Community, it became independent in 1960. Population: 4,902,000 (1984.). Capital: N'Djamena. ▷

CHAIN REACTION A process in which ATOMS are split up by bombarding them with neutrons. In splitting, the atoms release neutrons, which cause other atoms to split. A chain of reactions builds up in this way, and

▼ The Mayan civilization flourished in Central America between AD 500–1000. Below, the ceremonial centre at Tikal, Guatemala.

CENTIPEDE Centipedes have been on Earth for a very long time. They are known to have been in existence for some 400 million years; some fossil centipedes have been found embedded in amber.

The longest centipede is probably the giant scolopender of South America. It can measure 300 mm (12 in) in length.

Centipedes are arthropods of the class *Chilopoda*.

CHAD: FACTS AND FIGURES
Principal rivers: Chari and Logone, both flowing into Lake Chad.
Chad is a large landlocked country, twice the size of France.
Official language: French.
Currency: CFA franc.
The country takes its name from Lake Chad, a shallow lake, the size of which varies from 26,000 sq km (10,000 sq miles) to about 10,400 sq km (4,000 sq miles), depending on the season.

CHALK The chalk which makes up the White Cliffs of Dover gave the Romans their name for England – 'Albion' from the Latin *albus* meaning 'white'.

CHAMELEON The chameleon's tongue may be as long as the animal's body. When at rest, the tongue is coiled up like a spring on the bottom of the mouth. It is shot out at amazing speed to catch insects which become stuck to a sticky secretion at the end of the tongue.

The colour of a chameleon's skin changes if the animal is disturbed or if the amount of light changes. The chameleon has an outer transparent skin, and underneath this are four layers of colour cells: a layer of red and yellow cells, a layer of white and a layer of blue cells. The inner layer is a brown pigment called *melanin* which can darken all the other colours. All the colour cells can change in size, so changing the mixture of colours in the animal's skin – if the yellow cells are enlarged, the chameleon looks more yellow.

much ATOMIC ENERGY is released in the form of heat. (See ATOMIC BOMB)

CHALK A soft, white LIMESTONE rock. It consists mainly of the shells of minute sea creatures and crystals of calcite. These are both forms of the chemical compound calcium carbonate. ◁

CHAMELEON Type of tree LIZARD living mainly in tropical Africa. Chameleons range in length from 5–60 cm (2 in–2 ft) and have a flattish body. Two unusual features are their eyes which move independently, and their long tongues which shoot out at great speed to catch itself food. Chameleons can change colour to match their surroundings. ◁

CHANG JIANG (Yangste River) Longest river in CHINA and ASIA. It flows 5470 km (3400 miles) from TIBET to East China Sea. It provides vital irrigation and hydroelectric power to the surrounding country.

CHAPLIN, CHARLES English-born film comedian and director (1889–1977) who made his role of 'the little tramp', with bowler hat, cane and moustache, famous all over the world. After spending over 20 years in exile from the United States, his adopted home, Chaplin returned in triumph. He was knighted two years before his death.

CHARCOAL A form of impure black CARBON. It is usually made by heating wood with little air present. Charcoal is used in GUNPOW-

▲ The term ceramics covers many different styles and finishes. Two distinct types are shown here. Left: a brightly painted ancient Greek vase from Corinth; and right: a finely detailed pottery camel, made in China during the T'ang dynasty (AD 618–907).

▼ Chameleons are well adapted to living in trees. They have excellent eyesight, and feet and tails which are capable of grasping firmly on to the branches.

DER, as a smokeless fuel, for drawing and for absorbing gases.

CHARGE, ELECTRIC In the ATOMS of an uncharged object, the negative charges of electrons cancel the positive charges of protons. An object becomes charged when this balance is disturbed, for example, by friction (see ELECTRICITY). The SI UNIT of charge is the COULOMB.

CHARIOT An open, horse-drawn vehicle used in warfare in ancient times. Two- and four-wheeled chariots were used by the Egyptians and the Sumerians, and were adopted by the Greeks and Romans. A chariot was usually driven by a charioteer and carried an archer or warrior. As a military arm, chariots were eventually replaced by CAVALRY.

CHARLEMAGNE King of the Franks, Holy Roman Emperor and one of the greatest rulers in history (c. 742–814). His talents as a warrior and administrator gave him control of a kingdom that, by the end of his reign, stretched from the North Sea to the Mediterranean and east to the Adriatic Sea. His empire fell apart after his death under the weaker rule of his sons and grandsons. (See ROME)

CHARLES I King of Great Britain (1600–1649; king from 1625), the second son of James I and Anne of Denmark. Economic difficulties brought Charles into conflict with Parliament, and in 1642 CIVIL WAR broke out

between the forces of the king and those of Parliament. He was eventually brought to trial in 1648 and was beheaded on January 30, 1649. (See CROMWELL, OLIVER) ▷

CHARLES II King of Great Britain (1630–1685; reigning king from 1660), the son of Charles I and Henrietta Maria. Charles II's accession to the throne in the RESTORATION of 1660, marked the return of Britain to a monarchy after the period of Cromwell's Protectorate and military dictatorship. (See CROMWELL, OLIVER)

CHART In NAVIGATION, a map showing the depth of sea and location of rocks, coasts, channels, buoys, harbours, and so on, for those piloting boats and ships.

CHATEAU The French word for castle, used to refer to a castle, large mansion or country house in France. The most famous of such buildings are those built from the 15th century onwards. These were elaborate residences with towers and moats built for decoration rather than defence. Some of the most famous are Amboise, Chambord, and Chenonceaux.

CHAUCER, GEOFFREY English poet (c. 1340–1400), best known for *The Canterbury Tales*, a collection of romantic and often bawdy adventures written in the English dialect that was to become the foundation for modern English. Chaucer's humanity and comic flair make him one of the great figures of ENGLISH LITERATURE.

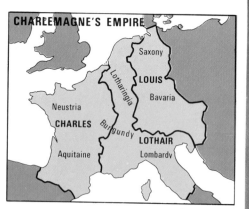

▲ A map of Charlemagne's empire after it was divided among his three grandsons.

◄ Charlemagne was probably the greatest warrior-king of the Dark Ages, and a great patron of the arts and scholarship. The son of Pepin the Short, he became king in AD 768. Charlemagne revived the idea of the Roman Empire in the West. On Christmas Day, in the year 800, Pope Leo III crowned Charlemagne the 'Emperor of the West' in St Peter's Basilica, Rome.

CHARLES There were seven Holy Roman Emperors named Charles, the first of whom was Charlemagne. They were Charles II, called the Bald (823-877, emperor from 875); Charles III, called Charles the Fat (839-888, emperor from 881 to 887); Charles IV, sometimes called Charles of Luxembourg (1316-1378, emperor from 1347); Charles V, emperor from 1519 to 1556); Charles VI (1685-1740, emperor from 1711); and Charles VII (1697-1745, emperor from 1742).

Three French kings called Charles were also Holy Roman Emperors: Charlemagne, Charles the Bald, and Charles the Fat. The other French kings of this name were: Charles III, the Simple (879-929, king from 898); Charles IV, called Charles the Fair, (1294-1328, king from 1322); Charles V, called Charles the Wise (1338-1380, king from 1364); Charles VI, called Charles the Well-Beloved (1368-1422, king from 1380); Charles VII, called Charles the Victorious (1403-1461, king from 1422); Charles VIII (1470-1498, king from 1483); Charles IX (1550-1574, king from 1560); Charles X (1757-1836, king from 1824 to 1830).

There were also four kings of Spain called Charles, the first, and greatest, being Charles I of Spain, who was also the Holy Roman Emperor Charles V. The others were: Charles II (1661-1770, king from 1665); Charles III (1716-1788, king from 1759); and Charles IV (1748-1819, king from 1788 to 1808).

There were also 14 Swedish kings called Charles and several kings of Naples.

CHEESE The characteristic texture and flavour of a cheese depends on how long it is left to cure. In general, a long curing period will produce a cheese with a crumbly texture and a sharp 'bite', while a short curing period will produce a cheese with a smooth texture and mild flavour.

No one knows who first began to make cheese, but there is a story about a nomad in the desert who

filled his saddlebag with milk and rode off on a long trip. The saddlebag was made from the lining of a calf's stomach. After he had been riding for some time the nomad tried to drink from the bag. A watery liquid came out, but no milk. Inside was a white mass which we now call cottage cheese. It had formed from the milk being acted upon by a chemical called rennet which is present in a calf's stomach.

Cheddar cheese took its name from the Cheddar area in Somerset, but today it is made in most temperate parts of the world, and has become important in international trade. Other British cheeses are: Cheshire, Double Gloucester, Derby, Leicester, Lancashire, Wensleydale, Stilton, Dunlop, Caerphilly and Blue Vinney.

▲ The beautiful chateau of Chenonceaux in France straddles the River Cher.

▶ The slim, lithe, long-legged cheetah runs faster than any other predator. It can outpace and kill the fastest antelopes.

CHEESE A food prepared mainly from cow's or goat's MILK. The milk is turned sour (curdled) by adding a small amount of acid or bacteria. This separates the milk into *curd*, a thick creamy substance containing most of the protein and fat in the milk; and *whey*, a thin watery liquid. The whey is drained off and the curd, the cheese, is cut into slabs, salted and left to harden and dry. There are many different types of cheese, depending on how they are prepared and how long they are left to ripen. Cheese can also be eaten fresh, as in cottage cheese. ◁

CHEETAH The world's fastest mammal. The cheetah, found mostly in East Africa, is a spotted cat-like animal. It has very long legs and over short distances can run faster than 110 kph (70 mph). (See CAT)

CHEKHOV, ANTON Russian dramatist and short story writer (1860–1904). His four most famous plays are *Uncle Vanya*, *Three Sisters*, *The Seagull* and *The Cherry Orchard*.

CHEMICAL ANALYSIS The process of testing a substance to find its chemical make-up. Analysis is used for many purposes. These

Che

► *Each year human beings swallow thousands of millions of pills intended to help cure everything from headaches and colds to contagious diseases. In a modern pharmaceutical factory, a major chemical industry, automatic pill-packing machinery counts out predetermined numbers of pills into hundreds of containers every hour.*

include checking the amount of alcohol in a motorist's blood or urine. Food analysts check food for impurities. *Qualitative* analysis is concerned with identifying substances. *Quantitative* analysis is for finding out the amounts of various substances present in a sample.

CHEMICAL INDUSTRY The vast range of products of the chemical industry includes paints, dyes, soaps and detergents, adhesives, fertilizers, pesticides, synthetic fibres and plastics. Basic raw materials, such as coal, petroleum and sea water, are used to make *starting chemicals.* From these, more complex substances are made by chemical reactions. Many physical processes are used too. These include grinding, EVAPORATION, DISTILLATION, and filtration and drying. *Heavy chemicals* are those manufactured in large quantities, such as caustic soda (sodium hydroxide) and SULPHURIC ACID. *Fine chemicals* are generally more complex and are produced in small quantities for specialized uses.

CHEMISTRY The science concerned with the preparation of ELEMENTS AND COMPOUNDS, and with the ways they react with one another. When man first learned to make fire, he was unaware that he was using a chemical REACTION to produce heat. He did not know that the wood he was burning combined with oxygen from the air to form the various substances that make up smoke and ash. The use of fire led to important discoveries that were to affect the whole world. Sometimes, strange glistening liquids would ooze from rocks heated by a fire. On cooling, they would solidify into lumps of metal. Copper was probably discovered like this in the Middle East, around 4000 BC. When man found how useful metals were for tools, weapons and ornaments, he sought to perfect ways of extracting them from their ORES. And he learned to make ALLOYS by mixing molten metals.

By the time of the Roman Empire, people had learned how to prepare many useful substances. Glass, dyes, coloured enamels, paints, varnishes, perfumes, ointments, medicines, poisons and other products were in great demand. But, although man was using chemistry, how it worked was a mystery. Various theories had been handed down from the Chinese, Indians and Greeks, but most of these were incorrect. The Greeks, for example,

had put forward the idea of four basic elements – earth, air, fire and water. And, even if a theory was correct, it was not always easy to prove it or to make use of it. This applied to the atomic theory of matter, originally taught in the 400s BC by a Greek called Democritus. More than 2000 years were to pass before this idea would be accepted. So, because of the confusion about chemistry, it became more and more associated with magic, trickery, fraud and religion, in a pursuit called ALCHEMY. This became extremely popular soon after the birth of Christ and persisted until the 1600s. Many alchemists tried to find the 'Philosopher's Stone' – a mythical substance that was supposed to change common metals into gold. They also experimented with various potions in an effort to produce the 'Elixir of Life' – a drink that would ensure a healthy and eternal life. However, some alchemists adopted a more logical approach to their science. They based all their knowledge on carefully planned experiments and would not accept a theory until it had been proved.

This trend eventually led to the start of modern chemistry in the 1600s.

In 1661, Robert BOYLE correctly explained the basic idea of ELEMENTS AND COMPOUNDS, although this theory was not widely accepted at first. In the 1700s, the French chemist Antoine LAVOISIER discovered why iron rusts and what happens when things burn. Previously it had been thought that substances lost something to the air during these processes. But Lavoisier showed that the substances actually combined with a gas in the air. And he named the gas OXYGEN.

In 1808, John DALTON published his theory explaining that elements are made up of atoms. Many new elements were being discovered at that time, and chemists made attempts at listing them in some logical order. Eventually, in 1869, Dmitri Mendeleyev con-

CHEMISTRY In medicine, the treatment of disease by means of chemicals is known as chemotherapy. Nowadays, we take it for granted that there are 'drugs' we can take for almost every ailment. However, this is a very recent state of affairs. The two main groups of chemotherapeutic substances are sulphur- and nitrogen-based drugs (sulphonamides), and antibiotics. The former group was discovered in 1930-35 by F. Mietzch, J. Klorer, G. Domagh and others; while Sir Alexander Fleming's discovery of the antibiotic penicillin in 1928 did not produce antibiotics useful for the treatment of infectious diseases until 1940. Before these two types of drugs came into use, only a few diseases could be treated by chemical substances. These included malaria (using quinine), syphilis (using mercury and bismuth) and sleeping sickness (using compounds of arsenic and antimony). The most recent developments in chemotherapy include the use of natural chemicals called hormones, and various tranquillizers – which have largely replaced brain surgery in the treatment of cases of mental illness.

structed the periodic table of ELEMENTS.

By 1900, the new understanding of chemistry had led to the establishment of a CHEMICAL INDUSTRY. This century, advances in PHYSICS have revealed much about atomic structure. This, in turn, has explained many properties of the elements. Since the 1940s, it has been possible to manufacture new elements using particle ACCELERATORS. ◁

▼ The fruit of the wild cherry tree can be eaten fresh or used in jams and liquers. The wood is used for crafting furniture and bowls.

Flowers and leaves

Wild cherry

Ripening fruit

▼ A quarter of the world's copper resources comes from Chile. This vast open cast copper mine is in Chile.

CHERRY Summer fruit that is yellow, red, purple or black according to variety. Cherries are mostly sweet, but the famous Morello cherry – widely used in cooking – is sour.

CHESS A game for two players, played on a checkered board with movable pieces, that demands great intellectual skill. Chess may have originated in India, and is played today in nearly all civilized countries. ◁

CHESTNUT Large deciduous tree with prickly fruits containing shiny, red-brown nuts (chestnuts). There are two kinds of tree, the horse chestnut with inedible nuts, and the sweet chestnut with delicious edible nuts.

CHEWING GUM A substance made from *chicle*, the gum-like juice of the sapodilla tree, which, with added sweeteners and flavourings, is used for chewing.

CHICKEN POX A common and usually mild infectious disease, caused by a VIRUS. It affects the skin with an itching rash of small, raised blisters.

CHILE A republic in SOUTH AMERICA, Chile has 11,878,000 people (1984 est.) and an area of 756,945 sq km (292,258 sq miles). The capital is Santiago. This long, narrow nation has deserts in the north, a Mediterranean-type zone in the centre and wet forests in the south. Mining is important. ◁

▼ Sweet chestnut can be eaten roasted and used to make flour or bread. Each husk which holds the nuts has radiating spines.

Immature fruit

nut

▲ Chinese workers lay the foundations for circular dwellings in the vast desert plains of Inner Mongolia.

CHIMPANZEE The most intelligent of the anthropoid apes *(Pan troglodytes)*, native to Africa. An adult chimp stands about 1.3 metres (4½ ft) high and weighs up to 68 kg (150 lb). In the wild, chimpanzees live in family groups, though each builds an individual sleeping platform in a tree. Chimpanzees have the ability to learn and solve problems, often using a 'tool' such as a stick or a stone. (See APE) ▷

CHINA The world's third largest country, the People's Republic of China contains more people than any other nation. Most people live in eastern China, especially along the coast and in the fertile Hwang Ho, YANGTZE and Si Kiang river valleys. The north-east has very cold winters and warm summers, but the extreme south-east has a wet tropical climate. The interior, called Outer China, has far fewer people. It contains bleak plateaux, many mountains, including part of the HIMALAYAS in TIBET, and deserts, which cover more than one million square kilometres (386,100 sq miles).

Most people are Han, or true, Chinese. Minorities, numbering around 50 million, include Manchus, Mongols, Tibetans and Uighurs. The minorities live mostly around the borders of the country. Religious belief is

◀ In ancient China, during the Shang dynasty (1500–1000 BC) chariot and horseback hunters used cheetahs to catch their prey.

CHIMPANZEE Scientists at the Institute of Primate Studies in Oklahoma, USA, have used a female chimpanzee called Washoe to investigate the ape's intelligence. Washoe was adopted by human parents when she was a year old, and from there on was taught a human lauguage: the American sign language for the deaf.

By the time she was three, Washoe had learned more than 30 signs. She could use them in a wide variety of situations and could also respond to sign-language commands. Two years later, Washoe knew over 150 signs, and her vocabulary was still improving. By that time she had also worked out how to combine signs to swear at humans who failed to do what she wanted.

CHINA If all the people in China stood on each other's shoulders they would make a chain three times longer than the distance between the Earth and the moon.

CHLORINE During World War I chlorine was used as a poison gas, both in its free state and in compounds such as phosgene.

CHLOROPHYLL Chlorophyll was first analysed in 1817 by two French chemists, Pelletier and Caventou. They named it chlorophyll from the Greek *chloros*, meaning 'green', and *phyllon*, meaning 'leaf'.

discouraged by the communist government. The traditional beliefs are Confucianism (see CONFUCIUS) and Taoism and there are Buddhists (see BUDDHISM), especially in Tibet, and Moslems, particularly in Sinkiang in the north-west.

The Chinese are mostly farmers and China produces more millet, rice, sorghum and tobacco than any other country. It is also a major producer of barley, cotton, ground-nuts, maize, silk, tea, timber and wheat. The Chinese also raise livestock and there is a large fishing industry. Since 1949 rural people have been encouraged to live in communes, which are groups of villages where the people work together and share the produce. China has large mineral reserves, many of which are unexploited. Manufacturing is developing, especially because the Chinese consider in-dustrialization, particularly the growth of heavy industry, to be essential in transforming China into a modern world power. It is already established in Manchuria, the Sichu-an basin, and in the larger cities, such as SHANGHAI and BEIJING.

China was the home of a great ancient civilization which goes back 3500 years. In 1912 China became a republic. From 1931 to 1945, China was partly invaded and ravaged by Japanese armies. From 1946 to 1949, Chinese nationalists led by Chiang Kai-shek (1887–1975) fought a civil war with the com-munists, led by MAO ZEDONG (1893–1976). After 1949 Chiang retired with his nationalist supporters to the island of Taiwan and main-land China was ruled by the communists. Mao introduced a centrally-planned economy and economic development was rapid. From the 1950s a serious rift developed between China and the USSR, and Mao accused the USSR of betraying true communism. After Mao's death, Deng Xiaoping (1904–) gradually emerged as the effective ruler of China (see COMMUNISM). ◁

CHIPPENDALE, THOMAS The most fa-mous member of a family of English cabinet-makers (1718–1779), whose name was given to the particular 18th century style of FURNI-TURE the family developed. Chippendale furniture is elegant and often makes use of elements from earlier styles, such as Re-naissance and Baroque.

CHIVALRY A code of ideal behaviour fol-lowed by knights of the MIDDLE AGES. Chivalry included such Christian values as honesty, courage, courtesy, modesty and honour.

CHLORINE A yellow-green poisonous, choking gas. Chlorine, symbol Cl, is used in the manufacture of bleach, hydrochloric acid and disinfectant. Small quantities of chlorine are used to kill germs in drinking water. ◁

CHLOROFORM A heavy, colourless liquid compound, used widely as a general ANAES-THETIC in the 19th century. It was discovered by Justus von Liebig (1831) and was first used as an anaesthetic in 1847, eventually replacing ETHER. Today its use is restricted to local anaesthesia.

CHLOROPHYLL Green colouring matter found in plant cells. Chlorophyll is essential for PHOTOSYNTHESIS – the process by which plants turn CARBON DIOXIDE and water into sugar, using light energy from the Sun. Chlorophyll makes this process possible by absorbing light energy and using it to power the various chemical reactions. Plants only make chlorophyll in the light; plants kept in darkness usually turn white or yellow. ◁

▼ *The predominant colour of the countryside is green. This is due to the chlorophyll contained in the chloroplasts, the plant cells, on the outer layer of the leaves of most plants. Plants need sunlight to make chlorophyll.*

CHOCOLATE A food made from COCOA beans, most often sold in bars or blocks. It may be eaten on its own or used to flavour other sweet mixtures such as cakes, ice cream and milk drinks. The cocoa tree is native to South America and the Caribbean, though today Ghana and Nigeria produce half the world's output.

CHOLERA A severe and often fatal infectious disease most often occurring in areas where there are unsanitary water supplies. Cholera is caught from infected food or water and causes acute stomach pains and diarrhoea.

CHOLESTEROL A white fatty STEROID alcohol, found in animal cells and body fluids. Cholesterol helps the body to absorb fats, vitamin D and various HORMONES. Carried in the blood-stream, cholesterol is necessary to help our bodies function, but too much cholesterol inside the ARTERIES may be a cause of heart disease.

CHOPIN, FRÉDÉRIC Polish-French pianist and one of the greatest composers of works for the piano (1810–1849). Altogether he wrote over 135 works for the keyboard.

CHRISTCHURCH The largest city in South Island, NEW ZEALAND (pop. 326,000). It serves the Canterbury Plains, from which wool, meat and dairy products are exported.

CHRISTIANITY The largest of the world's religions, founded by the followers of JESUS CHRIST after his crucifixion. They were convinced that he had risen from the dead and proclaimed him Lord and Saviour. They taught that those who followed Jesus would share eternal life with him.

To some extent Christianity grew out of JUDAISM, but it was at such odds with the Greco-Roman religions of its time that for many years Christians were persecuted by the Roman state, which made it illegal. Yet within 500 years of Jesus' death the majority of the population of the Roman Empire, including the emperors, were Christians. The early Church was organized into 'dioceses' headed by bishops. The Bishop of Rome, believed to be the direct successor of the apostle Peter, became the head of the Church, or POPE.

During the Middle Ages the Church became extremely wealthy and powerful. This led to a conflict of ideals and in the 16th century, Protestantism was born. Reformers such as Martin LUTHER and John CALVIN challenged the authority of the Church and stressed the authority of the BIBLE. The conflict led to the Counter Reformation and a series of religious wars, including the THIRTY YEARS' WAR, in Europe.

▲ The Christian faith centres around Jesus Christ, shown here with the Madonna and, at left, St John the Baptist, in a painting by Leonardo da Vinci.

Modern Christianity has had to come to terms with the new growth in scientific knowledge and the increased industrialization of society. At the same time, due to the growth of the European empires over the last few centuries, Christianity has spread and taken hold in many traditionally non-Christian parts of the world. (See CRUSADES; REFORMATION; ROMAN CATHOLIC CHURCH)

CHRISTIAN SCIENCE A religion that relies on the BIBLE as the ultimate authority and on spiritual healing as the central part of its

CHRONOLOGY In the past there have been many different ways of dividing up time. In ancient Greece and Rome, the cycles of the Moon were each given names, and 12 lunar months were called a year. However, 12 lunar months only add up to 355 days, so each year the same month fell during a slightly different season. By the time of Julius Caesar the month of March was happening in the middle of summer. So, in 46 BC Julius Caesar decreed that the year should go on for an extra three months in order to get the seasons back in their proper place. Later he introduced a solar calendar – based on the time it takes the Earth to go once around the Sun. His astronomers calculated this to be 365¼ days, so each year was made 365 days long with every fourth year being a leap year with an extra day to account for the quarters. This Julian calendar was quite successful, but it, too, was inaccurate. The solar year is in fact 365 days, five hours, 48 minutes and 46 seconds long – not 365 days and six hours. So, the Julian calendar was wrong by one day every 128 years. By the end of the 16th century, this error had become 10 days. In 1582, Pope Gregory decreed that Thursday, October 4, would be followed by Friday, October 15 to correct the error. Then he altered the system of leap years. Instead of these years falling on every fourth year when the year was divisible by four, he decreed that century years (those ending in '00') could only be leap years if they were divisible by 400. In fact, even this system is inaccurate, as it makes the length of the average year just 26 seconds too long. However, this will not add up to an error of a whole day for more than 3,300 years.

teaching. It was founded by Mary Baker Eddy in Boston, Massachusetts, in 1892. Today there are more than 3200 branches in 46 countries.

CHRISTMAS ISLAND An AUSTRALIAN territory in the Indian Ocean, important for its phosphate deposits. Population: 32,608.

CHROMIUM A hard, white metal that is highly resistant to corrosion. Parts of cars and bicycles are chromium plated to give them a protective, decorative finish. The metal is also used to make stainless steel and other corrosion-resistant ALLOYS.

CHROMOSOMES Threadlike, microscopic, paired bodies in living cells that consist of long chains of DNA. They carry the genes that determine the particular characteristics of each individual plant or animal. (See GENE; HEREDITY)

CHRONOLOGY The science of dating past events, as most often applied in archaeology, geology and history. Geological chronology is determined by studying the strata (layers) of rock. ◁

CHRONOMETER An extremely accurate CLOCK. An important navigational instrument used to determine longitude at sea or in the air when working out the position of a craft. (See LATITUDE AND LONGITUDE)

CHURCH A word used to describe the building used by most Christians for worship (from the Greek *kuriakos*, meaning 'belonging to the Lord'). Most churches are based on the Roman *basilica* – a long hall, flanked by aisles, with the altar and pulpit at one end. In the Middle Ages transepts were added to make

the church into the shape of a Latin cross. The buildings were lightened with the addition of flying buttresses, clusters of slender columns, and huge stained glass windows. Modern churches often depart from traditional styles, though the interior layout is usually the same. (See ARCHITECTURE)

CHURCHILL, WINSTON British Prime Minister and war leader (1874–1965). The son of Lord Randolph Churchill, he was educated at Harrow and Sandhurst and served with the

▼ Three very different styles of Christian church. Below, a simple white wooden church in Vermont, USA. Bottom right, the slender, graceful columns and vaults of Ely cathedral, built in the Gothic style. Bottom left, the modern interior of Le Corbusier's chapel at Ronchamp in France, uses light to create an effect inside the building.

army in India and Africa. He was a war correspondent in South Africa during the Boer War and entered politics in 1900. Between World Wars I and II he held several posts in government, but it was not until shortly after the outbreak of WORLD WAR II that Churchill took over the leadership of his country. As war leader he united the country behind the war effort with his bold and stirring speeches. He was defeated in the General Election of 1945 but served as Prime Minister again from 1951–56. He was knighted in 1953.

▷

CIDER An alcoholic drink made from fermented APPLE juice, usually from apples specially grown for the purpose. Rough, dry cider is often called 'scrumpy'.

CINEMA An entertainment and art form derived from the invention of the cinematograph, a machine that projected a series of images on to a screen to give the illusion of continuous movement.

The cinema was born in 1895, when the *cinématographe* was patented by Auguste and Louis Lumière. At first, films were like documentaries, recording news and events in the street, the home and the factory. But by 1902 films began to tell stories, and, realizing their commercial potential, film-making industries sprang up in France and the United States. Hollywood, California soon became the centre of the film industry. *The Jazz Singer* (1927) was the first 'talkie', or film with sound. America continued to dominate the film industry, though important work was done by directors in Germany, Sweden and Russia. The years after World War II saw a marked change in the kinds of films made. To the westerns, detective films and extravagant musicals of the '30s were added more realistic stories of everyday life, many, after 1945, coming from Italy. Britain's Ealing Studios became famous for comedies such as *Whisky Galore* and *Passport to Pimlico*. New directors with individual styles such as Ingmar Bergman, François Truffaut, Federico Fellini and Luis Buñuel, became popular in the 1960s, as the film industry's answer to television. In the 1970s, in a further attempt to compete with television, the film industry began experimenting with new technical effects: for example, by trying to create not only the sight and sound of the picture but also the feel of what is happening on the screen. But so far these methods have not been very successful.

CIRCLE A closed plane curve along which all points are an equal distance from the centre. The term also refers to the space within the curve.

CIRCUS A spectacle or entertainment made up of a variety of acts, including acrobatic displays, juggling and comic acts, and the presentation of trained animals. Circuses first appeared in the 18th century and were developed to colossal proportions by the American Phineas T. Barnum (1810–1891).

CIVIL RIGHTS The personal rights given to an individual by law. The Universal Declaration of Rights, passed by the UNITED NATIONS in 1948, lists the basic civil rights which should be available to all people in the world. ▷

CIVIL WAR The English Civil War (1642–1649) was the conflict between the King and PARLIAMENT that led to the supremacy of Parliament, and a final end to the belief in the 'divine right' of kings. CHARLES I had angered Parliament by his attempts to wield absolute authority and by his unpopular

▼ *During the 1930s spectacular Hollywood films were produced at enormous expense. Among them were musicals with extravagantly presented set pieces: this one, from* Footlight Parade, *was staged by Busby Berkeley.*

CHURCHILL Winston Churchill was famous for his rousing, patriotic speeches made during and after World War II. One of his most well-known quotations commemorates the airmen who resisted the might of the German Luftwaffe in the late summer of 1940. It reads: 'Never in the field of human conflict was so much owed by so many to so few.'

A later speech, made on March 5, 1946, at Westminster College, Fulton, USA, added a now familiar phrase to the world's vocabulary. Part of this speech reads: 'An iron curtain has descended across the Continent'. Churchill was referring to the dividing line between the communist states and the western democracies of Europe.

CIVIL RIGHTS In modern times the most successful campaign for civil rights was waged in the USA by black people in the late 1950s and '60s. As late as 1954 the US Supreme Court ruled that separate schools for black and white children were 'unequal and therefore unconstitutional'. This decision marked the beginning of the Civil Rights Movement, led mainly by Dr. Martin Luther King. Although the peaceful Movement was very successful, King was assassinated in 1968, and this destroyed the Movement. Violence and riots followed and continued into the 1970s.

CIVIL WAR Oliver Cromwell, the fearsome Puritan leader of the Parliamentary forces was clearly not a vain or fussy person. While having his portrait painted by an artist called Lely, he said, 'Remark all these roughnesses, pimples, warts and everything as you see me, otherwise I will never pay a farthing for it.'

CIVIL WAR (US) The American Civil War is often called the first of the modern wars. It featured such equipment as machine guns, iron-clad warships, telegraphs, railroads and a submarine that could sink a warship. As a result, the casualties and costs were astronomical. Of 1,556,000 Union soldiers who took part, 634,703 became casualties (of these 359,528 were killed); while of around 800,000 Confederate soldiers, more than 483,000 became casualties (of these 258,000 were killed). Altogether the American Civil War is reckoned to have cost over $15,000,000,000.

CLAM There are more than 12,000 species of clams, of which about 500 live in freshwater. They range in size from the 0.1 mm (0.004 in) of *Condylocardia* to the giant clam (*Tridacna gigas*) which can measure a metre (3 ft) across and is found in the Pacific and Indian Oceans.

▲ *Oliver Cromwell led the Parliamentary forces (Roundheads) against Charles I of England. After Charles' execution, Cromwell ruled the Commonwealth as Lord Protector.*

means of raising taxes. When, in early 1642, he attempted to arrest five prominent members of the House of Commons, Parliament gathered its forces and prepared for armed conflict. The Royalists (or Cavaliers), on the King's side, moved to the north of England, while the Parliamentary (Roundhead) forces under Oliver CROMWELL held the wealthier southern parts of England and the main ports. Important Parliamentary victories were won at Marston Moor (1644) and Naseby (1645). In 1647 Charles was handed into Parliamentary custody. He attempted to take advantage of the split in Parliament between the Presbyterians and Cromwell's Puritans by making terms with the Scots. For this he was branded a traitor, tried and executed in January 1649. The monarchy was temporarily abandoned, and Parliament ruled without a king until the RESTORATION of 1660. ◁

CIVIL WAR (US) The American Civil War was fought between the forces of the federal government (Union) and those of the 11 Confederate States of America from 1861–65. It began after 11 states seceded from the Union as a result of a long series of conflicts, the most important of which was the issue of SLAVERY. The South depended on slaves to work its profitable sugar and cotton plantations. Reformers in the North were opposed to the use of slave labour. The war broke out on April 12, 1861, when Confederate artillery fired on Fort Sumter, a federal garrison in

Charleston, South Carolina. The Confederate forces were led by General Robert E. Lee; the outstanding leader of the Union army was Ulysses S. Grant. Bloody battles were fought at such places as Manassas, Virginia, Antietam, Maryland, Gettysburg, Pennsylvania, Shiloh, Tennessee and Vicksburg, Mississippi. In Georgia, the Union General William T. Sherman captured Atlanta and then marched his army to the sea, cutting a path of destruction 97 km (60 miles) wide. The Confederate forces finally surrendered at Appomattox Court House, Virginia on April 9, 1865, bringing the war, and slavery, to an end. (See LINCOLN, ABRAHAM; UNITED STATES) ◁

CLAM Bivalve (twin-shelled MOLLUSC) inhabiting the shallows of the sea. Many species are edible. The giant clam of warm seas may be 1 metre (3 feet) across. ◁

CLAN A term, originally GAELIC, for a group of related families descended from a common ancestor. The clan system was particularly strong in SCOTLAND, where each clan took its name from the founder of the clan. Warfare and rivalry among the clans was once fairly common.

CLARINET Musical instrument in the woodwind family, popular since the 18th century. It consists of a long tube ending in a bell, with a flattened, reeded mouthpiece, and is popular as both a classical and jazz instrument.

CLASSIFICATION OF LIVING THINGS All living things – animals and plants – are divided into major groups according to their kind. These groups are then sub-divided again and again down to the single species (bluebell, snowy owl, grizzly bear, etc.)

The animal kingdom is arranged into about 21 major groups called *phyla* (singular *phylum*) such as Protozoa (single-celled animals), Mollusca (shell-fish), Arthropoda (animals – mostly insects – with jointed legs) and Chordata (back-boned animals). Most phyla are divided into classes: some of the classes mak-

▼ *The Giant clam is the largest of all bivalve molluscs. Its shell can be more than 1 metre (3 ft) across.*

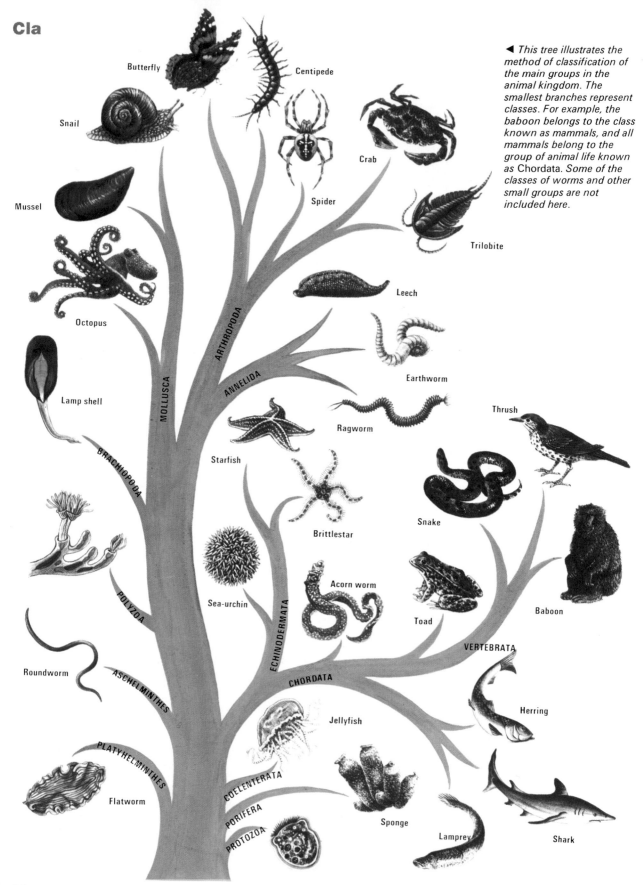

Butterfly

Centipede

Snail

Crab

Spider

Mussel

Trilobite

Octopus

Leech

Lamp shell

Earthworm

Thrush

Starfish

Ragworm

Brittlestar

Snake

Roundworm

Sea-urchin

Acorn worm

Baboon

Flatworm

Toad

VERTEBRATA

Jellyfish

Herring

Sponge

Lamprey

Shark

MOLLUSCA

ARTHROPODA

ANNELIDA

BRACHIOPODA

POLYZOA

ECHINODERMATA

CHORDATA

ASCHELMINTHES

PLATYHELMINTHES

COELENTERATA

PORIFERA

PROTOZOA

◄ This tree illustrates the method of classification of the main groups in the animal kingdom. The smallest branches represent classes. For example, the baboon belongs to the class known as mammals, and all mammals belong to the group of animal life known as Chordata. Some of the classes of worms and other small groups are not included here.

Snow and Tundra (Treeless)

Cold (Boreal Forest)

Temperate (Broad-leaved Woodlands)

Arid (Scrub and Desert)

Tropical Wet (Rain Forest)

CLASSIFICATION OF LIVING THINGS
To illustrate the enormous difficulties found in making any classification of living things, the following is the complete classification – followed by the category in brackets – of the timber wolf of sub-arctic Canada:
Animalia (Kingdom); Metazoe (Sub-kingdom); Chordata (Phylum); Vertebrata (Sub-phylum); Tetrapoda (Superclass); Mammalia (Class); Theria (Sub-class); Eutheria (Infraclass); Ferungulata (Cohort); Ferae (Superorder); Carnivora (Order); Fissipeda (Sub-order); Canoidea (Super-family); Canidae (Family); Caninae (Sub-family); no *Tribe* is described for this group; Canis (Genus); no *Subgenus* described for this group; Canis Lupus (Species); Canis Lupus Occidentalis (Sub-species).

ing up the phylum Chordata are Amphibia (AMPHIBIANS), Reptilia (REPTILES), Aves (BIRDS) and Mammalia (MAMMALS). Classes are further divided into orders, families, genera (singular genus) and species.

The plant kingdom consists of two major groups – *cryptogams* and *phanerogams* – which have various sub-divisions. Cryptogams, such as SEAWEEDS, FUNGI, MOSSES and FERNS, have no flowers or seeds. Phanerogams, also called spermatophytes, are seed-bearing plants. There are two sorts of spermatophytes: *gymnosperms* and *angiosperms*. Gymnosperms, mostly CONIFERS, have naked seeds, whereas angiosperms are flowering plants with seeds enclosed in a fruit.

This system of classifying living things, now used all over the world, was developed by a Swedish naturalist, Carl Linnaeus (1707–78).
◁

CLAW Hard, curved nail on the feet of some birds, reptiles and mammals. Claws are sharp and pointed and are used for scratching, tearing, seizing and clutching.

CLEOPATRA The most famous of several Egyptian queens of that name (c. 69–30 BC). Renowned for her beauty and wit, she charmed Julius CAESAR and went to Rome as his mistress until his death in 44 BC. In 37 BC she became the mistress of Marcus Antonius, (Antony), the Roman triumvir (one of three rulers). When the emperor Octavian declared

▲ The map above shows that the climatic regions of the world are roughly arranged by latitude. Most of the warm regions are near the equator, the cold ones near the poles, and the temperate regions are between them. However, within these belts the climates vary enormously. For example, mountains near the equator tend to have cold polar climates, while many deserts have extremely hot, dry climates even though they are thousands of kilometres north or south of the equator.

war against Antony, both Antony and Cleopatra committed suicide.

CLIMATE The overall effect, in a particular area, of such things as rainfall and temperature, that create the normal or average conditions for that area. It is distinct from the day-to-day atmospheric changes that we call the weather (see WEATHER FORECASTING). The world is divided into five climatic zones based on latitude: the tropical zone, two polar zones, and two temperate zones. (See LATITUDE AND LONGITUDE)

CLIMBING PLANT Thin-stemmed plant which uses a support to grow upwards to the light. Some plants climb by simply winding themselves round a neighbouring plant. They may, like the HOP twist clockwise or, like the BEAN, go anti-clockwise. Others, like the PEA, have slender shoots called tendrils, which wind round the nearest twig. A few have

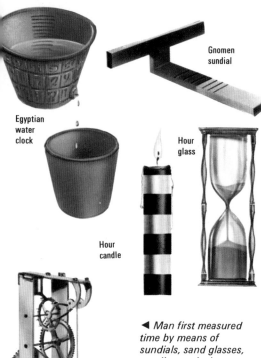

Gnomen sundial

Egyptian water clock

Hour glass

Hour candle

◄ *Man first measured time by means of sundials, sand glasses, candles marked at regular intervals, and water clocks. By the 1300s mechanical clocks were in use, and in the 1600s pendulum clocks appeared. However, a pendulum clock was useless on board ship – a problem eventually solved by the invention of the marine chronometer in 1759. A quartz clock is regulated by a vibrating crystal, while an atomic cesium clock is so accurate it should lose only 1 second in 1000 years.*

Galileo's escapement

Weight-driven clock

Atomic clock

Chronometer

Quartz watch

▲ *A famous race between the clippers* Ariel *and* Taeping. *They left Foochow in China on May 30, 1866, and reached England 99 days later.* Taeping *won – by just 20 minutes*.

special climbing aids. The IVY, for instance, holds onto trees and walls by means of tiny roots growing out of its stem.

CLIPPER SHIP The name given to a large sailing vessel developed in the 19th century in North America. It was built for speed, rather than cargo capacity, and was primarily used for transatlantic crossings and for shipping supplies and produce between Europe, America and Australia. (See SHIPS) ▷

CLOCKS Mechanisms used to mark the passage of TIME. Clocks are usually kept in one place, whereas watches are carried about.

One of the earliest devices for measuring time was the SUNDIAL, which showed the time of day by the position of a shadow, which moved around a marked surface as the Sun moved across the sky. The sandglass, invented c. AD 800, measured time as sand trickled from one glass chamber into another. In an hourglass, the sand took an hour to do this.

The first mechanical clocks, driven by weights, appeared around 1300 in Europe. The PENDULUM clock was developed in 1656 by Christian Huygens, a Dutch horologist, and by the end of the 17th century, 8-day, 1-month and even 1-year clocks had been invented. Pendulum clocks were gradually improved and made more and more accurate, but they were useless at sea on a rolling ship. Navigators needed an accurate clock in order to establish longitude when working out their position at sea. In 1759 John Harrison (1693–1776) made an extremely accurate portable timepiece for use on ships, which we now call a CHRONOMETER. Today, electric clocks containing vibrating crystals of quartz are some of the most accurate timepieces available. An atomic clock may vary less than a second in 1000 years more accurate than the rotating Earth itself. ▷

CLIPPER SHIP The record time of 89 days for a voyage between New York and San Francisco was set by the American clipper ship *'Flying Cloud'*. The transatlantic record was set by the British clipper ship *'James Baines'* which sailed from Boston to Liverpool in 12 days.

The all-time record for the greatest distance ever covered in a day by a sailing ship was set by an American clipper, *'Lightning'* which covered 436 nautical miles in one 24-hour period.

CLOCKS Until 1967, the measurement of time was based either upon astronomical cycles or mechanical vibrations (such as those of a pendulum or a quartz crystal). In that year, however, the frequency of an atomic beam of the element Cesium-133 was taken as the standard measure of time. This frequency – of 9,192.631770 megahertz (or units of 1,000,000 cycles per second) – henceforth became the definition of a second. The Cesium atomic clock installed at the National Physical Laboratory at Teddington, near London, is 'tuned' to an accuracy of one second in 1,000 years.

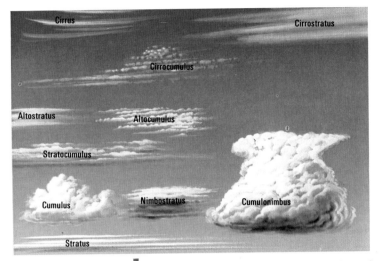

plants. These grew about 300 million years ago. Land movements eventually covered layers of decaying leaves and branches from the plants. Over the centuries, these layers were compressed and changed gradually into coal. The layers, called seams, vary in thickness from a few centimetres to 30 metres (100 ft). Products obtained from coal include coal gas, COKE, and chemicals used to make plastics, synthetic rubber, dyes and explosives.

COBALT A hard, silvery metal capable of withstanding high temperatures. It is used to make cutting tools, engine parts and magnetic ALLOYS.

COBRA The common name for a number of hooded poisonous snakes of the *Elapidae* family that range from Africa to Arabia, India, China, Malaya and the Philippines. ◁

COCOA Also called *cacao*. A South American tree with small yellow flowers and fleshy yellow pods containing seeds or beans. When roasted and powdered, the beans are used in making CHOCOLATE and cocoa powder for drinking. ◁

COCONUT Large oval hard-shelled fruit of the coconut palm. Coconuts are an important tropical crop, especially in south-east Asia. They have many uses: the juice is drunk; the kernel is eaten fresh or dried to form *copra* (copra yields coconut oil, and is used to make margarine, candles, soap, etc); and *coir* – the fibres from the husk – are made into rope and matting.

COD Important food fish from the north Atlantic. Cod are olive green or brown and can reach 1.8 metres (6 ft) in length and weigh up to 90 kg (198 lb). They are very prolific. A female can lay 8 million eggs at a time, but most are eaten by enemies so that only 6 or 7 reach maturity.

COFFEE Tall tropical shrub which bears red berries, each containing two greyish-green seeds or beans. These beans – dried, roasted and ground – are used to make the stimulating dark-brown drink. Most of the world's coffee is grown in Central and South America, particularly Brazil, and in Africa.

COINS Pieces of metal, usually of a uniform size, content and design, used as MONEY. They may be made of a variety of metals including gold, silver, brass, bronze, aluminium and nickel. Coins were first used in Asia Minor in the 600s BC. The Greeks and Romans used silver and gold coins. Today governments control the type and number of coins minted as part of their control of the national money supply. Most coins are made of the cheaper

COBRA Cobras are frequently used by snake-charmers, who make them rear up into their defensive posture with their hoods outstretched. As snakes are unable to hear high frequencies, a snake-charmer's cobra is actually made to sway in response to his or her movements, not the music from a pipe.
The cobra's bite is fatal to humans in about ten per cent of cases. However, the king cobra (or Hamadryad) is the world's largest poisonous snake. It is found from southern India to the Philippines and Indonesia and is often over 3.6 m (12 ft) in length. One specimen of over 5.6 m (18 ft) has been recorded.

The Indian cobra – which is usually around 1.7 m (5.5 ft) long – kills several thousand people every year, as it likes to visit houses at twilight to hunt rats.

COCOA Cocoa plants have been cultivated for more than 3,000 years in parts of tropical America. The Mayas, Toltecs and Aztecs sometimes used cocoa powder in a ceremonial drink, and also used the beans as currency. Christopher Columbus brought cocoa beans to Spain in 1502, and the secret of the cocoa drink reached Italy in 1606. From there it spread rapidly to France, and a Frenchman opened a shop selling cocoa drinks in London in1657. However, chocolate proper was not made for another hundred years.

▲ *High cirrus clouds, sometimes called 'mares' tails', are made of ice. Fluffy cumulus clouds usually mean fine weather, but layers of low stratus clouds bring rain. The dark, towering cumulonimbus are thunder clouds.*

CLOUDS Masses of tiny drops of water or ice crystals in the ATMOSPHERE, formed by the condensation of moisture in the air. The form clouds take varies greatly according to altitude and atmospheric conditions. Low clouds (to 2000 metres; 6500 ft) include *stratus, nimbostratus* and *cumulus* clouds. Medium clouds (2000–6100 metres; 6500–20,000 ft) include *altostratus* and *altocumulus*. High clouds (over 6100 metres; 20,000 ft) include *cirrostratus, cirrocumulus* and *cirrus*. (See WEATHER FORECASTING)

CLOVER Small plant growing wild in temperate countries. Its leaves are divided into three (a four-leafed clover is considered lucky) and its flowers are usually red or white. Clover is widely cultivated as a food crop (fodder) for animals.

CLOWN A CIRCUS performer who wears funny costumes and make-up and entertains between the acts at the circus, often by making fun of himself.

COACH A large four-wheeled vehicle, drawn by four or more horses, used for carrying a number of passengers. Similar to the CARRIAGE, coaches were usually larger and enclosed on all four sides, with a roof and windows. Stage coaches were the first real form of public transport, carrying people from town to town and changing horses at each stop, usually an inn.

COAL For centuries, coal has been an important fuel and source of raw materials. Coal is known as a FOSSIL fuel, for it consists of the fossilized remains of huge trees and other

metals, and are used for fractional parts of the basic monetary unit, such as the pound in Britain or the dollar in the USA. (See MINTING)

COKE A dark-grey porous solid produced from COAL, and containing about 85 per cent CARBON. Coke is used mainly in metallurgy for reducing ores to metals (see OXIDATION AND REDUCTION). Some coke is used as fuel.

COLD, COMMON An infectious respiratory disease characterized by such symptoms as sore throat, nasal discharge, coughing and sneezing, and probably caused by a group of VIRUSES. ▷

COLD STORAGE Any means of maintaining objects, such as perishable foods, at temperatures lower than their surroundings. Most cold storage, or REFRIGERATION, is achieved by mechanical or chemical means. The area cooled may be as small as a home refrigerator or as large as a refrigerated railway car or warehouse.

COLOMBIA A republic of SOUTH AMERICA. A Spanish colony until it gained independence in 1819. Population: 28,217,000. Capital: Bogotá. ▷

COLOSSEUM An amphitheatre built in ROME by the emperor Vespasian, beginning in AD 72. It held 50,000 spectators and was famed for gladiatorial combat and the killing of many Christians. ▷

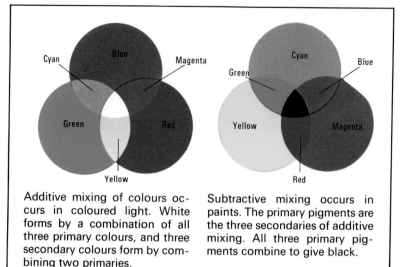

Additive mixing of colours occurs in coloured light. White forms by a combination of all three primary colours, and three secondary colours form by combining two primaries.

Subtractive mixing occurs in paints. The primary pigments are the three secondaries of additive mixing. All three primary pigments combine to give black.

COLOUR Our brain works out what we see in terms of colour. We see red when the LIGHT waves are relatively long. And we see violet when the waves are much shorter. Wavelengths between these extremes are interpreted as other colours of the SPECTRUM. A mixture of various wavelengths appears to us as a single colour, just as if the light were of a single wavelength. For this reason, colour is said to be a *subjective* quality – it is a description of the way we react to light, rather than an exact statement about the nature of the light.

White light is actually a mixture of light of various wavelengths. This can be demonstrated by splitting up sunlight into a spectrum of its component colours using a glass PRISM. The arcs of colour in a RAINBOW are formed in a similar way. In this case, the raindrops split up the white light.

For simplicity, white light is usually considered to consist of just three colours – red, green and blue. Known as the *primary colours of light*, these can be mixed to give virtually any other colour. The *primary colours of paint*, also called the *primary pigment colours*, are red, yellow and blue, or more accurately, magenta, yellow and cyan. The differences between mixing light (additive) and mixing paint (subtractive) are shown in the diagrams above.

COLOUR BLINDNESS The inability to distinguish one COLOUR from another. Colour blindness is an inherited trait, most often passed from mother to son. It was first recognized by the English chemist John DALTON (1766–1844).

◀ *The Colosseum in Rome, completed in AD 80, was the scene of gladiatorial and wild beast shows: men and animals were kept in quarters below the arena.*

COLD, COMMON Despite its name, this ailment is not brought on by exposure to cold conditions. However, the virus infection may be more likely to affect people whose resistance has been lowered by exposure or other stresses to their bodies. This idea is supported by the fact that people often receive and pass on the virus without ever 'catching' a cold themselves.

COLOSSEUM This most famous of all Roman arenas once featured the deaths of 2,000 gladiators and about 230 wild animals in a single 'celebration'. Until the law was repealed by the first Christian emperor, Constantine, in AD 326, a man could be condemned by the courts to face the wild beasts in the arena. In fact, the 'hunting' of wild animals in the Colosseum continued until AD 523, and that building served as a model for others at Pompeii, Verona, Possuoli, Capua and Pola in Italy, Syracuse in Sicily, Arles and Nimes in France, el-Djem in North Africa, and Dorchester and Caerleon in England.

COLUMBIA: FACTS AND FIGURES
Currency: Peso
Religion: Roman Catholic
Language: Spanish

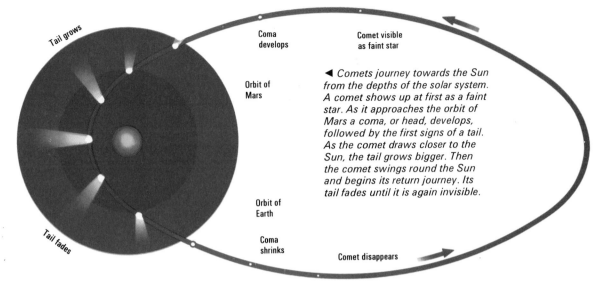

Tail grows

Coma develops

Comet visible as faint star

Orbit of Mars

◄ *Comets journey towards the Sun from the depths of the solar system. A comet shows up at first as a faint star. As it approaches the orbit of Mars a coma, or head, develops, followed by the first signs of a tail. As the comet draws closer to the Sun, the tail grows bigger. Then the comet swings round the Sun and begins its return journey. Its tail fades until it is again invisible.*

Orbit of Earth

Coma shrinks

Tail fades

Comet disappears

COLUMBUS, CHRISTOPHER On his second voyage to the New World in 1493, Columbus introduced sugar cane (native to southern Asia) to the island of San Domingo in the Caribbean. Sugar plantations were soon set up on other islands in the West Indies, and the need for a cheap labour force led to the large scale importation of African slaves. Sugar – and rum, a product of cane – are important to this day throughout the West Indies.

COMET The word 'comet' comes from the Greek *kometes aster*, meaning 'hairy star'. In fact, not all comets are bright and have long tails, but these were the only ones noticed by the Ancients. The most famous comet of all, Halley's, has had important historical connections. It appeared in 1066, and is depicted on the Bayeaux Tapestry. Then, in 1456 it caused great panic among Christians as its appearance coincided with the Turkish conquest of Constantinople (now Istanbul). It has since been calculated that this comet appears regularly every 76 years, the last appearance being in 1986.

COLUMBUS, CHRISTOPHER Italian explorer and discoverer of the New World (1451–1506). Born in Genoa, Columbus persuaded King Ferdinand and Queen Isabella of Spain to finance a sea voyage to Asia. Convinced that the Earth was round, Columbus was certain he could find a fast and direct route to Asia by sailing westwards. In 1492 he set out with three small ships, the *Niña*, *Pinta* and *Santa Maria*. On October 12 the expedition landed on a Caribbean island Columbus christened San Salvador, believing it to be part of Asia. He made four voyages in all, and died still believing he had reached Asia. (See AMERICA) ◁

COLUMN In ARCHITECTURE, a long, cylindrical or tapering vertical support, composed of a base, a shaft and a CAPITAL. The capital is often decorated.

COMBUSTION Another word for burning, a chemical REACTION that produces light and

heat. Combustion is a form of OXIDATION, as substances combine with oxygen when they burn.

COMEDY One of the two main types of DRAMA, the other being tragedy. Comedies in general are meant to amuse and entertain the audience, and often contain SATIRE.

COMET A heavenly body that periodically passes close to the Sun and becomes visible from the Earth. Most of the time, comets are a long way from us – usually beyond the edge of the SOLAR SYSTEM. Comets probably consist of frozen gases, ice and dust. ◁

COMIC STRIP A story told in a series, or 'strip' of pictures, especially popular with children. Comic strips originated in America but are now produced all over the world.

COMMON MARKET See EUROPEAN ECONOMIC COMMUNITY.

COMMUNISM A 20th-century political system based on common ownership of the means of production, the restriction or abolition of private property, and absolute equality, and practised in one form or another in a number of countries, notably RUSSIA and CHINA. (See MARX, KARL; STALIN, JOSEPH)

◄ *The brilliant Ikeya-Seki comet of 1965 just before sunrise. It was discovered by the Japanese amateur astronomers Kaoru Ikeya and Tsutoma Seki, and was one of the brightest comets of recent years. It came within 1,200,000 km (750,000 miles) of the Sun, and could be seen in broad daylight in some parts of the world. It orbits once in about 880 years, compared with Encke's comet which reappears once every 3.3 years.*

◄ Printed electronic circuits carry out the calculations in a computer. The computer is built up of many such boards, which can easil, be removed. This aids the location and repair of faults.

COMPANY An organization formed in order to conduct a business. Companies may be private or public. In Britain, companies that have limited responsibility for their debts must have the word *Limited* in their titles.

COMPASS A device for finding direction. The simple magnetic compass consists of a pivoted magnetic needle that points to the Earth's magnetic poles. The gyrocompass contains a GYROSCOPE that keeps it pointing in a fixed direction. Radio compasses are used

on aircraft to take bearings of transmitters in order to work out the aircraft's position.

COMPOUND See ELEMENTS AND COMPOUNDS.

COMPRESSOR A machine that provides a supply of compressed air. This can be used to operate pneumatic drills, paint sprays, sandblasting equipment and for pumping up tyres. Compressors are also used in REFRIGERATORS to convert refrigerant vapour into liquid.

COMPUTERS Devices for doing calculations quickly. Usually the term refers to electronic computers, but mechanical calculating devices have been around for thousands of years. Early man used pebbles to help him count his animals. This led to the invention of the ABACUS, a frame with counting beads on wires. In 1642, Blaise Pascal built a mechanical calculator with gear wheels and dials. Charles Babbage invented a much more elaborate machine in 1832. Unfortunately, the high-precision engineering required to make it was not available at that time. In 1944, Howard Aiken built a general purpose calculator using gear wheels driven by electric motors. Meanwhile, the more versatile electronic computer was being developed. The first one was completed in 1946 by J. Presper Eckert and John W. Mauchly. When working, it performed well, but it contained about 18,000 valves, and breakdowns were frequent. Since that time, the introduction of TRANSISTORS and INTEGRATED CIRCUITS has greatly improved the performance and reduced the size of electronic computers. They have also become much less expensive. ▷

CONCRETE A relatively cheap building material that is strong, waterproof, fireproof and easily shaped by casting. It is made from a mixture of CEMENT, fine aggregate (sand), coarse aggregate (rock chips or gravel) and water. Reinforced concrete has built-in steel rods to improve strength under tension.

CONDENSATION The change of state of a substance from a gas to a liquid or a solid state. For example, cooling steam makes it condense to form drops of water. Gases are

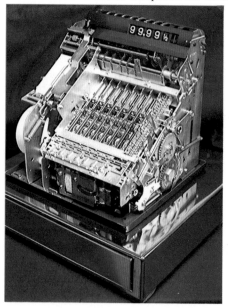

◄ A cash register is a mechanical digital computer. It contains wheels that turn to certain positions to represent numbers. Addition is accomplished by counting the number of turns that a wheel makes. Modern cash registers are usually electrically operated.

COMPUTERS Every computer has five basic parts. The input unit 'reads' the information fed into the machine; the data store holds this information, perhaps on a magnetic tape; the arithmetic unit picks out the required information and does calculations; a control unit takes charge of all these operations; and the output unit gives out the results.

Computers are now being used to create designs, to play chess, to translate from one language to another, even to compose music, but they still cannot think. They cannot solve any problem that man cannot solve because human beings have to give the computer all the information it needs for a calculation and instruct it how to work the calculation out.

Modern computers have led to the development of many astounding items of equipment. Among these are optical scanners which can 'read' more than 1,500 characters per second and 'feed' the information into a computer's memory. Some of these memories are able to store information up to 1,000,000,000,000 characters in a single wall-sized unit; while modern lasar memory stores can accommodate the same amount of information in only 5.6 sq m (60 sq ft) of floor space. On such systems, any information can be retrieved within a maximum of 8.6 seconds, and the lasar beam tracking system makes less than one error in every 10,000,000,000,000 selections. With the development of silicon 'chips', the possibility of being able to store 15,500 characters of information per square metre (100,000 per square inch) is now becoming a reality. For the future, scientists at the Bell Telephone Laboratories in the USA have discovered a 'magnetic bubble' computer memory. This uses lines of magnetism through certain crystals (e.g. garnets), and presents the possibility of being able to store more than 100,000,000,000 characters per square inch. Using this method even the largest, most refined computers in the world could be reduced to the size of suitcases!

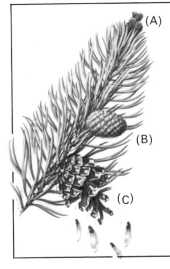

(A)
(B)
(C)

THE LIFE-CYCLE

In the type of conifer tree known as the pine, the male pollen cones are fairly small and soft, like short catkins. Young female cones (A) grow upright, with their scales open to allow pollen to reach the ovules. After pollination the scales harden and close, and the cone stalk bends so that the cone hangs suspended (B). Protected inside the closed cone, the pollen cells mature and fertilize the female reproductive cells. The ovules develop into seeds. When they are ripe the cone scales shrink and open (C) to release the winged seeds.

CONDOR The Californian condor is one of the world's rarest birds. Only about 40 individuals survive in the San Raphael Mountains near Santa Barbara in California, USA. As they only breed every other year and even then just lay one egg, the future of this species of New World vulture is obviously very much in the balance.

CONGO (ZAIRE) The Zaire River is so powerful its sediments are carried up to 280 km (173 miles) out into the Atlantic by currents that flow through the submarine Congo canyon. In the estuary this canyon is only 21 m (70 ft) deep, but where it cuts across the continental shelf of Africa its V-shaped walls are up to 1,100 m (3,600 ft) high, and its sides are more than 15 km (9 miles) apart. Finally, on the ocean floor at 2,650 m (8,700 ft) the sediments from the Congo Basin are spread out in a massive fan-shaped valley whose walls eventually reduce to around 30 m (100 ft) in height.

sometimes condensed by increasing their pressure.

CONDOR Large American bird of prey. All condor species have ugly bare heads, hooked beaks, long claws and huge wings. The black-and-white Andean condor with a wing span of up to 3 metres (10 ft) is one of the world's largest flying birds. ◁

CONDUCTION OF HEAT One of the processes by which HEAT can be transferred from one body to another.

CONDUCTOR, ELECTRICAL Any material that allows ELECTRICITY to pass through it is called a conductor. Metals are good conductors, the best being silver and copper. Substances that do not conduct electricity are called INSULATORS.

CONFUCIUS Chinese philosopher and founder of Confucianism (c. 551–479 BC), a way of thought which teaches tolerance and simplicity, and respect for family and society. Confucius believed that men should be virtuous and he taught that only virtuous men should govern a society. Confucianism was widely adopted by the ruling class in CHINA until the 20th century.

CONGO (ZAIRE) RIVER The second largest river in Africa (4370 km; 2716 miles long) and one of the largest in the world. It flows southwest through central Africa into the south Atlantic Ocean. The first European to discover the Zaire was the Portuguese navigator Diogo Cam (1484). It was most thoroughly explored by David Livingstone (1813–73) and Henry M. Stanley (1841–1904).

CONIFER Cone-bearing tree. Many well-known trees are conifers such as SPRUCE (Christmas tree), PINE, CEDAR and Yew. Instead of flowers, conifers produce their POLLEN and SEEDS in cones. They also have narrow, needle-like leaves and most types are evergreen. Conifers belong to cool countries, they form a great forest belt from Norway across to Siberia and they also cover Canada. Because they are quick-growing, they are widely planted for timber.

CONJURING The art of creating illusions and magical effects, using such skills as sleight of hand, levitation and escapology. (See MAGIC)

CONQUISTADORS Spanish soldier-explorers of the 1500s who conquered much of North, Central and South America for Spain. Adventurers motivated by greed for gold, religious zeal and a desire to conquer, the conquistadors often used cruel and ruthless methods to achieve their ends. (See AZTECS; CORTÉS, HERNANDO)

CONSERVATION The term used to refer to the careful management and preservation of natural resources, wildlife, historical monuments, and so on, so that they are not lost forever through carelessness. Conservation protects animal species in danger of extinction and natural resources, such as wood, that are important to man and the environment.

CONSERVATION LAWS The original conservation laws state that energy cannot be

▼ One of the ways in which we can conserve and protect species of wild animals, like these penguins, is by taking care of them and breeding them in zoos.

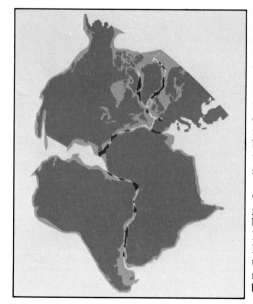

▲ *Continental shelves are the true boundaries of the continents. This map shows how well the continental shelves of continents on opposite sides of the Atlantic Ocean would fit together.*

created or destroyed, and that mass cannot be created or destroyed. In the early 1900s, EINSTEIN showed that energy and mass are different forms of the same thing. And it has since been shown that mass can be converted into energy (see ATOMIC ENERGY). As a result, we now combine the two laws and say that, in any system, the sum of the mass and energy (converted to the same units) will always remain the same. In other words, if some mass were destroyed, an equivalent amount of energy would be produced in its place.

CONSERVATISM A way of thought which is based on preserving established social institutions and traditions. Conservatives believe that societies develop in a natural way and that it is wrong to make any sudden or violent changes in our way of life. Conservatism became a particularly strong philosophy after the French Revolution and has been adopted by many people as a political viewpoint.

CONSTELLATIONS As seen from the Earth, STARS appear as distinct groups that we call constellations. Although the stars in a constellation lie in the same region of the sky, they may be greatly differing distances away.

CONTACT LENSES Lenses worn in contact with the eyeball, usually to correct eyesight defects. Some people wear tinted contact lenses to make their eyes look a different colour. ▷

CONTINENTAL SHELF Around the edges of the continents, the land shelves gently at first, forming a continental shelf, covered by a shallow sea. The shelf ends when the gradient changes and the steep, continental slope begins. The continental slope plunges down to the ABYSS. The continental shelves are parts of the continents. The continental shelf off the coast of north-west Europe is particularly marked, extending about 320 km (200 miles) beyond Land's End. But some other continental shelves are narrow. Continental shelves are rich fishing grounds.

COOK, JAMES British explorer and cartographer (1728–1779) who discovered HAWAII, brought AUSTRALIA and NEW ZEALAND into the British Empire, and charted a large part of the Pacific Ocean and its islands. Cook made three voyages to the Pacific, venturing as far north as the Bering Strait (1778) and south to below the Antarctic Circle (1774). ▷

COOK ISLANDS A group of 15 widely scattered islands in the south Pacific Ocean, self-governing in free association with New Zealand. About half the islands' population lives on Rarotonga, the seat of government. Population: 17,400 (1983). Land area 238 sq km (92 sq miles).

COPERNICUS, NICOLAUS Polish astronomer, often regarded as the father of modern ASTRONOMY (1473–1543). His fame rests upon his theory of a Sun-centred universe, which reversed the belief held for almost 20 centuries that the Earth was the central body of the universe. ▷

COPPER A reddish metal that is a good CONDUCTOR of heat and electricity. Copper is used to make water pipes and boilers and electric cables. But its main use is in alloys, especially BRONZE and BRASS.

CORAL Tiny marine animal consisting of a hollow tube with a mouth, surrounded by tentacles, at the top. The tentacles trap small

▼ *Brightly coloured corals appear like an underwater garden on the sea bed.*

▲ Coral grows in the warm waters surrounding an island; in this illustration the island has been formed by volcanic action.

▲ Coral continues to grow on the reefs as the island sinks or the sea rises.

▲ Once the island has completely disappeared, the coral reefs remain, forming a typical atoll.

CORK Cork is removed from the cork oak when the tree has reached a diameter of about 15 cm (6 in). Cuts are made around the stem with a special cutting tool in such a way as not to damage the underlying inner bark. The cork from the first stripping is usually of poor quality and is sometimes not used. Subsequent strippings, which take place once every eight to ten years, provide the material for an important industry in Portugal and Spain. Cork oak trees usually live for about 150 years.

Cork has long been recognized as a useful material. It is made up of millions of microscopic cells, bound together by natural resins. Each cell has a tiny amount of air trapped in it, so that more than 50 per cent of the volume of a piece of cork is captive air. This makes cork one of the lightest of all solid substances. Sheets of cork are used for heat insulation. Finely ground cork can be compressed and made into boards for insulation and sound absorption.

▲ Corals are tiny animals called polyps. All corals start as a single polyp with an opening at one end surrounded by tentacles. In the illustration above, the polyps on the left are open, showing the tentacle-fringed mouth, the polyps on the right are closed.

CRUSTACEANS and feed them to the mouth. At the base of the body tube, the coral forms a cup-shaped limestone skeleton. Some corals live alone, but the majority live in colonies built by budding (branches sprout from above the skeleton and develop their own mouth and tentacles; the skeleton grows up round the new branches). Budding eventually creates a colony made up of millions of corals and measuring many metres in length, width and height. Colonies form the basis of coral reefs. The outside of the reef is made of living corals while the rest consists of dead coral skeletons and other materials such as shell pieces. Solitary corals live in most seas but the reef-builders can only exist in warm tropical waters. (See ATOLL)

CORDUROY A cotton VELVET fabric with ridges, or 'wales', in the pile. It is made in various weights and widths of wale for clothes and upholstery.

CORK Protective layer of tissue lining the inside of BARK. The tissue consists of compact air-filled CELLS which form a water-tight and air-tight barrier to keep disease away from the stem. Bottle corks are made from the bark tissue of a special Mediterranean tree, the cork oak. ◁

CORNEA The tough, transparent outer covering of the eyeball. Its curvature affects vision: irregular curvature may cause the condition known as ASTIGMATISM. (See EYE)

CORNET A member of the brass family of musical wind instruments, similar to the modern trumpet but with a less brilliant, more controlled tone. It is most often used in brass bands.

CORONA In ASTRONOMY, the outermost part of the Sun's atmosphere. It is visible during a total ECLIPSE of the SUN, when it is seen as a halo of radiating pearly-white light.

▼ The Sun's corona can only be seen during a total solar eclipse, which never lasts for more than about 7 minutes. Normally, it is hidden by the light from the Sun's surface.

CORROBOREE A ceremonial or warlike dance of the ABORIGINES of Australia. Held at night by moonlight or by the light of bush fires.

CORROSION Damaging CHEMICAL action on the surface of metals or other substances. The most common form of corrosion is the rusting of iron or steel in damp air. Corrosion can be prevented by the application of paint or other surface coatings. (See RUST)

CORTÉS, HERNANDO Spanish explorer and CONQUISTADOR (1485–1547) who conquered Mexico by capturing the AZTEC capital, Tenochtitlán, and killing Montezuma, the Aztec emperor. ▷

CORTISONE A HORMONE produced by the ADRENAL GLANDS, one of the group of hormones called STEROIDS. It is an important aid to metabolism, helping to convert fats and proteins into GLUCOSE. Synthetic cortisone is used to treat a number of diseases, including rheumatoid arthritis and acute allergic diseases.

COSMETICS Scientific preparations applied to the body, and especially the face, in order to cleanse, beautify, or alter its appearance. The use of cosmetics goes back to ancient Egypt, Sumeria and Phoenicia, when paints, oils and unguents were used to decorate and perfume the body. Today the sale of cosmetics is big business. Their use by men as well as women has increased in recent years.

COSMIC RAYS See ELECTROMAGNETIC WAVES.

COSSACK A once-nomadic people who were settled on the frontiers of Russia in the 15th century as permanent frontier police. They became famous as skilled horsemen and served as cavalry in the army. Fiercely independent, however, they have, throughout their history, taken part in major revolts against various Russian governments. ▷

COSTA RICA A republic of CENTRAL AMERICA, with a land area of 50,700 sq km (19,575 sq miles). Produces coffee, bananas and timber. Population: 2,534,000; capital: San José. ▷

COSTUME The story of costume traces styles of dress throughout history in many different parts of the world. What people wear is first determined by such things as climate and degree of civilization, and is influenced by the art, political organization and economics of a particular society.

Costumes in the ancient world were based on the tunic, which developed into the soft

▲ *Cotton is harvested when the bolls ripen and burst open to form a fluffy white mass of long fine threads. In many places cotton is still picked by hand, though machines do the job in most large operations.*

folds of the Greek *chiton* and the Roman *toga*. The influence of the East through the BYZANTINE EMPIRE brought rich colours and patterns to clothing that was of finer materials and often decorated with jewels. Throughout the Middle Ages in Europe, the dress of ordinary people remained crude, but the wealthy dressed in fine silks and damasks from the East. The new wealth and reawakening of art during the RENAISSANCE brought with it a taste for sumptuous fabrics and often exaggerated styles.

Outrageous styles reached their peak in the 18th century. The reaction to these resulted in the simpler fashions of the early 19th century. Costume remained sober, though often elaborate, throughout the 1800s. The 20th century saw a social revolution in clothing styles, with more practical fashions for women and a uniformity of modern dress that has spread to most parts of the world. (See BYZANTINE ART; FASHION; JEWELLERY; SILK)

COTTON FIBRE from the seed of several species of the genus *Gossypium*, used as a textile material since 3000 BC. Cotton reached Europe in the 4th century BC, when Alexander the Great introduced it into Greece. It re-

CORTÉS On February 10, 1519, Cortés set sail from Cuba with just 508 soldiers, 100 sailors and 16 horses. His expedition was armed with flintlocks, arquebuses and bows. Despite their small number, this ill-armed force conquered the might of Mexico's Aztec empire. They did it with military skill, cunning and determination – which is clearly shown by the fact that Cortés ruled out any possibility of retreat by ordering all his ships to be destroyed.

COSSACK The word 'cossack' comes from the Turkish *Kazak* meaning 'adventurer' or 'free person', which reflects the origins of many cossacks who originally settled in the south and south-west of the Russian Empire as escaped serfs from both Poland and Russia.

COSTA RICA: FACTS AND FIGURES
Highest mountain: Chirripó Grande 3800 m (12,500 ft).
Religion: Roman Catholic.

Currency: Colon.
Official language: Spanish.

COULOMB Charles-Augustin de Coulomb (1736-1806) was a French soldier and engineer who became interested in investigating Joseph Priestley's Law of Electrical Repulsions. In 1785 he formulated what became known as Coulomb's Law, which states that 'the force between two electrical charges is proportional to the product of the charges and inversely proportional to the square of the distance between them'. His researches also explained friction in machinery, the working of windmills and the elasticity of metal and silk fibres.

COWBOY The word 'cowboy' is a direct translation of the Spanish *vaquero*, which is what the Mexican ranch hands of Texas called themselves before the arrival of the first American settlers in the 1820s and '30s.

▲ The cougar, or mountain lion, roams high up in the Rockies in North America, and the Andes in South America.

▼ A face mask shows the size of this robber crab. Immensely powerful, such a crab can escape from a tin crate, or a wooden box with sides 3 cm (over 1 inch) thick.

mained unimportant until the end of the 18th century, when, with the invention of Eli Whitney's cotton gin, which separated the seeds from the fibre, cotton cloth became the cheapest and most plentiful fabric available. Today cotton is still a popular fabric, despite the competition from man-made fibres. (See ARKWRIGHT, RICHARD; TEXTILES)

COUGAR Another name for the puma, or mountain lion (*Felis concolor*), a large member of the CAT family native to the Americas. It lives in open or mountainous country, preying on deer and other animals.

COULOMB The SI UNIT of electric CHARGE. It is the amount of electricity that flows through a conductor carrying a current of one AMPERE for one second. Coulombs are represented by the symbol C. ◁

COWBOY A man employed to look after a herd of grazing cattle on the North American plains in the 19th century. Skilful with rope, saddle, spurs and branding iron, he also earned a reputation for toughness and courage in his dealings with cattle rustlers and hostile Indians. The cowboy has become an American folk hero. ◁

CRAB A CRUSTACEAN with a hard shell and ten jointed legs. There are about 4500 species, varying in size from the pea crab, $\frac{1}{2}$ cm ($\frac{1}{8}$ in) wide, to the giant or spider crab of Japan, whose outstretched clawtips may span nearly 4 metres (13 ft). Most are marine species, but some are land animals.

▲ The ruins of Knossos in Crete. Many treasures of the Minoan civilization have been found here.

▲ A gold ring and a bull's head rhyton, or ritual vessel (below), both from Minoan Crete. The rhyton has onyx eyes and horns of gilded wood.

▼ Crested cranes perform elaborate courting dances consisting of graceful leaps and stiff-legged strutting. Cranes resemble herons, but whereas herons have fluffy plumage and fold their necks in flight, cranes have smooth, compact plumage and stretch their necks forward in flight.

CRANE Large long-legged bird found in many parts of the world. Most species have white or grey feathers and a loud trumpet-like call. They use their long, powerful bills for digging up roots and worms.

CRAYFISH Freshwater CRUSTACEAN. The crayfish (or crawfish), some 10 cm (4 in) long, is a brownish-green colour and lives in streams and ponds where it feeds off snails, insects and plants. It grabs its food with a pair of strong pincers.

CRETE This rugged island in the Mediterranean Sea is the largest island in GREECE. It has 457,000 people and an area of 8331 sq km (2444 sq miles). Crete was the home of the MINOAN CIVILIZATION and the excavations at Knossos, near the town of Heraklion, are impressive. Discoveries of early frescoes and pottery show high artistic achievement. ▷

CRIBBAGE A card game, usually for two players. Special counting combinations are formed, each player keeping his own score by moving two pegs along a cribbage board. ▷

CRICKET Small jumping INSECT. Crickets are night-time creatures, during the day they stay hidden in their burrows. They are famous for their song, made by rubbing their fore-wings together. In some countries, crickets are kept in cages as singing pets. ▷

CRETE One of Crete's most famous 'sons' is Domenico Theotokopoulos, who was born there in 1541. He studied and painted on his home island before moving on to Venice, Rome and Toledo. There he became world famous as the artist 'El Greco' – the Greek. Another famous Cretan is Nikos Kazantzakis, author of *Freedom or Death* and the epitome of Cretan spirit, *Zorba the Greek*.

CRIBBAGE This game was invented by the English poet, Sir John Suckling (1609-1642), although it was based on Noddy, an older game which also required a special scoring board.

CRICKET There are over 2,400 species of crickets, ranging in size from 3 to 50 mm (0.1-2 in). The males 'chirp' by rubbing a scraper on one forewing against a row of 50-250 teeth on the other forewing. The frequency of the sound they produce varies from 1,500 cycles per second in the largest varieties to over 10,000 cycles per second in the smallest. The purpose of the chirp is to attract females or warn off males.

CRIME *Crime and Punishment* written by the Russian Fyodor Dostoyevsky and published in 1866 is one of the greatest works of fiction in world literature. It deals with the belief that a criminal will always feel remorse for his or her crime.

CROCODILE The largest reptile in the world is the Estuarine crocodile which lives on coasts stretching in an arc from Australia, through Indonesia, the Solomon Islands and the Philippines to India, Sri Lanka and Pakistan. It eats all types of meat – dead or alive – and can be a serious danger to unfortunate humans. Estuarine crocodiles have been known to measure 9 m (29.5 ft) in length and weigh over 2 tonnes.

CRICKET Game played with a flat-fronted bat and a hard leather-covered ball, between two teams of eleven players. The national summer sport of Britain, it is also very popular in Australia, New Zealand, South Africa, the West Indies, India and Pakistan. Test matches are played each year between two of these countries.

CRIME Human behaviour which violates the laws of the community or nation in which it occurs. It is punishable according to those laws, which may vary greatly from one place to another. However, in most countries acts involving arson, burglary, forgery, murder and treason are considered crimes, and are punishable by imprisonment or some other punishment, depending on the laws of the community.

In the Middle Ages, a crime such as stealing a loaf of bread might be punishable by death. Now, on the whole, punishment is less harsh, but more acts are considered to be crimes. (See LAW) ◁

CRIMEAN WAR A war fought from 1853 to 1856 between Russia and the allied forces of Britain, France, Turkey and Sardinia. The allied forces, alarmed by Russia's increasing influence over Turkey, drove the invading Russian forces south into the Crimean Peninsula. A peace treaty was signed in Paris. (See NIGHTINGALE, FLORENCE)

▼ A scene showing the harsh conditions in which the Crimean War was fought. Most of the 650,000 casualties died from disease, exhaustion or bad leadership. The poor medical care given to British soldiers led the nursing pioneer Florence Nightingale to set up proper hospitals for them. At right, is a map of the Crimea on the Black Sea.

CROCHETING A decorative type of KNITTING, in which a single hook is used to work thread into looped patterns. It is often used for making bedspreads, bags, hats, scarves or fine lacework.

CROCODILE This REPTILE, found in tropical rivers, is the nearest living relative of the DINOSAUR. Crocodiles, up to 6 metres (20 ft) long, have a thick scaly skin. They spend most of their time floating just below the surface of the water or lying on the river bank in the sun. They are flesh eaters and live mainly on fish. Some crocodiles lay their white eggs in holes in the riverbank, others make nests. ◁

▲ Although crocodiles spend much of their lives in water, on land they can chase their victims with amazing speed. Sometimes they use their heavy tails to knock animals to the ground. In the water, the crocodile floats just below the surface, with only its eyes and nostrils showing. There it can breathe and watch for unwary prey.

Cro

▲ *The Cro-Magnon people of Europe wore clothes of scraped skin and often decorated themselves with ornaments of shell and bone. They created many cave paintings deep inside the cave systems of southern France and Spain.*

CRO-MAGNON MAN The name given to an early species of man who lived in Europe between 12,000 and 30,000 years ago. Named after a site in France where bones and other remains were discovered, the Cro-Magnons lived mostly in caves, sometimes building tents of skins inside. They wore clothes of skins and used tools of stone and bone. (See ANTHROPOLOGY)

CROMWELL, OLIVER Born in 1599, the son of a well-to-do landowner, he spent 20 years as a country gentleman and farmer in East Anglia before becoming a soldier, statesman and leader of the Puritan revolution.

Cromwell's first speech in PARLIAMENT, in 1628, fiercely attacked the High Church bishops. Grievances and antagonism mounted between Parliament and the king, CHARLES I, until in 1642 the CIVIL WAR broke out. Cromwell proved himself a brilliant, tough military leader. His well disciplined army, known as the New Model Army, defeated the Royalist forces and in 1649 Charles I was executed and England became a republic. Cromwell refused the crown and served as Lord Protector for five years, until he died in 1658. After his death the republic collapsed and CHARLES II became king. ▷

▶ *This magnificent prehistoric cave painting was dicovered by four boys searching for a dog in Lascaux, France. It is from the Cro-Magnon period.*

CROMWELL, OLIVER Oliver Cromwell died in Whitehall, London, on September 3, 1658. He was given a State funeral on November 23, but 13 days before this his body had already been secretly buried in Westminster Abbey. However, in 1661 – after the restoration of King Charles II to the throne of England – Cromwell's remains were dug out of his tomb. His embalmed body was hung up at Tyburn (now Marble Arch) – where criminals were executed – and later buried beneath the gallows. The former Lord Protector's head was stuck on a pole and mounted atop Westminster Hall where it remained throughout Charles' reign.

CROSS An ancient instrument of death by crucifixion, now the holy emblem of the Christian faith, signifying man's redemption through Christ's death on the cross. Various forms of the cross have developed throughout Christian history. (See CHRISTIANITY; JESUS CHRIST)

CROW A name for several species of *Corvus*, a genus of large perching birds. Two European varieties are the black carrion crow and the greyish hooded crow. Both are CARNIVORES, about 46 cm (18 in) long, and migrate south in winter.

CRUSADES Wars from 11th to 14th centuries, in which western European Christians set out to recover the Holy Land, especially

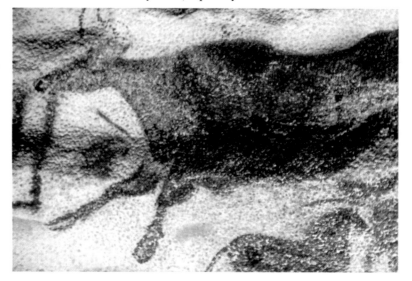

JERUSALEM, from Moslem rule. Confused by quarrels between different leaders, and desire for material as well as spiritual gain, the Crusades were all unsuccessful. (See ARABS; ISLAM; MOHAMMED; RICHARD I)

CRUSTACEAN CRABS, LOBSTERS, SHRIMPS and BARNACLES are all crustaceans. Most crustaceans have a hard, chalky shell and, except for a few species, like the woodlouse, nearly all of them live in the sea. The crustaceans have been called 'insects of the sea' because of their great number and variety. They range in size from microscopic floating creatures to giant lobsters weighing over 14 kg (30 lb). Small crustaceans form much of the PLANKTON – the drifting layers of plants and animals in the surface waters of the sea – and so feed many kinds of fish. They are also the main food of whalebone whales, the largest mammals alive.

CRYSTALS Solids that have solidified in definite geometric shapes (see GEOMETRY). Most solids can form crystals. Those that do not crystallize are termed *amorphous*. Large crystals can be grown by making a strong solution of a solid in water and letting it evaporate slowly. Tiny crystals form if EVAPORATION is rapid.

CUBA An island republic in the WEST INDIES, which has had a communist government since 1959. Cuba has 9,992,000 people and an area of 114,524 sq km (44,218 sq miles). The capital is Havana. Sugar, tobacco (especially Havana cigars), nickel and rum are important products. ◁

CUBA: FACTS AND FIGURES
Cuba is the largest of the Caribbean islands. It is about 1200 km (750 miles) long and 96 km (60 miles) wide.
Official language: Spanish.
Currency: Peso.
Highest point: Pico Turquino 1973 m (6473 ft), in the Sierra Maestra.
Principal river: The Cauto.
Religion: Roman Catholic.

▲ *The study of crystal shape is called* morphology. *The shape of a crystal tells us what the inside structure of the mineral is like. Some minerals can exist in more than one crystal form. Carbon, for example, is found in two very different crystal forms – graphite and diamond. Calcium carbonate also exists in two forms — as calcite and aragonite. Above is one of the guises in which calcite occurs — as pointed, honey-coloured crystals.*

▼ *Some of the more common crustaceans that may be found near the sea's edge are: prawn (1); stalked barnacles, here growing from a floating bottle (2); crawfish or spiny lobster (3); common lobster (4); spider crab (5); and squat lobster (6).*

◄ Marie and Pierre Curie in their laboratory in 1903, the year of their joint Nobel Prize as the discoverers of radium. Marie won a second prize for work on radium in 1911.

CUBISM An idea in painting, which attempted to show the three-dimensional nature of objects by breaking them down into basic geometrical shapes, such as spheres, cubes, cylinders and cones. Pablo PICASSO and Georges Braque led this movement in France in the early 1900s. (See ART) ▷

CUCKOO The Cuckoo family of birds is named after the two-note call of the common cuckoo – a bluish-grey bird which spends the summer in north Europe and the winter in Africa. Some types of cuckoo, including the common cuckoo, are brood-parasites, that is, they do not rear their own young. Instead, the female lays eggs in the nests of other birds and relies on the foster parents to hatch and feed the babies. ▷

CUCUMBER Long green-skinned fleshy vegetable which is usually eaten as salad. Cucumbers grow on creeping plants and are generally cultivated in greenhouses.

▼ The cuckoo's gaping beak triggers off its host's instinct to feed it, although the 'baby' is larger than its foster parents.

CUPID The god of love in Roman MYTHOLOGY, shown as a naked, smiling, winged boy, with a bow and arrows. Anyone wounded by one of his arrows would fall in love.

CURIE, MARIE AND PIERRE Famous French chemists and physicists, partners in marriage as well as research work. Marie (born Polish) lived from 1867–1934, and Pierre from 1859–1906.

In 1898, while studying URANIUM, the radioactive element in pitchblende, Marie discovered a probable new ELEMENT. Pierre joined her in her research and the same year they discovered polonium and RADIUM. In 1902 they isolated one gram of pure radium from tons of pitchblende, or uranium ore. In 1903 they shared the NOBEL PRIZE for physics with Henri Becquerel. After Pierre's death, Marie took over his professorship of physics at the Sorbonne, and in 1911 won the Nobel Prize for chemistry. ▷

CURRENT, ELECTRIC See ELECTRICITY AND MAGNETISM.

CYPRESS A CONIFER with hard wood and dense foliage. The cypress is a native of Greece, for although conifers generally grow in cool zones, some also thrive in hot dry climates. In Mediterranean countries, where the cypress is commonly planted for ornament, the tree's dark slender form is a very familiar sight.

CYPRUS An island republic in the east MEDITERRANEAN, Cyprus has 657,000 people and an area of 9251 sq km (3572 sq miles), it is the third largest island in the Mediterranean. The capital is Nicosia. The economy is largely agricultural, but mining is important. Conflict between Christian Greek Cypriots (77 per cent of the people) and Moslem Turks (18 per cent) led to the partition of Cyprus in 1974.

CZECHOSLOVAKIA A land-locked communist republic in eastern Europe. It has 15,459,000 people (1984 est.) and an area of 127,869 sq km (49,370 sq miles). The capital is Prague. The main groups of people are the Czechs (65 per cent of the total), who live in the west and centre, and the Slovaks (30 per cent), who live in the east. Farming is important, but the nation's wealth comes mostly from its many factories. Czechoslovakia, once part of the Austro-Hungarian empire, was created in 1918. It came under German rule between 1939 and 1945. A communist regime has ruled the country since 1948.

CUBISM This artistic movement was named after the derisive comments of the artist Henri Matisse and the critic Louis Vauxcelles, who scornfully described a 1908 painting by Georges Braque (Houses At L'Estaque) as being 'composed of cubes'.

CUCKOO. These birds use various ingenious ploys to successfully lay their eggs in a host bird's nest. These include matching their eggs' markings to those of the host bird; removing one of the eggs already in the nest so the host mother does not notice an addition to her brood; and the ejection by the young cuckoo of all other nestlings or eggs it finds in the nest when it hatches. This behaviour is quite instinctive.

CURIE, MARIE AND PIERRE The Curies were indeed a remarkable family. Not only did Marie and Pierre both share the Nobel Prize for physics in 1903, but also their daughter Irene and son-in-law Jean-Frederic Joliot shared the Nobel Prize for chemistry in 1935. Meanwhile, after Pierre's death, Marie – the first ever woman professor at the Sorbonne – had also been awarded another Nobel Prize (this time for chemistry) in 1911.

D

DACHSHUND Small dog with large drooping ears, short crooked legs and a very long body. Its name is German for 'badger dog' as it was once used for hunting badgers in central Europe.

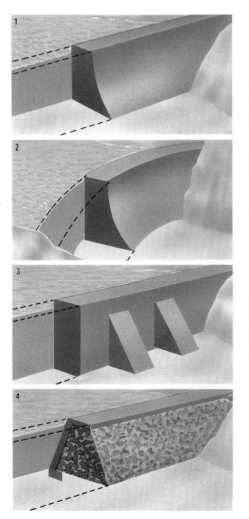

1. A gravity dam is a concrete or stone structure heavy enough to hold back the weight of the water it contains. The Grand Coulee Dam on the Columbia River is a gravity dam 170 metres (550 ft) high and over 430 metres (1400 ft) long.

2. Arch dams are built across rivers that flow through narrow canyons. Their curved flanks deflect the immense pressure of the water they contain against the canyon walls. These are the highest dams of all; the Nurek arch dam in the USSR is over 305 metres (1000 ft) high.

3. Buttress dams are relatively thin walled but are strengthened at regular intervals by buttress supports.

4. Earthen embankment dams are constructed by heaping earth and rock into a rough triangular shape across a river's course. These dams are often made with a core of clay and a covering of masonry or concrete.

DAFFODIL Spring plant growing from a bulb. Its yellow flower consists of a central trumpet surrounded by six petals. The daffodil, found wild in many parts of Europe, is a popular garden plant.

DAIRY INDUSTRY The production, distribution and sale of cows' MILK and products made from it. One-third of milk produced in Britain is made into BUTTER, CHEESE, cream, condensed milk or milk powder. The remainder is sold as fresh milk. Britain imports milk products from New Zealand, Canada and Europe.

DAISY Small European wild flower. The flower head – with a yellow centre and white rim – is made up of many tiny flowers, called florets. At night, the flower closes which explains its name: daisy means 'day's eye'.

DALI, SALVADOR A Spanish surrealist painter, born near Barcelona (1904–   ). His skill as an artist and the strange, dreamlike figures and scenes he portrays, make his paintings some of the most unusual in the contemporary period. (See SURREALISM)

DALTON, JOHN British chemist (1766–1844) who published an account of the atomic theory of matter in 1808. Dalton explained that the ELEMENTS consist of ATOMS, and that atoms of different elements combine to form compounds.

DAMS Barriers of rock, earth or concrete, for holding back water. The water may be released along pipes to operate HYDRO-ELECTRIC POWER generators. The reservoir of water behind a dam may also be used for IRRIGATION or general consumption.

Dan

▶ *Dance is one of man's earliest forms of self-expression. Here, one of a group of scarf dancers is giving a display in Hong Kong. Oriental dancers often wear beautiful and elaborate costumes and are renowned for the graceful movements of their hands and arms.*

DANCE Dancing is one of the most natural things we do. It consists of moving the feet and body in a rhythmical way. The simplest form of music for dancing is the pure rhythm of drum beats as in African tribal dancing. There are three main kinds of dances – religious and war dances, stage dances such as BALLET, and social dances, which people do for their own pleasure. Throughout history, dancing has been used to tell stories. The ancient Greeks considered dancing a great art, essential for physical health. Today, although 'ballroom' dancing remains popular, most people move freely in time to the music rather than follow set steps.

DANUBE, RIVER The Danube, EUROPE'S second longest river and a great trade route, rises in Germany and flows 2780 km (1730 miles) to the Black Sea. It passes through Austria, Czechoslovakia, Hungary and Yugoslavia. It also forms parts of Rumánia's borders with Bulgaria and the USSR.   ▷

DARWIN, CHARLES English naturalist (1809–1882) who pioneered the theory of EVOLUTION. As a young man, Darwin started to train as a doctor, then as a clergyman, but finally turned to natural history. In 1831 he joined HMS *Beagle* for a five-year scientific cruise. During the voyage, Darwin examined thousands of animals and plants and began to work out how they were related. On his return to England, he continued his research and in 1859 published his revolutionary ideas on evolution in a book called *The Origin of Species*. In a second book, *The Descent of Man* (1871) he traced man's ancestors back to ape-like creatures. Darwin went on writing and studying until his death in 1882.

DATE LINE An imaginary line around longitude 180° West (or East). When travellers cross the line from west to east, they gain one day. But they lose one day when crossing from east to west. This is because time is measured 180° east (plus 12 hours) or 180° west (minus 12 hours) of the prime MERIDIAN, or Greenwich mean time.

DA VINCI, LEONARDO See LEONARDO DA VINCI.

DEAD SEA A salty, inland lake on the Israel-Jordan border. Its shoreline is the world's lowest place on land, 393 metres (1289 ft) below sea-level.   ▷

DEAD SEA SCROLLS Ancient manuscripts, found between 1947 and the early 1950s in caves near the north-west shore of the Dead Sea. Written in Hebrew and Aramaic, languages of the ancient Jews, they include all

◀ *Charles Darwin in 1840. When he joined the* Beagle *expedition, Darwin was only 22 years old. He returned home five years later at the age of 27, and though he lived to be 73, he never again left England. He published* The Origin of Species *in 1859.*

DANUBE, RIVER The Danube carries enormous amounts of cargo in the ships and barges of many nations: Russian (738,632 tonnes), Yugoslavian (626,872 tonnes), Rumanian (403,352 tonnes) Hungarian (271,272 tonnes), Austrian (226,568 tonnes), Czech (201,168 tonnes), Bulgarian (198,120 tonnes) and West German (75,184 tonnes). However, it also carries a great deal of silt in its waters, especially in the delta – where over 80,000,000 tonnes of silt are deposited every year – constant dredging is needed to keep the river navigable. Despite this, the Danube's delta continues to grow into the Black Sea by 24.4-30.5 m (80-100 ft) every year.

DEAD SEA Because salty water is more dense than freshwater – and the Dead Sea is very salty indeed – it is quite possible for people to relax and read a newspaper while floating on the Sea's surface.

DEAFNESS There are three main types of deafness. Conductive deafness means that sounds are prevented from reaching the nerve cells of the inner ear by some sort of obstruction, like wax; while in nerve deafness the inner ear itself does not work as it should, due to damage from excessive noise or nerve infection. The third type of deafness is called 'functional', and it is usually a psychiatric problem caused by hysteria or fits.

DEBUSSY This French composer was a rebel throughout his life. As an anarchist, he overthrew the conventions of both society and music. As an artist, Debussy suffered from an over-sensitive nature. He invented a person called 'Monsieur Croche' to help him cope with his many conflicts. During one well-recorded conversation, Monsieur Croche asked Debussy (himself): 'What is the use of your almost incomprehensible art; is it not more profitable to see the Sun rise than to listen to the Pastoral Symphony of Beethoven?'

the books of the Old Testament except Esther, and are now kept in the Israel Museum in Jerusalem.

DEAFNESS It is very seldom that a person is completely deaf, and the degree of deafness depends to some extent on whether high or low sounds can be heard. When only low tones are heard, speech is difficult for a deaf person to understand. Children born deaf used also to be unable to speak – they were 'deaf-mutes'. Now, with new ways of amplifying sounds and phonetic teaching these children can be taught to talk.   ◁

DEATH Recent advances in medicine have made it more difficult to define the word 'death'. People have 'died' – their breathing and heart have stopped – but it has been possible to revive them by heart massage and artificial respiration. It is now believed that it is the stopping of the brain's activity which finally shows whether a person is dead or not.

DEBUSSY, CLAUDE A French composer (1862–1918), the first to write music in an impressionistic style. He broke away from traditional composition, to create poetical ideas and visual impressions in sound.   ◁

DECATHLON A two-day athletic contest of ten events held at the Olympic Games since 1912. The events are: the long jump, the high jump, discus throw, shot-put, javelin throw, pole vault, 110-metre high hurdle, and 100-, 400- and 1500-metre races.

DECLARATION OF INDEPENDENCE On July 4, 1776, delegates from the 13 British colonies in America adopted the Declaration of Independence, thus creating the 13 original states of the USA, independent of British government.

▲ General Charles de Gaulle, seen here with Haile Selassie, emperor of Ethiopia, was the founder and first president of the French Fifth Republic (1959–1969).

DEER Four-footed animals, many with antlers, found in Europe, Asia and America. Deer generally live among trees and eat leaves, shoots, grass and moss. Every year they shed their old antlers and grow new ones. There are many different kinds of deer ranging in size from the large ELK at 2 metres (7 ft) to the tiny South American pudu at 40 cm (16 in).

DEFOE, DANIEL A skilful English novelist, and often controversial writer of his times (1660–1731). His most famous work is *Robinson Crusoe*, a gripping tale of shipwreck and survival on a tropical island.

DE GAULLE, CHARLES A French military leader, politician, and president (1890–1970). He escaped to England in World War II, and led the Free French until liberation in 1945.

DELTA An area of alluvial land, built up from river sediments, at the mouths of some rivers, including the Hwang Ho, MISSISSIPPI and NILE. The world's largest is the GANGES-Brahmaputra delta in Bangladesh.

DELTA RAYS Electrons emitted by ATOMS when struck by cosmic rays. (See ELECTRO-MAGNETIC WAVES)

DEMOCRACY A form of GOVERNMENT organized by the people for the benefit of the

◀ North America's white-tailed deer lives in woods and thickets close to open meadows. As a startled deer runs, it lifts its tail, which has a white underside, as a warning to other deer.

1 Gila woodpecker
2 Elf owl
3 Kit fox
4 Rattlesnake
5 Gila monster
6 Desert tortoise

DENMARK: FACTS AND FIGURES
Official language: Danish.
Currency: Danish krone.
Highest point: Ejer Bavnehöj 173 m (567 ft). Denmark is a very low-lying country.
Denmark consists of the Jutland Peninsula, which is joined to Germany, and about 500 islands.
About one-sixth of the total population lives in the capital and leading seaport, Copenhagen (pop. 1,366,000).

DENSITY The densest naturally occurring element is Osmium, which was discovered in 1804 and of which one cubic foot would weigh 640 kg (1,410 lb, 22.59 g/cm³). Material with astronomically higher densities than this is, of course, believed to occur in 'black holes' in space.

DESERT The official definition of a desert is anywhere with an average of less than 25 cm (10 in) of rainfall, or other precipitation per year, or with more precipitation but a porous surface which does not retain enough moisture for plants to grow. About one eighth of the world's surface falls into the category of desert, and the Sahara – covering about 8,400,000 sq km (3,200,000 sq miles of North Africa – is the largest desert in the world.

DIABETES Throughout history – until 1921 – a person with diabetes faced almost certain death. In that year, however, three researchers (Sir Frederick Banting, Charles H. Best and John James Rickard Macleod) working at the University of Toronto, Canada, managed to isolate and identify the hormone insulin. This, they found, is produced naturally in the pancreases of healthy people, but is not produced by diabetics. By taking insulin from the pancreases of animals and injecting it regularly into their diabetic patients, these researchers found that the disease could be contained.

people. In most democracies representatives are elected by popular vote to express their followers' views in parliament.

DENMARK A small, prosperous north European monarchy, Denmark has 5,112,000 people (1984 est.) and an area of 43,069 sq km (16,629 sq miles). The capital, Copenhagen, stands on one of Denmark's many islands. The country is known for its dairy products, meat and other food exports, but manufacturing is now the chief industry. ◁

DENSITY The ratio of a body's mass to its volume. In SI UNITS, density is measured in kilograms per cubic metre (kg/m³). ◁

DENTISTRY Care of the teeth by a qualified dentist. This may involve the treatment of diseases and the correction of deformities of the teeth and mouth, drilling out decay and filling holes, and replacing lost teeth with bridges and dentures. Training to be a dentist takes five to six years.

DEODORANTS Substances that remove or disguise unpleasant smells in buildings or on the body. Antiperspirants are body deodorants that act by temporarily stopping perspiration.

DERBY, THE A famous English horse race run at Epsom over 1½ miles, open to three-year-old colts and fillies which must be entered for the race at least 18 months beforehand.

DESERT A barren region with scanty or no vegetation. Hot, dry deserts, such as the SAHARA, are in the tropics. Cold deserts, such as the ANTARCTIC, are barren because the low temperatures restrict plant growth. ◁

DESTROYER A small warship, usually between 90–120 metres (300–400 ft) long, used mainly to protect other ships and patrol areas. It is armed with torpedoes and guns of small or medium calibre. First built in 1893, it is now largely replaced by the smaller FRIGATE.

DETERGENTS See SOAPS AND DETERGENTS

DETONATOR A small explosive charge used to set off the main charge in bombs and other explosive devices.

◁ *As dark falls on a hot American desert the land and air soon cool. As the scorched ground cools, creatures that had hidden from the Sun's heat awake to feed. The gila woodpecker roosts on a saguaro cactus. The kit fox, one of the desert's predators, feeds on rabbits and rodents. Rattlesnakes and gila monsters also prey on rodents. The desert tortoise crawls from its burrow to browse on desert vegetation.*

DIABETES The cause of sugar diabetes is unknown, but it tends to be passed on in families. A lack of insulin in the blood makes it difficult for the body to use sugar for the production of energy. There are also several other types of diabetes. ◁

DIAMETER See CIRCLE

DIAMOND A form of the non-metallic element CARBON. When pure, a diamond is clear, but it often contains impurities that colour it. Naturally occurring diamonds are cut and polished to make valuable gemstones. Being the hardest known substance, diamond is used to make cutting tools. Some diamonds used in industry are made artificially from GRAPHITE. (See CARAT)

DICE Little cubes, each side marked with a different number of dots, from one to six. Dice are used in many games.

DICKENS, CHARLES One of the greatest writers of English fiction (1812–1870). At the age of 24 he became famous for writing comic adventures in *Pickwick Papers*. His early experiences and observations of poverty and hardship come across to the reader in novels such as *Oliver Twist*, *David Copperfield* and *Great Expectations*.

DICTIONARY A book in which people can look up the spelling, pronunciation and meaning of words, which are alphabetically arranged. Also given is an abbreviation, such as *n.* (for NOUN), or *adj.* (for ADJECTIVE), showing what part of speech each word is. Sometimes an example of the use of the word is given, and its history.

DIDGERIDOO A musical wind instrument, consisting of a pipe about 1½ metres (5 ft) long, made by North Australian ABORIGINES.

DIESEL ENGINE A type of INTERNAL COMBUSTION ENGINE, similar in many ways to the petrol engine. German engineer Rudolf Diesel invented this engine in the 1890s. It is now widely used to power buses, trucks and locomotives.

DIET Our diet is the total of all the foodstuffs we eat and drink to give us energy and the material for growth. The amount of food we need daily depends on many things – our age, our state of health, the kind of work we do, how tall we are, and how heavy we are. For good health we need a proper mixture of PROTEINS, FATS and CARBOHYDRATES, and we also need VITAMINS which we usually get from a normal mixed diet. And we need water in some form; it makes up 70 per cent of our body's total weight.

DIGESTION Digestion is the process by which food is broken down inside the body into a form that can be carried by the BLOOD to feed the CELLS. Digestion begins when we chew our food and produce saliva (see SAL-IVARY GLANDS). It continues in the STOMACH and then in the small INTESTINE. By the time food enters the large intestine nearly all the nutrients have gone into the blood. The remains are expelled via the anus.

DINOSAURS A large group of prehistoric REPTILES that lived during the Mesozoic era from about 225 million to 65 million years ago. The word dinosaur means 'terrible lizard', and some of them were indeed terrible. *Tyrannosaurus*, a ferocious flesh-eating giant was about 15 metres (50 ft) long and stood about 6 metres (20 ft) high on its strong back legs. Its huge mouth held dagger-like teeth. In contrast were the lumbering plant-eating dinosaurs such as *Brachiosaurus*, *Apatosaurus* (once called *Brontosaurus*) and *Diplodocus* with their long necks and tails and small heads. *Brachiosaurus* was the heaviest of them all; some individuals may have weighed as much as 100 tonnes, equal to 20 large elephants. The longest was *Diplodocus* at some 27 metres (88 ft). Other dinosaurs were encased in living armour. Some, like *Stegosaurus*, had large bony plates sticking out of their backs. Scientists still do not know why the dinosaurs quite suddenly died out.

DIPHTHERIA An infectious disease that attacks the throat and blocks the breathing passages. Injections against the disease have reduced the number of cases enormously.

DISCUS A round wooden plate, 21.9 cm (8$\frac{5}{8}$ inches) in diameter, thicker in the centre than at the edge. Athletes compete to throw the discus the greatest distance.

▼ Tyrannosaurus, *one of the most ferocious of the meat-eating dinosaurs, attacks the plant-eating, duck-billed* Corythosaurus.

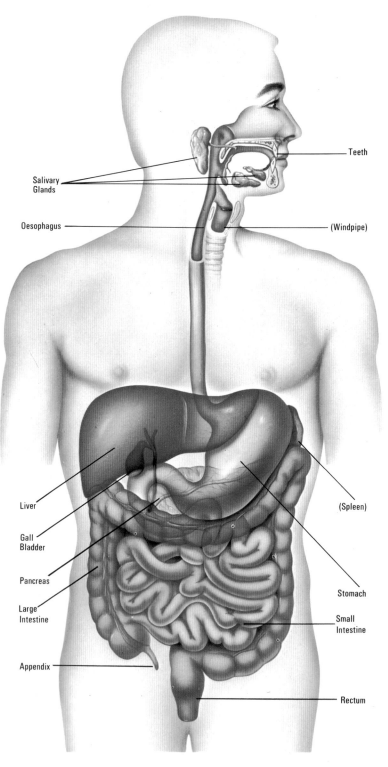

Teeth

Salivary Glands

Oesophagus

(Windpipe)

Liver

(Spleen)

Gall Bladder

Pancreas

Stomach

Large Intestine

Small Intestine

Appendix

Rectum

▲ The alimentary canal, or digestive tract (not to scale). An adult's digestive tract is about 9 metres (30 feet) long, beginning at the mouth and ending at the anus. Food is forced along the oesophagus, and other tubes of the digestive system, by an action called peristalsis, a series of muscular contractions.

DISRAELI, BENJAMIN Until 1858, people of the Jewish religion were prohibited from entering the British parliament. As Disraeli's parents were both Jewish, it was fortunate for their son's future political career that Isaac D'Israeli argued with his local synagogue in 1813. As a result, young Benjamin was baptized as a Christian four years later, and so was free to enter politics when he chose to do so in 1831.

DNA It has been estimated that all the DNA in a single, tiny human cell would, if stretched out, form a chain nearly a metre long, and would have about six million units of information on it.

DISINFECTANTS Chemicals used for killing germs as protection against disease. Chlorine is a disinfectant widely used to sterilize water.

DISNEY, WALT A producer of CARTOON films (1901–1966) with characters such as *Mickey Mouse, Donald Duck* and *Bambi*; real-life adventure films such as *Davy Crockett*, and nature films such as *The Living Desert*.

DISRAELI, BENJAMIN A British statesman and novelist (1804–1881) and Conservative Prime Minister for over six years. He was responsible for reforms which improved the conditions of working class people, and for policies which defended and increased Britain's colonial interests abroad. ◁

DISTILLATION A process for separating a mixture of liquids, or removing dissolved solids from a liquid. The process involves heating the original liquid and condensing the vapour given off (see CONDENSATION). Strong alcoholic drinks are made by distilling weaker alcoholic solutions to remove much of the water present.

DIVING Underwater diving is used for inspecting and repairing ships and harbours, or mining and drilling installations, and even gathering oysters and sponges from the seabed. A diver needs special equipment to breathe, and to protect his body from increased water pressure if he stays under for a long time and dives deep. (See AQUALUNG)

Diving is also a popular water sport in which the diver leaps from a platform or

▲ *The clumsy dodo could not fly. When men and their domestic animals came to its island home in the Indian Ocean, the dodo had no means of escape. By the end of the 17th century it had been completely wiped out.*

springboard, sometimes performing spins and turns in the air, before plunging hands and head first into the water.

DNA These letters are short for deoxyribonucleic acid. This is the chief material of the CHROMOSOMES found in the nucleus of every living CELL. Molecules of DNA are arranged in two spiralling bands. These bands of DNA control the HEREDITY of all animals and plants. They contain information which ensures that when cells divide the correct hereditary information is passed on to the new cells. ◁

DOCKS Constructed basins to receive vessels in ports for loading and unloading. Dry docks are enclosed basins from which water can be pumped so that ships can be repaired. Floating docks are mobile steel pontoons, sunk beneath ships. When water is pumped from their hollow chambers, the dock rises, lifting the ship with it.

DODO The dodo, now extinct, was a giant flightless bird with short stumpy legs and a large hooked beak. It used to live on the Indian Ocean islands of Mauritius and Réunion but had completely vanished by the end of the 17th century.

DOG Animal belonging to the *Canidae* family which includes the wolves, jackals and foxes. Dogs are flesh-eaters and good hunters – they are fast runners and have strong jaws and sharp teeth. The domesticated dog is one of man's earliest pets. They were probably even bred and trained by primitive people, for hunting and as protection from wild animals. Dogs are classified as sporting, non-sporting,

◀ *A diver helps raise the anchor of a sunken ship from the sea bed. Divers carry out many types of work under water – from salvaging vessels to repairing and maintaining oil rigs.*

hounds, terriers, working, or toys. All domestic dogs, in spite of their wide variety, belong to the same species, and are thought to have descended from the wolf.

DOLPHIN Small toothed WHALE found in nearly all the world's seas; a few live in tropical rivers. Most species are 2–4 metres (7–13 ft) long and grey or black in colour. Dolphins swim together in schools and feed mainly on fish. They are friendly animals and often follow ships for miles, leaping playfully out of the water. ▷

DOME A type of roof shaped like an inverted bowl, mostly used on religious buildings such as mosques and churches. The TAJ MAHAL at Agra, in India, carries a dome, as does St Paul's Cathedral, London, and the Pantheon, Rome.

DONKEY Domestic animal descended from the wild ASSES of Africa. Donkeys, usually brown or grey, are small sturdy creatures and are still used in many countries for pulling and carrying loads.

DON QUIXOTE The title, and hero, of a novel by the Spanish writer, Cervantes, written in the early 17th century. The confused hero sets out on his scraggy horse to perform heroic deeds, none of which actually occurs. ▷

DOUBLE STAR See BINARY STARS

DOVE Bird belonging to the PIGEON family. Doves are similar to pigeons, but smaller. In the Bible, it was a dove that brought Noah a sign of the flood's end; since then, the bird has been a symbol of peace.

DRAGONFLY Large carnivorous flying IN-SECT famous for its brilliant colours. Found

▲ *The gleaming gold dome on the Moslem Mosque of Omar in Jerusalem. Domes are a popular feature of Islamic architecture, and are often elaborately decorated with mosaic tiles. Modern domes are used for large exhibition halls and sports arenas.*

mostly in warm countries, the dragonfly spends its early life underwater but eventually leaves the stream or pond and reaches maturity on land. ▷

DRAINAGE This can mean the system used to lead away water and waste from buildings, from baths, sinks and lavatories (see SEWAGE).

It also means the system of collecting and taking away rain water from towns, or excess water from low-lying countryside, to make it workable for crop growing and other uses.

DRAKE, SIR FRANCIS A daring sailor, fighter and explorer (c. 1543–1596). His naval warfare against the Spaniards, backed by Queen Elizabeth I, helped England to become a major sea power. Drake was the first British seaman to sail round the world. In 1588 he took part in the defeat of the Spanish ARMADA in the English Channel. ▷

DRAMA An art form that tells a story, or expresses an idea, through the speech and action of the characters in a play.

Ancient Greek drama was already popular in the 400s BC. The outdoor theatre of Dionysus in Athens seated 14,000 people, and was used to perform tragedies – solemn, poetic and philosophic plays, often ending in the

◄ *Sir Francis Drake led many naval expeditions, particularly against the Spanish. From 1572 he took rich booty from treasure ships and Spanish possessions in the Americas. In 1588 Drake took part in the destruction of the Spanish Armada, shown at the left.*

DOLPHIN Dolphins use sophisticated methods of communication. Like humans, they produce and (with their ears) receive sounds, interpret them and build up mental ideas, maps and images. Recent studies on several species of dolphin – particularly the bottle-nosed dolphin of the Atlantic – have shown that it is possible for humans and dolphins to communicate. In fact, dolphins appear to be definitely interested in communicating with humans.

DON QUIXOTE The popularity of this comical elderly knight, whose head is filled with romantic ideas he is unable to fulfill, has led to the word 'quixotic' entering the language. This word describes someone who is full of lofty, but impracticable, ideals. Such people are often said to be 'tilting at windmills', based on one of Don Quixote's exploits where he mistakes the windmills for giants, and nobly challenges them to a joust.

DRAGONFLY These predatory insects are very fast fliers, and their wingspan may be up to 16 cm (6 in). In half an hour they can eat their own weight in food.

DRAKE When reading about the heroic exploits of this Elizabethan sailor, it is hard to imagine that his ships were little bigger than modern-day pleasure cruisers. In fact, when he set forth to pillage Spanish possessions in the West Indies and Central America in 1572, his two ships – the *Pasha* and the *Swan* – were just 71 and 25 tonnes respectively. The *Golden Hind*, in which he circumnavigated the world (1577-80) and returned loaded high with Spanish gold and silver, was a large merchant ship of its day, weighing about 101 tonnes.

DRUM Throughout history, drums have often been regarded as sacred instruments. In many cultures their manufacture is surrounded by ritual, and when they are first used, sacrifices are often made to them. This practice still occurs in East Africa, where new royal kettledrums are taken into service with the sacrifice of cattle. These drums are believed both to symbolize the king's power and offer him protection from supernatural forces. In Africa, as elsewhere, drums are often important message carriers and religious objects, as well as simple musical instruments.

DWARF Nowadays, dwarf humans are simply regarded as 'people of restricted growth'. In less sensitive times, however, they were often made into objects of curiosity or humour. In ancient Egypt and Rome, household dwarfs were 'kept' as curiosities, while in the Middle Ages, Italian, Spanish, Russian and German royal courts often kept dwarfs as entertainers or professional fools. In the 18th and 19th centuries, there was even a craze for 'dwarf weddings' in the Russian tsar's court.

death of the hero – and comedies – humorous plays based on happy thoughts, sometimes ridiculing or criticizing aspects of contemporary life.

Nowadays, drama is an extremely popular and varied form of art, practised by children in the classroom, and by actors on stage, screen, television and radio. (See ACTING)

DREAMS Unconscious thoughts and mental experiences which take place during sleep. We sometimes remember our dreams; they may be pleasant, extraordinary, or unpleasant and frightening, as in nightmares. Scientists can tell when people dream by using an electro-encephalograph, a machine which registers different 'brainwaves' in a sleeper. They can also observe rapid eye movements (REM), which occur when someone dreams.

People dream four to six times per night, and each dream lasts from 15 to 20 minutes.

DREDGING A method of mechanically clearing away earth from under water. The reasons are usually to clear or deepen canals and rivers, or entrances and channels to harbours and docks, so as to make them safe for shipping.

DRUGS Drugs are chemicals taken to prevent or cure disease. Opium, morphine and other narcotic drugs relieve pain. Sedatives calm us, the most common sedatives being the BARBITURATES which are used in many sleeping tablets. Tranquillizers calm anxiety without making us drowsy. The SULFA DRUGS and ANTIBIOTICS such as penicillin fight harmful bacteria in the body.

We also use the word drugs to mean habit-forming substances such as cocaine, MARIJUANA, ALCOHOL and NICOTINE.

DRUM A musical instrument, made of a cylinder (open at two ends), or a 'kettle' (open at one end) with the end or ends covered by a tightly stretched skin. The skin is struck to produce rhythms. ◁

DRY CLEANING A method of cleaning fabrics without using water. The term 'dry' is

misleading, as other liquids, such as trichloroethylene, are used to remove the dirt and stains.

DRY ICE Solid CARBON DIOXIDE, which is a gas at normal temperature and pressure. On cooling to $-78.5°C$ $(-109.3°F)$, it turns straight to dry ice without going through a liquid state.

DRY ROT The wooden parts of buildings are often attacked by a FUNGUS that causes the decay known as dry rot. At first, the fungus grows in the damp. But, once established, it can continue to survive on dry timbers.

DUCK Aquatic web-footed bird found by rivers and coasts all over the world. Some species feed off leaves, grass and seeds on land; others spend much time in the water, either eating surface insects or diving for fish. The most common duck is the northern hemisphere's Mallard, the ancestor of domestic ducks. Another well-known species, the Eider, comes from the Arctic seas of Canada and Siberia and is famous for its soft warm down.

DUNEDIN A port and manufacturing city on the east coast of South Island, NEW ZEALAND. It has a population of 112,000 (1983). The city has a Scottish atmosphere, and many people are of Scottish descent.

DWARF An unusually small human being, whose proportions are sometimes abnormal, but whose mental abilities are usually normal. This word can also refer to an unusually small animal or plant. ◁

DYEING The process of colouring cloth or other materials by soaking them in coloured solutions. Man has used natural dyes from plants and animals for thousands of years. The yellow dye saffron, for example, comes from crocus flowers. The manufacture of synthetic dyes started in 1856 with the production of the mauve dye *mauvein*.

DYNAMICS The branch of MECHANICS dealing with bodies in motion.

DYNAMITE A widely used EXPLOSIVE consisting basically of nitroglycerine absorbed in an inert earth called *kieselguhr*. Absorbing dangerous nitroglycerine in this way makes the explosive relatively safe to handle. The Swedish chemist Alfred Nobel invented dynamite in 1867.

◀ *Rectangles of dyed cloth are laid out to dry in an African village. Knots tied in the cloth before it is dipped into the dye produce the patterns.*

EAGLE Powerful bird of prey found all over the world. Many species are huge like the Steller's sea eagle from Siberia and the South American Harpy; both birds weigh about 6.5 kg (15 lb) and have wing spans of up to 2.5 metres (8 ft). All eagles eat flesh such as fish, birds or rabbits; some kinds are even strong enough to kill seals, deer and wolves. Eagles usually build their nests, called *eyries*, high on rocky crags or in tree tops and return each year to the same eyrie.

EAR Sense organ used for hearing and balancing. In simple animals the ear is often nothing more than a tiny pit lined with sensitive hairs; but in highly developed animals, like man, the ear is very complex. It has three parts: the outer, middle and inner ear.

▼ *A cutaway drawing of the ear. The ear has three distinct parts – the outer ear, the middle ear and the inner ear. Sound waves, or vibrations, are funnelled along the main canal to the eardrum, which vibrates in sympathy.*

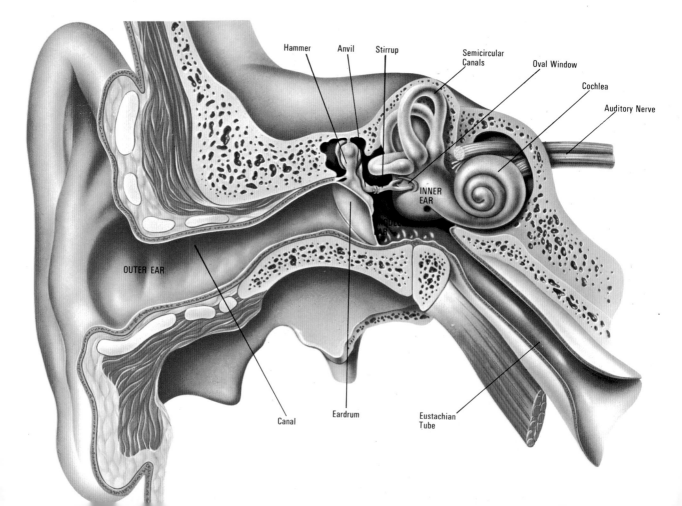

EARTHQUAKE The ancient Egyptians invented a simple seismograph to record earthquakes in AD 132, This used a free-swinging pendulum hung in a vessel 2.5 m (8 ft) high. When an earthquake occurred, the pendulum swung to and fro and indicated the force and direction of the 'quake.

ECHIDNA This animal, and the duck-billed platypus, are the world's only two monotremes, or egg-laying mammals. That is, they lay eggs like reptiles, but are warm-blooded and suckle their young like mammals. They are the most primitive of all mammals, and clearly show the evolutionary link with reptiles.

The outer ear consists of the *auricle*, a fleshy flap on the side of the head, and an opening, the *auditory canal*. Sound waves are gathered by the auricle and guided along the canal. The end of the canal is closed by a membrane called the *ear drum* which vibrates when hit by the waves. In the middle ear, three tiny bones magnify the drum's vibrations and pass them on to the inner ear. There, they are caught by the *cochlea* – a spiral cavity full of fluid – and sent by nerves to the brain to be translated into sounds. Also in the inner ear are three semicircular canals, filled with fluid, which give the sense of balance. (See DEAFNESS)

EARTH Our planet; the third from the SUN and the fifth largest in the SOLAR SYSTEM. It is slightly flattened at the Poles and revolves around the Sun in 365¼ days. The Earth is believed to have a central core of iron and nickel, surrounded by a layer of molten rock, then by a heavier layer of solid rock called the mantle. The outer crust is only a few miles thick. (See ROCKS)

EARTHQUAKE A tremor in the Earth's crust. Earthquakes occur when there are sudden movements along FAULTS beneath the surface. They are most common near the edges of the moving plates, into which the Earth's crust is split. They may cause great

▲ Some of the damage caused by the San Francisco earthquake of 1906. The city lies along the San Andreas fault, a crack in the Earth's crust on the west coast of America.

damage and loss of life. One earthquake in China killed about 800,000 people in 1556.
◁

EASTER The main Christian celebration in memory of the death and resurrection of JESUS CHRIST. Because it is based on the full moon, its date varies from March 22 to April 25. (See CHRISTIANITY)

EBONY Hard jet-black wood obtained from a family of trees growing in tropical Asia and Africa. Some of the world's best ebony comes from Sri Lanka. The wood takes a high polish and is used for carvings, cabinetwork and piano keys.

ECHIDNA This small egg-laying mammal is found only in Australia and New Guinea. The egg is laid in the mother's pouch where the young hatches and suckles for the first 6–8 weeks before coming out. Echidnas are covered with stubby spines. They have a long tubular mouth and a sticky tongue for licking up ants and termites. Their claws are strong for digging.   ◁

ECHO The repeat of a SOUND, caused by the reflection of its waves from a distant surface. From the time delay between the original sound and the echo, it is possible to calculate the distance of the reflecting surface. This principle is used in SONAR.

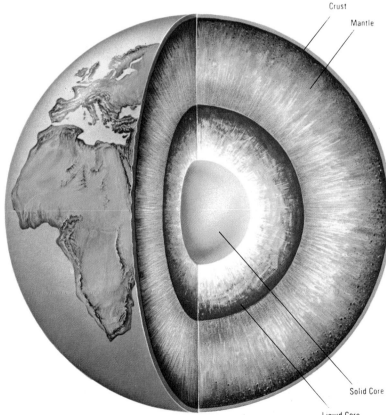

◀ The Earth is divided into three main zones – the crust, mantle and core. The continental crust reaches a depth of 60–70 km (37–43 miles) under mountains. The mantle (2900 km; 1800 miles thick) contains extremely dense rocks. The core is about 6920 km (4300 miles) in diameter.

Crust
Mantle
Solid Core
Liquid Core

Lunar eclipse

Moon

Solar eclipse

SUN'S
RAYS

Moon's shadow

Earth's shadow

ECLIPSE An eclipse of the Sun (solar eclipse) occurs when the Moon moves directly between the Earth and the Sun. In a total eclipse, the Moon completely obscures the Sun. Partial eclipses, in which only part of the Sun is obscured, are much more common. An eclipse of the Moon (lunar eclipse) occurs when the Earth's shadow falls on the Moon. The lunar eclipse may be partial or total. ▷

ECOLOGY The study of plants and animals in relation to their environment. Environment means surroundings, and includes the climate, soil, air and water as well as other plants and animals. Climate and soil are the most important aspects, as they control vegetation; in turn, vegetation influences animal life since animals eat plants. In this way, each of the world's major habitats or life zones – such as the Arctic TUNDRA, tropical rainforest, DESERT – has its own characteristic plants and animals. The ecologist studies plants and animals in the framework of their habitat; how their environment affects them and how, in turn, they affect each other and their surroundings. (See ADAPTATION; BIOLOGY)

ECONOMICS The study of the way in which people acquire money, and also the way they spend it. Economics studies the actions of businesses and of governments too. It also looks at the way changes in the cost of living, say in the price of bread, affect the amount people buy and whether they spend or save more as a result.

ECUADOR A republic straddling the equator in north-western SOUTH AMERICA. Ecuador has 9,115,000 people (1984) and an area of 283,561 sq km (109,483 sq miles). The capital, Quito, is located in the high, cool Andes region. About two-thirds of the people are farmers.

▶ *One of Thomas Edison's early phonographs. All records were cylindrical until 1887, when Emile Berliner invented the disc record.*

▲ *A solar eclipse occurs when the Moon passes between the Earth and the Sun. An eclipse of the Moon occurs when the Sun, Earth and Moon are lined up so that the Earth's shadow falls across the Moon.*

EDINBURGH The capital of SCOTLAND, Edinburgh has a population of 439,700 (1985 est.). This handsome city is a great commercial centre. It holds an annual international festival of music and the arts which was inaugurated in 1947.

EDISON, THOMAS American inventor (1847–1931) remembered in particular for the phonograph, which he invented in 1877. Perhaps his most important invention was the electric light bulb, with a glowing wire filament.

ECLIPSE In China in AD 213, the population was terrified when a total eclipse took place. They thought a dragon was trying to eat the Sun, and people ran into the streets shouting and banging drums to frighten off the beast. After a few minutes the Sun reappeared and all was well, except for the court astronomers, who were executed for failing to warn the emperor of the dragon's approach.

◄ *Eels spawn in the Sargasso Sea, in the western Atlantic. While still immature, the young travel to the rivers of North America and northern Europe, where they spend their adult lives. Then they return to the Sargasso Sea to spawn and die in turn.*

reach the coast, they swim over 6000 km (to 3720 miles) to the middle of the Atlantic – or Pacific – ocean where they lay their eggs, then die. The return journey by the young eels to the pond or river where their parents lived takes about three years. ◁

EGG Female reproductive CELL. Most animals reproduce sexually: this involves the joining together – fertilization – of a special female cell, the egg (ovum), and a special male cell, the sperm. After fertilization, the egg develops into a new individual. With some animals, such as birds and fishes, this development happens outside the female's body; in this case, the egg is protected by a shell and contains food (yolk) for the growing organism. With other animals, mostly MAMMALS, the egg develops inside the mother and is fed directly from her body and protected by it. (See REPRODUCTION)

EGYPT (ANCIENT) Ancient Egypt flourished for 3000 years in the fertile valley of the NILE. It was one of the greatest and most long-lived civilizations ever known. Records show that around 3100 BC, the first dynasty of PHARAOHS was founded after the Upper King-

ECUADOR: FACTS AND FIGURES
Area: Territory includes the Galapagos Islands, home of many rare and unusual animals.
Currency: Sucre
Religion: Roman Catholic
Language: Spanish

EEL Among the many varieties of eel, perhaps the strangest is the electric eel. It grows to around 2.75 m (8 ft) in length, and it can deliver a paralyzing shock of 200-300 volts from the electric organs that run along both sides of its body.

EGYPT (ANCIENT) The Great Pyramid of Cheops took 200,000 slaves 20 years to build, using over 2,500,000 stone blocks – some of which weigh up to 2.5 tonnes. The positioning of the blocks is so precise that on some facing stones a sheet of paper cannot be inserted in the joints. The fact that this massive structure is still standing after 4,500 years is proof indeed of the ancient Egyptians' remarkable engineering skills.

EDUCATION At its very simplest, education is about the way in which people learn about themselves and about the world around them. This is called informal education. It is what you learn from friends, from reading books and from everyday experiences.

Schools, colleges and UNIVERSITIES are described as formal education. For most people, it begins around the age of six. This kind of education teaches a mixture of general knowledge and special skills. Pupils learn how to read and write, and how to do maths. They also study history, the sciences, languages and geography. They may even learn skills that help them get jobs once they leave.

EEL Edible snake-like fish. Most eels live in the sea but there are several freshwater species found in rivers, lakes and ponds. Once in their lifetime, freshwater eels journey to the sea to breed. If their starting point is a pond, they wriggle overland to find a river. When they

▼ *An eider duck makes a nest among stones. Its eggs look like the stones for protection.*

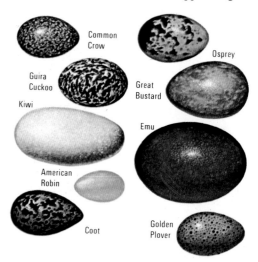

Common Crow
Osprey
Guira Cuckoo
Great Bustard
Kiwi
Emu
American Robin
Coot
Golden Plover

▲ *There is a great range of difference in the colour and size of birds' eggs. The kiwi lays enormous eggs for its size – each egg being one seventh of the bird's weight. Guillemots' eggs have a pointed end, so they always roll in a circle and not off the cliff edges where they are laid. Birds' eggs offer fine examples of protective colouring. Many field birds' eggs are speckled, to camouflage them on the ground where they are laid.*

▶ An astronomical painting on the ceiling of the tomb of the Egyptian pharaoh Seti I, showing the Sun's passage at night.

▲ The golden fan-holder of Tutankhamen, who was a child-pharoah of ancient Egypt from 1347–1335 BC.

dom vanquished the Lower Kingdom of the Nile Delta. The last dynasty ended when the Persians and the Greeks conquered the land in the 4th century BC.

The pharaoh, or king, was all-powerful. He was not just a man but a god. He owned all the land and was the nation's chief priest. He also ran the army, the government and the state's finances.

The Egyptians were fascinated by death and built huge tombs and PYRAMIDS to honour their dead. The tombs were filled with objects and models of all the things used in daily life, for they felt it necessary to take along into the afterlife everything that made living in this world pleasant. (See CLEOPATRA; PHARAOH; TUTANKHAMEN)   ▷

◀ A prosperous farm in ancient Egypt. Canals and dykes fed by the annual flooding of the Nile irrigated the crops of fruit, vegetables and wheat, as well as the vineyards. The leather pouch attached to a counter-weight was used to draw water, and called a 'shaduf'.

Several times during the Twentieth Egyptian Dynasty the workmen building a tomb for the pharaoh at Deir el Medinah on the west bank of the Nile were not paid their food and other goods on time. The men went on strike. They marched to the temple where supplies were kept, and sat down outside calling for bread. The workmen were able to get what they wanted because it was unthinkable that the pharaoh's tomb should not be finished.

One of the problems facing the builders of the Great Pyramid was how to achieve a level foundation for the huge structure. Engineers think that the Egyptians may have dug a trench all around the area to be built on. They then filled the trench with water and the water level gave them a perfect starting point. The south-east corner of the Great Pyramid is only half an inch higher than the north-east corner — and the two corners are 323 metres (1060 ft) apart.

◄ *Water from the River Nile is essential to Egypt. Irrigation canals lead water from the river to the farmland alongside it. About 95 per cent of Egyptians live in the Nile valley, which covers only 3 per cent of Egypt.*

EGYPT: FACTS AND FIGURES
Official language: Arabic.
Currency: Egyptian pound.
Religion: Moslem.
Only about 3 per cent of Egypt's area, the Nile valley and delta, has been settled and cultivated. The rest is desert. To the west of the Nile stretches the vast Libyan Desert, to the east lies the Arabian Desert.
The River Nile flows through Egypt for about 1488 km (925 miles). Its fertile valley is from 1.6 to 24 km (1 to 15 miles) wide.
The Suez Canal gives a sea passage from the Mediterranean to the Gulf of Suez. It is 162 km (101 miles) long.
Cairo is the largest city in Africa with a population of 11,500,000 (1985 est.). Alexandria has a population of 4,000,000 (1983 est.).

ELECTIONS The first-known law relating to elections was a 6th century Athenian decree which stated that in cases of 'civil turmoil', citizens must choose sides and so resolve the conflict quickly. Abstentions were not allowed, because too many would open the door to tyranny.

EGYPT An ARAB republic in north-eastern AFRICA, Egypt has 47,000,000 people (1983 est.) and an area of 1,001,449 sq km (386,662 sq miles). The capital is CAIRO. Most of Egypt is desert and most people are farmers in the narrow NILE valley. The chief crop is cotton, but manufacturing is increasing. In 1977–79 Egypt sought peace with Israel, following Arab–Israeli wars in 1948–49, 1956, 1967 and 1971. ◁

EIFFEL TOWER Towering 300 metres (990 ft) above Paris, the Eiffel Tower is the city's most famous landmark. It was built for the Exhibition of 1889 and named after its designer, Gustave Eiffel.

EINSTEIN, ALBERT German-American scientist (1879–1955) whose theories of RELATIVITY revolutionized PHYSICS. Einstein showed that NEWTON's laws of physics become more and more inaccurate as the speed of a body increases. Einstein also predicted that large amounts of energy could be produced by destroying a small mass. This forecast came true with the development of atomic physics (see ATOMIC ENERGY). Einstein won the NOBEL PRIZE for Physics in 1921.

ELASTICITY The property by which something returns to its original shape and size after being pushed or pulled out of shape. Rubber bands are not the only things that are elastic. Everything that is solid is elastic to some degree. A steel ball dropped on the floor

► *Albert Einstein was born in Germany, and worked in Switzerland and Germany before becoming a US citizen when his Jewish origins made life in Germany intolerable under the Nazi regime.*

will bounce to a small degree because the force of impact squashes the steel and the floor slightly out of shape. Because the steel is elastic, it regains its original shape and bounces. We use steel springs because of their elasticity.

ELECTIONS The way in which members of GOVERNMENT and other officials are chosen by those people who are qualified to vote. The vote is counted by a show of hands or by casting ballots, by machine or on slips of paper with the choice marked on them. ◁

ELECTRICITY AND MAGNETISM The ancient Greeks discovered that amber and certain other substances attracted light objects after being rubbed. Unknown to them, they had produced electric charges by friction, and the charges had caused the attraction. In the 1700s, many scientists built machines to produce high charges in this way. The electricity produced gave violent sparks and shocks, but its strength quickly died down. In 1752, Benjamin FRANKLIN showed that LIGHTNING was caused by charged clouds. This led to his invention of the lightning conductor for protecting tall buildings during thunderstorms. (See CHARGE, ELECTRIC)

In the 1790s, Alessandro Volta invented the electric cell and BATTERY. With the steady electricity supply these produced, scientists could carry out electrical experiments that

previously had been impossible. Passing a strong electric current through a wire was found to make it hot. While demonstrating this effect in 1819, Hans Oersted discovered that a nearby compass needle deflected every time he switched the current on or off. Oersted had discovered electromagnetism – the production of MAGNETISM by electricity. This inspired Michael FARADAY to invent the electric MOTOR in 1821, and the GENERATOR and TRANSFORMER ten years later. These important devices form the basis of today's vast ELECTRICITY SUPPLY systems.

ELECTRICITY SUPPLY In many power stations, coal, oil or gas are burnt to heat water. In nuclear power stations, the heat is produced by nuclear reactions (see ATOMIC ENERGY). The water is boiled and the steam is used to turn TURBINES linked to GENERATORS. The generated electricity is sent along cables at a very high voltage and relatively low current. This minimizes POWER losses in the cables. TRANSFORMERS reduce the voltage to suitable levels for domestic and industrial consumers. (See HYDROELECTRIC POWER) ▷

ELECTROLYSIS The breaking down of a liquid by passing an electric current through it. The liquid, called the *electrolyte*, may be a solution or a molten substance. Atoms in the electrolyte form charged IONS. The two *electrodes*, by which the current is passed through the electrolyte, attract differently charged ions (see BATTERY). This technique is used to extract some metals from their ores. Electroplating is another application of electrolysis.

ELECTROMAGNETIC WAVES RADIO waves are just one type of electromagnetic wave, or radiation. Such waves are generated by the movement of electrons or other charged particles. Electromagnetic waves can travel through space. This is why radio signals can be sent to and from other planets. It is also the reason why we can see stars and planets. For LIGHT is a form of electromagnetic radiation too. The only difference is that light waves are much shorter than radio waves – that is, they are of higher *frequency*. The other forms of electromagnetic radiation are cosmic

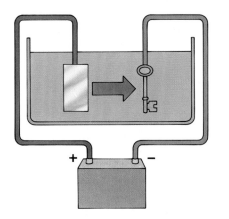

▲ *Electrolysis is the process of bringing about a chemical reaction by passing an electric current through a solution. One practical application is electroplating, as above, where a key is being coated with chromium from a solution of chromic acid.*

rays, GAMMA RAYS, X-RAYS, ultraviolet radiation, and INFRARED radiation (heat).

ELECTRON See ATOM

ELECTRONIC MUSIC Music produced by electronic devices instead of conventional mechanical instruments. Electronic musical instruments include various organs and the more versatile synthesizers. Devices called *oscillators* generate fundamental notes in the form of electronic signals. These are then modified to obtain the desired tonal quality. The electronic signals are amplified (strengthened) and reproduced on loudspeakers. ▷

ELECTRONICS A branch of technology involving the use of electrical circuits including CATHODE-RAY tubes, VALVES, TRANSISTORS or other semiconductor devices. William Crookes built a simple cathode-ray tube in

▼ *The electromagnetic spectrum is made up of energy that moves in a wave motion at a fixed speed – that of light. The only difference between the various kinds of rays is their particular wavelength. Visible light, the only rays we can see, is at the centre.*

ELECTRICITY SUPPLY As the traditional sources of fuel are becoming scarce, many scientists are turning to the sea as a source of power for the future. Research teams are working on the idea that floating generators can be placed around the coasts to convert wave movements into electrical energy. Some day, there will perhaps be lines of small floating generators many miles long, channelling power into the electricity grid system.

ELECTRONIC MUSIC The first person who attempted to 'synthesize' sound electronically was an American called Thaddeus Cahill. He worked from 1895-1906 on a machine he named the 'telharmonium'. However, his machine failed to sell because it was so cumbersome, very complicated and just not loud enough. (Unfortunately amplifiers and speakers had not then been invented.) In fact, it was not until 1934 that Laurens Hammond patented his 'Hammond Organ' – the forerunner of the modern electronic organ.

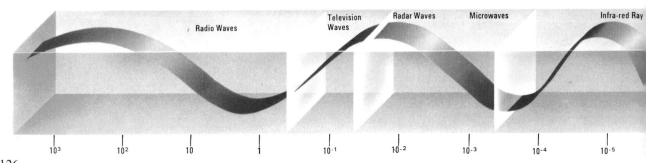

			Television Waves	Radar Waves	Microwaves		Infra-red Ray
Radio Waves							

10^3 10^2 10 1 10^{-1} 10^{-2} 10^{-3} 10^{-4} 10^{-5}

THE PERIODIC TABLE

The elements are listed here with their symbols and atomic numbers. Elements with chemically similar properties fall under one another – for example, copper, silver, gold. The elements from 89 to 105 (including uranium at 92) are increasingly similar and are not shown.

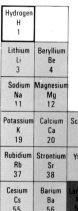

Hydrogen H 1																	Helium He 2
Lithium Li 3	Beryllium Be 4											Boron B 5	Carbon C 6	Nitrogen N 7	Oxygen O 8	Fluorine F 9	Neon Ne 10
Sodium Na 11	Magnesium Mg 12											Aluminium Al 13	Silicon Si 14	Phosphorus P 15	Sulphur S 16	Chlorine Cl 17	Argon Ar 18
Potassium K 19	Calcium Ca 20	Scandium Sc 21	Titanium Ti 22	Vanadium V 23	Chromium Cr 24	Manganese Mn 25	Iron Fe 26	Cobalt Co 27	Nickel Ni 28	Copper Cu 29	Zinc Zn 30	Gallium Ga 31	Germanium Ge 32	Arsenic As 33	Selenium Se 34	Bromine Br 35	Krypton Kr 36
Rubidium Rb 37	Strontium Sr 38	Yttrium Y 39	Zirconium Zr 40	Niobium Nb 41	Molybdenum Mo 42	Technetium Tc 43	Ruthenium Ru 44	Rhodium Rh 45	Palladium Pd 46	Silver Ag 47	Cadmium Cd 48	Indium In 49	Tin Sn 50	Antimony Sb 51	Tellurium Te 52	Iodine I 53	Xenon Xe 54
Cesium Cs 55	Barium Ba 56	Lanthanide series 57-71	Hafnium Hf 72	Tantalum Ta 73	Tungsten W 74	Rhenium Re 75	Osmium Os 76	Iridium Ir 77	Platinum Pt 78	Gold Au 79	Mercury Hg 80	Thallium Tl 81	Lead Pb 82	Bismuth Bi 83	Polonium Po 84	Astatine At 85	Radon Rn 86
Francium Fr 87	Radium Ra 88	Actinide Series 89-105															

Metals	Lanthanide series
Metalloids	Actinide series – 93 to 105 are man made.
Non-metals	
Inert gases	

ELEPHANT It takes 25 years for an elephant to grow to its full height.

The nearest relative of the elephant is the tiny rock hyrax, which is only about 30 cm (1 ft) long. It lives in Africa and the Middle East, and looks like a rodent; but it has hoofed toes rather like those of its giant relation.

At birth a baby elephant is about a metre (3 ft) tall and weighs about 90 kg (200 lb). The period between mating and the birth of a young elephant is about 22 months.

1879. The modern tubes used in TELEVISION and RADAR equipment work in the same basic way. Early RADIO equipment had limited range because no amplifying devices were available to strengthen weak signals. Amplification became possible in 1907 with Lee De Forest's invention of the triode valve. This enabled great improvements to be made in radio equipment and led to the development of a practical television system. The first electronic COMPUTERS, built in the 1940s, consisted of massive banks of equipment with thousands of valves. But the development of the transistor in 1948 enabled later computers to be drastically reduced in size. Further enormous reductions in the size and cost of electronic circuits have since been made possible with the introduction of microcircuits.

ELEMENTS AND COMPOUNDS Everything in the Universe is made up from fundamental materials called elements. Some substances, for example pure COPPER or CARBON, contain just one element. The air contains a *mixture* of various gaseous elements, mainly NITROGEN and OXYGEN. In a mixture, the elements exist separately and retain their own individual properties. *Compounds* consist

of two or more elements chemically combined. Most substances found on the Earth are compounds. Water, for example, is a compound of hydrogen and oxygen. The physical and chemical properties of a compound are quite different from those of the elements it contains.

Each element contains ATOMS with a specific atomic number. Elements with atomic numbers from 1 to 92 occur naturally. Other elements can be made artificially in nuclear reactions. (See CHEMISTRY)

ELEPHANT World's largest land MAMMAL, found in Africa and southern Asia. The elephant's unique characteristic is its long trunk used for carrying food and water to the mouth, spraying water over the body, lifting things and for smelling. Elephants feed off grass, leaves, and fruit, and usually live in herds. There are two species: the Indian elephant, widely used as a work animal, and the larger, fiercer African elephant. ◁

ELIZABETH I One of the best known of all English monarchs (born 1533), she ruled from 1558 to 1603. Hers was a reign of peace. She strengthened the position of the Anglican Church but soothed differences between Protestants and Catholics. She beat off a Spanish invasion attempt in 1588 (see ARMADA), yet kept out of long, costly wars. During her

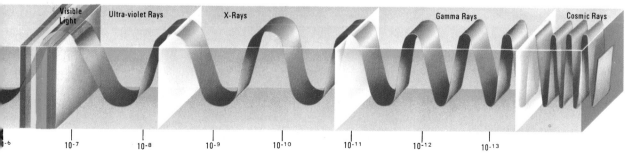

	Visible Light	Ultra-violet Rays	X-Rays			Gamma Rays		Cosmic Rays	
10^{-6}	10^{-7}	10^{-8}	10^{-9}	10^{-10}	10^{-11}	10^{-12}	10^{-13}		

reign, the country emerged as a leading world power and with a strong foothold in the New World. (See DRAKE, SIR FRANCIS)

ELIZABETH II The name of the reigning queen of Great Britain (born 1926). She came to the throne in 1952 after the death of her father, King GEORGE VI. She represents Britain to the world and upholds the dignity and traditions of the throne. She also takes an active interest in government affairs.

ELK Standing over 2 metres (7 ft) high, the elk is the largest member of the DEER family. It lives in northern Europe and Asia and is closely related to the MOOSE of N. America.

ELM Large deciduous tree found mainly in the northern hemisphere; it grows on open land rather than in forests. As elm wood is very tough and rot-resistant, it is often used for building boats and bridges. ▷

EL SALVADOR A mountainous republic in CENTRAL AMERICA, El Salvador has 5,228,000 people (1984) and an area of 21,041 sq km (8124 sq miles). The capital is San Salvador.
  ▷

EMERALD A type of rare and valuable GEM that can be more precious than diamond. Emeralds are a rich green colour. Most of the world's supply comes from Colombia in South America.

EMU Large flightless bird belonging to Australia. The emu is brown-grey and although it cannot fly it can run at over 60 kph (38 mph).

▶ *Electrical energy lights New York City, keeping the city as alive at night as it is by day. Most energy comes from burning natural fuels such as coal, gas and oil.*

◀ *An emu chick. Emus belong to the group of large, flightless birds that includes the ostrich of Africa. The emu is a grazing bird, and is killed off in many parts of Australia because it competes with cattle for the grass.*

Emus are disliked by farmers as the birds feed on grasses, plants and fruits and so damage crops and pasture land.

ENAMEL A hard, glossy substance resembling GLASS. It is made from sand and borax, with other compounds to make it opaque and to give it colour if required. Enamel is used for decorative effect or to protect surfaces from corrosion. The enamel layer on TEETH consists mainly of complex calcium salts. Some resinous PAINTS are also called enamels.

ENCYCLOPEDIA A book, or set of books, that contains a brief summary of a vast range of general knowledge or which deals with one branch of learning. The articles are usually arranged in alphabetical order and may be illustrated with pictures. The first great encyclopedia was the French *Encyclopédie* edited by Denis Diderot (1713–1784).

ENERGY Energy occurs in many forms – mechanical, chemical, electrical, nuclear and radiant. A wound-up clock spring has a store of mechanical energy. As the coiled spring slowly unwinds, it does useful WORK in turning the mechanism to drive the hands. The water behind a dam also has stored mechanical energy (See HYDROELECTRIC POWER). The water can turn TURBINES linked to generators to make electricity. Stored mechanical energy

ELM In the 1970s, the European elm population was decimated by Dutch Elm Disease. This is a fungus disease that is carried from tree to tree by the elm bark beetle, which lays its eggs in the tree. When a tree is infected it is doomed, and even mass felling and burning of infected trees failed to stop the spread of the disease. As the disease cannot affect trees less than 10 years old, it is to be hoped that when all the older, infected trees have been destroyed the fungus will also disappear. Then, a new generation of elms will once again be able to flourish.

EL SALVADOR: FACTS AND FIGURES
Official language: Spanish.
Currency: Colon.
Highest point: Santa Ana 2383 m (7,818 ft), a volcano.
Over 90 per cent of the people are 'mestizos', mixed white and Indian.
Chief river: The Lempa.
Coffee accounts for over half of the country's exports.
El Salvador is densely populated, with 260 people per sq km (670 per sq mile). It became an independent republic in 1839.

is termed *potential* energy. Mechanical energy occurs also as *kinetic* energy – energy of movement, as in a falling object. Chemical energy is released in certain chemical reactions – for example, when a fuel is burnt. Electrical energy is produced in cells and BATTERIES, or by GENERATORS. ATOMIC ENERGY, mainly in the form of heat, is produced in nuclear reactions. Radiant energy includes heat, light and other forms of electromagnetic radiation (see ELECTROMAGNETIC WAVES). The SI UNIT of energy is the JOULE. (See CONSERVATION LAWS)

ENGINEERING Various professions that apply scientific knowledge to the practical problems of making, operating, and maintaining engines, machines, structures, and other devices usual in everyday life. The main branches of engineering are civil, mechanical, chemical, mining, metallurgical, aeronautical, agricultural, marine and electrical. Engineering has played a vital part in our modern civilization. (See AERONAUTICS; BRIDGE; CHEMICAL INDUSTRY; ELECTRICITY SUPPLY; MACHINE TOOL; MINING; TUNNEL)

ENGLAND Part of the United Kingdom of GREAT BRITAIN and Northern IRELAND, England contains two main land regions: upland England and lowland England. There are three main uplands. In the north-east is the beautiful Lake District which contains Scafell Pike, England's highest peak. The Pennines form the rugged backbone of northern England. The third upland is in the south-west, including the windswept Exmoor and Dartmoor. Lowland England skirts the uplands in the north and south-west and also covers most of south-eastern England. It is a region of low chalk and limestone hills, including the Chilterns, Cotswolds and the North and South Downs in the far south-east. The hills are separated by fertile clay vales and basins. The longest river entirely in England is the THAMES. The largest island is the Isle of Wight.

Farming in England, with its rich soils and mild, moist climate, is scientific and highly productive. But comparatively few people work on farms and much food is imported. England's main wealth comes from manufacturing and international commerce and trade. Manufacturing began during the INDUSTRIAL REVOLUTION which started in the late 1700s. It was based on abundant local supplies of coal and iron ore.

England is the most densely-populated part of the BRITISH ISLES and most people live in cities and towns. The chief cities are LONDON,

▶ *One of the early figures in English literature was Geoffrey Chaucer, whose tales of the Canterbury pilgrims range from saints' lives and sermons to romances and bawdy stories of low life.*

Birmingham, Leeds, Sheffield, LIVERPOOL and Manchester. The English people are a blend of many peoples, including conquerors and settlers, such as the Romans, Angles, Saxons, Jutes, VIKINGS, Danes and NORMANS. Some later immigrants, such as the French Huguenots and Jews, settled in England to escape persecution. Most recently, people from the Commonwealth have made their homes in England (see BRITISH EMPIRE). England united with WALES in 1536 and with SCOTLAND in 1707. It is a country with many traditions, which reflect its complex history. (See ENGLISH LANGUAGE; ENGLISH LITERATURE; EUROPE) ◁

ENGLISH CHANNEL This stretch of water separates southern ENGLAND from FRANCE, linking the Atlantic Ocean with the Strait of Dover. Work on a rail tunnel under the Channel began in 1987.

ENGLISH LANGUAGE One of the most important languages in the world, it is second only to Chinese in the number of people who speak it. It is used the world over in films, radio, television, and in newspapers.

Modern English has its roots in Norman French, the speech of the VIKINGS who conquered England in the 10th century, and in the Old English of the Anglo-Saxons.

ENGLISH LITERATURE The entire body of books, pamphlets, newspapers and magazines that have been written in English. This includes POETRY and prose of every sort.

The earliest examples date from the late 6th century. They are ANGLO-SAXON poems written in Old English and telling of the struggles of Christianity to establish itself in a pagan land. The most famous is a poem called *Beowulf* written later, about AD 1000.

With the Norman conquest (1066), written English waned, not to re-emerge until the 14th century. Literature, written in the language known as Middle English, flowered again. Geoffrey CHAUCER's *Canterbury Tales* is the

▶ *This Eskimo girl has typical Mongoloid facial features. Her face is flat, with prominent cheekbones, flat nose, thin lips, straight black hair, and yellow-brown skin colour.*

most famous work of this time.

By the late 16th century, when SHAKESPEARE was writing his plays, modern English literature was in full bloom. Since then, the flow of work has increased tenfold. Perhaps the greatest contribution was the rise of the NOVEL, made popular today by the hundreds of paperback books found in all bookshops.

ENGRAVING A PRINTING process in which an image is cut into a hard surface, or plate, such as wood or metal. The design is first drawn on and then engraved by hand. Afterwards the plate is inked. Then it is covered with paper and passed through a press. The pressure transfers the image to the paper.

ENZYME A complex chemical made in living cells. In animals, enzymes speed up other chemical processes such as DIGESTION.
  ▷

EQUATOR An imaginary line encircling the Earth, the equator (0° latitude) is exactly halfway between the North and South Poles. The distance around the equator is 40,075 km (24,901 miles).

EQUINOX An occasion, which occurs twice every year, when the Sun is directly overhead at the EQUATOR. The spring equinox occurs on about March 21 and the autumnal equinox on about September 23.

ERMINE Small carnivorous animal 25 cm (10 in) long, related to the WEASEL. The ermine, also called stoat, lives in cool northern countries; its brown fur turns white in winter. White ermine fur was once used to trim the robes of royalty, peers and judges.

EROSION The wearing away of the land by running water, weather, ice and wind. Natural erosion continues slowly all the time. But, by destroying vegetation, man can greatly speed up the rate of erosion.

ESCALATOR A moving stairway for carrying passengers between the floors of a building. The stairs are built in the form of a flexible loop, which is driven by an electric motor. A moving handrail is provided for safety. ▷

ESKIMO Eskimoes are also known by the name Innuit, and are people who live

▶ *This stack in southern France, is all that remains of a natural arch. The power of the sea's waves has eroded away this part of the coastline, first forming an arch by wearing away the cliff from the bottom upwards.*

along the shores of North America, Siberia and the coasts of Greenland. There are several distinct groups of Eskimos, each with its own dialect and way of life. They used to depend entirely on the hunting of ARCTIC animals such as seals, walruses and bears for their livelihood. Now many Eskimos have left the old tribal life and have become skilled workers in towns bordering the Arctic. ▷

ESPERANTO A language invented by a Polish linguist in 1887. Intended as an in-

ENZYME A common commercial use for enzymes is in the production of alcoholic drinks, for which yeast and sugar are combined with water. Gentle heat is then applied and the enzymes in the yeast react with the sugar causing alcohol to form. The end result is either beer, wines or spirits.

◄ An Ethiopian herdsman and his son. Most Ethiopians are farmers or herdsmen. At left, Ethiopians winnow (separate) grain. Barley, durra (sorghum), maize and wheat are important crops.

ESCALATOR Although the first patent for an escalator was issued in 1859, it was never used. In fact, the first working escalator did not appear until 1899.

A modern escalator can handle up to 10,000 people an hour, and the longest 'moving sidewalk' is installed in the *Neue Messe Center,* in Dusseldorf, West Germany. It is 225 m (246 yd) long.

ESKIMO After their first contact with Europeans, previously unknown diseases like smallpox, tuberculosis, and influenza almost wiped out the Eskimo population. Now, with the help of modern medicines, the population is once again increasing. In fact, the Eskimos are now being closely studied, because two of the greatest killer diseases of Europeans – cancer and heart disease – are virtually unknown among them. This is despite their diet which is high in animal fats, substances that are often blamed for such ailments in the 'western world'.

ETHIOPIA: FACTS AND FIGURES
Official language: Amharic.
Currency: Ethiopian dollar.
Highest point: Ras Dashen 4620 m (15,150 ft).
Lake Tana is the source of the Blue Nile.
Ethiopia was formerly known as Abyssinia.
The major export is coffee.

ternational language, it is logical and easy to learn. After some early success, it has largely fallen into neglect.

ESTONIA A republic of the USSR, facing the Gulf of Finland. Estonia has a population of 2,600,000 (1976 est.) and an area of 45,000 sq km (17,375 sq miles). The capital is Tallinn. Estonia was Russian from 1721 to 1919, when it became independent. Soviet rule was fully restored in 1944.

ESTUARY The funnel-shaped mouth of a river. Tidal movements in an estuary cause the mixing of river and sea water, which affects the growth of flora and fauna. They are often the sites of major seaports.

ETCHING This is a form of PRINTING on paper, that makes use of acid to burn the lines of an image into a metal printing plate. By contrast, ENGRAVING uses a tool to dig out the lines. The design is then inked and made ready for printing.

ETHERS A group of complete organic chemical compounds (see ELEMENTS AND COMPOUNDS). One of these, *diethyl ether* ($C_2H_5OC_2H_5$), is the substance commonly called ether. It is used as a solvent and as an anaesthetic. (See ANAESTHESIA)

ETHIOPIA A republic in north-east AFRICA, Ethiopia has 42,441,000 people (1984) and an area of 1,221,900 sq km (471,778 sq miles). The capital is Addis Ababa. This mountainous country was ravaged by famine in the 1980s, and many thousands died.   ◁

ETIQUETTE An unwritten code of rules governing the way people should behave in social situations. Based on principles of politeness and good manners, forms of eti-

► The eucalyptus (gum tree) is a familiar sight in southern Australia. The name 'gum tree' comes from the sticky liquid which comes out of its bark. The leaves contain an aromatic oil, once popular for treating colds.

quette apply to many situations – from the way people treat each other, to how a formal occasion, such as a large banquet, should be organized.

ETRUSCANS People who built a flourishing civilization on the west coast of Italy between 700 BC and 300 BC, when they were finally conquered by Rome. They were a league of prosperous city-states; at first ruled by a king, they later became a republic. The Etruscans are famed for their superb sculpture and beautifully decorated tombs.

EUCALYPTUS Tall evergreen tree growing wild in Australia but also planted in many other countries. It is valuable for its oil, gum and reddish wood. Its long, leathery leaves are the staple food of KOALAS.

EUCLID A Greek mathematician who lived around 300 BC. Euclid's book *The Elements* was still being used as a standard geometry textbook earlier this century.

EUROPE The sixth largest continent, Europe is the most densely-populated of them all, with an average of 63 people per sq km (164 per sq mile). Europe was the birthplace of western civilization. Through conquest, colonization and emigration, European culture and technology have spread around the world.

Europe includes about 25 per cent of Russia and extends from the Ural Mountains to the

ARCTIC OCEAN

Murmansk

Narvik

NORWEGIAN SEA

Arkhangelsk

FAROE IS.

Trondheim

KJOLEN MOUNTAINS

SWEDEN

FINLAND

L. Onega

SHETLAND IS.

Tampere

Vyborg

L. Ladoga

NORWAY

Sundsvall

Helsinki

Bergen

Oslo

Stockholm

Leningrad

ORKNEY IS.

Stavanger

Vänern

Novgorod

Yaroslavl

Aberdeen

Vättern

Riga

NORTH SEA

Gothenburg

BALTIC SEA

Glasgow

Edinburgh

DENMARK

Moscow

Belfast

IRELAND

UNITED
KINGDOM

Copenhagen

Malmö

Gdansk

Kaliningrad

Smolensk

Dublin

Manchester

NETHER
-LANDS

Hamburg

Vistula

Minsk

UNION OF SOVIET

Cork

Birmingham

Amster
-dam

Poznan

Warsaw

SOCIALIST REPUBLIC

Cardiff

London

Elbe

Berlin

Kiev

Kharkov

Thames

Rhine

E.

ATLANTIC OCEAN

English Channel

Brussels

Bonn

GERMANY

POLAND

Dnepr

Brest

Le Havre

BELGIUM

W.

Frankfurt

Kraków

Dnepropetrovsk

Paris

LUX-

GERMANY

Prague

Nantes

EMBOURG

Stuttgart

CZECHOSLOVAKIA

CARPATHIANS

Dnestr

Loire

Seine

Munich

Vienna

Odessa

Saône

Bern

Zurich

AUSTRIA

Budapest

Prut

La Coruña

Bordeaux

FRANCE

Geneva

SWITZ-

LIECHTENSTEIN

HUNGARY

ROMANIA

Lyons

ERLAND

Santander

Rhône

Turin

Po

Milan

Zagreb

BLACK SEA

Oporto

Bilbao

Toulouse

MONACO

Venice

Trieste

Bucharest

Valladolid

PORTUGAL

Douro

ANDORRA

Nice

SAN MARINO

YUGOSLAVIA

Danube

BULGARIA

Lisbon

Ebro

Marseille

Florence

PYRENEES

Dubrovnik

Tagus

Madrid

Corsica

ITALY

ADRIATIC SEA

Sofia

Istanbul

Guidiana

Barcelona

Ajaccio

Rome

ALBANIA

TURKEY

Valencia

Bari

Thessaloniki

SPAIN

Naples

Tirana

Seville

BALEARIC IS.

Sardinia

Taranto

GREECE

Cadiz

Malaga

Cagliari

GIBRALTAR

Palermo

Messina

Athens

Sicily

Crete

MALTA

MEDITERRANEAN SEA

■ Capital Cities

0   100   200   300   400 miles

0   200   400   600 Kilometres

EEC As 40 per cent of all the world's trade stems from Europe, and because it seemed that competition between European countries would be a bad thing, economic relations have been re-organized under the EEC. However, the EEC was also formed in the hope that the countries of Europe would come closer together politically, and so end the wars which have ravaged the continent for the last 400 years.

EVEREST, MOUNT Attempts to climb Everest began with the opening of the Tibetan border in 1920. However, seven assaults on the north-east ridge, and then three on the south-east ridge, all failed. In 1953, Edmund Hillary and a Sherpa guide, Tensing Norgay ascended the south-east ridge to the summit. Since then many other ascents have been successful, including several by women and at least one solo climb.

EVOLUTION The concept of evolution is not a new idea. Hereclitus, an ancient Greek, believed that people evolved from fish-like creatures; and St. Augustine believed that the Biblical account of the Creation was symbolic – rather than literal – and that creatures must have evolved through the ages. Jean-Baptiste Lamarck was the first naturalist to come up with a theory of evolution in modern times. His *Philosophy of Zoology* was written in 1809. Twenty-eight years later, Edward Blyth actually mentioned in his essays the mechanism of 'natural selection'. However, it was not until 1871, when Darwin's *The Descent of Man* was published, that evolution and natural selection were accepted by the scientific world.

Atlantic Ocean. North-south, it runs from the Arctic TUNDRA to the warm lands bordering the northern MEDITERRANEAN. The climate is affected not only by latitude, but also by nearness to the sea. This means that, as one travels east from the mild Atlantic coastlands, so the climate becomes more severe. There are three main land regions. The northern uplands include Iceland, north-west Britain, Scandinavia and the Ural Mountains. This region is thinly-populated. The densely-populated central lowlands form an almost unbroken belt stretching from southern Britain to Russia. The third main region is the uplands of southern Europe, including the lofty ALPS.

The people of Europe belong mostly to the Caucasoid group. The chief religion is CHRISTIANITY and the main languages belong to the Indo-European group. About four-fifths of the world's business is conducted in three of these languages, English, French and German. Europe is highly industrialized and comparatively few people work on farms. Europe has rich coal and iron ore reserves, but many other metals and much oil are imported. The chief industrial regions are situated in and around the central plains, but other nations, such as Italy, have industrial centres. In the past, Europe has been the scene of much international rivalry and conflict. But, recently, European nations have been coming together, particularly in the field of economic co-operation.

EUROPEAN ECONOMIC COMMUNITY (EEC) Also called the Common Market, the EEC is an economic union of 12 European nations aimed at stimulating economic growth and eliminating trade barriers. It was set up in 1958 by Belgium, France, West Germany, Italy, Luxembourg and the Netherlands. Britain, the Republic of Ireland and Denmark joined in 1973, Greece in 1981, and Spain and Portugal in 1986. ◁

EVAPORATION The change of state that occurs when a liquid changes to a vapour. MOLECULES of the liquid break away from the surface.

EVEREST, MOUNT The world's highest mountain, Everest is in the HIMALAYAS, on the border between Nepal and China. It rises 8848 metres (29,028 ft) above sea-level and was first climbed in 1953. ◁

EVOLUTION The gradual development of one type of plant or animal from an earlier form. The theory of evolution states that today's species of plants and animals are descended from other forms that lived long ago. This process of change has been going on for millions and millions of years – ever since

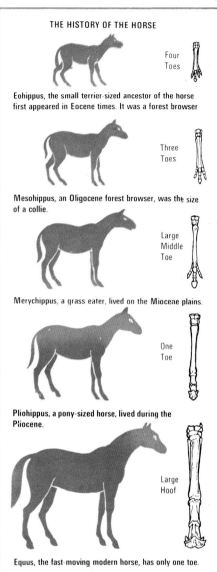

THE HISTORY OF THE HORSE

Eohippus, the small terrier-sized ancestor of the horse first appeared in Eocene times. It was a forest browser

Four Toes

Mesohippus, an Oligocene forest browser, was the size of a collie.

Three Toes

Large Middle Toe

Merychippus, a grass eater, lived on the Miocene plains.

One Toe

Pliohippus, a pony-sized horse, lived during the Pliocene.

Large Hoof

Equus, the fast-moving modern horse, has only one toe.

life first appeared on the Earth – and is still happening. Much of the evidence for evolution comes from FOSSILS. Rocks contain the remains of extinct plants and animals and so provide a family tree for species now living. In the case of the horse, for instance, fossils give a complete history of the animal's development from a little dog-like creature with four toes that lived 50 million years ago to the large one-toed animal living today. The explanation for evolution is based on the struggle for existence and the survival of the fittest. To exist, plants and animals must adapt to their surroundings and those which adapt best are most likely to survive. The theory of evolution was pioneered by the English naturalist Charles DARWIN. (See ADAPTATION) ◁

EXPANSION See HEAT

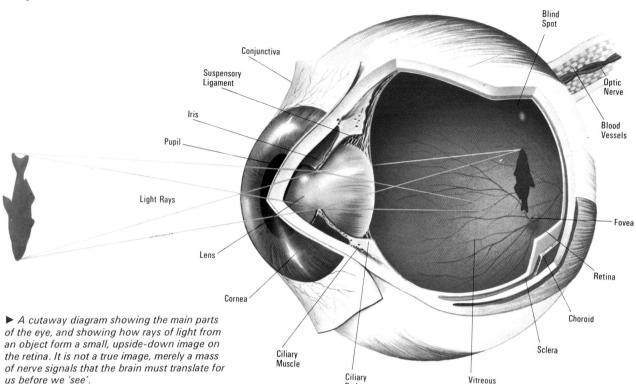

Conjunctiva

Suspensory Ligament

Iris

Pupil

Light Rays

Lens

Cornea

Ciliary Muscle

Ciliary Body

Vitreous Humour

Sclera

Choroid

Retina

Fovea

Blood Vessels

Optic Nerve

Blind Spot

▶ A cutaway diagram showing the main parts of the eye, and showing how rays of light from an object form a small, upside-down image on the retina. It is not a true image, merely a mass of nerve signals that the brain must translate for us before we 'see'.

EXPLOSION A sudden and violent increase in pressure, often caused by the production of large volumes of gas by chemical EXPLOSIVES. Shock waves travel outwards from the point of explosion and are heard as a bang. An *implosion* is the sudden rush of gas into a previously evacuated space.

EXPLOSIVES Chemicals that produce EXPLOSIONS when ignited or struck. Some of the most commonly used explosives include GUNPOWDER, TNT and cordite.   ▷

EXTRASENSORY PERCEPTION A person who has extrasensory perception, or ESP, is supposed to be aware of events that cannot be observed by the ordinary senses. The study of ESP includes telepathy and, clairvoyance.

EYE Sense organ used for seeing. For simple animals, such as jellyfishes and worms, seeing means reacting to light: the eye is a single nerve with a light-sensitive ending. In higher animals, the eye is more developed and contains a LENS so that seeing involves forming an image. Certain birds and mammals – including man – have very complex and efficient eyes. The human eye consists of the eyelids, which protect the eye and control the passage of light, and the eyeball itself. Light rays enter the eyeball through the CORNEA, a transparent layer at the front, and pass through the *pupil* to the lens. The pupil is a hole in the *iris* – a thin tissue curtain which gives the eye its blue,

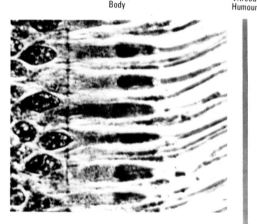

▲ The eye's retina is made up of millions of light-sensitive receptors, called rods and cones; shown here is a greatly enlarged section through a retina.

green, grey or brown colour and which regulates the size of the pupil so that the correct amount of light is received. The lens focuses the rays onto the *retina*, a light-sensitive screen connected to the BRAIN by the optic nerve. This nerve carries messages from the retina to the seeing part of the brain. (See GLASSES)   ▷

EYRE, LAKE A large, shallow, salty lake in South Australia. Lake Eyre is often dry in summer. Its area varies, but it covers about 9600 sq km (about 3700 sq miles).

EXPLOSIVES Whether the Chinese or the English discovered explosives is debatable. There are records of the Chinese using black powder (gunpowder) to fire stones from bamboo tubes in the mid-13th century. Meanwhile, in 1242, the Englishman, Roger Bacon, wrote clear instructions for the making of gunpowder.

EYE Some types of fish have 'four eyes'. When swimming on the surface, two half eyes see above the water and two half eyes see below the water.

Each eye of an insect may be made up of as many as 30,000 hexagonal lenses.

Man has two lids over each eye, one above and one below. The pink fold of skin at the corner of each eye is the remains of a third eyelid. Many animals have this third eyelid which moves across the eye to clean it.

F

FABLE A short, imaginary story that tells a moral at the end. Fables often have talking animals or objects in them to make their point. The most famous are those collected by AESOP, a Greek slave of the 6th century BC.

FAHRENHEIT A THERMOMETER scale in which the freezing point of water is 32° and the boiling point of water is 212°. The scale was devised by the German scientist Gabriel Daniel Fahrenheit (1686–1736).

FAINTING A sudden loss of consciousness caused by not enough BLOOD flowing to the BRAIN. Fainting is often preceded by dizziness and sickness and can be caused by pain, shock or fatigue.

FAIR A gathering of people who meet to do business, show and sell their products and to exchange information. Fairs today are also places of entertainment with fabulous exhibits, shops and restaurants. The biggest are known as World's Fairs.

FAIRY In folklore, a tiny creature with human features said to live in the woods and under hills. Fairies practise a gentle and mischievous magic.

FALCON Bird of prey related to the EAGLE. Some species of falcon inhabit nearly every part of the world. The most widespread is the peregrine. Peregrines live on high rocks and cliffs and feed off other birds which they catch in the air, swooping down on them at over 400 kph (250 mph). Another common falcon is the kestrel. Unlike other falcons, the kestrel catches its prey – mice, frogs, grasshoppers – on the ground and not in flight.

FAMILY A group of people who are closely related by MARRIAGE and by birth. The typical family is made up of a husband and wife, and their children. Usually, they live together. A wider sense of the family goes on to include grandparents, uncles and aunts and cousins. It may even extend to more distant relations and to dead ancestors.

FANG A long pointed tooth, especially the poison tooth of snakes such as vipers and cobras. A poison fang contains a thin tube open at both ends; the VENOM enters the fang at the base and is injected into the victim through the tip.

▼ Falconry is still practiced today, although it is not as popular a sport as it was in medieval times. This falcon is trained to take flight on command, chase game and return with its catch.

135

FARADAY, MICHAEL British scientist (1791–1867.) His first interests were in the field of chemistry, but it is his discovery of *electro-magnetic induction* by which he is best known. This led to the electric GENERATOR and the MOTOR. (See ELECTRICITY AND MAGNETISM)

FARMING The planting of crops and the rearing of animals for food began in the Middle East in about 8000 BC. Today, about one-tenth of the world's land area is cultivated arable (crop-growing) land. Another fifth is pasture, where animals can be grazed. But an enormous area is totally unproductive.

The world's chief food crops are CEREALS, or grains, including maize in warm regions, RICE in wet tropical countries, and WHEAT in cool, moist climates. In developing countries, many people practise subsistence farming, producing only enough food for their families' needs. But in developed nations farming is highly mechanized and yields are high. Farming methods are scientific and farmers often work together in co-operatives. Crop rotation (see ROTATION OF CROPS) is used and FERTILIZERS restore to the soil the nutrients taken by the crops. Plantation farming is a specialized type of farming which is employed mostly in the tropics. On plantations, only one crop, such as COFFEE or TEA, is usually produced.

The chief product of extensive pastoral farming, which is practised by nomads in some areas, is meat. Pastoral farming may also be intensive, such as on small dairy or POULTRY farms near large cities. (See DAIRY INDUSTRY) Mixed farms combine arable and animal farming. (See AGRICULTURE)

FASCISM A dictatorial type of GOVERNMENT such as that which existed in Italy under Benito MUSSOLINI. Fascism seeks very wide powers of control. It requires that an individual's wishes give way to those of the state, even if this means using armed force.

▷

▼ *Spraying crops with pesticides is an important part of modern farming. Pests such as maggots, beetles and locusts, and fungus diseases like potato blight, can reduce harvests by as much as one-third.*

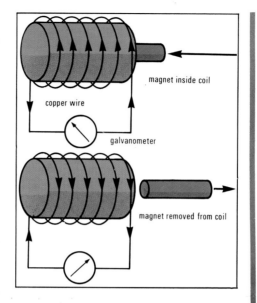

▲ *In 1831 Faraday demonstrated that when a magnet is moved in and out of a coil of wire a current is created in the coil. The galvanometer registering the current shows it flowing one way and then the other as the magnet is moved in and out.*

FASHION Those things that are popular at any particular time. Being 'in fashion' not only applies to clothes, but also to behaviour, manners, furnishings, hobbies, and even to attitudes and beliefs. Fashion changes all the time. Clothing styles are the best example. Dress lengths rise and fall, shoes go from rounded toes to pointed, and the shape of trouser legs flares and narrows. Such changes are greatly helped by ADVERTISING. But in the end, it is public taste that decides. A lot of changes seem to have no other cause than the simple craving for new experiences and styles.

FATS Fats help to make up one of the vital ingredients needed for a well-balanced diet. Two-thirds of our body warmth and energy comes from eating fats. (Other sources include CARBOHYDRATES and PROTEINS.) If we eat more fatty foods than we need we gradually become overweight. When fats are heated they turn into oils. Vegetable oils come from the seeds of plants; the SOYBEAN is one of the world's main sources. These vegetable oils have become the main raw material for MARGARINE and SOAP. Familiar animal fats are butter from milk, lard from pigs, and tallow from cattle and sheep.

FATHOM A nautical term, used to measure the depth of water. A fathom equals 1.8 metres (6 ft).

FAULT A fracture or break in rocks, along which the rocks have moved. The movements

FASCISM Fascism was a 20th-century phenomenon which dominated Europe from 1919 to 1944. The first movement was founded in Italy, led by Benito Mussolini. It grew out of a reaction to the carnage and futility of World War I and the subsequent rise of communism. The Italian fascist motto, 'To believe, to obey, to combat', was the direct opposite of the French Revolution's 'Liberty, equality, fraternity'. In fact, just as the French had blamed the power of the State for all their troubles, the Italian fascists blamed the freedom of the individual. In the end, by allying with Hitler in World War II, Mussolini led his country to defeat in 1944, and soon after he was murdered by his former supporters.

FAULT Geological faults in the Earth's crust are often a source of earthquakes. The city of San Francisco has learned to live with this danger as it is built on the giant San Andreas Fault – the largest fault in the world. Severe 'quakes were felt in the city in 1864, 1898, 1900 and 1906. The fire which followed the 1906 tremors raged for three days. In all, 700 people were killed, 28,000 buildings were destroyed and the total cost of damage was estimated at $500,000,000.

FEATHER The Japanese Long-tailed Fowl has the longest feathers of any bird, reaching over 9 m (30 ft).

FENCING Fencing was first practised as a sport in Egypt as early as 1360 BC. Its first governing body in Europe, however, was set up by England's King Henry VIII.

Fencing has been an Olympic sport since 1896, and there are regular world championships as well. A Frenchman, Christian d'Oriola, holds the record for the greatest number of world titles. Altogether he won four, in 1947, 1949, 1953 and 1954.

FERMI, ENRICO Fermi fled from fascist Italy in 1938, after travelling to Stockholm, Sweden, to collect his Nobel Prize. He was afraid that Nazi Germany might build and use an atom bomb, so he offered his services to the USA and was given the leadership of the Manhattan Project. This project led to the testing of the world's first atom bomb at Alamogordo, New Mexico, USA, on July 16, 1945. Soon afterwards, US bombers dropped atomic bombs on the Japanese cities of Hiroshima and Nagasaki and brought World War II to a sudden end.

FIG There are four types of fig: Caprifig, Smyrna, San Pedro and Common varieties. The Caprifig is usually inedible, but it is grown near other fig trees to attract the fig wasp. This minute insect (which is only 2.5 mm; 0.1 in long) is needed for the pollination of most types of figs, and the process is known as 'caprification'.

are usually vertical and sometimes horizontal. Faults can be clearly seen in exposed sedimentary ROCKS, because the rock layers on either side of the fault are displaced and do not match. Sudden movements along major faults cause EARTHQUAKES. ◁

FEATHER Only BIRDS have feathers. Feathers keep birds warm, help them to fly and to float – if they are aquatic. There are various types of feathers, the most obvious are *contour* feathers which cover the wings, body and tail. Each one has a stiff central shaft that supports a flat part, the vane. The base of the shaft is called the quill. ◁

FELDSPAR The most important group of rock-forming silicate minerals (see SILICON), found in most ROCKS. Feldspars make up a large part of the Earth's crust. Usually white or grey, when weathered they decompose into clay and soil.

FENCING The art of using SWORDS. Fencers use blunted weapons and wear protective masks and clothing. They score points every time one person's blade touches the other's body. There are three types of sword: the foil, the épée, and the sabre. ◁

FERMI, ENRICO An Italian-born American nuclear physicist (1901–1954). He was the first to achieve a nuclear CHAIN REACTION in 1942, and played a large part in the development of the American ATOMIC BOMB. (See NUCLEAR ENERGY) ◁

FERN Ferns are *cryptogams* – plants without flowers or seeds. They reproduce by scattering spores. Most ferns have feathery leaves and grow in moist shady places. They are found in

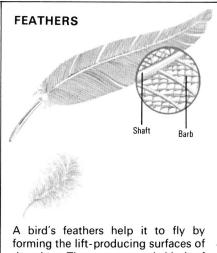

FEATHERS

Shaft   Barb

A bird's feathers help it to fly by forming the lift-producing surfaces of the wings. There are two main kinds of feathers. Strong, contour feathers cover the outer part of the body and the wings. Down feathers lie between the skin and contour feathers.

all parts of the world and vary greatly in size. Some are no bigger than mosses while others – in the tropics – are over 20 metres (66 ft) tall.

FERTILIZER A substance put into the SOIL to improve the quantity and quality of PLANT growth, usually by supplying NITROGEN, POTASSIUM salts and phosphates (see PHOSPHORUS). Organic fertilizers include animal manure and bone meal.

FEVER The normal temperature of the human body is 37°C (98.6°F). If a disorder makes it rise above this, the person is said to have a fever. Fever is not an illness itself, it is caused by injuries and infections.

FIBRE Thread made of natural or chemical materials. Most natural fibres come directly from animals or plants. Animal fibres include WOOL and SILK, while COTTON, FLAX and hemp are common plant fibres. Other natural fibres are processed by man: RAYON, for instance, is made from cellulose. There are many chemical fibres: the best-known is NYLON.

FIG Pear-shaped fleshy fruit grown in warm, dry lands especially in the Mediterranean region. Figs, green or purple in colour, are too delicate to keep easily and so much of the crop is canned or dried. The fig tree has a smooth grey trunk and large, shiny leaves. ◁

◀ *An Olympic fencing match between J. Hehn of Germany and I. Osztrics of Hungary. Today, fencing is thought of as an art form as well as a sport. It was first included in the Olympic Games in 1896.*

FIJI An island monarchy in the South Pacific Ocean. The 800 islands have 686,000 people (1984 est.) and cover 18,389 sq km (7100 sq miles). The capital is Suva. Sugar, coconut oil and gold are major products.

FILTER Most filters separate solids from liquids or gases. A kitchen sieve is a filter. The oil and air used in car engines is filtered to remove unwanted dust. Filter papers are used in the laboratory to separate solids from liquids. Light filters are made of materials that only let certain colours of light pass through them. Other colours are filtered out.

FINE ARTS Those arts whose products are most valued for their beauty and the enjoyment they give, rather than for any practical use they may have. As such, the term can apply to any decorative object. But usually, it is used to refer to what are called the design arts: drawing, graphics, PAINTING, SCULPTURE and ARCHITECTURE.

FINGERPRINTS The tips of your fingers have a network of swirling ridges on them called fingerprints. Each person in the world has a pattern that is unique. Police use fingerprints to make positive identifications of criminals they are seeking. Impressions of fingerprints can be gathered from the scene of a crime by a process called dusting. ▷

FINLAND A republic in northern EUROPE, Finland has 4,882,000 people (1984 est.) and an area of 337,009 sq km (130,120 sq miles). The capital is Helsinki. This cold land contains 35,000 or so lakes. Many occupy basins worn out by GLACIERS in the ICE AGE. Timber is the chief product. ▷

FIORD A long, deep, narrow and steep-sided sea inlet, which was worn out by GLACIERS. Fiords occur in glaciated areas, such as South Island in NEW ZEALAND, NORWAY, GREENLAND and CHILE.

FIR Evergreen coniferous tree with needle-like leaves. There are about 25 species of fir growing mostly in northern lands and on mountains farther south. They are important for timber. The Douglas fir, reaching 100 metres (330 ft), is one of the world's tallest trees.

FIRE See COMBUSTION; FLAME

FIREARMS Any weapon that uses an EX-PLOSIVE, like GUNPOWDER, to fire a bullet or a shell from a barrel is a firearm. Usually, big artillery weapons are not included. Rather, it is smallarms which are being referred to, such as pistols, revolvers, rifles, shotguns and submachine-guns that are carried by hand. Smallarms fire ammunition of less than 20 mm in size.

FIREFLY Type of beetle which can give off a yellowish-green light in the dark. There are about 2000 species of fireflies, found mainly in tropical countries.

FIRST AID On-the-spot care of the victims of accidents or sudden illnesses is called first aid. The most essential rules in first aid are to be sure the victims are out of further harm and to keep them calm and resting while you send for professional medical help.

First aid techniques are easy to learn and use. They will help you to care for people who have suffered cuts and burns; wounds such as broken bones and sprains; animal bites and stings, and also to deal with electrical shocks and poisoning. Many people keep a first aid kit around the house filled with bandages, dressings, salves and scissors.

FINGERPRINTS In 1880, Dr. Henry Faulds suggested that fingerprints be used as a means of identifying people. Previously he had observed that the fingerprint patterns present at birth remain the same throughout a person's lifetime. Although fingerprint identification seemed to be a new idea, soon afterwards a Mr. William Herschel wrote that he had used fingerprint identification of government pensioners and convicted prisoners for over 20 years! Not much happened until 1900, when a British government committee headed by Sir Edward Henry, was set up to investigate the possibility of introducing fingerprinting of criminals for identification purposes. The committee recommended that fingerprinting of criminals should be started, and shortly afterwards the practice was introduced throughout Britain and the USA.

▶ *Fiords such as this one in Norway are long, narrow inlets which were carved by glaciers during the Ice Age. When it ended, the deep, U-shaped valleys were filled by the sea.*

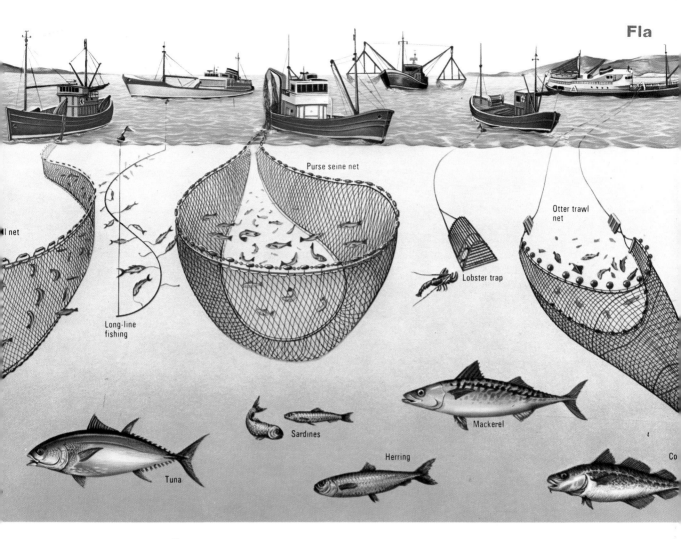

Purse seine net

Otter trawl net

ll net

Long-line fishing

Lobster trap

Tuna

Sardines

Herring

Mackerel

Co

FINLAND: FACTS AND FIGURES
Official languages: Finnish and Swedish.
Currency: Finnish markka (mark).
About two-thirds of the country is covered with forests, and timber and wood products form the mainstay of Finland's economy.
Chief rivers: The Torne, the Oulu and the Kemi, all flowing into the Gulf of Bothnia.
Helsinki (pop. 932,000) the capital and chief port, is icebound in winter, but the harbour is usually kept open by icebreakers.

FISH A VERTEBRATE (backboned) animal living entirely in water. There are two main groups. First, the *cartilaginous* fishes whose skeletons are made of gristly tissue; these all live in the sea and include SHARKS and skates. Most of today's fishes, however, belong to the second group, the bony fishes. These have real bone skeletons and often, an outer covering of thin SCALES. Some bony fishes, like carp and PERCH, are freshwater species. Others, such as MACKEREL and COD, live in the sea. Nearly all fishes, from both groups, have fins which together with the tail enable them to swim. Gills enable fish to breathe. As fish are aquatic they get their oxygen direct from the water. They take in water through the mouth and, as it passes over the gills, the dissolved oxygen is extracted. Most fish lay eggs that either go to the bottom or float on the water's surface. Some fish, like the COD, lay millions of eggs then swim away (most of the eggs are eaten by enemies); others lay only a few eggs but protect them until after they hatch. The freshwater stickleback even builds a nest.

FISHING For some people, fishing is a

▲ *Fishing techniques. From left to right: fishes such as cod are caught in gill nets; in long-line fishing, a series of baited hooks are attached to a long main line; the purse seine net is drawn around a school of fishes; lobsters are snared in traps; the otter trawl net traps bottom fishes.*

means of survival, or a daily job. But for most others it is a pleasurable pastime. Millions of amateur fishermen go out every year. The basic equipment (or tackle) is simply a rod, a reel, some line and several hooks and lures. Different equipment is used for different types of fishing; such as fly-fishing, trolling from a boat, surf-casting, deep-sea-fishing and ice-fishing. A fisherman must also know where and at what depth the fish lie and when they are hungry and feeding. He must know what sort of bait will tempt them and how to play a fish and land it once it is hooked.

FLAGS It is hard to believe how important a brightly coloured bit of cloth can be – unless it is a flag. Flags are symbols of many things. They represent nations, religious movements, international organizations, business com-

FLAGS OF THE WORLD

Afghanistan

Chile

Ghana

Jordon

Pakistan

Switzerland

Albania

China

Greece

North Korea

Paraquay

Thailand

Algeria

Colombia

Hungary

South Korea

Peru

Trinidad & Tobago

Argentina

Cuba

Iceland

Lebanon

Philippines

Tunisia

Australia

Cyprus

India

Liberia

Poland

Turkey

Austria

Czechoslovakia

Indonesia

Malaysia

Portugal

United Kingdom

Belgium

Denmark

Iran

Malta

Romania

United States

Bolivia

Ecuador

Iraq

Mexico

Saudi Arabia

Uruquay

Brazil

Ethiopia

Ireland

Morocco

Sierra Leone

USSR

Bulgaria

Finland

Israel

Netherlands

Singapore

Vatican City

Burma

France

Italy

New Zealand

South Africa

Venezuela

Canada

East Germany

Jamaica

Nigeria

Spain

Yugoslavia

Sri Lanka (Ceylon)

West Germany

Japan

Norway

Sweden

Zaïre

FLEA If humans had the same leaping abilities (relative to their size) as fleas, people would be able to jump clear over a four storey building. In fact, during their mighty leaps the average flea subjects itself to a force of 200 g (200 times the force of gravity) as it jumps up to 130 times its own height.

FLOUNDER These fish are interesting because they are not flattened from top to bottom as you would expect, but from side to side. As a result, what appears to be the top of the fish is in fact the whole of its left or right side. During the larval stage, the eyes of young flounders – which are in the normal positions at first – move over to either the left or right side of the body. This then flattens to produce either left- or right-eyed flatfish.

panies, armies and individual people. Some act as warnings or are signalling codes. The language of flags is complex. The study of flags and their meanings is called *vexillology*.

FLAME Hot, luminous gases or vapours caused by rapid COMBUSTION. When substances such as wool or coal reach their kindling or ignition temperature, gases are released which burst into flame. Flames differ according to the kinds of gases uniting. Dust can make a flame brighter.

FLAMINGO Large aquatic bird with long thin legs, graceful neck and exotic pink plumage. Flamingos live in vast flocks on marshes, shallow lakes and lagoons where they are usually seen wading rather than swimming. They feed on small creatures which they suck up from the water.

FLAX Plant grown in many parts of the world for its stem fibre and seeds. The fibre is made into LINEN, while the seeds yield linseed oil, used in paint and varnish. Flax is also planted in gardens for its attractive blue flowers.

FLEA Small wingless insect that lives on humans and other animals and feeds by sucking up their blood. The human flea is noted for its jumping; it can leap upwards as high as 20 cm (8 in). ◁

FLEMING, ALEXANDER British bacteriologist (1881–1955) who discovered PENICIL-

LIN. In 1928 he found the drug by accident, but he did not develop its use as an ANTIBIOTIC. (See BIOCHEMISTRY)

FLINDERS, MATTHEW A British naval explorer (1774–1814). In 1801 he took his ship, the HMS *Investigator*, on the first ever trip round Australia to chart its coasts. He is said to be the person who suggested Australia as the name for the new continent.

FLINT A variety of QUARTZ often found in chalk and limestone. Since it was easy to chip, primitive men made tools and weapons from it, and it was the earliest fire-starter as it makes sparks when struck against iron. Flint is used in the manufacture of ABRASIVES and earthenware.

FLOUNDER Type of European flatfish that lives in both salt and fresh water. It swims up rivers to feed but returns to the coast to breed. The flounder, weighing up to 2.7 kg (6 lb) is brownish on the upperside and pearl-white underneath. ◁

FLOUR The finely milled kernels of WHEAT, or indeed any other grain, are known as flour. About 125 million tonnes are produced every year. Most flour is made from wheat.

FLUORESCENCE The sending out of visible LIGHT by certain substances, when these substances are exposed to invisible radiation such as ultraviolet rays or X-RAYS. Energy absorbed by the substance from the ultraviolet or x-rays is sent out again at a longer wavelength in the visible part of the SPECTRUM.

FLUTE A musical instrument consisting of a hollow metal tube with holes bored in it. It is played by blowing across the mouth hole. Opening and closing the note holes varies the PITCH of the sound created by the vibrating column of air within.

FLY Flies form one of the largest insect groups. Unlike most other insects, flies have only two wings. They have a sucking mouthpart and feed off nectar and decaying substances. Some species, like the TSETSE and MOSQUITO, suck blood and so transmit serious diseases. Flies also cause illness by spreading germs and by laying their eggs – which turn into maggots – on food and animals. Using suckers on their feet, flies are able to walk upsidedown on ceilings.

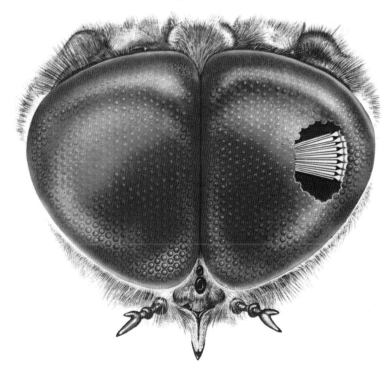

◀ *The fly's compound eye is made up of many units, each with its own hexagonal lens. Each tiny 'eye' looks in a slightly different direction. Though a fly can sense movement easily, it can only see objects as a rather blurred pattern of dots.*

FLYING DOCTOR SERVICE An Australian medical service that brings health care to remote villages and farms. Doctors and nurses are provided with planes to visit their distant patients. The service began in 1928.

FLYING FISH HERRING-like fish with large fins which can open like wings. To fly, these fishes swim along the surface reaching speeds of 56 kph (35 mph). Then, with a final tail-flick, they lift into the air, spread their fins and glide – without flapping their fins – for up to 400 metres ($\frac{1}{4}$ mile). They live in tropical seas and eat PLANKTON.

FLYING SAUCERS In June 1947, an unidentified flying object (UFO) was spotted in the USA. It had a disc or saucer-like shape, and the term 'flying saucer' was born. So far, UFOs have never been positively identified.
▷

FLYWHEEL A heavy WHEEL attached to a rotating shaft of a machine or engine. Its momentum tends to keep the shaft rotating at a steady speed.

FOG A mass of tiny droplets of water in the air. Fogs are like CLOUDS, but they occur at ground level. By international standards, fogs occur when the visibility is reduced to less than one kilometre (0.62 miles).

FOLKLORE Popular beliefs, legends and customs. Folklore is usually handed down by word of mouth as songs, stories, poems and rhymes. It also includes rituals and remedies; weather lore ('red sky at night, shepherd's delight'), and the casting of hexes and superstitions ('black cats are bad luck').

FOOD Substance needed by all living things for life and growth. Food contains CARBOHYDRATE and FAT for energy, PROTEIN for growth and tissue repair, and MINERALS and VITAMINS for the proper functioning of the various organs. Plants, through PHOTOSYNTHESIS, make their own food but animals have to rely on ready-made food: plants or other animals that have themselves eaten plants. Many animals eat only plants or flesh – they are herbivores or CARNIVORES – but humans generally eat some plant foods such as CEREALS, vegetables and fruit and some animal products. These include meat, eggs, butter, cheese and milk.

FOOD POISONING An often severe illness that comes from eating spoiled food. Signs of it are stomach-aches, vomiting and diarrhoea. It is caused by BACTERIA that have infected the food. Usually they do not change the way it tastes or looks, so are hard to detect. ▷

FOOTBALL A number of team ball games

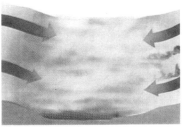

The cause of fog and cloud is the same, because fog is cloud at low level. When damp air near the ground cools enough for the water vapour to condense into water droplets, fog and mist occur. Cold air is heavy and sinks, so fog often rolls down hills into valleys.*

played in various parts of the world are called football.

Association Football or 'soccer' was born in Britain and is by far the most widely played and watched game in the world. It is played by two teams of 11 players with a round inflated ball. A game lasts for 90 minutes, with an interval at half-time. Players may use their feet, head or any other part of their body, except the arms and hands, to propel the ball. The goalkeeper may handle the ball within his own penalty area. The world governing body for soccer is FIFA (Fédération Internationale de Football Association). It was formed in 1904 and by the 1970s had 140 member countries. The major world tournament is the World Cup, held every four years.

Rugby Union Football grew out of the football game played at Rugby School in the 1820s. In rugby the emphasis is more on handling than kicking the oval-shaped ball. It is an entirely amateur game played on a pitch with a maximum width of 75 yards (69 metres). The 'H'-shaped goals are a maximum of 110 yards (100 metres) apart. A game lasts for 80 minutes and is played between teams of 15 players. The ball may be kicked, carried or thrown, but may not be thrown forward. Points are scored by touching the ball down by hand over the opponents' goal-line – a 'try'; by 'converting' this try – kicking the ball over the crossbar between the posts; by a drop-kick or a penalty kick. Rugby is played chiefly in Britain, France, New Zealand, Australia and South Africa.

Rugby League Football is a 13-a-side game played mainly in the north of England and Australia. The field is similar to that of Rugby Union, but the points scoring is slightly different. Rugby League is a professional game.

Australian Rules Football dominates the southern and western states of Australia. There are 18 players on each side, and goals and points are scored by kicking the ball through goal posts. It is played on an oval pitch, and the oval ball may be punched, palmed or kicked, but not thrown.

FLYING SAUCERS Although many people claim to have sighted flying saucers and other unidentified flying objects (UFOs), the authorities can usually find an explanation under any one of the following categories: unconventional aircraft; aircraft flying in unusual weather conditions, or with unusual flight patterns; high altitude balloons; artificial satellites; searchlights reflecting off clouds; flocks of birds; luminescent creatures such as fireflies; mirages; meteors; unusually bright planets; bright stars; and lastly the Aurora Borealis (Northern Lights).

FOOD POISONING One of the most dangerous forms of food poisoning is botulism. Over 50 per cent of all those who contract the infection die . . . mainly from respiratory failure. Botulism bacteria soon die when exposed to the air, but thrive in tins where the food is badly sterilized. When the bacteria are ingested by a human, they produce a toxin which attacks the central nervous system and which is very difficult to combat.

FORD, HENRY When he first set up in business – making chain-driven, two-cylinder automobiles – Henry Ford asked a banker for a loan. He was refused on the grounds that his idea of selling cars to 'farmers and shopgirls' was ridiculous. For the banker who told him to 'keep such day-dreams to himself', it must have been a sad day when Henry Ford drove his millionth car off the Detroit assembly line in 1915. In fact, Ford's production-line system was so efficient that in 1914 – when the average daily US wage was $2.40 – he was able to pay his workers a minimum wage of $5.00 a day.

FORGERY The greatest forgery of all time was that engineered in 1941 by the Secret Service of Nazi Germany. They planned to flood England with forged sterling, with the aim of undermining the value of the Pound and thus bringing about the downfall of the British government. £150,000,000-worth of £5 notes were printed, but only a few ever went into circulation in England.

American Football resembles in some ways the rugby codes. The main features are long forward passes and crunching tackles on any opposing player, whether he carries the ball or not. The teams consist of 11 players, with almost limitless substitution.

FORCE In MECHANICS, a force is any cause which changes the motion of a body, sets it in motion or brings it to rest. The SI UNIT of force is the Newton, which is defined as the force needed to give an acceleration of $1\,m/sec^2$ in mass of one kilogram. By NEWTON's law of motion, force is proportional to the rate of change of momentum of a body.

FORD, HENRY The famous MOTOR CAR builder (1863–1947) who founded one of the world's biggest companies. He built his cars on ASSEMBLY LINES using identical, interchangeable parts. He came up with the first cheap, popular car, the Model T. It sold 15 million models between 1908 and 1927. ◁

FOREIGN LEGION An elite French military unit first set up in 1831. It was manned by foreigners who served only outside France. The myth of legionnaires as tough, hard men with a past to hide, attracted recruits from many countries. Men from some 55 nations have served in its ranks.

FOREST Large area of land covered with TREES. There are three main types of forest:

▲ *The famous Model T Ford – the first mass produced automobile. Built between 1908 and 1927, it came in many versions – this is the 'Fordor' Sedan model.*

rain forest, deciduous forest and coniferous forest. Rain forest mostly occurs in tropical regions where both rainfall and temperature are very high. The trees, all evergreens, grow dense and tall and include such valuable species as MAHOGANY, TEAK and EBONY. Deciduous forests belong to warm temperate lands like Europe and the eastern USA; they consist of trees that shed their leaves in autumn such as the OAK, beech, ash and MAPLE. Coniferous forests, largely made up of PINE, FIR, SPRUCE and larch, grow in cool northern zones.

FORGERY A false copy of an object, made to deceive others; for example, forged signatures on cheques and forged banknotes. Forgeries of paintings and sculptures also exist. In the 1930s, a Frenchman passed off a bronze horse to the Metropolitan Museum of New York as an ancient Greek sculpture. The fake was only detected in 1967. ◁

FORGING The working of metals by heating, then hammering and rolling. Forging is more than a shaping operation because it improves the properties of the metal, making it stronger than similar parts made by other shaping operations.

FORK An eating utensil with a long handle and two or more prongs at one end for spearing food. Also a work tool, of the same design, but bigger, which is used for digging and lifting.

FORUM The open square in the centre of all ancient Roman cities. Here, business activity, shopping, public debates and pure gossiping took place. The most famous of all is the Forum in Rome.

FOSSIL Remains – or traces – of a living thing preserved in rock. Fossils, often many

◀ *The ruins of the Forum in Rome. The Forum was the centre of life in the city, an open market place that was surrounded by temples and monuments. In the foreground are the remains of the Temple of Vesta.*

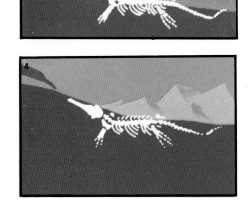

▲ *The history of a fossil. A marine reptile dies and its body sinks to the sea bed (1). Its flesh decays, but the skeleton remains (2). The skeleton is covered with mud and sand which gradually hardens into rock. The skeleton, too, turns to stone. Much later, earth movements cause the sea bed to buckle. The rocks are lifted up out of the sea (3) and the processes of erosion begin. Layer after layer is stripped off and the fossilized remains of the reptile are eventually exposed (4).*

millions of years old, include shells, skeletons, leaf outlines and footprints. They are formed when an animal or plant becomes buried – perhaps at the bottom of the sea or in a bog. Eventually, the surrounding mud layers harden into rock and the remains of the dead organism are preserved – fossilized – for all time. Fossils are important to man as they give a record of the Earth's history and show how plants and animals have developed; they provide vital evidence for EVOLUTION.

FOUNDATIONS The base of a building, bridge or tower by which the rest of the structure is held up. They are usually set deep in the earth.

FOUNTAIN A man-made stream or fall of water set in a wide basin. The water flows from pipes often set in pillars, sculptures or decorated marble. The tradition of throwing coins into fountains comes from the old habit of making offerings to the water gods.   ▷

▶ *The fennec fox of the Sahara has huge ears that help to keep it cool. Big ears help an animal to lose heat by acting like radiators. They also are an aid to hearing.*

FOX Flesh-eating animal of the DOG family with a pointed muzzle and long bushy tail, noted for its cunning. Foxes, found in most parts, live alone: they spend the day in their earths (holes) and hunt prey such as rabbits and partridges by night. The most common species is the northern hemisphere's reddish-brown red fox.

FOX TERRIER Small lively dog, first bred for unearthing FOXES, but now kept as a pet. Its white coat (smooth or wire-haired) has black or tan patches.

FRANCE The largest and one of the most beautiful nations in western EUROPE. Its history and culture are mirrored in the fine buildings, monuments, superb art galleries and museums in the cities, elegant palaces and *châteaux* (castles) and enchanting old towns.

FOUNTAIN Fountains have fascinated and entertained people throughout the ages. The French king, Louis XIV even loved them so much that he demanded that 1400 be built in the grounds of his palace at Versailles. They required more water than the whole of Paris, and at first gigantic systems of waterwheels and pumps were built to feed them. When this method became unreliable, two special reservoirs were built nearby and the fountains were supplied by aqueducts.

FRANCE: FACTS AND FIGURES
Area: 547,026 sq km (211,208 sq miles).
Population: 54,947,000 (1984 est.).
Largest cities: Paris (pop. 8,510,000), Lyon (1,170,000), Marseille (1,080,000).
Official language: French.
Currency: Franc.
Highest peak: Mont Blanc, 4810 m (15,781 ft), in the Alps.
Rivers: The Rhine forms the French border with Germany for about 160 km (100 miles). The longest navigable river entirely within France is the Seine, which flows through Paris. Other rivers are the Loire, the Garonne, and the Rhône. Farmland covers about half the country, and about 13 per cent of the people are employed in farming, fishing and forestry. France leads the world in quality wine-making.

FRANCO-PRUSSIAN WAR When the French army surrendered at Sedan in September 1870, the Germans marched on to Paris and laid siege to the city on September 20. This dragged on for four months, until an armistice was eventually signed on January 28. The French had been beaten, and this war was to shape the course of European history for the next 50 years. In January 1871, the German Empire was created, and the lingering animosity between France and Germany finally erupted once again with World War I in 1914.

FRANKENSTEIN Mary Shelley's *Frankenstein* was the forerunner of a now-common science-fiction theme, which symbolizes the catastrophic results of people's urge to control the elements. The first Frankenstein film was released in the USA in 1931, although earlier films – such as *The Golem* of 1915 – dealt with a similar theme. Now, there are dozens of variations on the Frankenstein film theme.

FREEMASONS This is the world's largest secret society. It has around 6,000,000 members, of whom about 4,000,000 live in the USA, and 1,000,000 in Britain.

FREEZING During World War II a new technique that was called 'freeze-drying' was used to store blood plasma. This same technique is now used to preserve many common foods, such as coffee, fruit juices, thin slabs of meat and small vegetables like peas. The food is first frozen and then thawed out slightly to release its moisture. The moisture is then evaporated off using large fans, and the result is dried food with less than 10 per cent of its original water content.

France was the birthplace of many of Europe's finest writers, artists, composers and philosophers.

The highest mountains are the French ALPS in the south-east. The Jura and Vosges mountains are also in the east and the PYRENEES in the south-west. The Massif Central is an upland in south-central France, and Corsica is a largely mountainous Mediterranean island. France also has fertile plains and river basins, such as those of the Dordogne, Garonne, Loire, Rhône-Saône and Seine.

France suffered greatly during the two world wars, but it is now one of Europe's most prosperous nations. Farming is important and food products are varied, because of the climatic differences between the regions. However, manufacturing is now France's chief source of wealth. Important centres include the capital, PARIS, Bordeaux, Lille, Lyons and Marseille. France is a republic and a founder member of the EUROPEAN ECONOMIC COMMUNITY.

Besides French, several other languages are spoken in France. German is spoken in the north-east, Breton in the scenic north-west peninsula, and BASQUE and Catalan in the south-west. Provençal is another language, spoken in the south-east. ◁

FRANCIS OF ASSISSI The founder of the Order of St. Francis (1182–1226), the largest order of monks in the Catholic Church. St Francis was a forceful man who gave up his worldly goods to lead a life of wandering, working and preaching the gospel.

FRANCO-PRUSSIAN WAR A brief war (1870–1871) during which the French were decisively beaten by the Germans led by PRUSSIA. Napoleon III of France was captured and Paris was besieged. When France surrendered, she lost the province of Alsace-Lorraine and had to pay Prussia five billion francs compensation. ◁

FRANKENSTEIN A man-made monster who runs amok and then causes his creator, Doctor Frankenstein, to die. Many films and books have dealt with this popular beast, the original being a novel by Mary Shelley, written in 1818. ◁

FRANKLIN, BENJAMIN A famous American printer, scientist, politician, writer and philosopher (1706–1790), he was a man of

▶ *Benjamin Franklin was a scientist as well as a statesman. In 1752 he demonstrated the electrical nature of lightning by flying a kite in a thunderstorm and drawing sparks from a key tied to the lower end of the kite string. Franklin's inventions included bifocal lenses and the harmonica.*

many careers and talents. His inventions include bifocal glasses and the lightning rod. He was America's first ambassador to France, and also signed its Declaration of Independence. (See ELECTRICITY AND MAGNETISM)

FREEDOM OF SPEECH A basic human right states that all people should be free to speak their opinions and beliefs in public, with no fear of being stopped by their government. Few governments have never violated this right.

FREEMASONS A worldwide organization that is a fraternity of men set up to help one another. Their brotherhood is strengthened by secret signs, rituals and legends about the order. ◁

FREEZING The process by which a substance changes from a liquid to a solid. If pressure is reduced, the freezing point of a liquid rises. ◁

FREMANTLE The chief port of western AUSTRALIA. Fremantle has a population of 23,580 (1985). It is about 19 km (12 miles) from Perth. Industries include shipbuilding, car assembling, fertilizer and soap making. Fremantle was founded in 1829.

FRENCH HORN A brass instrument made from metal tubing up to 5 metres (16½ ft) long and coiled in circles. It has three valves to change the tone. It was originally a French hunting horn in the 17th century.   ▷

FRENCH REVOLUTION A violent upheaval in France that began in 1789, when the king, Louis XVI, was deposed and executed. France became a republic for the first time. Its leaders struggled to give shape to the democratic ideals of liberty and equality. They failed, and the republic declined. It was replaced by the military dictatorship of Napoleon BONAPARTE.

FRESCO A PAINTING made on freshly laid, still wet plaster. The greatest time of fresco painting was during the RENAISSANCE in Italy. Huge MURALS showing scenes from the Bible were painted on the interiors of countless churches. The most famous are the scenes from Genesis showing the creation of man, painted by MICHELANGELO on the ceiling of the Sistine Chapel in Rome.

FREUD, SIGMUND Known as the 'father of modern PSYCHIATRY', Freud (1856–1939) was a well-respected Vienna doctor when he began his revolutionary theories on human nature. He was baffled by the side of human behaviour that seemed to make 'no sense'. He held that there was a deep unexplored part of the human mind called the unconscious. Tensions and forces within this shadowy world often led people to act in ways they could not explain. The science of PSYCHIATRY was a way to explore and treat problems that arose from the unconscious.

FRICTION Friction always occurs when two things are moved and rub against each other. There are two main kinds of friction. One is when a book slides across a table – sliding friction. The other is 'rolling' friction, the resistance produced when a wheel rolls along a road. By and large, the resistance of rolling friction is less than that of sliding friction. Without friction the world would be a strange place; the wheels of a locomotive would not grip the rails, nails and screws would not grip, bicycle and car brakes would not exist. Friction produces heat, which is often harmful. To reduce friction we oil machines and make things run on ball or roller bearings.

FRIGATE Originally a sailing warship of the mid-18th century, today frigates are small escort destroyers in the British Navy. In the US Navy they are large guided-missile destroyers.

▶ *Modern frigates are used to defend ship convoys, and as destroyers.*

FROM TADPOLE TO FROG
A frog starts as jelly-covered egg laid and fertilized in water early in the spring. The egg hatches into a tadpole: a tiny, limbless creature with a fish-like tail and gills for breathing oxygen dissolved in water. It feeds largely on algae. By summer, legs and lungs appear and tail and gills vanish. The tadpole has become a fully formed but tiny frog.

FROG Tailless AMPHIBIAN found in many parts of the world. Frogs have smooth slimy skins, protruding eyes, webbed feet and strong back legs for swimming and jumping. Well-known species include the Common Frog, which hibernates in mud underwater during the winter, and the Edible Frog (only its hind legs are eaten). There are also various Tree Frogs, especially in tropical forests, and Flying Frogs which can glide short distances using their broad webs as wings.   ▷

FRUIT Plant SEED and its surrounding case. Fruits, all shapes and sizes, can contain just one seed, but most have more. They are usually divided into two groups, dry fruits and

FRENCH HORN The modern French horn came into existence in 1818 with the invention of valves. Until then, various tunings had been achieved using lengths of tubing called 'crooks', which were inserted into the horn. Nowadays, three tuning valves give modern horns seven separate tunings, covering a chromatic range of 3½ octaves.

FROG The most dangerous frog in the world is undoubtedly the Arrow Poison Frog, found in Colombia, South America. Its skin secretes the most active known poison, called Batrochotoxin. One millionth of a gram of this is enough to kill a person.

DIFFERENT KINDS OF FRUIT
FLESHY FRUITS

Drupes
The fruit has a fleshy outer layer, and a hard inner layer (the stone). The actual seed is inside the stone. Blackberries and raspberries consist of several small drupes (drupels) lightly joined together.

Cherries

Plum

Peach

Raspberry

Blackberry

Orange

Tomato

Berries
The entire fruit is fleshy and contains many seeds. It is usually formed from several carpels, each segment of the fruit being formed from one carpel.

Grapes   Gooseberry

Pome
The true fruit is the core, the edible part is the swollen receptacle.

Apple

Pear

DRY FRUITS

Pea

Poppy

Dehiscent
These split open when ripe. Peas and beans have pods, each formed from one carpel. Poppies have capsules formed from several carpels.

Sycamore

Hazel

Wheat

Dandelion

Indehiscent
Indehiscent fruits do not split open when ripe. They therefore cannot germinate until the ovary wall (the woody or leathery 'coat') rots or is broken.

---

fleshy fruits. Dry fruits are ones which dry out as they ripen, like pea pods, acorns and sycamore keys. They often have some method of scattering their seeds: the pea pod, for instance, bursts open and shoots out its seeds while the winged sycamore key is carried away by the wind. In fleshy fruits, such as TOMATOES, GRAPES, BANANAS and CUCUMBERS, the case enclosing the seed is soft and pulpy. Animals and birds eat this juicy part but drop the seeds – often away from the parent plant.

FRUIT FLY Fly which lays its eggs inside fruit, especially fleshy stone fruits such as plums. The eggs develop into maggots which feed off the juicy flesh. Fruit flies are widespread and often do great damage to fruit crops.

FUEL See COAL; ENERGY; NATURAL GAS; HYDROCARBON; NUCLEAR ENERGY; OIL; SOLAR ENERGY

FUNGUS Plant without CHLOROPHYLL, roots, stem or leaves. As fungi have no chlorophyll, they cannot make food; instead some live off dead matter such as rotting leaves and wood, while others are PARASITES and feed off living plants and animals. Fungi are a mass of fine threads. In simple fungi, like MOULDS, these never take any definite shape – they just creep over and through whatever they are growing on. But in larger fungi, they grow into a toadstool to reproduce. Some toadstools, like the MUSHROOM and TRUFFLE, are edible; others, such as the Death Cap and red-and-white Fly Agaric, are poisonous. As well as being food, fungi are useful to man in other ways. YEAST and PENICILLIN, for example, are both fungi. In contrast, some parasitic species harm plants and animals.

FUR Short fine soft HAIR covering certain animals. The furred skins of many of these

▼ *Fly agaric fungi growing amongst leaf litter on the woodland floor. They feed on decaying matter and on tree roots.*

animals are used for making or trimming coats. Some valuable furs are ERMINE and MINK from North America and SABLE from Russia.

FURNITURE All the movable things with which you fill a room are known as furniture. Some fixed things, like cupboards and shelves, are also furniture. By and large, they are useful objects and not just decorations. They range from simple beds, tables and chairs to the most expensive and beautiful carpets and antique sideboards. Some pieces of furniture are so beautiful that they are very valuable works of art.

Modern furniture styles are very clean and uncluttered. They are made in wood, steel tubing, chrome, plastics, glass and with synthetic fabrics.

FUSE A safety device in an electric circuit. If there is a short circuit in an electrical appliance the current can rise to a dangerous level, wires can get too hot and start a fire. To prevent this happening, most plugs and devices have fuses in them. The fuse consists of a piece of thin wire that melts easily. If the current rises too high, the fuse melts and breaks the electrical circuit. It is important to use fuses of the right value. (See OHMS LAW)

FUSION, NUCLEAR When any substance gets hotter, its ATOMS move about faster and faster. The SUN is so hot that its atoms move very fast indeed, and they often collide with immense force. This impact is enough to overcome the forces that usually keep atoms apart, and the nuclei (centres) of the atoms strike each other. The nuclei fuse together and what is called *fusion* takes place. Light elements such as hydrogen and helium are involved in fusion. (*Fission* is the splitting up of *heavy* elements such as uranium and plutonium.) When fusion takes place a vast amount of energy is released, much more than from splitting atoms in fission. There is a limit to the power of a fission ATOM BOMB, and soon after World War II scientists began to wonder whether a bomb using fusion instead of fission could be made. Fusion works only at the temperature of the Sun, and the only way to make such temperatures on Earth was to explode an atom bomb. So the scientists used a fission explosion to set up fusion in ISOTOPES of hydrogen. They had made the HYDROGEN BOMB – but they are still trying to harness fusion for peaceful power. They hope to use *deuterium*, an isotope of hydrogen, as the source of fusion power, plentiful supplies of deuterium can be obtained from the sea. If controlled fusion becomes a reality, then fuel shortages and power problems will be things of the past. (See ATOMIC ENERGY; NUCLEAR ENERGY) ▷

▲ This French writing desk is a beautiful example of antique furniture. It was made in the 18th century, and is richly decorated with different coloured woods and gilt bronze mouldings.

▼ Scientists in a number of countries are trying hard to find a practical way of controlling fusion power. In the machine shown here, a beam of deuterium is being squeezed with enormous force in a strong magnetic field.

FUSION, NUCLEAR Thermonuclear bombs have given rise to the highest temperatures ever made by human activity. These temperatures are obviously very hard to measure, but they can certainly be measured in millions of degrees.

G

GAELIC LANGUAGE One of the ancient languages of the CELTS. It reached Ireland from Europe, and spread to Scotland and the Isle of Man. In Eire it is an official language, but only 5 per cent still use it regularly. *Clan* and *loch* are Gaelic words.

GAGARIN, YURI A Russian astronaut (1934–1968). In 1961 he orbited the Earth in *Vostok I*, so becoming the first man in space. (See SPACE EXPLORATION)

GAINSBOROUGH, THOMAS A famous English portrait painter (1727–1788). Largely self-taught, he painted over 500 of the fashionable people of his day, including GEORGE III, Benjamin FRANKLIN and Samuel JOHNSON. But his best-known work is just called *The Blue Boy*. He was a founder member of the Royal Academy.

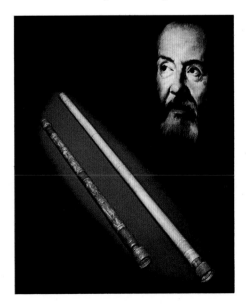

GALAPAGOS ISLANDS An island group in the Pacific Ocean, about 1050 km (650 miles) west of ECUADOR, which governs it. These volcanic islands cover a total of 7844 sq km (3029 sq miles) and there are about 5000 people. The islands contain many strange animals and some plants, which are found only there. A study of these animals helped Charles DARWIN to arrive at his theory of EVOLUTION.

GALAXY The Sun is just one of about 100,000 million stars in a vast spiral arrangement of stars that we call our Galaxy. In some parts of the night sky there are so many stars that they form the white band of light we call the MILKY WAY. Outside this great system of stars to which we and the Sun belong there are thousands of millions of other vast galaxies, some spiral in shape, others elliptical, and still others of no distinctive form.

GALILEO GALILEI An Italian scientist (1564–1642) who lived in an age when very few people had any knowledge of science. At the age of 18 he made his first great discovery. Sitting in Pisa cathedral he watched the swinging of a lamp suspended by a long chain. Common sense told him that wider swings would take a longer time than short swings, but when he timed the swings against the beat of his pulse he found that this was not so. All swings, large and small, took the same time (see PENDULUM). Later he carried out his famous experiment of dropping balls of different weights from the top of the Leaning Tower of Pisa. They all took the same time to reach the ground, showing that the weight of

◄ *Galileo with two of the telescopes he used to study the Sun and planets. His methods of careful observation and planned experiments formed the basis of modern science.*

149

objects made no difference to their rate of fall. Galileo made himself one of the first TELE-SCOPES, through which he saw the craters of the Moon, and in 1610 he discovered the moons of JUPITER revolving round their parent planet. He also discovered the phases of VENUS and said that Venus therefore revolved around the Sun. This supported the ideas of COPERNICUS, who had said that the Sun was the centre of the solar system. But it clashed with the ideas of the Church, and Galileo was made to renounce his Copernican ideas. In his lifetime Galileo had laid the foundations of modern science. ▷

GALL BLADDER Small pouch lying next to the LIVER and used for storing bile. Bile, a bitter green-yellow fluid, aids DIGESTION. It is secreted by the liver and stored in the gall bladder. During a meal, the gall bladder contracts and pushes bile out into the small INTESTINE where it helps to digest the food by breaking down fats.

GALLEON A type of large, square-rigged sailing-ship, built from the 16th to 18th centuries – especially by the Spanish, who used a heavy, cumbersome version for warfare and for trade with their American colonies.

GALLEY An open sea-going vessel powered mainly by oars, and used by Mediterranean nations from ancient times until the 18th century. Some designs had 5 men to each oar, and the largest war galleys held 1200 men. ▷

GALLSTONE Solid fatty lump that sometimes forms in the GALL BLADDER or bile duct (tube leading to the small intestine). Gallstones are painful and can cause illness; they are usually removed by surgery.

GALVANIZING A way of reducing the CORROSION of iron and steel by coating it with

▲ *Hindu pilgrims bathing in the Ganges. Since ancient times, Hindus have regarded this river as sacred, and believe that bathing in it will wash away their sins.*

a thin layer of ZINC. It is often used on corrugated steel sheets.

GALVANOMETER An instrument used to detect or measure small electric CURRENTS. It consists of a coil of wire suspended between the poles of a magnet. When current goes through the coil it rotates to a degree depending on the strength of the current.

GAMA, VASCO DA A Portuguese navigator (c. 1469–1524). In 1497–1498 he discovered the sea route to India via the Cape of Good Hope. This became Europe's main trade route to Asia until the opening of the SUEZ CANAL. ▷

GAMBLING Risking money in the hope of winning more. Popular forms of gambling are the football pools, and betting on horse races. Some games exist only so people can bet on them (e.g. ROULETTE).

GAMMA RAYS High frequency ELECTRO-MAGNETIC rays similar to, but more powerful than, X-RAYS. They can pass through iron 30 cm (1 ft) thick and are used in medicine to destroy CANCER.

GANDHI, MOHANDAS KARAMCHAND Indian social, political and spiritual leader (1869–1948). His programmes of peaceful protest helped bring about the independence of INDIA from Britain in 1947. He is thought of as 'father of his nation'.

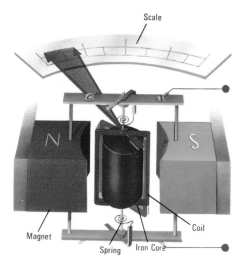

◀ *A galvanometer measures the flow of electrical current. The one shown in the picture is used in the moving coil ammeter and voltmeter.*

Scale

Magnet
N   S
Coil
Spring   Iron Core

GALILEO Even as a boy, Galileo tried to prove the truth of ideas that other people never questioned. This led him to spend his playtime building all sorts of devices. Galileo's father called him 'an absent-minded little star-gazer'.

GALLEY The last great battle fought by galleys happened at Lepanto off Greece in 1571. Over 200 Christian galleys and armed sailing ships beat a larger Moslem Turkish force of galleys, seizing 117 galleys and sinking 50 more. The Christians' use of sailing ships and cannon fire at once outdated ramming tactics and the galley that relied on them.

GAMA, VASCO DA When Vasco da Gama reached the port of Calicut in India, the end of his long journey eastward, he prepared gifts for the Hindu ruler. They included 12 pieces of striped cloth, 4 scarlet hoods, 6 hats, 4 strings of coral, a case containing 6 wash-hand basins, a case of sugar, 2 casks of oil and 2 of honey. When the ruler saw the gifts he laughed and declared them unfit to offer to a king. So da Gama sold his goods and collected a cargo of pepper, cinnamon, and ginger and set sail for home. When he reached Lisbon he had been away for over two years and only 55 of his original 170 men were still alive. But the sale of the cargo of spices was worth sixty times the cost of the expedition.

GARLIC People who dislike the smell of garlic should try sniffing ethyl mercaptan, one of the smelliest of 17,000 substances that have been tested. It reeks of garlic, onions, decayed cabbage and sewer gas.

GAS The most deadly gases are the so-called V agents. One droplet breathed in or falling on a person's skin could be enough to kill.

GAUGUIN, PAUL Gauguin's early life showed no sign of future painting genius. At school he made poor progress. Later he spent five years at sea as a second mate and stoker. Then he joined the stock exchange. He only took up full-time painting at the age of 35.

GAUL Julius Caesar spent nine years subduing Gaul for Rome. His main enemy was a chief called Vercingetorix. Caesar beat him in a siege where the Romans dug a system of trenches so large that the earth removed would have built a mound four-fifths the size of Egypt's Great Pyramid.

GANGES RIVER One of the greatest rivers of INDIA and BANGLADESH, the Ganges is sacred to Hindus (see HINDUISM). It flows about 2480 km (1540 miles) from its source in the HIMALAYAS to its mouth in the Bay of Bengal.

GARDENING Cultivating a plot of ground for pleasure (flowers, shrubs) or food (vegetables, fruit, herbs). Each nation has its own style of garden.

GARLIC Plant grown for its strong-tasting bulb, used as flavouring in cookery. Garlic is very popular in Mediterranean countries. ◁

GARMENT INDUSTRY Machines to cut and sew cloth, developed in the early 1800s, made possible today's mass-production of clothes. This is one of the world's major industries – its sales are helped by changing fashions from year to year.

GARNET A stone of many types and colours. Some – usually deep red – are used as GEMS, others as ABRASIVES in industry.

GARTER, ORDER OF THE The highest order of English KNIGHTHOOD, founded in about 1349 by King Edward III. Its emblem is a garter of blue velvet, with the motto *'Honi soit qui mal y pense'* ('Evil be to him who evil thinks'). There are only 25 such Knights at any one time, apart from royalty.

GAS One of the three states in which matter exists, the others being liquid and solid. The particles in a gas move about freely and spread out as widely as possible. If a quantity of gas is placed in a container, the gas spreads out until it fills the whole container. If the temperature of a gas is lowered, the particles in it move more slowly and stay closer together and the gas will become a liquid. If the temperature is lowered still further the liquid becomes a solid. Also, if a solid is heated it becomes first a liquid and then a gas – ice melts to water and water becomes steam. ◁

GAS MASK A mask to protect against harmful gases, especially in warfare. They were used by soldiers in World War I, and were issued to everyone in World War II, although no gas attacks in fact occurred.

GAS TURBINE An efficient type of engine perfected in the 1930s and used largely in AIRCRAFT. It usually has a single shaft which carries a series of fans, divided into two groups – the compressor and the turbine. Air is drawn in by the compressor fans and its pressure increased. The compressed air is mixed with fuel. This mixture is ignited and the expanding hot gases (see GAS) are forced against fans to drive the compressor and then against the power-producing turbine blades, where the mixture passes out as exhaust. In jet aircraft this exhaust is used to thrust the plane forward. Gas turbine engines are becoming more important in industry because they are compact and efficient. (See JET PROPULSION; TURBINE)

GAUGUIN, PAUL A famous French artist (1848–1903). Influenced by VAN GOGH, he developed a simple, colourful style of painting, and used it to depict the unspoilt life of the South Pacific. ◁

GAUL In Roman times, the part of EUROPE now covered by France and Belgium. Its inhabitants were CELTS, who at one time also overran northern Italy. But their power waned with the rise of Rome, and by 51 BC, Julius CAESAR had added all Gaul to the Roman Empire. ◁

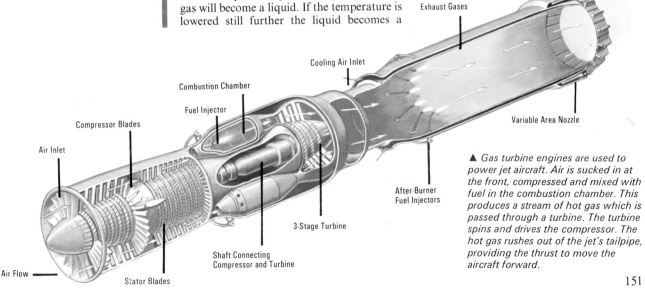

Exhaust Gases
Cooling Air Inlet
Combustion Chamber
Fuel Injector
Compressor Blades
Air Inlet
Variable Area Nozzle
After-Burner Fuel Injectors
3-Stage Turbine
Shaft Connecting Compressor and Turbine
Air Flow
Stator Blades

▲ Gas turbine engines are used to power jet aircraft. Air is sucked in at the front, compressed and mixed with fuel in the combustion chamber. This produces a stream of hot gas which is passed through a turbine. The turbine spins and drives the compressor. The hot gas rushes out of the jet's tailpipe, providing the thrust to move the aircraft forward.

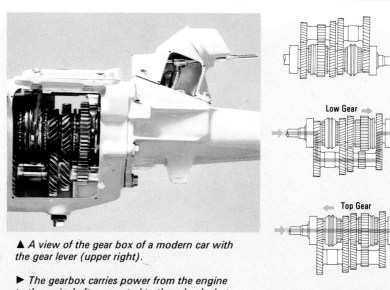

▼ Gear wheels turn at different speeds in proportion to the number of teeth they possess. The small wheel turns at four times the speed of the large one if it has one quarter the number of teeth.

Low Gear

Top Gear

Reverse Gear

▲ A view of the gear box of a modern car with the gear lever (upper right).

▶ The gearbox carries power from the engine to the mainshaft connected to the wheels, but changes the speed. At low gear, the engine turns the mainshaft at a slower speed. In top gear, the force is transmitted directly through the gear box; at low gear, it goes through the lower gear wheels. To reverse, a gear wheel called an idler turns the mainshaft in the opposite direction.

GAZA STRIP An area of land along the MEDITERRANEAN SEA coast in south-west PALESTINE. It was held by EGYPT after the first Arab-Israeli war of 1948–9, but it was taken by ISRAEL in another war in 1967.

GAZELLE Slender sandy-coloured ANTELOPE found on dry grasslands in Africa and parts of Asia. Most species have a white streak on either side of the face, and the male gazelle has tall sweeping horns. As with all antelopes, the horns remain for life (unlike deer whose antlers are shed each year).

GEARS A gear wheel is a wheel with teeth, that fit into the teeth of other gears and so turn them. It is used to transmit power from one rotating shaft to another, and it may change the speed or the direction of motion of the second shaft. Gears are most commonly used in cars to change the power ratio from the engine to the wheels.

GEELONG A city and port in Victoria, AUSTRALIA, about 70 km (43 miles) from Melbourne. It has 143,000 people (1984 est.). This busy city has a variety of industries.

GELATIN Substance obtained from animal skins and bones. Gelatin is hard, transparent and tasteless, and consists mostly of PROTEIN; it forms a stiff jelly when dissolved in water. Gelatin is used in cooking and photography.

GEM A precious stone. The most valuable gems are DIAMONDS and EMERALDS, followed by rubies and SAPPHIRES. Many others are 'semi-precious' (PEARLS are also valuable, but are not stones). The value of a gem depends on its size, colour and lack of flaws. Most types are cut into special shapes, to catch the light more brilliantly. Poor-quality gems can often be used in industry, and many of these are now made synthetically.

▼ The Springbok is closely related to the gazelle and inhabits the treeless plains of southern Africa. It is also the national and sporting emblem of South Africa.

GENERATOR By the late 1970s the largest generator was one of 1,300 megawatts capacity, being built in the United States. This output equals the electricity used by 1,300,000 one-bar electric fires. But Britain and America are both planning generators in the 2,000 megawatt range.

GENGHIS KHAN Legend has it that Genghis Khan was born with his right hand clutching a clot of blood as big as a knucklebone. This was supposed to be an omen of the killing he would one day bring about.

GENE Basic part of the HEREDITY process. A living organism inherits genes from its parents. Each gene causes the development of a certain characteristic such as the shape of a leaf, hair colour or height. There are hundreds, sometimes thousands, of genes in every cell; they exist in the nucleus where they are arranged along minute strands called CHROMOSOMES.

GENERATOR, ELECTRIC In a generator, mechanical energy is turned into electricity. The mechanical energy comes from some kind of engine or TURBINE, usually powered by oil or coal. A generator works because an electric CURRENT flows in a loop of wire when it is rotated between the poles of a magnet. Usually there are many loops of wire (the *armature*) which rotate on a shaft between electromagnets. The electromagnets create magnetic fields when current passes through them. The current generated in the rotating coils is collected by carbon 'brushes' which press against copper rings at the end of the shaft. ◁

GENGHIS KHAN A great MONGOL conqueror (c. 1167–1227). At 13 he succeeded his father as chieftain of an unimportant tribe. By 1206 he had united all the Mongols, and in 1213 began the campaigns that took him into China, Russia, India and Persia. At his death he ruled from Manchuria to the Caspian Sea. His empire was then divided between his four sons. ◁

GEOGRAPHY The study of the Earth's surface. Geography has various branches. Physical geography deals with land forms and scenery, and how they have evolved. Climatology studies weather and CLIMATE. Some geographers study SOILS, while others are concerned with how climate and soils interact with plants and animals.

Human geography deals with the interaction of people and their environments. Economic geography deals with natural resources, food production, the location of minerals and fuels and the distribution of industry. Urban geography is concerned with the location and growth of cities, and historical geography is the study of the geography of periods in the past. Because geographers are especially interested in the *distribution* of features on the Earth's surface, their chief tool is the MAP.

GEOLOGY The branch of science that studies the Earth's crust. Two of the main branches of geology are *petrology*, the study of rocks; and *mineralogy*, the study of minerals. The Earth has been in existence for thousands of millions of years and has undergone many changes. The result of these changes can be seen in the shape of the Earth's surface – its mountains, valleys, oceans and rivers; in the

▼ A generator produces electricity from mechanical energy. The growing demand for electricity makes it necessary to build larger generators.

Geo

fossilized remains of extinct animals, and in the presence of minerals such as coal, which is the compressed remains of primeval forests. All these things are studied by the geologist. (See EARTH; EARTHQUAKE; FOSSIL; MINERALS; ROCKS)

GEOMETRY The branch of mathematics that deals with points, lines, planes and volumes. Plane geometry deals with figures lying entirely in one plane (two-dimensional). Solid geometry deals with three-dimensional bodies, while spherical geometry deals with figures drawn on a spherical surface. (See CIRCLE; EUCLID; PARABOLA; PYTHAGORAS; SPHERE)

GEORGE, SAINT An early Christian, martyred in Palestine in AD 303. The old Greek myth of dragon-killing is linked with him. CRUSADERS brought his story back to England, and he was made patron saint of England in 1350.

GEORGE III King of Great Britain (born 1738, reigned 1760–1820). His reign saw such decisive events as the American REVOLUTIONARY WAR, the Napoleonic Wars, and the INDUSTRIAL REVOLUTION. But, though a dedicated ruler, George III suffered from attacks of madness, and from 1811 his son had to rule as Regent.

GEORGE IV King of Great Britain (born 1762, Regent 1811, reigned 1820–1830). He succeeded his insane father, GEORGE III. George IV was important as a patron of art and architecture, but his lack of interest in government, and scandals in his private life, greatly lowered royal prestige.

GEORGE V King of Great Britain (born 1865, reigned 1910–1936). After his father Edward VII, who loved fashionable society, George V seemed like a quiet country gentleman. At first he was almost unknown to his subjects, but gradually won their respect, especially in WORLD WAR I.

GEORGE VI King of Great Britain (born 1895, reigned 1936–1952). He became king unexpectedly, on the abdication of his brother Edward VIII. But he proved dedicated and well-intentioned, a good national leader through the crises of WORLD WAR II, Indian independence and rapid social change at home.

GERANIUM Popular name for two groups of plants. One group, found wild in woodlands and also cultivated in gardens, has pink, purple or blue flowers. The other group, with scarlet, pink or white flowers, is often grown indoors or in greenhouses.

▲ *The steep-sided Mosel (Moselle) Valley in western Germany. This region is famous for its excellent wines.*

GERMAN MEASLES Contagious but harmless disease, except in pregnancy when it can affect the baby. Symptoms include a sore throat, mild fever and red spotty rash.

GERMANY In 1945, Germany was occupied and divided into four zones under the Americans, British, French and Russians. BERLIN, the capital, was also split into four sectors. By 1948 the American, British and French zones had been joined together to form West Germany. But the Russian zone remained separate, with a communist government. West Berlin, although surrounded by East Germany, became part of West Germany. But the Russian sector of East Berlin became the capital of East Germany.

The northern part of Germany consists mostly of a broad plain, with generally infertile soils. The chief crops are potatoes and rye. The land rises in the south of both countries, although West Germany has a much larger area of uplands, including part of the ALPS in the far south. The uplands are warmer and often fertile and a great variety of crops are grown.

However, West Germany is chiefly an industrial nation and it has become western EUROPE's leading manufacturing country. The main industrial region was the Ruhr coalfield; the Ruhr is a tributary of the River RHINE. But today, many cities throughout West Germany have become major industrial centres. Before 1945, East Germany was a backward, farming region. But, with Russian help, it has now become a leading industrial nation. The main industrial centres and the best farmland, are in the south. ▷

EAST GERMANY: FACTS AND FIGURES
Area: 108,178 sq km (41,768 sq miles).
Population: 16,671,000 (1984 est.). East Germany ranks ninth in size of population and fifteenth in area among those nations entirely in Europe.
Language: German.
Religion: Christianity.
Capital: (East) Berlin (pop. 1,173,000).

WEST GERMANY: FACTS AND FIGURES
Largest cities: West Berlin (pop. 1,860,000), Hamburg (1,618,000), Munich (1,284,000).
Area: 248,577 sq km (95,976 sq miles).
Population: 61,181,000 (1984 est.). West Germany ranks first in size of population and ninth in area among those nations lying entirely inside Europe.
Language: German.
Religion: Christianity.
Currency: Deutsche mark.
Capital: Bonn.
Highest Point: Zugspitze, 2963 m (9721 ft).
West Germany is a member of the EEC.

GEYSER Waimangu, in New Zealand, was the greatest of all geysers. During its active period it spouted jets of water up to 460 m (1500 ft) into the air. One of the best known of all geysers is Old Faithful, in Yellowstone National Park, Wyoming, USA. It gets its name from the fact that it spouts water regularly once every 65 minutes for about five minutes.

GHANA: FACTS AND FIGURES
Among African nations, Ghana ranks twelfth in size and twenty-eighth in population.
Official Language: English, but Ewe, Twi, Fanti and many other languages spoken locally.
Religions: Animism, Christianity, Islam.
Currency: Cedi.
Principal river: The Volta, formed by the union of the White Volta and Black Volta.

GIBBON The gibbons (genera *Hylobates* and *Symphalangus*) are the smallest of the apes, and the least like man. Although their brains are comparatively large in proportion to their weight (which usually makes for intelligence), gibbons are not very intelligent. They are the most agile of all apes, swinging through the trees with amazing skill. They can walk on their hind legs without diffi-culty, balancing by holding their arms outstretched. Gibbons are very noisy, and love to call to each other.

GIBRALTAR The name of this famous rock comes from the Arabic *Gebel-al-Tariq,* which means 'Rock of Tariq'. In AD 711 the Berber leader Tariq used four ships to ferry 7,000 Moslem troops to southern Spain from North Africa. He seized Gibraltar, crushed a Christian army, and helped to start an age of Moslem rule in Spain that lasted in places for more than seven centuries.

GINKGO Fossil ginkgoes much like the one living species have been found in rocks that go back to Triassic times, when dinosaurs had just begun to roam the Earth.

GERM CELL Special cell for REPRODUC-TION. Animals, except very simple ones, have two kinds of germ cells: sperms, produced by a male, and eggs, produced by a female. When a sperm joins with an egg, a new individual is formed. Germ cells are also called *gametes*.

GEYSER A kind of hot spring from which hot water and steam erupt, often at regular intervals. A geyser may be caused when underground water is superheated by MAGMA, or by the action of gases in the water. ◁

GHANA A republic in West AFRICA, Ghana has 13,151,000 people (1984 est.) and an area of 238,537 sq km (92,100 sq miles). The capital is Accra. Formerly called the Gold Coast, the country became independent from Britain, as Ghana, in 1957. Most people are farmers and Ghana is one of the world's main producers of COCOA. ◁

GIBBON Small agile APE living in the forests of south-east Asia. Gibbons spend most of their time in the trees. Using their long arms, they swing from branch to branch so fast they can catch flying birds. As well as birds, gibbons eat fruit, leaves and insects. They are brown or black and are known for their unearthly two-tone call made in the early morning. ◁

GIBRALTAR A British territory on a rocky peninsula in southern Spain. It is an important fortress and tourist centre, the Barbary apes being a special attraction. Gibraltar has

28,000 people (1984 est.) and an area of 6.5 sq km (2½ sq miles). Frontier problems with Spain were resolved in the 1980s. ◁

GILA MONSTER Large LIZARD from the desert region of America. There are only two poisonous lizards in the world and the Gila is one of them. Coloured pink, brown and orange, the Gila is a stocky creature about 60 cm (2 ft) long; the poison gland is in its bottom jaw.

GILBERT AND SULLIVAN The creators of England's most famous comic OPERAS, including *HMS Pinafore* (1878), *The Pirates of Penzance* (1879) and the *Mikado* (1885). Sir William Gilbert wrote the stories and lyrics, Sir Arthur Sullivan the music.

GILDING The art of gluing GOLD leaf or powder as decoration on wood, metal, pottery, etc. Picture frames are often 'gilded' – though nowadays only with bronze dust.

GIN, COTTON A machine for cleaning seeds from freshly-picked COTTON. It was invented in the USA by Eli Whitney in 1793, and greatly increased cotton output.

GINGER Spicy root of the ginger plant. Although the root can be eaten fresh or preserved in syrup, it is generally dried and then used to flavour biscuits, cakes, curries, chutneys and many other foods. Some of the best ginger comes from Jamaica.

GINKGO Chinese tree with fan-shaped leaves, yellow flowers and apricot-like fruits containing nuts that are edible if roasted. Since ancient times in China and Japan the Ginkgo has been considered sacred and is therefore planted near temples. ◁

GIRAFFE The world's tallest animal. With its immensely long neck and legs, the giraffe stands over 5 metres (16 ft) high. It has a dark-spotted orange-red skin and a long tufted tail which acts as a fly whisk. Giraffes live on the dry African plains and feed on tree leaves, especially acacia leaves. They defend themselves by kicking powerfully.

GIRL GUIDES An organization for girls, founded in 1910 by Lord BADEN-POWELL (founder of the BOY SCOUTS) and his sister. In Britain there are three age groups: Brownie Guides (7–11), Guides (10–16) and Ranger Guides (14–20). The world Guide membership is over 6½ million.

◀ *Erupting geysers can reach heights of 30 metres (100 ft) or more. They are found in Iceland, the North Island in New Zealand, and Yellowstone National Park in the USA.*

GLACIER A body of ICE that moves down valleys under the force of gravity. (Ice sheets are even larger bodies of ice.) Glaciers have carved much of the world's most impressive mountain scenery. But they can be dangerous to climbers, especially if crevasses (cracks) are hidden by snow. ▷

GLADIATORS In ancient Rome, men who fought to the death for the entertainment of spectators. Most were slaves or criminals. The COLOSSEUM saw many such displays.

GLADSTONE, WILLIAM A great British politician (1809–1898) – four times Prime Minister to Queen Victoria. His main concerns were Irish Home Rule and social reform. His great rival was DISRAELI. ▷

GLAND Organ in an animal that makes and secretes substances needed by the body. There

▲ *Glaciers are formed high up in mountains when the weight of the snow squashes its lower levels into ice. Gravity forces this mass to slide slowly down the valleys. Melting glaciers are the source of many rivers.*

are two types of gland: *exocrine* and *endocrine*. Exocrine glands release their product through ducts (tubes) either into the INTESTINES or onto the body's surface; tear, saliva and sweat glands are all examples of exocrine glands. Endocrine glands discharge their substances, called HORMONES, directly into the blood stream. Hormones influence the growth and development of the body. One important endocrine gland is the THYROID; its hormone controls the rate at which the body uses oxygen and food.

GLASGOW A major city in central SCOT-LAND, Glasgow has a population of 762,000

GLACIER The longest glacier is the Lambert-Fisher Ice Passage, found in Antarctica in the 1950s. It extends for over 500 km (300 miles).

GLADSTONE, WILLIAM EWART The year of Gladstone's birth (1809) saw the birth of at least eight other famous men. They included the great American statesman Abraham Lincoln; Alfred Tennyson and three other writers; the composer Felix Mendelssohn; and Charles Darwin, who developed the theory of evolution.

GLASS People were coating soapstone beads with glass in Egypt 6,000 years ago. They made small, solid glass objects 4,500 years ago, and glass containers appeared 3,500 years ago. The earliest window glass dates from about 2,000 years ago.

(1981). It is a great commercial centre, with engineering, chemical and marine and aero engine industries.

GLASS One of the most useful materials of all, giving us not only windows, mirrors and containers, but also GLASSES, scientific LENSES, ornaments and, in fibreglass, a material strong enough for the hulls of boats. It is made from just sand, soda and lime, fused together at great heat. Shapes such as bottles are made by blowing air into tubes of hot glass. Decorative glass can be etched, engraved, or stained with colour. ◁

GLASSES (EYE) These work by bending rays of LIGHT before they reach the EYE (see LENS). This reinforces or corrects the work of the eye itself. Glasses (or 'spectacles') have

been known in Europe since about 1300.

GLAUCOMA A disease of the eye, marked by a hardening of the eyeball. It is fairly common after middle age, and, if untreated can lead to blindness. The disease usually requires surgery or treatment with drugs.

GLENN, JOHN HERSCHEL American astronaut (1921–   ). The first American to orbit the Earth, on February 20, 1962. The flight lasted 4 hours, 55 minutes.

GLIDING Flying in a winged AIRCRAFT without an engine. A glider is usually towed into the air by a normal aircraft, and released at 600–900 metres (2000–3000 ft). It then stays up by using rising air currents: either rising warm air ('thermals'), or 'slope winds'

▼ The drawing shows the position of the endocrine glands, and the chart names the hormones they secrete and their main function. For simplicity, both testes (male) and ovaries (female) are indicated, although they would not be present in the same body.

Pituitary
Thyroid
Parathyroids
Adrenals
Pancreas
Ovaries
Testes

THE ENDOCRINE SYSTEM

Pituitary Gland

Thyrotrophin	Controls activity of thyroid gland.
Corticotrophin	Regulates secretion from adrenal gland.
Gonadotrophin	Controls secretions from reproductive glands.
Growth hormone	Regulates general body growth.
Vasopressin	Regulates amount of water removed by kidneys.
Prolactin	Stimulates milk production in mother.
Oxytocin	Stimulates contractions of the womb at birth.

Thyroid Gland

Thyroxine	Controls rate at which food is converted into heat and energy in the cells. Essential for normal growth and for the proper working of the nervous system.

Parathyroid Glands

Parathormone	Stimulates release of calcium from bone, and regulates calcium level in the blood. Reduction of the hormone causes permanent contraction of muscles.

Adrenal Glands (composed of cortex and medulla)

Adrenaline (and Noradrenaline)	Produced by the medulla, these reinforce the effects of the sympathetic nervous system in response to fear, anger and excitement.
Cortisone	A steroid produced by the cortex, which helps fight stress and shock.
Aldosterone	From cortex; helps regulation of salt and water balance in the blood.

Pancreas

Insulin	Regulates body's use of glucose.

Ovaries (female reproductive glands)

Oestrogen	Controls development of secondary sexual characteristics, stops growth of long bones, and stimulates preparation of lining of womb at ovulation.
Progesterone	Prepares womb for pregnancy.* *During pregnancy the placenta produces hormones for the development of the foetus and the adaptation of the mother's body for pregnancy.

Testes (male reproductive glands)

Testosterone	Controls development of secondary sexual characteristics.

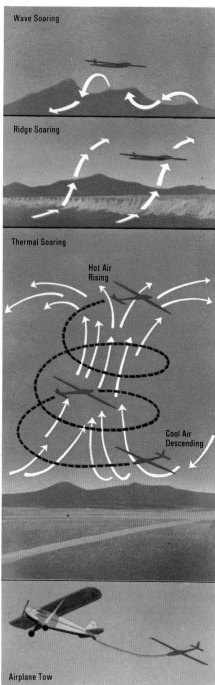

Wave Soaring

Ridge Soaring

Thermal Soaring

Hot Air Rising

Cool Air Descending

Airplane Tow

▲ *A glider stays airborne by riding on rising currents of air. Currents are formed in various ways. A range of hills can shoot air upward in a wave-like pattern ('wave soaring'); winds blowing against a cliff give a similar effect ('ridge-soaring'). Warm air rises, allowing 'thermal soaring'. The bottom picture shows a way of launching a glider — it is towed aloft by a light aircraft. A glider uses the height it gains from one air current to reach another one.*

rising off hills. Flights of over 70 hours have been made. The gliding altitude record is 14,102 metres (46,267 ft), and the distance record 1460 km (907 miles).

GLOBE A MAP of the world on the surface of a sphere – usually made by printing the map on segments of paper and then pasting them onto a solid base. It avoids the distortions of a flat map. The oldest known globe was made in about 1492; the biggest – 39 metres (128 ft) across – in France in 1824.

GLUCOSE Simple SUGAR found in many plants, fruits and HONEY. Glucose (or dextrose) is also produced from other sugars and starches during DIGESTION and is then absorbed into the blood and taken to the tissues.

GLYCERIN A colourless, odourless, liquid alcohol, used in the making of perfume, cosmetics, EXPLOSIVES, antifreeze mixtures, and in medicine. It is a by-product of SOAP-making.   ▷

GNAT General name for any small, thin two-winged insect with long delicate legs such as the MOSQUITO.

GNU Large African ANTELOPE. Antelopes are generally graceful, but the gnu, or wildebeest, with its thick neck, long face, small eyes and heavy horns, often appears ugly and awkward.   ▷

GOAT Mountain animal related to the SHEEP; its beard and strong smell distinguish the male goat from a sheep. Wild goats, found

▼ *A herd of gnus (or wildebeeste) in Kenya. The dry season forces huge herds to trek in search of grass and water. Gnus mate when they are migrating.*

GLYCERIN Glycerin was discovered by the Swedish chemist Carl Wilhelm Scheele (1742-1786). Scheele also found chlorine, oxygen (independently of Priestley), tartaric acid and many more elements and compounds. No other chemist has discovered so many new substances.

GNU Gnus are among the most abundant of East Africa's big mammals. Elephants roam in herds of over 100; buffalo herds range up to 600; but gnus and zebras form mixed herds 10,000 strong.

GOAT The domestic goat carries her unborn young for 21 to 22 weeks. One to three kids are born at a time, and they can follow after their mother a few hours after birth. The goat matures at six months and may live to an age of about 15 years.

The main wool-producing goats are the Angora and the Cashmere. The Angora goat of Asia Minor has spiral horns and long, white silky hair. Mohair cloth is made from this hair. India and Tibet are the homes of the Cashmere goat. Its soft, silky undercoat is used to make fine Cashmere cloth.

GOLD The largest gold-bearing nugget ever found was the Holtermann Nugget. It weighed 286 kg (630 lb) and came from New South Wales, Australia. The purest big nugget came from Victoria, Australia. Called the Welcome Stranger, it weighed about 73 kg (160 lb), of which 98.7 per cent was pure gold.

The biggest solid gold object in existence is the coffin of the Egyptian boy pharaoh, Tutankhamen. It weighs about 1110 kg (2450 lb).

Gold does not deteriorate with time because it does not tarnish. There are very few corrosives that have any effect on it, and it is not affected by water or air.

Thirty grams (1 oz) of gold can be drawn out to make a fine wire nearly 60 km (37 miles) long.

in the Middle East and central Asia, are agile, sure-footed creatures; they live in herds and eat grass and leaves. Domestic goats are descended from a Persian species. Goats provide milk, cheese, and leather (young kids). Some also provide excellent wool.

GOETHE, JOHANN WOLFGANG VON A great German writer (1749–1832). He was novelist, poet and playwright, as well as artist, statesman and scientist. His masterpiece was *Faust*: the story of a man who sells his soul to the Devil. His work began the Romantic movement.

GOLD Traditionally, the most precious metal – yellow and very heavy. The main mines today are in South Africa. Its pureness when processed is measured in CARATS – pure gold is 24 carat, but more often another metal has been added for strengthening. ◁

GOLDEN FLEECE The Greek legend of a sheep with golden wool, guarded by a dragon. Jason won the fleece by 'sowing' the dragon's teeth, and fighting the crop of men that sprang up.

GOLDENROD Flowering plant with a thin rod-like stem topped by a cluster of bright yellow flowers. It is very common in North America.

GOLDFISH Popular ornamental fish descended from a type of carp found in China. In the wild, goldfishes are a dull brown but most cultivated species are bright reddish-gold.

▶ *Panning for gold. Gravel from a stream bed is mixed with water, and light material is washed out, leaving any grains of gold in the pan.*

GOLD RUSH In the 1800s, discovery of GOLD often brought a flood of prospectors into undeveloped territory; towns sometimes sprang up overnight. The gold rush of California (1849) and the Yukon (1897) were the most famous.

GOLD STANDARD The system where a country guarantees to buy and sell GOLD at a fixed price, and its banknotes can be exchanged for gold coin. It was the basis of international trade in the 19th century, as the US dollar is today.

GOLF In golf, each player has his own ball, and set of clubs. He aims to get the ball into a series of holes, hitting it as few times as possible. A full game is 18 holes.

GOOSE Large web-footed bird related to DUCKS and SWANS. Geese usually live in flocks and spend much of their time on land, feeding off grass and other plants. There are two main groups: grey geese and black geese, both found in cold northern zones. The domestic goose comes from a grey species, the Grey Lag.

GOPHER Burrowing rodent (gnawing animal) of North America. One of the best-known kinds is the Pocket Gopher, 20 cm (8 in) long, named after its large cheek pouches used for carrying food to its underground home.

GORILLA Huge, heavily-built APE found in the forests of equatorial Africa. Gorillas, up to 180 cm (6 ft) tall, walk on all fours; they live in family groups and spend most of their time on the ground looking for food such as roots, leaves and fruit. At night, they sleep in nests, built of branches or undergrowth. In spite of their massive size, gorillas are peaceful and will only attack if provoked.

GOTH A Germanic people, probably from southern Sweden, who invaded the Roman Empire after AD 200. Pushed west by the HUNS, one branch (Visigoths) sacked Rome in AD 410, and finally set up a kingdom in Spain which lasted until the Arab conquest of AD 711. The others (Ostrogoths) reached Italy later, and were absorbed into the existing population.

GOTHIC ART AND ARCHITECTURE Gothic ARCHITECTURE was the main church style in Western Europe throughout the later MIDDLE AGES. It started in Normandy and Burgundy, and its typical features were tall pillars and spires, pointed arches, flying buttresses and rib vaulting. Chartres cathedral is a famous example. In England the style lasted from 1200–1575, but there was also a 'Gothic Revival' in the 19th century, when it was used for many public buildings, such as the House of Commons. Gothic ART was mainly concerned with the decoration of the Gothic churches, with stone carvings, tapestries, wall paintings and decorative iron.   ▷

GOUT Disease characterized by a painful swelling of the joints, which occurs when the body fails to break down certain PROTEINS. There is no cure, but gout can be controlled with drug treatment.

GOVERNMENT The body that directs the affairs of a group of people. It may be one man (e.g. a tribal leader) or a complex organization governing a whole nation (see CABINET; PARLIAMENT). A government sets down laws, and can use force to back up its authority. Governments may be weak or strong, active or inactive, dictatorial or democratic. (See DEMOCRACY; FASCISM; COMMUNISM)

GRAMMAR The rules by which a LANGUAGE works. They decide which words do which jobs (NOUNS, VERBS, ADJECTIVES, ADVERBS, etc); how to modify their meaning (man, men; go, gone); and how to put them together to say what you want (Dog bites man or Man bites dog).

GRAND CANYON A deep chasm in northwestern Arizona, in the USA. It is between 3 and 29 km (2–18 miles) wide and up to 1680

▲ *Part of the immense layered and eroded landscape of the Grand Canyon in northwestern Arizona. The canyon walls reveal different strata of rock, each marking a stage in the Earth's history.*

metres (5512 ft) deep. This superb canyon was carved out by the Colorado River.   ▷

GRAND NATIONAL The most famous STEEPLECHASE in the world, held at Aintree (near Liverpool, England) since 1839. It is run over 7 km 220 metres (4 miles 856 yards) with 30 jumps.

GRANITE Rock formed by the cooling and crystallizing of MINERALS which have been melted by the heat deep down in the Earth. Granite is mostly made up of FELDSPAR, QUARTZ, and MICA. It is used for buildings and monuments.

GRAPE Pale green or purplish-black berry growing in bunches on a VINE. Most grapes are used to make wine but some are cultivated as dessert fruit and some are dried and turned into currants, RAISINS and sultanas. Grapes mostly grow in warm temperate lands such as the Mediterranean zone, California, South Africa and Australia.

GRAPEFRUIT Large yellow citrus fruit, so named because it grows in grape-like bunches. Its acid juicy flesh, rich in Vitamin C, is often eaten for breakfast.

GRAPHITE A form of CARBON, graphite is one of the softest of all minerals. It has a flaky

GOTHIC ARCHITECTURE Examples of Gothic buildings in Europe include Milan Cathedral and the Doge's Palace, Venice (Italy); Burgos Cathedral (Spain); Wells, Westminster and Salisbury cathedrals (England); and Notre Dame de Paris (France).

GRAND CANYON American Indians have lived in and around the Grand Canyon since 1200 AD. One small tribe, the Havasupai, live today in a village at the bottom of the canyon.

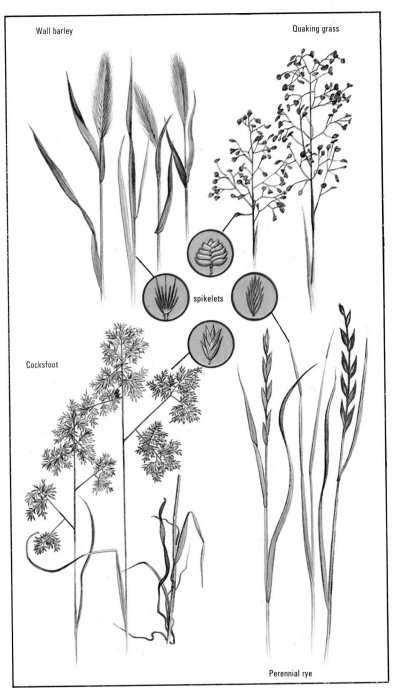

Wall barley

Quaking grass

spikelets

Cocksfoot

Perennial rye

◄ *Common grasses include wall barley found in waste lands; the delicate quaking grass found especially on roadside verges; cocksfoot grass found in dense clumps in rough grassland; and rye grass sown for pasture and lawns.*

all CEREALS such as WHEAT, RICE and OATS are cultivated grasses.

GRASSHOPPER Jumping insect related to the CRICKET. Grasshoppers live among grass and flowers near the ground and feed entirely on plants. Although most species can fly, they usually move by jumping and their hind legs are long and powerful. Many grasshoppers have a distinctive song, made by rubbing their back legs against their wings.

GRAVITY Gravity is the force which pulls everything towards the centre of the Earth. But the force of gravitation also applies to everything in the universe. NEWTON's law of gravitation says that any two objects are pulled towards each other with a force that is directly proportional to the product of their masses and inversely proportional to the square of the distance between them. In other words, the bigger their masses and the closer they are, the more strongly they are pulled together. This is why the Earth pulls us and everything on it with a strong force. To escape from this pull we need to build up a very high speed with powerful rockets – about 40,000 kph (25,000 mph). But spacecraft can be sent into orbit around the Earth at speeds less than this. The speed necessary to keep the craft in orbit depends on the height of the orbit. The higher the orbit, the less the craft is influenced by gravity, and therefore the lower the speed needed to counter gravity. In the

▼ *The force of gravity that the Moon exerts on any object is less than that exerted by the Earth, which has a greater mass than the Moon. Any object therefore weighs less on the Moon than on Earth.*

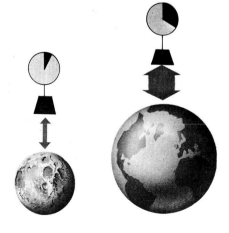

structure which makes it valuable as a LUB-RICANT. Graphite is chemically the same as diamond, the hardest of all minerals. It is used as the 'lead' in pencils.

GRASS Common flowering plant found all over the world. Grasses have long narrow leaves and dull flowers with no petals, bright colour or scent; their stems are nearly always soft and hollow. There are about 5000 species of grass. Some are vital to man: for example,

same way, the Moon is held in its orbit around the Earth by gravity. And it is gravitation that keeps the planets in their orbits around the Sun. (See ACCELERATION; FORCE; INERTIA; SATELLITE)

GREAT BARRIER REEF The world's largest CORAL reef, off the north-eastern coast of Australia. It consists of many small islands and underwater reefs. It is about 2000 km (1243 miles) long and, at its widest point, it is about 70 km (43 miles). It is a popular tourist region. ▷

GREAT BRITAIN The largest island in the BRITISH ISLES, Great Britain comprises the mainlands of ENGLAND, SCOTLAND and WALES, together with their offshore islands. The term, Great Britain, does not, however, usually include the Channel Islands and the Isle of Man, because these islands have their own governments.

Great Britain (or simply Britain) is also sometimes used as the name for the larger United Kingdom of Great Britain and

▲ *A typical English scene. Worcester cathedral, which has been much restored over the years but dates from the 11th century, overlooks a cricket field, where the country's favourite summer sport is in progress.*

▼ *How the Great Barrier Reef could have been formed. A platform of land off the Queensland coast slowly sank downwards along a fault. As the land sank, coral gradually built up to form islands and reefs.*

GREAT BARRIER REEF This great reef includes about 700 islands and is one of the largest wildlife sanctuaries in the world. It is estimated to be some 15,000 years old and is over 150 m (500 ft) thick at its deepest point. There are over 300 species of coral in the reef.

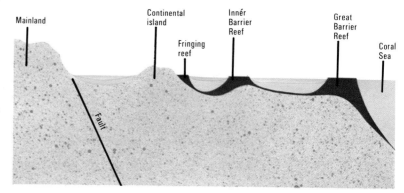

GREAT LAKES The Great Lakes are the remains of much larger lakes formed when a vast ice sheet melted as the last Ice Age ended. West of the Great Lakes once lay Lake Agassiz, three times the size of Lake Superior, largest of today's Great Lakes and the largest freshwater lake on Earth.

GREAT SALT LAKE This lake is too salty for fish. But some tiny animals can survive the brine. They include a brine shrimp. Brine shrimps' eggs laid in water that dries up can survive for years. They hatch when rainwater once more fills their pools.

GREECE (ANCIENT) An ancient Greek school had 60 to 100 pupils – all boys. They probably started early in the morning, about 7 am. From the age of about 6, a boy would be led off to school by a family slave. He learned to read and write, to play on the double flute (aulos) and on the lyre. A great deal of his schooling was sports training. The sons of wealthy parents went on after their ordinary schooling to attend the lectures of travelling teachers, called sophists (from the Greek word sophia, meaning 'wisdom').

Slavery had existed in Greece since the remote past, and was too long-established and too useful for the Greeks ever seriously to question it. Slaves worked in the house, in workshops and in the mines. They taught small children to read and write. Slaves had no political rights; they could not vote or hold any office. But they did not have to do military service, and, in Athens at least, were protected by law against ill-treatment. Above all, the Greeks thought of slavery as a way of leaving the citizen time to do the really important things in life – to serve in the Assembly, or on any of the committees by which his city was governed.

Northern Ireland. In this case, the Channel Islands and the Isle of Man are included. The United Kingdom had an estimated population of 56,582,000 in 1984, and an area of 244,046 sq km (94,227 sq miles). The capital of the United Kingdom is LONDON, but regional capitals include Belfast (Northern Ireland), Cardiff (Wales) and EDINBURGH (Scotland). (See EUROPE)

GREAT DANE Large strong dog of German origin, despite its name. It is quiet and good-tempered but can be very fierce and so makes a good guard dog.

GREAT DIVIDING RANGE A mountain range extending throughout eastern Australia. The mountains of TASMANIA are also part of the range. The highest peak is Mount Kosciusko at 2230 metres (7316 ft).

GREAT LAKES A group of interconnected freshwater lakes around the Canada–USA border. The lakes, in order of size, are Superior, Michigan, Huron, Erie and Ontario. The combined area is about 245,300 sq km (94,710 sq miles). The lakes are linked to the Atlantic by the St Lawrence River. ◁

GREAT SALT LAKE A lake in northwest Utah, USA, covering about 3900 sq km (1500 sq miles). It has no outlet and incoming water is steadily evaporated, making the lake much saltier than the oceans. ◁

GREAT WALL OF CHINA A fortified wall in north-central China. It was first built around 300 BC to defend China against invaders from the north-west. It is about 2400 km (1500 miles) long.

GRECO, EL The nickname of Domenico Theotokopoulos (1541–1614), a famous artist. Born on Crete, he worked mainly in Spain, and is best known for his religious paintings.

GREECE (ANCIENT) The birthplace of Western civilization – but never united under one ruler until it was conquered in its decline. The earliest Greek civilization was the MYCENAEAN, a tribal Bronze Age culture which had links with the MINOAN CIVILIZATION of Crete. It flourished from 1600 to 1200 BC, but was destroyed by waves of invaders. A 'dark

▼ The Great Wall of China. It was built under the Ch'in dynasty to keep out Mongolian and Turkish raiders. It consists of a brick-faced wall of earth and stone, with square watch towers.

▲ *A Greek colonizing expedition, about 500 BC. The site of a new city would have been chosen with defence in mind. Traders, already attracted by the presence of a new colony, have drawn up their ships on the beach.*

age' followed, lasting to about 800 BC. During this, many people from the mainland set up cities on the coast of Asia Minor, and on the mainland the great 'city states' emerged (ATHENS, SPARTA, Thebes). But the mountainous terrain prevented any movement towards national unity. Instead the Greeks took to the sea, and from about 750 BC became a great trading people, with an economy based on olives, grapes and imported grain. Colonies grew up at trading points throughout the MEDITERRANEAN and the Black Sea. Some of them became very rich and important.

All these Greek cities were linked by their common language, beliefs and traditions, but they often fought with one another. The earliest city states were ruled by kings. But in many of them the growth of wealth spread political power wider – first to rich land-owners and merchants, and then to the people as a whole. This DEMOCRACY was possible because of the small size of the 'states': everyone could meet in one place to debate public affairs.

Greek culture reached its peak after 600 BC, with a flourishing GREEK LITERATURE and the beginnings of European science and philosophy (see ARISTOTLE; SOCRATES; PLATO; EUCLID; ARCHIMEDES). The threat of Persian conquest was beaten off, after 500 BC, with famous victories at Marathon, Salamis and Platea. But quarrels between the city states led to Greek decline. In long struggles, the power of Athens was destroyed by Sparta, then

Sparta's by Thebes, until MACEDONIA (the country to the north) was able to extend her power over all Greece (under her Greek-speaking ruler Philip II and his son ALEXANDER THE GREAT). Finally, in 146 BC, Greece was annexed by ROME – although Greek culture survived and in fact dominated the later Roman Empire. ◁

GREECE A republic in south-eastern EUROPE, Greece attracts over two million visitors every year. Many go to the country to see the magnificent ruins of ancient Greece. They can also enjoy the hot dry summers and mild winters, while travelling on the mainland or around the many beautiful islands in the MEDITERRANEAN SEA. The largest island is CRETE.

Agriculture employs more than half of the working population. But two-thirds of the land is mountainous and many soils are thin and infertile. Processing farm products and manufacturing are now important in the cities and towns, including ATHENS, Piraeus and Salonika. Greece also obtains much revenue

GREECE: FACTS AND FIGURES
Area: 131,944 km (50,944 sq miles).
Population: 9,896,000 (1984 est.). Greece ranks fourteenth in size of population and twelfth in area among those nations lying entirely inside Europe.
Language: Greek.
Religion: Christianity.
Currency: Drachma.
Capital: Athens.
Highest point: Mt. Olympus, 2,917 m (9,570 ft) above sea-level.

164

GREEK LITERATURE A comedy by Aristophanes (448-330 BC) has the longest word in literature. It contains 170 Greek letters (182 in its English form). The word describes 17 ingredients making up a recipe.

GREENLAND Norsemen discovered Greenland about 1,000 years ago. But no one explored its inland ice-cap until the 1800s. The Norwegian Fridtjof Nansen led the six-man team that completed the first crossing of the island in 1888.

from its large merchant navy, which contains more than 3300 ships.

From 1453 to 1822, Greece was part of the Turkish Ottoman empire. After defeating Turkey in the Greek war of independence, Greece became a monarchy in 1830. Apart from two breaks (1924–35 and 1941–44), it remained a constitutional monarchy until 1973, when it became a republic. ◁

GREEK LANGUAGE Many of our scientific words (*cosmos*, *atom*, *biology*) are based on Greek. The language has actually passed through many forms: early dialects; classical Greek; Middle-Eastern Greek; and the two forms of modern Greek (literary and conversational). But so much has stayed unchanged that speakers a thousand years apart might still understand each other.

GREEK LITERATURE The oldest literature of Western Europe – beginning with HOMER and reaching a peak in the 5th century BC, with the poet Pindar; the dramatists

▼ *The Acropolis of Athens, crowned by the Parthenon. It was built during the 4th century BC, a magnificent complex of temples and statues.*

AESCHYLUS, Sophocles, Euripides and Aristophanes and the historians Herodotus and Thucydides. In fact, Greek writers established almost all the types of LITERATURE still known today. ◁

GREENHOUSE Glass building in which plants can be grown throughout the year. The glass keeps out the cold and wet but allows light – vital for PHOTOSYNTHESIS – to pass through.

GREENLAND The world's largest island. Greenland, in the North Atlantic Ocean, covers 2,175,600 sq km (840,000 sq miles). Administratively, Greenland was a county of Denmark. It was given home rule in 1979. It has 53,000 people (1984 est.). About 85 per cent of Greenland is buried by a vast ice sheet. ◁

GREYHOUND Fast-running dog with a slender body and long powerful legs. Greyhounds are used for hunting hares and for racing – in a greyhound race, the dogs chase a mechanical hare round an oval track.

GRIEG, EDVARD A major Norwegian composer (1843–1907), often inspired by

country songs and dances. He won fame in 1876 with his music for the play *Peer Gynt*.

GRIFFIN In ancient MYTHOLOGY, the griffin was a strange winged creature with an eagle's head and a lion's body. It is a common symbol in HERALDRY.

GRIMM, BROTHERS Jacob (1785–1863) and Wilhelm (1786–1859), German specialists in language and folklore, world famous for their collection of old fairy stories for children.

GROUSE Large game bird from the northern hemisphere. Grouse usually nest on the ground and feed off buds, seeds and insects. There are about thirty species, mostly grey, brown or black in colour.

GUATEMALA A republic in CENTRAL AMERICA, Guatemala has 7,740,000 people (1984 est.), and an area of 108,889 sq km (42,042 sq miles). The capital is Guatemala City. This tropical country produces coffee. The people are mostly Indians or they are of mixed Indian and Spanish descent. ▷

GUIDED MISSILE A rocket- or jet-propelled missile with an explosive warhead. A guided missile is controlled in flight by radio or automatic guidance system. These missiles were developed by the Germans during World War II (the V-1 and V-2). Since then, advances in electronics have increased accuracy of missiles such as American *Polaris* and *Minuteman* which can home in on targets over thousands of miles.

GUILLOTINE An instrument for beheading people, named after a Dr Guillotin. His design was first used in the FRENCH REVOLUTION, and is still the official form of execution in France and some other countries.

GUINEA A developing republic in West Africa. Formerly a French colony, it gained independence in 1958. Its chief resource is bauxite, but most people work on the land. ▷

GUINEA PIG Small tailless animal belonging to a family of South American rodents called cavies. Guinea pigs were first domesticated by the INCAS who bred them for food. Today, they are widely kept as pets. They are friendly creatures and feed off grass and roots.

GUITAR A musical instrument. The traditional Spanish guitar has a hollow wooden

▲ A male black grouse raises a patch of startling white feathers to attract a female. In the mating season, the males gather at special courting grounds called leks.

body and strings of gut, the modern electric version a solid body and metal strings.

GULL Seabird with long wings, web feet, mainly white plumage and a harsh cry. Gulls, found over much of the world, are strong swimmers and fliers. They feed off fish and floating refuse and usually nest in colonies on cliff ledges or the ground.

GUM Sticky substance made from the sap of certain trees such as cherry, acacia and eucalyptus. Gums harden when dry but are soluble in water. They are used in dyeing, medicine and ink-making.

GUN Any weapon that fires a BULLET or explosive shell. Smallarms include PISTOLS, RIFLES and shotguns, and date back to the matchlocks of the 14th century. Next in size are machine guns – still portable but not handheld – firing up to 1600 rounds per minute. Largest are artillery (or cannon). The first guns were probably cannons used by the

► The Gatling gun, invented during the American Civil War. It had six to ten barrels that fired in succession; they were turned by a hand crank.

GUATEMALA: FACTS AND FIGURES
Official language: Spanish, but several Indian dialects spoken.
Religion: Christianity.
Currency: Quetzal.
Highest point: Tajumulco, 4,210 m (13,812 ft), the highest peak in Central America.
The national emblem is the beautiful quetzal bird.

GUINEA: FACTS AND FIGURES
Area: 245,857 sq km (95,000 sq miles).
Population: 5,931,000 (1984 est.).
Official language: French.
Religions: Animism, Islam.
Currency: Syli.
Capital: Conakry.

GUTENBERG Gutenberg's printing press in Mainz was a simple wooden frame made from a wine press. The metal type letters were fixed in the base of the press, then these were inked with a special sticky ink. A sheet of paper was pressed down on the inked type and became a printed sheet. Gutenberg could print about 300 sheets a day.

In 1978, Texas University paid over two million dollars for a copy of Gutenberg's Bible, a world record for any printed book.

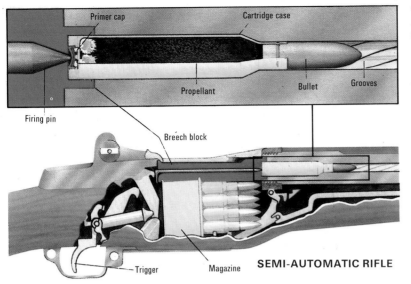

Primer cap
Cartridge case
Firing pin
Propellant
Bullet
Grooves
Breech block
Trigger
Magazine
SEMI-AUTOMATIC RIFLE

GUYANA A republic in north-eastern SOUTH AMERICA, Guyana has 936,000 people (1984 est.), and an area of 214,969 sq km (83,000 sq miles). The capital is Georgetown. Sugar cane, diamonds, gold and bauxite are the chief products. Forests cover large areas, with grass on the highest mountains. ◁

GYMNASTICS Physical exercise with gymnasium equipment. First practiced in ancient Greece, it is now also an OLYMPIC sport and emphasizes grace as well as strength. Equipment used includes the pommel horse, rings, parallel bars, and balance beam. ◁

GYPSIES A nomadic people, perhaps from the BYZANTINE EMPIRE. They entered Europe in the 14th century, and became linked with music and fortune-telling. True gypsies have their own language, 'Romany'.

GYROSCOPE A rapidly spinning wheel set in a frame which only touches another surface at one point. When the wheel is spun, its support may be turned in any direction without altering the wheel's original plane of motion. A spinning gyroscope will balance on the tip of a pencil without toppling, until the wheel begins to slow down. Then it will begin to wobble like a dying top. The gyro-compass and other navigational aids are based on the gyroscope.

GUYANA: FACTS AND FIGURES
Official language: English. Guyana is the only English-speaking country on the South American mainland.
Religions: Christianity, Hinduism, Islam.
Currency: Guyana dollar.

▲ *How a rifle works: pulling the trigger releases a spring which makes a firing pin strike the base of a cartridge. (The cartridge contains both explosive or propellant and a bullet.) The firing pin sets off the explosive and the gas produced by the explosion makes the bullet fly out of the rifle. Grooves inside the barrel make the bullet spin in flight. A chamber of cartridges is called a magazine.*

GYMNASTICS Apparatus: The *vaulting horse* is 1.6 m (5.25 ft) long, 35 to 37 cm (14 to 14½ inches) wide, and 1.35 m (4.4 ft) high. A springboard is used for take-off. The *pommel horse* is of the same dimensions as the vaulting horse, but it has two wooden handles (pommels) 40 to 45 cm (16 to 18 inches) apart. The height to the top of the pommels is 1.22 m (4 ft). The *horizontal bar* is 2.8 cm (1 inch) in diameter and 2.4 m (9.5 ft) long. It is 2.5 m (8.2 ft) from the ground. The *parallel bars* are wooden rails about shoulder-width apart, 3.5 m (11.5 ft) long and usually 1.6 m (5.25 ft) from the ground. The *rings* hang from ropes 2.4 m (8 ft) above the ground. The *balance beam* is a wooden beam 5 m (16.5 ft) long and 10 cm (4 inches) wide. The *asymmetrical bars* are two parallel bars. One is 2.3 m (7.5 ft) and the other 1.5 m (4.9 ft) from the ground. The space between the bars can be varied. Women carry out floor exercises to music.

Arabs around 1250. The first completely mass-produced handgun was the American Colt revolver. It was first used by American troops against the Indians. It was also the cowboy's favourite weapon. A gun's *calibre* is the measurement of the barrel diameter. (See FIREARMS).

GUNPOWDER An EXPLOSIVE made from saltpetre, sulphur and carbon. It is believed to have been invented in China about the 9th century, and did not reach Europe until the 14th century. Gunpowder revolutionized warfare but is now seldom used except in fireworks.

GUTENBERG, JOHANN A German printer (c. 1400–1468). He invented movable type, in which the letters of the alphabet are stamped on many separate little pieces of metal. The bits of type are put together to make words, and can be reused many times. (See BOOKS; PRINTING) ◁

▶ *Exercising on the horizontal bar. Gymnastics were highly developed in ancient Greece and Rome, and interest in the sport has revived during the last century. More recently, displays by such champions as Olga Korbut have increased its popularity.*

HADRIAN Roman emperor (born AD 76, ruled AD 117–138). He halted Roman expansion and concentrated on making government, law and communication more efficient. In Britain he is remembered for 'Hadrian's Wall'.

HAEMOPHILIA Disease in which the BLOOD does not clot normally; consequently, even small cuts can cause severe bleeding. Haemophilia is usually HEREDITARY and mostly attacks men; women seldom suffer from it.

HAIR Thread-like substance growing out of the skin of MAMMALS which provides warmth and protection. Hair can be short or long, thick or thin, straight or curly; some kinds of hair have special names such as fur and fleece. Many articles are made of hair ranging from paint brushes to carpets.

HAKA A MAORI ceremonial dance, which may include songs or chants. It is different from a war dance, as no weapons are held.

HALIBUT Large flatfish found in the North Atlantic and North Pacific. The halibut, up to 1.8 metres (6 ft) long, has its two eyes on the right side of the head. Halibut is an important food fish; also, the oil from its liver is rich in Vitamin D.

HAND The part of the body with which most primates (human beings and monkeys) touch and grasp. The hand, located at the end of the arm, consists of the wrist, palm and fingers. The fingers are moved by muscles in the forearm. Like the sole of the foot, the palm is protected by very thick skin.

HANDEL, GEORGE FRIDERIC A German-born composer (1685–1759), who settled in London and became a British subject. He is famous for the *Water Music* (1715) and for his oratorio the *Messiah* (1742). ▷

HANDICAPPED Having a physical or mental disability, such as BLINDNESS, weak-mindedness or deformity. On a world average, perhaps one person in seven has a handicap – but some have risen to fame despite disability.

HANNIBAL A great general (247–182 BC) of CARTHAGE in her struggle against Rome. He crossed the Alps and invaded Italy, beating the Romans at Cannae (216 BC), but later was defeated, exiled, and driven to suicide. ▷

HAPSBURGS A European royal family, rulers of Austria and often emperors of the HOLY ROMAN EMPIRE. With Charles V of Spain (1500–1558), their rule also covered Spain and

▶ *Rudolf of Hapsburg receives news of his election as German king in 1273. Though he ruled as Holy Roman Emperor, he was never actually crowned as such.*

168

HANDEL, GEORGE FREDERICK Handel could play the violin, oboe, organ, and harpsichord before he could talk. By the age of five he was already famous. At 11 he had written six sonatas for one bassoon and two oboes. At 16 he was writing operas.

HANNIBAL One record says that Hannibal had 50 elephants when he set off to attack Italy. Half way across France he had lost 13. He lost another 29 crossing the Alps. Seven of the eight survivors died, and only one survived Hannibal's 15-year campaign in Italy.

HARP In the late 1920s a British archaeologist in Iraq dug down into royal graves 4,500 years old. His finds included two mysterious holes in the ground. He poured liquid plaster in the holes, let it set, and then removed the soil. His plaster cast revealed the shape of one of the oldest known harps. Its wooden frame had rotted, but its fine gold fittings still survived.

HAWAII Geologists think that the Hawaiian islands formed when a part of the Earth's crust drifted over a hot spot underneath. Every million years or so molten rock burst upward from this spot and made a new volcanic island. The result is a row of islands. The youngest and highest lie at one end, and the oldest and lowest at the other end.

▶ *The brown hare, found on grasslands over most of the world. Because they live in the open, baby hares are furred and active, unlike baby rabbits, which are naked and blind.*

its empire, the Netherlands and Burgundy. The Hapsburgs held thrones almost continuously from 1273 to 1918.

HARBOUR A coastal stretch of water which provides shelter for sea-going vessels. Some are natural indentations in the coast, others, such as the Dutch harbour at ROTTERDAM, have been specially built.

HARE Large rabbit-like animal with long ears and long back legs. It is noted for its acute hearing and fast running. Hares, unlike RABBITS, live above ground in nests called *forms*. They are found in all parts of the world except Antarctica.

HARP A musical instrument, consisting of a triangular frame with 46 strings. Each string sounds only one note (although pedals in the base are now used to alter the PITCH).   ◁

HARPSICHORD A keyboard musical instrument. It is similar to a small grand piano, but its strings are plucked and not struck. It often has two keyboards. It was popular up to the 18th century, then gave way to the paino. It is now used again.

HARVEY, WILLIAM English physician (1578–1657), Royal Physician to both JAMES I and CHARLES I, and famous for his discovery of the circulation of the BLOOD and of the role of the heart as a pump.

HASTINGS, BATTLE OF One of the most famous of all battles (1066). It saw the defeat of Harold by WILLIAM THE CONQUEROR, and

the introduction of NORMAN rule to Saxon England. Battle Abbey marks the site.

HAWAII A group of tropical islands in the Pacific Ocean. Hawaii covers 16,705 sq km (6450 sq miles) and has 1,054,000 people (1985 est.). The capital is Honolulu. Hawaii became the 50th state of the USA in 1959.   ◁

HAWK Bird of prey with broad wings and a long tail. The best-known hawks are the small bluish-grey Sparrowhawk and the larger grey-brown Goshawk. Both are active by day when they hunt birds and small animals; they usually nest in trees.

HAYDN, FRANZ JOSEPH Austrian composer (1732–1809). He wrote over 100 symphonies – some of the best during visits to England. His music established many new patterns that later composers were to develop.

HAY FEVER ALLERGY which occurs in summer when plants are producing a lot of POLLEN. People who suffer from hay fever react to the pollen in the air by developing symptoms such as a running nose, sore mouth, watery eyes and blocked ears.

HEADACHE Continuous pain in the head. Many headaches last for only hours, but some last for days. They can be symptoms of physical illness like 'flu or malaria, or they can be caused by factors such as eyestrain, great heat or mental stress.

◀ *The Battle of Hastings, shown in this scene from the Bayeux tapestry. The soldier (far right) pulling an arrow from his eye, was long believed to be Harold. However, French history states that Harold was cut down by French horsemen. After his death his troops were soon beaten by William.*

Hea

▶ *The heart pumps blood continuously round the body. The human heart beats about 70 times a minute. It is able to do this throughout the 70 or 80 years of a person's life because the muscle is especially strong.*

HEARING AID Device worn by a deaf person to improve his hearing. The aid is like a tiny telephone with a microphone, amplifier and receiver. The receiver either fits into the ear or behind it.

HEART Hollow muscular organ which pumps BLOOD around the body. All but the simplest animals have some sort of heart. In most cases, this consists of a muscular bag divided into two or more chambers. Mammals, including man, have a four-chambered heart: two upper chambers, or *auricles*, and two lower chambers, or *ventricles*. Pure blood, carrying oxygen, is sent from the left ventricle to the various parts of the body and comes back, carrying CARBON DIOXIDE, to the right auricle. From the right auricle, the blood is driven into the right ventricle, and from there to the LUNGS where it gives up carbon dioxide and collects fresh oxygen. The pure blood returns to the left auricle then into the left ventricle, ready for another journey round the body. The tubes taking blood away from the heart are called ARTERIES and those bringing it back are called VEINS.   ▷

HEAT Heat is a form of ENERGY. It comes from the movement of ATOMS which are always in motion, constantly bumping into each other. But when a body has plenty of heat energy, the bumping movements of its atoms are fiercer and the body gets warm. The study of how heat works is called *thermodynamics*. Heat travels in three ways: by conduction through solids; mostly by *convection* in liquids and gases, where the hotter parts rise above the cooler parts and cause currents; and by *radiation* through space – the heat from a fire reaches us as waves which travel at the same speed as light. The SI UNIT in heat is the JOULE. (See CONDUCTION (HEAT); TEMPERATURE; THERMOMETER)

HEBREW LANGUAGE The language of the JEWS, both in Old Testament and modern times. It uses an alphabet of 22 consonants, with added marks for vowels. Spoken since 2000 BC, it is one of the oldest of living languages.

HELEN OF TROY In Greek MYTHOLOGY, the child of ZEUS and a human girl, Leda. Married to a Greek king, she ran away with Paris, prince of TROY, so starting the Trojan War.

HELICOPTER An AIRCRAFT with a horizontal *rotor*, which acts as both PROPELLER

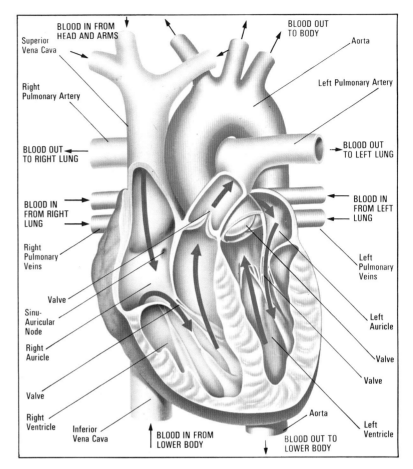

BLOOD IN FROM HEAD AND ARMS
Superior Vena Cava
BLOOD OUT TO BODY
Aorta
Right Pulmonary Artery
Left Pulmonary Artery
BLOOD OUT TO RIGHT LUNG
BLOOD OUT TO LEFT LUNG
BLOOD IN FROM RIGHT LUNG
BLOOD IN FROM LEFT LUNG
Right Pulmonary Veins
Left Pulmonary Veins
Valve
Sinu-Auricular Node
Left Auricle
Right Auricle
Valve
Valve
Valve
Right Ventricle
Aorta
Inferior Vena Cava
BLOOD IN FROM LOWER BODY
BLOOD OUT TO LOWER BODY
Left Ventricle

▼ *A Westland helicopter landing on the flight deck of an aircraft carrier. Helicopters are used by navies for anti-submarine and rescue duties. An early kind of helicopter was the autogyro, developed in 1923, but the first really successful design was built in 1939 by Igor Sikorsky.*

HEART A human heart beats 2,500 million times in 70 years. It pumps more than 1600 gallons of blood in a day, and more than 40 million gallons in a lifetime. Its day's work is equivalent to lifting a 1.3-tonne car to the roof of a 5-floor building.

The human heart is surprisingly small, considering the amount of work is called upon to perform. Its average weight, in an adult, is 225 g (9 oz). It is about 125 mm (5 inches) long, 90 mm ($3\frac{1}{2}$ inches) wide at its broadest, and 63 mm ($2\frac{1}{2}$ inches) thick. The rate at which the heart beats is controlled by two pairs of nerves, one from the spinal cord which speeds up the heartbeat and one from the medulla in the brain which slows it down. These nerve centres receive messages from other parts of the body and pass them along to the heart. Exercise and excitement speeds up the heartbeat; fear slows it down.

HELICOPTER Hundreds of years ago the Chinese made toy helicopters from tops with feathered arms. The first man-carrying helicopters were French and flew in 1907.

HELIUM Helium's name comes from the Greek word *helios*, meaning 'sun'. It was given this name because scientists knew that helium existed in the Sun before any was discovered on Earth. It was discovered on Earth in 1895 by William Ramsey. Most of our helium comes from natural gas. When the gas is cooled to a low enough temperature, all gases turn to liquid except helium, which can then be recovered.

HERALDRY So-called marks of cadency show a son's place in his family. A 'file' or 'label' marks an eldest son; crescent – second son; mullet (five-pointed star) – third son; martlet (a bird) – fourth son; annulet (a ring) – fifth son; fleur-de-lis (lilly) – sixth son; rose – seventh son; cross moline – eighth son; octofoil (eight-petalled flower) – ninth son.

The heraldic colours are, *gules* (red), *azure* (blue), *pourpre* (purple), *vert* (green), and *sable* (black), with two metals, *argent* (white or silver), and *or* (yellow or gold). There are also certain furs, of which ermine is the best known.

The 'charge' is a figure or symbol on the coat of arms. The lion, for example, is a common charge; it can be *rampant* (standing on a hind leg), *couchant* (lying down with head raised), *passant* (walking), or *dormant* (asleep).

HOW A HELICOPTER FLIES

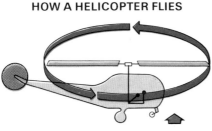

To fly upwards, all the helicopter's rotor blades are kept at the same angle or 'pitch'.

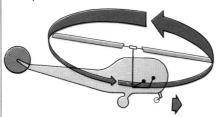

To fly forwards, the blades are tilted forwards and increase their pitch in moving towards the tail.

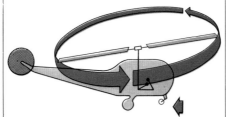

To fly backwards, the blades are tilted backwards and increase their pitch as they move towards the nose.

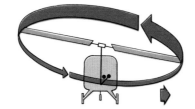

To move sideways, the blades are tilted in the direction the pilot wishes to travel.

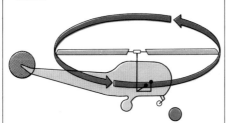

To hover, all the blades are kept at the same pitch. The helicopter's weight counters the rotor's upward pull.

and wings. This allows it to take off and land vertically; move forwards, backwards or sideways as the rotor is tilted; and even to hang stationary in the air. A small tail rotor prevents the body spinning (or there can be two main rotors, turning opposite ways). Uses for helicopters include passenger and troop transport, firefighting and life-saving. ◁

HELIUM The second most abundant chemical ELEMENT in the universe, but rare on Earth. It is a light gas with the chemical symbol He. Used to lift BALLOONS and AIRSHIPS it is preferred to hydrogen because it is non-flammable. It is also used in ROCKETS. ◁

HEMINGWAY, ERNEST American novelist (1898–1961), famous for his simple style and for his stories of tough outdoor life. He won the NOBEL PRIZE in 1954.

HENRY II King of England (born 1133, reigned 1154–1189). He restored order after the civil wars of Stephen and Matilda, and his marriage extended English claims in France. But his attack on the church law courts ended in the murder of Thomas à BECKET.

HENRY V King of England (born 1387, reigned 1413–1422). The son of Henry IV, he claimed the French throne, thus reopening the HUNDRED YEARS' WAR. He defeated the French at AGINCOURT (1415), conquered Normandy, and married Catherine of Valois.

HENRY VI King of England (born 1421, reigned 1422–1461, 1470–1471). A weak and sometimes insane ruler, his reign saw the loss of England's lands in France, a popular rising (1450), and the outbreak of the WARS OF THE ROSES. He was deposed 1465–1470, and finally imprisoned and murdered in 1471.

HENRY VIII King of England (born 1491, reigned 1509–1547), famous for his six marriages. To divorce his first wife, Catherine of Aragon, he broke with the ROMAN CATHOLIC CHURCH. This and his dissolution of the monasteries set England on the road to Protestantism. His reign also saw a great increase in the strength of the state and of the English navy.

HERALDRY The study of coats of arms, first used in medieval times to identify knights in battle (see KNIGHTHOOD). Later they were linked with families rather than knights alone. As well as a shield, designs often included a crest (helmet), motto, and even supporters (such as the lion and unicorn in the Royal Arms). Complex rules govern the designs, which in England are controlled by the Herald's College (founded 1484). Cities and even businesses now use coats of arms. ◁

HERB In BOTANY, a herb is a small plant with a fleshy (non-woody) stem; daisies and cabbages are both herbs. To most people, however, herbs are certain plants used for flavour in cooking. They include MINT, PARSLEY, rosemary, thyme and SAGE. Herbs are also used in medicine and in the perfume industry.

HEREDITY The passing on of physical characteristics from parents to offspring. It applies to all living things, and works through the CELLS that make them up. In the nucleus of each cell are thousands of tiny CHROMOSOMES, looking like chopped-up bits of string. On the chromosomes are the GENES, made of segments of an acid called DNA. The genes carry all the information that controls how the cells work. For example, one gene will decide what colour the cells in hair become: red, black, brown or blond. In fact, everyone inherits two genes for every characteristic – one from the father and one from the mother. But one gene will always be more powerful than the other one. This *dominant* gene decides the characteristic; the other gene is called *recessive*. This is why children can have, for example, hair that is a different colour to that of both their parents. They can inherit a gene that was recessive in their parents, but becomes dominant in them. (See MENDEL, GREGOR) ▷

HEROIN Drug made from MORPHINE. Although heroin is a powerful pain-killer, it is not used in medicine as it is too strong and dangerous. People obtain it illegally, however, and easily become addicted; heroin addiction often causes severe physical and psychological damage.

HERON Wading bird with very long legs, neck and bill (beak). There are over 60 species, found mostly in warm or hot regions. Herons

▼ *Many different herbs are used to improve the flavour of food. Some of the more common ones used in cooking are shown below.*

Sage
Mint
Thyme
Garlic
Parsley

BLUE EYES OR BROWN?

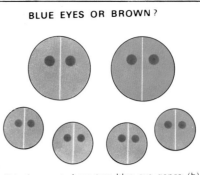

If both parents have two blue eye genes (b) each, all their children will have blue eyes.

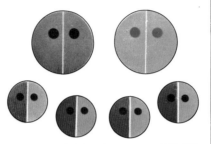

If one parent has two brown eye genes (B), and the other has two b genes, the children will all inherit one b and one B gene. But they will all have brown eyes because the B gene is dominant.

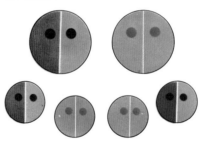

If one parent has a B gene and a recessive b gene, his own eyes will be brown. But if he marries a blue-eyed woman his children may have blue or brown eyes.

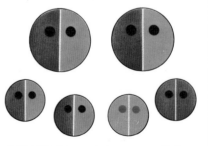

If the same man married a woman with brown eyes but with a recessive b gene, he might still have some blue-eyed children.

▲ *Heredity decides our physical characteristics, such as the colour of our eyes (as shown in this diagram), and hair. Heredity can even affect the length of our lifespan.*

HEREDITY Chance led the Austrian monk Gregor Mendel (1822-1884) to study plants and thus to learn the secrets of heredity. Mendel's father had a fruit farm, and the village school taught natural history. Mendel thus gained an early interest in plants. A quiet monastery life later gave him scope to carry out his now famous tests with garden peas.

Mendel discovered that if a man and woman carrying genes for both brown eyes and blue eyes have four children, three of the children will usually have brown eyes and one will have blue eyes. The gene for brown eyes is dominant over that for blue eyes. Similarly, dark hair is dominant over blond hair; curly hair over straight hair; prominent chin over ordinary chin; an easily tanned skin over a skin which does not tan easily; and unattached earlobes over attached earlobes.

Many defects and diseases are hereditary. They include baldness, cataracts of the eyes, diabetes mellitus, haemophilia, various allergies, and some types of mental deficiency and retardation.

HERON The heron belongs to the Ardeidae family, the most common species being the grey heron *Ardea cinerea*, the only species occurring commonly in Britain, and ranging from Madagascar to Northern Europe and western Asia. It is about 1 m (39 inches) long, with a grey back and white underparts. The wings are black-tipped and it has a crest of black feathers. The heron family also includes the bitterns and the egrets.

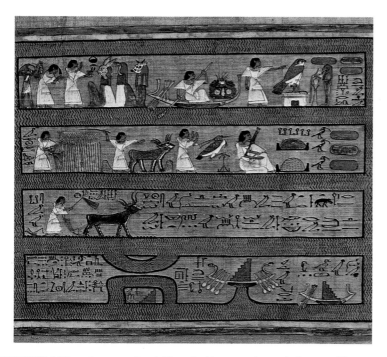

always live near water, feeding on fish and small animals. They nest at the top of tall trees. ◁

HERRING Important food fish from the North Atlantic and Pacific. Herrings – grey-green on top and silvery underneath – live near the sea's surface in huge shoals. Unlike most marine fish, whose eggs float on the surface, the herring lays its eggs on the seabed.

HIBERNATION Long deep winter sleep. Many small animals such as hedgehogs, SNAKES, SQUIRRELS, FROGS, SNAILS and earwigs, hibernate. At the start of winter they find a sheltered place – often underground – where they can sleep through the cold weather. Hibernating animals appear lifeless and their breathing rate and heartbeats are much slower than normal. During hibernation they do not feed but live off body fat stored during the summer. ◁

HICKORY Large North American tree belonging to the WALNUT family. Hickory wood is very hard and heavy and is used for tool handles and furniture. It also makes good charcoal. Some species have edible nuts.

HIEROGLYPHICS An early form of writing by pictures, especially that used in Egypt from 3500 BC to AD 200. The symbols all originally stood for objects or ideas, but later many were used for sounds, as in an ALPHABET. Egyptian hieroglyphics were written from right to left.

HIBERNATION A hibernating marmot may slow its breathing rate from 16 to 2 breaths per minute, and its heartbeats from 88 to 15 per minute. In a test, the temperature of a hibernating ground squirrel fell to almost freezing. The creature later woke up unharmed.

▲ *Hieroglyphics are a form of picture-writing. Those shown here are from an ancient Egyptian* Book of the Dead *(instructions to a dead person about the after-life).*

▼ *Many animals can only survive by hibernating throughout winter, when the weather is cold and food is scarce. Some are illustrated here (from top, left to right): newt, natterjack toad, adders, green toad, common toad, tortoise and woodchuck.*

▲ The Himalayas. A few people, such as the Sherpas of Nepal, are able to live in the mountains. The word 'himalaya' means 'home of the snows'.

HIGH JUMP An OLYMPIC event, using a bar suspended between two uprights. The bar starts at a set height, and is raised higher until no one can clear it. If a jumper fails at any height three times he must drop out.

HILLARY, EDMUND New Zealand mountaineer and explorer (born 1919). In 1953, with Sherpa Tensing, he was the first man to reach the summit of Mount EVEREST.

HIMALAYAS The loftiest mountain range in the world. The Himalayas extend around the edge of the Tibetan plateau. This vast range includes the world's highest peak, Mount EVEREST, and many other permanently snow-capped mountains, including Kanchenjunga, Lhotse and Makalu.

HINDUISM The religion and customs of the Hindus of INDIA. Hinduism had no single founder; it developed over many centuries, and is the world's oldest living religion. Its sacred books include the *Vedas* and the *Bhagavad-Gita*. Hindus believe in *reincarnation*: the rebirth of the soul in a succession of earthly lives, with our actions in past lives affecting our future fates. Popular Hinduism

▶ The hippopotamus is a very heavy animal, sometimes weighting as much as 4 tonnes. It is equally at home in the water or on land.

includes temples and festivals to countless gods (especially Vishnu the preserver and Shiva the destroyer). But to the educated these are all just aspects of one Supreme Spirit. Worship is mainly a family matter, within the framework of the CASTE system. Even weddings are held at home.

HIPPOCRATES A Greek physician (c. 460–c. 357 BC), often called the 'father of medicine' for his emphasis on scientific observation and reason. His Hippocratic Oath is still the basis of the oath taken by medical graduates.

HIPPOPOTAMUS Huge ugly animal found in the rivers and lakes of Africa. The hippopotamus has a thick hairless body, massive head and short, stout legs. It spends the day in water, where it can move fastest, but comes

HIPPOPOTAMUS The hippopotamus, *Hippopotamus amphibius*, is related to the pig. Adults measure 3 to 5 m (10 to 16 ft) in length, and about 1.5 m (5 ft) or more to the shoulder in height. They can weigh 4 tonnes. The skin on the body is about 40 mm ($1\frac{1}{2}$ inches) thick. The hippopotamus can remain under water for 8 to 10 minutes.

◄ A scene of destruction in Hirosnima after the atom bomb was dropped on the city. Thousands of people were killed at the time, and even today there are still many suffering the effects of radiation.

HIROSHIMA Below the explosion, stone and metal melted. Fires raged and the blast flattened everything within 3 km (2 miles) around. Within 5 km (3 miles), two in three of the city's 90,000 buildings were shattered. Blast, burns, or lethal rays killed anyone exposed within 2 km (1.2 miles) of the bomb.

out at night to look for grass and other plants to eat. In water, when the hippo submerges, it usually dives rear first. ◁

HIROSHIMA A Japanese city on Honshu island, Hiroshima was the target of the first ATOMIC BOMB, which was dropped on August 6, 1945, killing about 70,000 people. The population is now 898,000 (1984 est.). ◁

HISTORY The record of past human events. But because no one can know or tell everything, the historian must choose what seems to him important or significant. So in fact each age (and each nation) tends to have its own view of the past. Real historical writing began with the Greeks, Herodotus (c. 484–425 BC) and Thucydides (c. 471–401 BC). Modern historians use ARCHAEOLOGY, ECONOMICS and even PSYCHOLOGY, to understand the past.

HITLER, ADOLF German dictator (1889–1945). He was born in Austria, and spent his early life in poverty. In 1921 he set up the National Socialist German Workers' (Nazi) Party. In 1930 it began to attract support, enabling Hitler to become German Chancellor in 1932. He made Germany a one-party state with himself as *Fuehrer* (Leader); rebuilt her armed forces; annexed Austria and Czechoslovakia; and invaded Poland, so starting WORLD WAR II. He committed suicide in April 1945.

HOBART The capital of TASMANIA, Australia, Hobart has a population of 174,000 (1984 est.). It was founded in 1804 and was built on the estuary of the River Derwent. The city has various thriving industries.

HOCKEY Game played with wooden sticks and a ball, between two teams of eleven players. Developed in England, it became an Olympic event in 1908.

HOLLY Hardy evergreen tree with tough glossy leaves and bright red berries. In many countries, holly is a traditional Christmas decoration. Its hard white wood is used for carving and cabinet-making.

HOLLYWOOD A suburb of Los Angeles, in the United States, and centre of the film industry since 1911 (see CINEMA). It is now also the source of most US television entertainment.

HOLMES, SHERLOCK A fictional detective, famous for his amazing powers of observation and deduction. He was the creation of Sir Arthur Conan Doyle, and first appeared in the novel *A Study in Scarlet* in 1887.

HOLOGRAPHY A way of producing 3-dimensional images. Light from a LASER is split into two beams. One beam falls directly onto a glass photographic plate. The other

◄ Adolf Hitler attending a mass rally of the Nazi party. When Germany was defeated in the war, he killed himself to avoid capture.

▲ *The small British colony of Hong Kong is so crowded that thousands of people live in boats rather than on the land.*

half of the beam shines on the subject to be reproduced and then recombines with the first beam on the plate. There it makes a pattern called a *hologram*. When a laser beam passes through a hologram a 3-dimensional image is seen – an image that appears solid; as you walk around the image its perspective changes.

HOLY GRAIL In medieval legend, the cup used by JESUS CHRIST at the Last Supper. The story of the search for the Grail by King ARTHUR's knights inspired many early writers.

HOLY ROMAN EMPIRE The name given to the German empire founded by Otto I in AD 962 (it was seen as a revival of the old Roman empire). At its height it united Germany and most of Italy under one ruler. The empire continued in name till 1806; but it had lost most of Italy by 1300, while in Germany local rulers took over real power. After 1438 the position of Emperor was almost always held by a HAPSBURG.

HOMER The supposed Greek author of the epic poems *Iliad* and ODYSSEY. Legend depicts him as a blind wandering minstrel, living some time between 1050 and 650 BC.   ▷

HOMOSEXUALITY Sexual feeling towards a person of one's own sex. For many centuries homosexuality was widely condemned, but

▲ *The small British colony of Hong Kong is so crowded that thousands of people live in boats rather than on the land.*

recently society has become more tolerant. In some countries, however, homosexual acts are still illegal.

HONDURAS A mountainous, thinly-populated republic in CENTRAL AMERICA, Honduras covers an area of 112,088 sq km (43,277 sq miles) and has 4,232,000 people (1979 est.). The capital is Tegucigalpa. The people are mostly of mixed Indian and Spanish descent. Bananas are the chief product.   ▷

HONEY Sweet syrup made by BEES from flower nectar and stored in the hive as food for the growing LARVAE. Honey, white to dark gold in colour, is a good energy food for humans, as it contains simple sugars like GLUCOSE which are quickly digested.

HONG KONG A British colony on the southeast coast of China. This wealthy commercial centre has an area of 1045 sq km (403 sq miles) and 5,364,000 people (1984 est.). The capital is Victoria. In 1984 Britain agreed to hand Hong Kong back to China in 1997.   ▷

HOOF Hard growth, made of HORN, which protects the feet of certain animals such as horses, goats and zebras.

HOMER People once thought Homer's tales were fiction. But Heinrich Schliemann believed them to be true. In 1869, using Homer's *Iliad* as a guidebook, this German businessman decided that ruined Troy lay in a Turkish hillock called Hissarlik. Excavation of the mound later proved him right.

HONDURAS: FACTS AND FIGURES
Chief rivers: The Patuca, Ulúa, and Aguán, all flowing into the Pacific.
Official language: Spanish.
Currency: Lempira.
Religion: Roman Catholic.
Honduras has a long northern coastline of 560 km (350 miles) on the Caribbean and a very short 65-km (40-mile) southern coastline on the Pacific.

HONG KONG: FACTS AND FIGURES
Hong Kong island is only about 18 km (11 miles) long and 8 km (5 miles) wide at its broadest point.
Highest point: Victoria Peak 551 m (1809 ft).
Currency: Dollar.

HORSE An old statuette from Turkey shows that riding had begun by 1400 BC. Early horsemen had reins but lacked a saddle. For comfort they sat back near the broad rump.

HORSE RACING The English classic flat races are the 2000 Guineas and the 1000 Guineas, run at Newmarket over 1 mile (1.6 km); the Derby and the Oaks, run at Epsom over 1½ miles (2.4 km); and the St. Leger, run at Doncaster over 1 mile 6 furlongs and 132 yards (2.9 km). The 1000 Guineas and the Oaks are confined to fillies.

The most famous steeplechase is the Grand National, run at Aintree, Liverpool, over a distance of 4 miles 856 yards (7.2 km). There are 30 large fences.

▶ *A great deal of skill is required to control a horse in competitive events. Here, Princess Anne displays her fine horsemanship.*

HOP Tall climbing plant grown for its cone-like fruit. The cones – bunches of green scales – are used to make BEER.

HORMONE Chemical substance which regulates the body's activities. Hormones, mostly produced by GLANDS, make sure that cells, tissues and organs function properly. Two well-known hormones are *insulin*, which controls the amount of sugar in the blood (see DIABETES), and *adrenalin*, which gives the body extra strength and energy to fight – or run away – when danger threatens. Plants also have hormone-like substances, called *auxins*; these govern such processes as upward growth in stems and downward growth in roots.

HORN Semi-transparent, hard substance produced by the outer layer of skin. Nails, hoofs and beaks are all made of horn. So are the curved projections – called horns – which grow on the heads of cattle, sheep, giraffes and other animals; these horns are mainly used as weapons.

HORN, CAPE A rocky headland in a particularly stormy region at the southernmost tip of South America. It was discovered in 1616 by a Dutch navigator, William Schouten. Cape Horn is now part of Chile.

▼ *When choosing a horse or a pony to buy, it is necessary to know the 'points' of the animal. Here are some of the important ones.*

HORSE Hoofed, grass-eating animal used by man in all countries for pulling loads, carrying goods and for riding. Horses were first domesticated some 5000 years ago and there are now about 300 breeds in the world. In prehistoric times, wild horses roamed all over Europe and Asia but today only a very few survive in a remote part of Mongolia. Horses range in size from the tiny Argentinian

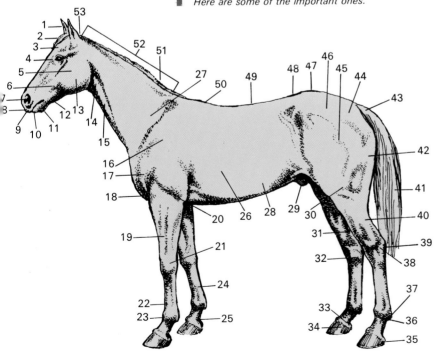

THE POINTS OF A HORSE

1 Ear	28 Belly
2 Forelock	29 Sheath
3 Forehead	30 Stifle
4 Eye	31 Shin
5 Cheekbone	32 Chestnut
6 Lower jaw	33 Coronet
7 Nostril	34 Hoof (wall of foot)
8 Muzzle	35 Heel
9 Upper lip	36 Ergot
10 Lower lip	37 Fetlock
11 Chin groove	38 Hock
12 Bars of jaw	39 Point of hock
13 Cheek	40 Gaskin
14 Gullet	41 Tail
15 Trachea (windpipe)	42 Buttocks
16 Shoulder	43 Dock
17 Breast	44 Hip joint
18 Pectoral muscle	45 Thigh
19 Forearm	46 Quarter
20 Elbow	47 Croup
21 Knee	48 Point of loins
22 Cannon bone	49 Back
23 Fetlock joint	50 Withers
24 Tendons	51 Mane
25 Hollow of heel	52 Crest
26 Girth	53 Poll
27 Base of neck	

Fallabella pony, under 70 cm (28 in) tall, to the giant English Shire draught horse – one of the world's strongest animals. (See EVOLUTION) ◁

HORSE RACING A sport popular as a basis for GAMBLING. In England it includes: flat races (e.g. the DERBY), held from March to November; and STEEPLECHASES in winter. Horses are handicapped by adding weights to the saddle. ◁

HOSPITAL Institution, staffed by doctors and nurses, for the treatment and care of people who are sick or injured. There are two main types of hospital. One, the general hospital, accepts all kinds of patients but treats them in specialized wards or units: for example, children are cared for in *paediatric* wards, old people in *geriatric* wards, expectant mothers in *maternity* wards and the mentally ill in *psychiatric* wards. The other type of hospital specializes in certain illnesses and disorders: there are, for instance, eye hospitals and psychiatric hospitals. Most large towns have a general hospital but specialized hospitals are usually confined to big cities. (See MEDICINE; SURGERY)

HOUND DOG used for hunting. Some hounds, such as beagles and foxhounds, hunt by following the scent; others, such as afghans and GREYHOUNDS, hunt by sight.

HOUSE FLY Common FLY found all over the world wherever man has settled. The house fly is particularly dangerous to health as it repeatedly vomits during digestion; in this way it passes on disease germs.

HOUSE OF COMMONS The lower but main house of the British PARLIAMENT, made up of 650 elected Members of Parliament (MPs). It votes on laws and government finances, and the chief members of its majority party form the GOVERNMENT (the Prime Minister with the Cabinet and other Ministers).

HOUSE OF LORDS The upper but less important house of the British PARLIAMENT, made up of about 790 hereditrary peers, 350 life peers, and some bishops and judges. Its powers are limited to making minor revisions to Bills (proposed laws).

HOUSE PLANT PLANT grown in a pot indoors for decorative purposes. Most plants chosen for indoor cultivation thrive in the

▶ *The housefly. It cannot eat solid food, so it pours a special juice onto food to make it liquid, the fly then sucks it up.*

warm atmosphere of the average room. Popular house plants include begonias, GERANIUMS and many species of CACTI.

HOVERCRAFT An air cushion vehicle designed to skim over the surface of water or land. A cushion of air is maintained between the craft and the surface by driving air at pressure under the hovercraft. This cushion supports the weight of the craft and keeps it clear of the surface. The hovercraft's air cushion is like a leaking tyre, in principle. Air must be pumped in continuously to maintain the necessary lift. Most craft are fitted with flexible skirts which contain the cushion of air. ▷

HOVERCRAFT The hovercraft was developed in Britain in 1959, following the experimental work of Christopher Cockerell (1910-   ). The first public hovercraft service was opened in 1962. In 1968, a car ferry carrying 30 cars and 250 passengers was launched for service across the English Channel.

The 'hover' principle is also being applied to other forms of transport such as hover trains.

▶ *A very popular house plant, Bryophyllum (Kalanchoe). It has a strange way of reproducing. Tiny plantlets form along the toothed edge of its thick, fleshy leaves, and then drop to the ground where they will develop into new plants.*

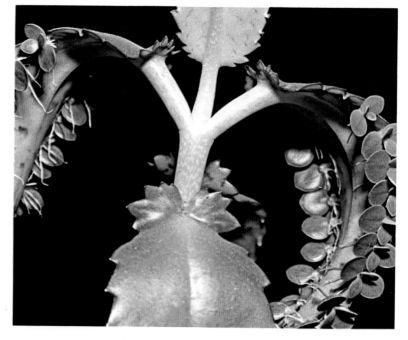

◄ A hummingbird hovers before a hibiscus flower. It rolls its tongue into a tube and sucks up nectar from the flower.

Hummingbirds feed on flower nectar, using their long fine bills and tube-tongues. When feeding, they hover over the flower and their rapid wing beats make a unique hum – hence their name. One species, from Cuba, is the world's smallest bird. ◄

HUNDRED YEARS' WAR The struggle between England and France, 1337–1453, over England's claim to the French throne. England's two main campaigns, under Edward III and HENRY V, brought victories at Sluys, Crécy, Poitiers and AGINCOURT. But England's resources of men and money were only a third of France's, and from 1429, JOAN OF ARC led a successful French revival. By 1453 only Calais was left in English hands.

HUNGARY A communist republic in eastern EUROPE, Hungary is a mostly low-lying country, drained by the River DANUBE and its tributaries. There is much fertile farmland, and grapes, maize, potatoes, rye, sugar-beet and wheat are important products. But manufacturing is now the most valuable activity, employing about 36 per cent of the working population, as opposed to 25 per cent in agriculture.

Before WORLD WAR I, Hungary, with Austria, was in command of the great Austro-Hungarian empire. Hungary became a separate country in 1919 and, in WORLD WAR II, it was one of the Axis powers. Soviet troops invaded Hungary in 1944–5 and a communist regime was established in 1947. ◄

HUNS A nomadic MONGOL people who entered Europe c. AD 373. Under the leadership

HUMMINGBIRD About 320 kinds have so far been discovered. During migration, some tiny hummingbirds spend 20 hours in the air, and make journeys of up to 800 km (500 miles) over water.

The smallest hummingbirds are no bigger than a bee. They beat their wings about 70 times a second during flight.

HUNGARY: FACTS AND FIGURES
Area: 93,030 sq km (35,919 sq miles)
Population: 10,665,000 (1984 est.).
Capital: Budapest (pop. 2,064,000).
Official language: Magyar.
Currency: Forint.
Religion: Roman Catholic, with Protestant minority.

HUDSON BAY A huge sea in north-central Canada. It is connected with the Atlantic and Arctic oceans and its area is about 114,930 sq km (44,375 sq miles). It was explored by Henry Hudson (c. 1550–1611) in 1610.

HUGO, VICTOR The chief writer (1802–1885) of the French Romantic movement, best remembered today for his novels *Notre Dame de Paris* and *Les Misérables*.

HUMIDITY The amount of moisture in the ATMOSPHERE. This moisture consists of tiny water particles moving about freely in the air. When we say a place is humid, we mean there is too much water vapour in the air. Hot, humid weather makes us feel hot and sticky. We may feel pleasantly warm at 29°C if the humidity is low, but far too hot if the humidity is high. Air conditioning makes rooms cooler and less humid.

HUMMINGBIRD Tiny brilliantly-coloured bird found in Central and South America.

► The Battle of Crécy (1346), the first major battle of the Hundred Years' War. Edward III's English force defeated Philip IV's French army near Abbeville, in France.

of Attila, their fearless fighting and amazing horsemanship nearly destroyed the Roman Empire. But their power was broken soon after Attila's deatl. in AD 453.

HUNTING Capturing or killing wild animals, once important as a source of food or a way of keeping down predators and vermin. Nowadays it is usually a sport, with the attraction either in the thrill of the chase or in the skill of stalking a wild creature.

HURDLING A foot race with hurdles to be jumped at set intervals. A competitor may knock over hurdles as he jumps them, but must stay in his own track throughout.   ▷

HURRICANE Low pressure air systems, also called *cyclones*. Hurricanes form over the oceans north and south of the EQUATOR. Fast, spiralling winds blow around the calm 'eye' (centre) of a hurricane. These winds which travel at more than 120 kph (75 mph), may cause much destruction when the hurricane nears land.

HYDROCARBONS Any of a vast number of important organic compounds (see ELEMENTS AND COMPOUNDS) which contain only HYDROGEN and CARBON. Hydrocarbons are obtained from oil and natural gas, and are used to make plastics and synthetic fibres.

HYDROCHLORIC ACID A strong ACID of great commercial importance. It is used in cleaning metal surfaces, in the manufacture of sugar and synthetic rubber, and in medicine.

HYDROELECTRIC POWER Electric power that comes from the energy of moving water. The water may be from a natural waterfall or a man-made dam. It is directed into water-TURBINES which drive electric GENERATORS. From the generators, electric current is sent through power cables to consumers. The amount of power produced depends on the rate of water flow and the distance through which it falls.

HYDROFOIL A boat which, at speed, rises out of the water supported on wing-like struts, or *foils*, that project from the lower hull. Only the foils touch the water once the boat is lifted, so FRICTION and drag are greatly reduced, allowing the hydrofoil to travel faster with less power.

HYDROGEN A colourless, odourless, tasteless GAS, and the lightest of all ELEMENTS. Its symbol is H. Although hydrogen makes up less than one per cent of the Earth's crust, it is

▼ *Most hydro-electric plants are in dams. Water is directed into water turbines which spin and so work a generator to make electricity.*

HURDLING The shortest hurdle race is the 110 m (120 yards), with 10 hurdles, each 1.07 m (3 ft 6 in) high. This is usually called the 'high' hurdles. The 'low' hurdles is raced over 200 m (220 yards) with 10 hurdles, each 76 cm (2 ft 6 in) high. In the 400 m (440 yard) hurdles, the 10 posts are 91 cm (3 ft) high. The men's steeplechase involved hurdles over 3000 m. Hurdling is also part of the men's decathalon and women's heptathlon competitions.

HYDROGEN Hydrogen is over 14 times lighter than air. It is the lighest substance so far discovered.

HYDROGEN Hydrogen was first described by Henry Cavendish in 1766. He called it 'inflammable air'. The name 'hydrogen', meaning 'water-former', was given by A.L. Lavoisier. Hydrogen is 14.4 times lighter than air, so it is used to fill balloons and formerly airships. But it is very flammable and caused the disaster in which the giant German airship *Hindenburg* burst into flames when about to land at Lakehurst, New Jersey, USA, in 1937. Hydrogen is a difficult gas to liquify; its boiling point is 252.5°C. It freezes solid at -259°C.

HYDROGEN BOMB In 1963 the Soviet Union claimed she had built a 100-megaton hydrogen bomb. A bomb like that could blast out a crater 30 km (19 miles) across and start fires ranging in a circle some 130 km (80 miles) in diameter.

HYPNOSIS The first man deliberately to hypnotize others was the Austrian doctor Franz Mesmer (1734-1815). He thought hypnosis was a kind of 'animal magnetism' flowing from one person to another. Mesmer grew rich trying to cure patients by hypnosis.

There is no clear proof that people can be made to do things that are not in their nature under hypnosis. It is doubtful whether an honest man can be made to act like a criminal by being hypnotized.

HYPOCHONDRIA A hypochondriac, scared of death and doctors, was the 'hero' in the last play by Molière, the great French playwright and actor (1622-1673). Molière was taking the leading part in the fourth performance of the play when he died of a haemorrhage.

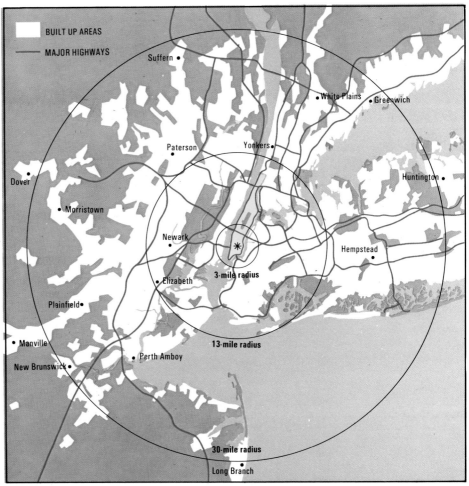

▲ *If a 10-megaton hydrogen bomb exploded over the centre of New York, Manhattan Island (21 km/13 miles long) would be totally destroyed. People would be burnt up to 48 km (30 miles) away.*

believed to be the most abundant element in the universe, making up a large part of the material in the stars. It is used in the manufacture of ammonia and margarine. ◁

HYDROGEN BOMB A nuclear weapon first exploded by the US in 1952. It uses the principle of FUSION instead of the fission of the original atomic bombs, and is therefore much more powerful. An atomic fission explosion is needed to trigger it off. (See NUCLEAR ENERGY) ◁

HYENA Savage dog-like creature found in India and parts of Africa. Hyenas hunt in packs by night and feed mostly on dead animals. When hunting they make uncanny laughing noises.

HYGIENE Science of health. Hygiene is concerned with preserving man's physical and mental well-being; it is often divided into personal hygiene, public hygiene and industrial hygiene. Personal hygiene deals with such matters as the care of teeth, hair and nails and the importance of exercise, sleep and diet. Public hygiene covers aspects affecting the health of the community; these include refuse disposal and water supplies as well as standards of cleanliness in places like restaurants and cinemas. Industrial hygiene refers to working conditions – air, space, light, heat, – in factories and offices.

HYPNOSIS The technique of creating a sleep-like trance. A hypnotized person can act much as normal, but his behaviour can be controlled by the person who has hypnotized him. (In deep hypnosis he may be made unable to feel pain.) The main use is in psychotherapy. (See PSYCHIATRY; PSYCHOANALYSIS) ◁

HYPOCHONDRIA A fear of becoming ill. A hypochondriac is always looking for signs of illness in himself, and seeking treatment for vague symptoms. It is usually a sign of psychological disorder. (See PSYCHIATRY) ◁

I

IBEX Species of wild GOAT living in the mountains of Europe, Asia and Africa; it has broader horns than the true wild goat.

IBIS Stork-like bird with a long, slender curved beak. Ibises, found world-wide in warm regions, usually live near water and feed on small animals.

ICE The solid form of water. Pure water freezes or ice melts at 0°C (32°F). Unlike most liquids, water increases in volume and so decreases in density as it freezes to a solid. So ice floats, with about seven-eighths of its volume below the surface.

ICE AGE The period of colder climatic conditions, in which ice sometimes covered much of Northern Europe and North America. There were four Ice Ages, with warmer periods in between. The first began over one million years ago, and the last only ended 20,000 years ago, and in fact it may be that we are just in one of the temporary warmer intervals.

ICEBERG A floating mass of ice. Icebergs weigh up to a million tonnes, and only a small part ($\frac{1}{8}$th to $\frac{1}{10}$th) shows above water. Even so, they can rise above the sea to 120 metres (400 ft).

ICE CREAM Nourishing frozen foodstuff made from sugar, fat and milk solids (or cream) with flavouring. The first ice-cream makers, some 5000 years ago, were Chinese; 4000 years later, the recipe was brought from China to Europe by MARCO POLO.

▶ A thick blanket of ice covers nearly all of Antarctica. Some peaks, called nantukas, rise through the ice. At the coast, the ice breaks off to form flat-topped icebergs.

▲ An ibex, one of several species of large-horned goats that live on the rugged mountains of Africa and Eurasia. Like other animals that live on mountains, the ibex has feet specially adapted to give extra grip on smooth rock when necessary.

THE ICE AGES

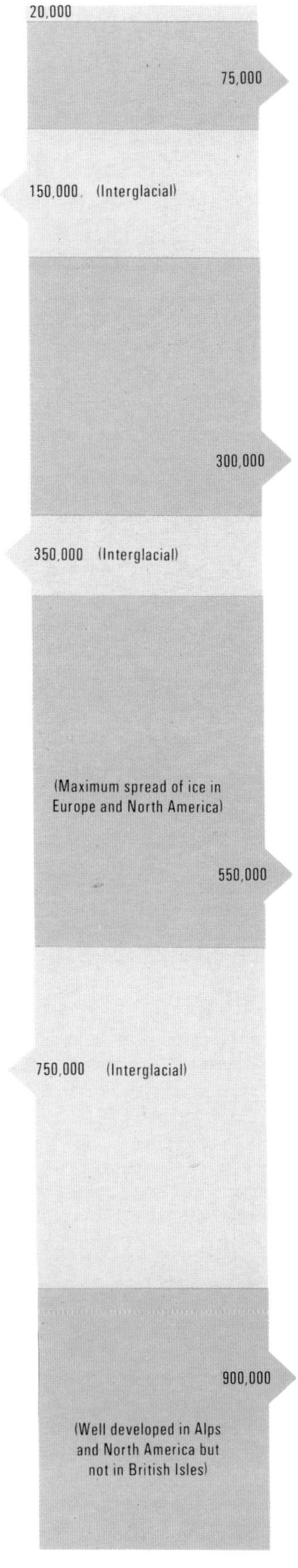

The vegetation was of a modern type, though it included many plants now found only in warmer regions. *Neanderthal Man* hunted hippos and other large animals.

Horses roamed the grasslands, often pursued by cave lions. Beavers gnawed at birch and aspen trees.

The huge straight-tusked elephant roamed the land, together with other large mammals. *Homo erectus* probably hunted these.

▲ *This chart shows what life was like in western Europe, and possibly North America too, during the Ice Ages and the periods in between (interglacials). While nothing could live in those areas completely covered with ice, many mammals managed to survive in the snowy wastes just to the south of the ice sheets. Man lived by hunting these animals. Conifers grew in many places, but in the colder regions probably only grasses and lichens could live. This chart does not show the earliest Ice Age (over 1 million years ago) as it only affected the Alpine regions.*

20,000

75,000

150,000   (Interglacial)

300,000

350,000   (Interglacial)

(Maximum spread of ice in Europe and North America)

550,000

750,000   (Interglacial)

900,000

(Well developed in Alps and North America but not in British Isles)

The sparse vegetation was mostly conifers and dwarf willows, while *Cro-Magnon Man* and the Arctic fox both fed on reindeer.

A woolly mammoth killed by the spears of *Neanderthal Man* gave a great deal of meat, and skins to make clothes.

During this period the land was like the Arctic of today. Musk oxen ate the scarce vegetation and were attacked by wolves.

Wild boars and brown bears lived in the forests around the tundra. Pines and spruces made up most of the forest.

ICE HOCKEY A game played on ice between two teams, using HOCKEY sticks to hit a rubber puck with the aim of scoring goals. Each team is of six players and a goalkeeper.

ICELAND An island republic in the North Atlantic Ocean. Iceland covers an area of 103,000 sq km (39,769 sq miles) and has a population of 240,000 (1984 est.). The capital is Reykjavik. Fish and whale products are the leading exports of this prosperous country. However, much of the land is covered by icefields and GLACIERS. There are also many active VOLCANOES, barren lava fields, and hot springs and GEYSERS. ▷

ICE SKATING Originally an outdoor winter pastime, today this is an international sport held on artificial indoor rinks, with both speed- and figure-skating events.

ICHTHYOSAUR Extinct dolphin-like REPTILE that lived in the sea about 200 million years ago. Ichthyosaurs were large, fast-swimming animals with paddle-shaped limbs.

ICON The name in the Eastern Orthodox Church for any picture or image of Christ, the Virgin Mary, an angel or a saint. Usually it is a painting on wood showing the human form in a flat, stylized way.

IGUANA Large LIZARD found in tropical America, Madagascar and Polynesia. Iguanas usually live in trees, often overhanging a river or lake. They are strong swimmers. If danger comes, they escape by diving into the water. Their food consists mainly of leaves, flowers and fruit.

ILLITERACY In developed nations, very few people cannot read and write. But illiteracy is a major problem in some developing nations. For example, some 80 per cent of all Africans over 15 are illiterate.

ILLUMINATED MANUSCRIPT A medieval hand-written BOOK decorated by monks with brightly-coloured designs. Usually the initial letter of each section is very large and elaborate. The *Book of Kells* (8th century) is a famous example from Ireland.

ILLUSTRATION A picture that adds in some way to a written work, by decorating, portraying or explaining it. The earliest illustrations in printed books were WOODCUTS. Today the illustration may have started life as a photograph, PAINTING, drawing, or ENGRAVING, before being printed in some way, either in black and white or colour (see PRINTING; LITHOGRAPHY). Common uses of illustration include advertisements, posters, maps, newspapers and magazines.

▲ Iceland's chief industry is fishing. Here, Icelandic fishermen are shown with their haul, enough to fill a hundred of their baskets.

▶ An illuminated letter 'B' from the Winchester Bible, which dates from the 12th century.

▼ Some specimens of the prehistoric ichthyosaur are so well preserved that the outline of the body can be clearly seen.

ICELAND: FACTS AND FIGURES
Language: Icelandic.
Religion: Lutheran.
Currency: Krona.
Iceland is the most westerly state in Europe. It lies just south of the Arctic Circle, about 800 km (500 miles) north-west of Scotland.
Highest point: Vatnajökull 2130 m (6950 ft).
The best known volcano is Hekla, which has erupted about 20 times since the 12th century.

IMPRESSIONISM The sketchy quality of Impressionist painting horrified art critics of the 1870s. One critic described how people rocked with laughter at the paintings. He thought the artists were a group of lunatics.

INCAS In 1532 the Spanish soldier-explorer Francisco Pizarro held the Inca emperor Atahualpa to ransom, demanding a room filled with gold. For months Indians scoured the Inca Empire for its treasures. Nine forges blazed for one month to melt them into plain gold bars. Then Pizarro treacherously killed Atahualpa.

IMPALA Reddish-brown ANTELOPE living in great herds in southern Africa.

IMPRESSIONISM A style of painting, begun in France in the 1860s. It tried to catch the immediate impression of a scene, through the different shades of light rather than the outlines of objects – often by using hundreds of tiny separate dots of pure colour. Well-known Impressionist artists include Manet, MONET, Degas and RENOIR. ◁

INCAS A South American ruling tribe whose empire lasted from c. 1200 until its destruction by Spanish CONQUISTADORS in 1532. Centred on modern Peru, their rule extended at its height from Ecuador to southern Chile. They formed a strict, ruthlessly efficient society, headed by a godlike emperor. Though writing and the wheel were unknown, architecture, metalwork and even surgery were well advanced. But the empire fell to Spanish firearms, cavalry and steel armour. ◁

INCENSE A mixture of various tree and plant saps, that burns with a sweet scent. It is usually made in stick or powder form, and used in religious ceremonies by Catholic and Orthodox Christians and by Buddhists.

INCOME TAX A tax on earnings, first introduced in England in 1799. A person may

▶ The isolated city of Machu Picchu became a refuge for the Incas after the conquest of the invading Spaniards.

▲ Inca religious ceremonies paid homage to the sun god Inti. He was represented with a human face on a ray-splayed disk. Human, as well as animal sacrifices were common to appease the gods.

earn a certain amount each year tax free, but must pay tax on every pound over that amount. The more he earns, the higher the rate of tax.

INCUBATION The process of giving a growing life ideal conditions of temperature and HUMIDITY. It usually refers to fertile EGGS awaiting hatching, but also to bacteria in a laboratory or weak babies in a hospital.

INDEPENDENCE, AMERICAN WAR OF
See REVOLUTIONARY WAR, AMERICAN

▶ *A typical busy street scene in Old Delhi. India became a republic in 1947 after about 150 years of British rule.*

INDIA The world's seventh largest country, the Republic of India is the second most populous. The population is increasing rapidly. Every year there are over 13 million extra people to feed, a major problem in a land where famines often occur. The diversity of languages and religions makes national unity difficult to achieve. More than 800 languages and dialects are spoken in India, although only Hindi and English are official languages. The chief religion, HINDUISM, is followed by 84 per cent of the people. Another 10 per cent are Moslems and there are sizeable groups of Christians, Sikhs, Buddhists and Jains.

There are three main land regions. The Himalayan mountain system extends along India's northern borders. The fertile northern plains, the most thickly-populated region, are drained by the GANGES and Brahmaputra rivers. The third region is the Deccan plateau in the south. Most Indians are poor farmers. Rice is the main food crop. Cotton, jute, millet, sugar cane, tea and wheat are other important products. Mining is underdeveloped, but manufacturing is increasing. The largest cities are CALCUTTA, Bombay, Delhi and Madras.

India, with PAKISTAN and BANGLADESH, was once part of the BRITISH EMPIRE. But, in 1947, the country split into two independent nations, the mostly Hindu India, and the Moslem Pakistan. War between these two nations over Kashmir ended in 1949, with India taking two-thirds of the disputed area. (See ASIA) ▷

INDIAN, AMERICAN See AMERICAN INDIANS

INDIAN OCEAN The third largest ocean, the Indian Ocean covers 73,426,000 sq km (28,350,000 sq miles). It lies between Africa, Asia, Australia and Antarctica. The average depth is 3960 metres (13,000 ft).

INDOCHINA The area in ASIA which now consists of three countries, KAMPUCHEA (Cambodia), LAOS and VIETNAM. From 1893 the region, called French Indochina, was ruled by France. Full independence was achieved in 1954. In 1975, following a long struggle, communist regimes were established in each of the countries.

INDONESIA A republic in south-east ASIA, Indonesia has 159,895,000 people (1984 est.). and a total area of 1,903,650 sq miles (735,000 sq miles). The capital is Jakarta. Indonesia is an island nation. Most people are Moslem farmers and rice is the main food crop. Coffee, copra, palm oil and kernels, rubber, tea and tobacco are exported. ▷

INDUSTRIAL REVOLUTION The sudden breakthrough in technical development and the use of MACHINE TOOLS in Europe (especially ENGLAND) from 1750 to 1850, and the effect this had on people's lives. The main

▼ *Vietnamese refugees running away from the scene of battle. Vietnam is one of the countries that make up Indochina. It was torn by a terrible war from 1954 to 1975, with the north fighting against the south.*

INDIA: FACTS AND FIGURES
Area: 3,287,590 sq km (1,269,345 sq miles).
Population: 745,012,000 (1984 est.).
Capital: New Delhi.
Official languages: Hindi, English.
Currency: Rupee.
Highest point: Nanda Devi, 7817 m (25,645 ft), in the Himalayas.
More than 800 languages and dialects are spoken.

◀The Industrial Revolution introduced the use of huge machines. They were often very dangerous, and many people working on them were injured. The picture shows a textile factory of the period.

INFANTRY Soldiers who fight on foot – the main combat force in most armies. Today their weapons include rifles, machine guns, grenades, mortars and even rocket launchers. They fight in scattered irregular formations to avoid giving too easy a target. (See ARMY)

INFLATION A period of rising prices. It can be due to demand for products exceeding their supply; or to a vicious circle of price and wage increases. It used to be linked with ECONOMIC growth, but today it often goes with high unemployment and stagnation.

INFLUENZA Infectious disease caused by a VIRUS. Influenza – or flu – often occurs in epidemics and can be serious. Its symptoms include a sore throat, high fever, and shivering and aching limbs.

INFRARED RAYS Invisible rays with a wavelength longer than that of red light and shorter than those of radio waves. Although invisible to the eye, infrared rays can be felt as heat. Photographic film that is sensitive to these rays is used in space and satellite photography, in botany and other sciences, and in the detection of crime. In the home we use infrared heat lamps and microwave ovens. (See ELECTROMAGNETIC WAVES)

INK The first inks were probably made by crushing berries in water. Today, as well as normal writing inks, there are marking inks, PRINTING inks, and special inks for ball-point pens.

INLAYING A type of decoration, made by cutting a design out of the surface to be decorated, and filling in the cut-out areas with a different material; e.g., decorating one wood with a differently coloured one.

INORGANIC CHEMISTRY Inorganic chemistry studies the properties of substances that do not contain CARBON and have never been part of a living thing. GLASS, IRON and SALT are examples of inorganic chemicals. The inorganic chemist is interested in the arrangement of bonds between ATOMS, in the arrangement of atoms in a MOLECULE, and in the way CRYSTALS are made.

INDONESIA: FACTS AND FIGURES
Official language: Bahasa Indonesia.
Currency: Rupiah.
Most Indonesians are Moslems, but there are large Hindu, Buddhist, and Christian minorities.
Two-thirds of the population of Indonesia live on the island of Java.

INVENTIONS were STEAM power (see WATT, JAMES), TEXTILE machinery, and improvements in metal processing. The results were factories and RAILWAYS – so creating large industrial towns, with new classes of owners and workers, and an expanding population with more banks and financial institutions, and greater overseas trade.

INERTIA The tendency of all bodies to resist changes in motion. A body at rest resists being set in motion. A body in motion resists being speeded up or slowed down. An external force must be applied to overcome this resistance, or inertia.

◀Chinese ink-makers preparing and mixing the ingredients (soot, oil, resin and gum). The Chinese began making ink around 1500 BC, for use with brushes rather than pens.

INQUISITION A ROMAN CATHOLIC tribunal (type of court) for the discovery and punishment of heresy. Founded in 1229, it was revived during the REFORMATION to fight Protestantism. The notoriously cruel Spanish Inquisition (1480–1834) was a separate body, under royal (not church) control.

INSANITY Legal term covering various illnesses of the mind. In LAW insane persons are considered incapable of doing certain acts, such as making a ·will, and are not held responsible for their actions.

INSECT Small animal with three body sections: the head, bearing a pair of feelers; the thorax, carrying three pairs of legs and, usually, two pairs of wings; and the abdomen. Also on the head are the eyes and the mouthparts. Most insects have *compound* eyes, made up of many tiny lenses; each lens sees just a fraction of the whole picture (see FLY). There are various types of mouthparts: biting insects, like WASPS and BEETLES, have strong external jaws and sharp teeth; sucking insects either have a long tongue like the BUTTERFLY, or a sharp piercing needle like the MOSQUITO. Insects breathe in a unique way; tiny tubes carry air from the surface to all parts of the body. There are about 35 million species of insects in the world. The majority of them have a remarkable life history divided into four very distinct stages: egg, LARVA, pupa and adult.　▷

INSECTICIDE Substance for killing INSECTS. Insecticides, mostly made from chemicals, are used on farms to protect crops and animals as well as in homes and public places, such as hospitals and restaurants.

INSOMNIA Inability to sleep. Insomnia is seldom an illness in itself; it is usually a symptom of some other physical or mental disorder such as indigestion or anxiety.

INSTINCT Inherited pattern of behaviour. Instinct plays an important part in the life of all animals. Spiders, for instance, are not taught to make webs, nor are beavers shown how to fell trees and build dams: they do these things by instinct. Instincts, like size or colour, are inherited and control many animal activities such as defence tactics, feeding habits, courtship, rearing of young, MIGRATION and HIBERNATION. (See INTELLIGENCE)

INSULATOR In ELECTRICITY, a substance such as rubber, plastic, porcelain or glass that

▶ Honey bees build their nest out of instinct. Like other animals, these insects are not taught how to live their lives. They are born with the instinctive knowledge.

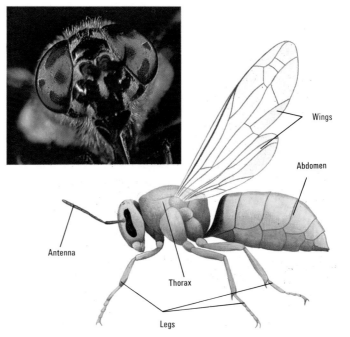

▲ Top: the face of a horsefly has large iridescent compound eyes, and beak-like piercing mouthparts. Above: side view of an inset showing the clear division of head, thorax and abdomen.

is a poor conductor. Most non-metals are insulators, and we use insulators to prevent electricity leaking into a place in which we do not want it. The opposite of an insulator is a conductor. (See CONDUCTION [ELECTRICITY])

INSURANCE A way of guarding against financial loss from risks such as fire, theft, accident and death. The idea is that many people pay small amounts of money (contributions) to an insurance company each year, so there is enough money to compensate (pay back) those who do lose. The insurance com-

INSECT Insect record holders include the goliath beetles (heaviest), a stick insect (longest), wasps called fairy flies (smallest), springtails (most plentiful), queen termites (longest lived), and cicadas (loudest). The flea is the champion of the insect world. It can jump 100 times its own height. This would be the same as a human being able to jump over 150 m (500 ft) straight up.

Queen

Worker

Insects are the most successful form of animal life on Earth. It has been said that there are more species of insect still waiting to be discovered than the total number of different species of all other animals put together. In a single acre of soil there may be four million insects. In the whole world there may be as many as 1,000,000,000,000,000,000 insects – over 300 million of them for each man, woman and child alive.

INSURANCE Hartford, Connecticut, USA is known as the insurance capital of the world, with some 50 multinational and national companies having their headquarters there. More insurance business is carried out there than anywhere else in the world.

INTELLIGENCE In 1967 a four-year-old South Korean boy, Kim Ung-Yong, spoke four languages, composed verse, and performed complex calculations. Experts rated his intelligence at 210 on a scale where 150 equals genius.

INTERNAL COMBUSTION ENGINE As early as 1680 the Dutch scientist Christian Huygens suggested an engine worked by an explosion in a cylinder closed by a piston. In 1826 Samuel Brown of London built an internal combustion engine that used atmospheric gas to power a vehicle. In 1876 the Germans Nikolaus Otto and Eugen Langen built the first four-stroke cycle engine.

▲ *The single miniature integrated circuit shown here is smaller than a thumbnail yet it contains 4096 'bits' of information for use in a computer.*

panies assess the various risks, and set the contributions (*premiums*) high enough to cover the likely loss and leave themselves a profit. ◁

INTEGRATED CIRCUITS Tiny electronic circuits which can contain TRANSISTORS and other components, formed on a single SILICON chip. Electronic engineers design the circuit in a large size. This is then reduced photographically until it takes up about as much space as a pinhead. Fine wires about 1/1000 cm thick are attached to the ends of the circuit so that it can be connected to other components of a calculator, COMPUTER, etc. Using integrated circuits, computers which twenty years ago occupied a whole room, can now be reduced to the size of a typewriter.

INTELLIGENCE Ability to reason and understand. Most animal behaviour is governed by reflexes (automatic responses to a stimulus such as heat or light) and by INSTINCT. Many human actions are similarly controlled: for example, a person jumps if someone sticks a pin in his arm; this is a reflex action, done without thinking. But human beings are able to think and are therefore able to act using reason and understanding: they have intelligence. The large APES, such as the chimpanzee and the gorilla, are also capable of intelligent behaviour, but their intelligence is far inferior to man's. Intelligence is linked with the size of the BRAIN and although an ape has a larger brain than all other creatures except man, it is still only half the size of the human brain. ◁

INTEREST A payment charged on borrowed money calculated at so much per cent (i.e. per £100) a year. So at 10 per cent, the charge on borrowing £50 over a year is £5.

INTERIOR DECORATION The decoration of the inside of a building in a particular style. The idea developed in the RENAISSANCE. Famous interior designers in the 18th and 19th centuries (the Adam brothers; William Morris) would design many items themselves (wallpaper, furniture, etc.), rather than just choose from existing designs.

INTERNAL COMBUSTION ENGINE Type of engine that operates by the combustion of a fuel-air mixture within the cylinders of the engine. There are two main types of internal combustion engine, the petrol engine and the DIESEL engine. In the petrol engine the fuel, a mixture of petrol and air, is ignited by an electric spark. The explosion in the top of the cylinder forces the piston downwards. The piston helps to turn a crankshaft. This kind of engine is used mostly in motor cars, and there are usually four, six or eight cylinders, firing one after the other. In the diesel engine, air is

▼ *The cylinder action of a petrol internal combustion engine.* Induction: *The piston moves downwards and the petrol/air mixture is drawn into the cylinder.* Compression: *The piston rises, compressing the mixture.* Power: *The sparking plug sparks, igniting the compressed mixture. The gases produced force the piston downwards.* Exhaust: *As the piston moves upwards again the burnt gases are forced out.*

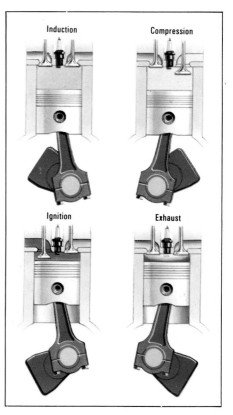

▶ *Each cylinder contains a piston, and as it moves, the connecting rods turn the crankshaft, which is connected by the transmission system to the wheels.*

drawn into the cylinder and compressed to make it hot. This hot air ignites the fuel oil injected into the cylinder. There is no spark. (See MOTOR CAR; MOTORCYCLE) ◁

INTESTINE Muscular tube through which food passes after the STOMACH. Man's intestine has two sections: small and large intestines. In the small intestine, DIGESTION is completed and the digested food is absorbed into the blood. The remaining undigested material goes into the large intestine where it loses its water before being passed out of the body as waste.

INVENTIONS A discovery is something that always existed, but was not known before. An invention is something new, thought up by men – from flint tools, the plough and the WHEEL, to TRANSISTORS, LASERS and COMPUTERS. Man is the only animal to invent things, and he does so for three main reasons: to make life better, to make money, and to make war. Inventions in power and machinery brought the INDUSTRIAL REVOLUTION. Those in products (record players, washing machines), have brought a revolution in comfort and enjoyment. Those in communications (cars, televisions, telephones), a revolution in how society organizes itself. Those in medicine (hypodermic needles, X-ray machines), a revolution in health. Before about 1900, most inventions were the work of individuals, acting alone. Now, most are the work of research teams of scientists and engineers. Of course, not all inventions are completely good. Some are simply new ways of killing people. Others, though useful, bring problems with them – such as the pollution caused by cars and lorries. But most inventions have made life easier and happier for many people. (See PATENT)

INVERTEBRATE Animal with no backbone. Invertebrates include INSECTS, CRUSTACEANS, WORMS, SNAILS and CENTIPEDES. As these creatures have no backbone and no internal bones, many of them have an outside skeleton or shell which gives protection, support and shape. In the animal kingdom there are some 1,200,000 species of invertebrate; they outnumber the VERTEBRATES (backboned animals) by about 30 to 1.

IODINE A grey-black crystal ELEMENT with the chemical symbol I. When heated it gives off a violet vapour. Iodine is found in SEAWEED and is essential for the proper working of the thyroid GLAND. ▷

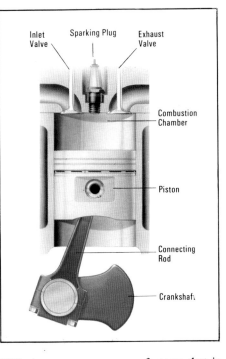

Inlet Valve — Sparking Plug — Exhaust Valve — Combustion Chamber — Piston — Connecting Rod — Crankshaft

ION An ATOM or a group of atoms that is electrically charged because it has gained or lost electrons. Ions can be made by radiation with X-RAYS or GAMMA RAYS, or by dissolving certain compounds in water.

IONOSPHERE A layer of the Earth's ATMOSPHERE starting at about 80 km (50 miles) up and ending about 500 km (300 miles) above sea level. It is called the ionosphere because the air at that level is highly ionized (see ION) by the Sun's ultraviolet radiation. The ionosphere is important because it reflects radio waves back to Earth which would otherwise be lost in space.

IRAN Formerly called PERSIA, and part of the great ancient Persian empire. Iran has 43,414,000 people (1984 est.) and an area of 1,648,000 sq km (636,296 sq miles). The capital is Tehran. Iran is the world's fourth largest oil producer, but more than half of the people are farmers. Wheat is the chief crop. ▷

IRAQ An Arab nation in the MIDDLE EAST, Iraq has 15,356,000 people (1984 est.) and an area of 434,924 sq km (167,925 sq miles). The capital is BAGHDAD. The valleys of the Tigris and Euphrates rivers, the birthplace of early civilizations, are still important farm areas in this largely desert nation. But oil is the main source of wealth. ▷

IRELAND The second largest island in the BRITISH ISLES, Ireland is divided into two parts. The Republic of Ireland has been independent since 1921. It lacks resources and many people

IODINE Iodine was discovered by Bernard Courtois in 1811 while he was analyzing the ashes of seaweeds. It is almost insoluble in water, but dissolves in alcohol, carbon tetrachloride and carbon disulphide. Iodine melts at 113.5°C and boils at 184.4°C.

IRAN: FACTS AND FIGURES
Official language: Persian (Farsi).
Currency: Rial.
Highest point: Mount Demavend 5670 m (18,600 ft).
Principal river: The Karun.
Religion: Mainly Shia Moslem, with minorities of Bahais, Sunni Moslem, Zoroastrians and Christians.
The interior of the country is made up of two large deserts – the Dasht-i-Kavir and the Dasht-i-Lut.
Since 1980 the country has been at war with its neighbour Iraq.

IRAQ: FACTS AND FIGURES
Official language: Arabic.
Currency: Dinar.
Rivers: Tigris and Euphrates.
About four-fifths of Iraq's people are Arabs. The Kurds form an important minority group. Iraq produces a large proportion of the world supply of dates.
Since 1980 the country has been at war with Iran.

IRELAND: FACTS AND FIGURES
Area: 83,014 sq km (32,052 sq miles).
Population: Republic of Ireland 3,535,000 (1984 est.); Northern Ireland 1,578,500 (1985 est.).
Capitals: Republic of Ireland, Dublin; Northern Ireland, Belfast.
The Shannon is the longest river in the British Isles. Most of Ireland has an annual rainfall of more than 100 cm (40 inches), and rain usually falls on more than 200 days a year. Dublin is in one of the drier areas, with only 69 cm (27 inches) of rain a year.

Bath with
portable paraffin
heater, 1882

Maughan's gas
geyser, 1868

Doulton's pedestal
water closet, c. 1888

Bramah's water
closet, 1778

DOMESTIC
INVENTIONS

Before the 20th century few
houses in Europe had baths
or inside lavatories. But
both had been invented at
various times in history.
Many familiar household
appliances (such as vacuum
cleaners, washing mach-
ines, spin driers) were
invented in the early 1900s.
People developed a passion
for 'gadgets', and when
King C Gillette invented his
safety razor it was an
instant success. His idea
was new and different and
especially useful to soldiers
and sailors.

Wizard vacuum
cleaner, 1912

Safety
razor, c. 1880

Washing machine,
1920

French radiator,
c. 1903

Modern electric
fan heater

Portable oil
stove, c. 1890

have emigrated in the last 140 years. But it is a beautiful country, where farming is the chief occupation.

Northern Ireland is part of the United Kingdom of GREAT BRITAIN and Northern Ireland. Protestants, who oppose unification with the mainly Roman Catholic Republic, form the majority. Since the late 1960s, animosity between Protestants and Roman Catholics has led to civil disturbances.   ◁

IRIS Plant with a *rhizome* (underground stem), sword-like leaves and brilliant flowers. It grows wild throughout the northern hemisphere. Iris flowers are all colours, hence the name 'iris' which is Greek for 'rainbow'.

IRISH WOLFHOUND Very tall dog developed in Ireland over 2000 years ago for hunting WOLVES and ELKS. Its rough, wiry coat is usually grey.

IRON A metallic ELEMENT with the symbol Fe, iron is the fourth most abundant substance in the Earth's crust. It is found in ores such as *pyrites*, *magnetite* and *haematite* and is usually manufactured in a BLAST FURNACE, where it is turned into STEEL or WROUGHT IRON.   ▷

IRON CURTAIN A term used in the western world to describe the barriers which have limited communications, trade and travel between the West and the communist countries of eastern EUROPE. It came into popular use when Winston CHURCHILL stated in a speech in 1946 that 'an iron curtain has descended across the continent'.

IRON LUNG Machine to aid breathing. An iron lung, or respirator, is used when the chest muscles are paralysed as in severe cases of POLIOMYELITIS. Except for the head, the patient's body lies in the lung which is a large metal box; air is pumped in and out of the box, forcing the patient's chest to rise and fall.

IRRIGATION The supplying of water for agriculture, where rainfall is too low. Primitive irrigation, along mud channels, was used in ancient EGYPT, MESOPOTAMIA and CHINA (especially in her RICE fields). Today vast DAMS are used to create artificial RESERVOIRS (as at Aswan in Egypt), and are often linked with HYDROELECTRIC POWER projects.

ISLAM One of the major world religions, also called Mohammedanism after its founder MOHAMMED (AD 570–632). Its creed is 'there is no God but Allah, and Mohammed is his Prophet'; its holy book is the *Koran*; and its basic duties are prayer, fasting, giving of alms, and pilgrimage to MECCA. Islam accepts much of the Bible, but emphasizes the oneness of

▲ In Ireland, peat has been used as a fuel for centuries. It is dug from bogs, as here, and dried before burning.

▲ The hostility between Catholics and Protestants in Ireland has led to many acts of violence. Here, in Northern Ireland, the detonator of a car bomb is set off by a controlled explosion.

▼ There are a thousand or so species belonging to the Iris family, including crocuses and gladioli. The Yellow Iris is found in river and ditch margins as well as marshy woods.

Wood iris

Ireland is the only country in Europe with a population less than it was 125 years ago. During the potato famine of the mid-1840s the population of Ireland was cut by half. Irish emigrants have played an important part in the history of North America. It is estimated that there are more people of Irish descent in New York City than there are people in Ireland.

IRON The largest iron mine on Earth is at Lebedinsky in the Soviet Union. Its reserves would be enough to keep the world supplied with iron ore for a generation. Brazil's reserves are greater still.

ISLAND The biggest group of islands is the 13,000 making up the Indonesian archipelago. Apart from the island continent of Australia, the five biggest individual islands in the world (in descending order) are Greenland, New Guinea, Borneo, Madagascar, and Baffin Island.

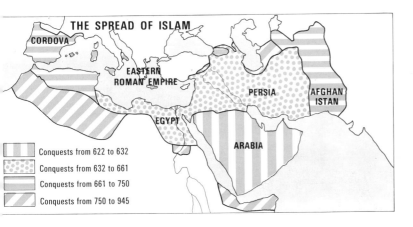

THE SPREAD OF ISLAM

CORDOVA

EASTERN ROMAN EMPIRE

EGYPT

PERSIA

AFGHAN ISTAN

ARABIA

Conquests from 622 to 632
Conquests from 632 to 661
Conquests from 661 to 750
Conquests from 750 to 945

ISOTOPE Botanists learnt how plants make food by supplying them with carbon dioxide gas containing the radioactive isotope of carbon. Detection devices showed the scientists how, when, and where plants absorbed and used the carbon.

ISRAEL: FACTS AND FIGURES
Area: 20,770 sq km (8019 sq miles).
Population: 4,194,000 (1984 est.).
Capital: Jerusalem.
Official languages: Hebrew, Arabic.
Currency: Pound.
Largest cities: Jerusalem (pop. 429,000), Tel Aviv-Yafo (pop. 327,000) and Haifa (pop. 226,000).
Lake Tiberias (Sea of Galilee) lies 212 m (696 ft) below sea level, entirely within Israel. Israel is a holy land for the Jewish, Christian and Moslem faiths.

▶ Followers of Islam make pilgrimages to Mecca, Mohammed's birthplace. Their object is the Ka'aba, the building shown here. It contains the sacred Black Stone, which according to tradition fell from heaven.

God and opposes the worship of saints and images. It inspired the ARAB conquests, and today there are about 430 million followers (called Moslems or Muslims) world-wide.

ISLAND A land area surrounded by water. The largest island is GREENLAND – Australia being regarded as a continent. Some islands are parts of the CONTINENTAL SHELF around continents. Others are VOLCANOES which rise steeply from the ocean depths. ◁

ISOTOPE The form of an ELEMENT that has neutrons added to or taken away from the nucleus of its ATOMS. Certain isotopes are radioactive, and these are very useful as their radioactivity allows them to be followed in various industrial processes. Isotopes are also used in medicine to track down and destroy diseased cells in the body. ◁

ISRAEL A republic in the eastern Mediterranean, Israel contains about one-fifth of the world's JEWS. But about 20 per cent of the population are ARABS. Israel, once part of PALESTINE, was established as a Jewish homeland in 1948, despite strong Arab opposition. Short Arab-Israeli wars occurred in 1948–9, 1956, 1967 and 1971, during which Israel took parts of Egypt, Jordan and Syria. In 1979 Egypt and Israel signed a peace treaty, and

◀ A very weak radioisotope and a phosphor that glows when struck by the isotope's radiation, is applied to the dial of a telephone, so that it can be seen in the dark.

◀ How radioisotopes are produced. Isotopes give off alpha, beta and gamma rays — the three kinds of radiation. Radioisotopes are therefore the most convenient source of radiation. They are made by bombarding a sample of a non-radioactive isotope with atomic particles. In the picture, a sample is being placed in position by manipulators. A beam of particles is then produced by the cyclotron (right) to strike the sample and change it into a radioisotope. The radiation is dangerous: the operator cannot enter the chamber, and the radioisotopes produced are packed in heavy boxes.

▼ *Israel's military leader, Moshe Dayan (wearing the eye-patch), holds a conference during the October War of 1973. Several times Israeli-Arab hostility has resulted in open war.*

▲ *Jerusalem, the capital of Israel. It is regarded as a holy city by Christians and Moslems as well as Jews. In the centre of the picture is the Dome of the Rock.*

Israel returned the Sinai Peninsula to Egypt. Israel is an industrious country. Its people have reclaimed desert, and set up thriving manufacturing industries. Cut diamonds, textiles, chemicals, machinery, fertilizers and fruit and vegetables are exported. ▷

ISTHMUS A narrow land bridge which connects two large land areas. For example, the Isthmus of PANAMA links North America to South America, and the Isthmus of Suez joins Africa and Asia.

ITALY A south European republic, Italy is noted for its beauty, the impressive ruins of the Roman empire (see ROME [HISTORY]), VATICAN CITY in Rome, and magnificent medieval cities, such as Florence and VENICE. Italy is also famed for its great achievements in the arts. It was the birthplace of the RENAISSANCE, and home of such great artists as LEONARDO DA VINCI and MICHELANGELO. Opera was born in Italy in the 1600s. Leading Italian composers of opera include Claudio Monteverdi (1567–1643), Gioacchino Rossini (1792–1868), Giuseppe Verdi (1813–1901) and Giacomo Puccini (1858–1924). La Scala, in Milan, is one of the world's great opera houses.

Between the Alps in the north and the

ITALY: FACTS AND FIGURES
Area: 301,225 sq km (116,304 sq miles).
Population: 56,983,000 (1984 est.).
Capital: Rome.
Highest point: Monte Rosa, 4638 m (15,217 ft) above sea-level.
Official language: Italian.
Currency: Lira.
Religion: Roman Catholic.
Volcanoes: Vesuvius, overlooking the Bay of Naples; Etna, in Sicily; and Stromboli, in the Lipari Islands.
Principal rivers: The Po, and Tiber and the Arno.
Largest cities: Rome (pop. 2,831,000; Milan (pop. 1,561,000); Naples (pop. 1,209,000); and Turin (pop. 1,069,000) (1984 est.).

◄ A market square in Rome, the capital of Italy. In the distance, the white dome of St Peter's Basilica can be seen. Many tourists visit Italy each year, attracted by the beauty of its historic cities as well as its Mediterranean beaches.

Italian peninsula which juts into the Mediterranean Sea is the broad Lombardy plain, an agricultural region drained by the River Po. The Apennine Mountains form the backbone of the peninsula, but there are also fertile basins, valleys and coastal plains. The southern part of the peninsula is relatively underdeveloped, as also are the islands of SICILY and Sardinia. Active volcanoes in the south include VESUVIUS, near Naples, Etna, on Sicily, and Stromboli, in the Lipari Islands. Much of Italy has hot, dry summers and mild, moist winters and about two-thirds of the country is farmland. But manufacturing is the most valuable industry, especially in the cities, such as Rome, Milan, Naples and Turin. Manufactured products include textiles, especially silk and wool; chemicals and motor vehicles. (See EUROPE) ◁

IVAN THE GREAT (Ivan III) Grand duke of Moscow (born 1440, reigned 1462–1505). His revolt against Russia's tartar overlords established Moscow's leadership of Russia and the official position of the Orthodox Church. He also drew up Russia's first law code.

IVAN THE TERRIBLE (Ivan IV) First tsar of Russia (born 1530, reigned 1533–1584). Gaining effective power at 14, he had himself crowned tsar in 1547. His rule extended Russian territory and reduced the power of the nobles. But from about 1560 he grew into a ferocious and unstable tyrant. ◁

IVORY A hard white substance that makes up the teeth of some animals. Ivory from elephant tusks is used for making piano keys and billiard balls and, particularly in China and India, for decorative carvings.

IVORY COAST A republic in West AFRICA. Formerly a French territory, it became independent in 1960. Farming is the most important industry, with coffee and cocoa the main products, accounting for over half the country's exports. ◁

IVY Climbing evergreen plant with shiny dark-green leaves. Ivy uses tiny roots, growing from its stem, to cling to walls and trees. Although the plant does not feed off the supporting tree, it does weaken and can even kill it. Since earliest times, ivy has been considered lucky and is often used for decoration, particularly at Christmas.

IVAN THE TERRIBLE A violent and passionate man, Ivan the Terrible killed his eldest son Ivan with a blow from his stick. The tsar died insane in 1584. During the last hours of his life he joined a very strict order of hermits, and died as the monk Jonah.

IVORY COAST: FACTS AND FIGURES
Area: 322,462 sq km (124,000 sq miles).
Population: 9,464,000 (1984 est.).
Capital: Abidjan (pop. 1,850,000).
Currency: CFA franc.
Official language: French.
Rivers: The Bandama, the Comoé, and the Sassandra.
Climate: Hot and humid, with heavy rainfall.
The Ivory Coast became a colony and was incorporated into French West Africa in 1904. It became an independent member of the United Nations in 1960.

◄ This ivory carving comes from Africa. Objects have been carved in ivory since prehistoric times in Europe, the Near East, and especially China and India. Ivory from the tusks of African and Indian elephants is the most valuable kind, as it is very hard and dense.

▼ Another example of an intricate ivory carving — a decorated compass.

JACKAL Small brownish DOG found wild in Asia and Africa. Jackals usually hunt at night, either alone or in pairs, and live on carrion, small animals and even plants and fruit.

JADE A hard stone used as a GEM. Usually green in colour, it may also be white, yellow or pink. Once the hardest material known. The Chinese, Aztecs and Maoris all used it for decorative carvings.

JAGUAR Large flesh-eating CAT from South America. The jaguar is very strong and can kill a man with one blow of its paw. Jaguars mostly live in forests where they hunt among the trees, springing from branch to branch and then jumping down on their victim.

JAMAICA A scenic, mountainous island in the WEST INDIES, Jamaica has an area of 10,991 sq km (4244 sq miles) and 2,301,000 people. The capital is Kingston. Jamaica

▼ *One of Jamaica's many fine beaches which attract thousands of tourists every year.*

▲ *An open jade ring made in China during the Han period, about 2000 years ago.*

became independent in 1962, with the British monarch as head of state. The country produces bauxite and various farm products. Tourism is an important industry.

JAMES I King of England and (as James VI) of Scotland. Born in 1566, the son of Mary Queen of Scots, he gained the Scottish throne on her abdication in 1567, and the English throne on the death of ELIZABETH I in 1603. But in England he upset Parliament and the Puritans with his attitudes on religion and royal authority. He died in 1625.

JAMES II King of England and Scotland (born 1633, reigned 1685–1689). He succeeded his brother CHARLES II, but was distrusted for his Roman Catholicism and use of royal power. In 1688 Parliamentary leaders invited William of Orange (see WILLIAM III) to take the throne. James fled to France, led an unsuccessful rising in Ireland, and died in exile in 1701.

JAPAN A prosperous island monarchy in eastern ASIA, Japan is a highly industrialized nation. It has a variety of light and heavy industries, producing such things as chemicals, electrical appliances and electronic machinery, food products, iron and steel, paper, ships and textiles. Japan has been the world's leading builder of ships since 1955 and, in 1974, it accounted for just over half of the world's launchings. It is the world's third largest crude steel producer and, in 1975, it manufactured over 10 million television sets, nearly 13 million radios and 7 million cameras.

Over 70 per cent of the people live in urban areas. The largest city is TOKYO. Farming is intensive on the 15 per cent of the land which is cultivable. Rice is the chief food crop. The main animal food is fish. Japan takes about one-sixth of the world's fish catch and leads in whaling.

Japan consists of four main islands, Hokkaido, Honshu, Shikoku and Kyushu. There are also about 3000 small islands. Much of the land is mountainous. There are many volcanoes and earthquakes are common.

Until the mid-1800s, Japan was an isolated feudal state. In the late 1800s, the country was rapidly modernized and industrialized. During WORLD WAR II, Japan became one of the Axis powers, but it surrendered in 1945.

▼ *A typical Japanese village built under one of the country's many volcanoes. Modern skyscrapers dominate the cities, but a number of people in the countryside still live in houses like these.*

▲ *Japanese girls in kimonos. Many people in Japan wear Western-style clothes at work and traditional dress at home and on special occasions.*

United States troops occupied Japan and introduced democratic institutions. The emperor declared that he was not 'divine' and became a constitutional monarch. ◁

JASMINE Ornamental shrub of Asiatic origin. In most species, the sweet-smelling flowers are either white or yellow. Some jasmines yield oils that are used in perfumes.

JAUNDICE Disease in which the skin and eyeballs turn yellow. Jaundice is caused by too much yellow bile pigment in the blood and often occurs when the bile duct is blocked by GALLSTONES.

JAVA A densely-populated island in southeast ASIA, Java contains nearly two-thirds of the population of INDONESIA, including the capital and largest city, Jakarta. This narrow, mountainous island has rich soils, and rice is the main food crop.   ▷

JAVELIN THROW An Olympic sport. The javelin is a thin lightweight spear. It is thrown for maximum distance, overhand, after a run-up. For a good throw, it must land point first and within a marked area.

JAZZ A type of American popular music, that began among the negroes of New Orleans c. 1880, and included memories of African tribal music. There have since been many styles, but jazz usually has strong rhythms and a simple structure, and emphasises improvization. It has greatly influenced other music. Famous jazzmen include Louis Armstrong, Duke Ellington and Charlie Parker.   ▷

JEFFERSON, THOMAS President of the United States. Jefferson (1743–1826) drafted the DECLARATION OF INDEPENDENCE, was ambassador to Paris, and founded the Democratic Party. He became Vice-President in 1796–1801, and President 1801–1809.   ▷

JELLYFISH INVERTEBRATE animal found in the sea. It has a round, semi-transparent soft body fringed with stinging tentacles. Food is caught by the tentacles and carried to the mouth, located underneath the body.   ▷

▼ A statue of Edward Jenner at work.

▲ The Portuguese Man O' War is a jellyfish that floats on the sea's surface. Its poisonous tentacles may be 12 metres (40 ft) long.

JENNER, EDWARD English physician (1749–1823). He discovered that a person who caught cowpox was immune to SMALLPOX, and so originated the use of VACCINE injections to protect against infection.   ▷

JERICHO An ancient city in the Jordan valley. Archaeologists have uncovered 17 levels of settlement, dating from 5000 BC or earlier. The BIBLE says that it was the first Canaanite town captured by the Israelites, and that its walls fell to a blast of their trumpets.

JERUSALEM The capital of ISRAEL, Jerusalem is an ancient city, which is holy for Christians, JEWS and Moslems. The city was divided between Israel and Jordan from 1948 to 1967, when ISRAEL took the entire city. The population is 429,000 (1984 est.).

JESUITS The largest religious order of the ROMAN CATHOLIC CHURCH. Called the Society of Jesus, it was founded by St. Ignatius of Loyola, with educational and missionary aims. The order was expelled from France, Spain and Portugal in the 18th century, suppressed by Pope Clement XIV in 1773, and revived as a worldwide order in 1814.

JESUS CHRIST Jewish religious teacher (c. 4 BC – c. AD 29), born in Bethlehem to Mary, and baptised by John the Baptist in AD 26 or 27. His message is summed up in the Sermon

JAVA Java is about 1060 km (660 miles) long and only 50 km (30 miles) to 160 km (100 miles) wide. Its population of nearly 70,000,000 makes it one of the most densely populated places in the world.

More than one quarter of Java consists of volcanic rock. It has no fewer than 112 volcanoes. The 35 active ones represent 1 in 13 of all active volcanoes formed on land. The highest one on the island is Semeru, 3660 m (12,060 ft).

JAZZ The first jazz record was made in 1917. It featured 'The Dark Town Strutters Ball' and 'Indiana'. The performers were the Original Dixieland Jazz Band.

JEFFERSON, THOMAS Jefferson learnt languages astonishingly easily. He mastered Greek, Latin, Spanish, French, Anglo-Saxon, and Gaelic. He used to study 15 hours a day, then take a two-mile run.

JELLYFISH There are three kinds of jellyfish: the *Medusae* or true jellyfishes; the *Siphonophores*, which are floating colonies of small sea animals hanging from the bottom of a gas-filled bag, (the Portuguese Man O' War is one of these); and the *Ctenophores* or sea-gooseberries. Jellyfish can be as big as 4 m (12 ft) in diameter, with tentacles more than 30 m (100 ft) long. About 95 per cent of a jellyfish is water, 4 per cent mineral salts, and only 1 per cent organic matter.

JENNER, EDWARD Jenner knew of a country belief that people who caught the mild disease cowpox from cows, were safe from smallpox. In 1796 he inoculated a boy called James Phipps with matter from a dairymaid's cowpox-infected hand. Six weeks later Jenner inoculated James with smallpox matter. The boy stayed well. Jenner's disease-prevention process is called vaccination from *vaccinia*, another word for cowpox.

JOAN OF ARC Joan claimed to be guided by the visions and voices of three saints whose statues stood in her village church. Some doctors think she simply suffered from a complaint which made her see and hear these things.

JOHNSON, SAMUEL As a boy, Johnson was cruelly thrashed by the Reverend John Hunter, headmaster of Lichfield Grammar School. Hunter beat any boy unable to answer a question. Surprisingly Johnson later claimed, 'no attention can be obtained from children without the infliction of pain'.

Johnson first became famous when his great *Dictionary of the English Language* was published in 1755 in two large volumes. It set the style for all dictionaries from that day to this. Johnson was the first to try to distinguish between all the separate meanings of every English word, and he was the first to illustrate the meanings with quotations. He also did much to standardize the spelling of the English language.

on the Mount. He entered Jerusalem in triumph in AD 29, acclaimed by some as the Messiah; but was arrested, condemned and crucified. His APOSTLES believed that he rose from the dead and ascended to heaven. This led to the foundation of CHRISTIANITY, in which he is seen as the Son of God.

JET PROPULSION Jet propelled AIRCRAFT have no propellers but get their thrust from the reaction to a jet of gas. If you blow up a balloon and let it go, it will fly across the room because the air you have put into it rushes out of the neck and pushes the balloon forward in the other direction. In a jet engine the gas jet is produced by burning fuel such as paraffin. The simplest jet engine is the ramjet, which has no moving parts. Most modern jets are turbojets or turbofans, which use a system of fans to bring about the compression of the incoming air. (See GAS TURBINE)

JEWELLERY Ornaments made mostly of GEMS and precious metals, and designed to be worn. Examples include necklaces, bracelets, brooches and earrings. Jewellery has been made since prehistoric times, when the bones and teeth of animals were used. There are many different styles and techniques for making jewellery.

JEWS A Semitic people who came to PALESTINE from MESOPOTAMIA in c. 2000 BC. Some became slaves in Egypt, and were led out by MOSES, who formalized their religion JUDAISM. They conquered all Palestine by c. 1000 BC, but split into two kingdoms and became dominated by a succession of outside empires, from Assyria to Rome. Finally, revolts against the Romans from AD 66 led to the destruction of the Temple at JERUSALEM and the complete dispersal of the people. Jews in medieval Europe were persecuted as the 'killers of Christ' (See JESUS CHRIST), and isolated

▼ *A gold brooch. This piece of jewellery was made in Crete about 3500 years ago.*

JET PROPULSION

▲ *A turboprop engine combines jet propulsion and conventional propellers. The arrows show the flow of air past the propellers and through the compressor and combustion chamber.*

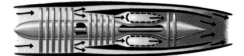

▲ *A turbojet engine sucks in air at the front. The air is compressed, then passed to the combustion chamber to burn the fuel. The hot exhaust gases thrust the engine forward.*

▲ *A turbofan engine is quieter and more powerful than other jet engines. It has a fan which pulls in extra air to bypass the combustion chamber.*

▲ *A ramjet, the simplest form of jet engine, has no compressor and only works properly at high speeds.*

in *ghettoes*; and in 1939–1945 the Germans under HITLER murdered over six million. In 1948 the foundation of ISRAEL gave the Jews a homeland in Palestine, and about 3 million now live there.

JOAN OF ARC French heroine (1412–1431) in the HUNDRED YEARS' WAR. Believing herself inspired by God, she led a French army against the English. Captured by the English, she was burnt for witchcraft and heresy. She was made a Roman Catholic saint in 1920. ◁

JOHANNESBURG The largest city in SOUTH AFRICA, Johannesburg has a population of 1,726,000. It is a great mining, manufacturing and financial centre, lying on the mineral-rich Witwatersrand ridge.

JOHNSON, SAMUEL English writer (1709–1784). After many years of poverty, he became famous for his *Dictionary*, his edition of Shakespeare, and his *Lives of the Poets*. But he is best remembered for his conversation and opinions, as recorded by his friend James BOSWELL in his *Life of Johnson*. ◁

JORDAN An Arab kingdom in the MIDDLE EAST, Jordan has 3,380,000 people (1984 est.) and an area of 97,740 sq km (37,738 sq miles). The capital is Amman. Most of the land is desert, but farmland exists in the moister uplands. The main export is phosphates. ▷

JOULE The SI UNIT of ENERGY and WORK, named after James Prescott Joule (1818–1889), the English physicist. The Joule is defined as the work done on an object by a FORCE of 1 newton acting through a distance of 1 metre. It can also be defined as the work done per second by a current of 1 AMPERE flowing through a resistance of 1 OHM.

JUDAISM Religion of the JEWS, formalized by MOSES. It teaches that there is only one God, and that the Jews are his special people, chosen to carry out his wishes. These wishes are summed up in the law of Moses, and set out in the *Torah*, or holy book. Jewish religious life is divided between home and SYNAGOGUE. Observances include circumcision, the Sabbath as a day of rest, and the holy days of Yom Kippur, Passover, Pentecost and Tabernacles.

JUJITSU The ancient Japanese SAMURAI skill of fighting without weapons, using throws and body locks. It is now much used by police and armed forces. Judo is the sport version.

JUPITER (GOD) The chief god of the ancient Romans. Also called Jove, he was the god of the sky and of battle, and reigned in Olympus as lord of heaven.

◀ A small silver statue of the Roman god Jupiter. The Romans left behind many relics of their religion and culture in the countries which once formed part of their empire.

JUPITER (PLANET) The largest planet in the SOLAR SYSTEM. Its orbit lies between those of MARS and SATURN. Around the giant planet is an atmosphere made up mainly of hydrogen. The main feature of Jupiter's atmosphere is its Great Red Spot, a huge oval mark thought to consist of a swirling mass of gases in a never-ending storm.

JURY A group of people (usually twelve) who have been called on to give a verdict in a court case. They must listen to all the evidence and, guided by the judge on points of law, must make a decision on the case. In English law at the present time, the decision does not have to be unanimous but is arrived at by a majority vote. The jury-system is used in Britain, the United States and most of the Commonwealth, although the rules governing its use vary from country to country.

▶ The size of Jupiter compared to the size of the Earth. Jupiter's diameter is ten times that of Earth's.

▼ Jupiter as seen from the Earth, showing bands of clouds. Jupiter has 16 satellites. The black spot just above the Great Red Spot is the shadow of one of them.

JORDAN: FACTS AND FIGURES
Official language: Arabic.
Currency: Dinar.
Religion: Moslem.
Jordan's only seaport is Aqaba on the Gulf of Aqaba. The River Jordan divides the country in two. The western bank is occupied by Israel. The Dead Sea, where the River Jordan ends, is nearly 393 m (1289 ft) below sea-level, the lowest point on the surface of the Earth.

K

KAMPUCHEA State in southeast Asia, formerly called Cambodia. It has an area of 181,300 sq km (70,000 sq miles), and 7,058,000 people (1984 est.). Formerly part of Indo-China, Kampuchea became independent in 1955. A Vietnamese-backed communist government took control in 1979. Civil war continued into the late 1980s. Capital: Phnom Penh.

KANGAROO MARSUPIAL (pouched MAMMAL) native to Australia, Tasmania and New Guinea. Kangaroos have strong hind legs with elongated feet, short front legs, a thick muscular tail and a small head. The females have a pouch in which the young are raised. The kangaroo moves by taking enormous leaps with its hind legs; it only uses its front legs for grazing. When it is not moving, the animal sits up on its back legs, balanced by its tail. Kangaroos eat grass and other green plants. There are many different species.

KARATE An oriental style of unarmed combat, using kicks and punches. As a sport, it involves both mock fights and formal examinations for the various grades of skill.

KEATS, JOHN Greatest of the English Romantic poets (1795–1821), and most famous for his *Odes*, all written in 1819: *To a Nightingale*; *To Autumn*; *On a Grecian Urn*; *On Melancholy*. He died in Rome of tuberculosis.

KELLY, NED Famous Australian outlaw (1854–1880). After wounding a constable in

◄ *A baby kangaroo with its mother. A kangaroo is blind and almost helpless when it is born. It crawls through its mother's fur to reach her pouch, which will be its home for the next nine months.*

▲ *John F. Kennedy was the fourth American President to be assassinated while in office.*

1878, he carried out several bank robberies, before being captured and hung. But many Australians have looked on him as a folk hero.

KENNEDY, JOHN F. President of the United States (born 1917). In the 1960 elections he defeated Richard Nixon, to become the youngest President ever, and the first Roman Catholic one. He dealt successfully with the Cuban crisis, forcing Russia to withdraw its nuclear weapons from Cuba, but at home his liberal policies made little progress. He was assassinated in November 1963.

KENYA A republic in East AFRICA, Kenya has 19,536,000 people (1984 est.) and an area of 582,646 sq km (224,961 sq miles). The capital is Nairobi. A beautiful country, it has magnificent national parks, and tourism is growing quickly. Formerly a British colony, Kenya became independent in 1963. Only 12 per cent of the land can be farmed. The rest is too dry. But farming is the chief industry, especially coffee and tea.   ▷

KIDNEY Complex organ which removes waste products from the BLOOD. Vertebrate (backboned) animals have two kidneys; each one consists of thousands of little tubes which filter the incoming blood. Useful substances are returned to the blood and re-enter the body's blood stream, but unwanted substances, including excess water, are kept back by the kidney. This waste matter, called *urine*, goes through a large tube, the *ureter*, to be stored in the *bladder*. From the bladder, urine passes out of the body. A person's two kidneys filter about 190 litres (40 gallons) of blood a day. As well as producing urine, kidneys secrete a hormone which controls the production of red blood cells; the kidneys also maintain the body's blood pressure.

KINGFISHER Brightly-coloured bird with a long pointed bill. Kingfishers are found all over the world. Some species are fishing kingfishers; they live near water and feed on fish. Other species, like the Australian kookaburra, are forest kingfishers; they live in wooded country, eating insects and small reptiles.

KIPLING, RUDYARD English writer (1865–1936). He is best remembered for his stories set in India, where he was born, and for his books for children (*Kim*, the *Just So Stories*, *The Jungle Book*).

KITE Bird of prey noted for its long wings, deeply forked tail and graceful flight. There are many species of kite throughout the world. Because of its magnificent gliding action, the kite has given its name to the man-made flying device.

KIWI Flightless, but fast-running, bird found only in New Zealand. The kiwi is about the size of a chicken, with brown or grey feathers, a long bill and no tail; it feeds on insects, worms and berries. Kiwis are night birds,

KENYA: FACTS AND FIGURES
Official language: English and Swahili.
Currency: Shilling.
Religion: Christianity.
Highest point: Mount Kenya 5199 m (17,058 ft).
Kenya has about 40 groups of African people, and some Asians and Europeans. The largest groups are the Kikuyu and the Luo.

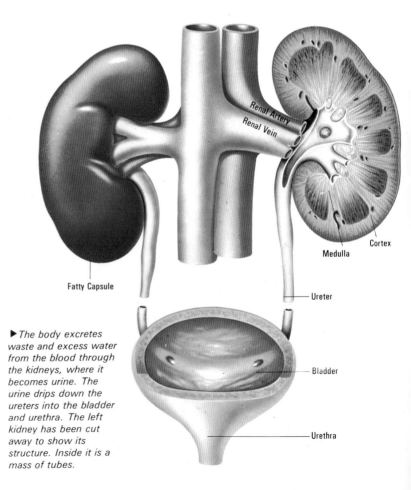

▶The body excretes waste and excess water from the blood through the kidneys, where it becomes urine. The urine drips down the ureters into the bladder and urethra. The left kidney has been cut away to show its structure. Inside it is a mass of tubes.

Renal Artery
Renal Vein
Cortex
Medulla
Fatty Capsule
Ureter
Bladder
Urethra

during the day they hide in burrows or dense undergrowth. ◁

KNIFE One of the first and most useful INVENTIONS – made by cavemen from sharpened pieces of flint and quartz. Uses today range from carving knives to paper knives, hunting knives and palette knives, from boy scout's pocket knife to surgeon's scalpel. ◁

KNIGHTHOOD Originally a knight was any mounted warrior who accepted the code of CHIVALRY. But later in the MIDDLE AGES the title of 'Sir' was only given to members of the Orders of knighthood – whether religious (like the Knights of St John) or royal (like the knights of the Order of the GARTER). ◁

KNITTING A way of interlacing thread or yarn so that it forms a fabric. It can be done with a machine or with hand-held needles (pointed rods, usually of plastic or metal). Wool is mainly used. The fabric is stretchy, and so can be used for buttonless garments (e.g. pullovers).

KIWI Kiwis are the sole surviving members of a group of wingless birds called moas. The largest moa lived on New Zealand's North Island and stood about 4 m (13 ft) high. It was probably the tallest bird that ever lived.

▲ *Kiwis hunt for food at night. They are nearly blind and use the nostrils at the tip of their long beaks to sniff out grubs.*

▶ *An early form of knife. This one was shaped from flint by people living in France or Spain over 10,000 years ago.*

▼ *Some knives are more decorative than useful. This ceremonial knife was made in Peru, about 600-700 years ago. The Peruvians were outstanding goldsmiths, but most of their work was destroyed by the Spanish conquerors 500 years ago.*

KNIFE No knives served a grislier purpose than the stone sacrificial knives of Mexico's Aztec Indians. Using sharp-edged flint blades, the priests hacked open living human victims and removed the hearts as sacrifices to the gods that they believed in.

KNIGHTHOOD The main British orders of knighthood are: The Order of the Garter (founded 1349); the Order of the Thistle (1687); the Order of the Bath (1725); the Order of St. Patrick (1788); the Order of St. Michael and St. George (1818); the Order of the Star of India (1861); and the Royal Victorian Order (1896). In 1917, the Order of the British Empire was started. This Order has Knights Grand Cross, Knights Commander, Commanders, Officers and Members.

Women who are given a rank similar to knighthood are called Dames.

KNOT (NAUTICAL) The unit of speed at sea: one knot is one nautical mile an hour. In theory a nautical mile is one minute of latitude – so it varies from one part of the globe to another. But in practice it is measured as 1853 metres (6080 ft).

KNOT (TYING) A way of tying rope, cord or thread. There are three main kinds of knot. *Hitches* are used for tying a rope to a ring, post, etc. *Bends* are used for tying the ends of two ropes together. *Knots* proper are used for tying up bundles, joining the ends of cords, or making loops or nooses. Common knots include the clove hitch and the reef knot. A knowledge of knots is vital to yachtsmen, mountain climbers, builders, etc.

KOALA Tubby tree-living MAMMAL from eastern Australia. Although koalas, with their thick grey fur and bushy ears, look like bears, they are not bears. They are MARSUPIALS: the young koala is reared in its mother's pouch which, unlike the KANGAROO's pouch, opens backwards. Koalas live on eucalyptus leaves and shoots.

KORAN The sacred book of ISLAM, said to have been revealed to the prophet MOHAMMED through the angel Gabriel. Its themes build on those of the Old Testament (see BIBLE), and its style has had a great influence on Arab literature.

KOREA Two nations in northeast Asia. Communist North Korea has 19,896,000 people (1984 est.) and an area of 120,538 sq km (46,540 sq miles). The capital is Pyongyang. The republic of South Korea has 40,578,000 people (1984 est.) and an area of 98,484 sq km (38,025 sq miles). The capital is Seoul.   ▷

KREMLIN The historic fortress at the centre of MOSCOW. It contains former palaces (now museums) and two cathedrals, and is the meeting place of the Supreme Soviet (PARLIAMENT) of the USSR (see RUSSIA). All the rest of old Moscow was destroyed by fire at different times.

KUBLAI KHAN A Mongol ruler (1216–1294), Kublai Khan was the grandson of the great GENGHIS KHAN. Under his rule, the Mongol empire reached its peak of power. Kublai Khan established his capital at Cambaluc, modern Peking, and encouraged art and trade. Among his visitors was MARCO POLO.

KUWAIT An Arab emirate in the MIDDLE EAST, Kuwait has 1,787,000 people (1984 est.) and an area of 17,818 sq km (6880 sq miles). The capital is Kuwait. This hot, dry country is one of the world's richest, being among the top ten oil producers.

▲ A koala lives in safety above the ground, eating the leaves and shoots of the gum or eucalyptus tree.

▼ Pusan, a busy port and the second largest city in South Korea. Korea was divided into two countries in 1945. They fought the Korean War from 1950 to 1953. Relations between them remain strained.

KOREA: FACTS AND FIGURES
Official language: Korean.
Currency: Won.
Climate: Hot, rainy summers; cold, dry winters.
About two-thirds of the people of Korea are engaged in farming.
South Korea hosted the Olympics in 1988.

L

LABOUR MOVEMENT The organization of workers in TRADE UNIONS to fight for higher wages and better working conditions, and to prevent UNEMPLOYMENT. Such movements have developed since the INDUSTRIAL REVOLUTION, when many workers began to live in industrial towns. Many political parties were set up with the support of the labour movement.

LACE An open fabric, plain or ornamented, and made from threads of linen, cotton, silk, silver, gold, nylon or, sometimes, wool. Lace-making began in Italy in the late 1400s.

LACQUER The RESIN of the lacquer or varnish tree. It is applied to wood, porcelain and metal to give a hard, smooth, transparent and shiny surface.

LACROSSE A fast team game borrowed from the North AMERICAN INDIANS. Each player has a stick with a net at one end. The aim is to get a ball into the other team's goal.

LADYBIRD Small, brightly-coloured BEETLE. There are about 5000 species of ladybirds in the world: most of them are oval-shaped and either red or yellow with black spots. Ladybirds are useful to man as they eat many insect pests.

LAKE An area of water enclosed by land. Freshwater lakes have outlets, such as rivers or streams. But some lakes are salty inland drainage basins.

LAMPREY Primitive eel-like creature found in both fresh and salt water. Although lampreys look like fish, they have no jaws and no SCALES. Some feed by sucking up small animals from the sea or river bed; others attach themselves to fish and feed on them by scraping off flesh.

LANGUAGE Language, both written and spoken, is our main means of communicating with each other. The word language comes from the Latin *lingua*, meaning 'tongue'. Most people learn their parent's language naturally, as children, by imitating the sounds made by older people and connecting them with the things they represent.

Early languages had complicated GRAMMARS, but few words. As they developed, the grammar usually became simpler and many words were added, mainly to account for the growth of new ideas. There are now about 2800 spoken languages, not including dialects, which are local forms of a language. The world's major languages, in terms of the number of speakers, are Chinese, ENGLISH, Russian, Hindi, Spanish and German. But English is the chief commercial or business language, followed by Chinese, French, Russian, Spanish and German.

◀ *Lampreys have existed for more than 300 million years. Lack of competition may be why their species has survived for so long.*

Lao

LAOS A communist republic in south-east ASIA, Laos has 4,019,000 people (1984 est.) and an area of 236,800 sq km (91,429 sq miles). The capital is Vientiane. Farming is the main occupation in this largely mountainous land.

LAPLAND A region, including parts of northern Norway, Sweden, Finland and Russia. Lapland is thinly-populated. Some Lapps are nomadic and follow the annual migrations of REINDEER. Other Lapps lead settled lives, living in villages.

LARK Small brown bird famous for its beautiful song. Larks live in open country and nest on the ground. There are many species; the majority belong to the deserts and plains of Africa.

LARVA Young INSECT. On hatching from the egg, some larvae, like those of GRASSHOPPERS and DRAGONFLIES, already resemble mature insects. During the larval stage, these young gradually change into complete adults. But others, such as young BUTTERFLIES, BEETLES and BEES, do not resemble the adult at all. For them, the larval stage is a time of eating and growing; then, they change into a pupa or chrysalis before turning into adults.

▷

LARYNGITIS Inflammation of the tissues lining the LARYNX. Laryngitis is caused by a germ or by an irritant such as tobacco smoke; it often results in loss of voice.

LARYNX Cavity in the upper windpipe (air passage in the throat) where sounds are produced. It is also called the VOICE box.

LASERS The word 'laser' is short for 'light amplification by stimulated emission of radiation'. A beam of laser light is very powerful, very narrow and it does not spread out as other LIGHT does – laser beams fired from the Earth at mirrors left on the Moon by Apollo astronauts, to give a very accurate measure of the Moon's distance, were only 3 km (nearly 2 miles) wide on reaching the Moon. Lasers behave in this way because the beams of light they send out are *coherent* – all the waves vibrate exactly together. The waves reinforce each other to produce light of great energy. Laser light is of a single wavelength, but each kind of laser produces its own wavelength.

▼ *The crystal at the heart of a laser produces a strong beam of light. The beam is reflected back and forth between mirrors until it is intense enough to shine through the half-silvered mirror.*

LARVA Some larvae are so different from their adult forms that they were long believed to be different creatures, and many still retain the names that were then given to them. Best known are the larvae of butterflies and moths (caterpillars) and flies (maggots).

LASER Some laser beams glow with a light a thousand times as bright as the Sun.

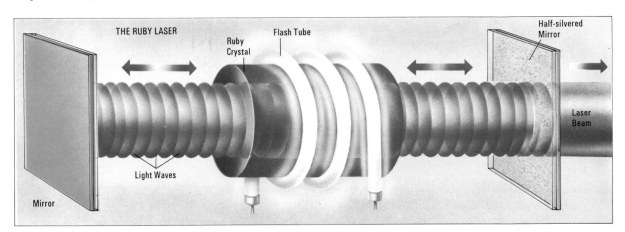

THE RUBY LASER

Ruby Crystal

Flash Tube

Half-silvered Mirror

Laser Beam

Light Waves

Mirror

◀ *Sparks fly as a laser beam cuts its way through a steel sheet. The laser's powerful beam is concentrated on a small area and can bore through almost anything, even a diamond.*

Some lasers produce invisible radiation such as INFRARED RAYS. Lasers can be used for cutting metals, drilling holes in diamonds, and measuring minute distances. They are also used in eye surgery and in HOLOGRAPHY. ◁

LATHE A MACHINE TOOL that cuts, grinds and polishes the surface of rotating pieces of metal, wood and plastic.

LATITUDE AND LONGITUDE These lines form networks on MAPS. Lines of latitude (parallels) are measured from the equator (0°) to the poles (90°N and 90°S). Lines of longitude (MERIDIANS) measure east and west of the prime meridian (0° longitude), which passes through Greenwich.

LATVIA A republic of the USSR (see RUSSIA), Latvia borders the Baltic Sea. It has a population of 2,587,000 (1984 est.) and an area of 64,000 sq km (24,711 sq miles). The capital is Riga. Russia ruled Latvia from the 1700s. A brief period of independence (1918–1940) ended when Soviet troops occupied the country.

LAUREL Dense evergreen tree from the Mediterranean region. True laurel – or bay – leaves are used for flavour in cooking; the leaves of the shrub called laurel are poisonous.

LAVA Hot molten rock which is erupted from VOLCANOES or from fissures (cracks) in the ground. Lava originates in large pockets of MAGMA deep underground. When it hardens on the surface, it forms rocks such as basalt. ◁

LAVA Lava flows cover 650,000 sq km (250,000 sq miles) of western India to a depth of up to 2,100 m (7,000 ft). In places there is a sandwich of up to 30 separate lava flows.

▼ *This lathe was invented by the British engineer Henry Maudslay in 1810 to produce accurate screws. Maudslay had to make the main screw by hand, so that the lathe could copy it for use in other lathes.*

LAVENDER Small Mediterranean shrub with fragrant narrow leaves and pale purple flowers. Lavender is cultivated on a large scale for use in the perfume industry.

LAVOISIER, ANTOINE LAURENT French chemist (1743–1794), the founder of modern CHEMISTRY. He investigated the processes of COMBUSTION and proved that AIR is a mixture of oxygen and nitrogen. He was executed during the FRENCH REVOLUTION. (See BIOCHEMISTRY)

LAW Any group of people needs to develop rules of behaviour to prevent some members of a community doing things which would injure other members, and they also need rules for settling disputes. The rules are, collectively, called the law. The GOVERNMENT makes law and ensures that it is enforced through the POLICE and the courts. Systems of law vary from country to country. Sometimes, laws vary from one part of a country to another.

LEAD A soft metallic ELEMENT with the chemical symbol Pb. Next to mercury, lead is the heaviest common metal. It is extracted chiefly from the mineral galena, and is used in paints, for the covering of cables and for the plates of car batteries.

LEAF Main food-producing part of a PLANT. In the presence of green CHLOROPHYLL and sunlight, a leaf makes food from carbon dioxide and water (see PHOTOSYNTHESIS). Most leaves consist of a blade and a stalk. The blade, full of green food-making cells, is usually broad and flat; underneath, it has tiny breathing holes, called *stomata*, which take in carbon dioxide and let out oxygen. The blade is supported by a skeleton of veins, carrying water to all parts of the leaf. The leaf stalk, linking the blade to the plant stem, is made up of tiny tubes which supply the veins with water from the roots and take food made by the leaf to other parts of the plant. Leaves generally grow in such a way as to trap the greatest possible amount of sunlight.

LEAP YEAR A year of 366 days which occurs when the year can be divided evenly by four. The extra day is February 29. Leap years are necessary because the CALENDAR year (365 days) is slightly shorter than the solar year. Century years are leap years only when they can be evenly divided by 400.

▶ *A Dutch law court in the early 18th century. Many courts are similar today. Here, a lawyer presents the case and another defends the accused (standing at right). The twelve people on the left, the jury, decide whether the accused is guilty. If guilty, the judge decides what the sentence will be.*

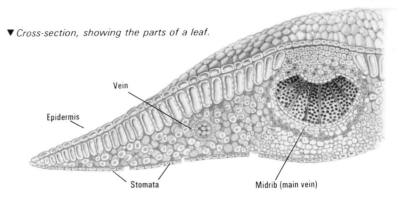

▼ *Cross-section, showing the parts of a leaf.*

Vein

Epidermis

Stomata

Midrib (main vein)

LEATHER Material prepared from the hide or skin of animals by removing the flesh and hair and then *tanning*. During tanning the skins are soaked in chemicals which prevent decay and give the leather flexibility and toughness.

LEBANON A republic in the MIDDLE EAST, Lebanon has 2,644,000 people (1984 est.) and an area of 10,400 sq km (4015 sq miles). The capital is Beirut. Commerce and trade, tourism and farming are the chief occupations.

▷

LEECH Blood-sucking worm, usually found in water. Leeches live on the blood or juices of other animals. They attach themselves to their victims by means of suckers at each end of the body; using sharp teeth they pierce the skin then suck out blood. In the past, doctors used leeches for blood-letting – taking blood from patients as a supposed cure for many illnesses.

LEEK Vegetable with a thick white stem and broad flat leaves; it is related to the onion but has a milder taste. The leek is the national emblem of Wales.

LEBANON: FACTS AND FIGURES
Official language: Arabic. Armenian, English and French are also spoken.
Currency: Pound.
Religion: About half the population is Christian, the other half is largely Moslem.
Rivers: The Orontes and the Litani.
During World War I, Lebanon was placed under French mandate. Its independence was proclaimed in 1941, but this did not become effective until 1944.

In normal sight, the lens in the eyeball focuses light rays on the retina to give a sharp image.

Short sight occurs because the lens brings parallel light rays from a distant object to a focus in front of the retina, making it look blurred. Short sight is corrected by wearing diverging lenses which push parallel rays further apart, so the eye lens can focus on the retina.

Long sight occurs because the lens tries to focus light rays from a nearby object behind the retina. This is corrected by wearing converging lenses which make the diverging light rays parallel or less diverging.

LENS The manufacture of lenses is a very specialized part of the glass industry. The glass used must be of exactly the right consistency, and the grinding must be carried out to a high degree of accuracy. A continuous stream of glass is usually drawn from a pot and cut automatically into pieces of the correct weight. The pieces of molten glass go into a mould and are pressed to the approximate shape of the required lens. These pieces of glass are annealed (heated and cooled to soften), and then ground to the correct thickness and curvature.

LEONARDO DA VINCI A brilliant artist, Leonardo nonetheless could not write normally. He wrote each line of words from right to left, reversing all the letters. Doctors call this *strephosymbolia*.

Among Leonardo da Vinci's inventions were the mincing machine, paddlewheels for boats, stonemason's saw, breech-loading guns, and pointed bullets instead of balls for ammunition.

LEMMING Small rodent (gnawing MAMMAL) found in cold northern lands. Lemmings are light-brown with dark markings. From time to time their numbers increase enormously; this creates a food shortage and forces the animals to migrate in thousands.

LEMON Small oval citrus fruit with a yellow skin and acid juice. Lemon trees are widely cultivated in southern Europe and the Middle East.

▼ Lemmings migrate at great speed and in large numbers. Many are killed but enough always survive to continue the species.

LENS A lens is a piece of GLASS or other transparent material, cut so that at least one surface is rounded. Lenses are used to *diverge* light (spread it out), or *converge* light (bring it closer together). *Convex* lenses make rays of light falling on them converge to a single point called the focus. *Concave* lenses make rays of light spread out. Lenses are used in cameras, TELESCOPES, MICROSCOPES and projectors. And they have important uses in eye GLASSES and contact lenses. ◁

LENT Part of the Christian year observed in the spring as a preparation for EASTER. It begins on Ash Wednesday and ends 40 days later (excluding Sundays) on Easter Sunday.

LEONARDO DA VINCI One of the most original and talented men of the Italian RENAISSANCE, Leonardo (1452–1519) is perhaps most well remembered as an artist, in particular for his paintings *The Last Supper* (1497) and the *Mona Lisa* (1503). But he was also a sculptor, architect, musician, inventor, civil and military engineer, botanist, astronomer, geologist and anatomist. He even designed flying machines. ◁

LEOPARD Fierce agile member of the CAT family found in southern Asia and Africa. Leopards, called panthers in India, are usually dark yellow with black spots. They hunt alone and at night. Often, they drag their kill – ranging from dogs to deer – up into a tree out of reach of lions and other preying beasts.

LEPROSY Disease occurring chiefly in tropical countries. Leprosy produces discoloured, lumpy skin, loss of feeling and, in severe cases, physical deformities and blindness, but it rarely causes death. It is successfully treated with drugs.

▼A self-portrait by Leonardo da Vinci. The anatomical drawing (right) shows Leonardo's abilities as both artist and scientist.

LESOTHO A mountainous, land-locked monarchy in southern AFRICA. Lesotho (called Basutoland until independence in 1966) has 1,470,000 people and an area of 30,335 sq km (11,720 sq miles). The capital is Maseru.   ▷

LETTUCE Vegetable growing close to the ground on a very short stem. Its large green leaves are usually eaten uncooked in salads.

LEUKAEMIA CANCER of the BLOOD in which the white blood cells increase at an uncontrolled rate. The result is a mass of abnormal cells which limits blood production and resistance to infection. Symptoms can be treated with x-rays and drugs, but there is still no cure for the disease itself.

LHASA Capital of TIBET (now part of China), Lhasa was once called the 'forbidden city'. It contains many Buddhist monasteries and temples. The population is about 120,000.

LIBERAL PARTY A political party which believes in the maximum individual freedom, although it supports government intervention to prevent poverty. But detailed Liberal policies vary. The first Liberal party was set up in Spain in the early 1800s.

LIBERIA A republic in West AFRICA, Liberia has 2,109,000 people (1984 est.) and an area of 111,369 sq miles (43,000 sq miles). The capital is Monrovia. Americans established Liberia in 1822 as a home for freed slaves.

LIBRARY A place where BOOKS are kept. The earliest libraries so far discovered were those of the ancient Babylonians and Assyrians who wrote on clay tablets. By the 1850s, the first public libraries were established in Europe and the United States.

LIBYA An Arab republic in North AFRICA, Libya has 3,624,000 people (1984 est.) and an area of 1,759,540 sq km (679,362 sq miles). The capital is Tripoli. Most of Libya is in the SAHARA but, beneath the hot sands, there are large oil reserves, forming Libya's chief re-

▲ A rainbow shows that white light is actually made up of many colours of light at different wavelengths. When sunlight passes through raindrops, it is broken up to form red, orange, yellow, green, blue and indigo violet bands. If the light is reflected again it forms a secondary bow, but this time with the colours in the reverse order.

source. Farmland is mainly on the Mediterranean coast.   ▷

LICHEN Plant organism in which special types of FUNGUS and alga (a very simple plant) live and work together. The tiny algae, bound up in the fungus threads, make food by PHOTOSYNTHESIS for themselves and the fungus. In turn, the fungus provides the algae with water, which it absorbs from the air, and mineral salts, obtained from the rocks on which it grows. Lichens are yellow or grey and spread over rocks, walls, tree trunks and poor soil.

LIGHT Light is a form of ENERGY, as heat and sound are. We see things because light is reflected from them. Light is produced when an object gets extremely hot. The Sun is a fiery ball of incandescent gas. According to the wave theory, light radiates out from its source as a series of waves – rather like the ripples on the surface of a pool spread out from a stone's splash. The distance between any two successive crests (or troughs) is called the *wavelength* of the light. These wavelengths are very

◀ Lichen growing on a rock. Lichens can grow in extremely bare places, where little else is able to survive. In time they break down the rock to form soil in which other plants can grow.

LESOTHO: FACTS AND FIGURES
Official languages: English, Sesotho.
Currency: Rand.
Highest point: Mont-aux-Sources 3298 m (10,822 ft).
No European settlement is permitted in the country.

LIBERIA: FACTS AND FIGURES
Official language: English.
Currency: Dollar.
Climate: Equatorial, with rainfall exceeding 250 cm (100 inches) annually on the coast, decreasing inland.
Iron ore and rubber are the chief resources, but Liberia also earns money from its large merchant navy, which consists almost entirely of ships registered under a 'flag of convenience'.

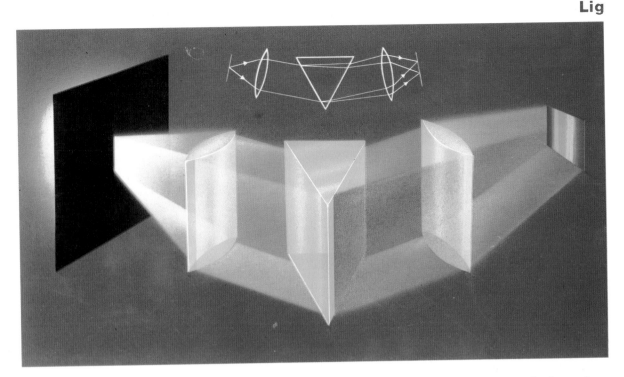

LIBYA: FACTS AND FIGURES
Official language: Arabic.
Currency: Dinar.
Religion: Moslem.
The country is largely desert, with farming possible only in two narrow strips around Tripoli and Benghazi.
Libya became an independent kingdom in 1951. The monarchy was overthrown by a military coup in 1969.

LIGHT Instruments called spectroscopes help astronomers to study light from the stars. The kinds of light a star emits can show the substances that it contains and how fast it is moving toward or away from us.

LIGHTHOUSE The first famous lighthouse was the Pharos of Alexandria in Egypt. It was built about 300 BC. At 120 m (400 ft) high this was one of the Seven Wonders of the World.

▲ *A spectrum of colours is formed when a beam of light passes through a prism. In a spectrometer, the light first passes through a slit and then an image of the slit is formed by passing the beam through two lenses. In between the lenses, a prism splits up the light into its basic colours. A series of images of the slit in the different colours forms, overlapping to give the spectrum.*

small – only a few millionths of a centimetre. The number of waves passing a point in space every second is the *frequency* of the light. And light travels at an enormously high speed – about 300,000 km per second (186,000 miles per second). The wavelength of light also determines its colour. For example, red light has a longer wavelength than blue light. When white light from the Sun, which consists of a mixture of many wavelengths, is passed through a glass prism, each wavelength is refracted to a slightly different extent. As a result, a prism can split white light into its component colours, or SPECTRUM. A rainbow is made up of the colours of the Sun's spectrum. (See ELECTROMAGNETIC WAVES) ◁

LIGHTHOUSE A building with a strong flashing light which warns ships of the danger of approaching land or rocks. Most are tall, often round or eight-sided, and are usually built on high ground along a coastline or on

▶ *Lighthouses are usually operated in shifts by three keepers, but some of the more isolated ones are now operated automatically.*

an island, so that they can be clearly seen from the sea. They must be strong structures to withstand stormy seas. Many are equipped with fog signals and radio beacons. ◁

LIGHTNING A lightning flash is simply a large spark of ELECTRICITY – a current flowing between a cloud and the earth, or between

▶ A streak of lightning flashes over a harbour at night. Lightning was once thought to be generated by gods, such as Jupiter and Thor, but we now know that it is a gigantic electrical spark.

clouds. The blinding flash and the clap of thunder are the effects of disturbances of the air by the electrical discharge.

LILAC Shrub or small tree grown in many parts of the world for its fragrant white or purple flowers.

LILY Plant, growing from a BULB, with showy white, yellow or red flowers. The lily family is large: as well as true lilies, it includes the hyacinth, bluebell, TULIP, ONION and asparagus.

LIMESTONE Limestone is one of the most common types of SEDIMENTARY ROCKS. There are many different kinds of limestone which not only look different but are in fact of a different composition and origin. Limestone is an important raw material for industry. It is used in vast quantities in the STEEL- and GLASS-making industries and to make cement and lime.

LINCOLN, ABRAHAM One of the greatest leaders of the UNITED STATES, Lincoln (1809–1865) became President in 1861. He ensured that the Union was preserved during the American CIVIL WAR. He was assassinated in Ford's Theatre, in Washington DC.

LINDBERGH, CHARLES A leading American aviator, Lindbergh (1902–1974) made the first solo trans-Atlantic flight in the *Spirit of St Louis*, in May 1927. (See AIRCRAFT)

▼ Charles Lindbergh at the window of the French Aero Club in Paris after his epic trans-Atlantic flight in May 1927.

LINEN Yarn and cloth made from FLAX. Linen is widely used for making dresses, sheets, and so on. The ancient Egyptians wrapped their dead in linen before burial.

LINOLEUM A floor covering made of powdered wood or cork, mixed with linseed oil, and then spread on hessian or felt paper. It was invented by a Briton, Frederick Walton.

LINOTYPE A machine for setting type, invented by Ottmar Mergenthaler (1954–1899). It originally set a complete *slug* or line of metal type. Modern Linotype machines are used for photographic typesetting.

LION Largest member of the CAT family, found in Africa and also parts of Asia. Lions are sandy-coloured with a large square

▼ A lioness rests during the day. Lionesses hunt for prey while the male lions stay behind to guard their territory.

LION Lions seldom specialize in hunting people. But in the early 1900s, the two maneaters of Tsavo killed and largely ate 135 Africans and Indians building a railway to what is now Uganda. The lions were eventually shot, stuffed, and put in a Chicago museum.

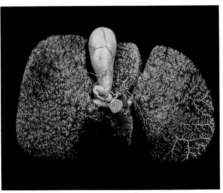

LISBON In 1755 Lisbon suffered one of the worst earthquakes ever known in Europe. The shock unleashed huge waves that swept in from the sea. Between them, waves and 'quake killed many thousands and destroyed much of the city.

LISZT, FRANZ As a boy Liszt was delicate. Once when he was ill his father felt so sure he would die that he even ordered the local carpenter to make a coffin. In fact Liszt lived to be almost 75.

LIVER The liver is the largest gland in the human body. It weighs between 1.4 and 1.9 kg (3 and 4 lbs).

head, tufted tail, powerful forelegs, and (males only) a flowing mane. They sleep during the day and hunt at night mostly for antelope and zebra. Lions live in prides – groups of up to 30 animals. ◁

LISBON The capital of PORTUGAL, Lisbon is a major seaport on the River Tagus estuary. This ancient city has 1,612,000 people. ◁

LISTER, JOSEPH English surgeon (1827–1912) who founded antiseptic SURGERY. He was the first to use carbolic acid to prevent infection in the operating theatre, and he discovered that instruments could be sterilized by heat.

LISZT, FRANZ A great Hungarian composer and a celebrated pianist, Liszt (1811–1886) combined folk and gypsy music in his famous *Hungarian Rhapsodies*. ◁

LITERATURE Everything written, from NEWSPAPER articles to the plays of William SHAKESPEARE or the fairy tales of the Brothers GRIMM is literature. However, the term is also used to distinguish between well-written material and work of a lesser quality. Imaginative literature can be divided into several areas, such as DRAMA, NOVELS, POETRY and SCIENCE FICTION. Non-fiction, such as books on HISTORY, is based on events that have actually

▼ *Aladdin's Cave, a limestone cave in the Cheddar Gorge. Limestone is a soft rock, easily dissolved by streams and underground rivers. Many caves and grottos in limestone regions have stalactites and stalagmites, formed by water dripping through the limestone.*

▲ *A model of the blood vessels of the liver. The gall bladder, shown in yellow, stores bile. Two arteries feed blood into the liver. The red artery (centre) and dark blue veins are those of the liver's normal blood supply. The hepatic artery (shown centre in pale blue) carries food from the digestion system. Excess carbohydrates and other materials, including some vitamins, are stored in the liver. Unwanted material is converted into urea and excreted as urine. The liver also destroys worn out red blood cells and stores iron.*

happened. The ancient SUMERIANS may have written the earliest literature, about 5000 years ago. Between the 900s and 300s BC, literature reached great heights in ancient GREECE. It included the famous poems of HOMER. With the invention of PRINTING, literature became available to almost everyone. Students often concentrate on a national literature, such as GREEK LANGUAGE AND LITERATURE or ENGLISH LITERATURE.

LITHOGRAPHY A PRINTING process using the flat surface of a stone or metal plate, which is based on the principle that oil and water do not mix. Hence, if a design is applied to a flat surface with a greasy material and then the surface is washed, greasy ink will be absorbed only by the greasy parts of the surface and will be repelled by the wet parts. Prints are then taken from the inked-in design.

LITHUANIA A republic of the USSR (see RUSSIA), bordering the Baltic Sea. Lithuania has 3,539,000 people (1984) and an area of 65,000 sq km (25,097 sq miles). The capital is Vilnius. Lithuania was independent from 1918 to 1920.

LIVER Large important organ found in all VERTEBRATES and some INVERTEBRATES. The liver is often called the body's laboratory as it makes and stores many vital substances. For example, it manufactures bile – a digestive fluid (see DIGESTION; GALL BLADDER), urea – a waste product, and various blood proteins. The liver also stores essential materials such as

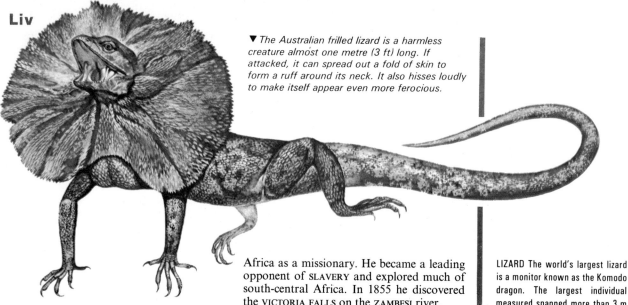

▼ *The Australian frilled lizard is a harmless creature almost one metre (3 ft) long. If attacked, it can spread out a fold of skin to form a ruff around its neck. It also hisses loudly to make itself appear even more ferocious.*

PROTEINS, MINERALS, VITAMINS and glycogen (reserve CARBOHYDRATE). ◁

LIVERPOOL A major seaport and industrial centre in north-western ENGLAND. Liverpool has a population of 540,000.

LIVINGSTONE, DAVID A great Scottish explorer, Livingstone (1813–1873) went to Africa as a missionary. He became a leading opponent of SLAVERY and explored much of south-central Africa. In 1855 he discovered the VICTORIA FALLS on the ZAMBESI river.

LIZARD REPTILE, related to the snake and found mainly in warm countries. Most lizards have a body covered with small overlapping scales and four limbs – but some, like the slow worm, are legless. They usually lay eggs and feed on animal matter such as insects. There are some 2000 lizard species in the world, including the CHAMELEON, IGUANA, gecko and skink. (See GILA MONSTER) ▷

LIZARD The world's largest lizard is a monitor known as the Komodo dragon. The largest individual measured spanned more than 3 m (10 ft) and weighed twice as much as an average man. Komodo dragons live on a few small Indonesian islands, where they kill and eat goats and small deer.

Among the European lizards illustrated here, the Ocellated lizard is the largest, being some 23 cm long, with a tail which doubles its length. Lizards are found in roadside banks, stone walls and sand dunes, among other dry places. Food consists of insects, fruit and birds' eggs.

Ocellated lizard

Common wall lizard

Male

Female

Sand lizard

Male

Female

Viviparous lizard

LLAMA South American domestic animal, related to the CAMEL but smaller and with no humps. Llamas are very sure-footed and are widely used in the ANDES for transport. They are also kept for their meat, milk and thick wool.

LLOYD'S A British INSURANCE firm that deals mainly in marine (shipping) insurance. But Lloyd's will also insure almost anything, including singers' voices and dancers' legs.

LOBSTER Large CRUSTACEAN with two great claws, found in northern coastal waters. It hides amongst rocks and only crawls out at night to find food such as crabs, worms and fishes. Alive, lobsters are bluish-black but turn bright red when cooked.   ◁

LOBSTER The largest lobster is the North Atlantic species, found mostly in American waters. There have been several catches of lobsters weighing more than 14 kg (30 lbs).

▲*Top: Most live lobsters are bluish-black, but the Norwegian lobster (above) is red. Lobsters have five pairs of legs, the front pair ending in large, strong pincers. The lobster uses these to seize and crush its prey. Most lobsters are caught in special pots. They have to be eaten very fresh and are usually boiled alive.*

LOCOMOTIVE The inventor of the *Rocket* began as a poor, uneducated cowherd. Becoming fireman on a colliery engine, George Stephenson discovered how it worked by taking it apart to clean it. Yet at 18 he could still not read or write. He learnt by taking three nights' spelling lessons a week, for a weekly cost of about 1p. Later he similarly studied mathematics.

The first really successful locomotive, Stephenson's *Rocket* had much in common with all steam locomotives that followed it. It was built as a unit and had a horizontal boiler. The boiler was tubular, and the exhaust steam was used to cause a forced draught up the funnel. The *Rocket's* maximum speed was 48 kph (30 mph), the fastest man had ever travelled on land.

LOCK AND KEY Methods of protecting property. Simple wooden locks were developed in ancient Egypt. There are now several kinds. The Yale lock contains a series of pins and drivers, which are all raised only when the correct key is inserted. Combination locks have no key. They are worked by a dial which is turned backwards and forwards to release the *tumblers*, which hold the bolt.

LOCOMOTIVE Machines used to push or pull trains. They can be powered by STEAM, DIESEL or ELECTRICITY. Steam locomotives need time to build up pressure. Diesel locomotives can be quickly stopped or started, and use fuel more efficiently than steam locomotives. The most powerful diesel locomotives are diesel-electric. The engine drives an electric generator and the electric power produced is fed to traction motors geared to the driving wheels. Electric locomotives stop and start quickly, and produce no smoke or

▼ *When a door is locked a bolt or bar moves out of the lock and fits into a slot in the door frame. In this lock, springs keep a set of levers in position so that the bolt cannot move. When the key is turned the levers are raised and line up to free the bolt.*

LEVER-TUMBER LOCK

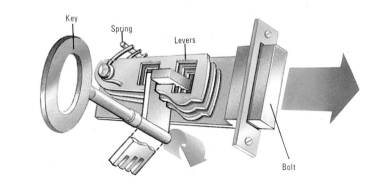

Key

Spring

Levers

Bolt

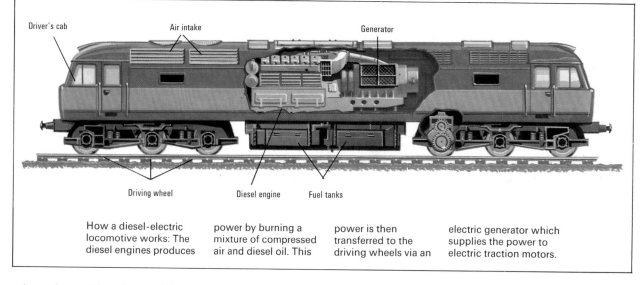

Driver's cab Air intake Generator

Driving wheel Diesel engine Fuel tanks

How a diesel-electric locomotive works: The diesel engines produces power by burning a mixture of compressed air and diesel oil. This power is then transferred to the driving wheels via an electric generator which supplies the power to electric traction motors.

exhaust fumes. They also need less maintenance. Two French electric locomotives hold the rail speed record of 330.8 kmh (206.6 mph). Most locomotives pick up the electric current from an overhead wire via a sprung arm called a *pantograph* on top of the engine body. Others pick up current from an insulated third rail.

The first steam locomotive was built in 1804 by a British inventor, Richard Trevithick (1771–1833). The first really successful one was the *Rocket*, built in 1829 by another Briton, George Stephenson (1781–1848). Electric locomotives were pioneered by the German firm of Siemens and Halske in the late 1800s. Diesel locomotives were first used in 1912. (See RAILWAYS) ◁

▶ *A powerful diesel locomotive pulls its carriages – many with observation rooms – through the Rocky Mountains.*

▶ *'Locomotion No 1' designed by George Stephenson, opened the Stockton to Darlington Railway in 1825 – and opened up the prospect of mass passenger and freight rail transport generally. This train went about 24 km/h (15 mph).*

Adult Locust (gregarious)

▲ *Locusts are a kind of grasshopper. Only the adults can fly; the younger hoppers keep to the ground. They are called gregarious because they move around in large swarms. Locusts on the move (at left) eat everything they can find and produce devastating damage. They can be controlled by spraying their breeding grounds with insecticide and killing them before they begin to swarm.*

LOCUST Type of GRASSHOPPER found in hot countries. Locusts move across the countryside in great swarms of a million insects or more. They eat all the vegetation in their path and can thus destroy vast areas of crops.

LONDON Capital of the United Kingdom of GREAT BRITAIN and Northern IRELAND, London is a great commercial city, standing on the River THAMES. It contains many places associated with events in British history, including the Houses of PARLIAMENT, WESTMINSTER ABBEY, the Tower of London, and so on. London was founded by the Romans. It was largely rebuilt after the Great Fire of London (1666). It has 6,767,500 people (1985). Its population is falling.   ▷

LOOM A machine used for WEAVING cloth. In a simple loom, the *warp* (lengthwise) threads are held in wooden frames and are lifted to allow the *weft* (crosswise) threads to be woven in. Looms were hand-operated until the late 1700s, when the power loom was invented by Edmund Cartwright (1743–1823). This machine speeded up the process.   ▷

LOS ANGELES A sprawling city on the Pacific coast of southern California in the UNITED STATES. Los Angeles, with its suburbs, has a population of 12,373,000 (1984). It includes HOLLYWOOD, the centre of the American film industry.

LOUIS Between 814 and 1824, there were 18 French kings called Louis.
Louis I (778–840), called the Pious, was the son of CHARLEMAGNE and succeeded him as Holy Roman Emperor.
Louis IX (1214–1270) led two CRUSADES to the Holy Land and was made a saint in 1297.
Louis XIV (1638–1715), known as the 'Sun King', believed in the absolute power of kings and, under him, France became the strongest power in Europe.   ▷

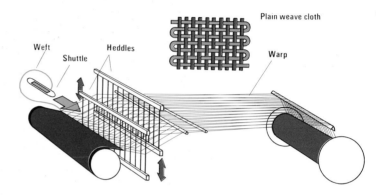

Weft · Shuttle · Heddles · Warp · Plain weave cloth

▲ *A loom. In plain weaving the warp passes through eyelets in the wires of two frames, or* heddles, *with half the threads running through one heddle and half through the other in an alternate pattern. Different weaves or patterns are made by threading the warp through the heddles in different orders.*

▼ *St Paul's Cathedral in London was designed by Sir Christopher Wren after the Great Fire of 1666 had destroyed most of the medieval city. St Paul's was bombed during World War II, but survived intact. The huge dome of this Anglican cathedral can be seen for miles around, and is one of London's most famous landmarks.*

LONDON Each year London sinks 0.3 cm ($\frac{1}{8}$th inch) into its foundations. But the land it stands on is sinking too. In a century the level of the Thames will rise 600 cm (2ft). Already, extra high tides could flood much of London. Only the Thames Barrier at Woolwich, completed in 1982, prevents this. It is the largest river barrier in the world.

LOOM In the 1700s French inventors devised ways of making a loom weave a pattern automatically. Warp threads of different colours were woven by a row of needles, that passed through a pattern of holes punched in a roll of paper. Where there were no holes, no needles could pass. After one passage of the weft, the paper moved on to show a new set of holes. These let through warp threads of a different set of colours.

LOUIS XIV No European king lived in more splendour than Louis XIV. An extravagant dresser, Louis wore elaborate wigs, and shoes with diamond-studded heels. He hired a small army of men to build, furnish and lay out the gardens of the vast palace at Versailles.

The building of Versailles took 50 years, no expense being spared. The gardens covered an area of over 100 ha (250 acres) and it is said that 4 million bulbs were brought from Holland each year to add colour.

In the gardens Louis built a Grand Canal 1.5 km (1 mile) long, on which guests sailed in ornamental boats. There were fountains and waterfalls everywhere, all powered by a large pumping station. By 1682, the entire French court had moved to Versailles. The palace housed over a thousand courtiers, with four times that number of servants.

Since the French Revolution of 1789 the great palace of Versailles has been only a museum.

LOUIS XVI After the French Revolution, Louis XVI and his family tried to escape from France disguised. They almost got to the frontier. Then an old soldier recognized Louis from his likeness on a bank note. The royal carriage was stopped, and Louis forced to return to Paris. Nineteen months later the revolution's leaders voted by 387 to 334 to kill him for treason.

LOUSE In 1528 the tiny body louse decided a war. Louse-borne typhus broke out among French troops besieging a Spanish army in Naples. In just 30 days half the French army had died, and the rest was defeated. Lice had made Spain's ruler master in Europe.

▶ *Louis XIV (1638-1715) was one of France's most powerful kings, and was responsible for the building of the magnificent palace at Versailles near Paris. This print shows Louis XIV receiving homage from a duke.*

▼ *This portrait of Louis XIV was painted by Hyacinthe Rigaud, and reflects the pomp and wealth of the 'Sun King'.*

Louis XVI (1754–1793) was executed in the FRENCH REVOLUTION. ◁
Louis XVIII (1755–1824) was given the throne when Napoleon was defeated in 1814.

LOUSE Wingless, blood-sucking insect. There are about 3000 species; some live as PARASITES on birds, others on mammals, including man. Many lice spread disease; one type found on humans carries typhus. ◁

LOUVRE The world's largest art MUSEUM, the Louvre is a beautiful building in PARIS. It holds about 275,000 works of art, including the *Venus de Milo* and LEONARDO DA VINCI'S *Mona Lisa*. The main parts of the Louvre were built in the reign of LOUIS XIV.

LUBRICANT A substance that is used to cut down the FRICTION between two surfaces. Fluid lubricants include oils and greases. Solid lubricants include GRAPHITE and talc.

LUMBERING The growing, tending and exploitation of FORESTS. Usually forests are grown for a supply of WOOD. But they may also be planted to prevent soil EROSION and to conserve water supplies.

Lun

LUNG Breathing organ found in man and many other animals. Air-breathing VERTE-BRATES have two lungs, usually in the upper part of the body. Air, from the nose or mouth, travels down the windpipe, through the two *bronchi* (tubes connecting the windpipe to each lung) and into the lungs. In the lung, the bronchial tube divides and re-divides many times until the air is being carried by millions of tiny tubes called *bronchioles*. Each bronchiole ends in a minute balloon called an *alveoli*, or air sac. The walls of the air sac contain hair-like vessels – *capillaries* – carrying blood. Oxygen spreads, or diffuses, through the air sac walls into the capillaries; at the same time, carbon dioxide diffuses from the blood into the lungs. (See RESPIRATION)

LUTE A stringed musical instrument introduced to Europe from Asia in the late 1200s. Modern European lutes have a pear-shaped body, with a flat top and several pairs of strings.

LUTHER, MARTIN The leading Protestant leader of the REFORMATION and the first German reformer to break with the ROMAN CATH-OLIC CHURCH. Luther (1483–1546) believed

▼*Lumbering has been an important industry in North America for hundreds of years, but it is a dangerous job with a high death rate.*

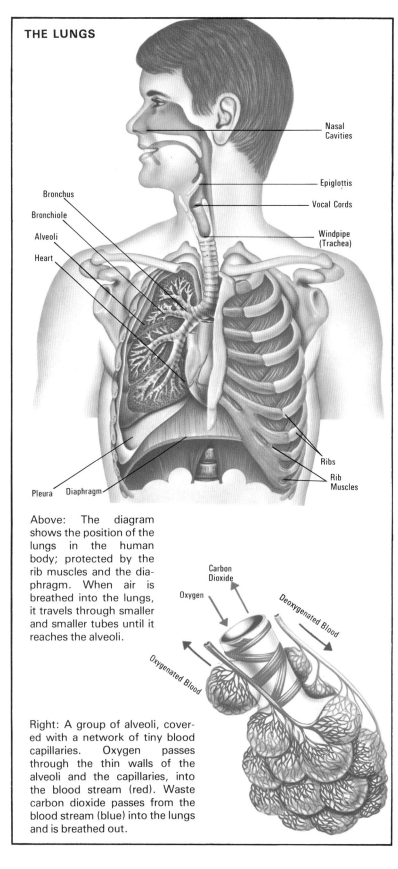

THE LUNGS

Nasal Cavities

Epiglottis

Vocal Cords

Windpipe (Trachea)

Bronchus

Bronchiole

Alveoli

Heart

Ribs

Rib Muscles

Pleura   Diaphragm

Above: The diagram shows the position of the lungs in the human body; protected by the rib muscles and the diaphragm. When air is breathed into the lungs, it travels through smaller and smaller tubes until it reaches the alveoli.

Carbon Dioxide

Oxygen

Deoxygenated Blood

Oxygenated Blood

Right: A group of alveoli, covered with a network of tiny blood capillaries. Oxygen passes through the thin walls of the alveoli and the capillaries, into the blood stream (red). Waste carbon dioxide passes from the blood stream (blue) into the lungs and is breathed out.

LUTHER, MARTIN Luther was a pupil at a school where boys spied on each other. They told the teacher who swore, spoke German, or broke other rules. Each week the teacher caned every guilty pupil once for each piece of misbehaviour. Luther often got 15 strokes.

LUXEMBOURG: FACTS AND FIGURES
Official languages: French and Luxembourgish.
Currency: Franc.
Religion: Roman Catholic.
Highest point: Buurgplatz 558 m (1835 ft), in the Ardennes.
Rivers: The Moselle, Sûre, Attert, and Alzette flow through the country.
Climate: The average temperature in July is about 17°C and about 0°C in January. Rainfall varies from 100 cm (40 inches) in the south-west to 30 cm (12 inches) in the south-east.

that men could be saved only if they believed in God, and that good deeds were not enough. (See CHRISTIANITY) ◁

LUXEMBOURG A Grand Duchy in western EUROPE. Luxembourg has 383,000 people (1984 est.) and an area of 2586 sq km (998 sq miles). Its capital is also named Luxembourg. French is the official language although most people speak a dialect of German. This rich nation has large iron ore reserves. Throughout the 20th century a considerable number of immigrants from Italy and other European countries have settled in the country. ◁

LYNX Wild CAT, about 75 cm (2½ ft) long with tufted ears and a fringe of hair on the cheeks. The lynx lives in forests where it hunts small animals by night. Lynxes run little, but are good walkers, climbers and swimmers and have exceptionally keen sight. The small lynx of North America, with a reddish-brown coat is called a bobcat or wildcat.

LYRE A musical instrument popular in ancient Greece, the lyre contained a hollow sounding board from which two arms projected. Strings extended from the sounding board to a crosspiece joining the arms. The lyre was also known in other ancient civilizations, including Assyria and Egypt, and in medieval Europe.

LYREBIRD Brown pheasant-like bird belonging to the forests of southern Australia. The bird takes its name from the cock's tail feathers which rise to form a magnificent fan in the shape of a LYRE.

► The European lynx was almost wiped out by hunters, and by farmers protecting their livestock from being attacked. The European lynx is now only found in Scandinavia, where it is protected by law.

▲ Martin Luther, the German monk, who questioned many of the teachings and practices of the Roman Catholic Church. As the Protestant movement grew, it also achieved political power, and for hundreds of years Europe was involved in religious wars and persecutions.

◄ Part of a 5th-century Greek vase showing an Athenian boy being taught to play the lyre. the lyre originated in Asia Minor, it was the forerunner of the harp.

M

MACAO Small Portuguese territory on the coast of southeast China, near Hong Kong. It has 343,000 people (1984 est.) and an area of 16 sq km (16 sq miles). In 1987 Portugal agreed to hand back Macao back to China in 1999.

MACAW Large brightly-coloured PARROT found in the tropical rainforests of Central and South America. Many species have gaudy green, blue, red or yellow feathers. The largest, the scarlet macaw, is over 90 cm (3 ft) long.

MACBETH A king of Scotland and the main character in SHAKESPEARE's play. Macbeth succeeded Duncan I, whom he killed in 1040. Macbeth was killed in 1057 by Malcolm III.

MACEDONIA A region in the BALKANS, Macedonia is divided between Bulgaria, Greece and Yugoslavia. In the 300s BC, it was a powerful kingdom under ALEXANDER THE GREAT.

MACHINE TOOL A power-driven machine, such as a LATHE, which operates by removing material – wood or metal – from the object that is being machined. Machine tools have many uses, e.g. for drilling, boring, and cutting threads for screws.

MACKEREL Slender, streamlined fish with a wide-forked tail. Mackerel, found in all the world's seas, swim in great shoals up to 40 km (25 miles) long and feed on PLANKTON in the surface waters. They are important food fish.

MADAGASCAR An African republic, Madagascar, which is also the world's fourth largest island, has an area of 587,041 sq km (226,656 sq miles) and 9,731,000 people (1984 est.). The capital is Antananarivo.

▲ A street in Macao, a tiny Portuguese territory and trading centre.

MADEIRA ISLANDS A Portuguese district in the Atlantic, off Morocco. Area: 796 sq km (307 sq miles); population: 251,000.

MADRID The capital of SPAIN, Madrid is near the centre of the Iberian peninsula. It has 3,188,000 people (1984). Its art gallery, the Prado, is one of the world's finest.

MAGELLAN, FERDINAND A Portuguese mariner, whose name in Portuguese was Fernão de Magalhães, Magellan (1480–1521)

◀ The route taken by Magellan's expedition, 1519–1522 — the first circumnavigation of the world. The left-hand map shows the route up to Magellan's death in the Philippines. The right-hand map shows the return route followed by the remainder of the expedition.

222

served Charles V of Spain. In 1519 he set out with five ships to find a western sea route to Asia. He was murdered in the PHILIPPINES, but one of his ships returned to Spain in 1522, the first to sail around the world.

MAGIC The belief that by doing or saying certain things, nature can be controlled and people can be influenced supernaturally. Magic was closely associated with primitive religions. Magic rites were supposed to bring success in hunting, warfare, and so on.

MAGMA Hot molten ROCK within the EARTH's crust or around the top of the mantle. Magma appears on the surface as LAVA or as burning-hot fragments during volcanic eruptions.

MAGNA CARTA A document which the leading barons of ENGLAND compelled King John to sign in 1215. The *Magna Carta* (Great Charter) secured the rights of the barons and made the king answerable to the law. It promised a fair trial and justice to everyone.

MAGNESIUM A light silver-white metallic ELEMENT. Its chemical symbol is Mg. It burns brilliantly when set alight, so it is used in fireworks. The hydroxide of magnesium is the familiar 'milk of magnesia', an antacid for stomach disorders. Most magnesium is obtained from sea water.

▼ *Many volcanoes are composite cones* **1**, *composed of alternate layers of ash, dust, rock fragments and lava. The volcano's vent* **2** *connects the crater to an underground reservoir of molten rock called* magma **3**. *Secondary vents cut through the volcano, causing lava flows on the surface* **4**. *Sloping sheets of magma push up through rock strata and solidify to form dykes* **5**. *Horizontal or nearly horizontal sheets of magma, solidified underground, are called* sills **6**.

Mag

MAGNETISM Magnetic compasses were in use in Europe by about AD 1200, but the Chinese are believed to have noticed long before that a suspended magnet always points in the same direction. A magnet can be used as a COMPASS because the Earth itself is a huge magnet that attracts the ends of any other magnet, pulling it in a north-south direction. The end of the magnet that points north is called the north pole; the other end is the south pole. It is a basic law of magnetism that similar poles repel and unlike poles attract each other – north attracts south but repels another north. IRON is the strongest magnetic metal; others are NICKEL and COBALT. These metals can be made magnetic by subjecting them to a magnetic field, either by stroking them with another magnet or by placing them inside an electric coil. Electric currents produce magnetic fields. If a wire is wound round a piece of iron and electric current is passed through the wire, the whole becomes an electromagnet. Also, when a wire is moved in a magnetic field, ELECTRICITY is generated in the wire. (See GENERATOR) ▷

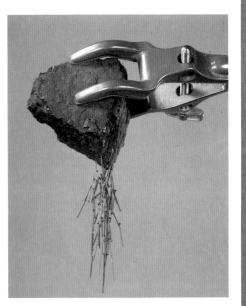

▲ *Lodestone is a type of iron ore that is naturally magnetised. Here, a piece of lodestone picks up a chain of pins.*

▼ *By shaking iron filings on to a magnet, the magnetic field can be seen as the filings align themselves along the field lines of (top) a bar magnet and (bottom) two magnets.*

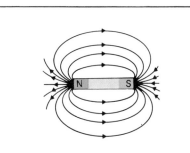

▲ *The magnetic field lines that exist around the poles of a bar magnet, where the lines of force meet halfway between the poles.*

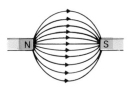

▲ *The magnetic field lines created by two opposite poles run from the north pole of one magnet to the south pole of the other.*

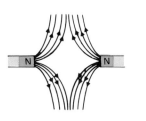

▲ *The magnetic field lines caused by two like poles will bend to avoid each other.*

MAGNETISM Iron oxide particles in clay act as magnets aligned with the Earth's magnetic north and south poles. Baking the clay stops the particles changing alignment. But the Earth's north and south poles shift position at a known rate. Thus, experts comparing the magnetic patterns in fresh clay and old, baked clay, can date baked clay objects that are thousands of years old. Archeologists call this archaeomagnetic dating.

The Chinese first used magnets to foretell the future. But they were using them on ships by AD 1100. In 1119 one Chinese writer wrote: 'The captain finds the ship's position by looking at the stars at night, by looking at the Sun by day, by looking at the south-pointing needle in cloudy weather'.

According to Pliny, the great early Roman naturalist, magnetic rock was discovered by a shepherd called Magnes, who found that his shoe-nails and iron-shod staff were attracted to the rock on Mount Ida, in Asia Minor. Others think the word 'magnetism' comes from a district in Greece called Magnesia where magnetic rock is found.

MALAWI: FACTS AND FIGURES
Official languages: English, Nyanja-Chews, Tumbuka.
Currency: Kwacha.
Malawi was once called Nyasaland. It includes part of Lake Malawi, which is called Lake Nyasa in neighbouring Tanzania. Almost all the people of Malawi are Bantu.

MALAYSIA: FACTS AND FIGURES
Official language: Malay.
Currency: Dollar.
Highest point: Mount Kinabalu, 4,100 m (13,455 ft) in Sabah. While 60 per cent of the area of Malaysia is in Borneo, more than 85 per cent of the people live in Malaya.
Climate: Hot and humid all through the year, average rainfall being over 250 cm (100 inches).
The capital, Kuala Lumpur, has a population of 938,000.

MALI: FACTS AND FIGURES
Official language: French.
Currency: Mali franc.
Chief river: The Niger.
Most people live by breeding livestock or by farming.

MALTA: FACTS AND FIGURES
Official languages: Maltese and English.
Currency: Maltese pound.
The main island of Malta is only 28 km (17½ miles) long and 13 km (8 miles) wide. The republic of Malta includes the smaller islands of Gozo and Comino.

▲ The shiny, dark green leaves and waxy flowers of the magnolia of North American forests. Botanists think the magnolia was among the first flowering plants, because of its primitive flower structure. Species may be evergreen or deciduous.

MAGNITUDE In ASTRONOMY, a measure of the brightness of a STAR or other heavenly body. Small magnitude numbers correspond to bright stars, the brightest of all having negative numbers. The very bright star Sirius, for example, has a magnitude of -1.45. The faintest stars, visible only with the most powerful telescopes, have magnitudes of more than 20.

MAGNOLIA Beautiful tree or shrub famous for its large, pale fragrant flowers which bloom very early in spring, often before the dark green leaves appear. Most species of magnolia are native to Asia or North America.

MAHOGANY Tall tree growing in tropical Africa and America. Its hard red wood, which has attractive markings and takes a high polish, is used for making furniture.

MALAGASY REPUBLIC See MADAGASCAR

MALARIA A disease which occurs mostly in tropical and subtropical areas. Malaria is caused by tiny PROTOZOA which are transmitted from infected to healthy people by the female *Anopheles* MOSQUITO. It causes recurring bouts of fever and great weakness.

MALAWI A republic in southern AFRICA. Malawi (called Nyasaland until independence in 1964) has 6,839,000 people and an area of 118,484 sq km (45,747 sq miles). Tobacco and tea are the main products. Capital: Lilongwe. ◁

MALAYA A peninsula with offshore islands in south-east ASIA, Malaya was formerly a British territory. It achieved independence in 1957 and became part of MALAYSIA in 1963.

MALAYSIA A monarchy in south-east ASIA, Malaysia consists of mainland MALAYA and Sabah and Sarawak on BORNEO. It has 15,193,000 people (1984 est.) and an area of 329,749 sq km (127,317 sq miles). The capital is Kuala Lumpur. The main peoples of this farming nation are Malays and Chinese. The country was established in 1963. ◁

MALI A republic in West AFRICA, Mali has 7,973,000 people (1984 est.) and an area of 1,240,000 sq km (478,767 sq miles). The capital is Bamako. Tuareg nomads live in the north, with black African farmers in the south. ◁

MALTA An island republic in the MEDITERRANEAN SEA, Malta (independent since 1964) has 380,000 people (1984 est.) and an area of 316 sq km (122 sq miles). The capital is Valletta. ◁

MAMMALS The most highly-developed class of animals on Earth and, as they have larger brains than any other living creature, they are the most intelligent. They are VERTEBRATES but differ from other backboned animals by their growth of hair and secretion of MILK. All mammals have hair – ranging from hedgehog spines to sheep's wool – although some, such as the hippopotamus and man have very little. And all mammals feed their young on milk from the mother's body: 'mammal' comes from *mamma* which means milk-secreting organ. There are three groups of mammals: *monotremes* – mammals such as the duck-billed platypus, that lay eggs; MAR-

◀ The earliest mammals appeared during the Mesozoic Era, 225 million years ago. Mammals such as this Morganucodon were hardly bigger than the eggs of the great dinosaurs with whom they shared the Earth. Mammals stayed small until the end of the Mesozoic; only in the Cenozoic Era did they grow and flourish.

REPTILE V MAMMAL

Reptiles give birth by laying eggs. Most mammals give birth to live young and provide food and care for them.

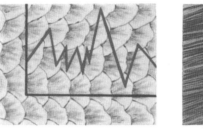

A covering of hair helps the mammals to maintain a constant body temperature. The scales of reptiles give no such insulation.

Air must pass through a reptile's mouth as it breathes, so it cannot breathe while feeding. In mammals the air passes direct to the back of the mouth. The mammals' brain (grey) is also larger than in the reptile.

The reptile's teeth can only gather food, but mammals have cusps for crushing their food.

▲ *Modern representatives of two kinds of mammal. The mice (above) are among the most successful* placentals, *having spread to all parts of the world. The koalas (top) are* marsupials. *The cubs emerge from the pouch after about six months and are then carried on the mother's back.*

SUPIALS – mammals, like KANGAROOS and KOALAS, that rear their young in pouches; and *placental* mammals which keep their babies inside the female's body for a relatively long time. Man is a placental mammal. The 5000 species of mammals alive today vary in size from the giant Blue Whale to the tiny shrew.

Mammals are the only vertebrates with a single bone in the lower jaw. Biologists have found fossils with this feature dating from the period of the dinosaurs, some 200 million years ago. These first mammals probably survived the changes that killed the great reptiles, because they had already developed fur and warm blood. From these ancient creatures, the size of rats, a vast variety of mammals developed, suited to widely varying conditions in nearly every part of the world. Present-day mammals show greater variety of forms than any other group of animals. ▷

MAMMALS Scientists divide the mammals into various 'orders'. Some of the main orders are: *Marsupalia* (the pouched mammals); *Edentata* (armadillo, sloth); *Carnivora* (dog cat, lion, seal); *Cetacia* (whale, dolphin); *Perissodactyla* (horse, zebra, rhinoceros); *Artiodactyla* (pig, cow, camel, sheep, goat, deer); *Rodentia* (squirrel, rat); *Lagomorpha* (rabbit, hare); *Insectivora* (mole, hedgehog); *Primates* (tree shrew, monkey, ape, man).

MAMMOTH Near Pavlov in Czechoslovakia archaeologists found a bone heap containing the remains of more than 100 mammoths. They believe that Stone Age hunters had caught and killed the huge beasts in pitfall traps.

MAMMOTH Huge prehistoric elephant with shaggy hair, powerful trunk and fierce curved tusks up to 4 metres (13 ft) long. Mammoths first appeared 3 million years ago and lived in parts of Europe, Asia and America. They died out around 8000 BC. ◁

MANATEE Large, grey-brown sea cow, up to 2.5 metres (8 ft) in length, found in tropical rivers and coastal waters on both sides of the Atlantic. Manatees are heavy, torpedo-shaped animals with flippers and a strong, flat tail. They feed on seaweed and other water plants. Manatees were hunted for their meat, oil and skin and are now quite rare.

MANCHURIA A region in north-east CHINA. Manchuria has many heavy industries, based on abundant reserves of coal and iron ore. Winters are very cold and summers mild.

MANDOLIN A musical instrument with four or five pairs of strings, the mandolin (or

▶ Woolly mammoths long deep-frozen in the Siberian tundra, have been discovered in recent years still intact. This baby one, known as 'Dima' was found in the late 1970s.

◀ Mammoths were Ice Age mammals that found sufficient food on the fringes of the great ice sheets. Their thick fur kept them warm and their reserves of fat stored around their shoulders supplied extra nourishment. Early human hunters wiped them out over 10,000 years ago.

Man

mandoline) is played with a *plectrum*, a small piece of wood, metal or plastic.

MANGANESE A hard, brittle metallic element – symbol Mn. Its chief use is in making ALLOYS such as hard manganese steel. It is also used in dry batteries, fertilizers and glass manufacture. ▷

MANGO Juicy fruit of a tropical evergreen tree. Mangoes, about the size of apples but heavier, have a soft, juicy yellowish flesh. They can be eaten when they are ripe or used green for pickles.

MANGROVE Tropical tree or shrub which grows along low-lying muddy coasts and estuaries in Africa, Asia and South America. At high tide only a floating mass of grey-green leaves is visible, but at low tide, trunks, supported by a maze of roots, appear.

MAORI A Polynesian people who travelled by canoe from Pacific islands to NEW ZEALAND in the 1300s. The Maoris were prosperous until the land wars with the British in the mid-1800s. They now have full CIVIL RIGHTS and number about 258,000 (1976 est.).

MAO ZEDONG (or Mao Tse-tung), great revolutionary leader of China (1893–1976). He led the peasants to defeat the Nationalist leader Chiang Kai-shek. He established the communist Chinese People's Republic in 1949 and became its chairman. ▷

MAP An accurate representation of the Earth's surface, or part of it. Most maps are drawn to scale so that distances can be measured off them. Topographic maps are small-scale maps, showing natural and man-made features, together with the height of the land, depicted by contours. Large-scale maps

MANGANESE The metal was discovered by Johann Gahn in 1774. About 95 per cent of all manganese is used in the production of steel. To make a tonne of steel, about 6 kg (13 lbs) of manganese is used. Manganese does not exist naturally in its pure state, but more than a hundred different manganese ores are known, most of them found in Russia. Many meteorites contain a quantity of manganese.

▶ Contours are lines on maps that join places of equal height above sea level. The numbers represent the height in metres. The left-hand diagram shows the shape of the land represented on the map by the contours.

▼ To find a distance on a map, you must first find the map scale. Some maps have a graphic scale — a line divided into kilometres. This map's graphic scale shows that one cm on the map represents 40 km.

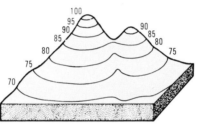

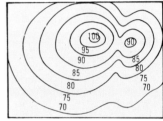

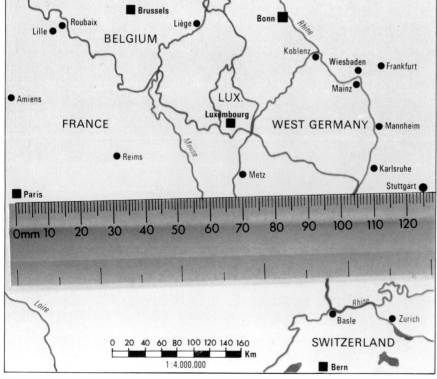

MAO ZEDONG In 1934–1935 he led 90,000 Communists on a 368-day march through China to escape Nationalist forces. His army crossed 18 mountain ranges and covered 9,650 km (6,000 miles) in what was the longest military march ever. Rearguard fighting killed four-fifths of Mao's army.

MAP The first map to be printed appeared in AD 1472. But one source says the oldest map known is about 5,800 years old. It is a clay tablet with a scratched outline of the River Euphrates in what is now northern Iraq.

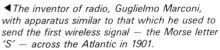
◀ *The inventor of radio, Guglielmo Marconi, with apparatus similar to that which he used to send the first wireless signal — the Morse letter 'S' — across the Atlantic in 1901.*

MARCONI, GUGLIELMO The importance of the new wireless in saving life at sea was first shown in 1899. In that year, the East Goodwin Sands lightship was rammed in fog, and help was summoned in time by wireless.

Marconi was awarded the Nobel Prize in physics in 1909; in 1912 he lost his right eye in a car accident. In 1929 the Italian government made him a *marchese* (marquis). Marconi was a Fascist; when he died in 1937 he was in charge of scientific research under Mussolini.

MARIE ANTOINETTE There is a story that in 1789 the women of Paris marched on the palace of Versailles to try and make Louis XVI give way to their demands for a better government. When Marie Antoinette was told that the women outside the palace were hungry and had no bread, she said 'let them eat cake'. This story of the queen's callousness was spread about during the French Revolution, but there is no evidence that she ever made the remark.

MARIJUANA Marijuana has many regional names. In western countries, it is often called pot. Other names include bhang (India), dagga (South Africa), hashish (Arabia) and kif (North Africa).

are called plans. Special maps show many things, such as population distribution, weather conditions and even the incidence of diseases. ◁

MAPLE Deciduous tree native to the northern hemisphere. In autumn, its leaves turn spectacular shades of yellow, orange and red. There are many different species. One, the sugar maple, is tapped for its sweet syrup. The maple leaf is the emblem of Canada.

MARATHON A long-distance race of 42.19 km (26 miles, 385 yards), the Marathon has been an event in the OLYMPIC GAMES since 1896. It was named after a soldier's run from Marathon to ATHENS in 490 BC to bring news of a Greek victory over the Persians.

MARBLE A metamorphic ROCK formed when LIMESTONE is subjected to great heat and pressure. It is often used by sculptors. It is easy to shape and takes a high polish.

MARCONI, GUGLIELMO The inventor of wireless TELEGRAPHY (RADIO), Marconi (1874–1937) produced a wireless telegraph

system in 1895. In 1901 he established communication with Canada from England. ◁

MARCO POLO A Venetian merchant explorer, Marco Polo (1254–1324) penetrated the Chinese empire of Kublai Khan. He set out in 1271 with his father and uncle on a 3½-year overland journey across Asia to Peking. He travelled widely in the service of Kublai Khan. On his return to Venice in 1295, he wrote an account of his travels.

MARGARINE A butter substitute, margarine is made from vegetable fats and oils, usually with vitamins A and D. It was developed during the FRANCO-PRUSSIAN WAR.

MARIA THERESA Born in Vienna, Maria Theresa (1717–1780) became empress of Austria, Hungary and Bohemia in 1740. An able ruler, she introduced many reforms while striving to keep her lands intact.

MARIE ANTOINETTE The wife of LOUIS XVI of France. Marie Antoinette (1755–1793) became unpopular because of her extravagance and support of Austrian interests. She was executed in the FRENCH REVOLUTION. ◁

MARIGOLD Garden plant belonging to the DAISY family, with bright yellow or orange flowers. Many species originated in Mexico.

MARIJUANA A narcotic DRUG made from the sap or dried leaves of the hemp plant (*Cannabis sativa*), which is native to India. Marijuana may cause mild hallucinations. Its use is prohibited in many countries, partly because users may turn to stronger drugs. ◁

MARLIN Large fish found in tropical oceans; it is related to the SWORDFISH. Some

◀ *The caravan of the Venetian explorer Marco Polo, taken from an old Catalan manuscript. Marco, his father, Nicolo Polo, and his uncle Maffeo Polo, travelled to Cathay (China) from 1271 to 1275. They stayed there in the service of Kublai Khan until 1292, when they set out for home. They reached Venice again in 1295.*

species of marlin weigh over 500 kg (half a ton) and grow to 3.5 metres (12 ft) in length.

MARRIAGE A publicly recognized contract between a man and woman. Marriage is a way of providing a secure life for children. Marriage laws vary from country to country according to the religions and customs. For example, Moslems practise polygamy and a man can have up to four wives. In most societies, marriage is sanctified by religious ceremonies.

MARS (GOD) The son of JUPITER and Juno, Mars was the Roman god of war. Among the gods, Mars ranked second only to Jupiter. He was regarded as the father of ROME and his son, Romulus, was its legendary founder. The month of March was dedicated to Mars.

MARS (PLANET) The fourth planet from the Sun. It is about half the size of the Earth and takes 687 days to orbit the Sun. White polar caps increase and diminish with the seasons. The *Viking* spacecraft's mission in 1976 failed to settle the question as to whether there is any life on Mars. The planet's thin atmosphere is composed mainly of CARBON DIOXIDE. ▷

MARSUPIAL MAMMALS with pouches. A young marsupial is born very undeveloped and very small (a baby kangaroo is as tiny as

▲ *The surface of Mars, the 'Red Planet', photographed by* Viking 1 *on July 21, 1976. The scene is one of loose rocks up to a metre or so across, scattered over a dusty surface.*

▼ *The koala, one of the world's marsupials, rides on its mother's back for six months after leaving her pouch.*

MARS (PLANET) The temperature on Mars varies from −70°C to 30°C during the day. Its rotation period is 24 hours 37.5 minutes. Mars has two small moons, Phobos and Deimos, which were first seen in 1877. The land surface of Mars is dominated by huge volcanoes and massive gorges, far more impressive than anything on Earth. The planet's atmosphere is only about a hundredth part as thick as our own. Like Earth, Mars probably has a large iron core.

MARSUPIAL The smallest is probably the Kimberley flat-skulled marsupial mouse of Western Australia. Its body is less than 4.5 cm (1.75 in) long. The largest species is the Red kangaroo from south and east Australia. From nose to tail males measure up to 2.7 m (8 ft 11 in.).

MASK Masks found in Africa in the 1800s were used in religious rites and ceremonies. Many Europeans condemned them as crude. But artists, such as Pablo Picasso and Amedeo Modigliani, collected them. The abstract nature of these masks strongly influenced a new European art movement, called cubism.

MASTODON In North America fossil mastodons have turned up in bogs and swamps, and on the beds of lakes, rivers, and the sea. Specimens deep-frozen in Alaskan bogs have been so well preserved that we can still see the coats of red-brown hair that insulated them from Ice Age cold.

MATCHES Early types of match included the French phosphoric candle, invented in 1780. This was a paper strip dipped in phosphorus and stored in an airtight glass tube. When the tube was broken the paper burst into flame. Matches of modern type date from 1827.

MECCA was a holy centre of the Arabs even before Mohammed's birth. From all Arabia pilgrims came to offer homage to the *Ka'aba* or 'cube', a shrine containing a black meteorite. They thought that many gods made this shrine a home. Moslems believe in one God, but the *Ka'aba* is still the Moslems' major meeting place in Mecca.

2 cm [1 in]) and cannot possibly look after itself. Instead, it crawls into its mother's pouch and stays there for several months, feeding off its mother's milk. The female's milk glands open into the pouch. The young animal does not leave the pouch for good until it is able to fend for itself. Except for the OPOSSUMS of America, all the world's marsupials live in Australia. They include KANGAROOS, wallabies and KOALAS. ◁

MARX, KARL Possibly the most influential political thinker and writer of modern times. Karl Heinrich Marx (1818–1883) saw history as a series of class struggles which would end when the workers overthrew their masters. His major work, *Das Kapital*, formed the basis for the beliefs of modern COMMUNISM..

MARY The mother of JESUS CHRIST, the Blessed Virgin Mary was betrothed to Joseph, a carpenter, when an angel told her that she would give birth to Jesus. Her virginity is an important belief of the Christian Church.

MARY I A devout ROMAN CATHOLIC, Mary I (1516–1558) became queen of England in 1553. Her marriage to Philip II of Spain involved England in European wars. Her attempts to restore Roman Catholicism led to the execution of many Protestants.

MARY, QUEEN OF SCOTS The last ROMAN CATHOLIC ruler of Scotland, Mary (1542–1587) was also heir to the Protestant ELIZABETH I of England. Until her execution, she was the centre of plots to overthrow Elizabeth.

MASK A covering for the face to disguise the wearer's features. Masks were worn by actors in ancient China and Greece to express character or emotions. In some parts of the world masks are associated with magic and are worn in rites and ceremonies. ◁

MASS In PHYSICS, mass is the quantity of MATTER in a body. A cricket ball has more mass than an apple, although they look the same size. Mass should not be confused with weight. Weight is the force with which a body is attracted to the Earth by gravitation. A cricket ball weighs more than an apple on Earth. In space neither would have any weight, but the cricket ball would still have a greater mass. Weight varies from place to place. Mass is the amount of matter in something and does not vary.

MASTODON Extinct elephant-like animal with a furry coat, massive teeth and short sturdy legs. Mastodons, smaller than today's elephants, first appeared in North Africa about 40 million years ago, then spread to

other parts of the world. They died out some 8000 years ago. ◁

MATCHES Small sticks of wood or cardboard tipped with a substance containing phosphorus sulphide, which catches fire by FRICTION when drawn over any rough surface. In *safety matches* part of the burning material is in the tip and part is in a striking surface on the box. ◁

MATTER The stuff of which everything is made is called matter – solids, liquids and gases. A vital property of matter is its MASS, and all forms of matter have gravitational attraction (see GRAVITY). People used to think that the total amount of matter in the universe was constant; that matter could neither be created nor destroyed. But Albert EINSTEIN showed that matter and energy could be interchanged. The mass of an object in motion is greater than its mass at rest. (See ATOM)

MEASLES A highly contagious disease, caused by a VIRUS. Symptoms include fever and coughing. A blotchy rash appears in a few days. Patients are isolated for 10–14 days.

MECCA The chief holy city for Moslems (see ISLAM), Mecca, in Saudi Arabia, was the birthplace of the Prophet MOHAMMED. Many pilgrims visit Mecca every year. Population: 463,000 (1983 est.). ◁

MECHANICS The branch of PHYSICS that deals with the effect of forces acting on bodies. It is usually divided into two branches – statics and DYNAMICS. Statics deals with stationary bodies, dynamics deals with particles and bodies in motion.

MEDALS Pieces of metal attached to a ribbon which commemorate events or are given as awards for distinguished service in war or peace. Medals were introduced around the 1400s. Famous medals include the Victoria Cross (Britain), the Croix de Guerre (France), the Iron Cross (Germany), the Medal of Honor (USA) and the Hero of the Soviet Union (USSR).

MEDICI An Italian family and rulers of Florence from the 1300s to the 1700s, the Medici derived their power from their wealth, made in commerce and banking. Lorenzo the Magnificent (1449–1492) was a famous patron of the arts. His son became Pope Leo X (1475–1521). Both Catherine (1519–1589) and Marie de' Medici (1573–1642) became queens of France.

MEDICINE The prevention of disease, the science of healing and the relief of PAIN. Probably the most important part of a

Med

▶Early students of medicine often had to carry out dissections of the human body in secret, because of Church opposition. But by the mid-17th century, anatomy was an accepted study, as shown here in Rembrandt's The Anatomy Lesson (1632).

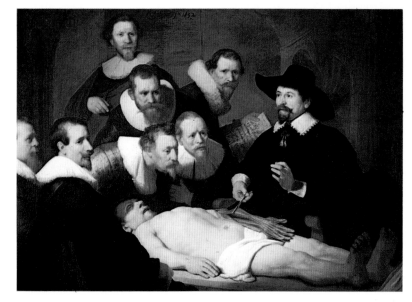

doctor's work is diagnosis, by which the doctor finds out a patient's illness from studying the symptoms. Medicine became a science in Europe through the work of HIPPOCRATES in ancient Greece. The writings of another Greek, Galen (AD 129–199) dominated medical thought until the 1500s, when the science of anatomy made great advances in our knowledge of the human body, and William HARVEY made a number of discoveries about the circulation of BLOOD. In the late 1700s, Edward JENNER performed the first vaccination against SMALLPOX. In the 1800s, the use of anaesthetics (see ANAESTHESIA), ANTISEPTICS and PASTEUR's discoveries about microorganisms in the air were major steps forward. And the 1900s have seen many more advances, including the wide use of ANTIBIOTICS, VACCINES, blood transfusions and, most recently, organ transplants. (See SURGERY)

▼ Modern medicine is now so advanced that we can build machines that serve as parts of the body. This heart/lung machine takes over from the patient's heart and lungs during an operation. Without such machines it would not be possible to perform certain types of open heart surgery.

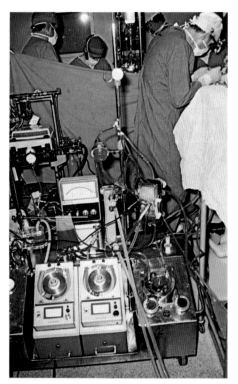

MEDITERRANEAN SEA An inland sea which borders southern EUROPE, North Africa and south-west Asia. It is connected with the ATLANTIC OCEAN by the narrow Strait of GIBRALTAR in the west, and with the Black Sea in the north-east. Parts of the Mediterranean include the ADRIATIC, Aegean and Ionian seas. The Mediterranean covers 2,965,500 sq km (1,145,000 sq miles). The largest islands are SICILY, Sardinia, CYPRUS, Corsica and CRETE.

MELBOURNE The capital of the state of VICTORIA, Australia, Melbourne stands on Port Phillip Bay. It is a major commercial centre, with a population of 2,865,000 (1983 est.). It was founded in 1835.

MELON Creeping or climbing plant grown in warm climates for its large juicy fruit. There are many different kinds of melon with skin and flesh of various colours and textures. Melons can be eaten fresh or made into jams and pickles.

MEMORY The term used for our ability to store and recall past experience. We tend to forget things easily soon after we have learned them, then more slowly as time goes by. It has also been shown that quick learners remember things better than do slow learners. PSYCHOLOGISTS say that we make ourselves forget certain things such as painful experiences.

MENDEL, GREGOR Austrian discoverer of the natural laws of HEREDITY. Mendel (1822–1884) was a botanist and a monk. His discoveries were based on a study of peas. He found that some inherited characteristics were dominant and some were recessive. He published his results in 1866, but his work was unrecognized until 16 years after his death.

METEOROID The largest known meteorite weighed 59 tonnes and measured nearly 3 m (9 ft) long. It fell in south-west Africa, near Grootfontein. An Antarctic depression 240 km (150 miles) across may have been made by the largest meteoroid ever to hit the Earth.

MENDELSSOHN, FELIX A German composer. Mendelssohn (1809–1847) composed symphonies, overtures, songs, and oratorios. One of his most often performed works is his violin concerto.

MENOPAUSE Also known as the 'change of life'. A term for that period in a woman's life, usually between the ages of 40 and 50, when her reproductive organs gradually cease to function.

MENTAL ILLNESS Sickness of the mind. Mental illnesses include disorders caused by disease or brain damage. Functional disorders include psychoses, such as depression, and neuroses, such as phobias. (See PSYCHIATRY)

MERCURY (GOD) In Roman MYTHOLOGY, Mercury was the messenger of the gods. He

▼ An artist's impression of the sun-baked surface of Mercury seen in close-up. The cracks are caused by the extreme variation between day-time and night-time temperatures, and the craters are the result of the impact of meteorites early in the planet's history.

was usually shown as an athletic young man, wearing a winged cap and winged sandals, and carrying a winged staff entwined with snakes.

MERCURY (METAL) The only metal that is liquid at room temperature, mercury's chemical symbol is Hg. Often called quicksilver, it is used in THERMOMETERS and BAROMETERS. It forms ALLOYS called amalgams with most metals; silver and gold amalgams are used to fill teeth. The main source of mercury is cinnabar.

MERCURY (PLANET) The closest planet to the Sun, and the smallest in the SOLAR SYSTEM. In 1974 *Mariner 10* passed within 800 km (500 miles) of the planet and showed it to have a strong magnetic field, a thin atmosphere made up partly of HELIUM, and craters similar to those on the Moon.

MERIDIAN Any line of longitude (see LATITUDE AND LONGITUDE). The prime meridian (0° longitude) passes through Greenwich Observatory. Other meridians are measured east and west of the prime meridian.

MERMAID A legendary sea-maiden with the body of a beautiful woman, but with a scaly, fish-like tail instead of legs. Mermaids were supposed to lure sailors to their death.

MESOPOTAMIA A region between the Tigris and Euphrates rivers, now mostly in IRAQ. It was the centre of several early civilizations, including that of the SUMERIANS.

METEOR See METEOROID

METEOROID A solid body that has broken away from a COMET. Meteoroids are always entering the Earth's atmosphere, but friction usually burns them up before they reach the ground. This gives rise to bright streaks called *meteors* or *shooting stars*. Large meteoroids that hit the Earth are called *meteorites*. A very few of these make huge craters when they hit the ground. ◁

METEOROLOGY The study of the changing conditions in the ATMOSPHERE and the causes of weather. One of the main jobs of a meteorologist is WEATHER FORECASTING. Scientific meteorology began with the ancient Greeks. In the 1600s, scientific instruments, such as BAROMETERS and THERMOMETERS, were developed and observations became more precise. Today meteorological stations are scattered around the world, on land and at sea. At these stations, regular measurements are made of conditions at ground level and in the upper atmosphere. Data also comes from weather SATELLITES, RADAR, and so on. The measurements are collated and analyzed at forecast centres.

METRIC SYSTEM The decimal system of weights and measures in which the metre is the unit of length, the gram is the unit of weight, and the litre is the unit of capacity. In the decimal system each unit is ten times as large or small as the next unit. The prefixes used to indicate magnitude are, *mega,* million; *kilo,* thousand; *hecto,* hundred; *deca,* ten; *deci,* tenth; *centi,* hundredth; and *milli,* thousandth. Most countries of the world either use or are introducing the metric system. ▷

MEXICO A Latin American republic, Mexico has 76,792,000 people (1984 est.) and an area of 1,972,547 sq km (761,606 sq miles). The capital is Mexico City (pop. 14,750,000). Most Mexicans are descendants of American Indians and Spaniards, who conquered the area in the early 1500s. Farming, oil and natural gas are important. ▷

MICA Any of various transparent or coloured mineral silicates (see SILICON) that can be split off in paper-thin leaves. Mica used to be used in large quantities for stove and lamp windows where transparent heat-resisting material was needed.

MICHELANGELO A great sculptor and painter of the Italian RENAISSANCE. Michelangelo Buonarroti (1475–1564) had a lifelong interest in the human figure. His interest was expressed in his early work, including the statue of *David* (now in Florence Academy). His paintings include the great FRESCOES in the

▲ *Michelangelo's* Pietà, *the carved figures of the Madonna and the dead Christ, is in St. Peter's Basilica in Rome. The artist began this sculpture when he was only 23.*

▲ *Sound waves travel into a microphone and strike a thin plate called a diaphragm. The diaphragm vibrates and connects to a device which produces an electric signal. This signal then passes to the amplifier and speakers.*

Sistine Chapel, in the VATICAN. He also designed the dome of St Peter's Basilica. ▷

MICROFILM A space-saving photographic film used for copying documents at such a reduced size that the film has to be magnified for viewing. It is used for storing records, books and newspapers. (See PHOTOGRAPHY)

MICROPHONE An instrument in which SOUND waves are turned into electric currents so they can be recorded or transmitted along wires or on RADIO waves. Different types of microphones are used for different purposes. The most common is the microphone used in TELEPHONES. A simple microphone consists of a piece of soft iron with a coil of wire round it. This electromagnet is placed close to a thin disc of metal called a *diaphragm*. The diaphragm vibrates as the sound waves from your voice strike it and this causes changes in the strength of the MAGNETISM of the electromagnet. This in turn causes electric current to flow through wires joining the microphone to the recording apparatus. The current changes at the same speed as the sounds that caused it changed. At the reproducer there is another electromagnet and diaphragm. The varying current makes the receiver diaphragm vibrate in the same way as the microphone diaphragm. So it reproduces the sound that strikes the microphone. (See ELECTRICITY)

MICROSCOPE An instrument that is used to magnify the appearance of small objects. If we say that the magnification of a microscope is × 100, the image is 100 times larger than the

METRIC SYSTEM The metric system was devised in 1790 when the French Revolutionary government decided that the metre should be one ten-millionth of the distance between the Equator and the Pole on a meridian passing through Paris. In 1798 three standard metres were made in platinum, one of them being kept in the French archives. Some time later it was decided that these metres were not accurate enough and a prototype metre was marked on a bar of platinum-iridium alloy. The metre was defined as the distance between two fine lines engraved on the bar when the bar was at a temperature of melting ice, with the bar resting on two rollers 0.571 metres apart. The metre is now defined as 1,650,763.73 wavelengths of the orange-red light given off by krypton 86, a rare gas found in the atmosphere.

MEXICO: FACTS AND FIGURES
Official language: Spanish.
Currency: Peso.
Highest point: Pico de Orizaba, 5,700 m (18,700 ft), the third highest mountain in North America.
Rivers: Rio Grande, Rio de las Balsas Pánuco, Grijalva, Santiago, and Conchos.
Largest lake: Lake Chapala 1,080 sq km (417 sq miles).
Religion: Roman Catholic.

MICHELANGELO Michelangelo is famous for the beauty of the figures that he carved and painted. Yet his own nose and face were disfigured when he fought with a fellow apprentice. The youth had criticized a painting by Michelangelo.

MICROSCOPE One of the first people to use microscopes to add to human knowledge was the Dutchman Anton van Leeuwenhoek (1632-1723). Leeuwenhoek's studies showed that fleas and mussels hatched from eggs and were not born from sand or mud as people had supposed.

MIDAS Legend says that Midas lost his magic power to turn everything he touched into gold, by bathing in the River Pactolus and so escaped starvation. This is supposed to be why people later found grains of gold lying on the river bed.

MIGRATION Long-distance animal migrations include those of the albacore (a fish). One tagged off California was caught near Japan less than a year later. It had swum nearly 7,900 km (4,900 miles). But the champion migrant is the Arctic tern. One bird ringed in the Arctic was recaptured 10 months later in Australia. It had flown 19,300 km (about 12,000 miles).

object viewed. The simplest microscope is a magnifying glass. But the microscopes used in scientific laboratories are much more complicated. They contain a number of LENSES, and tiny details of animals, plants and other objects can be seen. The highest magnification possible using glass lenses and ordinary light is about × 1600. For higher magnifications the electron microscope is used. It uses a beam of electrons (see ATOM) which is focused on the object, just like LIGHT waves. Magnifications of about × 2,000,000 can be achieved. ◁

MIDAS A king of Phrygia, in Asia Minor. Midas, according to Greek legend, was given the power by the god Dionysus to turn everything he touched (even his food) into gold. ◁

MIDDLE AGES A term used by European historians for the period between the fall of the Roman empire in the AD 400s, the end of ancient times, and the 1400s, when the RENAISSANCE marked the beginning of modern times. European states in the Middle Ages were based, economically, on AGRICULTURE, under the feudal system. The ROMAN CATHOLIC CHURCH, the sole religious authority, exercised great influence in maintaining European unity. (See CATHEDRAL; CHIVALRY; CHRISTIANITY; GOTHIC ART AND ARCHITECTURE; KNIGHTHOOD)

MIDDLE EAST A region including 16 nations in south-west ASIA and Egypt in AFRICA. ISLAM is the chief religion, but CHRISTIANITY is important in CYPRUS and LEBANON. Most people in ISRAEL are Jewish.

MIDNIGHT SUN Because the Earth's axis is tilted, the Sun shines at midnight for at least one night every year at places north of the Arctic and south of the Antarctic circles.

MIGRAINE A severe, prolonged and recurrent HEADACHE. Migraine is often accompanied by disturbed vision and nausea. DRUGS and special DIETS are forms of treatment.

MIGRATION Many mammals, birds, fish, insects and other animals move from one region to another at certain times of the year and return at other times. This regular movement between two places is called migration and is usually connected either with breeding or feeding. SALMON live in the sea but swim up river to breed. In winter, when the Arctic TUNDRA is frozen, CARIBOU move south into the forests in search of food and shelter. SWALLOWS, breeding in north Europe fly 11,000 km (7000 miles) to South Africa to find winter warmth and insect food. Insects themselves are great travellers: the monarch butterfly migrates between Canada and Mexico. ◁

MILK A major FOOD which aids growth and good health. Milk contains CARBOHYDRATES, FATS, MINERALS, PROTEINS and VITAMINS. The milk of many animals, notably cows, goats and sheep, is used for human consumption. PASTEURIZATION makes it safe to drink.

MILKY WAY The Sun is only one of countless millions of STARS that make up our GALAXY. This galaxy, to which we and the Sun belong, is sometimes called the Milky Way because on a clear night part of it can be seen as a misty band of stars stretching across the sky. Our galaxy is shaped like a flat spiral of stars. There are millions upon millions of other galaxies far away from our Milky Way system.

▼ Parts of the Milky Way are so thick with stars that they take on a cloudy appearance. The bright streak in the picture is the track of a man-made satellite.

MILLET Important CEREAL crop. Millet is cultivated as a basic food in the drier regions of Africa and Asia – especially in India and China. In other parts of the world, it is grown for animal fodder.

MILLIPEDE Small worm-like animal with a tough outer skeleton, segmented body and two pairs of legs on almost every segment. Millipedes are slow, nocturnal creatures that feed on decaying plants. There are about 8000 species. Most of them, when disturbed, curl up into a tight coil.

MILNE, A. A. A British author, Alan Alexander Milne (1882–1956). He wrote the popular children's novels *Winnie the Pooh* (1926) and *The House at Pooh Corner* (1928). He also wrote children's verse.

MILTON, JOHN One of England's great poets and an important political writer. Milton (1608–1674) wrote the poems *Paradise Lost* (1667) and *Paradise Regained* (1671). ▷

MIME A silent form of ACTING, used by masked actors in ancient Rome. Mime has been continued into the 20th century by such performers as Marcel Marceau (1923–   ).

MINARET The tower of a mosque, a minaret is among the most beautiful features of MOSLEM architecture. From a minaret, the muezzin (crier) calls people to prayer.   ▷

MINERALS Minerals are the materials of which the EARTH's crust is made. ROCKS are made of minerals. Most common minerals are solid and made up of CRYSTALS, but there are exceptions. Some people say oil is a mineral, and water is also strictly speaking a mineral. There are also several mineral gases. The most important minerals are those from which we get useful metals. These are called ORES.

MING DYNASTY A period in Chinese history between 1368 and 1644. It was founded by Chu Yuan-chang, a Chinese monk, who overthrew the MONGOL Yuan dynasty. The Ming dynasty, which is noted for its literature and porcelain, was replaced by the Manchu dynasty.

MINIATURE PAINTING The art of PAINTING detailed but very small pictures, such as miniature portraits which were produced in Europe in the 1500s and 1600s.

MINING The extraction of valuable materials from the Earth's crust. *Open-cast* mining involves the removal of top layers by power-shovels and then the extraction of MINERALS or COAL near the surface. DREDGING is used to mine alluvial deposits. *Underground*

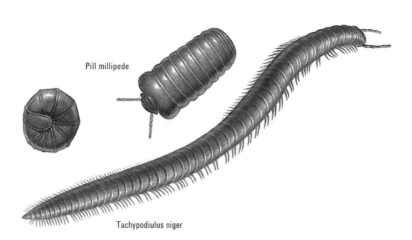

Pill millipede

Tachypodiulus niger

▲ The pill millipede, as its name suggests, is much more compact than its relatives, and is often confused with woodlice. It curls up like a watch spring when disturbed. It is about 50 mm long.

▼ Quartz is the most common mineral in the world. Most grains of sand are quartz. Pure quartz is translucent, but impurities give it many different colours.

MILTON, JOHN Milton spent years writing *Paradise Lost*, one of the greatest poems in the English language. All he got for it was £5 down and £5 more when the first small batch of printed copies had sold out. After Milton died his widow sold all rights to further royalties for just £8.

MINARET The world's tallest minaret, the Qutb Minar, near New Delhi, India, was built in 1193. It is 72.5 m (238 ft) high. The Arab explorer Ibn Battutah (1304-1368) said that it had 'no equal in all Islam.'

MISSISSIPPI RIVER With its tributary, the Missouri River, the Mississippi is the longest river system in North America, draining one-third of the United States. Each year it dumps 270 million m³ (350 million yd³) of mud, sand, and gravel in the sea. This helps to enlarge the Mississippi Delta.

MOHAMMED Mohammed was about 40 years old when he felt himself called to be a prophet of God. He said that an angel told him to preach the words of God to the Arabs in their own language. These words became part of the *Koran,* the book that is the foundation of the Moslem religion. The contents of the *Koran* were revealed to Mohammed bit by bit during the remainder of his life.

Mohammed was one of many famous men who suffered from fits. Others included Alexander the Great, Julius Caesar, King Alfred, and Napoleon. Edward Lear, artist and inventor of nonsense rhymes, suffered up to 18 fits a day.

MOLE Moles are in the *Talpidae* family. They are the master burrowers of the insectivores. A mole can dig its way through 14 m (45 ft) of soil in an hour – and in the mating season it can dig through 36 m (150 ft). Moles' eyes are capable only of distinguishing light and dark.

mining is costly and can be dangerous, but deep shafts and tunnels reach rich deposits far beneath the surface. OIL and NATURAL GAS are mined by pumping them to the surface.

MINK Cat-sized amphibious MAMMAL with a brown coat and bushy tail. Minks, found wild in North America and Europe, generally live in river banks and feed on small creatures such as frogs, water birds and fish. They are also bred on special farms for their valuable glossy fur. (See AMPHIBIAN)

MINNOW Small freshwater fish belonging to the carp family. Most species are under 15 cm (6 in) long and have a speckled back and silvery belly. Minnows are caught in nets and used as live bait for larger fish.

MINOAN CIVILIZATION A BRONZE AGE culture based on CRETE, named after the legendary King Minos of Crete. The Minoan civilization was Europe's first major civilization. It flourished between 2500 and 1450 BC. The Minoans grew rich through trade in grain, wine and olives from their fertile farmlands, and in the pottery, carved stone and textiles made by their skilful craftsmen. A TIDAL WAVE, generated by a volcanic eruption, is thought to have destroyed the Cretan civilization.

MINT Hardy strong-scented plant used in the kitchen for flavouring many foods. Mint is a popular HERB and easy to grow. Varieties include spearmint, peppermint and applemint.

MINTING The craft of making coinage. COINS are made from a variety of metals, including copper, nickel and silver. Each coin has its date of manufacture and its value stamped on it. The *mint* is the place where money is coined.

MIRROR A mirror is made of a flat sheet of GLASS on the back of which is sprayed a thin layer of silver or ALUMINIUM. A coat of paint on top of the metal layer prevents it being scratched. Light is reflected from the metal through the glass. Mirrors made of polished metal were used in the Iron Age, and the ancient Egyptians had silver and bronze mirrors about 2500 BC.

MISSISSIPPI RIVER This river flows about 3780 km (2350 miles) from its source in Minnesota, in the north-central USA, to its mouth on the Gulf of Mexico. ◁

MISSOURI RIVER The chief tributary of the MISSISSIPPI RIVER in the USA. The Mississippi-Missouri system is one of the world's longest, at 5970 km (3710 miles).

MISTLETOE Evergreen plant with shiny white berries which grows as a PARASITE on trees, especially apple trees. For centuries, mistletoe was considered magical and is still surrounded by superstition. Today, it is widely used as a Christmas decoration.

MITE Microscopic arachnid. Many mites live as PARASITES on animals and plants and so spread disease and damage crops.

MIXTURE When powdered iron and sand are stirred together they form a mixture. The iron can easily be separated from the sand by using a magnet. When such substances are mixed together they do not change. They can always be separated from each other (see ELEMENTS AND COMPOUNDS). AIR is a mixture of gases such as NITROGEN, OXYGEN, etc. These gases can be separated from the air. Liquids can also be mixtures. This is why medicine bottles often bear the instruction 'Shake the Bottle'; if left standing, the various ingredients in the mixture separate, the densest falling to the bottom.

MOCKINGBIRD Long-tailed, greyish-brown song bird belonging to the Americas. The mockingbird is so called because it mimics the cries of other birds and mammals.

MOHAIR The fine, white hair of the Angora GOAT. Mohair is used to make fabrics, including smooth, long-wearing clothes, draperies and furniture upholstery.

MOHAMMED The founder of ISLAM. Mohammed (AD 570–632), also called Muhammad or Mahomet, was born at MECCA, Arabia. In 610 he received his first vision and he proclaimed himself the 'Prophet of God' in 616. A plot to kill him led to his flight (*Hegira*) to Medina in 622. But he conquered Mecca in 630 and was recognized by the Meccans as the Prophet. ◁

MOLE Small burrowing MAMMAL with velvety grey-black fur. Moles live underground and have strong forelimbs for digging tunnels; they push the loose soil up into a heap – molehill – on the surface. Their eyes are small and weak and they rely on their keen smell and hearing to find food, mostly worms and grubs. ◁

MOLECULE When a number of ATOMS join together to form a stable and definite structure, they have formed a molecule. A molecule is the smallest part of a compound that is still the compound (See ELEMENTS AND COMPOUNDS). WATER is a compound made up of oxygen and hydrogen atoms; each water molecule has in it two hydrogen atoms and one oxygen atom. If any of these three atoms is removed, we no longer have a water molecule.

▶ *Water consists of many separate molecules. Each one is made up of two hydrogen atoms (blue) and one oxygen atom (yellow) joined together by covalent bonds.*

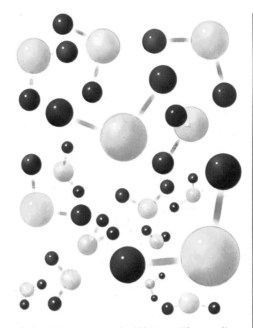

Before the identification of atoms it was thought that molecules were the smallest particles of nature. Some organic molecules may contain thousands of millions of atoms.

MOLLUSC Any of a varied group of soft-bodied animals, most of which have a hard protective SHELL. SNAILS, SLUGS, OYSTERS, MUSSELS, SQUID and OCTOPUSES are all molluscs. The body of a typical mollusc is divided into a powerful foot, a soft mass of internal organs above the foot, and shell-producing tissue called the 'mantle'.

MONACO A tiny principality in south-eastern FRANCE. Monaco has 28,000 people and an area of 189 hectares (467 acres). It is a famous MEDITERRANEAN resort. ▷

MONET, CLAUDE A French IMPRESSIONIST painter. Monet (1840–1926) produced masterly landscapes showing the changing effects of light at various times of the day.

MONEY Items which are units of value and the common medium of exchange in a community. Early peoples used salt, nails and cocoa beans as money. And cattle and cowrie shells are still used in some places. The earliest known COINS are Chinese. Coins appeared in

▼ *Monet's Lady With Umbrella. Claude Monet was the only Impressionist artist fully recognized in his own time.*

Asia Minor around 600 BC. The earliest banknotes were made in China in the AD 800s.

MONGOLIA A communist republic between China and the USSR in central ASIA. Mongolia has 1,820,000 people and an area of 1,565,000 sq km (604,250 sq miles). The capital is Ulan Bator. Much of the land is desert.
                                                          ▷

MONGOLS Nomadic Asian herdsmen, the Mongols founded a great empire which stretched from CHINA to the borders of eastern Europe. GENGHIS KHAN, a Mongol chief, was the first to unify the war-like Mongols. He took northern China in 1215 and then swept west into Russia and Persia. His grandson, KUBLAI KHAN (1216–94), completed the conquest of China. In the 1300s, the empire began to break up and the MING DYNASTY succeeded the Mongols in China in 1368.

MONGOOSE Snake-killing MAMMAL from Africa and Asia. Mongooses are long-bodied creatures, about one metre ($3\frac{1}{2}$ ft) in length, with short legs, sharp muzzle and bushy tail. They usually have speckled brown or grey fur.

MONKEY MAMMAL belonging to the same animal order as APES and man, the Primates. Monkeys are mostly long-tailed creatures with man-like arms, legs, hands and feet. Most species live in the forest regions of warm countries. South American monkeys – unlike ones from Africa and Asia – can swing from branches by their tail. The only monkeys found in Europe are the tailless Barbary apes of Gibraltar. ▷

MONORAIL A RAILWAY with a single rail which is usually elevated. The cars are either

MONACO: FACTS AND FIGURES
Official language: French.
Currency: Franc.
The principality has a customs union with France and an interchangeable currency. After the Vatican, it is the world's smallest sovereign state.
Most of Monaco's revenue comes from the tourist industry, the gambling casino, and the international car rally. There is also some income from stamps.

MONGOLIA: FACTS AND FIGURES
Official language: Mongol.
Currency: Tugrik.
Religion: Buddhism.
Chief rivers: The Selenga, which drains into Lake Baikal, and the Kerulen, which drains into the River Amur.

MONKEY The noisiest of all monkeys is the howling monkey of South America. In the males, a bone at the top of the windpipe is enormously developed, forming a resonant sound-box. The howls, which keep other howling monkeys away from each group, can be heard for miles.

Monkeys and apes groom one another both in order to keep clean and as a way of preserving social harmony within the troop.

MONORAIL The first monorail system was built in 1901 at Wuppertal in Germany. It is still operating. The fastest monorail journey was made by an unmanned rocket-driven sled in New Mexico in 1959. The sled reached nearly 5,000 kph (nearly 3,100 mph).

MOON: FACTS AND FIGURES
Diameter at the equator:
3476 km (2160 miles).
Gravity: One-sixth of Earth's gravity.
Mean density: 3.34 (water =1).
Turns on axis in 27.32 days.
Orbits Earth in $27\frac{1}{3}$ days.
Escape velocity: 2.4 km/second (1.5 miles/second).

The near side of the Moon has more 'seas' than the far side, which is almost entirely covered by mountainous regions.

Radio-isotope dating of a piece of Moon rock brought back by the *Apollo 12* astronauts has found it to be 4.6 thousand million years old, making it the oldest rock yet found on the Moon or on Earth.

MOOSE One moose may need to eat five tonnes of shoots and bark to take it through the winter. Herds will stamp deep snow into flat 'yards' where they can reach low-growing shoots and berries.

suspended from the rail or run above it. Driving wheels may make contact with the side of the rail. ◁

MONSOON A wind system in which prevailing summer and winter winds are reversed in direction. In India, the well-known summer monsoon brings heavy rainfall.

MONTREAL An industrial and commercial city in CANADA. Montreal, in Quebec province, has a population of 2,862,000 (with its suburbs). It is a major transport centre.

MOON The Earth's only natural SATELLITE, and our nearest neighbour in space. It orbits the Earth at an average distance of 384,400 km (238,900 miles). The month, based on a complete cycle of the Moon's phases from full moon to full moon, has been a unit of time since earliest recorded history. The average time between full moons is $29\frac{1}{2}$ days. The Moon always turns the same face towards Earth. Its surface has thousands of craters, most of which were probably formed by meteorites (see METEOROID) from outer space. On July 20, 1969, *Apollo 11* astronauts Neil Armstrong and Edwin Aldrin became the first human beings to walk on the surface of the Moon. Experiments carried out during this and later Moon flights have taught us much about the Moon. We now know that our neighbour is made up of much the same elements as are some volcanic rocks on Earth,

but they contain no water. (See ECLIPSE; SOLAR SYSTEM; TIDES) ◁

MOORE, HENRY A great British sculptor. Henry Moore (1898–1986) who worked in wood, stone and bronze. His figures are semi-abstract, but they convey pathos and tragedy. His drawings, such as those of people sheltering from air raids, are also impressive.

MOORS A nomadic people of North Africa, the Moors (named from the Latin *Mauri*) joined with the ARABS in the so-called Moorish invasion of Spain in the AD 700s.

MOOSE Large, dark brown DEER found in the cold northern forests of Alaska and Canada. The male carries huge, flattened antlers up to 2 metres ($6\frac{1}{2}$ ft) across. Moose are very similar to the European and Asian ELK. ◁

MORAY EEL Large, fierce EEL found in warm seas, especially near coral reefs; many species are brightly coloured. Morays hide by day and feed at night, using their sharp teeth to catch fish and other water creatures.

▼The Apollo astronauts took stunning colour photographs of the Moon from space. During the first circumlunar voyage in December 1968, the Apollo 8 astronauts took a view of the nearly full Moon that we can never see from Earth (left) and a photo of the lunar highlands (right).

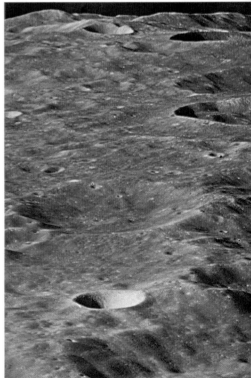

MORMONS Members of the Church of Jesus Christ of Latter-day Saints. Mormons follow the *Book of Mormon*, which they believe was revealed by God to Joseph Smith (1805–1844).

MOROCCO A monarchy in north-west AFRICA, Morocco has 21,408,000 people (1984) and an area of 445,500 sq km (172,395 sq miles). The capital is Rabat. Morocco contains much of the Atlas mountain range and part of the SAHARA. Phosphates are the most valuable product, but most people are farmers. ▷

MORPHINE A DRUG obtained from the OPIUM poppy, morphine is used by doctors to relieve pain. But it is a dangerous, habit-forming drug and its sale is restricted.

MORSE CODE A system of sending messages by wire or radio. The Morse Code was developed by Samuel Morse (1791–1872). Letters are coded by dots, dashes and spaces.

MORTAR A GUN designed to fire shells in a high trajectory, such as over hills. The barrel is a steel tube, with a firing pin at the bottom, supported by two adjustable legs.

MORTGAGE A method of borrowing money. Mortgages may be obtained from BANKS or building societies for house purchases. The mortgage is a security for the loan.

MOSAIC A decoration made by fitting together pieces of coloured MARBLE, stone, glass or some other material. The pieces, called *tesserae*, are set in cement. Some mosaic floors in Greek and Roman times were made up of elegant patterns. Others depicted scenes. Beautiful mosaics also adorn many BYZANTINE and Italian churches. ▷

MOSCOW Capital of the USSR (see RUSSIA) on the River Moskva, population 8,537,000 (1984). The country's industrial, cultural and political centre, Moscow became the national capital in 1547 under the first tsar, IVAN THE TERRIBLE, and remained so until 1712. It became the capital again in 1918, after the Revolution. Places of interest include the KREMLIN and Red Square with Lenin's tomb and the 16th century St Basil's Cathedral. Among the theatres are the Bolshoi and the Moscow Arts.

MOSES In the BIBLE, a Jewish leader, law-giver and prophet. According to the Old Testament, Moses (c. 13th century BC) led the JEWS out of captivity in Egypt so that they might find the 'Promised Land' (PALESTINE). Moses received the Ten Commandments from God, and formalized the Jewish religion (see JUDAISM).

MOSLEM ART From AD 633, the ARABS built up a great empire. As ISLAM spread, a

▼*A diagram of Morse's electric telegraph system (1882). From the 1770s there were many experiments with telegraph systems. But Morse invented a code to translate messages over the wires which was simple to use, and so his method was adopted.*

MOROCCO: FACTS AND FIGURES
Official language: Arabic.
Currency: Dirham.
People: Mainly Berber, with some Arabs.
Highest peak: Djebel Toubkal, 4,165 m (13,664 ft). in the High Atlas mountains.
Largest city: Casablanca (pop. 2,409,000), the leading seaport. Morocco produces 20 per cent of the world's phosphates. In 1956 Morocco gained its independence from France.

MOSAIC The world's largest mosaic adorns four walls in the National University, Mexico City. It depicts historical scenes. The two largest walls cover 1203 sq m (12,949 sq ft).

▼*Beautiful wall mosaics at the ruins of the Roman city of Pompeii include this one, warning visitors to 'beware of the dog'.*

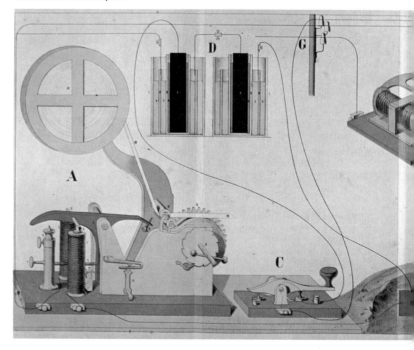

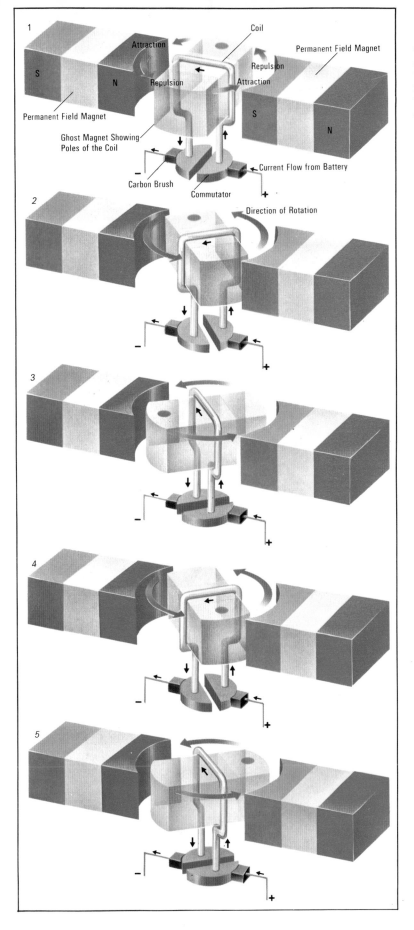

1

Attraction

Coil

Repulsion

Permanent Field Magnet

S

N

Repulsion

Attraction

Permanent Field Magnet

S

N

Ghost Magnet Showing Poles of the Coil

Carbon Brush

Current Flow from Battery

Commutator

–   +

2

Direction of Rotation

–   +

3

–   +

4

–   +

5

–   +

Mot

distinctive Moslem art evolved. The supreme art form was ARCHITECTURE. Book illustrations, CALLIGRAPHY, glassware, metalware, POTTERY and rug-making were also important. Life-like images were banned and so decorations took stylized or abstract forms.

MOSQUITO Small two-winged FLY with long legs and slender body. Although mosquitoes are found all over the world, most types live in tropical countries. The females of many species are blood-sucking and, in this way, they can transmit organisms that cause deadly diseases such as MALARIA and yellow fever. Mosquitoes breed in water.

MOSS Common, tiny non-flowering plant which grows in dense spreading clusters. Mosses are very simple plants and were among the earliest land plants. They reproduce by means of airborne spores. Although some species prefer dry conditions, most mosses need a moist environment and are found on damp rocks, tree trunks and on the ground in shady woods.

MOTION SICKNESS A feeling of nausea and vomiting experienced by some people when they are travelling. The sickness is caused by the effect of motion on the fluids in the inner EAR. Drugs are used to treat it.

MOTOR A machine in which electrical energy is turned into mechanical energy. A motor is the reverse of a GENERATOR. In the simple motor, electric current is passed through a coil of wire placed between the poles of a magnet. This produces a force in the wire, which makes it move. Current has to be supplied to the coil through a *commutator*. The commutator reverses the direction of the current after the coil has made half a rotation. If there were no commutator, the coil would stop after half a turn. The change in direction of the current pushes the wire through another half rotation, and so on (see diagram). Real motors have many coils of wire, and the commutator has many segments, one for each coil. Electric motors have many uses, from

◀ *The sequence of events during one rotation of a simple motor. For clarity, the coil has been shown as a single loop of wire. When a current flows through the coil, a magnetic field is set up, represented here as a ghost magnet.* **1** *The magnetic fields interact, and forces of attraction and repulsion cause the coil to turn.* **2** *The poles of the coil are almost in line with the poles of the magnets.* **3** *The commutator reverses the current flowing through the coil, thus reversing the magnetic poles of the coil.* **4** *Forces of attraction and repulsion keep the coil turning.* **5** *The poles of the core again pass those of the magnet, the current through the coil reverses, and the coil keeps turning.*

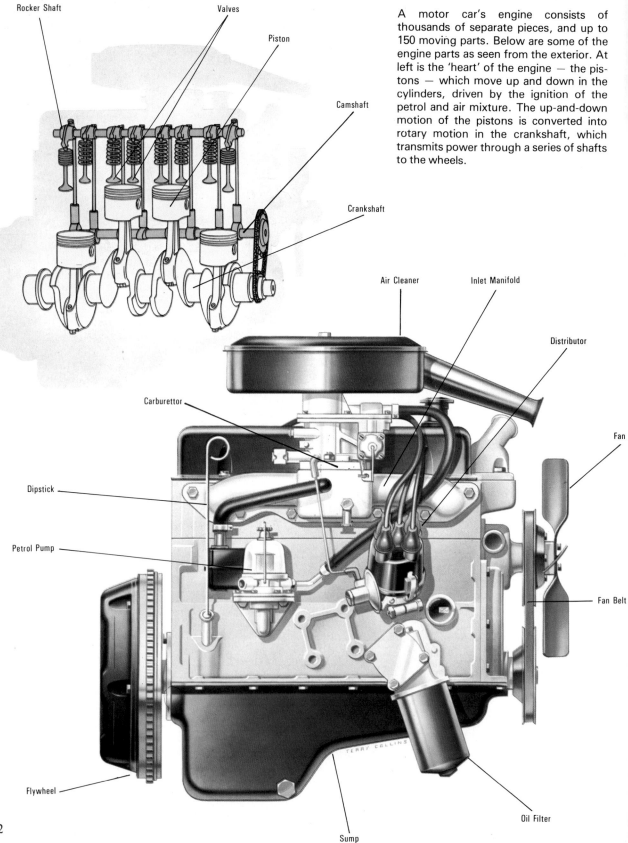

Rocker Shaft

Valves

Piston

Camshaft

Crankshaft

PARTS OF A MOTOR CAR ENGINE

A motor car's engine consists of thousands of separate pieces, and up to 150 moving parts. Below are some of the engine parts as seen from the exterior. At left is the 'heart' of the engine — the pistons — which move up and down in the cylinders, driven by the ignition of the petrol and air mixture. The up-and-down motion of the pistons is converted into rotary motion in the crankshaft, which transmits power through a series of shafts to the wheels.

Air Cleaner

Inlet Manifold

Distributor

Fan

Carburettor

Dipstick

Petrol Pump

Fan Belt

Flywheel

Oil Filter

Sump

TERRY COLLINS

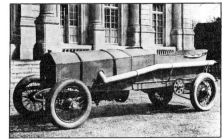

MOTOR CAR The production of passenger cars in 1984 was as follows: United States 7,622,000; Japan 7,073,000; West Germany 3,788,000; France 2,910,000; Italy 1,439,000; USSR 1,296,000; Spain 1,174,000; Canada 1,033,000; UK 909,000; Australia 371,000.

Almost 38 per cent of the world's motor cars are in the United States. About one third of all American car-owning families have more than one car.

▲ *Left: the bodywork of this 1909 Fiat shows the lingering influence of the horse-drawn carriage. Centre: A German Mersserschmitt bubble car of the 1960s. The car is reminiscent of an airplane cockpit, with passenger directly behind driver. Right: the original 'Chitty-Chitty-Bang-Bang', 1921 with aero-engine for racing.*

those in electric shavers to huge industrial motors that drive heavy machinery or electric trains.

MOTORBOAT A boat driven by any engine except a steam engine. The two main kinds are outboard and inboard motorboats. HYDROFOILS may be used to lift the hull above the water.

MOTOR CAR In 1885, two German engineers, working independently, produced vehicles which can be considered the forerunners of today's cars. These men, Karl BENZ and Gottlieb Daimler, used INTERNAL COMBUSTION ENGINES fuelled by petrol. In 1913 Henry FORD in the United States introduced the first successful way of producing cars quickly and cheaply. The cars moved down a line of workers who each assembled a certain part. Cars are still made in this way. The power for the car comes from an internal combustion engine which burns a mixture of petrol and air in cylinders. Most engines have four or six

▼ *The Rolls Royce Corniche. In the motoring world, Rolls Royce means fine engineering.*

cylinders. Inside the cylinders are pistons which are forced down by the burning gases and turn a crankshaft. At one end of the crankshaft is a heavy flywheel which smooths out the motion of the engine. From the crankshaft, the power goes through a clutch which is a device for disconnecting the engine from the propeller shaft which takes the drive to the wheels. (The wheels that are driven can be either at the front or the back.) The driver uses GEARS to make the car go faster or slower for the same engine speed, and to reverse. Some cars have automatic transmission that changes gear automatically. All cars need a BATTERY which is charged from the engine. The battery provides power for the starter motor, the lights, the horn and the windscreen wipers. Some cars and most lorries have a DIESEL engine which burns diesel oil. ◁

MOTORCYCLE A two-wheeled vehicle propelled by an INTERNAL COMBUSTION ENGINE. Motorcycle engines have one to four cylinders and the size of the engine is given in c.c. (cubic centimetres) of the cylinders. The engine power generally varies between 50 and 1000 c.c. The first true motorcycle was invented by the German Gottlieb Daimler (1834–1900). Motorcycling is now a popular pastime and racing has become a major spectator sport.

MOULD Simple FUNGUS consisting of a mass of fine fluffy threads that cover the dead

▲ *Mountains in the harsh Polar regions of the southern hemisphere support little life.*

organic matter – such as bread, cheese, leather – they are growing on. One species of mould is used to make the blue veins in Gorgonzola and Stilton cheeses. Another mould produces the powerful germ-killer, PENICILLIN.

MOUNTAIN CLIMBING An adventurous sport which requires special training and equipment. Mountain climbing became popular in Europe in the 1850s and 1860s, when most of the Alpine peaks were scaled. The Himalayan peaks were mostly tackled in the 1900s.

MOUNTAINS High, rugged land masses whose summits cover small areas by comparison with their bases. *Fold mountains*, such as the ALPS, ANDES and HIMALAYAS, have been squeezed up by plate collisions in the Earth's crust. *Block mountains* are areas of land which have been raised up between FAULTS. *Volcanic mountains* are composed of LAVA, volcanic ash or both. Many mountains rise from the ocean floor. The tips of some emerge as ISLANDS. ▷

MOUSE Small rodent (gnawing MAMMAL) with bright eyes, sharp teeth, a pointed muzzle, long naked tail and a grey or brown coat. Its diet is mainly vegetarian. Mouse populations increase rapidly; one mouse has about 40 babies a year and, when the young are 12 weeks old, they can themselves breed.

MOZAMBIQUE A republic in southeast AFRICA with 13,602,000 people (1984 est.) and an area of 783,030 sq km (302,330 sq miles).

The capital is Maputo. Mozambique became independent from Portugal in 1975. ▷

MOZART, W. A. A great Austrian composer. Wolfgang Amadeus Mozart (1756–1791) began composing when he was five. He later wrote 13 operas, including *Don Giovanni* (1787) and *The Magic Flute* (1791), 15 masses, 41 symphonies, superb concertos and much chamber music. ▷

MULE Sturdy MAMMAL bred from a male DONKEY and a mare (female horse). Mules are still used in many parts of the world to pull and carry heavy loads.

MULTIPLICATION The mathematical operation that is a shortened way of repeatedly adding a number to itself. Thus, 4 × 3 is 3 added to itself four times.

MUMPS A contagious disease, usually among children. Mumps is caused by a VIRUS, which inflames the SALIVARY GLANDS. One attack usually gives immunity for life.

MURAL A wall PAINTING, usually inside but sometimes outside a building. Murals may be FRESCOES or oil paintings. Prehistoric cave paintings were early murals (see ART). The greatest European murals, such as those by MICHELANGELO, were painted during the RENAISSANCE.

MURRAY-DARLING SYSTEM An Australian river system, important for IRRIGATION and HYDROELECTRIC POWER. The Murray River is 2575 km (1600 miles) long. The Darling, a tributary, is 2740 km (1702 miles) long.

▼ *Wolfgang Amadeus Mozart gained international fame as a child prodigy at the keyboard. Though he died when he was only 35 he left a vast amount of music.*

MUSCLE MAN

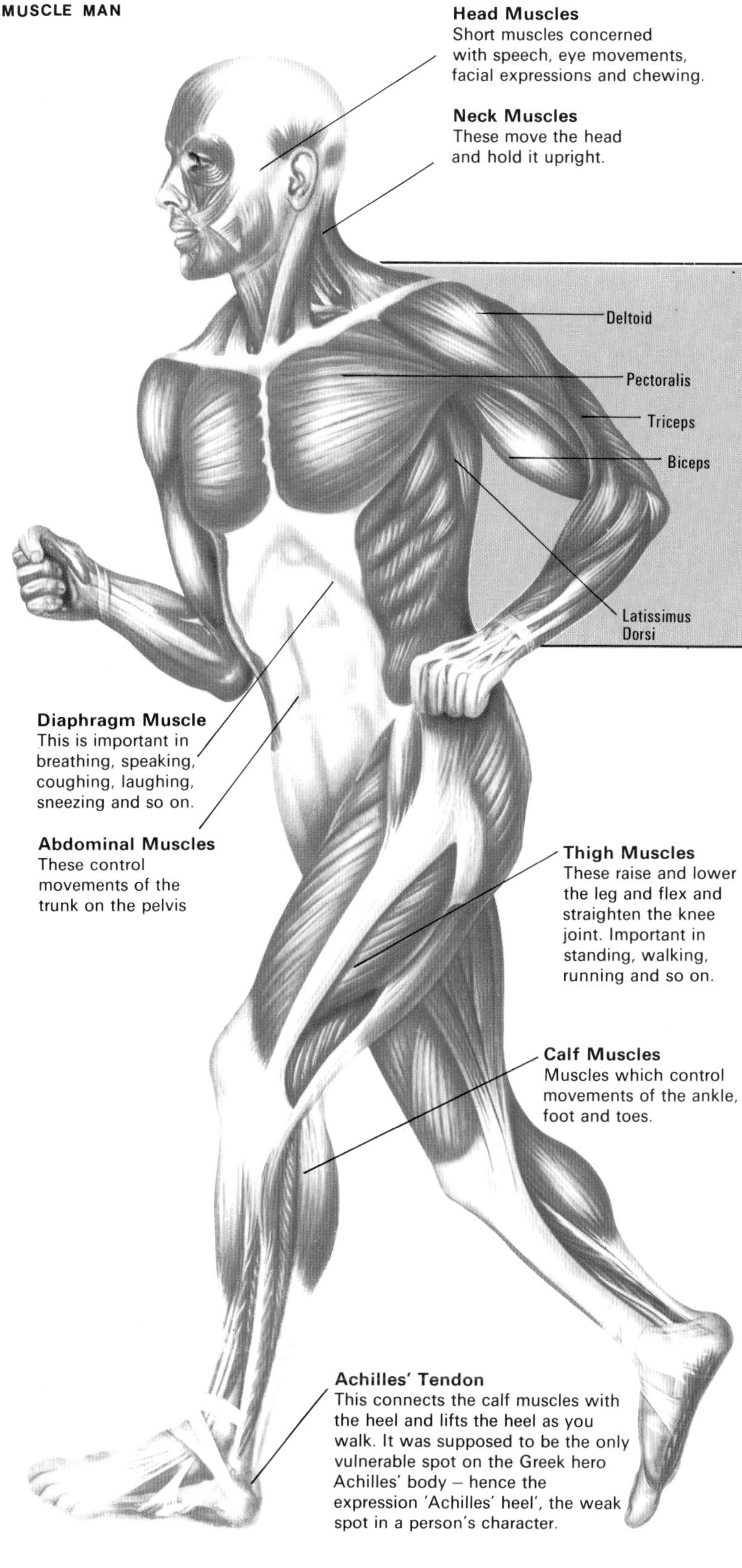

Head Muscles
Short muscles concerned with speech, eye movements, facial expressions and chewing.
Neck Muscles
These move the head and hold it upright.
Deltoid
Pectoralis
Triceps
Biceps
Latissimus Dorsi
Diaphragm Muscle
This is important in breathing, speaking, coughing, laughing, sneezing and so on.
Abdominal Muscles
These control movements of the trunk on the pelvis
Thigh Muscles
These raise and lower the leg and flex and straighten the knee joint. Important in standing, walking, running and so on.
Calf Muscles
Muscles which control movements of the ankle, foot and toes.
Achilles' Tendon
This connects the calf muscles with the heel and lifts the heel as you walk. It was supposed to be the only vulnerable spot on the Greek hero Achilles' body – hence the expression 'Achilles' heel', the weak spot in a person's character.

Muscle Power

A muscle can, when necessary, lift up to 1000 times its own weight. Scientists have calculated that there is enough power in the muscles of a man to lift a weight of 25 tons (25·25 tonnes). Put another way, a man could exert a force equal to six horsepower – but every single muscle in his body would be needed.

Muscles of the Arm and Shoulder

The biceps muscle flexes, or bends, the arm. The deltoid lifts the arm. The teres behind the shoulder and the latissimus dorsi pull the arm down and back. The pectoralis muscle pulls the arm forward and across the front of the body. Muscles in the forearm extend and flex the fingers, while rotator muscles enable us to rotate hand and forearm. So, to pick an object off the table: deltoid and pectoralis lift and move the arm forwards; the triceps lowers the forearm and rotator muscles turn forearm and hand; flexor muscles in the forearm bend the fingers (to grasp the object); and finally the biceps lifts the arm up.

Muscle Tone

Muscles used for moving are always partially contracted, ready for immediate action. Even when a person is standing or sitting still, many muscles must be contracted to hold him upright and preserve his balance: for example, those surrounding the spinal column and joining it to the skull. This is known as muscle tone. If muscles lose their tone, through lack of use or for any other reason, the body becomes limp and floppy.

MUSCLE Tissue that is used to control body movements. The human body has about 640 muscles. Some are voluntary, that is, people control them consciously (i.e. when walking or lifting things). Some, such as those in the STOMACH, are involuntary. They move without any conscious effort.

MUSEUM A place where original objects are collected and displayed. Museums include art galleries, natural history museums, science museums, folk museums, and so on.

MUSHROOM Type of edible FUNGUS. The mushroom, like other toadstools, exists for most of the year as a mass of fine threads; but in autumn, the threads grow together and upwards to form the stem and cap. Often the word 'mushroom' is used to describe any non-poisonous toadstool that is good to eat.

MUSIC The art of combining sounds made by instruments or the human voice to express thought or emotion in an organized form.

Three important elements of music are melody, harmony and rhythm. In Europe, vocal music, such as church plainsong, was the chief musical form until the late MIDDLE AGES. Instrumental music developed in the 1500s and OPERA in the 1600s. Classical concertos and symphonies were developed in the 1700s by such musical geniuses as J. S. BACH, Josef HAYDN and W. A. MOZART. Ludwig van BEETHOVEN was a master of the classical tradition and the romantic styles which emerged in the early 1800s. The 1900s has been a period when a wide variety of music has reached a bigger audience than ever before, principally via the radio and record player. It has also been an age of experimentation, with the development of atonal and ELECTRONIC MUSIC. (See ORCHESTRA)

MUSIC BOX A clockwork instrument that plays tunes. Developed in Switzerland in the late 1700s, music boxes were installed in such everyday objects as powder boxes and jewellery boxes.

MUSK Brown, strong-smelling oily substance obtained from a gland in the male musk deer and used for making PERFUME and SOAP. The musk deer is a small, hornless animal from the mountains of central Asia.

MUSKET A military FIREARM, in use from c. 1540– c. 1840. It was muzzle-loading and smooth-bore. Matchlocks, wheellocks and flintlocks were all different versions of it, as the firing mechanism was improved.

MUSSEL Small MOLLUSC found mainly in the sea, although there are also some freshwater species. Mussels are *bivalves*: that is, their shell is in two parts and hinged together. Like other bivalves, they feed by filtering tiny particles from the water. The best-known species is the edible mussel which lives in dense clusters on coastal rocks; its shell is blue-black.

MUSSOLINI, BENITO Italian dictator (1883–1945). He founded the Fascist Party in 1919 (see FASCISM), was made Prime Minister in 1922, and made himself dictator from 1925. He changed many instititutions, invaded Ethiopia, conquered Albania, and took Italy into WORLD WAR II on Germany's side. In 1943 he was made to resign, but was rescued by German paratroopers and set up a state in northern Italy. He was killed as he tried to flee the country in 1945.

MUSTANG Small half-wild HORSE roaming the plains of Central America and the southwest US. Mustangs are probably descended from the horses brought to Mexico by Spanish conquerors in the 16th century.

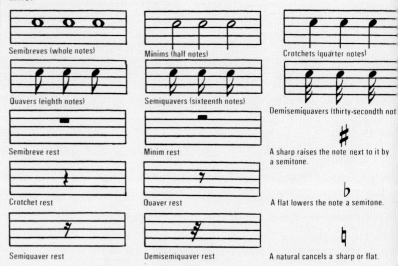

MUSIC SYMBOLS AND NOTATION

A *stave* or *staff* is a set of 5 parallel lines on which music is written down. *Bar lines* are upright lines on the stave, dividing it into *bars*, or *measures* of musical time.

The *clef* sign at the beginning of each stave fixes the name and pitch of the notes written on that line of the stave.

Semibreves (whole notes)

Minims (half notes)

Crotchets (quarter notes)

Quavers (eighth notes)

Semiquavers (sixteenth notes)

Demisemiquavers (thirty-secondth not

A sharp raises the note next to it by a semitone.

Semibreve rest

Minim rest

A flat lowers the note a semitone.

Crotchet rest

Quaver rest

Semiquaver rest

Demisemiquaver rest

A natural cancels a sharp or flat.

MUSTARD Plant with bright yellow flowers and pods containing white or black seeds. The seeds of some varieties are used in cooking. The seeds are either added whole, as flavouring, to various dishes, or they are crushed into a hot-tasting powder which is then mixed to a paste with water and eaten with certain foods.

MYCENAEAN CIVILIZATION The first civilization of ancient GREECE, named after one of its great palaces at Mycenae. It was a society of warrior princes, living by trade and piracy, and speaking a form of Greek. It had links with the MINOAN CIVILIZATION of Crete, and flourished c. 1600–1200 BC, but was destroyed by invaders soon after this.

MYRTLE Evergreen shrub or small tree with glossy blue-green leaves and fragrant white flowers. Oil from the leaves and flowers is used to make PERFUME.

MYTHOLOGY Myths are stories about supernatural beings and happenings. Mythology means a collection of myths, and also the study of myths. All primitive peoples and early civilizations had such stories. They helped explain (for example) how the world began, and how certain customs and beliefs grew up. Closely related to myths are legends, which often have some basis in fact. ▷

MYTHOLOGY Mythical characters that do not have separate articles in this book. When there is a Roman equivalent of the Greek name, the character is listed under the Greek name, with the Roman in parentheses.

Ajax: Greek warrior; killed himself when Achilles' arms were awarded to Odysseus.

Artemis (Diana): Twin sister of Apollo; goddess of the Moon and a famous huntress.

Athene (Minerva): Goddess of wisdom and war, daughter of Zeus and Metis; sprang fully grown and armed from her father's head.

Dionysus (Bacchus): God of wine and fertile crops.

Hector: Son of Priam; chief hero of the Trojans; slain by Achilles.

Helen of Troy: Fairest woman in the world; cause of Trojan War.

Heracles (Hercules): Strongman who performed 12 labours to be free from bondage.

Pan (Faunus): God of woods and fields; part man, part goat.

N

NAIL Hard growth, made of HORN, at the end of the fingers and toes. Animals such as man, elephants and apes all have nails. Many other animals have equivalent horny growths in the form of claws, talons and hoofs.

NAPOLEON BONAPARTE See BONAPARTE, NAPOLEON

NARCISSUS A spring plant, grown from a BULB, with long sword-shaped leaves and a flower containing six petals round a central trumpet. Narcissi, mostly white or yellow, grow wild in many countries and are cultivated in gardens throughout the world. Species with long trumpets are usually called DAFFODILS.

NARWHAL Small WHALE, about 5 metres (17 ft) long, found in the Arctic Ocean. Narwhals swim together in great schools and feed mainly on cuttlefish and squid. The male narwhal has a twisted tusk some 3 metres (10 ft) long.

NATO The North Atlantic Treaty Organization founded in 1949. It links the countries of North America and western Europe in a mutual defence pact, so an attack on one is an attack on all. The headquarters are in Paris, but the United States contributes most of the pact's armed forces.

NATURAL GAS A mixture of gases produced naturally from organic matter below the Earth's surface. It is widely used as a fuel. Natural gas consists mainly of methane (80 to 95 per cent) and it is usually found in oil fields. To produce natural gas, drilling has to take place as for oil. It is then piped to a refinery, where unwanted substances are removed before it is supplied to homes and factories.

NAUTILUS Sea animal with a soft body inside a hard, spiral shell. The shell is lined with a shiny substance called mother of pearl.

◄ A natural gas field at Hass R'Mel, in Algeria. Below: the most common rock structure — an anticline — in which natural gas and petroleum collect.

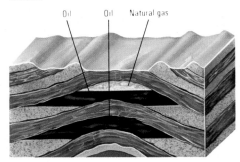

The nautilus lives on the sea bed of the South Pacific and Indian oceans.

NAVIGATION The setting of a course for a ship, plane or spacecraft. Navigation at sea was originally based on watching the positions of the Sun, Moon and stars. Navigational aids were developed in the Middle Ages and new inventions and improvements have continued since then: the COMPASS, astrolabe, quadrant, SEXTANT, speed log, CHRONOMETER, CHARTS and BUOYS. Today RADIO, RADAR and other electronic aids play a big part, and in air navigation these are all-important. Space navigation is based on star observation backed by COMPUTER analysis. (See CLOCKS)

NAVY A nation's warships. For a long time they were just merchant ships, used for fighting when the need arose. The first permanent navy was probably that of ROME, set up in 311 BC. In England, ALFRED THE GREAT built some warships to use against the Vikings, but the modern British Navy was not founded until the reign of HENRY VIII. Today the largest navies of the world are those of the United States and the Soviet Union, and the emphasis has passed from BATTLESHIPS and aircraft carriers to SUBMARINES armed with nuclear missiles.

NEANDERTHAL MAN A primitive type of man who lived 100,000 to 30,000 years ago, during the Paleolithic period of geology. His remains were first discovered in 1856. He was shorter than modern man, very powerfully built with heavy brows. These people cooked their food, sewed animal skins to make clothing, and buried their dead with bunches of flowers. (See ANTHROPOLOGY). ▷

NEBUCHADNEZZAR King of BABYLONIA (reigned 605–562 BC). He defeated the Egyptians, brought Palestine and Syria into his empire, and took many captive Jews to Babylon after they had attempted to revolt.

NEBULA A name originally given to all kinds of misty objects in the sky. The real nature of these objects could not be discovered with the telescopes of the early astronomers. Some, we now know, are distant GALAXIES; others are star clusters and clouds of dust and gas within our own galaxy.

NECTARINE Type of PEACH. Nectarines taste like peaches but they are smaller and have a smooth skin instead of a fuzzy one.

▼ *Neanderthal Man wore animal skins to keep out the cold, and hunted animals with stone pointed spears. He often competed with cave bears for shelter.*

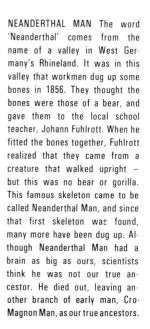

NEANDERTHAL MAN The word 'Neanderthal' comes from the name of a valley in West Germany's Rhineland. It was in this valley that workmen dug up some bones in 1856. They thought the bones were those of a bear, and gave them to the local school teacher, Johann Fuhlrott. When he fitted the bones together, Fuhlrott realized that they came from a creature that walked upright – but this was no bear or gorilla. This famous skeleton came to be called Neanderthal Man, and since that first skeleton was found, many more have been dug up. Although Neanderthal Man had a brain as big as ours, scientists think he was not our true ancestor. He died out, leaving another branch of early man, Cro-Magnon Man, as our true ancestors.

◄ *An artist's impression of Neptune, seen from one of its two moons, Triton. Triton may be one of the largest moons in the solar system. The other moon is called Nereid and it is tiny. From Neptune, Earth would seem a dim speck near the star-like Sun. (It is nearly 4,350 million kilometres away.)*

NETHERLANDS: FACTS AND FIGURES
Official language: Dutch.
Currency: Florin (Guilder).
Religions: Protestant and Roman Catholic.
Highest point: Vaalser Berg 322 m (1057 ft).
Area: 40,844 sq km (15,770 sq miles).

Population: 14,420,000 (1984 est.).
Capital: Amsterdam (pop. 994,000).
Chief port: Rotterdam (pop. 1,025,000), the world's busiest port.

In the last 700 years, the Netherlands has suffered about 140 flood disasters. The last great flood occurred in January 1953. A terrible storm in the North Sea, combined with high tides, raised the level of the water so that the sea burst through the dykes (sea walls). Over four per cent of the country was flooded and about 1800 people were drowned. More than 30,000 houses were destroyed.

NEPTUNE The length of a year on Neptune is 165 Earth years. The inter-planetary space probe Jupiter 2 is set to fly past the planet in 1989.

NEST The Long-tailed tit makes a beautifully crafted nest out of cobwebs, lichen, hair and moss. It then lines it sometimes with up to 2,000 feathers. The nest shape is domed with a minute entrance at the top – but the tit's amazing flexibility allow easy entry.

NEEDLE A small, pointed instrument – especially one used for sewing, but also those used for knitting, playing records, acting as pointers on compasses or dials, etc.

NEEDLEWORK Any work done on cloth with a needle and thread. It includes purely practical work (sewing, patching) now often done with a SEWING MACHINE, but also various kinds of decorative work, such as CROCHETING, embroidery, needlepoint and petit point.

NELSON, HORATIO British admiral (1758–1805). He joined the navy when he was 12, and became a captain at 20. The victory of Cape St Vincent made him a national hero. He defeated the French at the Battle of the Nile (1798) and the Danes at Copenhagen (1801). Given the Mediterranean command, he chased the French to the West Indies and back, before defeating the joint French and Spanish fleets at Trafalgar (1805), where he was killed.

NEON An ELEMENT, and one of the most useful of the rare gases. Its chemical symbol is Ne. Neon is used for lighting; neon tubes give a brilliant orange-red light. The gas is obtained by distilling liquid air.

NEPTUNE (GOD) The Roman god of the sea. Many of the stories about him are borrowed from the Greek sea god, Poseidon.

NEPTUNE (PLANET) The second outermost planet of the SOLAR SYSTEM. It takes about 165 years to travel round the Sun and can never be seen from Earth without a telescope. It has two orbiting moons, Triton and Nereid. ◁

NERO Roman emperor (born AD 37, reigned 54–68), notorious for his vanity, cruelty and corruption. He was eventually overthrown by a military revolt and committed suicide.

NERVOUS SYSTEM The system of nerves that runs throughout the body. It consists of three main parts. First there is the *central nervous system* (CNS): the BRAIN, and the great bundle of nerves leading to the brain called the spinal cord (see SPINAL COLUMN). This is the part that makes decisions. (Some emergency actions, called *reflexes*, are decided in the spinal cord and not in the brain.) Second, there are the *peripheral nerves*. These take messages to the CNS from all parts of the body, and take back the orders that control the body's actions. Third, there is the *autonomic nervous system*, which is rather separate. It governs the automatic functions of the body, like the heartbeat, that are not under complete conscious control.

NEST Structure built by an animal generally as a shelter for its young. Many creatures, from ANTS to APES, build nests, but the most elaborate nests in the animal kingdom are those made by BIRDS. Birds build their nests in all kinds of places, ranging from the tops of tall trees to underground holes, and use all sorts of materials, such as twigs, grass, leaves, mud, moss and hair. Most nests are cup-shaped but some also have a roof to give the eggs extra protection. Birds only use nests for breeding and not as permanent homes; but some species, like storks, return every year to the same nest. ◁

NETHERLANDS A densely-populated monarchy in western EUROPE, the Netherlands is a country which has been largely reclaimed from the sea. Nearly half of the land is below sea-level. The reclaimed *polders* are rich farmland. Arable farming is extensive and live-stock, dairy and poultry farming are especially important. But much of the nation's wealth now comes from manufacturing, although most raw materials have to be imported. The Netherlands is a member of the EUROPEAN ECONOMIC COMMUNITY. ◁

NEWCASTLE A city in NEW SOUTH WALES, Australia. It is also an important port on the mouth of the Hunter River. Newcastle's iron and steel industries use coal from the New-castle-Cessnock field. The city has a population of 414,000 (1984 est.).

▲ *Covered with mud and wearing grotesque headmasks, tribesmen from the New Guinea highlands perform a ritual ceremony.*

NEWCASTLE UPON TYNE A major industrial city on the River Tyne in north-eastern England. Newcastle is the centre of a coal-mining region. Population: 282,200.

NEW GUINEA A large island divided between INDONESIA (West Irian) and Papua New Guinea. Papua New Guinea, in the east, was ruled by Australia until independence in 1975. This tropical mountainous country has an area of 475,300 sq km (183,514 sq miles) and 3,425,000 people (1984 est.). The capital is Port Moresby. Papua New Guinea also includes islands in the Bismarck Archipelago and part of the Solomon Islands.

NEW SOUTH WALES The most populous Australian state, New South Wales has an area of 801,428 sq km (309,433 sq miles) and 5,436,900 people (1984). The capital is SYDNEY. Other cities include NEWCASTLE and Wollongong. The state's prosperity is now based on manufacturing, but mining, notably at Broken Hill, and farming, especially sheep farming, are important. Captain COOK explored the coast in 1770. The first British settlers arrived in 1788.

NEWSPAPER A daily or weekly publication giving the news and commenting on it. The first English weekly appeared in 1621, the first daily in 1702, but newspapers did not achieve a mass readership until the 19th century. Britain has the highest newspaper readership per head of population in the world.

NEWT Small, lizard-like AMPHIBIAN. Newts have similar life stories to FROGS; they are born in streams and ponds, spend their adult life on land, but return to water to breed. Most species are brown with dark markings and have an orange belly with black spots.

NEWTON, ISAAC English scientist (1642–1727) – the founder of modern PHYSICS. He put forward the law of GRAVITY, explained the movement of the planets around the Sun, developed the mathematical techniques of CALCULUS, and did important groundwork in MECHANICS, optics and ACOUSTICS. His ideas on the universe lasted till the time of EINSTEIN. ▷

NEW YORK CITY The greatest city in the UNITED STATES of America, New York City has a population (including its suburbs) of 17,807,000 (1984). It is an important seaport,

NEWTON, ISAAC Isaac's father wanted him to be a farmer like himself. But the boy let cows stray while he studied. His disappointed father sent him to university. There, Isaac discovered the binomial theorem when he was only 21.

NEW YORK CITY FACTS
New York City has some of the world's largest structures of their kind. It holds the biggest office building (the World Trade Center); the largest commercial hotel (the Waldorf Astoria); the largest museum (the American Museum of Natural History); the largest railway station (Grand Central Terminal); the longest single-span bridge (the Verrazano-Narrows Bridge); and the largest port (New York Harbor).

NILE The huge Aswan High Dam on the Nile now stores the river's annual flood waters so that they can be used in the hot months when the Nile is low. The dam is 109 m (364 ft) high and holds 169,270 cubic metres of water. It was completed in 1970.

situated at the mouth of the Hudson River, and is one of the world's leading financial, commercial and industrial centres. New York is noted for its cultural life and its many fine museums and theatres. The first European settlement there was established by the Dutch in 1613. ◁

NEW ZEALAND An independent monarchy within the Commonwealth of Nations, New Zealand is an island nation in the South Pacific Ocean. There are three main islands: North Island, South Island and Stewart Island, together with various smaller islands. The most densely-populated is North Island, a land of rolling hills and low mountains, including three active volcanoes. Volcanic steam is used to generate electricity. South Island is mountainous, with a mostly rugged coastline.

The MAORIS, who now form 8 per cent of the population, reached New Zealand in the 1300s, replacing the small Moriori tribes on North Island. The Dutch seaman Abel Janszoon TASMAN (1603–1659) sighted New Zealand in 1642, but nothing came of his discovery. Captain James COOK rediscovered and mapped New Zealand's coasts in 1769. In 1839 a settlement was established at what is now Wellington, by the British New Zealand Company. New Zealand became a British colony in 1841. Land disputes between settlers and the Maoris led to fighting in the late 1840s and again in the 1860s. But, after a gold rush in 1861, immigration increased quickly. Today, 91 per cent of the people are of European, mostly British, origin. In 1907 New Zealand became a self-governing dominion in the BRITISH EMPIRE.

The people now enjoy a high standard of living. Sheep and cattle farming are the main industries and butter, cheese, meat and wool dominate the exports. But manufacturing is increasing quickly in the cities, including AUCKLAND, WELLINGTON and CHRISTCHURCH. ◁

NIAGARA FALLS These scenic falls on the Canada-USA border include the Horseshoe Falls, 48 metres (158 ft) high, and the American Falls, 51 metres (167 ft) high.

NICARAGUA A republic in CENTRAL AMERICA, Nicaragua has 3,162,000 people (1984 est.) and a total area of 130,000 sq km (50,193 sq miles). The capital is Managua. ◁

NICKEL A tough, hard, silvery-white metal ELEMENT with the chemical symbol Ni. It is widely used in the form of plating and in ALLOYS. It is electroplated on to metals such as steel to protect them from CORROSION, and is added, with chromium, to steel to make it stainless. Its alloy with copper, *cupronickel*, is used for 'silver' coins.

NICOTINE A highly poisonous substance found in the TOBACCO plant. One grain of pure nicotine could be fatal for an adult. It is used as an insecticide.

NIGERIA A republic in WEST AFRICA, Nigeria has 92,038,000 people (1984 est.), more than any other African nation. The area is 923,768 sq km (356,669 sq miles) and the capital is Lagos. The people are divided into about 250 groups, the largest being the Hausa and Fulani in the north, and the Ibo and Yoruba in the south. Conflict led to a civil war (1967–70). Since then, revenue from oil has been used for rapid national development. ◁

NIGHTINGALE Small, brown bird famous for its beautiful song which is usually heard in the late evening or early morning. Nightingales live in damp shady woodlands and feed on insects. They breed in Europe but spend the winter in Africa.

NIGHTINGALE, FLORENCE British hospital reformer (1820–1910), famous for her work in the CRIMEAN WAR. She established the modern nursing profession.

NILE The world's longest river, the Nile flows 6670 km (4145 miles) from its source in the East African highlands to its outlet in the MEDITERRANEAN SEA. Its waters are important for irrigation in SUDAN and EGYPT. ◁

NITRIC ACID An extremely corrosive ACID, capable of dissolving most metals. It is used chiefly in making explosives, fertilizers, dyes and drugs.

◄ *The largest boiling lake in the world is in the Waimangu Valley, New Zealand, a country of hot springs and geysers.*

NITROGEN A colourless, tasteless gas. It is an ELEMENT with the symbol N. The Earth's ATMOSPHERE is nearly four-fifths nitrogen. It is essential to life for plants and animals. Plants get their nitrogen from compounds in the soil. These, in turn, get their nitrogen from the air or from fertilizers and decaying matter. Animals obtain nitrogen by eating plants or by eating other animals. The way in which nitrogen passes from the soil to plants and animals, and then back to the soil again, is an important part of the balance of nature called the *nitrogen cycle*. Nitrogen is used for making ammonia, fertilizers, explosives and plastics.

NOBEL PRIZES Alfred Nobel, a Swedish chemist and millionaire (1833–1896), donated funds in his will for a series of annual awards. These awards are known as the Nobel Prizes. The five original prizes were for chemistry, physics, medicine, literature and peace. They have been awarded annually on December 10 since 1901, to individuals of any nationality, for outstanding work in these areas. A prize for economics was added in 1968. They are regarded as the highest awards in their fields.

NOISE Noises are sounds that are unpleasant or unwanted. Harsh noises differ from pure musical tones in the fact that their wave vibrations are random and irregular. Often they are also high in pitch, like the squeak of chalk on a blackboard. Excessively loud noise can cause pain, and if we have to listen to loud noise for some length of time our hearing can be permanently damaged. People are becoming increasingly aware of the dangers of 'noise pollution' in modern life. (See SOUND)

NOLAN, SIDNEY Australian artist (born 1917). His paintings show different aspects of Australian life: the deserts of the outback and its explorers and inhabitants – especially the bandit Ned KELLY.

NOMADS People who have no permanent home and move about constantly in search of food and pasture for their herds. Nomads are found mainly in Africa and Asia, the Arab BEDOUIN being the best known.

NORMAN ARCHITECTURE The main style of ARCHITECTURE in England from the Norman Conquest to the end of the 12th century. Its typical features include massive stone walls, rounded arches, and buttresses that only project a little way from the face of the building. It is a branch of ROMANESQUE

▶*The homes of Saharan nomads are light and portable, and can be easily erected. The fence of matting is both a windbreak and a wall to keep out drifting sand.*

▶*Norman architecture is characterized by rounded arches, as in this 12th-century ambulatory at Peterborough Cathedral.*

architecture. Famous examples include the Keep of the Tower of London, and the Cathedrals of Winchester, Durham and Ely.

NORMAN CONQUEST William of Normandy, claiming to be the rightful heir to the throne, invaded England in 1066 and defeated King Harold at the Battle of Hastings. He became William I or WILLIAM THE CONQUEROR (1027–87). Normans became the ruling class.

NORMANS The VIKINGS (Norsemen) who invaded north-west France and adopted French language and customs. Their rule over Normandy was acknowledged by the French king in AD 911. From there, in the 11th and 12th centuries, they conquered England, parts of Wales and Ireland, southern Italy, Sicily and Malta. They also took an important part in the CRUSADES. Gradually they became absorbed through inter-marriage with local populations, and they ceased to be a separate people after the 13th century.

NORSEMEN See VIKINGS

NORTH AMERICA A continent which includes CANADA, GREENLAND, MEXICO, the UNITED STATES and the countries of CENTRAL AMERICA and the WEST INDIES. North America is the third largest continent, with an area of 24,257,000 sq km (9,366,000 sq miles). The population is about 357 million. The highest peak is Mt McKinley, in Alaska, which rises 6194 metres (20,320 ft) above sea-level. The MISSOURI RIVER is the continent's longest river.

▷

NORTH AMERICA The lowest point in North America is Death Valley, California, 86 m (282 ft) below sea-level. Death Valley is also the hottest place on the continent, a temperature of 56°C (134°F) having been registered there on July 10, 1913.

Nome ●

Alaska

Fairbanks ●

Anchorage ●

Mackenzie

Greenland

Baffin Is

*Great
Bear L.*

● Whitehorse

● Juneau

*Great
Slave L.*

Churchill ●
Hudson Bay

CANADA

Rocky

Edmonton ●
Vancouver ●
● Calgary

L. Winnipeg

PACIFIC OCEAN

Seattle ●

Mountains

Regina ●
● Winnipeg

Quebec ●
Montreal
Ottawa ■
● Halifax

St. Lawrence

Portland ●

Missouri

L. Superior

Toronto ●
L. Ontario
Boston ●

Minneapolis ●
● St Paul

L. Michigan
L. Huron
Detroit ●
L. Erie
Cleveland ●
New York ●

San Francisco ●

Salt Lake City ●

USA

Milwaukee ●
Chicago ●
Pittsburg ●
Philadelphia ●

Colorado

Denver ●

Indianapolis ●
Columbus ●
Baltimore ■
Washington DC ■

Las Vegas ●

Kansas City ●
● St Louis

Los Angeles ●

Santa Fe ●

BERMUDA

San Diego ●

Phoenix ●
Albuquerque ●

Red

Memphis ●

Mississippi

Tucson ●

El Paso ●

Dallas ●

Atlanta ●

Jacksonville ●

ATLANTIC OCEAN

Sierra Madre

Rio Grande

San
Antonio ●
Houston ●
New Orleans ●

G. of California

Monterrey ●

Miami ●

Gulf of Mexico

Nassau ■
BAHAMAS

MEXICO

Havana ■

Guadalajara ●

Mexico City ■

CUBA

**DOMINICAN
REP**
San Juan

HAITI
Port-au-Prince ■

**PUERTO
RICO**
Santo
Domingo

BARBADOS

JAMAICA
Kingston ■

Caribbean Sea

BELIZE
Belmopan ■

**TRINIDAD &
TOBAGO**
Port-of-Spain

GUATEMALA

HONDURAS

Guatemala City ■

Tegucigalpa ■

San Salvador ■
EL SALVADOR

NICARAGUA

Managua ■

**Panama
Canal Zone**

San Jose ■
COSTA RICA

Panama ■
PANAMA

NORTH AMERICA

■ Capital Cities

```
0        500        1000 miles
|----|----|----|----|----|
0    500   1000    1500 kilometres
```

▲ Baron Nils Nordenskjöld, geologist and explorer, navigated the Northeast Passage in his ship the Vega in 1878-9.

NORTHEAST PASSAGE A route, sought by various explorers, between Europe and Asia, via the icy Arctic Ocean. It was finally sailed by the Swede Nils Nordenskjöld (1832–1901) in 1878–1879.

NORTHERN TERRITORY A thinly-populated and mostly arid Australian territory. Northern Territory has an area of 1,347,519 sq km (520,280 sq miles) and 138,900 people (1984). The capital and chief port is Darwin.

▼ Norway's long coastline is lined with deep fiords formed during the Ice Age, when glaciers etched steep U-shaped valleys that were later filled by the sea.

NORTH SEA A sea between Britain and the mainland of western EUROPE, the North Sea has an area of about 6475 sq km (2500 sq miles). It is a fishing area, and oil and natural gas are extracted from the underlying rocks.

NORWAY A monarchy in north-west EUROPE, Norway is a mountainous land, with a coastline deeply indented by FIORDS. Part of Norway is north of the Arctic Circle and most people live in the south. Forests cover large areas, and only about 3 per cent of the land is farmed. Mining and manufacturing are the most important sectors of the economy, and oil now comes from the NORTH SEA. However, most of Norway's electricity is generated at hydroelectric power stations. Norway became a separate independent nation in 1905. ▷

NOSE Part of the face or head used by man and many other VERTEBRATE animals for breathing and smelling. The nose contains two openings, the nostrils; air is taken in through the nostrils and passes into the narrow tubes, called nasal passages, which connect with the throat. The sense of SMELL is located in the upper part of the nose. There, special nerve endings react to the vapours and scents given off by most substances. ▷

NOUN A word that is used as the name of something. Common nouns are the names of types of things (e.g. *boy, dog, mountain, team*). Proper nouns are the names of individual things (e.g. *John, Rover, Everest, Arsenal*).

NORWAY: FACTS AND FIGURES
Official language: Norwegian.
Currency: Norwegian krone.
Area: 324,219 sq km (125,182 sq miles).
Population: 4,140,000 (1984 est.).
Capital: Oslo (pop. 643,000).
Highest point: Galdhopiggen 2468 m (8087 ft).
Religion: Lutheran.
Much of Norway is uninhabited, a part of the country lying north of the Arctic Circle.

NOSE Noses come in many shapes and sizes, varying with the racial group as well as from one individual to another. A nose is Roman if it is straight, Grecian if it is straight and continues to the forehead without any depression, aquiline if it is convex, and retrousé if it is concave.

NOVA In addition to nova explosions, there are other, much bigger explosions in stars which we call 'supernovas'. A supernova explosion may be 10,000 times as great as a nova explosion, but they are much rarer occurrences. Only three visual supernovas have been recorded in our Galaxy. One was seen in China and Mexico in 1054, one was observed by the Danish astronomer Tycho Brahe in 1572, and one was seen by the German astronomer Kepler in 1604. The supernova of 1054 was visible even in the daytime. It gave rise to the Crab nebula, the gases of which are still flying outwards at about 1500 km per second (900 miles per second).

NOVA A STAR that suddenly increases in brightness, usually by several thousand times. This 'flare-up' is caused by an explosion in the star. It may make the star visible for the first time, hence the term 'nova', meaning 'new'. After the explosion, the star slowly returns to its normal state. ◁

NOVA SCOTIA A Canadian province bordering the North Atlantic, Nova Scotia has 883,800 people (1986) and an area of 55,491 sq km (21,425 sq miles). The capital is Halifax.

NOVEL A long story in prose, about imaginary people and events. Usually there is one main character who is the hero or heroine. As well as novels about people living ordinary, everyday lives, there are crime novels, science-fiction novels, historical novels, etc. (See LITERATURE)

NUCLEAR ENERGY An ATOM is a tiny particle of matter, made up of a nucleus surrounded by electrons. The nucleus is itself only a tiny part of the whole atom, yet the two parts of the nucleus, the proton and the neutron, are bound together by forces of enormous strength. When the neutron and the proton are separated this force is released in the form of ENERGY. This is how nuclear energy is produced. The atom's nucleus can be broken apart by bombarding it with other nuclear particles in huge 'atom smashers' or ACCELERATORS called *cyclotrons* and *synchrotrons*. But the atoms of certain elements can split by themselves without being bombarded in accelerators. The atoms of URANIUM, for example, can do this. Uranium-235 is an ISOTOPE of uranium. If a lump of uranium-235 is larger than a certain size, all its atoms split in a fraction of a second and enormous amounts of energy are given off as an explosion. Uranium-235 is used to make ATOMIC BOMBS. But this CHAIN REACTION, as it is called, can be controlled in a *nuclear reactor* to give us useful nuclear energy. The centre of the reactor is called the *core*. Here the uranium is housed inside rods. Around the rods is placed a *moderator*, a substance such as graphite or water that slows down the neutrons. In case the chain reaction starts to go too quickly,

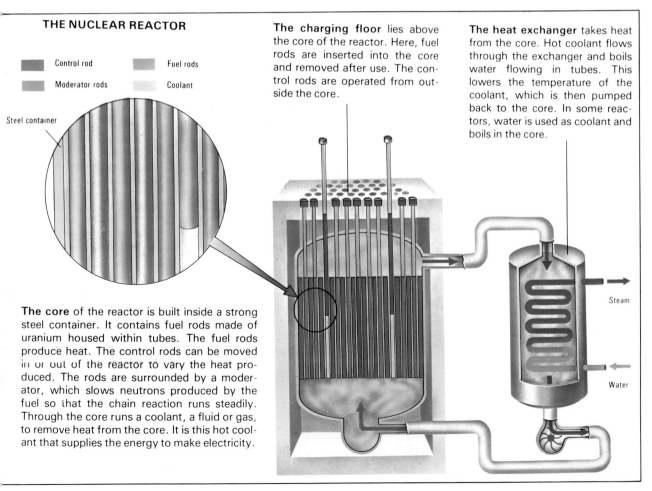

THE NUCLEAR REACTOR

Control rod
Moderator rods
Fuel rods
Coolant

Steel container

The charging floor lies above the core of the reactor. Here, fuel rods are inserted into the core and removed after use. The control rods are operated from outside the core.

The heat exchanger takes heat from the core. Hot coolant flows through the exchanger and boils water flowing in tubes. This lowers the temperature of the coolant, which is then pumped back to the core. In some reactors, water is used as coolant and boils in the core.

Steam

Water

The core of the reactor is built inside a strong steel container. It contains fuel rods made of uranium housed within tubes. The fuel rods produce heat. The control rods can be moved in or out of the reactor to vary the heat produced. The rods are surrounded by a moderator, which slows neutrons produced by the fuel so that the chain reaction runs steadily. Through the core runs a coolant, a fluid or gas, to remove heat from the core. It is this hot coolant that supplies the energy to make electricity.

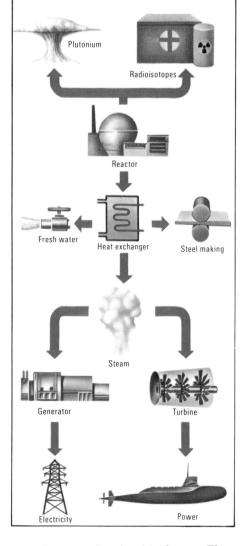

USING NUCLEAR POWER

A reactor is at the centre of every nuclear power system. It can produce plutonium or radioisotopes directly by irradiating elements with neutrons. Otherwise, the reactor's heat is used via a heat exchanger, although steam can be obtained directly from the reactor.

Plutonium

Radioisotopes

Reactor

Fresh water

Heat exchanger

Steel making

Steam

Generator

Turbine

Electricity

Power

▲ *A view inside the core of a nuclear reactor. The tubes contain fuel rods, control rods, moderator and coolant to remove heat from the core.*

control rods are also placed in the core. They are made of metals such as cadmium or boron that absorb neutrons, and they can be moved in or out of the core. To remove the heat produced in the uranium rods, a liquid or gas coolant is pumped through the core. When this coolant leaves the core it goes to a *heat exchanger*, where it gives up its heat before returning to the core. This heat is used to drive TURBINES which in turn drive large GENERATORS. The electricity produced by the generators is fed into the national network of electricity supply lines. (See FUSION)

NUT Popular name for a plant fruit which consists of a hard or leathery shell containing a kernel. Many kernels are edible, such as the ALMOND, Brazil and sweet CHESTNUT. In BOTANY, a nut is a plant fruit which contains only one seed and which does not open on ripening to distribute the seed.

NUTMEG Hard seed of a tropical fruit used as a spice. The nutmeg tree, an evergreen, is native to Indonesia. Another spice, mace, comes from the outer part of the nutmeg fruit. ▷

NUTRITION The study of the food needed by the body, and how it is used. For human beings a well-balanced diet needs to include PROTEIN, CARBOHYDRATE, FAT, VITAMINS, SALT and other MINERALS, and water. It must also give as many CALORIES of energy as are needed. ▷

NYLON A type of PLASTIC with widespread uses, especially in the form of fibre. In 1928, an American chemist called Dr Wallace Carothers started to search for materials suitable for making synthetic fibres. Ten years later, he announced his discovery of the material now called nylon. It is made from benzene (obtained from coal), oxygen, nitrogen and hydrogen. Nylon's excellent elastic properties make it especially suitable for stockings and tights. Clothes made from nylon drip-dry quickly and resist creasing; nylon carpets are hardwearing; and nylon ropes are strong and rot-proof. An important use for rigid, moulded nylon is in the manufacture of bearings and gears. Unlike metal components, these rarely require lubrication.

NUTMEG The nutmeg tree grows up to 21 m (70 ft) high. It first fruits at 8 years old, yields a full crop by 25 years, and remains fruitful for 60 years or more.

NUTRITION In addition to carbohydrates, fats and proteins, very small quantities of about twenty minerals are needed by the body. Some, such as calcium and iron, are needed for the formation of certain tissues (bones and teeth need calcium; the red cells of the blood need iron). Others are vital to certain processes such as the conduction of nerve impulses (sodium and potassium); the contraction of muscle fibres (calcium); the control of growth (iodine); and the production of enzymes (phosphorus, copper, cobalt, zinc, manganese and molybdenum). Minute quantities of fluoride prevent tooth decay. Many other minerals are also present in the body, but as yet no one knows for certain what they all do.

We also require a lot of water, as water makes up about 70 per cent of the body.

O

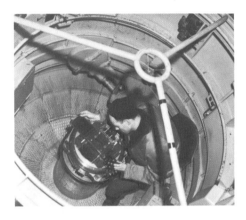

▼ Mount Stromlo Observatory, near Canberra, Australia. Note the silver-domed buildings housing the telescopes. At night the domes open to expose the telescopes to the heavens. There are more than 200 major observatories, or astronomical research stations, scattered throughout the world. Above: an astronomer sits in the observer's cage at the top of the telescope tube.

OAK Well-known tree found in most parts of the world, except in very cold zones. There are over 300 species of oak. Some, like the Common and Turkey Oaks are deciduous; others, like the Holm and Cork Oaks, are evergreen. Many oaks are large, sturdy trees with hard, strong wood. Some species live for hundreds of years. The oak fruit is called an acorn.

OASIS A place in a desert where water appears on the surface. Some oases are springs. The largest oases are river valleys, such as that of the NILE in Egypt.

OATS Important CEREAL crop grown in cool climates, often as fodder for animals. Oats are also eaten by man in various prepared forms such as oatmeal and breakfast foods.

OBELISK A stone monument, in the shape of a tall pillar: four-sided, narrowing upwards, and topped by a small pyramid shape. Cleopatra's Needle in London is an example.

OBOE Musical instrument of the woodwind family, especially used in an ORCHESTRA. It has two reeds and a nasal tone, and is played held vertically. Its range is nearly three octaves.

OBSERVATORY A place from which observations are made, usually of heavenly bodies. Major observatories are built in places where optical sightings will be least affected by atmospheric conditions. Dry, mountainous regions are, therefore, ideal. Relatively little dust is found at high altitudes, and dry regions have few clouds. Conditions are even better in outer space, but launching and running a major observatory in space would be extremely expensive. However, many useful observations have been made from the Russian *Salyut* and American *Skylab* general-purpose space laboratories. Fortunately, as-

257

▲ *The waters of an ocean are never still. The surface is whipped into waves by the wind.*

tronomers no longer have to rely on optical TELESCOPES alone. For, since the 1940s, RADIO ASTRONOMY has provided a vast range of information, impossible to discover by visual means.

OCEANS Vast areas of salt water that surround the continents. Oceans cover about 71

▼ *On a larger scale, the waters are moved by great currents that sweep across the oceans, profoundly affecting the world's climate.*

per cent of the Earth's surface. Although they are all interconnected, geographers distinguish three main oceans: the PACIFIC, ATLANTIC and INDIAN. The Antarctic and Arctic oceans are extensions of the other three. The waters of the oceans are constantly circulating because of ocean currents, which are caused by winds and differences in density. (See TIDES)
▷

OCTANE RATING The quality of petrol is described in terms of its octane rating. In a petrol engine, low-grade fuel may ignite prematurely, making the engine run unevenly with a knocking noise. Octane numbers range from 0 to 100 and refer to the fuel's anti-knock

OCEANS: FACTS AND FIGURES
Pacific
Area: 165.7 million sq km (63.9 million sq miles).
Average depth: 4267 m (14,000 ft).
Greatest depth: 11,033 m (36,198 ft) in the Marianas Trench.
Atlantic
Area: 81.6 million sq km (31.5 million sq miles).
Average depth: 4267 m (14,000 ft).
Greatest depth: 8381 m (27,498 ft), in the Milwaukee Deep.
Indian
Area: 73.4 million sq km (28.3 million sq miles).
Average depth: 3960 m (13,000 ft).
Greatest depth: 7725 m (25,344 ft) south of Java.
Arctic
Area: 14 million sq km (5.4 million sq miles).
Average depth: 1280 m (4200 ft).
Greatest depth: 5333 m (17,500 ft) north of Svalbard.

About 35 parts in every 1000 parts of ocean water consist of dissolved salts. The most abundant elements in sea water are sodium and chlorine. Only 10 other elements make up more than one part per million of sea water. They include sulphur, magnesium, calcium, potassium, bromine, boron, and strontium.

In the tropics, the ocean surface is a warm 25°C, but deep down the temperature is close to freezing. Polar fishes such as Greenland sharks can thrive 3,000 m (10,000 ft) below the warm surface off California.

The average temperature of all the water in the oceans is 3.8°C. This low average is caused by the coldness at great depths. From the surface down to 50 m (164 ft) the temperature is about 27°C, then there is a sharp fall to about 10°C at 400 m (1312 ft), and 5°C at 900 m (3000 ft). At depths greater than 5000 m (16,500 ft) the temperature drops to 1°C.

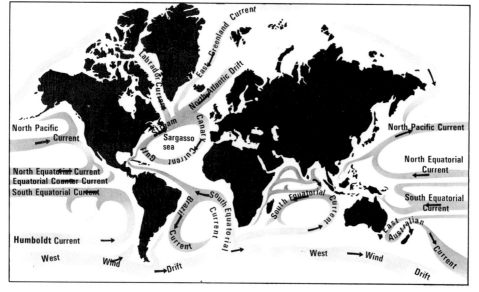

OCTOPUS The largest octopus is the Pacific octopus, which can measure up to 9.7 m (32 ft) from the tip of one tentacle to the tip of the opposite one.

The octopus takes on the same colour as the rocks or sand in which it is hiding. It can change colour in a flash to confuse its enemies. Stories of swimmers being attacked by octopuses are almost all unfounded. The octopus is a timid creature. But some octopuses can inject a most powerful venom, the deadliest of all being the blue-ringed octopus of the Pacific. Its venomous bite can kill a man within two hours. However, a bite from most octopuses will only result in a slight swelling.

OHM'S LAW Georg Ohm thought that the flow of electricity through a wire was something like the flow of water through a pipe. To make water flow, work must be done by a pump. To make electricity flow through a wire there must be a difference of potential or voltage between the two ends of the wire. This difference is measured in *volts*. Ohm also measured the amount of electricity (the current) that passed through a wire in a second. The unit of current is the *ampere*. Ohm found that there was a link between the voltage and the current. When the voltage was doubled, the current doubled too. He also found that if the voltage remained the same, the current was halved if a wire of twice the resistance was used. In other words, current, measured in amperes, is equal to voltage, measured in volts, divided by resistance, measured in ohms.

▼ The common octopus can be up to 3 m (10 ft) across its eight extended arms. Its bag-like body is usually grey-brown. It has 8 arms each with two rows of suckers. It can give a painful bite if handled. It lurks in rocky crevices on the seabed.

quality. Petrol with a high octane number is, therefore, unlikely to cause knocking.

OCTOPUS Sea creature, found all over the world, with eight long arms growing out from its head. These arms are used for walking on the ocean bed and for catching food, mainly crabs and shellfish. The octopus hides from enemies by changing its shape and colour. If discovered, it squirts out an inky fluid, then escapes under cover of this black screen. ◁

ODYSSEY An epic poem by the Greek poet HOMER. It tells the story of the wanderings of Ulysses (Odysseus), a Greek hero, as he tries to return home to his kingdom of Ithaca after the Trojan War. The word is now also used to describe any long journey, or story of such a journey.

OEDIPUS Legendary Greek king of Thebes. He unintentionally killed his father and married his mother – as an oracle had predicted. Sophocles wrote two famous Greek dramas, or 'tragedies', on the subject.

OHM The SI UNIT of electrical RESISTANCE. The resistance between two points on a conductor is one ohm (Ω), if a current of one AMPERE flows when a potential difference of one VOLT is applied across them.

OHM'S LAW An important electrical law, first demonstrated by the German physicist Georg Ohm in 1827. It states that, in a conductor, the ratio of the voltage (**V**) across its ends to the current (**I**) flowing through it is equal to its resistance (**R**). In symbols, this is expressed as: $\mathbf{R} = \mathbf{V/I}$. ◁

OILS Greasy chemical compounds which dissolve in ETHER, but not in water. Usually the term refers to substances that are liquid at normal room temperatures; solids being referred to as FATS. Oils are obtained from various animal, vegetable and mineral sources. *Fixed oils*, which do not evaporate easily, are obtained mostly by squeezing animal or vegetable substances, such as fish or seeds. Such oils vary greatly in their drying properties. Some, called 'drying oils', form a hard surface film when left in contact with the air. This makes them suitable for use in paints and varnishes. Drying oils include linseed (obtained from flax seeds), sunflower and poppyseed. *Volatile oils* evaporate quickly. Some, such as lavender, have a pleasant smell and are used in soaps and perfumes. Others, such as clove, are used to flavour foods and medicines. Animal and vegetable oils have widespread uses, but man's most important

source of oils is the mineral petroleum.

Scientists think that petroleum was formed from the decayed remains of tiny plants and animals that lived in the sea millions of years ago. Many petroleum regions have since become land masses owing to movements in the Earth's crust. Petroleum is extracted by drilling wells to a depth of several kilometres. The crude oil obtained is a black mixture so valuable to man that it is sometimes called 'black gold'. Refineries separate it into petrol, diesel oil, fuel oils, lubricants, asphalt and many other substances. Other industries use petrochemicals (chemicals made from pet-

▲ *Oil deposits are now being mined from under the sea as well as on land, using offshore drilling rigs like the one shown here.*

roleum) for numerous products including plastics, drugs, antiseptics, anaesthetics, cosmetics, fertilizers and detergents.

OLIVE Small oval fruit with a hard stone and bitter oily flesh. Olives are either eaten ripe, when they are black, or unripe, when they are green and pickled in brine. Oil, used in cooking, is pressed from the ripe fruit. Olive trees, found mostly in Mediterranean lands,

OLYMPIC GAMES Host cities since World War II:
1948 London, England
1952 Helsinki, Finland
1956 Melbourne, Australia
1960 Rome, Italy
1964 Tokyo, Japan
1968 Mexico City, Mexico
1972 Munich, West Germany
1976 Montreal, Canada
1980 Moscow, USSR
1984 Los Angeles, USA
1988 Seoul, South Korea
1992 Barcelona, Spain

are evergreen with silvery-green leaves and a twisted, gnarled trunk.

OLYMPIC GAMES The original Games were held in ancient GREECE, at Olympia. They took place every four years, from before 776 BC to AD 396. At first there were just foot races, but later there was boxing, wrestling, and chariot and horse races. The modern Games have been held every four years since 1896 (except in wartime) and in a different country each time. They are supervised by the International Olympic Committee, and there are many more events (team sports, water sports, weapon sports etc). The Winter Olympics feature snow and ice sports. From 1994 the Winter and Summer Olympics will alternate every two years. All Olympic competitors should be amateurs. ◁

ONION Strong-tasting edible BULB grown as a vegetable. Onions have a brown, papery outer skin surrounding a mass of white, fleshy leaves. They are grown throughout the world and are eaten raw, cooked and pickled.

ONYX A form of the mineral *silica* (see SILICON). It is distinguished by straight parallel bands of different colours (mainly milk-white, black and red). Onyx is often used for CAMEOS.

OPAL A form of the mineral *silica* (see SILICON), and found in STALACTITES in volcanic rock. Usually it is opaque, but precious opal has many tiny cracks from which crystals of another substance give out brilliant colours.

OPERA A type of DRAMA, performed on a stage, but with singing in place of speech. The music is usually thought to be more important than the acting. Some operas also use dancing and spectacular stage effects. Opera started in Italy in the late 16th century, and rapidly became a popular entertainment. Since then the greatest operas have come from Austria (MOZART), Germany (Wagner) and Italy itself (Verdi). There is also light opera, which is humorous and combines songs and speech. ◁

OPIUM A DRUG made from the juice of a type of poppy. From it, in turn, come the drugs MORPHINE and HEROIN. Opium has medicinal uses. Many tribal communities in Asia grow opium illegally, and are dependent on it.

OPOSSUM American MARSUPIAL. Opossums look like large rats. They are active at

▶ *A fine example of a gem opal. The reddish-orange colour is characteristic of the variety called fire opal. The milkiness of some opals is caused by the presence of tiny gas bubbles. Precious opals are usually given a smoothly rounded finish to show off their colour.*

night and sleep by day. Most species live among trees and are expert climbers.

OPTICS See LENS; MICROSCOPE; MIRROR; PRISM; TELESCOPE

ORANGE Popular citrus fruit grown in most subtropical countries. It is round with tart, juicy flesh divided into segments and a tough reddish-yellow outer skin. There are two main types of orange: the sweet orange which is eaten raw or squeezed for its juices; and the bitter, or Seville orange, which is used for making marmalade. The orange tree is evergreen and has fragrant white flowers. ◁

ORANG-UTAN Reddish-brown APE from the swampy forests of Indonesia. In Malay, its name means 'jungle man'. Orangs have short, weak legs but long, powerful arms; they live in trees, swinging slowly from branch to branch. Their diet consists mainly of fruit and leaves.

▼*A male orang-utan shows the large, grasping hands which allow him to swing so easily through the trees of his native jungle.*

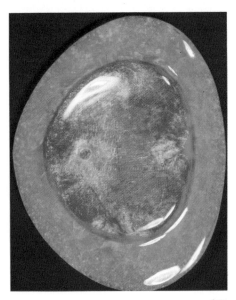

Orb

ORBIT The path of one body moving completely around another body. Planets move in orbits around the Sun, and the Moon and numerous artificial satellites orbit the Earth. The shape of these orbits is elliptical – like a circle that has been squashed to some extent. The *perigee* is a body's closest distance and the *apogee* its farthest distance from the body it orbits. In ATOMS, one or more electrons orbit a nucleus.

ORCHESTRA A large group of musical instruments and their players, under the control of a conductor. The standard modern orchestra has about 90 instruments, in four sections: *strings* (violins, violas, cellos, double basses); *woodwind* (flutes, oboes, clarinets, bassoons, with a piccolo, cor anglais, bass clarinet and double bassoon); *brass* (French horns, trumpets, trombones and a tuba); and *percussion* (side-drum, bass drum, timpani, cymbals and triangle).

ORCHID One of the world's most fascinating flowers. An orchid bloom consists of six petal-like segments; one segment, called the lip, is much larger than the others and has a special colour or shape. Most orchids are found in the tropics. These often have richly-coloured exotic blooms and grow in the jungle tree tops; but there are many species in other parts of the world.

ORE A ROCK or MINERAL from which useful amounts of an ELEMENT, usually a metal, can be obtained. Some ores are simply heated until the molten metal runs out. Gold, silver and copper can be obtained in this way. In other ores, the metals exist as compounds, being chemically combined with other elements, such as oxygen or sulphur. Iron, for example, is found as iron oxide, and copper is often found as copper sulphide. The pure metals are obtained from compound ores like these by chemical treatment or by ELECTROLYSIS.

ORGAN (INSTRUMENT) A large musical instrument. It has tall pipes through which air is blown, controlled by keyboards, knobs and pedals. Organs are often found in cathedrals and large churches. There are now also small home electric 'organs'.

OSCILLOSCOPE An electronic instrument that displays electric signals as patterns on the screen of a CATHODE-RAY TUBE. Sound waves, for example, can be studied by connecting the signal from a microphone to the oscilloscope. With no input signal, the oscilloscope displays a horizontal straight line. This is formed by a spot of light sweeping continually across the screen. When an input signal is connected, this deflects the spot vertically. Hence the spot traces out a pattern of the input signal.

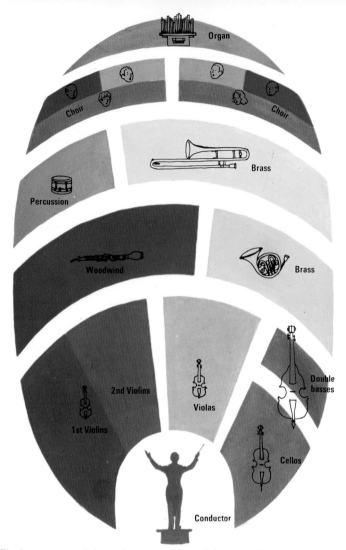

▲ The instruments of the orchestra, and one of the ways they are often arranged on stage. A large block on the conductor's left is made up of first and second violins, generally playing different parts. The cellos and double basses have heavier tones, so fewer of them are needed to achieve a good balance of sound. There are often only two to four of each wind instrument. Orchestras vary in size from string or chamber groups with under twenty players to those with a hundred or more.

▶ The colourful mineral crystals shown opposite are attractive to look at. But, more important, they are all valuable ores which can be processed into the metals on which our industrial civilization depends.

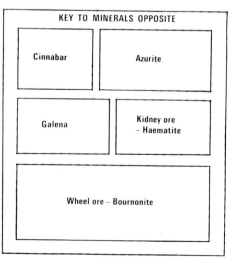

KEY TO MINERALS OPPOSITE

Cinnabar	Azurite
Galena	Kidney ore – Haematite
Wheel ore – Bournonite	

OSMOSIS The process by which liquids pass through a porous *membrane* (skin) until the fluid on both sides of the membrane is equal. This is how PLANTS take in water through their roots, and how the BLOOD stream absorbs food from the digestive tract.

OSPREY Large fish-eating bird of prey found in most parts of the world; it is brown with a white head and underparts. Ospreys take their food from both fresh and salt water.

OSTRICH Largest living bird. Ostriches have long legs and necks and stand up to 2.5 metres (8 ft) tall; they cannot fly but are very fast runners. Ostriches live in the dry bush of East Africa. In some parts of the world, they are bred on farms for their feathers and skins. ▷

OTTER Flesh-eating water animal found in many parts of the world. Otters have slim bodies, short legs, webbed feet and thick fur – usually brownish. They are strong, swift swimmers and can also move quickly on land. As well as fish, they eat creatures such as rabbits, frogs and ducks.

OWL Bird of prey found in all parts of the world. Owls have soft feathers – usually grey or brown – short tails, large heads and big round eyes. Most species live in trees and spend the day sleeping and the night hunting. Their diet consists mainly of mice, voles and rats. (See CARNIVORE) ▷

OXIDATION AND REDUCTION Oxidation is a chemical REACTION in which a substance combines with oxygen or loses hydrogen. In reduction, a substance loses oxygen or gains hydrogen. The terms are sometimes used more generally to include any reaction in which an atom loses electrons (oxidation) or gains them (reduction).

OXYGEN The life-supporting gas making up about one-fifth of the AIR by volume.

▼ Otters swim fast by wagging their powerful tails and using their webbed feet as paddles. In the water they show up as three distinct humps – head, arched back, and tail tip.

Humans and other land animals absorb oxygen from the air they breathe (see RESPIRATION). Fish absorb dissolved oxygen from the water. Oxygen is a chemical ELEMENT obtained commercially by separation from liquid air. Substances burn by combining with oxygen. Extremely hot flames are produced in WELDING torches by burning other gases with pure oxygen. (See OXIDATION AND REDUCTION; OZONE)

OYSTER Sea animal with a soft fleshy body enclosed in a hinged, two-part shell. Species exist in nearly all the world's seas. The fleshy part is a popular sea food. (See PEARL)

OZONE A form of OXYGEN in which each MOLECULE contains three atoms instead of the usual two. Ozone is formed from normal oxygen by electrical sparking, and is responsible for the characteristic smell sometimes noticed near electric motors. Ozone is used as a sterilizing agent and bleach. An ozone layer in the ATMOSPHERE absorbs much of the Sun's harmful ultraviolet radiation.

▼ An eagle owl. Being a bird of prey, an owl has large, forward-facing eyes with extra-sensitive retinas. These allow it to see in very dim light. The owl uses its talons and curved beak to kill small mammals and birds.

OSTRICH The ostrich is the only bird with only two toes on each foot. The male makes a loud booming roar during the mating season. The female lays as many as 10 large white eggs in a shallow hole scooped in the sand. Ostriches are greedy eaters, their main food being berries, plants and seeds; but sometimes they swallow stones, cans and other objects to help digest their food. They can live for up to 70 years. It is not true that the ostrich buries its head in the sand to 'hide' from danger. If cornered they can do considerable damage by kicking with their powerful legs.

OWL Owls surprise prey by their silent flight. This is due to flight feathers with tooth-like outer edges that help to muffle the sound of flapping flight. Engineers have fitted similar teeth to jet aero-engines' exhaust ducts to cut down the noise made by hot, escaping gases.

P

PACIFIC OCEAN The largest and deepest ocean, the Pacific covers 165,722,970 sq km (63,986,000 sq miles). It was named the Pacific, meaning *peaceful*, by the Portuguese navigator Ferdinand MAGELLAN.

PAIN This is the brain's response to nerve messages sent from *pain receptors* in the different parts of the body. The result is unpleasant, but vital for survival. If we could not feel pain, we would not know when we were ill or injuring ourselves. (See BRAIN; NERVOUS SYSTEM)

PAINT This is used to decorate and protect surfaces such as wood, metal and plaster. It is made up of a PIGMENT, which gives it its colour; a *binder* (such as oil, latex or resin) which dries on contact with air; and a *solvent* (water or spirit) to make it flow.

PAINTING This ART dates back to the paintings of animals done by prehistoric man on the walls of caves. Some paintings in fact are still done directly onto walls (these are called MURALS or FRESCOES). But most are painted on canvases – pieces of fabric stretched tight on wooden supports. They are then hung on walls in homes, offices, art galleries,

▼ *Turner's painting of* Ulysses Deriding Polyphemus *(1829). Turner was fascinated by skies, clouds and water, sometimes using them for supernatural effects.*

museums, etc. The type of paint usually used is oil paint. This was developed in the Netherlands in the 15th century. Other paints include WATER COLOURS and synthetic acrylic paints. A painter may choose any subject, including scenes from history, religion and MYTHOLOGY; individual people (portraits); landscapes and seascapes; animals; scenes from everyday life; still lifes (flowers, bowls of fruit, etc); and abstract patterns of shapes and colours (see ABSTRACT ART). A painting can be built up gradually, with successive layers of paint – the traditional technique. Or it can be created more directly, as if the painter is 'drawing' with the paint. In either case, the finished painting aims to use colour, texture and design to create an effect. ▷

PAKISTAN A Moslem nation in southern ASIA, Pakistan has 93,286,000 people (1984 est.) and an area of 803,943 sq km (310,404 sq miles). The capital is Islamabad. The north and west are mountainous. Most people are farmers who live in river valleys, such as that of the Indus. From 1947, when it became independent, to 1971, Pakistan in-

▲*Picasso's painting of* Guernica, *inspired by the bombing of a Basque town in 1937. It is painted in shades of grey and black, in the distorted 'surrealist' style.*

▼ *A self-portrait by Rembrandt. This painting, like the one by Turner on the previous page, shows the artist's interest in the effects of light and shade. These qualities were later adopted by the Impressionists of the 19th century.*

◄ *These pictures of bison are among the earliest ever made. About 20,000 years ago, Stone Age men painted them on the walls of a cave in Lascaux, France. These primitive artists used pigments made largely from mineral oxides; these were mixed with animal fat, water or blood.*

PAINTING The oldest known paintings are animal outlines sketched in European caves by Stone Age hunters. One bison head at Altamira in Spain may be 25,000 years old. The oldest landscape painting is about 8200 years old. It shows the early town of Catal Hüyük in what is now Turkey.

PAKISTAN: FACTS AND FIGURES
Official language: Urdu, although it is spoken by only about 10 per cent of the people. Punjabi is more widely spoken.
Currency: Pakistani rupee.
Religion: Islam.
Chief rivers: Indus, Sutlej, Chenab, and Ravi.
Largest cities: Karachi (pop. 5,103,000), Lahore (2,922,000), Faisalabad (1,092,000), and Rawlpindi (806,000).

cluded BANGLADESH (then East Pakistan). But a bitter civil war led to the break-up of the country. ◁

PALESTINE The Biblical Holy Land, Palestine now belongs mostly to ISRAEL. The Romans took Palestine in 63 BC and, in the AD 70s, they crushed Jewish opposition and many JEWS emigrated. The area came under Moslem Arab rule in the 600s. In 1882 a group of Zionist pioneers settled in Palestine and Israel was established in 1948. Parts of Palestine in neighbouring Arab nations were taken by Israel during Arab-Israeli wars.

PALM TREE Tropical tree having a tall straight trunk topped with a cluster of large fan-like or feathery leaves. There are about 1500 species. Many of them are useful to man: for example, dates, coconuts and raffia all come from palms.

PANAMA A republic in CENTRAL AMERICA, Panama has 2,134,000 people (1984 est.) and an area of 75,650 sq km (29,209 sq miles). The capital is Panamá. This tropical, farming nation is cut in two by the PANAMA CANAL Zone. ◁

PANAMA CANAL An important waterway connecting the Atlantic and Pacific oceans,

the Panama Canal is 81.63 km (50.72 miles) long. It was built by the United States and was opened in 1914. The Panama Canal Zone is still administered by the United States.

PANCREAS A large GLAND, about 18 cm (7 inches) long, lying behind and below the stomach. It releases digestive juices into the small intestine, and it also produces a HORMONE (insulin) · which is important in the body's use of sugar (see DIABETES).

PANDA Asian MAMMAL related to a raccoon. There are two kinds of panda. One, the Red Panda, is the size of a large cat and lives in the Himalayas. It has a thick black and red coat and spends most of its time in trees; it is active at night and feeds on bamboo, fruit and nuts. The other, the Giant Panda, is a bigger, bear-like animal found in the bamboo forests of western China. It has white fur, with black legs, shoulders, ears and eye patches. The Giant Panda moves slowly; it rests by day and shuffles around at night eating bamboo shoots, small mammals and fish.

PANTHER See LEOPARD

PAPER The material used for writing, PRINTING, wrapping and many other things. It was invented in China in AD 105, and reached Europe via the Arabs. Paper is made from vegetable fibres (usually wood). The fibres are mixed with water and reduced to a pulp. The pulp goes into a mesh mould and is then pressed and dried to form a sheet.

PAPUA NEW GUINEA See New Guinea.

PAPYRUS A material for writing on, made in ancient Egypt from a type of reed. The pith of the reed was cut, beaten into thin strips, and pressed together into sheets which were rolled onto rods.

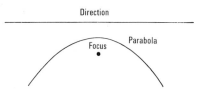

PARABOLA A curve traced out when a point moves in such a way that its distance from a point, called the *focus*, is equal to its distance from a straight line, called the *directrix*. BULLETS and other projectiles move in paths resembling parabolas. If there were no air resistance, such flight paths would be exactly parabolic in shape. (See BALLISTICS)

◄ *The giant Panda is still an endangered species and survives in the wild only in remote bamboo forests of China.*

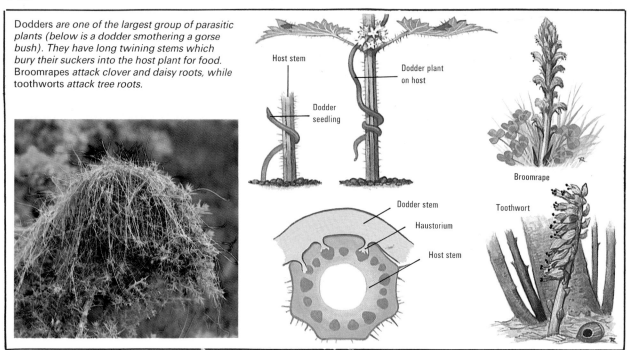

Dodders *are one of the largest group of parasitic plants (below is a dodder smothering a gorse bush). They have long twining stems which bury their suckers into the host plant for food.* Broomrapes *attack clover and daisy roots, while* toothworts *attack tree roots.*

Host stem

Dodder plant on host

Dodder seedling

Dodder stem

Haustorium

Host stem

Broomrape

Toothwort

PARAFFINS Also called alkanes, a group of inflammable hydrocarbons. The paraffins methane, ethane, propane and butane are gases under normal conditions. Liquid paraffins are known as paraffin oils. The liquid commonly called paraffin, or kerosine, is a mixture of these oils. Solid paraffins are called paraffin waxes.

PARAGUAY A land-locked republic in SOUTH AMERICA, Paraguay has a population of 3,477,000 (1983 census) and an area of 406,752 sq km (157,048 sq miles). The capital is Asunción. Farming, especially cattle-rearing, is the main occupation and meat is the chief export. Forestry is also important. ▷

PARASITE Animal or plant that gets its food from another living animal or plant. Parasites usually weaken and sometimes kill their 'host'. Some animal parasites live inside the host's body: the tapeworm, for example, attaches itself to the host's intestines and steals the digested food. Others, such as the FLEA, hang on to the skin and live by sucking blood. There are also two kinds of plant parasite. Those such as the MISTLETOE have leaves but no roots; they only take water from the host and use it to make their own food. But other plants have no roots and no leaves – just flowers – and these depend entirely on their host for nourishment.

PARCHMENT A material for writing on, made from the skin of animals like sheep and goats. It was used for books and documents before the introduction of PAPER.

PARIS Capital city of FRANCE, Paris has 8,707,000 people, including its suburbs. It is a major cultural centre, with a university, art galleries, theatres, and so on. The many

▼ *The Eiffel Tower, Paris's most memorable landmark, was built in 1889. It is a 400-metre (1,312 ft) iron structure.*

PARIS Paris lies on the River Seine, 177 km (110 miles) from the sea at Le Havre. It is the most densely populated city in Europe.

The city is the presidential seat. The Elysée Palace, once the home of Madame de Pompadour, is the official home of the President of the Republic. The Assemblée Nationale (Chamber of Deputies) is the head chamber of the French parliament. The Palais du Luxembourg is used for sittings of the senate.

The University of Paris (Sorbonne) was founded in 1253 for 16 poor students of theology.

The Bibliothèque Nationale is the oldest of Europe's national libraries and contains more than six million books. The Cathedral of Nôtre Dame on the Ile de la Cité is one of the most beautiful Gothic structures in Europe. The 300-m (990-ft) Eiffel Tower is the tallest building.

PARLIAMENT Although it dates back for seven centuries, the British Parliament is not the oldest. Iceland's Althing goes back to AD 930, but was abolished between 1800 and 1843. The Parliament with the longest unbroken history sits in the Isle of Man's Tynwald Court, and may be more than 1000 years old.

The founder of the first English Parliament was a French baronial leader, Simon de Montfort. Simon defeated Henry III in battle, and tried to rule with help from the barons, knights, and people chosen to speak for the towns. They met in Parliament in January 1265. Seven months later, Simon himself was killed in a battle with Henry's son Edward. Edward's own Model Parliament of 1295 became a model for later ones.

superb buildings include Nôtre Dame Cathedral, on an island in the River Seine. Industries are varied. Parisian perfumes and women's fashions are world-famous ◁

PARLIAMENT The governing body of Great Britain. It dates back to 1265, but only became more powerful than the king in the 17th and 18th centuries. In the 14th century it was divided into the HOUSE OF COMMONS and the HOUSE OF LORDS. Parliament now meets at the Palace of Westminster, in London. Elections for Members of Parliament (that is, members of the Commons) must be held at least once every five years. ◁

▲ The Queen sits enthroned in the House of Lords for the traditional opening of Parliament. The real power of the monarchy and the House of Lords has been reduced over the years. Law-making and government are controlled by the House of Commons.

PARROT Tropical bird with a stout, sharply-hooked beak, found mainly in southeast Asia, Australia and South America. There are about 500 species; many of them are brightly coloured and many are good mimics, able to copy other sounds, especially human voices. Parrots generally inhabit trees and feed on fruit and nuts; they can live for fifty years.

PARSLEY Popular herb grown in temperate lands. Its fine, curly leaves are either used fresh to decorate foods, or they are used fresh or dried as a flavouring.

PARTHENON The famous temple at ATHENS, built 447–438 BC. It was so called because it was dedicated to the goddess Athena Parthenos (meaning 'the Virgin'). It was reduced to ruins in 1687, when the Venetians bombarded Athens (then held by the Turks). Part of the Parthenon's beautiful sculptured frieze was acquired by Lord Elgin and is now in the British Museum.

PARTRIDGE Common game bird, related to the PHEASANT, and found in Europe, Africa and Asia. Most species of partridge are brown or grey and live on the ground rather than perching in trees.

PASSOVER An important Jewish religious festival, lasting eight days and held in springtime. It commemorates the escape from Egypt under MOSES. There is a ritual meal in the home on the first evening. (See JUDAISM)

PASTEURIZATION A process for preserving food by heating it before packaging. The heat kills many of the BACTERIA and other micro-organisms that cause disease or spoilage. The process was developed by the French scientist Louis PASTEUR in the 1800s and named in his honour.

PASTEUR, LOUIS French scientist (1822–1895) who discovered some of the important roles played by micro-organisms (minute living organisms). He thus founded the science of microbiology. Pasteur found out how tiny YEAST cells cause the fermentation of sugars to alcohol. He also discovered that similar processes turn wine to vinegar and make milk go sour. To prevent foods being spoilt in this way, Pasteur devised the heating process now called PASTEURIZATION.   ▷

PATENT A document giving an inventor the exclusive right to make and profit from his INVENTION for (in England) 16 years. He may choose to sell this right to others.   ▷

PATHOLOGY The study of diseases or abnormalities of the body. Pathologists take tiny samples of body cells, and look at them under the microscope, to see if there is any disease and whether treatments are working. They also do *post-mortem* examinations on dead bodies, to decide the causes of death.

PAVLOV, IVAN Russian researcher into PHYSIOLOGY (1849–1936). He won a NOBEL PRIZE in 1904 for work on digestion. But he is mainly remembered for his work with animals which revealed an unconscious process of

PASTEUR, LOUIS At 17 Louis gained the lowly job of school usher. His task was just keeping order. But one pupil had a microscope that Louis borrowed to study insects. This sparked off his interest in tiny life forms – a hobby that became a career and in time made him famous.

PATENT In 60 years the great American inventor Thomas Alva Edison patented no fewer than 1100 inventions. Yet he claimed that genius was '1 per cent inspiration and 99 per cent perspiration'. It took him two years and thousands of experiments to find an effective lamp filament.

PEACOCK The name peacock is also used for some other kinds of pheasant. One is the green peacock of South-east Asia. Others include the Congo peacock which lives in Africa.

PEANUT In a normal year three nations produce more than half the world's peanuts. In one recent year their shares of the world output were as follows: India 28 per cent; China 15 per cent; United States 9.5 per cent.

The peanut plant *(Arachis hypogaea)* is the strangest member of the pea family. When its small, yellow, pea-like flowers have faded, it does a very peculiar thing. It pushes the tips of the small stalk-like organs into the ground. These work their way under the soil until they are about 10 cm (4 inches) below the surface, where they develop into pods and ripen. They are then ploughed up for marketing.

▼Louis Pasteur carried out research into rabies, among other diseases. In 1885 he successfully inoculated a child bitten by a rabid dog. He is pictured here (centre) in his clinic.

The food value of peanuts is very high. It has been calculated that a kilogram of peanuts has as much protein as a kilogram of steak, plus more carbohydrate than a kilogram of potatoes, plus a third of the fat content of a kilogram of butter.

PEAR In a normal year seven nations produce about two-thirds of the world's pears. In one recent year their shares of the world output were: Italy 20 per cent; China 14 per cent; United States 9 per cent; Japan 7 per cent; Spain 6 per cent; France 6 per cent; West Germany 4.5 per cent.

PEARL Ancient Romans prized pearls so highly that their rulers allowed only people of a certain rank to wear them. Only a special group of traders were permitted to deal in pearls. They were known as *margaritarii* – from the Latin world *margarita*, meaning pearl.

The Japanese are expert at 'cultivating' pearls by putting small beads of mother-of-pearl (shell material) inside the oyster. This bead is then covered naturally with pearl. There are large oyster farms for this industry.

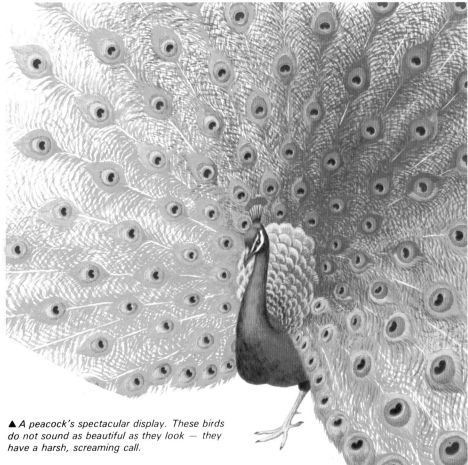

▲ *A peacock's spectacular display. These birds do not sound as beautiful as they look — they have a harsh, screaming call.*

'learning by association'. This greatly influenced modern PSYCHOLOGY.

PEA Climbing plant cultivated for its seeds which are eaten as a VEGETABLE. The round seeds – peas – are contained in a long pod and picked when they are unripe and green. Most pea plants have white flowers but some species have brightly-coloured ones and are grown for ornament.

PEACH Large roundish fruit with a hard stone surrounded by sweet juicy flesh and a yellow-red fuzzy skin. Peaches grow in warm climates and ripen in late summer. Although they are delicious eaten raw, they do not keep well and many are canned; more so than any other fruit in the world.

PEACOCK Male peafowl. Peafowl, found wild from India through to Indonesia, live in jungle lands near water. The peacock is a brilliant blue with a long train of feathers that spreads out into a magnificent fan; the peahen (female) has no train. Peafowl have been domesticated for centuries. They were once bred for food but are now kept for ornament in gardens and parks. ◁

PEANUT Important crop grown in warm parts of the world. Peanuts, also called ground nuts, develop underground. They are covered by a red, papery skin and contained in wrinkled, yellowish pods. The nuts are full of PROTEIN and are either eaten raw or turned into peanut butter. They also produce oil, used for manufacturing margarine and soap, and they can be made into cattlefeed. ◁

PEAR Juicy, cone-shaped fruit. Pears are related to apples and are grown in temperate climates. They are mostly eaten raw or canned. ◁

PEARL A precious GEM – the only one that is not a stone. It is found in some kinds of OYSTER and other shellfish. These produce a chalky substance called *nacre*. If this hardens round a foreign body inside the shell (e.g. a piece of grit), it forms a pearl. ◁

PECTIN A mixture of various CARBO-HYDRATES. It is found in the cell walls of fruits, especially ripe ones, and is used for making jams and jellies set.

PEKING See Beijing.

PEKINGESE A small dog with long hair and a curly tail. The breed originated in China. The chinese regarded pekingese as royal.

PELICAN Large white or brown water bird, found by estuaries and swamps in warm regions. Pelicans have a small head, short legs, massive body, long neck and a giant beak with a big pouch. The beak and pouch act as a fishing net. Although pelicans are clumsy on land, they are superb swimmers and fliers.

PENDULUM A weight hanging from a fixed point (on a chain, rod, etc), and able to swing freely. The rate it swings at (i.e. the number of swings a minute) is set by the length it hangs by. Pendulums were used in CLOCKS, so they could be controlled accurately.

PENGUIN Flightless, fish-eating sea bird found in the southern hemisphere, especially the Antarctic. There are 17 species ranging in size from the little Blue Penguin of Australia (50 cm/20 in tall) to the great Emperor Pen-

▶ *Both these species of Pelican breed in swamps and marshes in the eastern Mediterranean. The white species has flesh-coloured feet while the Dalmation has grey feet.*

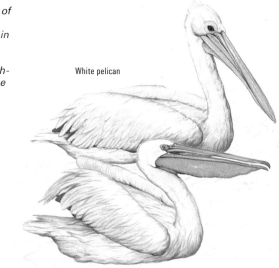

White pelican

Dalmatian pelican

guin of Antarctica (over 1 metre/3 ft tall). All species have grey or black backs and white fronts. Their paddle-like wings are used for swimming; on land, they have an upright, waddling walk.

PENICILLIN A substance used in medicine to kill BACTERIA. It can be given in a pill or by injection. Penicillin is a natural substance, extracted from certain moulds (FUNGI). It was discovered by Sir Alexander FLEMING in 1928.

PENTATHLON five-part competition in which contestants have to run, high jump, swim, shoot, and horse jump. The name comes from the Greek *pente* (five) and *athlon* (contest).

PEKING MAN was a prehistoric species of mankind that lived around Beijing (formerly known in the West as Peking) about 375 years ago. The remains of Peking Man, known to scientists as *Homo erectus pekinensis*, were found in the 1920s about 48 km (30 miles) from Beijing. Similar fossils have since been found in other parts of China.

▲ *An Emperor Penguin shielding its young chick from the Antarctic cold.*

PENTATHLON

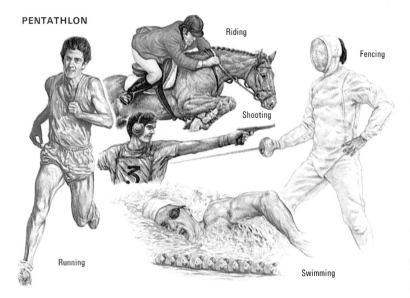

Riding

Fencing

Shooting

Running

Swimming

PENGUIN Emperor Penguins breed farther south than any other backboned animal, and may be the only birds that never step on land. On sea ice in the Antarctic autumn, each male incubates one egg between his feet and belly. For weeks he starves, losing up to one-third of his weight. Then the female takes over to complete the hatching.

PERFUME One perfume may have 16 ingredients. Some of these could be odours of synthetic origin, for instance: carnation, jasmine, lily of the valley. These come respectively from oil of cloves, oil of citronella, and coal tar. Other odours could be natural, for instance: mimosa, sandalwood, styrax, vetiver. These come respectively from blossom, wood, resin, root.

PERISCOPE Archaeologists in Italy have used periscopes to help them explore hundreds of tombs made by the ancient Etruscans. An archaeologist would bore a hole in a tomb roof, then lower a periscope fitted with a camera. In this way, he could quickly find out if a tomb contained wall paintings or other items worth full-scale excavation.

▲ *Different souces of perfume. Essential oils are tiny drops of liquefied leaves, stems, roots and wood. Flower oils, animal extracts and alcohol are also used as perfume ingredients.*

PEPPER Common hot-tasting SPICE obtained from the dried berries (peppercorns) of the tropical pepper plant. Peppercorns, black or white, are either used whole or ground into powder. The large green-red fruits of the tropical Capsicum shrub are also called peppers. They are cooked or eaten raw in salads.

PEPSIN One of the ENZYMES that form part of the digestive juices (see DIGESTION). It comes from the lining of the stomach, and helps in the digestion of PROTEIN.

PEPYS, SAMUEL British diarist (1633–1703). He followed a successful career in the Admiralty, but his famous diary concentrates on his private life. It covers the years 1660–1669, and was written in a private shorthand only deciphered in 1825.

PERCH Common European freshwater fish; it has an olive-brown or yellowish back with dark bars and a white belly. Perches generally swim in shoals and are easily caught as they are greedy fish and readily take the bait.

▼ *The perch lives in lowland rivers, lakes and ponds, close to tree roots or weed beds. It eats insects larvae, shrimps and other fish.*

PERFUME Perfume is used to give a pleasant scent to the body. The ancient Egyptians made perfume by soaking fragrant wood in water and oil, and then rubbing the liquid on their bodies. Today, expensive perfumes are still made from plant and animal oils, but cheaper ones usually have synthetic ingredients (mainly coal tar products). ◁

PERIODIC TABLE See ELEMENTS AND COMPOUNDS

PERISCOPE A device used in SUBMARINES. It consists of a long tube with mirrors inside, and it allows those inside a submarine to see above water level without having to bring the vessel to the surface. A simple periscope has two sloping mirrors, one above the other. Light from an object strikes the top mirror, which reflects it to the bottom mirror. This mirror reflects the light into your eyes, and you see an image of the object. ◁

SUBMARINE PERISCOPE

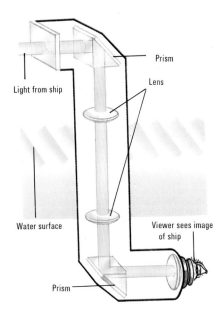

Prism

Lens

Light from ship

Water surface

Viewer sees image of ship

Prism

PERPETUAL MOTION The action of a machine that would go on running for ever without new supplies of energy from outside. Many people have tried to invent a perpetual motion machine, but in fact it is an impossibility. Such a machine would contradict the laws of THERMODYNAMICS. ▷

PERSIA Now known as IRAN. Persia ruled over a great empire which flourished from the 6th to the 4th centuries BC, and extended from Asia Minor and Egypt, eastward to the borders of India. It was captured by ALEXANDER THE GREAT and after his death the empire was divided between his generals. The area of Persia itself changed hands a number of times until the AD 600s, when it became part of the world of ISLAM.

PERTH The capital of WESTERN AUSTRALIA, Perth has 969,000 people (1983). It is a commercial and marketing centre. Its port, FREMANTLE, is the state's chief port. Perth has a pleasant climate and tourism is important.

PERU A mountainous republic in tropical SOUTH AMERICA, Peru has 19,198,000 people (1984 est.) and an area of 1,285,216 sq km (496,225 sq miles). The capital is Lima. The INCA civilization dominated the area until the Spaniards destroyed it in the 1530s. Today, farming, fishing and mining are important. ▷

PETER THE GREAT Tsar of Russia (born 1672, reigned 1682–1725). He tried to re-organize Russia on western-European lines, and built St Petersburg (Leningrad) as its new capital.

PETROLEUM See OILS

PEWTER An ALLOY of tin and other metals, used for making bowls, candlesticks, mugs and ornaments. Traditionally it was 10 to 25

▼ Colossal statues of the pharaoh Ramesses II, outside the temple at Luxor in Egypt.

▲ Peter the Great of Russia. He began the modernization and westernization of his vast country, and by often ruthless methods made it an important power in Europe.

per cent lead, and the rest tin. Nowadays it is 5 to 20 per cent antimony, 1 per cent copper, and the rest tin: 'Britannia metal', rather than true pewter.

PHARAOH The title given to the kings of ancient EGYPT. It meant 'great house', and originally applied to all the royal household. After about 950 BC it came to mean the king alone. The Egyptians regarded their pharaoh as both a god (Horus, the falcon god, in human form) and the son of a god (Ra, the Sun god). In theory he owned all the land and people of Egypt, but in reality his power was limited by the priests and nobles.

PHEASANT Common long-tailed game bird, found in many parts of the world. The male's plumage has bright metallic colours. Pheasants spend most of their time on the ground, scratching the earth for seeds and insects. They have strong legs and can run very fast.

PHILIPPINES An island republic in south-east ASIA. The Philippines has a population of 53,351,000 (1984 est.) and an area of 300,000 sq km (115,831 sq miles). The capital is Manila. Farming is the chief industry. ▷

PHILOSOPHY This is the study of knowledge, and of such basic questions as: 'What is reality?'; and 'What are good and evil?'. It tries to give a consistent picture of life, and to make a person think more carefully. To do these things it draws on logic, observation and belief. European philosophy dates back to

PERPETUAL MOTION The British Patent Office will not accept an application for a patent that claims perpetual motion, on the grounds that such an idea is against all the laws of physics.

At first thought, some devices such as self-winding watches might appear to be perpetual motion machines. But all such things need an input of energy of some sort – the self-winding watch gets its energy from the movements of the wearer's wrist, which gets its energy from the food the wearer eats, etc.

A device in the Clarendon Laboratory at Oxford University comes close to being a perpetual motion machine. Two voltaic piles are connected at their upper ends. At the bottom of each pile is a small bell, and a small brass ball suspended by a thread oscillates from one bell to the other. It has been doing this without stopping since 1840 – but, like all machines, it will stop in the course of time.

PERU: FACTS AND FIGURES
Official languages: Spanish and Quechua.
Currency: Gold Sol.
Religion: Roman Catholic.
Chief river: Amazon.
Largest cities: Lima (pop. 5,258,000), Arequipa (447,000), Callao (441,000).
Peru is the third largest South American nation, and is dominated by the Andes Mountains.
About one in four of the population speaks Indian languages only.

PHILIPPINES: FACTS AND FIGURES
Official language: Filipino.
Currency: Peso.
Religion: Roman Catholic.

The Philippines is an archipelago of 7107 islands, stretching about 1770 km (1100 miles) along the south-eastern rim of Asia. Eleven of the islands account for about 94 per cent of the total land area and population. The largest islands are Luzon and Mindanao. The Philippines is the only Christian nation in Asia. It became an independent republic in 1946, having been under the control of the USA.

PHOSPHORUS Poisonous white phosphorus is a soft crystalline substance, rather like wax in appearance, and with an odour like garlic. It melts at 44°C and boils at 280°C. When exposed to air it ignites spontaneously at from 35° to 40°C, or by friction, producing a dense white smoke. Red phosphorus is made by heating white phosphorus to about 250°C, in the absence of air. It is completely stable and non-poisonous. Its melting point is about 600°C.

White phosphorus was at one time used for making matches, but this is no longer allowed because of its poisonous nature and because many fires were started by rats gnawing at the matches.

ancient GREECE. It has played an important part in science, politics, education and religious thought.

PHOENICIANS The people who lived in the coastal lands of the Lebanon from c. 3000 BC. They were organized into city states, such as Tyre and Sidon, and were skilled seamen. From the 12th century BC they began to trade all over the Mediterranean and beyond, and founded colonies such as CARTHAGE. They also invented the first ALPHABET.

PHOENIX A mythical Arabian bird. It was supposed to burn itself to death every 500 years, and was then miraculously reborn from its own ashes.

PHONETICS The branch of the study of languages that deals with pronunciation. It uses special *phonetic alphabets*, to cover all the different sounds that languages use.

PHOSPHORUS A non-metallic ELEMENT that occurs as various *allotropes* (different physical forms). White or yellow phosphorus is a waxy, poisonous, inflammable solid. It catches fire spontaneously in air, so is usually kept under water. When heated, it changes to red phosphorus. This form is non-poisonous and does not ignite spontaneously. Under extreme pressure, white phosphorus changes to a black form. Phosphorus is essential to life and occurs in bones as calcium phosphate. Phosphorus was used to make matches, and phosphorus compounds are used as detergents and fertilizers. ◁

PHOTOGRAPHY When you take a photograph, light enters the camera through a LENS and reaches the film inside. The surface of the film is coated with chemicals that are sensitive

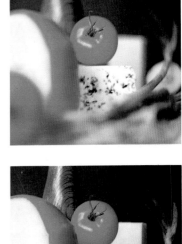

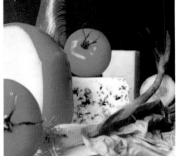

▲ *In photography it is important to focus the camera lens properly, otherwise the image in the photograph will appear fuzzy and distorted. In the examples above, the top photograph is only partly in focus, but the whole of the bottom picture is sharp and each item can be clearly seen. Some cameras have special fittings which help to bring a whole picture into focus.*

▼ *William Fox Talbot (1800-1877) invented the calotype (or talbotype) process. This produced a negative, from which several copies could be made. Here, some of his assistants are seen using this process.*

to light, and so the scene outside is recorded on it. Later the film is *developed* and treated with other chemicals so it is no longer responsive to light. This gives a *negative*, from which the final photograph is printed. Photographs can be in black and white or colour, and are used in books, newspapers and scientific studies, as well as for family 'snaps'.

PHOTON Radiant energy exists only in whole numbers of units called *quanta*. For energy produced as ELECTROMAGNETIC WAVES, the unit, or quantum, is the photon. (See QUANTUM THEORY)

PHOTOSYNTHESIS Process by which green plants turn CARBON DIOXIDE and water into sugar. The carbon dioxide enters the plant through its LEAVES and the water is taken in by the roots. Photosynthesis, which means 'building with light' only happens in the presence of sunlight and a special green col-

▶In photosynthesis, carbon dioxide passes into air channels in the leaf, where it dissolves in water and passes into the cells. Chlorophyll 'catches' energy from sunlight and uses it to break down molecules of water and carbon dioxide and to rebuild them into glucose and oxygen.

ouring matter, called CHLOROPHYLL. The chlorophyll absorbs light energy from the Sun and uses it to power various chemical reactions that convert the carbon dioxide and water into sugar. During the process, oxygen is given off. Photosynthesis mostly takes place in the leaves. (See CARBON CYCLE) ▷

PHYSICS The science dealing with MATTER and ENERGY. Physics can be split into various branches. MECHANICS deals with objects and forces, and is subdivided into statics (sta-

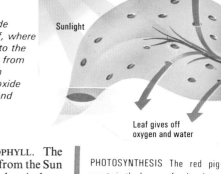

Sunlight

Leaf gives off oxygen and water

PHOTOSYNTHESIS The red pigments in the leaves of red and purple maples and the copper beech absorb light, but cannot use its energy for making food. Instead, the light produces heat. Thus in full sun the leaves of such varieties of plants are more likely to be scorched than those of green varieties.

Photosynthesis is possible because a leaf exposes a lot of moist cells to the air in order to absorb carbon dioxide. But this also means the leaf loses water by evaporation. In one summer's day a beech tree may lose water weighing nearly five times as much as its own leaves. In temperate climates as much water is lost from plants this way as flows out to the sea from rivers.

PICASSO, PABLO It is said that Picasso could draw before he could talk. At 14 he spent one day on an art school test that took most people a month to prepare. By 16 he had passed all the tests Spain's art schools could offer.

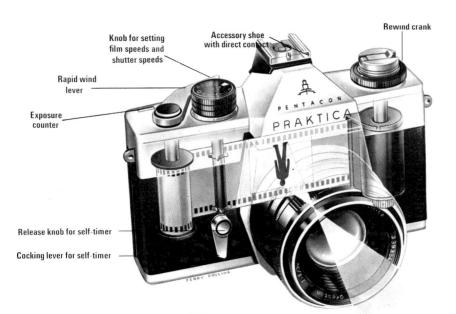

Knob for setting film speeds and shutter speeds

Accessory shoe with direct contact

Rewind crank

Rapid wind lever

Exposure counter

PENTACON PRAKTICA

Release knob for self-timer

Cocking lever for self-timer

TERRY COLLINS

This German camera takes 35mm film. The speed of the film is set on the control on the left. It has its own built-in light meter; otherwise, many photographers check the light of a subject with a separate battery-powered meter. Shutter speed settings vary from one second to one-thousandth of a second. The basic lens arrangement can be screwed off and replaced by special lenses such as a telescopic lens for making distant objects appear closer.

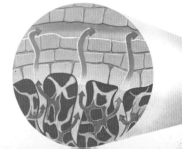

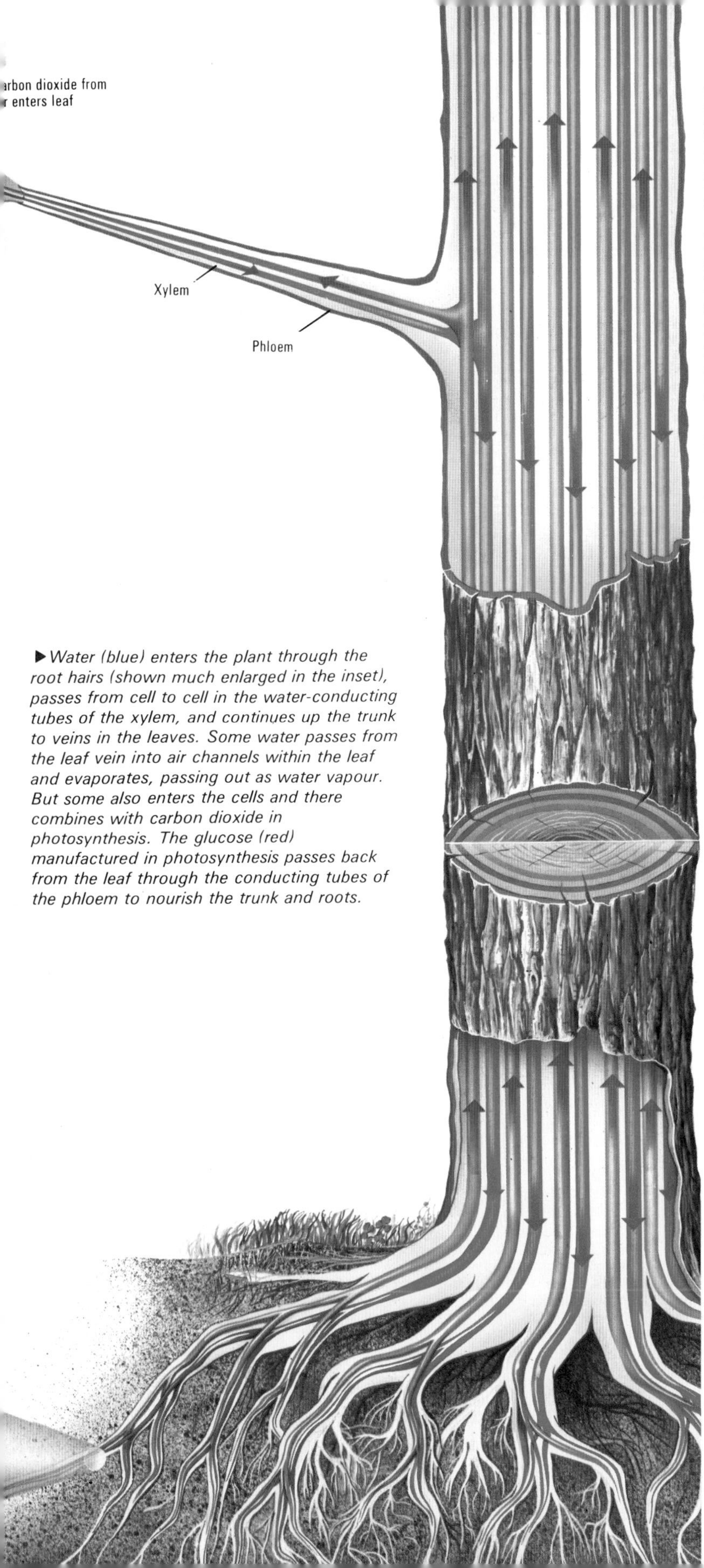

Xylem

Phloem

▶ *Water (blue) enters the plant through the root hairs (shown much enlarged in the inset), passes from cell to cell in the water-conducting tubes of the xylem, and continues up the trunk to veins in the leaves. Some water passes from the leaf vein into air channels within the leaf and evaporates, passing out as water vapour. But some also enters the cells and there combines with carbon dioxide in photosynthesis. The glucose (red) manufactured in photosynthesis passes back from the leaf through the conducting tubes of the phloem to nourish the trunk and roots.*

arbon dioxide from
r enters leaf

tionary objects) and dynamics (moving objects). Other branches of physics are HEAT, LIGHT, SOUND, and ELECTRICITY AND MAGNETISM. Nuclear physics is the study of the physical properties of ATOMS and their constituent particles.

PHYSIOLOGY The study of the processes of life in human beings, animals and plants. For example, it studies RESPIRATION and DIGESTION, and PHOTOSYNTHESIS in plants. HARVEY's work on the circulation of the blood founded modern physiology. But it was not put on a full experimental basis until the 19th century. Today physiology involves several scientific disciplines, including biophysics, BIOCHEMISTRY and neurology.

PIANO A keyboard musical instrument. The keys connect with padded hammers that strike wires inside. The first design was built in 1709 (forerunners were the virginals and clavichord). There are two types: the upright piano, with vertical strings; and the concert or grand piano, with horizontal strings.

PICASSO, PABLO Spanish artist (1881–1973). He had his first public exhibition at 16. Settling in Paris, he helped found the revolutionary style called CUBISM, and rapidly became the most famous and versatile of modern painters. His huge output includes collages, CERAMICS, ballet sets, MURALS and sculpture, as well as hundreds of paintings. ◁

PICCARD, AUGUSTE Swiss scientist (1884–1962), designer of air BALLOONS and BATHYSCAPHES. In 1931–32 he ascended by balloon to 16,764 metres (55,000 ft), making some important discoveries about cosmic rays. In 1960 his son used one of his bathyscaphes to descend to 11,521 metres (37,800 ft) below sea-level.

PIG Important farm animal bred throughout the world; it has a stout, heavy body covered with rough, bristly hair. Man has kept pigs for about 5,000 years. They provide meat, and their fat, skin and hair are used to make products like lard, leather and brushes.

PIGEON Medium-sized bird found all over the world. There are many species; most of them are soft shades of grey, brown or pink and inhabit woodlands. They mainly feed on nuts, seeds, buds and leaves and often do great damage to crops. Large numbers of pigeons have also moved into towns and cities, where they have become pests.

PIGMENT Anything used to give colour, e.g. to paints, plastics, etc. The skin contains a pigment called *melanin*. The more melanin there is, the darker the skin's colour.

PIKE Fierce-looking freshwater fish from the northern hemisphere. Pike are yellowish-green and measure up to 1.5 metres (5 ft) in length. They are greedy, vicious creatures and will attack and eat fish as large as themselves.

PINE Evergreen coniferous tree with needle-like leaves (see CONIFER). There are about 200 species of pine, all growing in the cooler parts of the northern hemisphere. Pine is a valuable timber tree. Its pale wood is mostly used for furniture, construction work and paper pulp. Some species are also tapped for resin from which TURPENTINE is obtained.

PINEAPPLE Large tropical fruit with a thick yellow-red skin, juicy pale-yellow flesh and spiky leaves growing out of the top. Pineapples are so named because they look like pine cones. They are eaten raw or canned.

PIRANHA Savage freshwater fish from tropical South America. Piranhas, about 30 cm (1 ft) long, are carnivorous. With their strong jaws and sharp teeth, they attack and tear the flesh off other fish and mammals – even men.

PIRATES Robbers of ships and their cargoes at sea. Pirates were common from ancient times until the 19th century, and survived until recently in the China Seas. But the 17th and 18th centuries were the great age of piracy. Arab pirates from North Africa patrolled the Mediterranean and the eastern Atlantic, while Englishmen such as Henry Morgan and Captain Kidd raided Spanish shipping in the West Indies. ▷

PISTOL A small FIREARM, held in one hand when firing. There are two main types. The revolver has a rotating chamber, holding up to 6 bullets. This turns with the trigger action, bringing a fresh bullet into place behind the barrel. The automatic pistol holds the bullets inside its body, and works by gas or recoil action.

PITCH (MUSIC) The sharpness of a musical note – i.e. whether it is higher or lower than another. A NOISE has irregular vibrations, but a musical *note* has regular ones, and the rate of these per second give it its pitch.

PITUITARY GLAND An important GLAND at the base of the brain, about the size of a pea. It has two halves, both producing HORMONES. The hormones from one side control all the other glands in the body, and also affect growth. Those from the other control, among other things, the body's water balance.

PLAGUE A deadly disease, carried to man by some types of rat fleas. It caused millions of deaths in medieval Europe and was known as the Black Death. It is still found in tropical countries.

PLANETARIUM A device for showing the movements of the planets and other heavenly bodies. Early planetariums, called *orreries*, were small mechanical models of the SOLAR SYSTEM. The modern planetarium is a domed building containing a complex assembly of optical projectors. These throw images of the stars and planets onto the inside of the curved ceiling, which represents the sky.

PLANETS In our SOLAR SYSTEM, nine major planets orbit the Sun. Details of individual planets are given in the accompanying table. In addition, there are numerous minor planets, or ASTEROIDS. ▷

PLANKTON Plankton is the name given to the microscopic plants and animals that live in the surface layers of oceans, seas and fresh waters. These floating organisms are important as they provide rich food for many fish and other water creatures.

PLANT Life on Earth consists of plants and animals. Although most animals are able to do many more things than plants – such as moving, seeing and hearing – there is one very important thing they cannot do: animals cannot make food, while some plants – green plants – can. (By PHOTOSYNTHESIS green plants use the Sun's energy to turn carbon dioxide and water into sugar.) Because of this, animals need plants to survive. They either feed directly on plants or on other animals that have themselves eaten plants. Plants are therefore a

▼ *In the key to the picture opposite, the numbers refer to the following planets (which are shown to scale): 1 Mercury; 2 Venus; 3 Earth; 4 Mars; 5 Jupiter; 6 Saturn; 7 Uranus; 8 Neptune; 9 Pluto.*

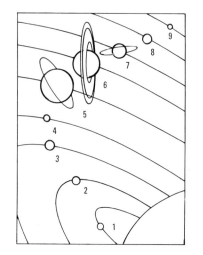

PIRATES England's Edward Teach, called Blackbeard, was one of the fiercest pirates. He fought with lighted matches framing his face. He scared friends by firing pistols under the table and setting pots of sulphur alight. In 1718 in his last fight he suffered 25 wounds and was shot dead. His head was put on a pole and shown to the Virginian settlers whom he had terrorized.

PLANETS: FACTS AND FIGURES
Mercury: Mean distance from Sun 57.7 million km (36 million miles); equatorial diameter 4828 km (3000 miles); circles Sun in 87.9 days.
Venus: Mean distance from Sun 107.8 million km (67 million miles); equatorial diameter 12,391 km (7700 miles); circles Sun in 224 days.
Earth: Mean distance from Sun 149.58 million km (92.95 million miles); equatorial diameter 12,757 km (7927 miles); circles Sun in 365.26 days.
Mars: Mean distance from Sun 227.9 million km (141.6 million miles); equatorial diameter 6790 km (4219 miles); circles Sun in 687 days.
Jupiter: Mean distance from Sun 779.1 million km (484.3 million miles): equatorial diameter 142,745 km (88,700 miles); circles Sun in 11.86 years.
Saturn: Mean distance from Sun 1426 million km (886.1 million miles); equatorial diameter 120,858 km (75,100 miles); circles Sun in 29.46 days.
Uranus: Mean distance from Sun 2870 million km (1783 million miles); equatorial diameter 47,152 km (29,300 miles); circles Sun in 84.01 years.
Neptune: Mean distance from Sun 4493 million km (2793 million miles); equatorial diameter 50,210 km (31,200 miles); circles Sun in 164.79 years.
Pluto: Mean distance from Sun 5898 million km (3666 million miles); equatorial diameter approx. 6400 km (approx. 3980 miles); circles Sun in 247.70 years.

vital part of the living world.

There are over 350,000 kinds of plants. They can be divided into two main groups: plants that bear seeds and those that do not. The seed-bearing group is the largest and consists mainly of CONIFERS and flowering plants. Seed-bearing plants have well-developed roots, stem and LEAVES and produce FRUITS which contain the seeds. Plants without seeds are much simpler. In some, like FUNGI, the plant body is not separated into root, stem and leaf; others, like MOSSES, have stems and leaves, but no proper roots. (See BIOLOGY) ▷

PLASTER A coating put on walls and ceilings, to give a surface for decoration. It is made from certain CEMENT powders, mixed with water and (usually) sand.

PLASTICS It is difficult to imagine what our lives would be like without plastics. A great many plastics are in common use, each with different properties. All plastics can be shaped easily when heated, and they all have long-chain MOLECULES – molecules made up of a chain of repeated small units. Such substances are called *polymers*, and most of them are made from PETROLEUM products. Plastics react to heat in one of two ways. Some soften and melt, and only return to a solid state when they cool. These are called *thermoplastics* and are used to make things like bowls and buckets. Others remain quite rigid when re-heated after they are formed; these are *thermosetting* plastics. They remain rigid because their long molecule chains are criss-crossed.

Most plastic products are made by moulding. In injection moulding, thermoplastic chips are heated until they melt; then the melted plastic is forced into a water-cooled mould under pressure. This method of making things from plastic is very widely used. In blow moulding, air is blown into a blob of molten plastic inside a hollow mould, forcing it against the walls of the mould. Thermoplastics can also be shaped by *extrusion*. In extrusion, molten plastic is forced through a shaped hole or 'die'. Fibres for man-made TEXTILES and sheet plastic may be made in this way.

Thermosetting plastic products can be made by compression moulding. Thermosetting powder, the molecules of which have not yet criss-crossed into a rigid plastic, is placed in the lower half of a mould. The mould is heated and the plastic powder molecules start to criss-cross. Before this reaction is complete the top half of the mould is forced down onto the lower one and the plastic is pushed into shape between the two halves.

PLATINUM A precious, silvery metallic ELEMENT. Its high resistance to CORROSION

makes it suitable for use as electrical contacts and in scientific apparatus. Platinum is sometimes used as a *catalyst* to speed up chemical reactions without itself undergoing permanent change. ▷

PLATO Greek philosopher (c. 428–c. 348 BC). As a follower of SOCRATES, Plato took over and developed his philosophy. He wrote thirty surviving 'dialogues', including the *Symposium* (on love), the *Phaedo* (on the immortality of the soul) and the *Republic* (on politics). He also founded a school of philosophy in Athens.

PLATYPUS Odd-looking dark brown furry animal found only in Australia and Tasmania. It is about 45 cm (18 in) long and has short legs, webbed feet and a wide, flat bill. The platypus is the world's most primitive MAMMAL. It has a very simple brain and, unlike any other mammal except the spiny anteater, it lays eggs; but because the platypus feeds its young on milk, it is a true mammal. The platypus lives in burrows in the banks of streams and pools, and eats small water creatures. ▷

PLAYING CARDS These reached Europe c. 1320. A modern pack has 52 cards, in four *suits* (hearts, spades, diamonds, clubs). Each suit has ten numbered cards and three court cards (King, Queen and Knave or 'Jack').

PLUM Sweet roundish fruit with juicy flesh and a hard central stone. Plums can be green, yellow, red, blue or purple according to species. Some varieties are eaten raw, others cooked. Plum trees grow in temperate lands.

PLUMBING The pipes that bring water to a house or building, circulate hot and cold water

▼*The platypus, often called the duck-billed platypus, feels for its food in the mud with its bill, which is really a soft, sensitive snout.*

PLANT The first land plants evolved just over 400 million years ago. Unlike the limp aquatic algae that they came from, they had tubes to draw up water and stiff stems to help them stand erect in open air. But they lacked leaves, roots, or flowers.

PLATINUM Platinum was discovered in 1735 by Antonio de Ulloa in gold-bearing deposits in Colombia. It was called 'platina' from the Spanish *plata*, 'silver', because it resembles that metal. Platinum now costs about three times as much as gold.

Platinum is almost twice as heavy as silver. It melts at 1769°C and boils at about 3800°C. The resistance of platinum to corrosion leads to its extensive use in chemical and electrical instruments, and in jewellery, when it is sometimes alloyed with gold to make 'white gold'.

PLATYPUS Captive platypuses prove hard to keep. New York City's Bronx Zoo kept one individual that ate a frog, two eggs, a handful of mealworms, 24 crayfish, and 200 earthworms in one day. Only Healesville, Victoria, has bred the animal, and kept one that reached the age of 17.

▶ The chart shows the seven major divisions of plant life (indicated by the horizontal lines). The coloured bars, running from top to bottom, show the different ways that these divisions can be grouped.

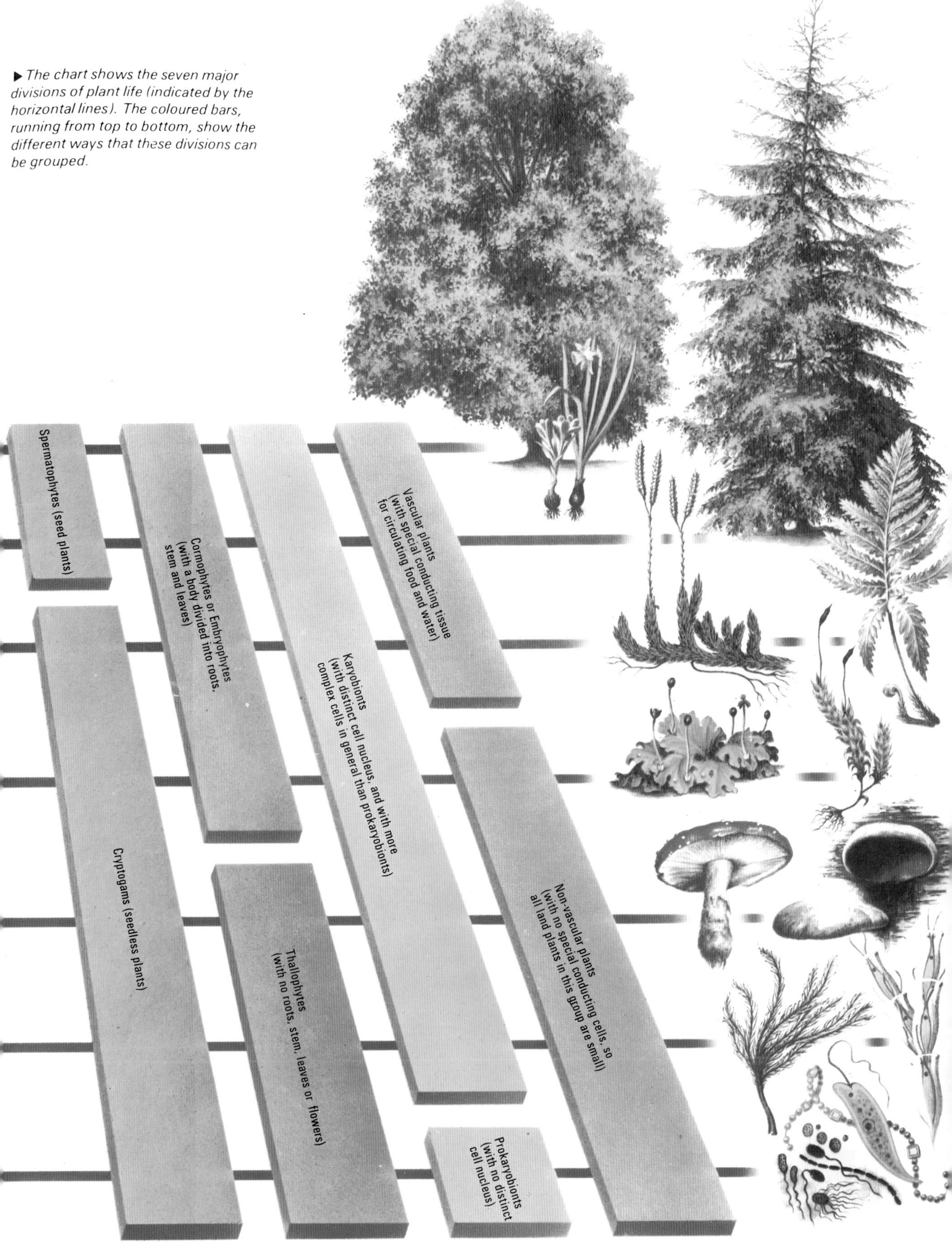

Spermatophytes (seed plants)

Cormophytes or Embryophytes (with a body divided into roots, stem and leaves)

Vascular plants (with special conducting tissue for circulating food and water)

Karyobionts (with distinct cell nucleus, and with more complex cells in general than prokaryobionts)

Cryptogams (seedless plants)

Thallophytes (with no roots, stem, leaves or flowers)

Non-vascular plants (with no special conducting cells, so all land plants in this group are small)

Prokaryobionts (with no distinct cell nucleus)

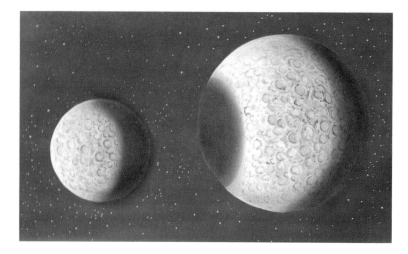

▶ *Pluto's one known moon is called Charon and is about half the size of the planet. Charon and Pluto orbit so closely together that they often produce eclipses of the distant sun. Pluto was discovered by an American astronomer Clyde Tombaugh in 1930.*

through its rooms, and take waste water away. Modern houses have three pipe circuits: one for the cold tap water, one for the hot, and one for the central-heating radiators. Problems with plumbing can include blockage, air locks, corrosion and cracking due to frost.

PLUTO (GOD) In Roman mythology, the god of the dead, and brother of Neptune and Jupiter. Most of the stories about him are borrowed from the Greek god Hades.

PLUTO (PLANET) A small planet of diameter 6400 km (3980 miles), normally the outermost of the known planets in the SOLAR SYSTEM. However, its orbit periodically crosses inside that of Neptune, which has temporarily become the farthest planet from the Sun.

PLUTONIUM A silvery, radioactive metallic ELEMENT. The isotope plutonium-239 (see ATOM) is used as a nuclear fuel to produce ATOMIC ENERGY by the process of fission. A little plutonium is found in some uranium ores. But plutonium is generally produced artificially by bombarding uranium or neptunium in nuclear reactors. (See NUCLEAR ENERGY)

PLYWOOD A building material, made up of thin layers of wood glued together. The grains in adjacent layers run at right angles to each other. This gives great strength, and reduces warping, twisting and swelling.

PNEUMONIA An inflammation of the lungs, due to infection. The spongy lining of the lungs swells, blocking the air spaces. It is now effectively treated by ANTIBIOTICS.

POETRY Poetry is LITERATURE in which special techniques have been used to give an exciting and rhythmic effect. Almost all poetry uses *meter* (regular patterns of rhythm), and much of it uses rhyme. Other important techniques are *alliteration* (words beginning with the same letter) and *assonance* (words with the same vowel sounds, although they do not actually rhyme). The main kinds of poetry are lyric (which deals with personal emotion), dramatic (as in plays), and narrative (as in ballads and epics).

POINTILLISM An ART movement that flourished in France in the mid-1880s. Small dots and brush strokes of pure colour are applied

so that the eye blends the colours together when the painting is viewed from a distance. George Seurat and Paul Signac painted in this manner.

FAMOUS POETS

Homer, Greek (c. 9th century BC) — *The Iliad, The Odyssey*
Virgil, Roman (65-68 BC) — *The Aeneid*
Dante Alighieri, Italian (1265-1321) — *Divina Commedia*
Geoffrey Chaucer, English (c. 1340-1400) — *Canterbury Tales*
Pierre de Ronsard, French (1524-1585) — *Odes*
William Shakespeare, English (1564-1616) — Sonnets
John Donne, English (1572-1631) — Songs and Sonnets
John Milton, English (1608-1674) — *Paradise Lost*
Jean de la Fontaine, French (1621-1695) — *Fables*
Johann von Goethe, German (1749-1832) — *Faust*
William Blake, English (1757-1827) — *Songs of Innocence and Experience*
Robert Burns, Scottish (1759-1796) — *The Jolly Beggars, The Two Dogs*
William Wordsworth, English (1770-1850) — Lyrical Ballads, *The Prelude*
Samuel Taylor Coleridge, English (1772-1834) — *The Ancient Mariner*
George Byron, English (1788-1824) — *Don Juan*
Percy Bysshe Shelley, English (1792-1822) — *The Skylark, Adonais*
John Keats, English (1795-1821) — *Odes*
Victor Hugo, French (1802-1885) — *Odes*
Alfred Tennyson, English (1809-1892) — *In Memoriam, Morte d'Arthur*
Walt Whitman, American (1818–1892) – *When Lilacs Last . . .*
Emily Dickinson, American (1830–1886) – *Poems*
W. B. Yeats, Irish (1865-1939) — Poems, 1895
Robert Frost, American (1874-1963) — Collected Poems, 1930
Rainer Maria Rilke, German (1875-1926) — Lyrics
T. S. Eliot, American (1888-1965) — *The Waste Land*
John Betjamen (1906–1984) English – *Summoned By Bells*
Dylan Thomas, Welsh (1914-1953) — Collected Poems, 1934-52
Robert Lowell, American (born 1917) — *Lord Weary's Castle*
Philip Larkin (1930–1985) English – *High Windows*
Ted Hughes (1930–) English – *Poems*

POISON Some of the most powerful poisons are produced by animals. The venom from one species of Australian snake could kill 300 sheep. One gram of poison from the skin of one species of South American frog could kill 100,000 people.

POLAND: FACTS AND FIGURES
Official language: Polish.
Currency: Zloty.
Religion: Roman Catholic.
Chief rivers: Vistula, Oder, and Bug.
Largest cities: Warsaw (pop. 1,649,000), Lodz (849,000), Kraków (740,000), and Wrolaw (636,000).

POMPEII The Roman writer Pliny the Younger described what happened when Vesuvius destroyed Pompeii. Pliny saw the ground shake; the sea sucked back and then hurled forward; great tongues of flame spurt from the black cloud that boiled up from the volcano. Ashes fell and darkness closed in. Thick ash had cloaked the ground like snow.

POISON A substance causing illness or death if swallowed or (in some cases) put on the skin. There are three types: corrosives, such as acids; irritants, affecting stomach and bowels (e.g. arsenic); and narcotics, affecting the nervous system (e.g. cyanide). ◁

POLAND A communist republic in eastern EUROPE, Poland has 36,914,000 people (1984 est.) and an area of 312,677 sq km (120,725 sq miles). The capital is WARSAW. The best farmland is in the south, but Poland is now an industrialized nation. Despite its communist government, the proud and independent Poles are still predominantly Roman Catholics. ◁

POLAR BEAR A large creamy-white BEAR of the Arctic Circle. They spend their time on floating ice or in the water. Adults grow to a length of 2.7 metres (9 ft) and weigh up to 726 kg (1600 lb). Polar bears differ from other bears in having smaller, more pointed heads and longer necks.

POLE VAULT An OLYMPIC sport – a form of high jump in which a pole is used to help lift the body. The poles used are fibreglass and are 4–5 metres (12–16½ ft) long. The world record for pole vaulting is over 6 metres (19 ft).

POLICE The force responsible for maintaining law and order, protecting life and property, and catching criminals. They also control traffic. The police in Britain were founded by Sir Robert Peel in 1829, and are organized as separate local forces.

▼ One way of pollinating a flower. As the bee collects nectar from the flower, pollen from the anthers, the tips of the stamens, is brushed on to its body. When the bee reaches the next flower, some of the pollen is rubbed off and lands on the sticky surface of the stigmas.

POLIOMYELITIS A VIRUS infection that can attack the central NERVOUS SYSTEM, and cause paralysis. It is now effectively prevented by VACCINES given to all children.

POLLEN Yellow powder at the tip of a flower stamen (the male organ of plant REPRODUCTION). Pollen contains the male reproductive cells and, before a flower can form seeds, these male cells must unite with the female cells which are inside the carpel (the flower's female organ of reproduction). This happens when pollen is carried – usually by insects or the wind – from the stamen to the stigma, the sticky top of the carpel. This process is called pollination. (See BIOLOGY)

POMPEII An ancient Roman city about 23 km (14 miles) southeast of Naples which was buried in AD 79 by a massive volcanic ◁

▲ Excavation has shown that the homes of rich Pompeiians had peaceful central courtyards. These let light and air into the houses.

▶ Homes in Pompeii were heated by three-legged, charcoal-burning stoves.

eruption of Mount VESUVIUS. It lay buried under a thick blanket of ash for almost 1700 years. What were to become the largest archaeological excavations ever, began there in 1748 and continue to this day. They have revealed a wealth of evidence about daily life in ancient ROME. ▷

POODLE Small lively dog with a black or white curly coat; the coat is often clipped. Poodles were originally Russian gundogs but they are now kept as pets all over the world.

▲ A street in Pompeii. Many finds have been left in place, so the town is a museum as well as a monument to the Roman Empire.

▼When the blanket of ash settled over Pompeii, it encased the bodies of its victims. As a body decayed, the exact outline of its shape remained, fixed in a hard ashy shell. By forcing liquid plaster into the hollows that remained, archaeologists have made these lifelike models.

Lombardy poplar

▲ The quick growing Lombardy poplar provides ideal shelter-belts as well as an attractive ornament to parks and gardens. It grows to 36 metres (118 ft). Its name refers to the region of Italy where it is produced.

POP ART Short for 'popular art', it was an artistic movement that thrived in the 1950s and 1960s. Pop artists made use of images that came from everyday life, such as cans of soup.

POPE The head of the ROMAN CATHOLIC CHURCH; the Pope is accepted by all Catholics as the representative of JESUS CHRIST on Earth. He lives and rules in the VATICAN CITY, a small area within the city of Rome. Pope means 'father' and was the name originally taken by the bishops of Rome. There have been Popes for over 1900 years; ever since the time of St Peter, the first bishop of Rome.

POPLAR Tall, deciduous tree of the northern hemisphere. Most species grow in damp places and have broad trembling leaves which make a lovely rustling noise in the wind. Poplars are fast-growing and are often planted for ornament or to give shelter. The wood is used for matches, boxes and PAPER pulp.

POP MUSIC Short for 'popular music', it refers to the tunes we hear every day on the radio or sing ourselves, rather than to classical music or jazz. Today's pop music is a mixture of traditional folk songs, spirituals, ballads and rock 'n roll.

POPPY Common plant with grey-green leaves and showy white, orange, red or purple flowers. Two well-known kinds are the corn poppy, which colours the summer fields with

Clues to the lost site of Pompeii emerged as early as the 16th century. Men cutting a water channel through the mound that hid the town discovered bits of carved marble and a Roman coin. But the city's excavation that began in 1748 was only a treasure hunt for silver, gold, and statues. People were slow to value Pompeii for what it told them about daily life in Roman times.

POP MUSIC The best selling album of all time is *Thriller* by black singer Michael Jackson. It had sold between 50–55 million copies by the late 1980s. The film soundtrack *Saturday Night Fever* is the next best-selling record, followed by Fleetwood Mac's *Rumours*.

PORCELAIN Fine early pieces of porcelain cost so much to buy that forgers copy them and sell the copies as originals. Because few old Chinese porcelain pieces survive intact, forgers break and mend imitations to make them seem old. At one time most French Sèvres porcelain bought by collectors may have been forged.

PORCUPINE In 1969 a pair of Himalayan porcupines escaped from a wildlife park in Devon. By 1973 porcupines were stripping bark from nearby conifer plantations. By then the original pair had founded Britain's first wild breeding colony of porcupines.

PORPOISE There is some confusion over dolphins and porpoises. They are both small toothed whales – they are both mammals. But porpoises are tubbier, with a rounded head, a triangular dorsal fin, and rounded front flippers. Dolphins have a beak-like snout and a dorsal fin that curves back. Both porpoises and dolphins are famous for the interest they take in human beings. They both follow ships for miles. Although they can stay under water for 10 minutes at a time, they must come up to breathe. This is why schools of porpoises break water every few minutes.

scarlet, and the opium poppy, which produces the drug OPIUM.

PORCELAIN A very fine type of POTTERY. The Chinese developed the art of making porcelain using *kaolin*, a very pure form of clay that remained white when fired; and *petuntse*, which helped the clay turn hard and glass-like at a low temperature. Porcelain is hard and does not absorb water like earthenware. It became known in Europe only in the late 17th century. ◁

PORCUPINE Large rodent covered with long, sharp, black and white spikes called quills. Porcupines in Europe, Asia and Africa live mainly on the ground, but the American species are tree-creatures. ◁

▼ *Porcupines raise their spines when they sense danger. Very few animals attack them, but some manage to turn the porcupine over and attack its soft underbelly.*

▲ *This elaborate porcelain vase and cover were made at Sèvres in France about 1785. At this time Sèvres was the leading porcelain factory in Europe; work there began in 1768. The classical painting, which shows Jupiter and Callisto, is adapted from a picture by the artist Boucher. Sèvres work is distinguished by its rich colours and heavy gilding; it is now very valuable.*

PORPOISE Small (1.5 metres/5 ft long) tubby, toothed WHALE of the northern seas. Porpoises have a black back and whitish belly; they swim together in great schools and feed on fish. ◁

PORTUGAL A republic in south-western EUROPE, facing the Atlantic Ocean. Portugal has 10,164,000 people (1984) and an area of 92,082 sq km (35,553 sq miles). The capital is LISBON. Portugal has a pleasant climate and tourism is an important industry. The country was prominent in the Age of Exploration in the 1400s and it once ruled a large empire. But

◀ *Fishing boats approach the shore of a Portuguese fishing village. The sardine catches of the Atlantic are very important to the country's economy.*

most people are now poor farmers. Cork, sardines, wine and wood pulp are exported.

PORTUGUESE MAN O' WAR Bluish-purple JELLYFISH found mainly in tropical seas. It has trailing tentacles up to 12 metres (40 ft) long, which are equipped with powerful stinging cells.

POSITRON A particle with the same MASS as an electron (see ATOM) and an equal, but opposite (positive) electrical charge.

POSSUM (or Phalanger) The name given to a group of Australian MARSUPIALS; the group includes the well-known KOALA. Phalangers all live in trees and have thick furry coats. They are commonly called possums because they look like the American OPOSSUM.

POSTER A form of announcement to the public. Usually it consists of a brief message written or printed on paper or card. The first posters were notices painted on walls in Greece and Rome. In 1761, Louis XV of France ordered that posters should be fixed to walls rather than protrude into the streets and endanger people. In the 1960s decorative posters became accepted as a form of art and

many people now frame them and hang them on the walls of their homes and offices.

POST OFFICE A place where mail is collected, sorted and distributed. The sale of postage stamps was started in 1840 and franking machines, which stamp a symbol onto the letter or parcel showing that postage has been paid, were first used in 1922. Post Offices are usually run by the government. The first postal system ever was begun by King Darius of Persia (c. 558–486 BC).

POTASSIUM An extremely reactive metallic ELEMENT. When placed in water, it reacts violently and bursts into flames. Because it reacts so quickly with oxygen or water, it is stored under oil. Potassium compounds are used in medicine, photography, explosives, soaps and dyes, and as fertilizers.

POTATO Plant grown in cool lands for its edible tuber (swollen underground stem). The tubers, potatoes, are oval-shaped and hard with pale flesh and a brown or reddish skin; they are usually eaten cooked. Potatoes are native to South America. They were discovered there by the Spanish conquerors in the 16th century and brought to Europe. Today, after wheat, rice and maize, potatoes are the world's most important food crop. ▷

POTENTIAL ENERGY This is the energy possessed by a body because of its position. If you lift a weight from the floor you have to do work to raise it. But this work is not wasted. The weight has more energy than it had when it was on the floor. This stored energy is called potential energy. If you let the weight fall it loses its potential energy. Because it falls it gains kinetic energy (see ENERGY).

POTTERY Objects formed from soft clay and fired in a hot oven or kiln to harden. They can be useful everyday objects like plates and cups, ornamental pieces like vases and statues, or even industrial products like bricks and tiles. Pottery has been made since prehistoric

▲ *Postal sorting offices now use machines to speed the mail on its way. For example, the 'glacis' is a machine which separates letters from parcels.*

▶ *A variety of post boxes. The very first one was erected in Jersey in the Channel Islands, in 1852.*

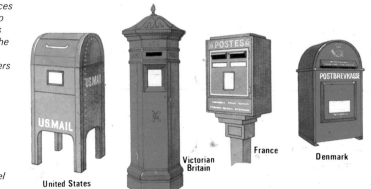

United States

Victorian Britain

France

Denmark

POULTRY The ordinary domestic hen has been derived from many crossings of four Asian wild fowls of the genus *Gallus*. But selective breeding over the centuries has produced a very different bird. The jungle fowl usually produces only one clutch of eggs a year, whereas a good modern layer produces around 200 eggs. (Over 350 eggs from a single bird have been recorded.) It is now possible to produce a 1.5 kg ($3\frac{1}{2}$ lb) liveweight broiler chicken in 7 weeks, using about 1 kg (2 lb) of feed per pound of meat. Turkeys are usually marketed when 5 to 6 months old. At this age the average female bird weighs between 5 and 7 kg (10 to 16 lb) and the male 7 to 11 kg (16 to 25 lb).

▲ *Pottery is one of mankind's oldest crafts. This pottery model of women making bread is from the ancient Greek city of Thebes.*

times when clay was shaped and dried in the sun before being hardened in an open fire. (See CERAMICS; PORCELAIN; TERRA COTTA) ◁

POULTRY Domesticated birds kept for their meat and eggs. Chickens are the most common poultry birds; others include DUCKS, geese (see GOOSE) and TURKEYS. ◁

POWER The rate at which WORK is done or ENERGY used. The SI UNIT of work is the WATT. One horsepower is equal to 745.7 watts.

PRESBYTERIAN A Protestant church of British origins, and based on the teachings of John CALVIN, the French reformer and lawyer. It is a moderate church based on the New

Testament (see BIBLE) and it regards all its ministers as equal in rank. Its European counterpart is the Reformed Church. The Presbyterian Church is the national church of Scotland.

PRINTING A way of reproducing words and pictures by pressing an inked pattern on paper, fabric or metal. The chief methods of printing are letterpress, LITHOGRAPHY and photogravure. Letterpress is the oldest and began in Europe in the 15th century with Johann GUTENBERG. (However, this kind of

▼ *An offset printing press uses a system of inked rollers (containing the four 'process' colours of magenta/red, cyan/blue, yellow and black) to transfer the coloured ink to the large cylinders holding the four printing plates. The ink is transferred or 'offset' from the plate and on to the paper.*

OFFSET COLOUR PRINTING PRESS

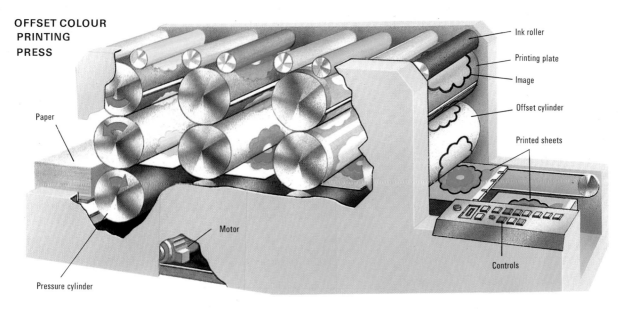

Ink roller

Printing plate

Image

Offset cylinder

Printed sheets

Controls

Motor

Paper

Pressure cylinder

printing was known in Japan as early as AD 770.) Each letter or piece of 'type' is set on a small stick of metal which carries a line of type. A number of these lines are then locked together into a frame. For more than 400 years, *typesetters* placed the bits of type in position by hand. Then they inked it and pressed paper on top. Modern typesetting is done by computers, producing a paper copy of the type ready for making plates to print by LITHOGRAPHY. (See BOOKS AND BOOKBINDING; PUBLISHING). ▷

PRISM A solid block of transparent material used in various instruments to disperse (split up) or reflect LIGHT or other rays. Optical instruments, such as prismatic binoculars, use glass prisms. Quartz prisms are used for ultraviolet rays (see ELECTROMAGNETIC WAVES) as these are mostly absorbed by glass.

PRISON A secure building where people are confined while they wait for trial or in which they serve their sentences after being found guilty. Most prisons are patrolled by guards and have barred windows and doors to keep prisoners from escaping. ▷

PRONGHORN Shy antelope-like animal found in North America. It is about 90 cm (3 ft) tall, with branched horns, a brown coat and white markings. Pronghorns are not true antelopes as they shed their horns every year and antelopes do not.

PRONOUN A word mainly used as an alternative to a NOUN. By using pronouns, we can refer to ourselves and other people and things without having to repeat their names all the time. Instead of saying Mr Smith, the pronoun *he* or *him* can be used. The English language has about 100 pronouns.

▲When white light is passed through a prism, it is refracted (bent), and split into the different colours: red, orange, yellow, green, blue, indigo, violet.

▲ In modern lithography, the printing surface or plates — often prepared photographically — are fitted round a cylinder in a high-speed rotary press.

▼The pronghorn is in a family all by itself. It is distinguished by its hollow horns, found on both male and female. These are shed in autumn after the mating season, and grown again the following spring.

PRINTING Early Chinese and Japanese printing was done from blocks of wood carved with full-page carvings of text or pictures. By AD 1030 the Chinese could build up a page of type from movable pieces. But the 10,000 characters in their script made typesetting slow. Not surprisingly printing from movable type first caught on in Europe, where a script of only 26 letters made typesetting simpler and faster.

Fast modern printing machines make it possible to produce millions of copies of a newspaper in just a few hours. On some Sundays, presses in London have produced as many as nine million copies of one British newspaper. Printing morning and evening editions in several cities has helped daily sales of one Japanese newspaper to exceed twelve millions.

▶A woodcut printed by William Caxton in the 1480s. A picture was cut into a wooden block, inked, and then stamped by hand on to the paper. In Europe, this printing process was first used for making playing cards.

PRISON The largest prison system of all time was that of the Soviet Union under Joseph Stalin, who ruled from 1929 to 1953. The hundreds of prisons and prison camps held up to twelve million prisoners – equivalent to more than the entire population of present-day Belgium, Sweden, or Greece. Most were not criminals. They were simply people whom Stalin's government feared or disliked.

PROPELLER For thousands of years people have lifted water by turning a spiral enclosed in an open-ended tube. But the first screw propeller for use in ships was one made in 1796 by the American inventor John Fitch. His propeller was a spiral that revolved on a rod. The first successful ship's propeller with blades dates from 1837. Its inventor was John Ericsson, a Swede living in England.

PROTEINS Some foods are rich in protein but poor in the kinds of amino acids our bodies need. For instance, weight for weight, soybean flour and peanuts have more protein than cheese, fish, beef, milk, or eggs. But the last five have a higher percentage of useful amino acids than the first two.

PROTOZOA Some protozoan parasites can cause serious illness. One is an amoeba – a tiny creature resembling a speck of jelly. This amoeba feeds on red blood cells and causes amoebic dysentery. But not all amoeba-like protozoans that enter the body are harmful. The mouth amoeba lives in the mouths of three out of four of us, yet we never know it is there.

PROPANE A colourless gas, formula C_3H_8, belonging to a group of hydrocarbons called PARAFFINS. Propane is inflammable and widely used as a fuel, either by itself or mixed with butane.

PROPELLER An assembly of twisted blades used to propel some aircraft and ships. Engines turn the propellers, which act on the air or water to produce a driving thrust for the vessel. In effect, the propellers screw their way through the air or water. (See HELICOPTER) ◁

PROTEINS Chemical compounds forming an essential part of every CELL in plants and animals. Proteins perform a wide range of important tasks. For example, most HORMONES and all ENZYMES are proteins that control chemical processes in living organisms. Proteins from one organism sometimes enter an animal's body and cause illness. But the foreign proteins, or antigens, stimulate the formation of other proteins called ANTIBODIES. These combine chemically with the antigens, making them harmless. Our

▼ Some early designs of ships' propellers developed in the 19th century. 1 An experimental screw of 1836 (during trials half the blade snapped off and the vessel being propelled gathered speed). 2 The double propeller invented by John Ericsson. 3 Ericsson's improved version of his invention – the first modern-type ship's propeller.

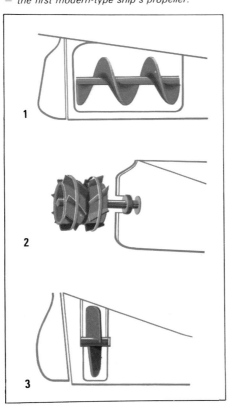

bodies obtain protein from foods such as meat, milk, eggs, fish, soybeans and nuts. In the process of DIGESTION, these are broken down into substances called AMINO ACIDS. The body then builds up other proteins from these acids. ◁

PROTON See ATOM

PROTOPLASM Jelly-like substance that is the basis of all living things. All plants and animals are made up of CELLS and all cells are made of protoplasm. The protoplasm in the centre, or nucleus, is called *nucleoplasm*, and the protoplasm outside the nucleus is called *cytoplasm*. Protoplasm contains water, PROTEINS, FATS, CARBOHYDRATES and MINERALS.

PROTOZOA Lowest division of the animal kingdom. Protozoans, the members of this group, are all microscopic, one-celled animals and either live in water or inside other animals. ◁

PRUNE Dried PLUM. Special types of plum are grown for processing into prunes. Generally, prunes are soaked before being cooked.

PRUSSIA This was the kingdom of the Prussians that lay on the south-east coast of the Baltic Sea. Its capital and biggest city was Berlin. For many years, until the unification of GERMANY in 1871, Prussia was the most powerful kingdom of all the German states. (See FRANCO-PRUSSIAN WAR; SEVEN YEARS' WAR)

PSYCHIATRY A branch of medicine that deals with mental disorders and diseases. Its goal is to relieve the problems of people who suffer from distress, anxiety, or depression to such a degree that they cannot function normally. Modern psychiatry treats people by discussing their problems, by teaching them skills to cope with everyday life, and also by using drugs to ease their symptoms. (See PSYCHOANALYSIS; PSYCHOLOGY)

PSYCHOANALYSIS A method of investigating the working of the human mind and of treating mental disorders, first begun by Sigmund FREUD in 1896. Psychoanalysis treats people by exploring their past history and examining their thoughts and feelings about themselves and their world. It seeks to deal with the problems that arise out of the unconscious side of the mind, but about which most of us are generally unaware. (See PSYCHIATRY; PSYCHOLOGY)

PSYCHOLOGY Coming from the Greek word *psyche*, meaning mind or soul, psychology is the science of how the mind works. It deals with the way people and animals

▲ Although puffins spend much of their time at sea, they do come ashore to breed. In the breeding season, their bills grow larger and become brightly coloured. A female will lay just one speckled egg in a burrow in the soil.

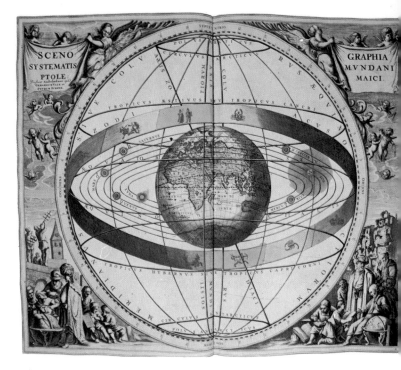

▲ The universe according to Ptolemy, as shown in the Harmonia Macrocosmica (1708) by Andreas Cellarius. At the centre is the Earth, around which circle the Moon, Sun and planets. The broad bands show the constellations of the zodiac. Ptolemy's theory was accepted right up until the 16th century, when it was challenged by Copernicus.

▼ The simple pulley mechanism is a great aid in construction work. Here, medieval builders are seen using the winch and pulley for hoisting small loads.

learn, think and react to what their senses tell them. It also examines the way we reason and make decisions. Psychologists may work as researchers and study the way messages are carried to and from the BRAIN. They may also work as teachers or in clinics where they see and treat patients (see PSYCHOANALYSIS). Other psychologists carry out large-scale studies of hundreds of people to find out their attitudes, their reactions and the way they behave in certain situations. An important branch of psychology deals with the behaviour of animals.

PTOLEMY, CLAUDIUS A famous Greek-Egyptian scientist (c. AD 100–170) who lived in Alexandria in Egypt. From his astronomical studies he concluded that the Earth was the centre of the universe, and that the sky was a sphere within which hung the Sun, Moon, stars and planets. (See ASTRONOMY)

PUBLISHING The preparation and presentation of written and illustrated material. Up to 150 years ago, publishers were usually printers and booksellers too. Today, their job is to take a written manuscript, edit it into a form suitable as a book or a magazine and then to have it printed, advertised and sold to the public. (See BOOKS AND BOOKBINDING; PRINTING)

PUFFIN Small black and white fish-eating sea bird, about 30 cm (12 in) long. During the

PUFFIN Puffins are members of the auk family *(Alcidae)*. They breed in colonies and the females lay a single speckled egg in holes excavated a metre into the turf, or in abandoned rabbit burrows. The plumage of both sexes is glossy black on the back and white underneath. The feet are webbed and bright orange. Their gait is a rolling waddle.

Old sailors' names for puffins are sea parrot, bottle nose, coulter-neb, and pope.

PULSARS Pulsars are thought to be rapidly rotating neutron stars, comprised of tightly packed neutrons — particles found at the centre of atoms. A pulsar is so dense that it has a mass of between 1.4 and about 3 times that of the Sun, though its diameter may be only 24 km (15 miles) as opposed to the Sun's diameter of 1,392,000 km (865,000 miles).

PUNIC WARS Until the early 1970s no one had found a warship from the Punic Wars, or indeed any other ancient warship. Then the British archaeologist Honor Frost excavated two off Sicily. Both were about 37 m (121 ft) long, narrow, and armed with pointed rams. Sixty-eight oarsmen had rowed each craft which also carried 68 fighting men. Carpenters' marks proved the boats to be Punic. Other finds show that they had been prefabricated as part of a mass-production process. They sank about 255 BC while the first Punic War was raging.

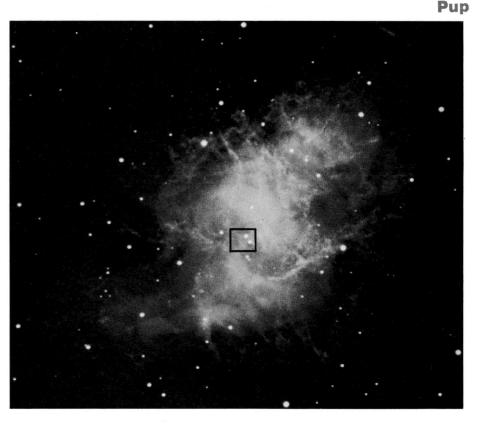

▲ *This pulsar was discovered in the Crab nebula, in the constellation of Taurus.*

breeding season its bill is bright red, blue and yellow. Puffins live in the north; they breed on rocky cliffs and islands but often spend the rest of the year out at sea. ◁

PULLEY A wheel, usually with a grooved rim to take a rope or cable. The pulley is a simple machine enabling work, such as hoisting a load, to be done more conveniently. An arrangement of several pulleys, as in the block and tackle, enables heavy loads to be moved with relatively little effort.

PULSARS Stars that emit pulses of radio waves at regular intervals. The first pulsar was discovered in 1967 by astronomers at the Mullard Radio Astronomy Observatory, Cambridge, England. From a certain point in space, their radio telescope picked up bursts of radio signals that lasted about 1/30 second and repeated every 1.34 seconds. Pulsars are thought to be extremely small – about 24 km (15 miles) across – and only one has been observed by optical telescope. This pulsar, situated in the Crab NEBULA, emits bursts of light and X-rays, as well as radio waves. ◁

PULSE The rhythmic throbbing of an ARTERY as the heart beats and pumps blood through it. It can be felt at the wrist, neck,

temple, armpits and ankle. Pulse waves travel about 6–9 metres (20–30 ft) a second.

PUMA See COUGAR

PUMPKIN Large orange-coloured fruit which grows at ground level on a trailing plant. It is used in cooking and is also fed to animals. In the US, pumpkin pie is a traditional dish on THANKSGIVING DAY.

PUMPS Machines for moving fluids (liquids or gases). *Reciprocating pumps* have a piston moving to-and-fro in a cylinder. Devices called valves control the flow so that the fluid moves in one direction only, not back-and-forth. In *rotary pumps*, fast-turning propeller-like blades make the fluid flow. *Centrifugal pumps* contain turning vanes that make the fluid rotate. CENTRIFUGAL FORCE causes the moving fluid to pass along an outlet pipe.

PUNIC WARS Three Punic Wars were fought by CARTHAGE and Rome for the control of the western Mediterranean, between 264 BC and 146 BC. The Romans won, though at great cost, and totally destroyed Carthage in revenge, razing it to the ground. ◁

PUPPET Miniature human or animal figures that are usually hand-held. Glove puppets are slipped over the hand and worked by moving the fingers. Puppets can also be worked by

▲Europeans of average height standing beside African pygmies of average height. It is thought that pygmies are descended from the earliest inhabitants of Africa.

strings from above, or by rods from below. The most famous of all puppets are the couple, Punch and Judy.

PYGMY Small, dark-skinned people who live in the hot equatorial forests of Africa. The men are seldom taller than 1.5 metres (5 ft) and the women are even smaller. They have negroid features and live in small bands that survive by hunting game in the forests. ▷

PYRAMID A geometric solid shape with a square or polygonal base and triangular sides that meet at a point. The volume of a pyramid can be found by multiplying the area of the base by the height, and dividing by three.

PYRAMIDS Huge monuments of solid stone built by the ancient Egyptians as burial sites for their PHARAOHS. They were made from giant blocks of stone weighing as much as $2\frac{1}{2}$ tonnes each. The stones were quarried miles away and dragged to their final site next to the Nile. The tombs of the pharaohs were a network of tunnels and chambers guarding their mummified bodies. (See ARCHITECTURE; EGYPT) ▷

▶The pyramids of Giza in Egypt. Pyramids were always built in the desert, as the fertile land was needed to grow food. Each pyramid was intended to house the preserved body (mummy) and possessions of its owner. It guarded them and was thought to assist the soul on its journey to the Next World.

PYRENEES A mountain range which runs along the French-Spanish border. The highest peak is Pico de Aneto, 3404 metres (11,168 ft) above sea-level. The small state of Andorra nestles in the Pyrenees.

PYTHAGORAS A Greek mathematician of the 6th century BC who laid the roots of modern GEOMETRY. He was one of the first to believe that the Earth was a sphere.

PYTHON Large non-poisonous snake up to 9 metres (30 ft) long, found in Africa, Asia and Australia. Most species have brown and yellow patterns. Pythons are very strong and kill their prey – all kinds of animals – by squeezing them until they are asphyxiated.

PYGMY African pygmies are one of several groups of small negroid peoples. Others live in remote forests of South-east Asia. People once thought they were all survivors of a population scattered by immigrant peoples of normal size. But blood tests show that African and Asian pygmies are unrelated.

PYRAMIDS: FACTS AND FIGURES
Oldest: Step Pyramid at Saqqara, Egypt – built about 2650 BC.
Tallest: Great Pyramid at Giza, Egypt – originally 146.6 m (481 ft) high.
Largest: Quetzalcóatl, at Cholula, Mexico – containing about 3,300,000 cu m (4,300,000 cu yd) of material.

QUAIL Small game-bird, related to the PAR-TRIDGE and found in most parts of the world. Quail prefer open country and, if disturbed, they run for cover rather than fly. They feed on seeds and insects.

QUANTUM THEORY A theory developed by the German scientist Max Planck in 1900, to explain the emission of radiant energy. Planck originally developed the theory to explain why ultraviolet radiation failed to obey another law. He suggested that radiant energy is emitted in units called *quanta*. He stated that the energy (E) of a quantum is given by the formula: $E = hf,$ where f is the frequency of the radiation and h is a constant known as Planck's constant. (This is equal to 6.6256×10^{-34} JOULE seconds.) We now know that this theory applies to all forms of radiant energy and that the quantum of energy is the PHOTON. The quantum theory formed the basis of the study known as quantum mechanics, which deals with small-scale physics concerning, for example, the electrons and nuclei in ATOMS.

QUARKS Tiny particles which some scientists think may be the building blocks of which all other atomic particles are made. It is possible that tiny protons and neutrons may be made up of quarks, but no such particle has so far been found. (See ATOM)

QUARTZ A common MINERAL consisting of crystalline silica (silicon dioxide), formula SiO_2. Its purest form, known as rock crystal, is colourless and clear. But most quartz is white and opaque. Varieties coloured by impurities include rose quartz, smoky quartz, citrine (yellow), and amethyst (purple or violet). These and other varieties are used in jewellery. Being harder than steel, quartz is a useful abrasive. Slices of quartz tend to vibrate at fixed frequencies when suitable electrical signals are applied to them. Because of this, quartz crystals are used to regulate electronic watches and CLOCKS. Quartz also produces electricity when subjected to mechanical stresses. This property, known as the *piezo-electric effect*, is used in some record-player pickups.

QUASARS The term quasar is an abbreviation of *quasistellar*, meaning 'seemingly a star'. For over a century, quasars appeared in photographs of the heavens. But no particular interest was aroused as they appeared to be ordinary stars. However, we now know that quasars are most unusual objects. They appear to be extremely distant, yet they are remarkably powerful sources of radio waves, giving out hundreds of times as much energy as our whole GALAXY. Yet other evidence suggests that quasars are only about one-millionth the size of our Galaxy. Since 1960, when the first quasar was discovered, hundreds more have been located. Some can be seen using an optical telescope, while others can be detected only by radio telescope. Some astronomers think that quasars are typical galaxies in the early stages of their evolution.

QUEENSLAND The second largest state in AUSTRALIA. Queensland has 2,505,000 people (1984) and an area of 1,727,522 sq km (667,000 sq miles). Broad plains are in the west, but the GREAT DIVIDING RANGE overlooks the coast in the east. The chief occupation is farming, especially cattle- and sheep-rearing. Sugar-cane is the chief crop on the northern coast. Mining is also important and BRISBANE is a manufacturing centre.

QUININE A strong, bitter-tasting substance made from the bark of the cinchona tree. It was used as a medicine to treat MALARIA.

R

RABBIT Small brownish-grey MAMMAL with long ears and a very short tail. Rabbits have spread from Europe to all parts of the world. They live together in great numbers in underground burrows and come out at dusk and dawn to feed on grass and other plants.

RABIES An infectious, often fatal disease. Rabies attacks the central NERVOUS SYSTEM. It is spread by the bites of infected dogs or wild animals. The VIRUS is present in their saliva.

RACCOON Common American MAMMAL about 90 cm (3 ft) long with greyish fur. Raccoons are tree creatures and live in forests, often near streams. They hunt by night and eat anything – animals, fish and plants. Near towns they take scraps from rubbish heaps and bins. ▷

RACE A race is a group of people who have certain important physical features in common. The three main races of the world are the Caucasian, the Negroid and the Mongoloid. Caucasians have light-coloured skins, straight or wavy hair, narrow noses and prominent chins. Negroids have dark skins, tight, curly hair, broad noses and thick lips. Mongoloids

▼*The Chinese are part of the Mongoloid racial group, while the black African (below left) belongs to the Negroid race. Below right, a European Caucasian.*

RACCOON The raccoon swims well. At one time people used to think the animal always washed its food before eating. But this 'washing' is just a paddling movement of the front feet, and occurs whenever the animal enters water, even without food.

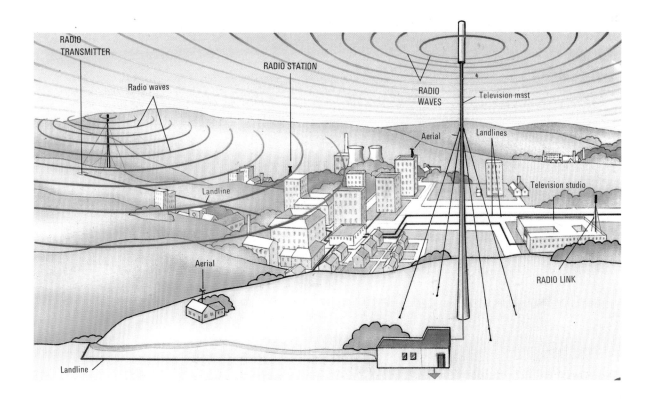

RADIO TRANSMITTER

Radio waves

RADIO STATION

RADIO WAVES

Television mast

Aerial

Landlines

Aerial

Landline

Television studio

RADIO LINK

Landline

RADAR A radar operator calculates the distance of the reflecting object, such as an aircraft, by measuring the time that elapses between the sending of the radio signal and the return of a tiny fraction of the electrical energy of this signal in the form of a radio echo. He can also determine the direction of the aircraft and its height above the ground so that even in dense fog or complete darkness he can establish its position. Radar can also detect the presence of a mass of ice particles or raindrops in the atmosphere, or even a sharp boundary between air masses, and as such can be used to detect weather conditions.

have dark, straight hair, high cheekbones and a yellowish skin tone; a small fold of skin on the upper eyelid gives their eyes an almond shape.

RADAR A term standing for RAdio Detection And Ranging. It is a system for locating distant objects by transmitting RADIO signals and detecting their reflections. The reflected signals are displayed as images on the screen of a CATHODE-RAY TUBE. Sea and air navigators use radar to study their surroundings, especially when visibility is bad. And flight controllers use it to observe the planes they guide in and out of airports. Some aircraft use radar altimeters for direct measurement of their height above the ground. Radar also plays an important part in watching for enemy missiles and aircraft in early-warning systems. ◁

RADIATION Any form of energy radiated from a source. (See ALPHA PARTICLES; BETA PARTICLES; ELECTROMAGNETIC WAVES; GAMMA RAYS; SOUND)

RADIO The use of certain ELECTROMAGNETIC WAVES to carry information, such as MORSE CODE, speech, or music. Radio waves are also used in RADAR equipment for detecting distant objects, and in TELEVISION to carry sound and vision signals.

The idea of transmitting radio waves was conceived by the Scottish scientist James

▲ A radio station sends out music or speech as an electric signal which is changed into radio waves via the transmitter. Your radio aerial picks up the radio waves and the radio converts this to sound. Radio waves also carry sound and vision signals for television.

▼ Marconi, one of the great radio pioneers. In 1901 he sent signals across the Atlantic from Cornwall, England to Newfoundland.

Clerk Maxwell in 1865. He thought that there must be some way of making an alternating (back-and-forth) electric current produce electromagnetic waves. But it was the German scientist Heinrich Hertz who discovered how to do it. In 1887, Hertz made a spark jump the gap between the ends of two metal rods. When

Rad

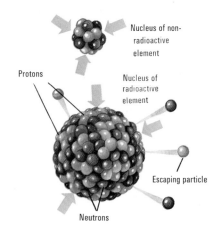

▲ *Inside an atom is the nucleus (centre) made up of minute particles (protons and neutrons) packed tightly. If there are too many particles packed together some breakaway from the nucleus creating radioactivity.*

Labels in diagram: Nucleus of non-radioactive element; Protons; Nucleus of radioactive element; Escaping particle; Neutrons

this happened, another spark jumped the gap in a nearby metal ring. Energy had been transmitted to the ring in the form of radio waves.

Among those to hear of Hertz's simple, but important experiment was a young Italian student called Guglielmo MARCONI. Using the ideas of Hertz and others, Marconi built a simple transmitter and receiver. When he switched on the transmitter, a bell rang in the receiver. The year was 1894, and the range of this simple equipment was only about 4 metres (13 feet). But, within two years, Marconi had increased the range to about 3 km (2 miles). And, in 1901, he succeeded in transmitting signals across the Atlantic.

By this time, wireless TELEGRAPHY – the use of radio for sending Morse Code signals – had proved itself a worthy rival to the electric telegraph. And wireless telephony – the transmission of speech by radio – was soon to become an alternative to the TELEPHONE. This important development was made possible by Lee De Forest's invention of the *triode valve* in 1906. With the new valve, circuits were designed to enable speech, or other sounds, to be superimposed on a radio signal. Sets for receiving the signals ranged from simple crystal sets with headphones to much more complex and sensitive sets with several large, glowing valves.

Besides its use as an alternative to the telephone, radio had much more to offer. For it provided an excellent means of communicating with and entertaining the public at large. So, in the 1920s, radio broadcasting stations started to spring up, and an ever-increasing audience listened to the pro-

grammes. Since those days, amazing changes have taken place in the field of radio. The development of the TRANSISTOR in the 1940s enabled the size and cost of equipment to be greatly reduced, while reliability was increased. As a result, small, cheap, portable receivers became available for the masses. Today, through the miracle of radio, almost everyone in the world, from Eskimos in the Arctic wastes to desert tribesmen, can be informed of major world events.

RADIOACTIVITY The nuclei of certain ISOTOPES (see ATOM) are unstable and tend to disintegrate (break up) to form different nuclei. In this process, charged ALPHA PARTICLES or BETA PARTICLES are emitted and a new element is formed. Substances that undergo such changes are said to be radioactive, and the process of change is called radioactive decay. The time taken for half the atoms in a radioactive substance to decay is called the half-life of the substance. In some cases, this is less than half a second, while, for one RADIUM isotope, it is 1620 years. When a substance undergoes radioactive decay, it changes into another element. Thorium, for example, gradually decays to form lead. The radiation emitted by radioactive substances can be harmful to man. But small doses are used to advantage in some forms of medical treatment.   ◁

RADIO ASTRONOMY The investigation of heavenly bodies using the radio waves they emit instead of the light they emit or reflect. A radio TELESCOPE consists essentially of a large aerial, usually dish-shaped, and an assembly of amplifiers and recording equipment. Some bodies can be studied by optical telescope as

RADIOACTIVITY The alpha particles given off by radioactive substances are not a great hazard to human life. The particles are, in fact, stopped by the outer layer of the skin. Beta particles are more penetrating and can get inside the skin. But there is a third kind of radiation when atomic nuclei change – gamma rays. Gamma rays are not streams of tiny particles like alpha and beta rays. They are a form of very strong X-rays, and, like X-rays they can easily penetrate matter. They pass right through the human body and can cause harm to the atoms in the body.

▼ *A radio telescope has a very large hollow or concave dish which reflects the signals from space onto the radio receiver.*

▲ *Two steam engines are needed here to pull their heavy load up a steep incline. Such scenes are rare as more countries electrify their lines.*

RADIOCARBON DATING People, animals and plants are all slightly radioactive. They contain a fixed proportion of a radioactive form of carbon called carbon-14 or radiocarbon. When a person, animal or plant dies, no more radiocarbon is formed in the remains, and the amount left slowly emits beta particles and decays. Its half-life is 5570 years. The date when the animal or plant died can be found by measuring the amount of carbon-14 left in the remains. Radiocarbon dating can be used to date remains up to about 40,000 years.

RADIUM This metallic element is extremely rare. It is found only in beds of uranium ore. Even the richest uranium beds will only yield a single gram of radium for every four tonnes of ore. The yearly world output is only 60 grams.

RAILWAY The first regular passenger-carrying railway ran between Liverpool and Manchester in northwest England, and opened in 1830. Another of George Stephenson's locomotives, the famous *Rocket*, won a competition for the best engine for the line.

Today there are about 1,250,000 km (785,000 miles) of track in the world. This is enough to girdle the Earth more than 30 times.

well as by radio telescope. But many bodies can be detected only by radio telescope. Such bodies include most of the PULSARS.

RADIOCARBON DATING A technique for estimating the age of ancient objects that were once alive, such as wood. A living tree acquires a radioactive isotope (see ATOM) that decays at a known rate after the tree has been cut down (see RADIOACTIVITY). So, by measuring the amount of radioactive isotope present, the age of the wood can be estimated. (See ARCHAEOLOGY) ◁

RADISH Small roundish edible root with a strong peppery taste. Most kinds are either red or white and are eaten raw in salads.

RADIUM A rare, radioactive metal (see RADIOACTIVITY) first isolated by Madame CU-

RIE in 1910. It is produced by the radioactive decay of URANIUM and is found in pitchblende and other uranium ores. The radiation from radium is used to treat CANCER. ◁

RAILWAY Railways existed long before steam LOCOMOTIVES. As early as the 16th century, wooden rails were used in coal mines for horse-drawn wagons. Wagons with flanged wheels, to keep them on rails, came into use in the 1750s.

The first public railway on which a STEAM ENGINE was used ran between Stockton and Darlington, in northern England. It opened in 1825. The engine was *Locomotive No. 1* built by George Stephenson.

In the past 100 years, railways have spread to all parts of the world. Most modern trains are pulled by DIESEL or electric locomotives, although in some places steam engines are still used. ◁

▼ *The French railway's* Train à grande vitesse *(TGV) is the fastest regular passenger train averaging a speed of 210 km/h (130 mph) between Paris and Lyons.*

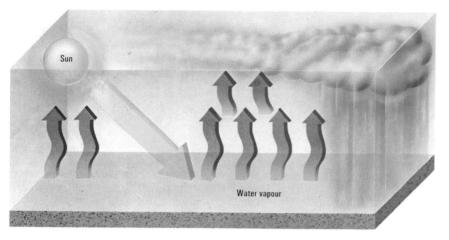

Sun

Water vapour

RAIN This is caused by water vapour in the air cooling, condensing into droplets and falling to the ground. Rain is part of the water cycle in which water in seas, lakes and rivers EVAPORATES, forms clouds and then falls back to Earth. ▷

▲ *Rain occurs during the continual exchange of water between the Earth and the atmosphere, called the water cycle. The Sun's heat causes water to evaporate from seas, rivers and lakes. The vapour condenses into clouds in cool air and returns to the ground as rain or snow.*

RAINBOW A many-coloured arch of LIGHT formed by the play of sunlight on tiny raindrops. When a beam of sunlight strikes a drop, the drop acts as a PRISM to split the beam into different colours. Folklore says that at the end of every rainbow lies a pot of gold. ▷

RAISIN Dried GRAPE. Raisins are produced from special large, white, sweet grapes and are used in cooking for making puddings, cakes and biscuits.

RALEIGH, WALTER A dashing adventurer (1552–1618) of the court of ELIZABETH I of England. Raleigh was one of the first to bring TOBACCO back to Europe from America. He was a soldier, explorer, historian and a poet. ▷

RASPBERRY A fruit that is closely related to the blackberry, and made up of a number of tiny round parts called *drupelets* that are red or yellow-white in colour.

RAT A rodent that is found all over the world in huge numbers. It is well adapted to scavenging on human litter and thrives wherever there are people. Rats spread diseases including the dreaded bubonic PLAGUE that wiped out a quarter of Europe's population in the 14th century.

RATTLESNAKE A poisonous snake of North America. Its sound comes from a number of dry, loose horny bits of skin on the tip of the tail that rattle as the tail vibrates. ▷

RAVEN A large black bird of the crow family, that grows up to 64 cm (25 in) in length. Ravens feed on carrion and small animals and live as long as 26 years. They can be recognized by their hoarse croaking cry. ▷

RAYON The name given to various man-made TEXTILE fibres containing CELLULOSE, a substance found in the walls of plant cells. The two main types of rayon are made from threads of cellulose itself (*viscous* rayon), or from threads of cellulose acetate.

REACTIONS, CHEMICAL A chemical reaction is said to take place when chemical changes occur in one or more substances. In *decomposition*, for example, a substance splits up to form two or more simpler substances. In other reactions, ELEMENTS combine to form more complex substances called compounds. Sometimes two compounds react to form two new compounds. Reactions of this kind are called *double decomposition*. A *reversible* reaction is one in which a change in physical conditions can convert the products of the reaction back into the original substances.

RED CROSS An international organization founded in 1863 for the care of soldiers wounded in war. Its emblem is a red cross on a white flag. Its headquarters are in Switzerland and it has branches in most countries of the world.

RED SEA A branch of the INDIAN OCEAN, the Red Sea separates north-eastern Africa from Arabia. The SUEZ CANAL links the Red Sea with the MEDITERRANEAN. The Red Sea has an area of about 440,300 sq km (170,000 sq miles). Its width across ranges from 210 to 400 kilometres (130–250 miles). ▷

REINDEER

female, summer

male, summer

refrigerator acts as a heat pump, maintaining the interior at a low temperature by conveying heat to the outside. In a typical refrigerator, this is done by using a low-boiling-point liquid called a refrigerant. It is pumped through a tube in the cabinet, where it absorbs heat and vaporizes. The vapour is then compressed and passed into a condenser at the back of the refrigerator. There it turns back to liquid and gives up the heat absorbed from inside. This process repeats, gradually lowering the temperature inside the refrigerator. ◁

REINDEER A large type of deer that lives in the far north of Europe, Asia and America. Both the males and females have antlers, which is unique in the deer family. The Lapps, a nomadic people, depend on the herds of reindeer that roam the Arctic tundra, for their clothing, meat and milk. This area is poor in vegetation and both reindeer and Lapps keep on the move. (See LAPLAND).

RELATIVITY In 1905, Albert EINSTEIN published his *Special Theory of Relativity*. This appeared to show that the physical laws established by Isaac NEWTON could not be applied to bodies moving at speeds approaching that of light. For, said Einstein, length, mass and time all change according to a body's VELOCITY. In fact, at the velocity of light, a body would have no length and infinite mass. And, for that body, time would stand still. Many scientific observations made since

RAVEN These large black birds are said to be omens of everything from death and disease to bad luck and even bad weather. Armies used to dread being followed by ravens as they marched into battle, for they were taken to be a sign that there would be many corpses to scavenge.

RED SEA The Red Sea is famous for the miraculous crossing by the Israelites fleeing from the Egyptians. Archaeologists now think that any such crossing is more likely to have been made near the Great Bitter Lake, which is north of Suez and the Red Sea.

REFRIGERATOR No one knows when it was discovered that liquids in porous pots kept cool if left in a wind. The liquid seeps through the pot, evaporates. and the wind absorbs the warm vapour. Heat is therefore continually removed from the contents of the pot.

▲ *Wild reindeer eat grasses in summer and young shoots in winter. They can swim strongly if they need to.*

REED Belonging to the GRASS family, reeds grow in marshes all over the world from the tropics to the Arctic. They are used for fencing, woven furniture and for thatching.

REFORMATION The great religious upheaval of the 16th century. It was a revolt against the practices of the established ROMAN CATHOLIC CHURCH in Europe. Much of northern Europe became Protestant as a result. The split with the Catholic Church was marked by much violence and bloodshed as people struggled to give expression to their religious beliefs. Many felt disillusioned with the Church and sought a simpler, 'purer' form of worship. The Reformation was also a struggle between the power of the POPE and the kings of several nations. (See LUTHER)

REFRACTION The bending of LIGHT when it passes from one medium to another. Light is refracted when, for example, it passes from air to water, or vice versa. Light passing into an optically denser medium is bent towards the normal – a line perpendicular to the surface of the material. LENSES and PRISMS both bend light by the process of refraction.

REFRIGERATOR An enclosure for keeping foods or other substances cool. In effect, the

▼ *The refrigerant in a refrigerator absorbs heat on changing from gas to liquid form. Electricity, via the pump, supplies the power for evaporation and condensation.*

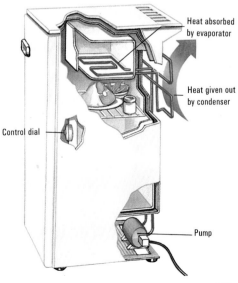

Heat absorbed by evaporator

Heat given out by condenser

Control dial

Pump

this theory was published have confirmed Einstein's predictions. In 1916, Einstein published his *General Theory of Relativity*, dealing with accelerating bodies and gravitational fields. This theory suggests that gravitation is a property of space – a 'curvature' caused by the presence of matter. (See ATOMIC ENERGY)

RELIGION The word that describes the various beliefs human beings have about God and the way in which they practice these beliefs.

There are many kinds of religions. Primitive people usually had many gods. They worshipped the forces of nature, the rocks, trees and animals. Later religions built temples and shrines to their gods and collected religious objects that were symbols of their power. Learned men or priests conducted religious ceremonies and upheld all the rules of their religion. The main religions of today: CHRISTIANITY, ISLAM, JUDAISM, BUDDHISM, HINDUISM and Confucianism (see CONFUCIUS), all have elaborate ways of worshipping God, including churches, temples, holy places, law books and priests. ▷

REMBRANDT, HARMENS VAN RIJN One of the most famous of Dutch painters

▶ *The dome of Florence Cathedral, designed by Brunelleschi, is a fine example of Renaissance architecture. Brunelleschi was a pioneer of early Renaissance architecture, during the period 1420 to 1506. He was the first architect to construct a dome over such an enormous space. The sculptor Donatello and the painter Masaccio worked with Brunelleschi on the cathedral.*

(1606–1669). His enormous output included about 700 paintings, several thousand drawings and many etchings. He was the favourite portrait painter of his time in Amsterdam, and in spite of failing sight he continued to paint until his death. ▷

RENAISSANCE The word means 'rebirth' and it describes the great revival in learning, LITERATURE, PAINTING, ARCHITECTURE and science that took place from the 14th to 16th centuries in Europe. Trade, navigation and exploration also flourished during this

JUDAISM

Jewish people number about 15 million, of whom 6 million live in the USA.

◀ *The Menorah, symbol of the Jewish faith.*

◀ *A stone cross, symbol of the Christian faith.*

CHRISTIANITY

Christians number about 1000 million, though many do not actively practise the religion. More than 500 million are Roman Catholic. Protestants, Anglicans and Episcopalians number more than 300 million. The Orthodox Churches claim 120 million.

◀ *An Eastern Orthodox bishop.*

ISLAM

Moslems number over 500 million. There are two main branches — Sunni Islam which accepts the *Koran* and traditions of

Mohammed; and Shia Islam (mostly in Persia) which accepts only the *Koran*.

◀ *The crescent moon, symbol of Islam.*

BUDDHISM

Buddhists number 250 million, and live mainly in China and other parts of Asia.

◀ *A statue of the Buddha.*

HINDUISM

Hindus number nearly 500 million and live mainly in India.

◀ *A Hindu carving.*

EASTERN ASIA

Shinto is an ancient religion of Japan. Taoism was founded in China in the 500s BC.

◀ *A Japanese pagoda.*

◀ The Ambassadors, *painted in 1533 by the German artist Hans Holbein. He has made this double portrait a summary of Renaissance thought as well as a picture of the two men, one a courtier and the other a bishop, both of whom were at one time ambassadors. Between these two figures, powerful men of state and Church, lies a collection of objects, some from the world of the arts, others from the then developing sciences; the well-rounded Renaissance man did not specialize in one field only. The repose of the picture is shattered by the extremely distorted skull in the foreground — a reminder of the inevitability of death.*

RESISTANCE When an electric current passes through a wire that has a high resistance, the metal in the wire becomes hot. The higher the resistance of the wire the hotter it becomes. It is this effect that gives us electric fires and light bulbs. The wire in the electric fire becomes red hot; that in the light bulb becomes white hot.

RESPIRATION A person at rest breathes in and out some 13 times a minute. With each breath, about 500 cc (30 cubic inches) of air is taken in.

period. Columbus discovered the Americas.

The Renaissance began in Italy and soon spread to the rest of Europe. It was marked by a great admiration for ancient Greece and Rome. People looked to the past for inspiration as new discoveries and ideas led them to question their own world.

RENOIR, PIERRE AUGUSTE A French painter (1841–1919) of the Impressionist school. Renoir was born the son of a poor tailor and his first job was painting designs on porcelain to pay his way to art school. His paintings are well-loved for their joy and gaiety. (See IMPRESSIONISM)

REPRODUCTION The ability of all living things, whether plants or animals, to produce more life like themselves. Humans give birth to babies, chickens lay EGGS and flowers produce SEEDS and POLLEN. The most usual way among higher animals is for the male to produce sperm and the female to produce an egg; the two must combine before new life is formed. (See GERM CELL; SEX)

REPTILES A group of cold-blooded animals that lay eggs on land, and in a few cases give birth to live young. They include ALLI-

GATORS and CROCODILES, TURTLES, SNAKES and LIZARDS. Millions of years ago, reptiles in the shape of DINOSAURS were the most important form of life on Earth. Today they are surpassed by birds and mammals. ◁

RESERVOIR A large quantity of stored water. Some reservoirs are man-made lakes, created by the building of DAMS across river valleys. Others are natural lakes.

RESIN Natural resin is a sticky gum that oozes from trees. Rosin, the best known, comes from pines. It is used in making paint, paper, soap and ADHESIVES.

RESISTANCE The property of a conductor (see CONDUCTION [ELECTRICITY]) to resist the flow of an electric CURRENT. Silver and copper, being good conductors, have relatively low resistance. The OHM (Ω) is the SI UNIT of resistance. The resistance (R) of a conductor carrying a current (I) is given by the equation $R = V/I$. ◁

RESPIRATION The process by which OXYGEN is carried to the body cells and CARBON DIOXIDE waste is removed. Oxygen is taken from the air by the LUNGS and absorbed by the blood, where it is carried to all parts of the body. Carbon dioxide is exhaled when we breathe out. ◁

RESTORATION This was the return of the monarchy to England in 1660 after Cromwellian rule with the accession of CHARLES II. The term is also used to describe the period that followed. (See CROMWELL, OLIVER)

REVOLUTIONARY WAR, AMERICAN The struggle by the 13 American colonies to gain their independence from Britain (1775–83). The war ended with the founding of the UNITED STATES of America. The colonies were used to a great deal of freedom and resented the tax burdens placed on them by the English king without first consulting them. The heavy-handed response of the British led to the outbreak of fighting. (See BOSTON TEA PARTY; BRITISH EMPIRE)

RHESUS FACTOR Most people have a protein known as a Rhesus (Rh) factor in their BLOOD. These people are called rhesus positive. But some people do not have this factor. They are the rhesus negative group. Special care is needed when an Rh negative woman has a child fathered by an Rh positive man.

RHESUS MONKEY A small, lively monkey native to the forests of south-east Asia. It is often used in scientific experiments.

RHEUMATIC FEVER A disease that used to be very common among children. The patient suffers from pain in the limbs, a high temperature and a sore throat. It is dangerous because it can lead to heart disease.

RHEUMATISM The name given to a group of diseases which cause pain in the muscles and joints and makes them stiff and hard to move. There is no simple cure for it.

RHINE, RIVER West Germany's leading economic waterway. The Rhine rises in SWITZERLAND and flows 1290 km (800 miles) through industrial areas in West GERMANY to the North Sea, via the NETHERLANDS. ▷

RHINOCEROS One of the heaviest of all land animals, a large male may weigh up to $3\frac{1}{2}$ tonnes. The rhinoceros that lives on the plains of Africa is often hunted for its horns which are believed by some people to have magical powers.

▶ In Asia terraced rice paddies have been cut into the hillsides. A complicated system of dykes and pumps is used to flood the fields. Ox-drawn ploughs then prepare the soil for the young rice shoots which are planted by hand. Rice is the main food in many parts of India, China, Indonesia, Malaysia and Japan.

▲ Africa has two species of rhinoceros — black and white, but both are really grey. These are white rhino.

▶ The River Rhine (opposite) rises in Switzerland and flows to the North Sea. A wide variety of goods are transported by boat from mountainous southern Germany and the Ruhr industrial region to the North Sea. The southern highlands bordering on the Rhine are very fertile. Cereals, hops, sugar beet, tobacco and grapes are all produced there.

RHODESIA See ZIMBABWE

RICE A starchy CEREAL grain which is the chief food of about half the people in the world. It yields more food per acre than any other grain and is grown in flooded paddy fields. ASIA produces some nine-tenths of the world's output.

RHINE, RIVER There are many romantic legends linked with this river. One is of a beautiful young maiden with flowing golden hair who sat on a rock in the middle of a fast flowing stretch of the Rhine Gorge. She sang to passing boatmen. Her voice was so beautiful that it would lure them to their doom on the rocks. Today, a large rock in the river is named the Lorelei after the lovely siren who is said to have sat there. In 1986 the river sufferered serious pollution from chemical spillage.

RICHARD I Known as Richard the Lion Heart (1157–1199), he succeeded his father, HENRY II, to the throne of England in 1189, and was crowned a second time after his return from the Third Crusade in 1194. He spent much of his reign out of the country on CRUSADES to the Holy Land.

RICKETS A disease which is caused by the lack of Vitamin D, found in sunlight and cod liver oil, without which the body cannot build strong healthy bones. It especially affects children.

RIFLE A GUN that fires a bullet along a rifled (spirally grooved) barrel. The grooves give the bullet a spin that steadies it in flight. Rifles came into use in the 15th century.

RNA The abbreviation for *ribonucleic acid*, a complex organic substance found in many types of VIRUS. RNA is one form of nucleic acid; the other is DNA.

ROADS Ancient roads were developed for carts and wagons from the paths and tracks people had formerly trod on foot. The Romans built superb roads of stone that were even arched at the centre for drainage. One of the greatest roads of the ancient world was the Persian Royal Road from Susa to Smyrna. It was 2857 km (1775 miles) long. ASPHALT paved roads have been known since the early 1800s when John McAdam devised a tar, stone and sand mixture for road surfaces. ▷

ROBIN A small bird in the thrush family, with rusty-orange feathers on its throat and breast. It often makes its home in towns and gardens.

ROBIN HOOD The legendary hero of many English ballads. He was a daring and gallant

▲ *Robots are used in production lines, particularly in vehicle manufacturing, for welding, painting, loading and unloading.*

outlaw who robbed from the rich to give to the poor. He is said to have lived in Sherwood Forest at the end of the 12th century.

ROBOT The word robot is a modern one coming from the Czech for 'forced labour'. Robots are devices that do some of the work of human beings. They are used a great deal in industry and science to do tasks that are dangerous or repetitive. Robots may handle hot or radioactive devices. These are simply a pair of arms and fingers operated by a human

▼*A motorway intersection in Germany, the country that pioneered fast intercity roads.*

ROADS The Romans were the greatest road builders of the ancient world. They laid out over 80,000 km (50,000 miles) of road across their far-flung empire. The best roads were remarkable feats of engineering. They had thick beds, over a metre (3 ft) deep made of rock slabs, stones, gravel and sand layers.

The longest motorable road in the world is the Pan-American Highway system which runs from northern Alaska to Brazil, via Santiago, Chile and Buenos Aires, Argentina. There are some gaps in the system however.

ROCKETS The largest American rocket ever built was the Saturn V. It stood 110 m (363 ft) high on its launching pad and weighed 2.7 million kg (6.1 million pounds). Its engines developed a thrust of 3.4 million kg (7.5 million pounds); enough to place a 127,000-kg (140-ton) payload into orbit around the Earth or to hurtle 45,000 kg (50 tons) to the Moon.

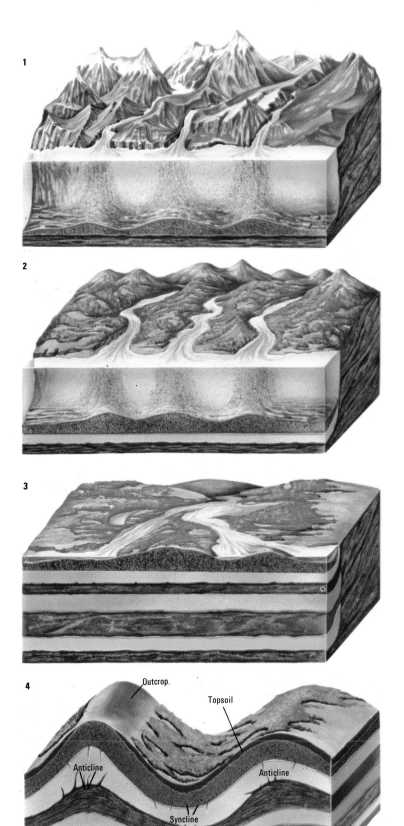

(see RADIOACTIVITY). Other robots are programmed to do jobs such as welding cars on assembly lines. They are operated by computers. In SCIENCE FICTION films and stories, robots often look like humans and are able to talk and think.

ROCKETS The first rockets were used in warfare by the Chinese in the 1200s. Like the rockets now used as fireworks, these missiles were propelled by GUNPOWDER. Gases produced by the fast-burning chemicals were forced from the back of the rockets, causing them to be propelled upward. In the same way, if you stand on a trolley and throw bricks from it, the trolley will move in the opposite direction. The action of throwing the bricks produces an equal and opposite reaction force that thrusts the trolley forward. The important difference between the rocket and the jet engine is that the rocket does not take in air (see JET PROPULSION). This enables it to operate in outer space, where a jet would cease to function. In fact, rockets are the only known means of propelling space vehicles. Spacecraft are usually launched by a three-stage rocket. A large booster rocket provides power for lift-off. After burning out, the booster separates and drops away, leaving a smaller, second-stage rocket to take over. This too drops away after use. Then an even smaller, third-stage rocket gives the spacecraft the final boost it needs to enter space. During later stages of the mission, small rocket engines control the spacecraft. (See page 306) ◁

ROCKS Rock is the substance that forms the Earth's crust. It is made up of mixtures of MINERALS. Rocks are divided into three main types: igneous, sedimentary, and metamorphic. Igneous rocks are formed when molten lava from volcanic eruptions turns solid. Granite, obsidian, basalt and pumice are igneous rocks. Igneous rocks make up about four-fifths of the Earth's crust. Sedimentary rocks are igneous rocks that have been worn away by rivers, seas, wind and rain. The worn-away particles of these rocks are carried away and deposited, for instance, at the bottom of the sea. After millions of years these particles are compressed to form sedimentary rocks. Sandstone and limestone are sedimentary rocks. The third main kind of rock is metamorphic rock. This rock is formed by the action of great heat and pressure on igneous

◀ Stages in the formation of sedimentary rocks: 1 Rivers begin to wear away newly formed rocks, carrying sediment to the sea. 2 and 3 The landscape gets flatter and the rivers widen as erosion continues. Layers of sediment build up in the sea. 4 Massive earth movements fold the crust in which the sedimentary layers have now been compacted into hard rock — sedimentary rock.

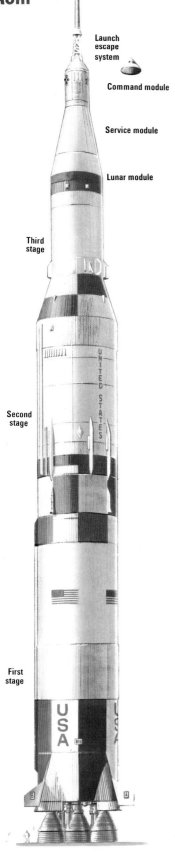

Launch
escape
system

Command module

Service module

Lunar module

Third
stage

Second
stage

First
stage

USA

and sedimentary rocks inside the Earth's crust. Marble is a metamorphic rock formed from limestone.

ROMAN CATHOLIC CHURCH The Catholic Church is the original Christian Church and is still by far the largest. Its leader is the POPE who lives in the VATICAN in Rome. The Church traces its history back to the College of the APOSTLES of the 1st Century AD. Catholics view their Church as the authority that enshrines the teachings of JESUS CHRIST and ensures that the faithful receive spiritual leadership and protection. (See CHRISTIANITY; REFORMATION)

ROMANESQUE ART A great ART movement that flourished in western Europe in the Middle Ages. The art of this period (the 11th and 12th centuries) was romantic and spiritual in its content. Its central themes were religious. It was also a style of ARCHITECTURE that was heavily influenced by Roman traditions, notably the use of rounded ARCHES.

ROMANIA A communist republic in southeastern EUROPE. Romania has 22,897 people (1984 est.) and an area of 237,500 sq km (91,699 sq miles). The capital is Bucharest. Farming is important, but manufactured goods are the main exports. Romania was created in 1861 from a union of Moldavia and Walachia. After World War II, a communist government took power. All industry is state-owned and the state farms own 90 percent of the land.

ROME Today the capital of ITALY, Rome was once the centre of a great empire. It is believed to have been founded in 733 BC, on the east bank of the River Tiber. At first Rome was a republic and ruled by elected consuls. As it grew more powerful it overran the whole Mediterranean. Julius CAESAR consolidated and governed the power of Rome until his assassination in 44 BC. After his death, his adopted son Augustus established the Roman Empire and made himself its first emperor.

The city flourished and the golden age of Roman culture began. Riches and tributes poured into the city and a great number of magnificent buildings and monuments were erected, the ruins of which still stand today. With the collapse of the empire in AD 476, the city declined. It was sacked during the wars of the Germans and the Byzantines, but regained its importance at the end of the 5th century when it became established as the centre of

◀ *The* Saturn V *rocket, developed for the Apollo missions, is the largest in the world. All that returns to Earth after a space mission is the little command module containing the astronauts (top right).*

ROMANIA: FACTS AND FIGURES
Official language: Romanian.
Largest cities: Bucharest (pop. 1,979,000), Brasov (334,000).
Currency: Leu.
Chief river: Danube.
Religion: Rumanian Orthodox Church, with a Roman Catholic minority.
The Transylvanian Alps and the Carpathian Mountains form a semi-circle through the centre of the country, separating the plains in the east and south from the Transylvanian plateau in the north-west.

ROME At the height of the Roman Empire in the 3rd century AD, the city of Rome had a population of a million. It was the largest city in the world. A thousand years later, Rome had declined to barely 35,000 inhabitants. Today, it is again a flourishing capital city. Over 2½ million people make their home there.

St Peter's in Rome is the world's largest church. It covers 2.5 ha (6 acres), is over 200 m (700 ft) long, and 140 m (450 ft) wide across the transepts. It is built on the site of an earlier church. The present St Peter's was begun in 1506 and finished in 1626. The great dome was designed by Michelangelo.

Rome is in about the same latitude as New York, but it does not often have snow or frost. The average temperature for the year is about 16°C (61°F). Its hottest month averages about 25°C (77°F), and its coldest about 7°C (44°F). Most of Rome's rainfall comes in winter.

▲ Roman houses and warehouses at Ostia, an ancient harbour town at the mouth of the River Tiber.

▼ A cutaway view of a Roman public bath. The water was heated by an underground furnace called a hypocaust. Each room was a different temperature — the hottest of all was the steam room.

▲ Wealthy Roman families had the walls of their rooms painted with detailed landscapes and fantasy scenes.

Christianity. (See BYZANTINE EMPIRE; PUNIC WARS; VATICAN CITY) ▷

ROOSEVELT, FRANKLIN Elected as the President of the USA four times, Roosevelt (1882–1945) led his country out of the great economic Depression of the 1930s, and through the difficult years of World War II.

ROSETTA STONE An ancient Egyptian stone on which a message was carved in three languages. It provided the key to deciphering HIEROGLYPHIC writing. The stone was found in Rosetta, Egypt, in 1799 by a soldier in Napoleon's invading army. Today it sits in the British Museum in London. ◁

ROTATION OF CROPS A system of planting different crops which are grown in rotation in the same field. This allows the soil to rest and be restored so that it can remain in use and give high yields.

ROTTERDAM Europe's busiest port and a major manufacturing city in the NETHERLANDS. Rotterdam has 1,025,000 people including its suburbs. A canal links it to the NORTH SEA.

ROULETTE A gambling game played in casinos involving a spinning wheel and a small ball. The wheel is divided into 37 numbered compartments. The one in which the ball comes to rest pays to the person who bet on it.

RUBBER Natural rubber comes from rubber trees in the form of a milky white liquid called *latex*. The inner bark of the tree is cut or 'tapped' and the latex oozes out. Today, most rubber is made synthetically from petroleum and coal products.

RUBENS, PETER PAUL A Flemish painter (1577–1640) who worked on huge canvases that were full of light and colour. He trained in Italy and did many paintings for the Spanish and French courts. He travelled to many countries as a diplomat, and was knighted in London in recognition of his talents.

RUHR A West GERMAN industrial and coal-mining region around the valley of the River Ruhr, a tributary of the RHINE. The Ruhr includes the cities of Essen, Dortmund and Duisberg. It became important in the mid-1800s, during the INDUSTRIAL REVOLUTION.

RUM A liquor that is distilled from the fermented products of sugar cane. It originated in the West Indies around 1650 and was called rumbullion at the time. Until 1970, British sailors in the Navy received a regular daily ration of rum.

RUSSIA The popular name for the Soviet Union or, officially, the Union of Soviet Socialist Republics (USSR). Russia is the world's largest country. It extends nearly half way around the world and is larger than all of South America. Over 60 languages are spoken within its boundaries. Because of its diverse population, the USSR is divided into 15 republics, the largest of which is the Russian Soviet Federal Socialist Republic (RSFSR), which is also called Russia. But, here, the term Russia refers to the entire country.

The European part of Russia, west of the Ural mountains and the Caspian Sea, covers only about one quarter of the nation. But over 70 per cent of the people live there. European Russia has much fertile farmland, especially in the UKRAINE. It also contains most of the nation's great industrial and mining centres, together with the two largest cities, MOSCOW and Leningrad. Asian Russia is less developed and vast areas are too cold or too dry to support more than a few people.

Russia has enormous natural resources. It leads the world in producing chromium, iron, lead and manganese, and is second only to the USA in coal, oil and natural gas production.

The country was ruled as an empire from the 1500s to 1917. Imperial Russia was renowned for its great literature, music, ballet, and so on. In 1917, the Bolshevik communists, under Vladimir Ilyich Lenin (1870–1924), seized power. Despite the destruction caused by World War I, the revolution and subsequent civil war, and by World War II, the communists have made Russia one of the world's super-powers. Progress has been especially marked in the state-owned manufacturing industries and in technology. Russia was the first nation to enter the Space Age, when *Sputnik I*, an artificial satellite, was launched into orbit around the Earth on October 4, 1957. The development of agriculture has been less successful. (See COMMUNISM) ▷

RUST A reddish-brown coating that forms on naked iron or steel if left out in wet. It is caused by a chemical process called OXIDATION which occurs when metal is in contact with air and moisture. A coat of oil, grease or paint can prevent rusting.

RUTHERFORD, ERNEST The famous New Zealand scientist (1871–1937) who helped to lay the foundation of modern nuclear physics. He developed the theory that explains the shape of ATOMS and their orbiting particles called electrons. He was awarded the NOBEL PRIZE for Chemistry in 1908. (See NUCLEAR ENERGY)

RYE A CEREAL grain that, with barley, is one of the hardiest grown. It is used to make flour and to distil whisky, gin, vodka and kvass.

ROSETTA STONE When the Rosetta Stone was found in 1799 no one had been able to decipher the ancient Egyptian hieroglyphics. One person whose imagination was stirred by the finding of the stone was a young Frenchman, Jean-Francois Champollion. Champollion knew that the Rosetta Stone's inscriptions were translations of one text, written to mark the crowning of Ptolemy V in 196 BC. He proceeded by working out the sound equivalents for all the hieroglyphs. But the key to the grammar of the language lay in his knowledge of Coptic, a language that survived only in the Coptic Church in Egypt. In 1822, 14 years after he began, Champollion finally completed his decoding of ancient Egyptian. His success was a triumph of deciphering, for hieroglyphics bore no relation to any modern alphabet.

RUSSIA: FACTS AND FIGURES
Official language: Russian is the native tongue of 60 per cent of the population, and is spoken as a second language by the rest.
Currency: Rouble.
Religion: Officially, religions are not encouraged, and it is estimated that 70 per cent of the population follow no religion. About 18 per cent of the people are Russian Orthodox, and there are small groups of Moslems, Roman Catholics and Jews.
Chief rivers: The Volga, Dnieper, Dniester, Don, Ob, Yenisey, Lena and Amur.
Largest cities: Moscow (pop. 8,537,000), Leningrad (4,827,000), Kiev (2,409,000), Tashkent (1,986,000).
Highest peak: Communism Peak (formerly Stalin Peak), in the Tadzhik SSR, 7495 m (24,590 ft).
Capital: Moscow.
Area: 22,402,000 sq km (8,649,460 sq miles).
Population: 275,000,000 (1984 est.).

Above: Shoppers mill around
the ornate gallery interior of
Moscow's largest department
store GUM. Above right: A very
high percentage of the work
force are women, particularly in
heavy industries. Centre: Chess
is a national pastime. Russia
produces world champions in
the game.

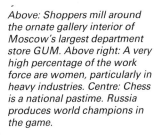

▲ Russian agriculture has been
considerably modernised, but
still relies on imported foods.

▶ Huge military parades are
held in Red Square, Moscow
on May Day (May 1).

S

SABLE A small, carnivorous mammal of the weasel family, valued for its dark fur. It belongs to Siberia, but because of hunting it is now rare in its wild state. A typical adult sable is about 51 cm (20 in) long, including its tail.

SABRE-TOOTHED TIGER A prehistoric carnivorous mammal. In its largest form it was bigger than a modern lion, and had two canine teeth 20 cm (8 in) long in its upper jaw, for slashing at its prey.

SACCHARIN A white crystalline substance, 300 times as sweet as sugar, discovered in 1879. It has no food value, and so is used in the diets of diabetics and slimmers.

SAFFRON A type of crocus. The dried *stigmas* of its flowers give us the powder called saffron. This is used as a flavouring in food and also as a yellow dye. It takes 100,000 flowers to make 1 kg (2 lb) of saffron.

SAGE A perennial herb belonging to the mint family. The leaves are used in cookery as a seasoning (e.g. in stuffing for poultry).

SAHARA The world's largest hot DESERT. The Sahara covers about 8.4 million sq km (3.2 million sq miles) in North AFRICA. The only settled people live around oases (see OASIS), although some nomads travel around with their camels. The Sahara contains oil and natural gas deposits. ▷

SAILING The use of wind to propel a boat. Once the chief form of power at sea, today it is

◀ *The sabre-toothed tiger was one of the early members of the cat family. It lived during the Pleistocene, nearly 2 million years ago. The tiger's name comes from its two long, curved canine teeth.*

▶ *An oasis in the Algerian Sahara. Oases occur where the water is near the surface. The existence of such luxurious growth as soon as water is present shows that the desert is basically very fertile.*

SAHARA The Sahara is almost as large as the United States. Its greatest length from east to west is greater than the distance from New York to San Francisco, and it varies from 1300 km (800 miles) to 2200 km (1400 miles) from north to south.

The average altitude of the Sahara is between 300 m (1000 ft) and 760 m (2500 ft) above sea-level.

Throughout the Ice Age, the Sahara was fertile grassland on which prehistoric men hunted elephant, buffalo and hippopotamus. Relics of these men include stone tools and rock carvings on walls of caves and sheltered cliffs. The Sahara became a desert about 2000 BC.

mainly a sport. *Fore-and-aft* rigging is almost universal: triangular sails mounted on booms and gaffs, in line with the boat's keel. (Many old types of vessel used square rigging: square sails hanging from spars at right angles to the keel.) This has affected many sailing techniques. With fore-and-aft sails, careful trimming (adjustment of the angle of the sails) allows sailing across the wind (reaching) to be faster than sailing with it (running). Also the manoeuvre of tacking into the wind becomes possible. (See BOATS AND BOATING)

SALAMANDER A type of small AMPHIBIAN. Salamanders must keep their skin moist and live in water, or wet climates. They can re-

▼*The fire salamander owes its name to an old legend that it could not be hurt by flames. No one knows quite how this strange myth first arose.*

▲*Sailing ships like this East Indiaman were sturdy and almost as well armed as warships. But they were slow, with a top speed of only 9 or 10 knots. They eventually gave way to the new, faster clippers.*

grow a lost limb or tail. Old legend believed that the 'fire salamander' could live through fire and even put it out.

SALIVARY GLANDS Three pairs of GLANDS in and near the mouth. The *saliva* they produce keeps the mouth moist and helps us soften and swallow food. It also contains ENZYMES which begin digesting CARBOHYDRATES. The sight or thought of food can stimulate the glands into action. They produce about 1.75 litres (3 pt) of fluid a day.

SALMON A fish prized as a food. It hatches in freshwater streams, makes its way to the sea, and remains there for about three years before migrating back upstream to its birthplace to breed. This difficult upstream migration can involve journeys of up to 5000 km (3100 miles) and spectacular leaping of rocks and small waterfalls.

SALT The substance sodium chloride, very important in the human diet and as a food preservative, and universally used as a flavouring. It is obtained from sea water and from deposits in rocks. (See SALTS)

SALTS Chemical substances that are compounds of an ACID and a base. For example, hydrochloric acid and caustic soda unite to give *sodium chloride* (common SALT) and water. Salts formed from hydrochloric acid are called chlorates; from sulphuric acid, sulphates; from nitric acid, nitrates; and so on. The Earth's crust contains many salts of natural origin. Salts are among the most important of chemical compounds, widely used in industry and agriculture.

SALVATION ARMY A Protestant body involved with social and religious work among the poor. Founded as the Christian Mission, it was given its present name soon after, in 1878. It is organized on military lines, with ranks and uniforms, and holds outdoor services. It has about 1½ million members throughout the world.

SAMURAI The members of the warrior caste of JAPAN from the 12th to 19th centuries. They followed a strict code of behaviour called *bushido* (the way of the warrior).

SAND This is made up of tiny grains of MINERALS – mainly QUARTZ – eroded from rocks. The grains have been carried (by water, wind or ice) into deposits in shallow water or low-lying land. Sand is an important building material, it is used in CEMENT, mortar and PLASTER.

SANDPIPER A group of birds in the snipe family, found on estuaries and seashores all over the world. The common sandpiper breeds in summer in Britain and most other European countries, but winters in warmer countries.

SANDSTONE ROCK formed from grains of sand and a binding material (such as clay, silica, iron or lime). It varies greatly in strength. Soft sandstone is sometimes crushed as a source of SAND. Hard sandstone makes a useful building and paving material.

▲One method of producing salt is by flooding coastal hollows, called salt pans, and letting the sun evaporate the water.

SAN FRANCISCO This beautiful city and seaport on the Pacific coast of the USA has 5,685,000 people, including its suburbs. It is in an earthquake zone, and was largely rebuilt after a great earthquake in 1906. ▷

SANITATION Measures taken to promote public health, by preventing the spread of germs. The most important are water purification and SEWAGE disposal. (These are the chief concern of sanitary engineers.) Others include food HYGIENE, refuse disposal, inspection of factory and other premises, and control of insects and rodents.

▼One of San Francisco's famous cable cars, built to climb the many steep hills of this beautiful harbour city.

SAN FRANCISCO On April 18, 1906, San Francisco was struck by a severe earthquake. The water system was damaged, and the fires that followed the earthquake raged for three days. The entire heart of the city was burned out and about 500 people were killed.

San Francisco's Chinese quarter is considered to be the largest Chinese settlement in the Western world, numbering about 50,000 people.

▲A Samurai warrior wore highly decorative armour, both to protect him and to make him appear more ferocious.

SATELLITES America's Space Shuttle, first flown in 1981, can lift about 150,000 kg (150 tonnes) of cargo and up to seven passengers into satellite orbit. After being launched by its two solid-fuel boosters, (which parachute back to Earth for recovery), the Shuttle reaches orbit. It ejects its payload at a rendezvous with the satellite or space station being serviced, and then glides back to Earth. The only piece of equipment which cannot be re-used is the large fuel tank, which is jettisoned. There are plans for some 560 Shuttle missions.

Isaac Newton was the first man to discuss the laws governing the flight of artificial satellites in his *Principia,* published in 1687. But it was not until October 1957 that the first artificial satellite was successfully put into orbit. This Russian satellite was named *Sputnik I.* It weighed only 84 kg (184 lb) and had a diameter of 58 cm (23 inches). There are now almost 5000 pieces of hardware orbiting the Earth as satellites.

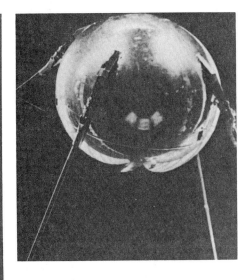

◀*The Space Age began on October 4, 1957, when the Soviet satellite* Sputnik 1 *was launched. Only 58 cm (23 in) across and weighing 84 kg (184 lb), it started the 'space race'.*

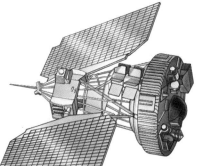

▼*A Nimbus weather satellite, one of a series of satellites designed to record and transmit details of weather conditions on a world-wide scale.*

SANSKRIT The literary language of ancient INDIA, dating from c. 1500 BC. It is the language of the sacred books of HINDUISM, and of works of poetry, philosophy, law, grammar and medicine. Several modern Indian languages are descended from it, including Hindi and Urdu.

SAPPHIRE A transparent blue stone, highly valued as a GEM. It is a form of aluminium oxide, and the hardest MINERAL known apart from diamond. The best sapphires come from Sri Lanka and Burma. Artificially-made ones are widely used in industry.

SARACEN Originally the Greek and Roman name for the people of north-west Arabia. In medieval Europe it was used to describe MOSLEMS, whether Arabs, Moors or Turks.

SARDINE A small fish of the HERRING family, familiar as a canned food. It lives in large shoals off the coasts of Europe. The main fishing grounds are around Spain and Brittany.

SARGASSO SEA An area of the North Atlantic Ocean, between the WEST INDIES and the AZORES, which is covered by seaweed. Its name comes from the Portuguese *sargaco* (seaweed).

SATELLITES A body that moves in ORBIT around another body is called a satellite. The Moon, for example, is the Earth's natural satellite. But most satellites are man-made devices launched into space by powerful ROCKETS. Manned spacecraft may become temporary satellites during space missions, but most artificial satellites are unmanned. Some carry scientific instruments for studying the stars and planets. Others send back information about the world's weather. Communications satellites enable radio, television and telephone signals to be transmitted around the curvature of the Earth. Signals beamed from one part of the Earth are received by the satellite and retransmitted to a receiving station. ◁

SATIRE A form of writing that sets out to ridicule a person or group, or society in

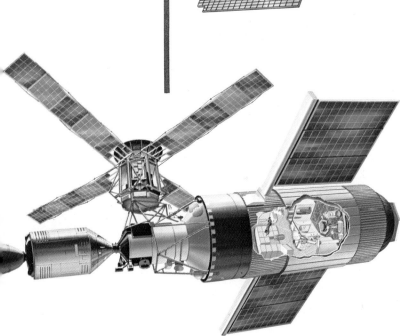

◀ Skylab, *the most ambitious and highly successful manned satellite project was launched from the United States in 1974. Three different crews took turns to man this orbiting space laboratory.*

When Voyager I passed by Saturn in November 1980, it discovered that there were many more bands to the planet's ring system than had been thought. It used to be thought that there were 5 or 6 distinct rings. Voyager showed that there are hundreds. It also discovered that the outer ring is braided in a most peculiar way. The rings are made of solid particles of ice and rock. It is thought that they may have been formed by a moon drifting too close to the planet and disintegrating under the force of Saturn's gravitational pull.

The density of Saturn is very low, possibly less that that of water.

Saturn's ninth moon, Phoebe, is the smallest, and is peculiar in that it revolves around the planet in a retrograde direction, travelling from east to west instead of from west to east as all the others do.

general – or even the whole human race! It makes fun of behaviour and beliefs that seem stupid, deluded or hypocritical. Satire dates back to the comedies of ancient Greece, and its tone may be gentle (as with the poet Alexander Pope) or cruel (as with Jonathan SWIFT). Modern satire pokes fun at leading politicians on television and radio as well as in magazines.

SATURN A large planet distinguished by the beautiful ring system around it. The rings probably consist of dust, rock, ice and frozen gas. Excluding these particles, Saturn has 15 known satellites. The planet has a cloudy atmosphere consisting mainly of hydrogen and helium. ▷

▲ *Saturn's rings are made up of pieces of ice rock and dust in narrow ringlets. They form a perfectly flat band 20 times the Earth's diameter.*

▼ *The surface of Titan, one of Saturn's moons. beneath its thick foggy atmosphere.*

314

SAUDI ARABIA: FACTS AND FIGURES
Official language: Arabic.
Currency: Riyal.
Largest cities: Riyadh (pop. 1,793,000), Jidda (983,300), Mecca (463,000) (1983 est.).
Religion: The vast proportion of the population is Sunni Moslem.
There are no permanent rivers.
Saudi Arabia is the world's third largest oil producer and it exports more than any other nation.
Saudi Arabia pumps nearly 8.5 million barrels of crude oil every day. Beneath its desert sands lie an estimated 170 thousand million barrels of reserves; just under a quarter of the world's total.

SAWFISH The sawfish is a member of the ray family. Its saw, which is sometimes two metres (6 ft) long, has about 25 pairs of long, sharp teeth along its edges. The female gives birth to about 20 living young. The fish slashes with a side-to-side motion among shoals of smaller creatures, but seldom attacks fish as big as itself.

▲ Millions of Moselms from around the world make their pilgrimage, called the Hajj, to Mecca, Muhammad's birthplace.

SAUDI ARABIA An oil-rich, desert nation in south-west ASIA, Saudi Arabia has 11,093,000 people (1984 est.). Area: 2,149,690 sq km (830,000 sq miles). Capital: Riyadh. ◁

SAVANNA The name for a tropical type of vegetation, consisting of grassland with scattered trees. The largest areas are in AFRICA. The *llanos* and *campos* of South America are other examples of savanna vegetation.

SAW A cutting tool, used by carpenters and builders. It has a metal blade with sharply-pointed teeth along one edge, and is used for cutting materials such as wood, metal and plastics. There are both handsaws and 'power saws' (run by electric or petrol motors).

SAWFISH A large fish found in shallow tropical waters. It has a long nose edged on both sides with sharp teeth, and it uses this to dig or slash for food. It can grow to over 7 metres (23 ft). ◁

SAXONS A group of barbarian tribes, originally from north Germany. Their name may have come from a short sword, the *seax*, which was their national weapon. In the 3rd and 4th centuries AD they spread south, and eventually invaded Roman territory. They often raided the coast of England, and in c. AD 450 they invaded it, together with the Angles and Jutes. They beat the Roman-British CELTS, and by AD 500 most of England was in ANGLO-SAXON hands (with the Saxons mainly in the south – Essex, Sussex and 'Wessex'). Their various local kingdoms lasted until the Danish (VIKING) invasions. Meanwhile on the Continent, Saxons had settled as far south as the coast of GAUL. But later, in AD 772–804,

CHARLEMAGNE made a series of expeditions that broke the power of the Continental Saxons. They were incorporated into his Frankish empire and forced to convert to Christianity.

SAXOPHONE A wind musical instrument invented by Adolphe Sax (1814–1894), and used in jazz bands and orchestras. It has a single reed, is made of brass, but is part of the woodwind family.

SCALES (FISH) Little plates of bony material, that cover the body surface of many FISH. They protect it from drying, and are covered with a mucus that stops water being absorbed into the fish's body.

SCALLOP A shellfish found all over the world, especially in shallow waters. It is mobile and it propels itself through the water by clapping together the two halves of its shell, so forcing out the water between them.

SCARAB A type of dung BEETLE, held sacred by the ancient Egyptians. It collects dung in small pellets, which it rolls underground, and

▼ There are 20,000 species of scarab beetle. This is the South African dung beetle.

▶ *The Van de Graff generator is one of science's spectacular achievements. It produces high voltages for bombarding atoms in nuclear accelerators. Electric charges produced by the generator are transferred to a dome at the top (out of the picture), where the charge can build up to several million volts. Here, the dome has been connected to a steel ring. A steel girder placed near the ring causes the generator to discharge, and bright streams of 'lightning' flow between the ring and the girder.*

in these it lays its eggs. The Egyptians regarded it as a symbol of eternal life and rebirth.

SCHIZOPHRENIA A serious mental illness. Some sufferers become totally inactive; others are violently emotional, or fearful of persecution. Hallucinations can occur. It may be due to a physical disorder affecting the brain. Treatment with drugs can give some help.

SCHOONER A SAILING vessel used for trading, developed in the American colonies in the 18th century. It had a specially streamlined hull, and all its sails were of fore-and-aft rigging.

SCIENCE Knowledge obtained through systematic observation, experiment and reasoning. The main branches of science are ASTRONOMY, BIOLOGY, CHEMISTRY, GEOLOGY, MEDICINE, PHYSICS and mathematics. All scientists try to find reasons for the observations they make. Having found a possible reason for some phenomenon, experiments are performed to test the theory. As a result, the theory may be rejected or may become established as a law of science. This is known as *scientific method*. But even so-called laws may after a while be disproved when new evidence is discovered. For example, we now know that NEWTON's laws of motion are not quite true. Although they are quite satisfactory for most purposes, they do not apply to bodies moving at extremely high speeds. EINSTEIN's *Special Theory of Relativity*, published in 1905, showed that changes were needed in Newton's laws for fast-moving bodies (see RELATIVITY). Established scientific laws should not, therefore, be regarded as the absolute truth. They are merely the best available explanation of observed events and may be changed later if the need arises.

SCIENCE-FICTION A well-known form of imaginative LITERATURE. Usually set in the future, it deals with such subjects as space travel, time travel, the arrival of space travellers on Earth, and what future societies will be like. Modern science-fiction dates from Jules Verne (1828–1905) and H. G. WELLS. It has become very popular since World War II.

SCORPION Scorpions may have been among the first land animals; their fossils date back to Silurian times. They give birth to live young, about seven at a time. These tiny creatures at once mount their mother's back and ride around in safety there for the first week of life. It is commonly believed that scorpions will commit suicide by stinging themselves to death if they are trapped by a ring of fire and can find no escape.

SCOTLAND Scotland extends over an area of 79,000 sq km (30,400 sq miles). It has a population of 5,146,000 including 186 inhabited coastal islands. Most Scots, however, live in a narrow belt in the south that is centred on Glasgow (pop. 762,000) and Edinburgh, the capital, (439,700). The highlands and the far north are very sparsely settled. Much of the land is rugged and mountainous. The highest peak in the United Kingdom, Ben Nevis (1343 m/4406 ft), lies here. The discovery of oil in the North Sea off the north-east of Scotland has brought new prosperity to the area.

SEA The biggest lakes in the world easily outrank the smallest seas in size; Lake Superior, for example, has an area of 82,350 sq km (31,800 sq miles). One of the smallest seas, the Dead Sea on the border of Israel and Jordan is only 70 km (45 miles) long. The main difference between seas and lakes is that the former are salty. The Dead Sea is the saltiest of all. It does not have any outlets, and its high rate of evaporation – 1 cm ($\frac{1}{2}$ inch) a day – means that incoming fresh water soon vanishes. It is too salty by far for any fish to live there – thus its name.

▲ *Scorpions are poisonous arachnids that live in hot deserts. When threatened, they raise their tails, which contain the poison, in an aggressive posture.*

SCORPION A creature related to the spider and found in hot countries. It varies in length from 1.2 to 15 cm ($\frac{1}{2}$ in–6 in) and has a poisonous sting in its tail. The poison of some scorpions can be fatal to humans. ◁

SCOTLAND Part of the United Kingdom of GREAT BRITAIN and Northern Ireland. Scotland has three main regions: the highlands in the north; the central lowlands; and the southern uplands. There are also many islands, including the Hebrides, Orkneys and Shetland Islands. Manufacturing and mining are the most valuable sectors of the economy. The chief industrial zones are in the central lowlands, especially around Scotland's largest city, GLASGOW. The central lowlands also contain the best farmland. Scotland united with England and Wales in 1707. But the Scots have retained their own traditions and culture and some Scots favour independence. ◁

SCOTLAND YARD The headquarters in London of the Metropolitan POLICE, and the national base of the CID (Criminal Investigation Department) and of criminal records. The name comes from the address of the original offices.

SCOTTISH TERRIER A breed of dog established in the 19th century. A small rough-haired terrier, good at hunting, and also known as the Aberdeen Terrier or Scottie.

SCOTT, WALTER Scottish poet and novelist (1771–1832). After early success as a poet, he wrote the long *Waverley* series of historical novels (*Waverley, Rob Roy, The Heart of Midlothian*, etc.). These gave him a reputation throughout Europe as a leader of the Romantic movement in literature.

SCULPTURE The making of three-dimensional shapes as works of ART. Traditionally, sculptors carved their works out of stone or (especially in tribal societies) out of wood. They usually chose living things as their subjects: human beings, gods and goddesses, animals. Almost all the ancient civilizations produced sculpture of this kind. In Europe the tradition began in Greece, and continued in Rome and RENAISSANCE Italy. In the 20th century there have been a number of new developments. Sculptors have been influenced by 'primitive' art, from Africa and the South Pacific. They have tried new materials: metal, glass, plastic, and even pieces of discarded 'junk'. And, influenced by ABSTRACT ART, some sculptors have concentrated on making abstract shapes (including *mobiles* – hanging collections of shapes that move in the wind). Important English sculptors of the 20th century include Jacob Epstein, Barbara Hepworth and Henry MOORE.

SCYTHE An agricultural implement, used for harvesting. It has a long curved cutting blade, and a long wooden handle with two short bars for the hands. It was developed by the Romans as an improvement on the earlier sickle.

SEA A part of an OCEAN or a large sea, such as the MEDITERRANEAN, or a large area of salt water, which may be completely enclosed by land, such as the CASPIAN SEA.

Seas influence the climates and the ways of life of people in coastal regions. This is partly

▼ *Half Figure, by the British sculptor Henry Moore, is one of several examples of his work on show in the Tate Gallery, London.*

Sea

SEA ANEMONE Sea anemones are polyps of the phylum *Coelenterata*, which includes the jellyfish. They belong to the class *Anthozoa*, and there are about a thousand species. The most brilliantly coloured species are found in tropical waters. When a small fish touches one of the sea anemone's tentacles it is paralyzed; the fish is then drawn into the creature's body cavity, where it is digested.

SEA HORSE Unusual among fish, it is the male sea horse that carries the eggs until they hatch. It keeps them in a pouch in its abdomen. They are placed there by the female. After 40-50 days, up to 200 young may hatch out.

because the sea heats and cools more slowly than the land or the air. Hence, coastal regions generally have fairly mild climates. Currents in seas also transport relatively warm water to cool regions and relatively cold water to warm regions. Onshore winds are warmed or cooled by the seawater and their effects are felt on land.

About $3\frac{1}{2}$ per cent of seawater consists of dissolved ELEMENTS. By far the commonest of these elements are sodium and chlorine, which together form salt. Because of the salt content of seawater, it is easier to swim in a sea than in a freshwater lake. ◁

▲ *A huge wave, caught at its peak, gives a dramatic impression of the power of the sea.*

▼ *The flower-like sea anemone is, in fact, a soft-bodied animal. At its centre is a mouth surrounded by stinging tentacles. The tentacles paralyze small sea creatures, which the anemone then pulls through its mouth into its stomach.*

SEA ANEMONE Small sea creature that lives in shallow water, attached to rocks or half-buried in the sea bed. It has a short tubular body, fringed at the mouth with tentacles with which it stings its prey (shrimps, tiny fish, etc). ▷

SEA HORSE A small fish found in many parts of the world. It has a delicate bony body,

SEAL Seals and sea lions are *pinnipeds* or fin-footed animals that spend almost all their lives in water, but have evolved legs with fins on the ends, rather than true fins, like the whales. They can shuffle around on shore, and breed on beaches in great colonies called rookeries. There are 32 species of pinnipeds, forming three groups: *Eared seals* (family Otariidae) include the sea lions and the fur seals, which are still hunted for their coats. *True seals* (Phocidae) have no outer ears. Their rear flippers are useless on land, so they pull themselves along with their front limbs. They include the common seal, harp seal, monk seal, and the sea elephants. *Walruses* (Odobenidae) have no external ears, but they do have hind limbs that can be used for locomotion when they come ashore. Their main distinguishing feature is the male's pair of long white tusks.

The longest mammal migration is by the Alaska seal *(Callorhinus ursinus)*, which does a round trip of 9600 km (6000 miles).

◄ In spring a seal cow has a single pup, like this young elephant seal. The mother is always able to find her pup, even though there are hundreds of pups in the rookery.

▼ Sea lions in the Galapagos Islands. These playful creatures have ears on the outside of their heads, while true seals do not.

with a horse-shaped head. It hangs upright in the water, often holding to seaweed stems with its tail. There are about fifty different species. ◁

SEAL A group of sea-mammals that live in coastal waters, especially near the Poles. They have flippers for swimming, eat fish, live in herds and communicate by 'barking'. They range in size from 1.4 metres (4½ ft) up to 6 metres (20 ft) for some elephant seals. Seals are still hunted for their meat, hides, blubber and bone, as they were by the ESKIMOS. ◁

SEA LION A sea-mammal very similar to the SEAL, but with fur over its body. (Also, unlike the true seal, it has ears.) Sea lions are hunted for their skins, and are also popular in zoos and circuses.

SEASONS Periods of the year with distinctive CLIMATES. Seasons occur because the Earth's axis is tilted at 23½°. Hence, as the Earth rotates around the Sun, the northern and southern hemispheres are, in turn, tilted towards and away from the Sun. For example, on June 21, the northern hemisphere is tilted

▼ The Earth's axis is not vertical, so each hemisphere is alternately tilted towards and away from the Sun, giving rise to the seasons.

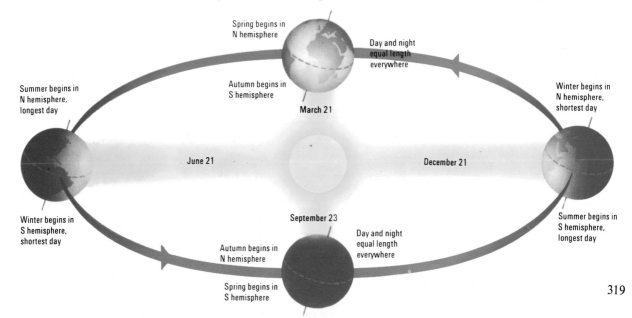

Spring begins in
N hemisphere

Day and night
equal length
everywhere

Autumn begins in
S hemisphere

March 21

Summer begins in
N hemisphere,
longest day

Winter begins in
N hemisphere,
shortest day

June 21

December 21

Winter begins in
S hemisphere,
shortest day

September 23

Summer begins in
S hemisphere,
longest day

Autumn begins in
N hemisphere

Day and night
equal length
everywhere

Spring begins in
S hemisphere

Sea

▶ *The prickly sea urchin is similar in build to a starfish, with spines, a mouth under its body and tube feet.*

towards the Sun, so that the Sun is directly overhead at the Tropic of Cancer. This is the summer solstice in the northern hemisphere, but it is winter in the southern hemisphere.

SEA URCHIN A class of small sea animals: INVERTEBRATES with brittle external skeletons. They are round, heart-shaped or shield-shaped, and covered with hard spines that help with movement and defence. Most live on rock surfaces. Some are edible.

SEAWEED Sea plants (algae) of many different types, growing from the high-tide mark on shore right down to depths of 183 metres (600 ft). Most are green, red or brown. Many kinds of seaweed are edible and some are valuable for fertilizing the soil. Others are used in making such varied products as iodine, ice cream, soap and glass. ▷

SEDIMENTARY ROCKS ROCKS made from fragments of older rocks (or sometimes from fragments of the shells of dead creatures, as with CHALK). The fragments settle as *sediment* on the sea bed before becoming stuck together as new rocks. Usually they are fused together by the weight of new sediment on top, but they can be cemented together by another material. Sedimentary rocks now cover most of the Earth's land surface. ▷

SEED At the centre of a seed is a tiny embryo of a new plant, complete with root, shoot, and one or more special leaves. Around this there is usually a stock of food cells for the embryo – the *endosperm*. Then there is the hard outside – the *testa*. Seeds are spread in many different ways: by the wind, by sticking to animals, by being eaten by birds, etc. But they need good conditions of soil, moisture and temperature before they will begin to grow (*germinate*). (See PLANTS)

SEAWEED Long ribbony strands of Pacific giant kelp may grow to 60 m (196 ft) and more in length. It can grow at a rate of more than 40 cm (16 inches) in a day. Usually seaweeds are anchored to rocks on the sea floor, though some types drift freely. The great mass of seaweed found in the Sargasso Sea has been carried there by currents and wind.

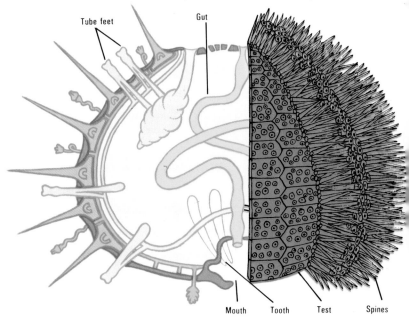

Tube feet — Gut — Mouth — Tooth — Test — Spines

▲ *This cutaway view of a sea urchin shows the hard 'test' that forms a case around the body. The spines project from the test, and a mouth equipped with powerful teeth opens beneath the centre of the body. The tube feet poke from tiny holes in the test.*

SEISMOGRAPH An instrument for recording the strength of EARTHQUAKES. It produces an ink line on a paper tape. Any ground tremors show up as jagged sections in the line. Separate tapes show horizontal and vertical movements.

SEQUOIA A group of North American CONIFERS. There are two types. The Californian redwood is the tallest known tree, reaching 111 metres (364 ft). The giant sequoia is the largest known tree, reaching over 10 metres (35 ft) diameter – and also one of the oldest (living more than 3500 years).

SEDIMENTARY ROCKS Given enough time, sediments may accumulate in beds that are thousands of metres thick. In the Grand Canyon in Arizona, the Colorado River has cut a course through sedimentary rocks to a depth of over 1.6 km (1 mile), exposing rocks that were laid down more than 600 million years ago.

SEED STRUCTURE

The two illustrations below show a dicotyledon seed (bean), and a mono-cotyledon seed (corn). Most of the space in a seed is taken up by its food store — the cotyledons in the bean; the endosperm in the corn.

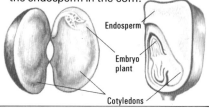

Endosperm

Embryo plant

Cotyledons

Great Pyramid

Pharos Lighthouse

Tomb of Mausolus

Hanging Gardens of Babylon

Statue of Zeus

Temple of Diana

lossus of Rhodes

▲ *The Seven Wonders of the Ancient World (left to right). Top: Pyramids of Egypt, the only 'wonder' that has survived; Pharos of Alexandria, a lighthouse near Alexandria in Egypt; Tomb (Mausoleum) of King Mausolus of Asia Minor (300 BC); Hanging Gardens of Babylon. Bottom: Colossus of Rhodes; Temple of Diana at Ephesus; Statue of Zeus.*

SEWING MACHINE In the first sewing machines a single continuous thread was used to form a chain stitch. The chain stitch was, however, slack and weak, and if the thread broke, the stitching came undone. So, in 1846, the American Elias Howe developed a lockstitch machine which was the basis for Isaac Singer's patent of 1851 and for all future machines.

Today's sewing machines use over 2000 different techniques for specific operations. Some of the processes have been automated so that several different sewing operations are now performed simultaneously.

SERUM The fluid part of the BLOOD – left as a clear yellowish liquid when the blood corpuscles and fibrin have been removed. It can be seen as the fluid inside blisters. It contains PROTEINS, sugars, fats and ANTIBODIES. Serum from immune people helps to cure victims of snake bite and provides protection against tetanus.

SEVEN WONDERS OF THE WORLD In classical times these were judged to be: the PYRAMIDS of Egypt; the 'hanging' (elevated) gardens of BABYLON; the temple of Diana at Ephesus; the statue of Zeus at Olympia; the mausoleum at Helicarnassus; the colossus of Rhodes (a statue); and the Pharos (lighthouse) at Alexandria. All were man-made.

SEVEN YEARS' WAR The war of 1756–63, with Britain and PRUSSIA fighting France, Austria and Russia. It came about through the colonial rivalry between Britain and France, and the European rivalry between Prussia and Austria. The victories of Wolfe at Quebec and Clive at Plassey resulted in the British conquest of Canada and the founding of her Indian empire. The success of Prussia, under Frederick II, made her the dominant power in central Europe.

SEWAGE Human waste, made up of URINE and *faeces*, with water to carry it. It is led through underground sewers to *sewage works*, where it is treated to remove BACTERIA. The purified sewage can be made into fertilizer, but it is usually just piped into rivers or into the sea. In some countries (e.g. China) human sewage is saved for use as manure on the land.

SEWING MACHINE A machine for sewing cloth, leather and other materials, mainly popularized by the American, Isaac Singer (1811–1875). There are home and industrial versions. Many are now powered by electric motor, rather than by hand or treadle (foot pedal). ◁

SEX Some very simple creatures reproduce by splitting in two (like the AMOEBA) or by growing a bud that develops into a new adult.

But most living things use sexual reproduction. This means that an offspring can only
be made by uniting male and female CELLS.
Sometimes male and female cells come from
different parts of the same adult – as with
many plants (see BIOLOGY). But usually they
are made by different male and female adults –
as with men and women. From ADOLESCENCE,
men begin to produce male cells (sperm) in
their *testes*, and women begin to produce
female cells (ova) in their *ovaries*. When a man
and a woman make love, in sexual intercourse, the sperm flow through the man's
penis into the woman's body. If one of the
sperm unites with an ovum, the resulting
combination of cells begins to grow into a new
human being inside the woman. She is then
said to be *pregnant*, and if all goes well she
gives birth to a baby nine months later. (See
REPRODUCTION)

SEXTANT An optical instrument used to
measure the angles of heavenly bodies above
the horizon. Finding the angle of the Sun
above the horizon enables a ship's navigator
to work out his LATITUDE.

SHAKESPEARE, WILLIAM The greatest
English dramatist (1564–1616). Born in
Stratford-on-Avon, he married Anne Hathaway in 1582. He is said to have joined a group
of actors, and from 1589 was an established
playwright in London. He wrote a great

▲ *Sharks sometimes carry 'passengers' —
remoras use a sucker on their heads to attach
themselves to the shark's body. The shark gives
the remora transport to its feeding grounds
and the remoras eat the shark's leftovers.*

number of plays including comedies (such as
Much Ado about Nothing and *As You Like It*);
tragedies (*Macbeth, Hamlet, King Lear*); English histories (*Henry IV, Richard III*); classical
histories (*Anthony and Cleopatra*) and the
final 'fantasies' (*The Tempest, A Winter's
Tale*). He also wrote poems including *Venus
and Adonis* and the *Sonnets*. ▷

SHAMROCK The name for some types of
CLOVER. St Patrick was supposed to have used
one in his preachings, to illustrate the doctrine
of the Holy Trinity. Because of this it has
become the badge of Ireland.

SHANGHAI The greatest Chinese port,
handling about 50 per cent of her overseas
trade, and CHINA's largest city. Shanghai's
population is 11,940,000 (1982). The port is
sited by the Chang Jiang estuary. It was
developed by European powers, when they
began trading with China in the 19th century.

SHARK A type of fish with a cartilage
(gristle) skeleton. They range from the 1.5–
metre (5–ft) dogfish to the 15–metre (50–ft)
whale shark. Some feed on PLANKTON, but

SHAKESPEARE, WILLIAM Shakespeare has probably been quoted
more often and more widely than
any other writer. The *Oxford Dictionary of Quotations* devotes
more pages to his words even
than to quotations from the *Bible*.

Very little is known about Shakespeare's life, but some dates are
known: In 1582 a licence was
issued for his marriage to Anne
Hathaway of Shottery; in 1583, a
daughter, Susanna, was born; in
1585, twins, Hamnet and Judith,
were born; in 1592 came the first
reference to Shakespeare as an
actor and playwright, written by
Robert Greene on his deathbed· in
1593 *Venus and Adonis* was published; in 1596, his son Hamnet
died; in 1596, his father was
granted a coat-of-arms; in 1597,
he purchased New Place in Stratford; in 1603, he and his players
were honoured by James I; in
1607, his daughter Susanna married; in 1609, the *Sonnets* were
published; in 1616, his daughter
Judith married; and in 1616, he
died on April 23 and was buried in
Stratford on April 25.

SHARK Sharks will eat almost
anything that is available. One
Great White caught in Australia
had its stomach opened to reveal
a chunk of horsemeat, a paint-
scraper, a sack, the forequarters
of a dog, the hindquarters of a pig,
half a ham and eight legs of mut-
ton.

wooden raft dugout canoe (c. 6000 BC) Egyptian boat with sail (c. 1500 BC) Viking longboat (c. 1000 AD) Spanish galleon (16th century)

SHEEP By far the most common animals in Australia are sheep. Over 150 million are grazed, roughly 10 sheep for every Australian man, woman and child.

SHELLAC Large quantities of shellac were once used in the making of gramophone records. Nowadays, synthetic vinyl is used.

SHIPS The first known ship was built about 4500 years ago in Egypt. It was a sea-going vessel of about 30 metres (100 ft) in length. The first known steamboat made a 15-minute trip on the river Saône in France in 1783. The first steam passenger ship was Robert Fulton's *Clermont,* which began operating in the United States in 1807. The first known iron ship was the British *Vulcan,* a sailing vessel built in 1818. The first iron steamship was the British *Aaron Manby,* in service in 1821. (Steel ships came about 60 years later.) The first steamer to cross the Atlantic using entirely steam power was the British *Sirius* in 1838. The first propeller-driven ship was the *Robert F. Stockton.* Its screw propeller was developed by John Ericsson, a Swede in England, and put to commercial use by him in the United States in 1839. The longest passenger liner ever built was the *France,* later renamed the *Norway.* She was built in 1961 with a total length of 315.66 m (1036 ft).

many are CARNIVORES and a few (such as the Great White shark) will attack man. Sharks are found all over the world, but are more common in tropical waters. In some areas they are hunted as a sport. ◁

SHEEP A common farm MAMMAL (originally found wild in parts of Asia, Africa and America). Sheep can be kept on poor land, or grazed in rotation with crops on good soil. They give meat and wool, and the milk and skin may also be used. In medieval England, sheep were a major source of wealth. Today they are reared in large numbers in Australia, New Zealand and South Africa. ◁

SHELLAC A product made from a resin produced by female lac insects. The resin is found on the twigs of trees in India and the Far East. Shellac is left after a wax and a red dye have been extracted. It is used as a protective finish on wood and plaster. ◁

SHELLS A shell is the tough protective layer on the outside of some animals and around the seeds of some plants. Animals with shells include tortoises, turtles, lobsters, crabs, and especially MOLLUSCS (snails and shellfish). Their shells are built up in layers from the inside. The layers are formed by a fluid produced by special glands. Mollusc shells can be *univalve* (spiral) or *bivalve* (two halves hinged together). Plants whose seeds have shells include the various nuts.

SHERRY A white wine which has been fortified with brandy. It has an alcohol content of 16-22 per cent. True sherry comes only from the Cadiz province of Spain, but imitations are produced in South Africa, Cyprus and elsewhere.

SHIPS The earliest ships were probably those built by Mediterranean peoples – the Egyptians, MINOANS and Phoenicians (see PHOENICIA). By Roman times there were two main types: long narrow war GALLEYS, powered mainly by oarsmen; and broad-beamed cargo sailing ships. Later, VIKING longships were the first to be designed for rougher seas. In medieval times the rigging of sails was improved, and the first triangular fore-and-aft sails appeared on the Mediterranean (see SAILING). By the Renaissance multi-decked

▲*For thousands of years people have used shells as decoration, often stringing them into necklaces and bracelets.*

ships had developed (see GALLEONS), and the first permanent battle fleets (see NAVY). Over the next 300 years, wooden sailing ships became highly specialized. This led to the warships of Napoleonic times, fast trading SCHOONERS and passenger packet-ships, and finally the clipper ships of the tea and wool trades.

In the 19th century ship design was revolutionized by the use of steam power and iron hulls. By 1840 iron had largely replaced wood, while the first Atlantic crossing powered entirely by steam was made in 1838. Also by 1850 the PROPELLER had taken over from the paddle wheels used by the first steam ships. The great age of the tramp steamer and the ocean liner followed. In the 20th century, DIESEL engines displaced steam. Modern cargo vessels include giant oil tankers, dry bulk

▼*Early boats were rafts and dugout canoes. The Egyptians put sails on to their reed boats and made use of wind power. Sailing ships developed over centuries, reaching their peak with the clipper ships of the 19th century, before steam power took over and metal hulls replaced wooden ones. Today, the great liners are like floating hotels.*

Clipper ship
(c. 1850)

Paddlesteamer
(c. 1840)

Luxury liner
(1967)

carriers and container ships. Among warships the BATTLESHIP has given way to the aircraft carrier and more recently, the nuclear SUB-MARINE. ◁

SHOT PUT An OLYMPIC event. It involves throwing a heavy metal ball as far as possible with one hand. The ball weighs 7.3 kg (16 lb) for men, 4 kg (8 lb, 13 oz) for women. The throw is made from inside a marked circle.

SHRIMP A small sea-creature – one of the CRUSTACEA. It is about 5 cm (2 in) long, lives on the sea bed, and spends much of the time buried in the sand. Shrimps are edible, and are commercially important in Japan and the southern United States.

SIBERIA A vast region in north-east RUSSIA, Siberia covers about 13,468,000 sq km (5,200,000 sq miles). Much of Siberia is bleak and thinly-populated. But, in recent years, many industries have been established there.

SICILY A large, rugged Italian island in the MEDITERRANEAN. Sicily has an area of 25,708 sq km (9926 sq miles) and 5,000,000 people (1984). The capital is Palermo. ▷

SILICON After oxygen, silicon is the most common ELEMENT in the Earth's crust. It is found in QUARTZ, which is a form of the compound silica (silicon dioxide). Silicon also occurs in compounds called *silicates*. The element is used in steels and other alloys. Pure crystalline silicon is used to make TRANSISTORS and complex electronic micro-circuits.

SILK A natural fibre, from the cocoon of the silkworm moth. One cocoon gives a strand of silk 610–915 metres (2000–3000 ft) long. Four strands twisted together make a usable thread. The larva of the moth feeds only on white mulberry leaves, and spins its cocoon about a month after hatching. Fifty per cent of the world's silk output is Japanese; China and India make most of the rest. ▷

SILVER A precious metal used for JEWEL-LERY and once used for COINS. It is found as the free metal as well as in the form of compounds. Light-sensitive silver compounds are used in photography. And silver nitrate is used in silver plating and to 'silver' mirrors. Nuggets of silver weighing over a tonne have been found in Mexico.

SINGAPORE A prosperous republic in south-east ASIA. Singapore has 2,529,000

▲ Silver has long been one of Man's favourite decorative metals. This silver plate from Persia dates from about AD 200. The image of the mounted archer could be finely detailed because silver is soft and easily worked.

▶ The Egyptian King Psusennes of the Twenty-first Dynasty (about 1000 BC) was buried in this silver coffin made in his image. The casket is solid silver except for the gold cobra on the king's forehead.

SICILY This island, the largest in the Mediterranean, contains one of the few active volcanoes in Europe. Mount Etna, soaring to 3222m (10,700 ft) in eastern Sicily, last erupted in 1950.

SILK The first mention of silk in history is in 2600 BC when the emperor of China had his wife investigate to see if silkworm fibres could be made into cloth. It takes 3000 silkworm cocoons to make a single pound of silk thread.

SINGAPORE: FACTS AND FIGURES
Official languages: Malay, Chinese, Tamil and English.
Currency: Dollar.
People: About 74 per cent of the population is Chinese, 14 per cent Malays, and 8 per cent Indians and Pakistanis.
Religions: The Chinese are mainly Buddhist, the Malays and Pakistanis are Moslems, and the Indians are Hindus.
Largest city: The city of Singapore has a population of 2,517,000.
Formerly a British colony, Singapore was part of Malaysia between 1963 and 1965.

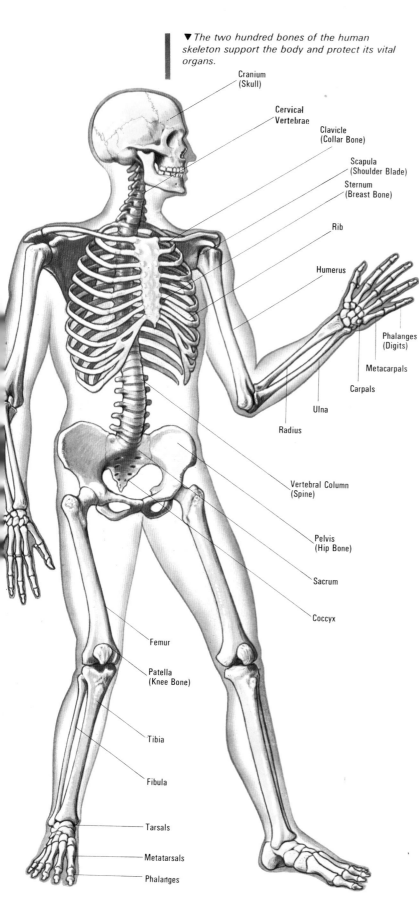

▼ *The two hundred bones of the human skeleton support the body and protect its vital organs.*

Cranium (Skull)

Cervical Vertebrae

Clavicle (Collar Bone)

Scapula (Shoulder Blade)

Sternum (Breast Bone)

Rib

Humerus

Phalanges (Digits)

Metacarpals

Carpals

Ulna

Radius

Vertebral Column (Spine)

Pelvis (Hip Bone)

Sacrum

Coccyx

Femur

Patella (Knee Bone)

Tibia

Fibula

Tarsals

Metatarsals

Phalanges

people (1984 est.) and an area of 581 sq km (244 sq miles). The capital is also called Singapore. It is a busy port. ◁

SINUS The sinuses are four cavities in the bone of the skull: one in the forehead, one just behind and below this, one in the cheeks and one behind the NOSE. They all connect with the nasal cavity (the inside of the nose). The sinuses help to warm, moisten and filter the air we breathe in. Infection of the sinuses (sinusitis) is quite common during colds, but is seldom serious.

SIPHON A tube for transferring liquid from one vessel to a lower one. Once it is full of liquid, the difference in pressure at the ends of the tube ensures a continuous flow.

SI UNITS Units used in the *Système International d'Unités*, a system derived from the metre-kilogram-second system (M.K.S.). SI has now replaced the centimetre-gram-second (c.g.s.) and the foot-pound-second (f.p.s.) systems for scientific and many other purposes.

SKELETON The bones of the body. Some INVERTEBRATES (e.g. crabs) have an external (outside) skeleton. But VERTEBRATES, such as man, have an internal (inside) skeleton. The human skeleton has over 200 bones. Together they make up the skull and SPINAL COLUMN; the breastbone and ribs; the pelvis (hip); and the limbs. This gives a rigid framework for the flesh, anchor-points for the MUSCLES, and protection for the internal organs. The bones of the skeleton also manufacture blood cells, and store calcium and phosphorus. (See BONE)

SKIING The art of travelling across snow on skis. These are long narrow pieces of wood, plastic or metal, which are attached to the feet. They curve upwards at the front, and slide easily over the snow. Hand-held pointed sticks are used to help push the skier along. Although still a way of travelling in snow-bound country, skiing today is mainly a sport.

SKIN The skin acts as a barrier to infection, and prevents the body losing water and heat too rapidly. It has two layers. The outer part (*epidermis*) is a protective layer of dead cells. It is constantly being rubbed away and replaced from beneath. The inner part (*dermis*) contains blood and lymph vessels, nerve ends, hair roots, sweat glands and sebaceous (fat) glands. The skin will normally heal itself when cut, but it can be troubled by infection and ALLERGY.

SKIN DIVING Going underwater without a full DIVING suit and breathing line. Strictly, a skin diver uses just a face mask, fins, and a snorkel tube; he must come back to the surface to breathe. But the term is also used for *scuba* divers, who carry a self-contained breathing apparatus working from compressed-air tanks. (See AQUALUNG)

SKUNK A North American MAMMAL, related to the BADGER. It is bushy-tailed and about the size of a cat. The skunk is notorious for being able to spray out a foul-smelling fluid, to defend itself. The spray comes from special glands and can reach up to 3.5 metres (12 ft).

SKY What we see when we look up is a section of the Earth's ATMOSPHERE, with the immensity of space beyond. The blue colour is due to the atmosphere, which splits up the Sun's light like a SPECTRUM, and scatters the blue part of the light more than the rest. Without an atmosphere, the sky would look black, except for the Sun, Moon and stars. ▷

SKYSCRAPER A very tall building of many floors, built around a framework of steel. The style developed in the United States in the late 19th century, especially in NEW YORK and Chicago where building land was expensive.

SLAVERY The condition of people who are not only forced to work for others but are also owned by them like a piece of property. The ancient Greeks and Romans kept slaves. Although the slave trade was prohibited by British law as early as 1807, it continued in parts of the world as late as the 1970s. (See CIVIL WAR [US]) ▷

SLAVS The most numerous ethnic and linguistic group of people in Europe. The Slavs were a tribe that migrated from Asia in the 2nd and 3rd centuries BC. Today, they are mostly found in eastern and south-eastern Europe. They speak many different, but related, tongues. Those nationalities of Slavic origin include Russian, Ukrainian, Polish, Czech, Slovak, Serb, Bulgarian, Macedonian and Croat.

SLEEP A temporary state of unconsciousness during which time the mind and body are refreshed. The energy lost during the day is made up during sleep. Breathing and heartbeat slow down and the body temperature drops. A newborn baby sleeps almost 24 hours a day. An adult needs only seven to eight hours of sleep a day. (See DREAMS)

SLOTH A tree-dwelling MAMMAL found in tropical America. It is a sluggish creature that

▶ The typical posture of a three-toed sloth. It spends almost all its time hanging upside-down in a tree, hardly moving at all.

◀ The Empire State Building in New York City was for some time the world's highest building. The solid bedrock of Manhattan Island allows such skyscrapers to be built safely.

sleeps all day, often hanging upside down, and moves very slowly when it roams at night.

SLUG A crawling land MOLLUSC, related to the SNAIL but with little or no shell. It eats vegetable matter, and is regarded as a pest in the garden.

SMALLPOX One of the world's most dreaded diseases, it is often fatal. Those who don't die are left with pockmark scars on their skin. It has been almost stamped out by vaccination. (See VACCINE)

SMELL One of the five human senses. Like TASTE, it uses nerve endings that respond to chemicals (rather than to pressure, heat or light). But while taste responds to solid and liquid chemicals, smell responds to gases and vapours. In higher animals the smell receptors (olfactory nerves) are set in mucous membrane in the NOSE. Some animals use smell to find food and avoid enemies, and to recognize

SKY The blue colour of the sky changes when there are more dust or water particles in the air. The colour becomes paler and whiter. By contrast, the setting Sun makes the sky seem red. Its rays have farther to travel through the atmosphere. Blue light becomes so scattered that only the red remains to be seen.

SLAVERY In Moslem countries in former times, slaves were sometimes recruited as soldiers and as government officials. In some cases, as with the Mamluks in Egypt, they became so powerful in these posts that they were able to take control from their former masters.

Garden snail

Strawberry snail

Roman snail

Kentish snail

Round-mouth snail

Garlic grass snail

Brown-lipped snail

Two-toothed door snail

Great ram's horn

SNAIL Most snails feed on plants, but a few are carnivores. They eat earthworms.

SNAKE Snakes are deaf. They have no ears comparable to ours. On the other hand, they are able to taste their surroundings in a way we cannot. Their flickering tongues pick up tiny particles from the air and carry them to sensing pits in the roof of their mouth.

▲ *Snails have two pairs of tentacles, usually with eyes at the tips of the longer one.*

their own home territory. In some moths, the males can smell the chemicals released by females at a distance of several miles. The human sense of smell is much weaker, but it can still detect tiny quantities of a scent, and identify over 10,000 different odours.

SMELTING The process by which metal is separated from its ORE by heating to a high temperature. The earliest metal known to have been smelted is COPPER, in about 5000 BC.

SMOG A word combining 'smoke' and 'fog' and used to describe the heavily polluted air often found around cities and factories. At its worst, it can lead to death. In 1909, more than 1000 smog deaths occurred in Glasgow. (See AIR POLLUTION)

SNAIL A gastropod MOLLUSC that glides on a flat body and carries a shell on its back into which it can retreat. The largest, the giant land snail of the tropics, has a shell up to 20 cm (8 in) long. ◁

SNAKE A REPTILE without eyelids or legs. It has a long narrow body covered with a scaly skin which it sheds several times a year. Snakes move by wriggling along the ground or swinging their body in loops. They swallow their food whole – small mammals, lizards, birds, eggs, insects and fish. Some have poison glands which release deadly VENOM into hollow or grooved FANGS which they inject into their victims when they bite. The biggest

snakes grow to some 10 metres (33 ft) in length. Snakes live all over the world, except for the Polar regions, New Zealand, Hawaii and Ireland, where, it is said, Saint Patrick drove them out. ◁

SNOOKER A game played on a billiards table with 15 red balls, 6 coloured balls and a white cue ball. The object of the game is to sink the balls into the table's pockets in a certain order so as to score points.

SNOW In its frozen state in the air, water may turn into crystalline flakes of snow before falling to Earth. Snowflakes are six-sided crystals. They have a regular geometry but there are thousands of variations in their detail.

SNOWY MOUNTAINS SCHEME An IRRIGATION and HYDROELECTRIC POWER scheme in south-east Australia, in which the headwaters of the south-flowing Snowy River are diverted into the east-flowing MURRAY and Murrumbidgee rivers, providing water for an arid region.

SOAPS AND DETERGENTS Organic chemical compounds used to remove dirt and grease. When dissolved in water, soaps and detergents form chains of ATOMS. One end of each chain attaches readily to dirt or grease particles, making them relatively easy to remove. Soaps form insoluble grey scum when dissolved in hard water. But this problem has been largely overcome in modern detergents.

SOCCER See FOOTBALL

Woodland and mixed grasses   Tall bunch grass   Short grass and shrubs

A

B

C

PRAIRIE SOIL   **CHERNOZEM SOIL**   **CHESTNUT BROWN SOIL**

SOLUTION There is no limit to the proportions in which two liquids or solids may be mixed, but a liquid can hold only a limited proportion of a particular solid. When it has dissolved as much as possible, the solution is said to be 'saturated'. In certain circumstances a solvent may be induced to take up even more of the solid, making a 'supersaturated' solution. But this kind of solution is unstable, and generally a small vibration or the addition of a solid impurity will cause the extra solute to be thrown out.

SOCRATES A Greek philosopher (c. 470 –399 BC) who laid the foundations of much of western thinking. His method was to take nothing for granted but to ask endless questions in the search for the truth. His teachings were unacceptable to the people of Athens and he was sentenced to death by drinking the poison hemlock.

SODIUM A silvery-grey metal (Na), so soft that it can be cut with a knife. It is the sixth most abundant ELEMENT in the Earth's crust. One of the most widespread sodium compounds is the chloride, common salt (NaCl). Sodium belongs to the group of alkali metals, so-called because they react with water to form hydroxides which are strong alkalis. The bicarbonate is an ingredient of baking powder, and the hydroxide is used in the making of soaps, detergents, aluminium and textiles.

SOIL The layer of ground in which plants grow. It is usually between 15–23 cm (6–9 in) deep. Beneath it is the subsoil and below that rock. Soil acts as a reservoir for water and nutrients. It also absorbs and breaks down the waste that plants accumulate near their roots.

SOLAR ENERGY Energy radiated by the Sun can be collected and put to use. It can be converted to electricity by photoelectric cells. Artificial satellites use this technique to provide the electricity they require. Solar energy is also used for domestic heating. Usually the radiant energy is made to heat water, which is then stored in an insulated tank. The heat is

▲ Three different kinds of soil that occur in areas of increasing dryness. Soils have three layers, or 'horizons'. The **A** horizon contains grains of rock and organic materials. The **B** horizon often contains materials dissolved from the A horizon. The **C** horizon overlies the bedrock.

▼ The world's largest solar furnace is in the French Pyrenees. The curved, polished mirror focuses the Sun's rays to produce temperatures of around 3000°C.

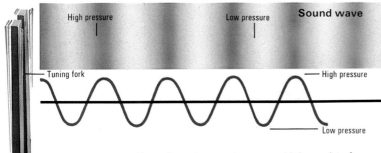

▲ *Sound moves in waves which consist of bands of high or low pressure. The bands of pressure strike the ear drums making them vibrate. Signal are then sent via nerves to the brain which distinguishes them as sound.*

SOUND The speed of sound changes with the type of material through which it travels. Thus from a mile in five seconds in air, the speed increases in water to a mile in one second and in iron rails to about a mile in a third of a second.

released, when required, through a system of hot-water radiators.

SOLAR SYSTEM The SUN and the system of PLANETS and other bodies orbiting around it. These include the COMETS and ASTEROIDS. All the orbiting bodies in the solar system move in nearly the same plane. This is why the Sun, Moon and planets all appear to move across the same part of the sky. This zone, called the zodiac, is divided into 12 regions, which are named after CONSTELLATIONS.

SOLE A flatfish found in temperate and tropical seas, and occasionally in freshwater. It lives on the seabed and has two small eyes, both on the upper side of its head.

SOLUTION A mixture produced when one substance (the solute) dissolves in a liquid (the solvent). Solid solutions, which include AL-LOYS, are solids containing two or more thoroughly mixed substances. ◁

SONAR An abbreviation for SOund NAvigation and Ranging, equipment using SOUND waves to detect submerged objects or find the depth of water under a ship. Sounds are transmitted from the bottom of a ship and are reflected back by objects under the water. The echoes are picked up and displayed on the screen of a CATHODE-RAY TUBE. The images produced indicate the time taken for the sound echoes to bounce back, and so the depth of the objects or the sea-bottom.

SONIC BOOM A disturbing bang, like an explosion, heard on the ground when an aircraft flies faster than the speed of sound. The boom is caused by shock waves set up by the aircraft. Sometimes the waves are powerful enough to shatter windows.

SOUND A sensation experienced when certain vibrations are received by the EAR. Sounds are produced by vibrating objects, such as guitar strings, the column of air in an organ pipe, bells or a shattering pane of glass. When a body vibrates, it compresses and stretches the surrounding air. The pressure variations produced pass through the air in wavelike fashion, rather like vibrations passing along a long, slack spiral spring. Each part of the air (or spring) moves to and fro, transmitting the vibrations to the next part. The frequency of a sound, expressed in hertz (Hz) is the number of waves produced each second. Sound frequencies range from about 20Hz to about 20,000 Hz. The wavelength of a sound is the distance between the tops of adjacent waves.

▼ *This diagram shows the main belt of the minor planets as well as a few which have more unusual orbits.*

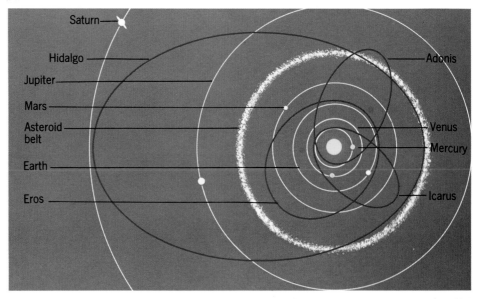

Sound travels at a velocity of 332 metres (1120 feet) per second in air at 0°C (32°F). The frequency (**f**), wavelength (λ) and velocity (**v**) are related by the equation $\mathbf{v} = \mathbf{f}\lambda$. ◁

SOUND REPRODUCTION In radios, record players and tape recorders, sound is reproduced on loudspeakers. They convert electrical signals, matching the SOUND waves, into physical vibrations. These vibrations resemble those produced by the objects that made the original sounds. Hi-fidelity equipment can reproduce sound with life-like clarity.

SOUTH AFRICA A republic in southern AFRICA, in which black Africans form 70.2 per cent of the population; Europeans, 17.5 per cent; Coloureds, 9.4 per cent; and Asians, 2.9 per cent. The Europeans control the political and business life of the nation and the government operates a controversial racial policy, called 'separate development' or *apartheid*. This involves allocating 13 per cent of the country for black African occupation, while the Europeans retain the rest.

Farming is important and there are vast mineral deposits, but manufacturing is the leading activity. The first European settlement was established in 1652. Modern South Africa came into being in 1910 when the four provinces, Cape Province, Natal, Orange Free State and Transvaal were united. ▷

SOUTH AFRICAN WAR See BOER WAR

SOUTH AMERICA The fourth largest continent, South America contains 13 nations. Spanish is an official language in nine of them, but Portuguese is the official language of the largest nation, BRAZIL. Dutch is used in Surinam; English in Guyana; and French in French Guiana. The language differences reflect the colonial history of the continent. The original people were South American Indians, including the INCAS. The population now consists of Indians and the descendants of European settlers and African slaves. Many are of mixed origin.

The continent includes tropical areas in the north and cool temperate zones in the south. South America contains the world's largest rain forest, in the AMAZON basin, the lofty ANDES MOUNTAINS in the west, and the Atacama desert, the driest place on Earth. There are also vast grasslands, where livestock-rearing is important. Most people are poor farmers, but mining is important in BOLIVIA (tin), CHILE (copper), VENEZUELA (oil), and other places. Manufacturing is increasing, particularly in ARGENTINA and Brazil.

SOYBEAN A bushy plant, native to Asia but now grown all over the world. The soybean is

▲ This modern recording studio contains a wide range of equipment. Sounds can be modified or backed with other instruments.

▲ At a recording session, the music is recorded on tape and the tone, volume and sound mix are achieved by electronic controls.

▼ A market in La Paz, Bolivia. La Paz is Bolivia's seat of government, but the city of Sucre is the official capital.

SOUTH AFRICA: FACTS AND FIGURES
Official languages: Afrikaans and English.
Currency: Rand.
Religion: Chiefly Protestant.
Chief rivers: Orange and Limpopo.
Largest cities: Johannesburg (pop. 1,726,000), Cape Town (1,491,000), Durban (961,000), Pretoria (739,000).
Population: 31,586,000 (1984 est.).
Area: 1,221,037 sq km (472,000 sq
Capitals: Cape Town (legislative), Pretoria (administrative), and Bloemfontein (judicial).
South Africa became a republic and formally withdrew from the British Commonwealth in 1961.

SOUTH AMERICA

Barranquilla
Caracas
Maracaibo
Orinoco
Medellin
VENEZUELA
Georgetown
Paramaribo
Cayenne
Llanos
GUYANA
SURINAM
FRENCH
GUIANA
Bogotá
ATLANTIC OCEAN
Cali
COLOMBIA

Quito
ECUADOR
Manáus
Belém
GALAPAGOS IS.
Amazon
Guayaquil
Fortaleza
PERU
Selvas
Chiclayo
Recife
Trujillo
BRAZIL

Callão
Salvador
Lima
Cuzco
BOLIVIA
La Paz
ANDES
Brasilia
Cochabamba
Oruro
Paraná
Sucre
PACIFIC OCEAN
MOUNTAINS
Brazilian Highlands
PARAGUAY
Rio de Janeiro
Gran Chaco
São Paulo
Asunción
ATACAMA DESERT
Pôrto Alegre
Córdoba
Mt Aconcagua
URUGUAY
Valparaiso
Rosario
Montevideo
Santiago
Buenos Aires
ARGENTINA
La Plata
CHILE
PAMPAS
Colorado
Bahia Blanca
ATLANTIC OCEAN

■ Capital Cities

0   500   1000 miles

0   500   1000   1500 kilometres

Chubut

Patagonia

FALKLAND IS.

**Tierra
del Fuego**

Cape Horn

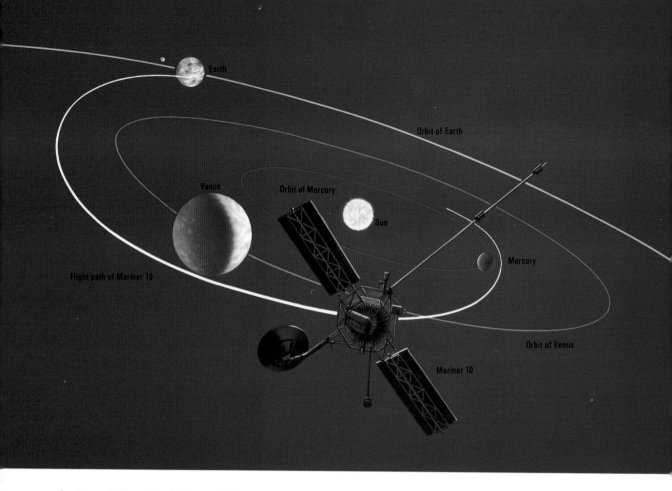

grown for its seeds (beans), which are rich in PROTEIN and are of great commercial value. Oil from the seeds is used for margarine, soaps, enamels and varnishes. Soybean meal provides a base for livestock feeds and a protein concentrate. ▷

SPACE EXPLORATION On October 4, 1957, the Russians sent the first artificial SATELLITE into orbit around the Earth. Called *Sputnik I*, it measured only 58 cm (23 in) in diameter, and weighed a mere 84 kg (184 lb). America's first satellite, launched the following year, was smaller still. But, from these beginnings, the world's two major powers quickly developed a wealth of expertise in space travel and exploration.

The first space traveller to orbit the Earth was a dog called Laika. It was launched in the Russian satellite *Sputnik II* only a month after the flight of *Sputnik I.* Information from instruments connected to the dog was transmitted back to Earth. This enabled scientists to see how the animal stood up to the stresses of launching and the weightless conditions in

▲ *The flight trajectory of* Mariner 10, *the first spacecraft to make use of the gravitational pull of one planet — Venus — in order to reach another — Mercury. It was* Mariner 10 *which transmitted the first close-up photographs of Mercury, in March 1974. Twin solar-cell panels supplied the electricity to power the instruments.*

SOYBEAN Most soybeans are made into oil, about one-fifth of the entire bean being oil. Over 90 per cent of the oil goes into edible products such as cooking oils, margarine, and shortening.

▶ *The Earth, photographed by the* Apollo 17 *astronauts in December 1972. Practically the entire African continent is visible, as is the Antarctic ice cap.*

▲An excellent view of the Apollo 17 command and service module, showing the exposed instrument bay, the SIM. Apollo 17 was the longest Moon mission to date, lasting 12½ days.

▲Astronaut and geologist Harrison Schmitt collects Moon samples beside a massive boulder at the Taurus-Littrow landing site. In the foreground is the lunar rover.

space. Experiments like this paved the way for the first manned satellite. On April 12, 1961, the Russian Yuri GAGARIN became the first man to orbit the Earth. His spacecraft, *Vostok I*, returned safely after making one complete circuit. The first American in orbit was John GLENN, who made three circuits in his *Friendship 7* spacecraft on February 20, 1962.

During the next few years, developments in space technology were rapid. Both the Russians and Americans launched numerous

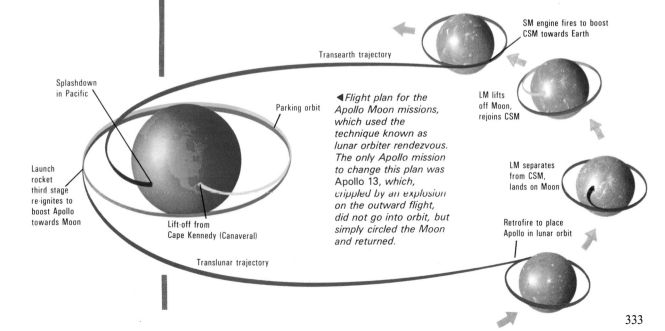

SM engine fires to boost CSM towards Earth

Transearth trajectory

LM lifts off Moon, rejoins CSM

Splashdown in Pacific

Parking orbit

◀Flight plan for the Apollo Moon missions, which used the technique known as lunar orbiter rendezvous. The only Apollo mission to change this plan was Apollo 13, which, crippled by an explosion on the outward flight, did not go into orbit, but simply circled the Moon and returned.

LM separates from CSM, lands on Moon

Launch rocket third stage re-ignites to boost Apollo towards Moon

Lift-off from Cape Kennedy (Canaveral)

Retrofire to place Apollo in lunar orbit

Translunar trajectory

◀ *The second man on the Moon, Edwin Aldrin, photographed by the first, Neil Armstrong, in July 1969. The lunar module and Armstrong are reflected in Aldrin's visor.*

and collected samples of rock and soil for analysis back on Earth. The Russians obtained samples from the Moon too, but achieved this using unmanned probes.

In 1976, two American *Viking* probes soft-landed on Mars. Experiments were carried out on soil samples and radioed back to Earth. Scientists had hoped to discover if any form of life was present, but the results were inconclusive. In 1981 the Americans successfully launched the first Space Shuttle *Columbia*, but in 1986 the shuttle *Challenger* exploded on lift-off, killing its crew. The programme was suspended for many months. (see ASTRONAUTS). ▷

SPAIN A monarchy which occupies most of the Iberian peninsula in south-western EUROPE. It also includes the BALEARIC ISLANDS in the Mediterranean and the CANARY ISLANDS in the Atlantic. Mainland Spain consists mostly of a tableland, between 600 and 900 metres (2000–3000 ft) above sea-level. Mountain ranges include the Sierra Nevada and the PYRENEES.

Farming is the chief industry. Barley, fruits, grapes, olives, potatoes, wheat and vegetables are grown. Livestock, especially sheep, cattle, pigs and goats, are also important. Coal, iron, zinc and other minerals are mined. Manufacturing is important in the cities, such as MADRID and Barcelona. Tourism is a major industry and, every year, 30 million visitors enjoy Spain's sunny climate, beaches, beautiful cities and ancient castles.

Spanish (Castilian) is the official language. There are also three other important languages: Catalan, BASQUE, and Galician. Many people who speak these languages want a greater degree of independence for their regions.

Spain has been conquered many times by such peoples as the Carthaginians, Phoenicians, Romans, Visigoths and Moors. Christian rule was restored in Spain in the 1200s. In the 1500s Spain became the world's

SPACE EXPLORATION The reports from *Voyager 1*, the spacecraft that dipped to within 278,000 km (172,400 miles) of Jupiter in March, 1979, show that the planet is a ball of seething gas and liquid swirling violently around a core of rock. After a 640 million km (400 million mile) journey across space, the tiny craft turned its 11 cameras onto Jupiter and spotted dozens of churning storms. Most are about 9600 km (6000 miles) across but the biggest, the Great Red Spot; is a shifting storm over three times the size of the Earth's diameter.

SPAIN: FACTS AND FIGURES
Area: 504,782 sq km (195,000 sq miles).
Population: 38,333,000 (1984 est.).
Capital: Madrid.
Official language: Spanish.
Religion: Roman Catholic.
Currency: Peseta.
Chief rivers: Ebro, Guadalquivir, Duero.
Largest cities: Madrid (pop. 3,188,000), Barcelona (1,755,000), Valencia (752,000), Seville (654,000).
In 1977 the people of Spain voted in the first free election in 41 years.

manned and unmanned Earth satellites. And unmanned craft called space probes were sent to investigate the Moon, Mars and Venus. The Moon, being relatively close to the Earth, was of particular interest. Early Moon probes were designed to crash onto the Moon, sending back close-up pictures during descent. By 1966, Russia and America had both developed techniques for soft landing probes on the lunar surface. For the first time, pictures and other information were transmitted direct from the Moon. And other probes were sent into orbit around the Moon to photograph the side always hidden from us on Earth. The Russians then concentrated on developing more and more complicated unmanned space probes.

Meanwhile, the Americans pursued a more difficult task – sending men on a return trip to the Moon. Success came in July 1969, when astronaut Neil Armstrong became the first person to walk on the Moon. This historic achievement was watched by about 600 million television viewers. On the Moon, Armstrong and fellow astronaut Edwin Aldrin carried out various scientific experiments

▶ *A magnificent hilltop castle overlooking a village in the Spanish province of Almería. Architecture in Spain owes much to the Islamic influence of the Moors.*

SPARTA The citizens of Sparta were famous for the importance they placed on military skills, on discipline and on obedience. They were superb professional soldiers who spent their entire life in regular training. In 480 BC, King Leonides of Sparta and a heroic band of 300 men managed to hold a huge army of 180,000 Persians and allies at bay for three days at the narrow mountain pass of Thermopylae before being surprised from behind and wiped out.

SPEAR In the Middle Ages, a Knight who rode into the lands of another lord carrying his spear point forward was declaring his intentions to be hostile. But if he carried his spear slung backwards over his shoulder, it was a gesture of peace.

SPECIFIC GRAVITY Mercury is the densest of all liquids at normal temperatures. It has a specific gravity of 13.6. Lead can float on it like cork on water.

▲ A statue of a running girl, thought to be Spartan. Spartan girls trained as athletes to prepare them to be mothers of warriors.

▼ Spears, like the ones carried by warriors on this Greek vase, are one of man's oldest weapons.

◀ The Roman theatre at Meridia in Spain. The Romans extended their culture, including their love of theatre, to all parts of their vast empire.

most powerful nation. It acquired a great overseas empire, which it lost in the 1800s and 1900s. Spain suffered a bitter civil war in the 1930s and it became a dictatorship led by General Francisco Franco (1892–1975). However, after Franco's death, a constitutional monarchy was established, with Juan Carlos I as king. ◁

SPARROW A small seed-eating bird found all over the world. It is noisy, bold and has a quick, darting flight. There are three kinds, the house sparrow, the tree sparrow and the hedge sparrow.

SPARTA The capital of Laconia in ancient GREECE, founded in the 9th century BC. Sparta was a city dedicated to the military arts. Its ruling class forged it into a powerful state which rivalled Athens, but its power declined when ALEXANDER THE GREAT conquered all of Greece. ◁

SPEAR A long-handled weapon with a sharp weighted head that is used for throwing or thrusting. It was first used for hunting and fighting in the STONE AGE. BRONZE AGE people smelted the first metal spearheads. ◁

SPECIFIC GRAVITY The DENSITY of a substance compared with the density of water at 4°C (39°F). If, for example, a substance is twice as dense as water, then it has a specific gravity (S.G.) of 2. ◁

▼ A group of house sparrows splash about in a pool of water. Bathing is usually followed by preening and oiling.

SPECTROSCOPE An instrument used to split LIGHT into a SPECTRUM of its component colours. By using a spectroscope to analyze starlight, astronomers can find out which elements are present in the STAR. For each element emits its own distinct pattern of light.

SPECTRUM The whole range of ELECTRO-MAGNETIC WAVES is known as the electromagnetic spectrum. And any mixture of electromagnetic waves can be separated into a spectrum of its component frequencies. White light, for example, can be split up by a PRISM to form separate coloured bands. Rainbows are seen when raindrops split up sunlight in this way.

SPHERE A solid figure traced out when a semi-circle rotates about the diameter joining its ends. The volume of a sphere of radius r is $\frac{4}{3}\pi r^3$, and its surface area is $4\pi r^2$.

SPHINX In MYTHOLOGY, a fabulous monster of the ancient world with a winged lion's body and a human or animal head. Sphinx statues have been found in Egypt, Greece, Crete and Turkey. The Egyptian sphinx heads were usually images of gods or kings. Those in Greece were of young women. The Greek sphinx sat by the wayside, it was told, asking riddles of travellers, whom she devoured if they could not answer correctly.   ▷

SPICE An aromatic vegetable product used to improve the flavour of food and drink. Spices may be the leaves, berries, nuts, seeds or bark of a plant.

SPIDER The name given to 30,000 species of animals that are all *arachnids*. Spiders have eight legs and two main body parts. They all have VENOM glands but most are not poisonous to humans. Spiders make silk in the spinnerets found on the underside of their abdomen. They use it to build webs and traps in which their prey is caught. The largest, the giant bird-eating spider of South America, has a legspan of up to 25 cm (10 in). (See TARANTULA)   ▷

SPIDER MONKEY A large, lanky and very agile forest dweller of Central and South America. They roam in bands, living mainly on fruit and occasionally birds and insects. Their name comes from their long, spider-like limbs.

SPINACH A leafy green vegetable with a very high iron and vitamin A and C content. Both the leaves and the seed stalks are cooked and eaten.

▶ *A spider's web is covered with a sticky liquid which securely traps small insects.*

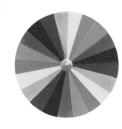

THE COLOUR SPECTRUM

A spectrum of white light is made up of the colours of the rainbow. If a piece of card is painted with bands of these colours (top) and the card is then spun very fast, the colours appear to the eye to mix together and give white (bottom). This shows that 'white' light is actually a mixture of colours.

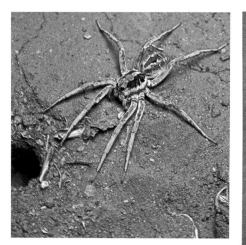

▲ *A wolf spider by its burrow. These desert spiders rely on speed and strength to catch and kill their victims.*

SPHINX The riddle of the Greek sphinx was the following: 'What walks on four feet in the morning, on two feet at noon and on three feet in the evening?' Oedipus, the only person to guess correctly, answered that it was Man. As a baby he crawled on all fours, as an adult he walked upright and as an old man he used a stick to help himself along.

SPIDER Very small spiders are known as 'money spiders' because they are thought to be a sign that good fortune will come to anyone who finds them on their clothes.

SPINAL COLUMN There are 33 vertebrae in the spinal column, but some of them grow together. The first vertebra, the *atlas*, supports the skull. All the vertebrae are held in place by ligaments. The top end of the column is the *cervical* region (the neck), below that is the larger *thoracic* region (the chest), below that is the *lumbar* region (the lower back), then comes the *sacral* region (the hips), and the column ends in the *cocygeal* or tailbone.

SPLEEN In past times it was believed that a person's character could be traced to different parts of the body. Someone given to bad moods, ill-humour and melancholy was said to be ruled by his spleen.

SPONGE The natural sponges used in baths are the soft skeletons of recently living animals. Once sponges have been collected from the seabed, the inner jelly-like flesh is left to dry and decay. Then the sponges are beaten to clean out the remains and hung to air and dry.

SPRUCE Most newspaper is made from spruce wood; the most common being that of Black, White and Red spruce trees. Most Christmas trees are Norway spruce.

SPINAL COLUMN This is a flexible column of bone running from the neck to the lower small of the back in man, or to the tail in animals. It is made up of a chain of small bones called VERTEBRAE. It protects the spinal cord of nerves and stiffens the body as well as being the anchor for many muscles. It is also known as the backbone. (See NERVOUS SYSTEM; SKELETON) ◁

SPINET A musical instrument of the HARPSICHORD family. Either triangular or wing-shaped, it is played by a keyboard. The wires are plucked by a quill instead of being struck, as with a PIANO.

SPLEEN The main organ of the body for filtering the blood. The spleen is found on the left side of the abdominal cavity, just below the diaphragm. It is about the size of a fist. (See diagram in DIGESTION) ◁

SPONGE One of the simplest forms of ocean animal life, sponges are INVERTEBRATES. There are about 5000 species in the sea. Their basic form is plant-like and for a long time they were believed to be plants. The skeletons can hold an enormous amount of water. The most common kind of sponge is the type widely used in homes. ◁

SPORE The part of a flowerless PLANT that is responsible for its reproduction. Spores are spread by the wind. They can remain dormant for many years before sprouting into a new plant.

SPRINGS Mechanical devices, usually metal, that store energy when distorted. In

◀ *The spruce is one of the* gymnosperms, *an important plant group that provides about 80 per cent of the world's timber.*

CLOCKS and watches, a spiral spring stores energy when wound up. This energy is used to turn the mechanism, when the spring slowly unwinds. In some vehicles, springs separate the body from the wheels. On passing over a bump, energy that would otherwise give the body a severe jolt is absorbed by the springs, thus ensuring a smoother ride.

SPRUCE A member of the PINE family of trees. Spruce trees grow as far north as the Arctic Circle. They can be identified by their downward hanging cones (those of FIR trees grow upward). ◁

SQUASH A game played by two players, with racquets and a small black rubber ball, inside a four-walled court. It is based on a 19th century British game called 'rackets'.

▼ *These are the tube sponges from the Caribbean. Sponges are attached to the sea bottom, on rocky crevices and overhangs. They expel waste and reproductive products through the hole at the top. Their walls are perforated and they take in food through holes in the walls.*

SQUID A sea MOLLUSC related to the OC-TOPUS. It has a slender body and a square-shaped head and ten long 'arms'. Squids move through the water by JET PROPULSION. They take in water through their gills and squirt it out through a forward pointing funnel, so that they glide through the sea backwards. If frightened, they shoot a cloud of inky liquid into the water. The giant squid of the Atlantic Ocean may grow up to 15 metres (50 ft) and is said to have attacked ships.

SQUIRREL A rodent with a soft, bushy tail that is found all over the world. Red and grey squirrels are the most common kinds. They live in holes in trees or on the ground and feed mainly on seeds and nuts.   ▷

SRI LANKA Formerly called Ceylon, Sri Lanka is a pear-shaped island republic off the south-east tip of India. It has 15,606,000 people (1984 est.). Its area of 65,610 sq km (25,332 sq miles). The capital is Colombo. The chief products are tea and rubber.   ▷

STAINED GLASS Coloured pieces of GLASS that are used in making ornamental windows. True stained glass, used in the 14th and 15th centuries, was made by adding metal oxides while the glass was in the melting pot. In the 16th century designs were painted onto the glass in enamel paints and then heated. The pieces of glass were put together in a many coloured pattern or scene and held with strips of lead. The first stained glass was made by the Romans.

▲ Women pick tea on a Sri Lanka tea plantation. Plantation agriculture was introduced by Europeans who colonized and settled in tropical areas. Today, many plantations are operated by the local people.

▼ The grey squirrel is native to North America. It was imported to Britain, where its numbers have grown so large it has almost replaced the native red squirrel.

▼ The ten 'arms' of the squid are lined with disc-shaped suckers. With its excellent eyesight, the squid is a fearsome predator, often hunting in schools.

SQUIRREL In the tropics of Asia there is a type of squirrel that is able to 'fly'. It has a large loose flap of skin along each side that stretches from its fore legs to its hind legs. When it leaps, the flaps open out and it sails like a tiny glider from branch to branch.

SRI LANKA: FACTS AND FIGURES
Official language: Sinhala. English is the second language.
Currency: Rupee.
Largest cities: Columbo (pop. 1,412,000), Jaffina (121,000), Kandy (107,000).
Sri Lanka (formerly Ceylon) became independent of Britain in 1948, with dominion status within the Commonwealth. In 1972 it became a republic within the Commonwealth.

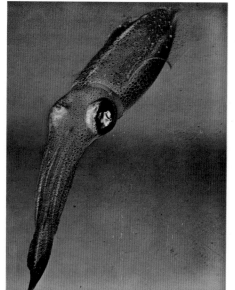

◀ *Stalactites hanging from the roofs of limestone caves are impressive and beautiful features. They are fairly fragile and often break off before they get very long.*

▼ *Tens of thousands of stars make up this globular cluster known as Hercules star cluster M13. The weak, yellow stars are about 10,000 million years old.*

has been paid. The price of postage depends on the weight of the item, the distance it travels and the way it goes. The hobby of collecting stamps is known as *philately*. (See POST OFFICE) ◁

STARCH An important FOOD substance formed in plants. Starch is abundant in CEREALS and root crops, such as potatoes. The body breaks down starch, a CARBOHYDRATE, into various sugars, which provide energy. In industry, starch is used to stiffen textiles.

STARFISH A sea-living INVERTEBRATE that has five or more arms around a disc-like body. It can lose an arm and grow another to replace it. The largest starfish grow up to 60 cm (2 ft).

STARLING A bird with glossy black feathers and a long bill for catching insects. Starlings also do great damage to crops of fruit and grain.

STARS Heavenly bodies giving off vast amounts of light or other radiant energy

STAMPS Stamp collecting is a very popular hobby. With so many collectors bidding for them, old and rare stamps have become especially valuable. One of the most expensive single stamps ever to be sold was a one cent issue from British Guinea in 1856. It changed hands for $280,000 in 1970.

STARS From Earth only 7000 stars can be seen in the night sky by naked eye. All are in the Milky Way. With powerful telescopes, millions of others can be made out. In all, there are at least 100,000 million stars in our galaxy.

The nearest star to Earth (other than our own Sun) is Proxima Centauri. It is 4.2 light years away.

STALACTITE AND STALAGMITE Stalactites are long, icicle-like stone features which hang from the roof of a LIMESTONE cave. They consist of calcite deposited from dripping water. Stalagmites are similar, but they grow upwards from the cave floor.

STALIN, JOSEPH The head of the Communist Party and the leader of the Soviet Union for a quarter of a century until his death (1879–1953). He was infamous for the ruthless way he ran the country, but was successful at defeating Germany in World War II and made his nation a major world power. (See COMMUNISM)

STAMPS Sticky labels that are put onto letters and parcels to show that their postage

▶ *The sunstar is a starfish that lives around coasts and in rock pools. Starfish, like other echinoderms ('hedgehog skins'), walk with a tube foot system.*

produced by nuclear fusion reactions (see ATOMIC ENERGY). Some stars are thousands of times greater than the Earth. The Sun is a relatively small star called a dwarf. BINARY STARS consist of two separate stars orbiting around a common point. PULSARS are stars that emit pulses of energy. ◁

STATISTICS The science of collecting figures, studying them and drawing conclusions about their meaning. For example, a bus company might count how many people travel by bus to work each day to help decide what kind of buses and how many to run on its routes.

STEAM ENGINES When water is heated and turns into steam, it expands to about 1600 times its former size. Steam engines use the energy of expanding steam to drive a piston in a cylinder. This to-and-fro motion can be turned into a rotary motion to turn wheels. Steam can also be used to turn the blades of a TURBINE, and this turning motion can be used to propel ships or turn the shafts of an electric GENERATOR.

STEEL IRON with a carbon content of up to about 1.5 per cent. The carbon is present in the form of a compound called *cementite* (iron carbide). Adding carbon to iron increases the strength and hardness of the metal, and these qualities are adjusted by a heating process called tempering. Steel is made by first removing carbon and other impurities from molten iron or scrap steel and then adding an accurately measured amount of carbon. Stainless steel and other steel ALLOYS are made by adding carbon and metals such as CHROMIUM, MANGANESE and TUNGSTEN.

STEEPLECHASE A horse or foot race over a course with obstacles such as fences or ditches. In the past, the goal of such a race was a church steeple. ▷

STEROIDS Chemical compounds (see ELEMENTS AND COMPOUNDS) found naturally in the body and which affect the way people grow and develop. Synthetic steroids are sometimes taken by people, such as athletes, who wish to build up their strength.

STETHOSCOPE A medical instrument used by doctors for listening to the sounds made by the human body. It was invented in 1816, and at first was simply a wooden cylinder with holes. ▷

STOCK EXCHANGE A marketplace for buying and selling stocks, shares and bonds that are issued by business companies or by governments. The prices for which they are traded rise and fall depending on the demand.

▲ A steel casting emerging from an annealing furnace. Annealing is a form of heat treatment which relieves stresses in the metal, making it less brittle.

▼An automatic rolling mill for sheet steel. A red hot, thick steel slab enters at one end and is progressively reduced in thickness by a series of rollers.

▼The French physician René Laënnec invented the stethoscope about 1816. Below, Laënnec's stethoscope (top) beside a modern one used today.

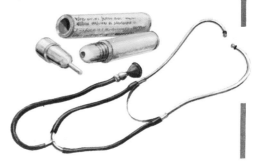

STEEPLECHASE This kind of race is said to have started in Ireland in 1803 when a high-spirited party of fox hunters raced each other in a straight line over fields and hedges to a distant church steeple.

STETHOSCOPE The word 'stethoscope' comes from the Greek 'chest, I examine'. A doctor used to put his ear on his patient's chest to listen to the heart and lungs. But in fat patients it was difficult to hear distinctly enough to diagnose accurately. René Laënnec, a French doctor, solved the problem in 1816 by using first a roll of paper and then a wooden cylinder. He put one end of the roll to the patient's chest, the other to his ear. This was the first stethoscope.

◄ Residents play ice hockey in front of their modern apartments in Stockholm, Sweden's capital.

▼ The stomach is just one key organ that aids the digestion of food. Food is churned up in the stomach for some time before it passes on to the large intestine in small amounts.

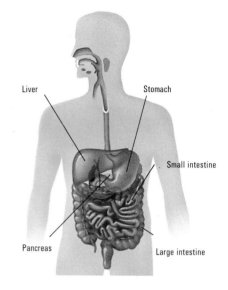

Liver
Stomach
Small intestine
Pancreas
Large intestine

If many people want to buy a share, its price goes up. If few do, its price drops until buyers are found.

STOCKHOLM Capital of SWEDEN. Stockholm stands on a group of islands on the Baltic Sea coast. This handsome industrial city has a population of 1,420,000.

STOMACH A main organ for digesting food. In human beings, the stomach is a pear-shaped sac. At one end it is connected by the *oesophagus* to the mouth. The other end is joined to the small INTESTINE. The stomach breaks down food by kneading it with digestive juices. It turns it into a semi-fluid mass called *chyme*. (See DIGESTION)

▼ Mammoth hunters of the Stone Age. Such groups made their clothes and tents from animal hides.

STONE AGE A period in the history of mankind when weapons and tools were mostly made of stone. They consisted of crude axes, knives and spears that were chipped into shape. Stone Age tools over two million years

old have been found. In some isolated parts of the world, people using stone tools still exist. The Stone Age was followed by periods when people began using metals. The first of these was the BRONZE AGE.

STONEHENGE A prehistoric circle of standing stones on Salisbury Plain in Wiltshire, England. It was probably constructed as a place of worship to the Sun and Moon, between 1800 BC and 1400 BC. An outer ditch and bank surrounds a ring of stones, with an inner horseshoe of stones and an altar at the centre. ▷

STORK A long-legged wading bird with a long neck, large bill, broad wings and short tail. It may grow up to 1.5 metres (5 ft) tall. Storks are voiceless but can make a noise by clattering their bills when excited.

STRAWBERRY A small plant belonging to the rose family, with white flowers and delicious red fruit. Strawberries grow wild in fields and are also raised on farms.

STRONTIUM A reactive metallic ELEMENT found as various compounds including the carbonate (strontianite) and the sulphate (celestine). The metal is extracted by ELECTROLYSIS. Because it reacts strongly with air or water, it is stored under oil. The radioactive ISOTOPE strontium-90, present in the fall-out from nuclear bombs, is a health hazard as it is readily absorbed by the body. Strontium compounds are used in fireworks to give a crimson flame.

STUARTS The Stuarts were a Scottish family who inherited the crown of Scotland in 1371, and the crown of England in 1603. The first Stuart king was Robert II. The last Stuart to claim the British throne was Bonnie Prince Charlie who died without heirs in 1788. The family had a history of sudden death. Seven Stuart kings came to the throne as minors, their parents having died suddenly.

STURGEON A toothless, sharklike fish that grows up to 3½ metres (12 ft). It is valued for its roe (eggs) which is sold under the name of CAVIAR. There are about 25 different species of fresh and saltwater sturgeon.

▲ The megalithic circle at Stonehenge is thought to have been a place of worship, but it may also have been an astronomical observatory for predicting solar and lunar eclipses and for establishing an accurate calendar.

▼ White storks migrate from Africa to Europe every spring, where they will often build their nests on the roofs of houses.

STONEHENGE The largest of the main Stonehenge upright stones weighs about 50 tonnes. These giant stones, archaeologists believe, were dragged some 32 km (20 miles) from near Avebury on the Marlborough Downs. The stones were carefully dressed, and erected in a circle, with lintels on top, each lintel weighing about 7 tonnes. The lintels were held to the uprights with mortise and tenon joints, and to each other with tongue and groove joints. This part of the construction took place about the 15th century BC.

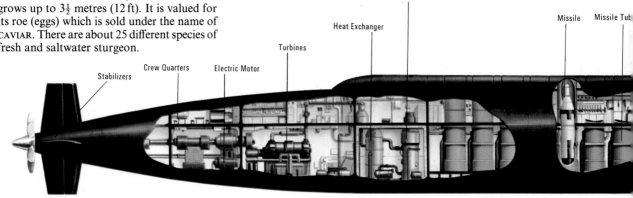

Nuclear Reactor

Heat Exchanger

Missile   Missile Tub

Turbines

Crew Quarters   Electric Motor

Stabilizers

SUBMARINE The first submarine ever to operate successfully was a tiny leather-covered vessel that was propelled by rowing. It had 12 oars. It could operate up to a depth of 5-6 m (16-19 ft) and was reinforced with iron against the water pressure. It was first demonstrated in the Thames in 1620 during the reign of King James I. It could stay underwater for up to several hours.

▶ A submarine is made to sink or float by filling the space between the inner and outer hulls with more or less water.

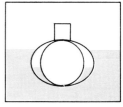

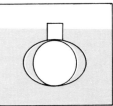

SUDAN: FACTS AND FIGURES
Official language: Arabic.
Currency: Sudanese pound.
Religion: Islam.
Largest cities: Omdurman (pop. 526,000), Khartoum (476,000).
Chief rivers: The Blue Nile and the White Nile join at Khartoum.
Sudan was proclaimed an independent republic in 1956.

▲ "America's new armoured torpedo boat, the Holland," 1898. Used by the British and American navies, the Holland submarine had petrol engines for surface running and an electric motor for use when submerged.

SUBMARINE A SHIP that can operate on the surface and under the water. It is powered by either batteries, diesel engines or by nuclear fuelled reactors. Submarines equipped with guns and TORPEDOES were used very effectively as weapons in both World War I and II. They destroyed thousands of tonnes of shipping. Small submarines are also used for underwater research and exploration and to carry out underwater work on ships, cables and oil rigs. ◁

SUDAN The Democratic Republic of Sudan is the largest country in AFRICA. It has an area of 2,505,813 sq km (967,500 sq miles) and a population of 20,945,000 (1984). The capital is Khartoum. The north and centre are desert, but cotton flourishes on irrigated land. ◁

SUEZ CANAL An international waterway linking the MEDITERRANEAN and RED SEAS, the Suez Canal was opened in 1869. It is 162 km (101 miles) long. It was closed between 1967 and 1975, because it had been blocked by wrecks during the Arab-Israeli war of 1967.

SUGAR One of a group of CARBOHYDRATES, usually having a sweet taste. Sugars are important to plants (see PHOTOSYNTHESIS), and are vital to human life as they are easily digestible and provide an immediate source of energy (see GLUCOSE). The form of sugar commonly used as a foodstuff comes mostly from sugar cane, a tall grass-like plant grown in the tropics, and from sugar beet.

SULPHA DRUGS These are synthetic chemicals that were discovered in 1935 to be a powerful substance for killing BACTERIA. They were widely used to treat infections and were the first of the 'miracle drugs', so-called because of the wide number of uses they had. Today they have been widely replaced by ANTIBIOTICS such as penicillin.

SULPHUR A non-metallic ELEMENT existing naturally as a yellow crystalline rock, often found in the region of volcanoes and hot springs. Plastic sulphur is formed by pouring molten sulphur into cold water. Flowers of sulphur is a fine powder made by condensing sulphur vapour. Sulphur is used to make drugs, gunpowder, SULPHURIC ACID and numerous chemical products.

SULPHURIC ACID An extremely corrosive, colourless, oily acid widely used in the chemical industry. The acid reacts with various metals and compounds to form salts

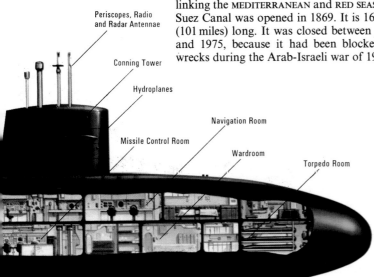

Periscopes, Radio and Radar Antennae
Conning Tower
Hydroplanes
Navigation Room
Missile Control Room
Wardroom
Torpedo Room

◀ A cutaway drawing of a nuclear submarine. The rounded bow and tapering tear-drop shape give the craft maximum speed, stability and control. The missiles it carries are housed in the centre of the submarine.

Sum

▶ *Two main methods are used to produce sulphuric acid — the chamber and the contact processes. The chamber, or lead-chamber process, is so called because the acid is formed in large chambers of sheet lead. The essential reaction is the oxidation of sulphur dioxide (SO_2) in moist air, in the presence of oxides of nitrogen. The top diagram shows the lead-chamber method.*

Most acid today is made by the contact process (bottom). A mixture of sulphur dioxide and air is passed over a heated catalyst, whereupon the sulphur dioxide is converted to sulphur trioxide, which is cooled before passing through a dilute acid spray. It reacts with water in the spray to form more acid, and concentrated acid collects at the foot of the tower. The catalyst for the contact process is usually platinum.

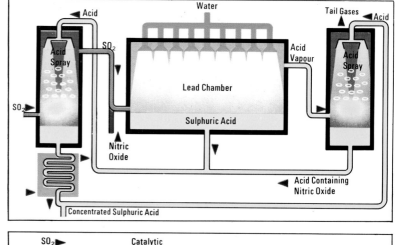

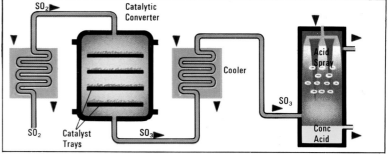

called sulphates. Ammonium sulphate is an important fertilizer. Dilute sulphuric acid is used in car batteries.

SUMERIANS A civilization that flourished in the southern part of BABYLON some 5000 years ago. From about 3000 BC to 1900 BC the Sumerians were the most important nation of the Middle East. They were the first people to write down their language in a script known as *cuneiform*. They wrote on clay tablets that were baked to harden, and were kept in libraries.

SUN The Sun is the central body in the SOLAR SYSTEM and the nearest STAR to the Earth. Compared with other stars, the Sun is relatively small and dim. Astronomers describe it as a yellow dwarf. But, because it is only 150 million kilometres (93 million miles) away from us, the Sun appears large and bright. Heat, light and other forms of ELECTROMAGNETIC WAVES are produced by nuclear reactions in the Sun's core. A little of this energy reaches the Earth, thus making life possible on our planet. At its core the Sun's temperature is about 15,000,000°C (27,000,000°F), while its surface temperature is a relatively cool 6000°C (11,000°F). Roughly round in shape, the Sun has a diameter of about 1,392,000 km (865,000 miles). It consists of gases, mostly hydrogen (90 per cent) and helium (8 per cent). ▷

SUNDIAL A device for telling the time of day by the position of the shadow of an upright rod (gnomen) on a flat surface, which is marked with the hours of the day. The shadow moves around the marked surface as the Sun moves across the sky. (See CLOCKS)

SUNFLOWER A tall plant that can grow as high as 3.5 metres (12 ft). Its huge yellow flowers have seeds that are rich in an oil used for cooking, soap and paints.

▼ *A spectacular eruption, or prominence, on the Sun, photographed from the American Skylab space laboratory.*

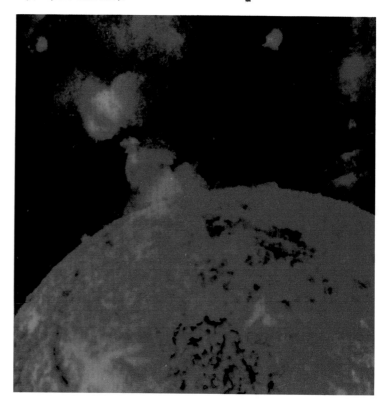

SUN The Sun emits a truly stupendous amount of energy – about 9 hp for every square centimetre of its surface. The Earth receives a mere .00017 hp per square centimetre. The rest is radiated into space.

SUPERSONIC FLIGHT One of the problems of supersonic flight is that raindrops encountered at such high speeds can scar metal and penetrate cockpit windows. This is one of the reasons why supersonic airliners fly so high (around 17,000 m/50,000 ft) in order to travel above any rain-bearing clouds.

SUNSPOTS Relatively dark markings that appear from time to time on the Sun's surface. They may last for months or disappear within a few hours. Sunspots appear dark because their temperature is about 2000°C (3600°F) lower than the surrounding temperature. The cause of sunspots is unknown, but their occurrence reaches a peak every eleven years and is associated with surface eruptions called flares and prominences.

SUPERSONIC FLIGHT Supersonic means faster than the speed of SOUND. At sea level, this is about 1220 km (760 miles) per hour. At higher altitudes, the air is thinner and the speed of sound decreases. Supersonic speeds are often expressed in terms of a Mach number; i.e. the speed in relation to the local speed of sound. A rocket travelling at Mach 3, for example, is moving at three times the local speed of sound. When an aircraft flies at supersonic speed, shock waves build up and are heard as 'sonic booms' on the ground. These sometimes break windows and cause other damage. Aircraft designed for supersonic flight have a pointed nose and swept-back wings to reduce problems with shock waves. ◁

SURGERY A branch of MEDICINE that deals with injury and disease mainly by operating

▼ *The nose of the supersonic airliner* Concorde *narrows to a point to produce the least resistance in the air.*

▲*The flowers of the sunflower are composite. They are made up of a number of tiny florets — each one a complete flower in miniature, with its own reproductive organs.*

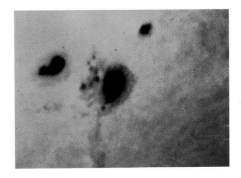

▲ *Sunspots are about 2000°C cooler than their surroundings, and so appear black in photographs of the Sun.*

Sur

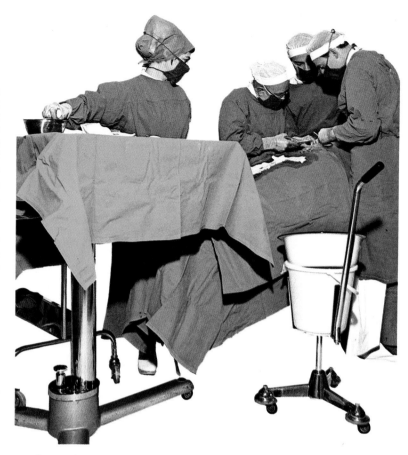

▶An operation in a modern hospital theatre. The skill of the surgeon and the latest equipment ensure the patient has the finest treatment. Early surgery was a much more haphazard procedure.

on the body with instruments. Surgeons can cut away diseased parts, remove objects that have lodged themselves in the body and repair broken tissues. Early surgeons dealt mainly with blood-letting, the lancing of infections and the removal of limbs. They made no use of painkillers. Today surgeons can replace kidneys, transfer hearts, repair bone with metal or plastic pins, remove organs, graft skin and carry out many other operations.

SURREALISM An ART movement that began in Europe at the time of World War I. It grew out of a feeling held by many artists that the world was no longer sane. Surrealists tried, through painting, sculpture and literature, to create images that came from dreams – from beyond the 'reality' of everyday life. (See DALI, SALVADOR)

SURVEYING The measurement and mapping of the Earth's surface. Surveys are used to locate and define features such as rivers, lakes and coastlines, and to show the height of land areas. Surveying is also used in marking out property boundaries. (See MAP)

SWALLOW A fork-tailed bird with pointed wings enabling it to swoop and dart at high speed as it feeds on insects while in flight. It spends a great deal of its life in the air.

SWAN A graceful long-necked bird with powerful wings and paddling feet. Swans spend much of their time floating and feeding on the water. They form mating pairs for life. ▷

SWEDEN A monarchy in north-west EUROPE. Sweden is a mountainous and thinly-populated country. However, it is extremely prosperous and its people enjoy one of the world's highest standards of living.

The cold north lies above the ARCTIC Circle and includes part of the region called LAPLAND. The most important place in the north is the region around the towns of Gällivare and Kiruna, where rich deposits of iron ore are mined. Mining and manufacturing are Sweden's leading industries. Ship-building, machinery and steel products are all important. Industrial centres include STOCKHOLM, Gothenburg, Malmö and Norrköping. Sweden lacks coal and most electricity comes from HYDROELECTRIC POWER stations. Forestry is

another major industry, but farming is confined to the south, which has warm summers.

The country is known for its many scientists and inventors. One of them, Dr Alfred Nobel (1833–1896), founded the NOBEL PRIZES. Sweden has been neutral for over 150 years. Political stability has enabled its governments to introduce an advanced system of social welfare. Neutral Sweden also plays an important part in international affairs. ▷

SWAN According to old legends, swans sing an especially haunting song just before they die. The term 'swan-song' has since come to refer to the last work or performance by an actor, musician, singer or painter.

▶A swan preens by running its beak through its feathers. This removes dirt and parasites and keeps the feathers smooth.

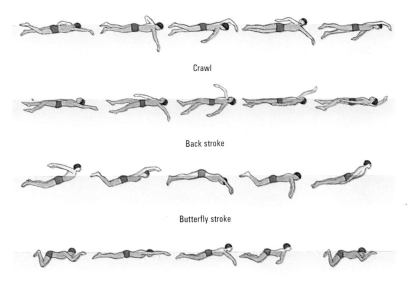

Crawl

Back stroke

Butterfly stroke

Breast stroke

◀ The four main methods of swimming. The crawl is the fastest stroke as the body cuts through the shallowest amount of water. It was developed in Australia in the early 1900s from a swimming style used by natives of the South Seas. The breast stroke was used as long as ago as the 1500s.

SWEDEN: FACTS AND FIGURES
Area: 449,964 sq km (173,732 sq miles).
Population: 8,337,000 (1984 est.).
Capital: Stockholm.
Official language: Swedish.
Currency: Swedish krona.
Religion: Lutheran.
Largest cities: Stockholm (pop. 1,420,000), Gothenburg (699,000).
About half the country is wooded, and lakes cover about 9 per cent of the area.

SWITZERLAND: FACTS AND FIGURES
Area: 41,288 sq km (15,941 sq miles).
Population: 6,442,000 (1984 est.).
Capital: Bern.
Official languages: French, German, Italian.
Currency: Swiss franc.
Religions: About half the population is Roman Catholic and half Protestant.
Chief rivers: Rhine and Rhone.
Largest cities: Zurich (pop. 840,000), Geneva (372,000), Basel (365,000).
Perpetual Swiss neutrality was guaranteed by the Congress of Vienna in 1815. The country maintained its neutrality during World Wars I and II.

SWEET POTATO A tropical plant of the morning glory family, its swollen, thick tuberous roots are eaten like potatoes. In Japan, they are used for their starch and to make an alcoholic drink.

SWIFT The fastest of all the small birds, swifts can reach 110 kph (70 mph) in flight. They are known to eat, drink, bathe and mate while in flight.   ◁

SWIFT, JONATHAN An Irish-born writer, poet, churchman and political journalist (1667–1745), he became the dean of Saint Patrick's Cathedral in Dublin. In 1726, he published his most famous book, *Gulliver's Travels*. In it, he poked fun at many human weaknesses.

SWIMMING The art of propelling oneself through the water. It is the best activity for

▼ A large store of cheeses in Switzerland, a country noted for its high quality dairy products.

exercising the entire body. The main styles of swimming are the breaststroke, the crawl and the backstroke. Swimming comes naturally to many animals, but has to be learned by humans. Swimming competitions were known from the 1st century BC, and it had become fashionable as early as the 17th century – schools in Japan were ordered to include swimming by that time.

SWITZERLAND A federal republic in south-central EUROPE, Switzerland is divided into 25 small cantons (states). The powers of government are split between the cantons and the national government. The scenery is breath-taking. The ALPS and the Jura mountains cover about two-thirds of the country. There are superb waterfalls, deep valleys and beautiful lakes. Lakes cover about one-fifth of the land. Farming is limited by the rugged nature of the land, but cheese, butter, sugar and meat are all important products. Switzerland lacks minerals and many raw materials are imported. The nation is best known for its skilled craftsmen, who make extremely accurate scientific instruments, watches, and so on.

There are three main languages. German is spoken by 74.5 per cent of Swiss nationals; French by 20.1 per cent; and Italian by 4 per cent. Romansch, a language related to ancient Latin, is spoken by about 1 per cent. In the past, the Swiss fought many wars to maintain their independence. However, Switzerland has been neutral for over 100 years. It does not belong to the UNITED NATIONS, although it has joined some of the UN's specialized agencies.
◁

SWORD A hand weapon that has a metal blade and a handle, and usually a guard to protect the hand. It is used for cutting and thrusting and may be held with either one hand or two. The blade may be straight and sharpened on one or both sides – or curved. Swords have long been the symbols of military rank, and are still worn by officers on ceremonial occasions.

SWORDFISH A gamefish with a long, flat sword-shaped snout of bone that is strong enough to pierce the planks of a boat. Its maximum length can be as much as 6 metres (20 ft) and it can weigh up to 450 kg (1000 lb).

Syd

▶ *The modern, dramatic shape of the Sydney Opera House is a feature of the city's harbour area. It was designed by the Danish architect Utzon.*

SYDNEY The capital of NEW SOUTH WALES, Australia. Sydney has 3,335,000 people (including its suburbs) and is Australia's oldest city. It is a major port with a superb harbour and is a cultural and industrial centre.

SYMBIOSIS State in which two animals or plants live together to the advantage of both. Symbiosis is a partnership. An example of symbiosis occurs in LICHEN where fungi and algae benefit each other. Another is the case of the Nile crocodile and the Egyptian plover. The plover eats the leeches that cling to the crocodile. In this way, the plover gets food and the crocodile is freed from PARASITES. ▷

SYMPHONY A piece of music – the most important form of composition for a full ORCHESTRA. It was developed by HAYDN and others in the 18th century, and perfected by

▲ *The symbiotic relationship between the hermit crab and the sea anemone helps both creatures. The anemone eats scraps of food left by the crab, and in turn protects the crab with its stinging tentacles. Below, another form of symbiosis. In this case, the sea anemone's tentacles provide the clownfish with shelter. In return, the clownfish guides other fish within the anemone's reach.*

▼ *An aerial view of Sydney, the largest city in Australia and the capital of New South Wales. Sydney began as a convict settlement, set up by the British in 1788.*

MOZART and BEETHOVEN. Traditionally it is in four separate sections (movements) which contrast with each other.

SYNAGOGUE A Jewish place of worship, used for services, prayer, education and various ceremonies. It is usually built to point towards Jerusalem. (See JUDAISM)

SYRIA An Arab republic in the MIDDLE EAST, Syria has 9,934,000 people (1984 est.) and an area of 185,180 sq km (71,498 sq miles). The capital is Damascus. Cotton, grown in irrigated river valleys, is the chief crop. But much of Syria is barren semi-desert. ▷

SYMBIOSIS One unexpected partnership is between seagulls and lizards in the Dalmatian Islands off the coast of Yugoslavia. Several lizards may be found sheltering under the wings of each young gull before it learns to fly. In return, the lizards eat the gulls' body parasites.

SYRIA: FACTS AND FIGURES
Official language: Arabic.
Currency: Syrian pound.
Religion: Mainly Sunni Moslem.
Chief rivers: Euphrates and Orontes.
Chief cities: Damascus pop. 1,112,000), Aleppo (985,000).
Syria became an independent republic in 1945, having been a French mandate since 1920.

TABLE TENNIS A game played on a table measuring 2.7 metres by 1.5 metres (9 ft by 5 ft), using a net, a celluloid ball and solid bats with rubber faces. Each player tries to keep hitting the ball back across the net, so that it bounces on the table on the opponent's side. The game developed about 1880 and is popular in most countries, especially China and Japan.

TAIWAN An island republic off CHINA. Taiwan has 19,012,000 people (1984 est.) and covers 35,961 sq km (13,885 sq miles). The capital is Taipei. Taiwan (previously known as Formosa) is ruled by Nationalist Chinese, but China claims it.

TAJ MAHAL One of the most beautiful buildings in the world – the tomb built for his wife by the emperor Shah Jehan, at Agra in northern India. It took about 18 years to complete (1630–1648), and 20,000 workmen were involved.

▲ *Like many other historic buildings in the world, the Taj Mahal is suffering from corrosion due to climate and pollution.*

TANK A military fighting vehicle. A tank is completely enclosed and heavily armoured, and runs on caterpillar tracks. It is armed with a large gun firing shells, fitted to a revolving turret, plus usually one or more machine guns. The crew is normally four or five. Tanks were first used in World War I (from 1916), but their full potential was not realized until the success of the German tank-borne invasion of France in World War II.

TANZANIA A republic in East AFRICA, Tanzania has 21,062,000 people (1984 est.) and an area of 945,087 sq km (364,000 sq miles). The capital is Dar es Salaam. This mainly farming nation contains Africa's highest mountain, Kilimanjaro, as well as Serengeti and Ngorongoro national parks.

TAPESTRY A decorative TEXTILE, traditionally made of wool. It is made by passing coloured threads through fixed *warp* threads

British Mk IV
Male 2324 tank

◄ *The tank was introduced by the British in 1916, during World War I. It could operate on the roughest ground and could destroy enemy machine-gunners.*

349

Tar

(see WEAVING), to give a colourful scene or pattern. Tapestries have been made since ancient times, and were widely used in the Middle Ages for covering walls and furniture.

TAR A thick, dark, sticky material obtained from coal, wood and various fats and oils. It is used as a protective covering on ROADS. Tar is also an important source of phenol (carbolic acid), toluene (toluol) and many other chemicals.

TARANTULA Large black south European SPIDER named after the town of Taranto in Italy; it has a slightly poisonous bite. In the Middle Ages, people thought the tarantula's bite was very dangerous; its victim was supposed to die of melancholy – unless cured by music. Musicians played a series of lively tunes – tarantellas – to tempt the victim to get up and dance and so sweat out the poison.

TASMAN, ABEL Dutch navigator (c. 1603–1659). On his voyage of 1642–1643 he discovered TASMANIA, NEW ZEALAND and the Tonga and Fiji Islands. Tasmania, originally called Van Diemen's Land, was renamed in his honour in 1853.

TASMANIA A mountainous island state of Australia, Tasmania has 440,000 people (1984 est.) and an area of 68,332 sq km (26,383 sq miles). The capital is HOBART. Tasmania is often called the 'apple isle'. But mining, livestock-rearing and manufacturing are important industries.   ▷

TASMANIAN DEVIL Small flesh-eating MARSUPIAL found only in Tasmania. The Tasmanian Devil, black with a white chest band, has a short body (70 cm/28 in), short legs, a large head and strong teeth. It hunts by night.

TASTE One of the five human senses. The hundreds of taste receptors on the TONGUE's surface detect the four basic kinds of flavour:

THE ORGANS OF TASTE AND SMELL

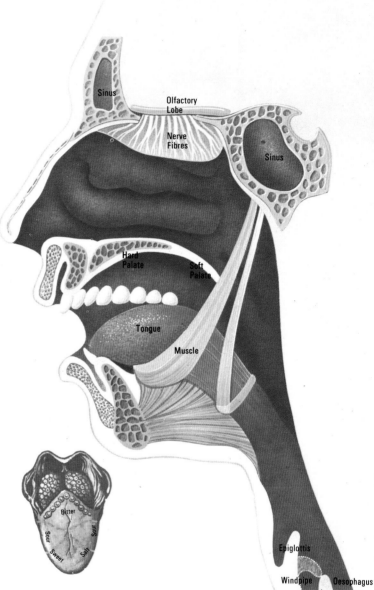

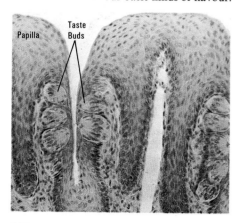

▲ Cutaway diagram of the head showing the nasal cavity and the mouth. The smell receptors are embedded in the lining of the roof of the nose. The four main kinds of taste bud are distributed over the tongue so that different areas taste different flavours.

◄ A highly magnified section through the taste buds. They are located on the sides of tiny lumps, or papillae, on the tongue. The sensation of flavour is a combination of taste and smell.

TASMANIA Tasmania was discovered in 1642 by the Dutch explorer, Abel Tasman, who named it Van Diemen's Land. It was annexed by the British in 1802, and there was a penal settlement at Port Arthur until 1852. There is a higher proportion of forest land in Tasmania than in any other part of Australia.

TEA When left to its natural growth, the tea plant reaches a height of 6 to 9 m (20 to 30ft). The best tea is grown at altitudes of 900 to 2000 m (3000 to 7000 ft). Tea is usually grown from seeds; the young plants are replanted about 1.2 m (4 ft) apart, and when they grow they are continually cut back to a height of about 1 m (3 ft) so that the pickers can reach all the leaves. The first leaves are plucked after 3 to 5 years' growth, only new leaves being taken.

TEETH Human beings get their first teeth when they are six to nine months old. The first teeth appear over a period of two or three years until the child has 20 teeth, 10 upper and 10 lower. There are 32 permanent teeth; the first of these, usually molars, appear about the age of six or seven. The last teeth to grow are the wisdom teeth (the four back molars). They can appear at any time between the ages of 17 and 21, or not at all in some people.

TELEPHONE In the 1980s there were 134,000,000 telephones in the United States, more than any other country in the world. There were 93,000,000 in Japan; 30,100,000 in West Germany; 28,000,000 in the United Kingdom; 26,400,000 in Russia; 18,000,000 in France; 8,200,000 in Australia; and 1,900,000 in New Zealand.

sweet, sour, bitter and salt. More subtle differences actually depend on help from the sense of SMELL.

TEA A drink made from the leaves, buds and shoots of the tea bush, grown chiefly in China, northern India, Sri Lanka and Japan. The pickings are dried, heated, and may be fermented. The drink is made by soaking them in boiling water. Tea reached Europe in 1610. It is the world's most widely used beverage. ◁

TEAK A tropical evergreen tree found in India, Burma and Thailand. It can grow to a height of 46 metres (150 ft). It has a very hard durable wood, used in shipbuilding and for furniture and flooring.

TEETH Hard, bone-like structures attached to the jaws of most VERTEBRATES except birds. There are usually two rows of teeth, one in the upper jaw and one in the lower jaw. Teeth are basically used for biting, tearing and chewing food. An animal's teeth are adapted to its diet. Gnawing creatures such as RATS have sharp pointed teeth; grazing creatures, such as HORSES, have flat grinding teeth. Teeth are not only used for eating. Some CARNIVORES, such as HYENAS, use their teeth to catch prey. BEAVERS use their teeth to fell trees, and ELEPHANTS use two of their teeth – grown out as long tusks – for digging and fighting. ◁

TELEGRAPHY Various techniques for sending messages in code. Before the 1800s, visual or audible signals were used for conveying messages between distant points. Electric telegraph systems were introduced in the 1800s. Samuel Morse devised a method of sending messages using long and short pulses of electricity to represent letters and numbers (see MORSE CODE). Radiotelegraphy is the transmission of telegraph signals by RADIO.

TELEPHONE A device for sending speech over wires by turning sound into electrical

▼ The first telephone receiver, patented by Alexander Graham Bell in 1876.

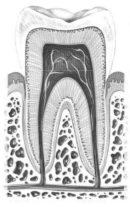

◁ The structure of a molar tooth. Above the gum is the crown and below it the roots. The outer layer of enamel is the hardest substance in the body. The next layer is made of a bone-like substance called dentine. Inside it is the pulp cavity which contains blood vessels and nerves.

impulses. The first practical telephone, patented by Alexander Graham BELL in 1876, represented a major breakthrough in communications. But Bell's instrument produced only a weak signal that was difficult to hear over long distances. However, others were quick to improve on the system, and the telephone soon became a commercial success in Britain and the United States. At first, telephones were used mainly by lawyers, bankers and large firms, often for communi-

▼ The telephone handset contains a small microphone in the transmitter (mouthpiece) and a small loudspeaker in the receiver (earpiece). As you speak, a diaphragm in the transmitter vibrates. Carbon granules translate the vibrations into electric current. The current travels to the earpiece of the receiving telephone, where it passes through the coils of an electromagnet. The current causes the electromagnet to vibrate another diaphragm. This sets up sound waves that reproduce the sound of your voice.

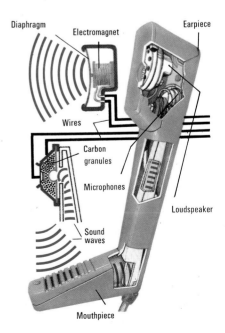

Diaphragm
Electromagnet
Earpiece
Wires
Carbon granules
Microphones
Loudspeaker
Sound waves
Mouthpiece

Tel

cation only between different departments of the same organization. Users called a switchboard operator who made the required connection. But, as more and more firms became subscribers, exchanges were established to interconnect them. The first automatic exchange was patented by Almon Strowger in 1889. Callers selected other subscribers by pressing three keys. Dial telephones were introduced in 1896. Since then, world-wide telephone networks have been established using landlines and communications SATELLITE links. (See MICROPHONE) ◁

TELESCOPES A Dutch optician called Hans Lippershey invented the telescope in 1608. Hearing of this useful device, the Italian

▲The giant Hale reflecting telescope at Mount Palomar Observatory in California. Its mirror is 5.08 m (200 in) in diameter. Reflecting telescopes can be made much bigger than refracting ones and can 'see' more clearly.

▼ The Hyades star cluster, photographed through a telescope and a prism. The prism splits up the light from each star into a spectrum. By studying this, astronomers can discover some of the star's characteristics.

▲ A model of Newton's reflecting telescope, invented in 1672, before he was 30 years old.

TELESCOPES The world's largest reflecting telescopes are the 6.02-m (237-inch) at the Academy of Sciences of the USSR, near Zelenchukskaya, in operation since 1976, and the 5.08-m (200-inch) at Palomar Observatory, Mount Palomar, California, USA, in operation since 1948. The largest refracting telescope is that with a lens diameter of 100 cm (40 inches) at Yerkes Observatory, Williams Bay, Wisconsin, USA, in operation since 1897.

TELEVISION In the 1980s the United States had 143,000,000 TV receivers; Russia had 75,000,000; Japan had 30,000,000; West Germany had 21,800,000; France had 19,000,000; the United Kingdom had 18,700,000; Australia had 6,500,000; and New Zealand had 922,000.

inventor GALILEO GALILEI built one for himself the following year. Although a crude instrument by today's standards, Galileo used it to make many important discoveries in ASTRONOMY. His telescope was of the refracting type – that is, it used lenses to bend light and thus produce a magnified image (see LENS). This type of telescope suffered from a defect called *chromatic aberration.* Coloured fringes could be seen around the images, and the problem became worse as the magnification was increased. Isaac NEWTON invented the reflecting telescope to overcome this defect. By replacing the main (objective) lens with a curved mirror, Newton managed to eliminate the unwanted coloration. Modern high-quality telescopes may be of the refracting or reflecting type. Today's refracting telescopes use compound lenses, made from elements of different types of glass cemented together, to prevent chromatic aberration. Large optical telescopes are usually of the reflecting type using a mirror, as huge lenses would tend to distort under their own weight. (See RADIO ASTRONOMY) ◁

▼ Inside a colour television camera are tinted mirrors which split up the light from the scene being filmed into three colours: blue, green and red. Each of these colour images is scanned separately by a special camera tube, then combined and transmitted.

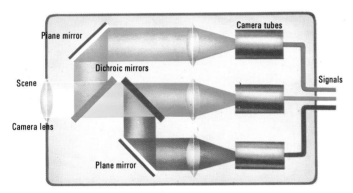

▼ Inside a colour television receiver, the signals for the three colours are separated out again, and each one controls the strength of an electron beam. The beams scan the television screen, which is coated with minute phosphor dots. These dots glow blue, green or red, and make up the colour picture.

Screen coated with phosphor dots

Perforated shadow mask

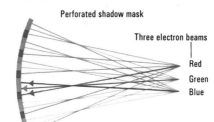

▶ An early television set, with the screen set into the lid. The BBC transmitted the first regular television programmes in 1936.

TELEVISION The basic theory of television was developed in the 1800s, but many years passed before practical television became possible. In 1880, the English scientists Ayrton and Perry put forward an idea called electric vision. They proposed using a number of photoelectric cells to convert each part of an image into an electric signal. The idea was that the signals would be sent over wires and used to light an array of tiny lamps at the far end. In this way, variations in brightness in the original image would be reproduced. One problem was that the system required hundreds of wires between the transmitting and receiving equipment. German scientist Paul Nipkow overcame this difficulty by devising a mechanical scanning system. Using a rotating perforated disc, he arranged for each part of the image to fall, in turn, on a single photoelectric cell. Only one pair of wires would be required to convey the signal, and one lamp and a scanning disc would be used to reconstruct the image. Unfortunately, there was a major problem. The signal produced by a photoelectric cell was too weak to light a lamp. So real progress in television had to wait for the invention of an amplifying device – the triode VALVE – in 1907. This enabled the weak signal from a photoelectric cell to be strengthened sufficiently to light a neon lamp.

Using Nipkow's mechanical scanning system, and valves for amplification, Scotsman John Logie Baird developed a practical television system in the 1920s. By this time, radio broadcasting services were being established, and some organizations started experimenting with television transmissions. In 1936, the British Broadcasting Corporation started the world's first regular broadcasts of scheduled television programmes. Besides using the Baird system, the BBC also tried another technique – electronic scanning, using spe-

Tem

cially designed CATHODE-RAY TUBES. This proved vastly superior, and the Baird system was soon abandoned.

All modern television systems use electronic scanning systems to analyze and reconstruct the pictures. In the television camera, a LENS forms an image of the studio scene on a camera tube. A beam of electrons (see ATOM) rapidly scans this image, line by line, and is made to vary in strength according to image brightness. The varying flow, or current, of electrons produced is called the vision signal. Sound and vision signals from the studio are transmitted together. In the receiver, a beam of electrons scans the screen of a picture tube, tracing out a series of lines across it. The vision signal is used to vary the brightness along the lines and thus reproduce the original scene. As scanning occurs so quickly, the viewer has the illusion of seeing a complete picture, although it is actually constructed bit by bit. In colour television, separate signals corresponding to the three primary colours of light are used to form a full-colour image on the screen of a specially designed picture tube. ◁

TEMPERATURE A measure of the hotness of a body. The Celsius (CENTIGRADE) and FAHRENHEIT temperature scales are the most commonly used.

TENDON Fibrous tissue joining a MUSCLE to a BONE. Tendons may be shaped as cords, bands or sheets, and may be short and thick or long and thin.

TENNIS A game played between two or four people on an open court divided by a net. A pressurized ball and strung racquets are used. Tennis is descended from 'real tennis' played in England and France in the 14th century. The modern game was devised in England in 1873. ▷

TENT A portable shelter, usually of canvas stretched over a frame of metal poles. Tents were originally made of animal skins or bark and have been used by wandering nomadic tribes since prehistoric times. Now mostly

▲ Suzanne Lenglen of France was the first really great woman tennis star. She dominated the game from 1919 to 1926.

used for CAMPING, modern tents may have plastic windows, built-in floors and zipper doors.

TERMITE INSECT found in warm parts of the world. Termites, like ants, are social creatures and live together in great colonies. There are about 2000 species of termite; most feed on wood and can do great damage to trees and buildings. Some species nest in old tree trunks; others build homes in huge mounds of soil cemented together by saliva. These mounds, which may be up to 6 metres (20 ft) high, are called *termitaria*. ▷

TERRA COTTA A type of baked clay, usually brownish-red in colour. It is used for statues, pottery, tiles and as a covering material on buildings.

TERRAPIN Popular name for a freshwater or tidewater TURTLE. One type of terrapin is a

▼ Blanding's terrapin is one of several North American terrapins living in ponds and rivers. It eats both plants and animals, and lays its eggs on land.

◀ Termites live in large colonies in warm countries. They build huge nests, often much taller than a man. The nests are rock hard and difficult to knock down. Many termites eat wood, and can damage houses. Queen termites may live for over fifty years.

TENNIS The singles court is 78 ft (23.8 m) long, divided by a net 3 ft (0.91 m) high at the centre and 3½ ft (1 m) high at the posts. It is 27 ft (8.2 m) wide. The doubles court is an additional 4½ ft (1.4 m) wide on each side. The service line is 18 ft (5.5 m) from the base line. Tennis balls are between 2½ and 2 5/8 inches (63.5 and 66.67 mm) in diameter and weigh between 2 and 2 1/16 ounces (56.7 and 58 grams). They must bounce to a height of between 53 and 58 inches (134.6 and 147.3 cm) when dropped from a height of 100 inches (254 cm) on to a concrete base.

The first rules of tennis were drawn up by the Marylebone Cricket Club in 1875, and the first Lawn Tennis Championships were played at the All England Croquet Club at Wimbledon in 1877, with rules very similar to those of today.

TERMITE The termites belong to the order Isoptera. The majority live in tropical regions, 56 species are found in North America, and there are none in Britain. They are often called 'white ants', though they are quite unrelated to the ants. They are closer to the cockroaches. Once inside the woodwork of a building, termites tunnel in all directions, never coming to the surface of the wood. The first sign of their presence may be total collapse of a wall or a piece of furniture.

TEXTILES Textiles are among the oldest man-made articles in existence. We have pieces of flax yarn from Stone Age lake dwellings, together with pieces of primitive looms. Fine linen cloths have been found in ancient Egyptian tombs, some of the mummy wrappings being as much as 20 m (over 60 ft) long and 1.5 m (5 ft) wide. The early Egyptian craftsmen often painted their fabrics.

THAILAND: FACTS AND FIGURES
Official language: Thai.
Currency: Baht.
Chief rivers: Chao Phraya, Mekong and Salween.
Largest cities: Bangkok (pop. 5,468,000), Songkhla (173,000).
Religion: Hinayana Buddhism is the religion of over 95 per cent of the population.
The word 'Thai' means 'free', and Thailand is the only South-east Asian nation that has never been colonized.

medium-sized turtle found along the Atlantic coast of the US and Mexico. It has a diamond-shaped pattern on its shell and eats both animal and vegetable food.

TEXTILES Traditionally a textile is a woven fabric (see WEAVING), but today all fabrics are classed as textiles (including knitted fabrics, felts and lace). The traditional materials used for textiles are WOOL, LINEN and SILK, and COTTON. But today many artificial fibres are made – some from wood pulp and cotton (e.g. RAYON and acetate), but most chemically from coal and oil (e.g. NYLON and polyester). Sometimes natural and artificial fibres are mixed in a fabric, to get the best of both. The output, quality and variety of textiles has been greatly increased by the mechanization of spinning and weaving. Other new developments include treatments to make fabrics flame resistant and easy to care for. Though most textiles are used in clothes, other textile products include boat sails, conveyor belts, fire hoses and typewriter ribbons. ◁

THAILAND A monarchy in south-east ASIA. Thailand (formerly called Siam) has 50,396,000 people (1984 est.) and an area of 514,000 sq km (198,457 sq miles). The capital is Bangkok. Important products include rice, maize, tapioca, rubber and tin. ◁

THAMES, RIVER The longest river wholly in ENGLAND. The Thames rises in the Cotswold Hills and then flows 338 km (210 miles) across southern England. It passes through much beautiful countryside before reaching

▼ The Royal Palace in Bangkok, resplendent with golden temples, spires and statues.

LONDON and its estuary, and then into the North Sea.

THANKSGIVING DAY (US) A public holiday in the UNITED STATES, held on the fourth Thursday in November. It was established by the American Pilgrim Fathers, to commemorate their first successful harvest. George WASHINGTON made it a national holiday.

THEOLOGY The study of RELIGION. It tries to deal with the nature of God and of man's relationship with him. Christian theology deals with the study of the BIBLE, the doctrines of the Church, the nature of 'right' and 'wrong', the different paths to God, the forms of public worship, and the defence of Christian beliefs against criticism. There is also *comparative religion*, which studies different religious beliefs throughout the world.

THERMODYNAMICS The study of energy-conversion processes involving heat changes. These processes are governed by three laws of thermodynamics. The first is the law of conservation of energy (see CONSERVATION LAWS). It states that energy can be neither created nor destroyed. If, for example, mechanical energy is used up, then the same amount of heat or other energy is produced. The second law of thermodynamics states that heat cannot, of its own accord, flow from a colder body to a hotter one. The third law deals with the properties of substances at absolute zero temperature ($-273.15°C$, or $-459.67°F$).

THERMOMETERS Instruments for measuring temperature. Most thermometers consist of a sealed glass tube with a bulb at one end. This contains MERCURY or alcohol, which

▼ Floating markets are lively trading places in Thailand. Bangkok has floating markets along its Klongs (canals) where fruit, vegetables, meat, crafts, clothes and other goods are sold.

expands or contracts with temperature changes. As a result, the liquid level in the narrow-bore tube rises or falls with the temperature. A calibrated scale on the tube indicates the temperature corresponding to any level of the liquid.

THERMOSTAT An automatic device for controlling temperature. The thermostat in many electrical appliances, such as electric blankets and irons, is a simple switch, the moving part being a bimetallic strip. It consists of two strips of metal that expand at different rates when heated. As the strips are bonded together, the uneven expansion causes bending. This movement switches off the electric current when the temperature rises beyond a certain point. After a short period of cooling, the bimetallic strip returns to its original position and switches the current on again. The thermostat's automatic switching action ensures that the temperature of the appliance is kept within certain limits.

THIRTY YEARS' WAR The war in Germany (1618–1648), between the Catholic HAPSBURG emperors and the Protestant princes. It was a power struggle as much as a religious war. The princes were aided by, in turn, Denmark, Sweden and France. In the end the Hapsburgs lost any real authority over the local princes, but the population and countryside had been devastated by the conflicting armies of paid mercenary soldiers.

THORIUM A dark grey radioactive metallic ELEMENT (see RADIOACTIVITY). It occurs in the

minerals monazite and thorite. Thorium is used in nuclear reactors to make the nuclear fuel uranium-233 (see NUCLEAR ENERGY). ▷

THROMBOSIS A blood clot in a blood vessel or in the heart, restricting the flow of blood. It can be due to infection or impaired circulation. A clot in the heart can cause a heart attack, one in the brain – a stroke and paralysis.

THYROID GLAND An important GLAND in the neck. It makes a HORMONE that helps growth and stimulates the body's *metabolism* (its rate of working). If the thyroid is too active it may enlarge, swelling the neck (goitre). If it is under-active it may cause a type of mental deficiency (cretinism).

TIBET A region of CHINA, Tibet occupies a high wind-swept plateau in south-central ASIA. Tibet was part of China in the 1700s and 1800s, but it became virtually independent in the 1900s. In 1950 China occupied Tibet. After putting down a revolt in 1959, the Chinese made Tibet an Autonomous Region in 1969. ▷

TIDAL WAVE A destructive wave caused by an EARTHQUAKE or a volcanic eruption in the oceans. It travels at up to 800 kph (500 mph). Tidal waves are not connected with tides. Scientifically, they are called *tsunamis*. ▷

TIDES Rises and falls in sea-level which occur twice every 24 hours 50 minutes, caused by the gravitational pull exerted on the oceans by the Moon and Sun. The highest, *spring*, tides occur when the Earth, Moon and Sun are in a straight line. The combined gravitational pull of the Moon and Sun makes high tides higher and low tides lower. The lowest, *neap*, tides occur when the Moon, Earth and Sun form a right angle. (See GRAVITY)

THORIUM The element thorium is about three times as abundant as uranium, and nearly as plentiful as lead. It has 13 isotopes, all radioactive. Thorium is almost as heavy as lead, and melts at about 1700°C. When heated in air, it burns with a brilliant white light, like magnesium.

TIBET Tibet has long been known as the 'forbidden land'. This title comes from the traditional opposition by the Tibetan leaders to the entry of Western visitors, especially to the capital, Lhasa – the 'forbidden city'. Tibet has also been called the 'roof of the world' because of its great height above sea-level.

TIDAL WAVE Although tidal waves travel across oceans at an extremely high speed, the height of the waves in the open sea is very low. The distance between the crests of the waves can be very long, perhaps 150 km apart. They can often pass under ships without their presence being noticed.

TIGER Tiger kittens number from 2 to 5 in a litter, but seldom are more than 2 raised. The gestation period is from 98 to 110 days, and the young remain with the mother for about 2 years. The biggest tiger is the Siberian; adult males can measure 4 m (13 ft), including the tail. All tigers belong to the species *Felis tigris*. Lions and tigers can interbreed.

TIN Cornwall was almost the only source of tin in the world until the 18th century, and remained an important source until 1928, when most of the mines were closed. The Phoenicians sailed from their Mediterranean home to Cornwall to get tin.

▼ *Spring tides are high because the gravitational pull of the Sun is combined with that of the Moon. Neap tides are low because the Moon and Sun are pulling at right angles to each other.*

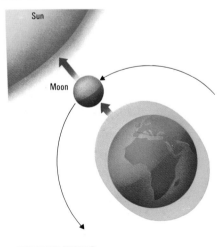

SPRING TIDES

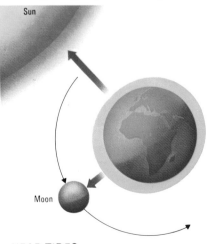

NEAP TIDES

◄ The Siberian tiger, larger and paler than the Indian one, is much prized for its skin. However, hunting restrictions may save it from extinction.

White tin is nearly as heavy as lead. When alloyed with less than 5 per cent of copper and sometimes 1 per cent of lead, it is known as pewter. Tin has 10 stable and 21 radioactive isotopes.

TITANIUM Titanium is a hard, lustrous, white metal that melts at 1675°C, boils at 3260°C, and is about half as heavy as copper. Future high-speed aircraft will probably have skins of titanium because of the metal's great resistance to heat and its comparatively low weight.

Titanium is present in the Sun and many stars, in the human body and in plants. It is the ninth most abundant element on Earth.

TIGER LIONS and tigers are the largest members of the CAT family. Tigers belong to Asia and have a reddish-yellow coat striped with black. They lie quiet during the heat of the day and hunt by night, usually alone. They kill and eat all kinds of animals, from monkeys to buffaloes, even men. Tigers are good swimmers, but poor climbers; yet they can spring up to a branch 6 metres (20 ft) high. ◁

TIME Our system of keeping time is based on periods determined by the movements of the Earth and Moon. The rotation of the Earth on its axis gives us the length of each day. The movement of the Moon around the Earth gives rise to the Moon's changing appearance, known as its phases. These repeat every lunar (Moon) month. And the Earth's period of rotation around the Sun determines the length of the year. For convenience, we have modified our CALENDAR so that each year contains exactly twelve months and exactly 365 days, or 366 days in LEAP YEARS.

As primitive man became more civilized, his life became more complicated. So, in order to plan his activities, he invented various time-keeping devices. These early CLOCKS included the sundial, water clock, sandglass and marked candle. Mechanical clocks appeared in the 1300s. These had only an hour hand, for it was not until the late 1600s that clocks were accurate enough to warrant having a minute hand. Today, extreme accuracy can be attained. Wrist watches regulated by tiny vibrating crystals remain accurate to within a few seconds over a period of several weeks.

The SI UNIT of time is the second, symbol s. Scientists now define the second as the time taken for 9,192,631,770 vibrations of a cesium-133 atom.

TIN A soft, white metallic ELEMENT found in the ore cassiterite. 'Tin' cans are made from steel coated with tin to make them corrosion resistant. Tin is also used to make solder and other ALLOYS. ◁

TITANIUM A silvery metallic ELEMENT found in various ores. Although these are abundant, titanium is expensive to produce because the extraction process is so complicated. The metal is used mainly as an ALLOY. ◁

TITIAN Italian painter (c. 1487–1576). His real name was Tiziano Vecello. He is famous for royal portraits of the HAPSBURGS Charles V and Philip II of Spain; for religious paintings such as the *Entombment of Christ*; and for mythological pictures such as *Venus and Adonis*. He also introduced new approaches to composition and use of colour.

TOBACCO Plant cultivated for its large broad leaves. Dried tobacco leaves are used to make cigarettes, cigars, pipe tobacco and snuff. Tobacco grows in warm, humid climates; some of the world's best cigar tobacco comes from the Caribbean.

TOBOGGANING A toboggan is a flat sledge curved up at the front, used for sliding over snow and ice. Tobogganing is both a child's game and an OLYMPIC sport.

TOKYO The capital of JAPAN. Tokyo is one of the world's largest cities. It has 11,676,000 people (1984 est.). The city is an industrial and business centre on Honshu Island. It was

◄ The modern city of Tokyo. Tokyo was rebuilt after the 1923 earthquake and again after heavy bombing in World War II.

badly damaged by an earthquake in 1923 and by bombing in 1945.

TOMATO Plant grown for its large, round red or yellow fruit which is eaten as a vegetable. Tomatoes belong to Central America but are now grown all over the world. They are cultivated outdoors in warm countries, and in glasshouses in cooler zones. ▷

TONGUE The tongue is used in tasting, swallowing and speech. It is a flap of muscle covered in mucous membrane that contains many nerves and TASTE buds. Its movement directs food towards the teeth or the throat, and also changes the shape of the mouth to help give the different sounds used in speaking.

TONSILS A pair of GLANDS at the back of the mouth. It is thought that they help to prevent infection entering the body via the throat. But they can become infected themselves, and are then removed by a minor operation.

TOPAZ A mineral that is valued as a GEM. It can be coloured yellow, white, blue or pink, and is mainly found in Brazil, Peru, Sri Lanka and Siberia.

TORNADO A severe storm. One kind of tornado is the whirlwind of the south-eastern United States. Although these tornadoes cover only a small area, winds may reach 650 kph (400 mph) and cause great destruction.

TORONTO Capital of Ontario province, in CANADA. Toronto has 3,067,000 people (including its suburbs). It is a major manufacturing centre and it has a fine harbour on the north-western shore of Lake Ontario.

TORPEDO An underwater projectile, used in sea warfare. It can be launched from a SUBMARINE, ship or aircraft. A torpedo is self-propelling and has an explosive head.

▼ *The toucan uses its huge beak to reach between the branches and pick fruit. It lives in the tropical forests of America.*

▲ *A whirling tornado sweeps over a town in Texas. Tornadoes are fairly common in the eastern United States.*

TORRES STRAIT A channel which separates Cape York Peninsula in north-east Australia from New Guinea. It was named after Luis Vaez de Torres, a Spanish captain, who discovered it in 1606. ▷

TORTOISE Slow-moving REPTILE with a box-like shell; the head and limbs can be pulled back into the shell. It is vegetarian and has no teeth. Tortoises first appeared on the Earth 200 million years ago and have changed very little. They are often confused with TURTLES. Generally, the name tortoise describes species living on land, and turtle describes species living in the sea. ▷

TOUCAN Large brightly-coloured bird with an enormous orange beak. Plumage colour varies according to species. It is usually a mixture of black and yellow, orange, red, blue, green or white. Toucans belong to the forests of tropical America. They live in flocks and feed mostly on fruit. ▷

TRADE UNION An association of workers, formed to protect their interests by getting higher wages, shorter hours and better working conditions. Modern trade unions began with the INDUSTRIAL REVOLUTION, and for many years their main struggle was simply to be allowed to exist. Some unions are just for certain craftsmen, others are for all the workers in an industry or on a type of job. Today many people in office jobs also have their own unions.

TRAGEDY A type of play (DRAMA) in which the hero (or heroine) is caught in a situation or course of action from which there is no honourable escape. It usually ends with the

TOMATO Indians of Central America grew the tomato for food in prehistoric times, but it was not until the 16th century that the Spaniards brought it to Europe. The tomato belongs to the same family as the deadly nightshade, and is rich in vitamins A and C.

TORRES STRAIT The Torres Strait is a meeting place for tides from the Indian and Pacific oceans, and this results in extremely fast-flowing currents. These, with coral reefs and sandbars, make the Strait a very dangerous place for shipping. Vessels sailing through the Strait take on a Torres Strait pilot.

TORTOISE The Giant tortoise is the longest-living animal – known to live up to 177 years – though it is thought that some bacteria may live many times as long. The Giant tortoise *(Testudo gigantea)* may have a shell 1.8 m (6 ft) long, and a weight of 225 kg (500 lb) or more.

The tortoise is the slowest moving of all the reptiles. Even when tempted with food, they cannot move faster than about 4.5 m (15 ft) in a minute.

TOUCAN There are about 50 or 60 species of toucan, covering an area from Argentina north to Mexico. The bird's 20-cm (8-in) beak is very strong, but light. It is paper-thin on the outside with a bone honeycomb. The toucan's tail is connected to its body with a kind of ball-and-socket joint. This allows the tail to be erected suddenly above the back.

TREE The world's largest living thing is the General Sherman, a giant sequoia tree in California, USA. It stands 83 m (272 ft) high, and is 11 m (36.5 ft) in diameter at its base. The General Sherman is also one of the oldest living things. Ring counts have proved it to be between 3500 and 4000 years old. The oldest trees are the bristlecone pines of Nevada, California and Arizona. They are nearly 5000 years old. The tallest trees are the California redwoods, which grow up to 111 m (364 ft) high. The tree with the thickest trunk is a Montezuma cypress in Mexico. It has a diameter of 12 m (40 ft).

Most of the timber produced today is soft wood. It takes between 50 and 60 years to produce a tree suitable for timber.

hero's death. Great tragedies were written in 5th century BC Athens (by AESCHYLUS, Sophocles and Euripides); in Renaissance England (by SHAKESPEARE) and in 17th century France (by Corneille and Racine).

TRANSFORMER A device used to transform ELECTRICITY from one voltage to another (see VOLT). A typical transformer consists of two coils of wire wound on the same iron core. Electricity is transferred from one coil (the primary) to the other (the secondary) by a process called electromagnetic induction. The voltage change is determined by the ratio of secondary coil turns to primary coil turns. If, for example, the secondary has twice as many turns as the primary, then the voltage will be doubled. Transformers can be used only with voltages that change in some way, and not with steady (direct) currents.

TRANSISTOR A small device used to amplify (strengthen) signals in electronic equipment, such as radio receivers and television sets. Practical transistors were developed by American scientists William Shockley, Walter Brattain and John Bardeen in the late 1940s. When it became possible to mass produce reliable transistors, they were used instead of VALVES in all kinds of electronic equipment. Transistors are much smaller than valves, more efficient and cheaper generally to produce. In a typical transistor, three electrical connections are made to a specially modified crystal of germanium or silicon. The regions to which the connections are made are called the emitter, base and collector. In operation, weak signal currents passed between the emitter and base cause corresponding, but much larger currents to flow from emitter to collector. Today, complex circuits containing thousands of transistors can be constructed cheaply on chips of silicon only a few millimetres square. This development has revolutionized electronics.

TRAWLING FISHING with a large bag-shaped net, dragged along the sea bottom. It is used to catch white fish such as haddock and cod. Modern trawlers are 31–52 metres (100–170 ft) long, and some have equipment for automatically processing the catch and refrigerating it.

TREE Although it looks very different from a cabbage or a carnation, a tree is a plant. The main difference is that trees are much taller than other plants and therefore need strong, woody stems – trunks – to support them. A tree has two main parts. The part above ground, the crown, consists of the trunk, branches, twigs and leaves. The part below ground consists of the roots. There are two kinds of trees: coniferous trees and broad-leaved trees. CONIFERS have needle-like leaves and, in place of flowers, produce their seeds in cones. Most conifers are evergreen (they do not lose their leaves in autumn). Broadleaved trees have flowers – though these are often not easy to see. Their seeds are contained in seed cases, berries or fruits. Some broadleaved trees, like MAPLES and POPLARS, are deciduous (they drop their leaves in autumn). Others, like the HOLLY and IVY are evergreen. ◁

TRIGONOMETRY A branch of mathematics concerned with the properties of triangles. It was originally developed to help ASTRONOMERS and NAVIGATORS with calculations involving angles and distances. Trigonometry is also used by today's scientists and engineers in problems involving repetitive changes or movements, such as vibrations.

TRILOBITE Small animal that lived on the sea bed about 600 million years ago. Trilobites became extinct after some 400 million years but many have been preserved as FOSSILS. They were distantly related to CRABS but looked rather like woodlice. They had several pairs of legs and a three-part body (head, middle and tail).

TROMBONE A brass wind musical instrument. Part of the brass tube from which it is made slides into another part, and this

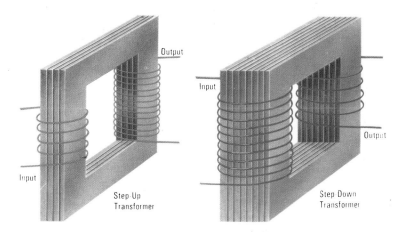

Output
Input
Output
Input
Step-Up Transformer
Step-Down Transformer

◀When electricity is sent over long distances, it goes through a transformer. The transformer steps up the voltage of the electricity. When the electricity reaches its destination, another transformer reduces (steps down) the voltage so that we can use it safely. The alternating current in the input coil makes the magnetic field in the core change constantly. This induces an alternating current in the output coil. The final voltage depends on the number of turns in the output coil. So a step-up transformer has more turns in the output coil and a step-down transformer has fewer.

changes the note. Trombones come in four different pitches: alto, tenor, bass, contrabass. (See PITCH)

TROUT Silvery-brown speckled freshwater fish found in rivers and lakes in many parts of the northern hemisphere. The trout belongs to the SALMON family. It is fished for food and for sport.

TROY An ancient city sited on the coast of modern Turkey. HOMER's epic poem, *Iliad*, tells how it was besieged by the Greeks for 10 years, and how it finally fell through a trick (the gift of a huge wooden horse with soldiers hidden inside). The story of Troy was thought to be imaginary until a German amateur archaeologist, Schliemann, discovered the site of the city in 1871–1894.

TRUFFLE Edible FUNGUS which grows underground. Truffles are cultivated in many parts of Europe and are a popular food. Because truffles grow underground, farmers use pigs to find them. The pigs are able to locate the fungi by smelling them and then dig them out with their snouts.

TRUMPET A brass wind musical instrument, also used at one time by armies for giving signals. Its tube is coiled to give a compact shape. VALVES and the action of the lips and breath give the different notes.

TSETSE FLY Brownish FLY found in tropical Africa. Using a piercing-sucking mouthpiece, it feeds on the blood of animals, including man. Tsetse flies are deadly pests as they carry and transmit fatal diseases, such as sleeping sickness in man and nagana in cattle.

TUATARA Lizard-like REPTILE found only on certain islands off the New Zealand coast. The tuatara is the most primitive reptile alive today. It spends the day in a burrow and comes out at night to search for insects and other animal food. Often, instead of digging its own burrow, the tuatara shares the home of a petrel or other seabird. ▷

TUBA A brass wind musical instrument – the largest and lowest-pitched of the brass range.

It is frequently used in bands and sometimes in ORCHESTRAS.

TUBERCULOSIS A disease caused by bacterial infection. One form is carried in infected milk, and attacks the bones and joints of young people. The other is spread by bacteria in the air, and usually attacks the lungs. Both have now almost disappeared in developed countries. ▷

TUDORS English royal dynasty (1485–1603), descended from a Welshman, Owen Tudor. His grandson, Henry Tudor, became HENRY VII by defeating Richard III at

▲ *The tuba (left) is a large brass instrument held vertically. The trumpet (right) is a tubular instrument. Some trumpets were known in ancient times and were made of horn, ivory or wood.*

▲ *The flower shown top left is a common tulip; the other three are new varieties that have been achieved by cross breeding. There are some 100 different species of tulip.*

◄ *The tuatara is the last living member of a prehistoric group of reptiles. It survived in New Zealand because it had few natural enemies, but it is now a threatened species.*

TUNGSTEN This steel-white metal has a melting point of 3420°C, higher than that of any other element except carbon. Tungsten is one of the heaviest substances, weighing almost twice as much as lead. The tensile strength of the metal is greater than that of any other substance. Its chemical symbol is W.

TUNISIA: FACTS AND FIGURES
Official language: Arabic, but French is widely spoken.
Currency: Dinar.
Religion: Moslem.
Chief river: Medjerda.
Largest cities: Tunis (pop. 774,000), Sfax (232,000).
Tunisia became a French protectorate in 1881, and won its independence in 1956.

the battle of Bosworth. He then married the eldest daughter of Edward III. This united the families of York and Lancaster, and so ended the WARS OF THE ROSES. His policy of strong and efficient government was continued by his son HENRY VIII. It was also carried on by the advisers to his young grandson Edward VI, and by his granddaughters MARY I and ELIZABETH I. The Tudor period saw the beginnings of the modern state, the rise of PARLIAMENT and the growth of naval power. ◁

TULIP Spring-flowering plant which grows from a BULB. The tulip has a long stem and a large, bell-shaped upright flower which is brightly coloured. Tulips, found wild in Mediterranean lands, are a popular garden plant. Producing tulip flowers and bulbs is an important industry in the Netherlands.

TUMOUR A lump in the body, made up of abnormal cells (cells growing without any normal purpose). Some tumours are malignant: they spread into the normal body cells and can travel to new parts of the body. These are called CANCERS and are highly dangerous.

TUNA Large fish, also called tunny, belonging to the MACKEREL family. It can grow to over 3 metres (10 ft). Tuna live in the warm waters of the Atlantic, Pacific and Mediter-

ranean. They are a favourite food fish and tuna fishing is a big industry in many parts of the world.

TUNDRA A bleak region between the icy north polar region and the coniferous forests. MOSSES, LICHENS and flowering plants flourish during the short summer. But it is too cold for trees, although some dwarf shrubs grow.

TUNGSTEN Also called wolfram, a hard white metallic ELEMENT. It is resistant to CORROSION and has a high melting point. Tungsten occurs in the minerals wolframite and scheelite. The metal is used to make electric light bulb filaments and is also used in various ALLOYS. ◁

TUNISIA A republic in North AFRICA. Tunisia has 6,937,000 people (1984) and an area of 163,610 sq km (63,170 sq miles). The capital is Tunis. Most of the people are farmers, but tourism is a major source of revenue. ◁

TUNNEL An underground passageway cut through rock or earth – usually so as to pass under a river or a range of hills. Modern

▼ The tunnel shield was invented by M.I. Brunel in 1843, to protect workers while they were boring through clay or soft rock.

tunnels are widely used for public transport systems beneath large cities. (See UNDER-GROUND RAILWAYS)

TURBINE A wheel turned by the force of a flowing liquid or gas. The first turbines were water wheels and WINDMILLS. Today's power stations use huge turbines to convert steam power to rotary motion for driving electricity generators. (See GAS TURBINE; WATER POWER)

TURKEY A republic which is divided between ASIA and EUROPE. Asian Turkey (also called Asia Minor) covers 97 per cent of the country. It consists mainly of plateaus and rugged mountains, bordered by broad coastal plains. The largest city, Istanbul, stands on the Bosphorus, which forms part of the channel which links the MEDITERRANEAN and Black seas and separates Asian from European Turkey.

The Turks once ruled the great MOSLEM Ottoman empire. This empire collapsed in World War I and Turkey was modernized in the 1920s and 1930s by its first president, Kemal Attaturk (1881–1938). Most of the people are farmers, but mining, especially for chrome ore, is important, and manufacturing industries are steadily increasing in number.

▷

TURKEY Large game bird native to North and Central America, now bred in many parts of the world for its meat. The first people to keep turkeys for food were the AZTECS of Mexico, then they were brought to Europe by the Spanish CONQUISTADORS. Turkey is traditionally eaten at Christmas in various countries and on Thanksgiving Day in the US. The domestic turkey is brown tinged with bronze.

▷

TURNER, J. M. W. English painter (1775–1851). He is best known for the almost ABSTRACT paintings of his later life, which captured dazzling effects of light, weather and water (e.g. in the railway painting *Rain, Steam and Speed*). Turner's work greatly influenced IMPRESSIONISM.

TURNIP Plant, grown for its roundish, white, edible root which is eaten as a VEGE-TABLE. Turnips grow best in cool climates. They are usually eaten cooked; the leaves may also be cooked and eaten as a green vegetable.

TURPENTINE A RESIN obtained from pine trees. It is used to produce oil (or spirits) of turpentine, a useful solvent (see SOLUTION). This oil is the substance usually referred to and sold as turpentine.

▶ *This Leatherback turtle is usually found in tropical waters. It may be up to 1.8 metres (6 ft) long, and can weigh more than 725 kg (1600 lb).*

▲ *Many people in Turkey today have a low standard of living. Although manufacturing is a developing industry, there is still much unemployment.*

TURQUOISE A mineral that is valued as a semi-precious GEM. It is blue or green, and found chiefly in Iran, Mexico and New Mexico. Turquoise was used in ancient Egypt c. 4000 BC.

TURTLE REPTILE with a box-like shell found mostly in tropical seas. Turtles are very similar to TORTOISES except that their limbs are paddle-shaped for swimming. They come ashore to breed and lay their eggs on sandy beaches. Most turtles are carnivorous and

TURKEY: FACTS AND FIGURES
Area: 780,576 sq km (301,382 sq miles).
Population: 48,265,000 (1984 est.).
Capital: Ankara.
Official language: Turkish.
Currency: Lira.
Largest cities: Istanbul (pop. 2,949,000), Ankara (2,276,000), Izmir (1,083,000).

TURKEY The domestic turkey (family Meleagrididae) is one of the most strangely named of birds. Turkeys originated in North America and were taken to Europe in the early 1500s. When the birds were introduced to England in about 1541, people thought they came from Turkey. The French name, *dindon,* means 'from India'.

TURTLE The largest marine turtle is the Leathery or Leatherback turtle (*Dermochelys coriacea*), whose shell may be 1.8 m (6 ft) long, with a flipper-to-flipper stretch of 3.6 m (12 ft), and a weight of more than 725 kg (1600 lb).

TUTANKHAMEN In 1922 the British archaeologist Howard Carter broke through the inner door of an ancient Egyptian tomb to find the most famous and the most valuable treasure in archaeological history. There were four rooms containing a gold throne, caskets, precious gems, furniture and clothing. In the burial chamber itself were four gold shrines, one inside the other, and a sarcophagus containing a nest of three coffins. The inner coffin was of solid gold, and in it was the mummified body of Tutankhamen. Over his face was a mask of gold, inlaid with lapis lazuli and blue glass. Although few facts are known about the reign of the young Tutankhamen, his is now the best-known name of all the pharaohs.

▲ *The death mask of Tutankhamen. It is made of polished gold set with lapis lazuli and strips of blue glass. Tutankhamen died after a reign of only about eight years.*

▲ *A gold shrine from the tomb of the young pharoah Tutankhamen showing the King with his Queen. This is one of the treasures found by Howard Carter in 1922.*

◄ *This little gold fisherman is another of the many treasures from the tomb of Tutankhamen. The tomb is the only royal burial to have been found unrobbed in the Valley of Kings. It has been very valuable to archaeologists in reconstructing Egyptian civilization at its height.*

feed on shellfish and other sea creatures. One species, the green turtle, is edible and is used to make turtle soup.   ◁

TUTANKHAMEN A young Egyptian PHARAOH who reigned for about eight years (c. 1361 – c. 1352 BC). He was the son-in-law of Akhenaten, a pharaoh who had tried to introduce a new religion recognizing only one god. Tutankhamen restored the old religion and moved his capital back to Thebes. He died at about the age of 19, and his tomb was discovered by archaeologist Howard Carter in 1922. It was filled with magnificent burial treasure, including a solid gold coffin.   ◁

▼ *Tutankhamen scatters his enemies, the Syrians. This scene from a painted chest found in his tomb shows vividly the effect the introduction of the chariot had on warfare in ancient Egypt.*

TYPHOID FEVER An infectious disease that attacks the digestive tract (see DIGESTION). It can cause internal bleeding with great danger to life. The bacteria responsible are found in the URINE of sufferers and others, in contaminated food and water, and can be carried by flies.

TYPHOON A tropical cyclone, or HUR-RICANE, which occurs in eastern Asia. These storms hit the PHILIPPINES and the south China coasts. They can cause great destruction.

TYRANNOSAURUS Fierce flesh-eating DINOSAUR which lived about 70 million years ago. Tyrannosaurus was the largest carnivorous animal that has ever lived on Earth. It was 15 metres (50 ft) long and stood 6 metres (20 ft) high. The monster walked on its back legs and had long, dagger-like teeth. ▷

TYRE A rubber tube filled with air, which is fitted around the wheel of a vehicle. The first rubber tyres, made in 1846, were solid. An air-filled (*pneumatic*) tyre had already been patented by then (see PATENT), but it was largely ignored and was 're-invented' by John Boyd Dunlop in 1888–90. It was soon fitted to all BICYCLES, and first appeared on a MOTOR CAR in 1895.

▼ *The violent world of dinosaurs.* Tyranosaurus *has a vulnerable* Corythosaurus *in its vice-like jaws.* Tyrannosaurus *stood taller than a giraffe and its head was the size of a new born calf. It weighed about 100 tonnes.*

TYRANNOSAURUS This huge creature must indeed have been a frightening sight. Each of its immensely powerful hind legs bore perhaps a four-tonne load – more than the entire weight of a rhinoceros. Its three big forward-pointing toes bore claws as long as carving knives. The creature's skull measured over a metre (4 ft), and each eye socket was big enough to hold a human head. Sabre-like teeth – some nearly the length of a man's hand – lined the jaws.

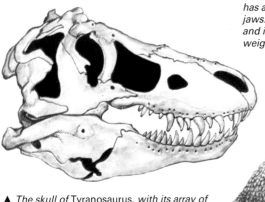

▲ *The skull of* Tyranosaurus, *with its array of sharp curved teeth.*

U

UGANDA A republic in East AFRICA. Uganda has 14,961,000 people (1984 est.) and an area of 236,036 sq km (91,134 sq miles). The capital is Kampala. Coffee, cotton and tea are the chief products. In 1971 an army takeover brought General Idi Amin to power. In 1979, Amin's government was overthrown with the help of Tanzanian troops.

UKRAINE A region in south-west RUSSIA, the Ukrainian Soviet Socialist Republic is Russia's chief farming area. It also has great reserves of coal and various metals and manufacturing is very important. The Ukraine has 50,667,000 people (1984) and an area of 603,700 sq km (233,089 sq miles). Capital: Kiev.

ULCER An open sore, usually with a flow of pus (infected fluid). It can be on the skin or in the digestive tract (e.g. in the mouth or stomach). An ulcer is usually due to infection or irritation. Gastric ulcers (in the stomach) are caused by irritation from the digestive juices, and must be treated by a very mild diet.

ULYSSES (ODYSSEUS) Ulysses is the Roman name for the legendary Greek hero Odysseus (see ODYSSEY). His adventures (as he tried to return home after the siege of TROY) included being captured by a race of one-eyed man-eating giants (the Cyclopes); resisting the fatal song of the Sirens; and having his men turned into pigs by the witch Circe.

UNDERGROUND RAILWAYS The world's first underground railway for public use was built in London in 1863. It was only four miles long and used steam locomotives, but it proved that underground railways could help to relieve traffic problems. In 1879 it was

▼ *Passengers at Baker Street Station where the first underground railway was opened.*

shown that electric trains were possible, which meant that deeper TUNNELS (less well ventilated) could be used. By 1898 the present system of motorized coaches had been developed. Today many major cities have underground railways, including London, New York, Paris, Tokyo and Moscow.

UNEMPLOYMENT Situation where people are out of work. Unemployment can be seasonal (due to work that only lasts part of the year), structural (due to a declining industry), or general (due to national economic conditions).

UNICORN A mythical animal with a body like a horse and a single straight horn set in its forehead. In the Middle Ages it became a symbol of purity and self-sacrifice.

USSR See RUSSIA

UNITED ARAB EMIRATES An ARAB nation consisting of seven emirates (states). The UAE has 1,267,000 people (1984 est.) and an area of 83,000 sq km (32,278 sq miles). Formerly called the Trucial States, this largely desert land is a major oil producer. ▷

UNITED NATIONS The international organization which works for peace and security throughout the world. The UN also has specialized agencies which deal with other matters, such as food and agriculture, health, labour, and so on. The UN was set up in 1945 by 51 nations. By the mid-1980s its membership had grown to 159.

The main organs of the UN, based in New York City, are the General Assembly, the Security Council and the Secretariat. The General Assembly consists of delegates from all member nations. It discusses international problems and each nation has one vote. The Security Council, with 15 members, is concerned mainly with keeping peace. The Secre-

▲ A cowboy on a ranch in Oregon, one of the three Pacific coast states of the USA. Oregon is the nation's largest producer of lumber, plywood and other wood products. It has some beautiful national forests.

▼ The white dome of the Capitol building in Washington DC. It was designed by William Thornton, who won a contest for its design in 1792. Washington was the first carefully planned city in the world.

tariat services the UN. Its head, the Secretary-General, is also a diplomat who can act on his own to solve problems, without having to refer them to the other organs of the UN. ▷

UNITED STATES A prosperous and powerful nation, the USA is the world's fourth largest country in area and population. It is a federal republic, with 50 states. Of these 49 are in NORTH AMERICA and one, HAWAII, is an island group in the central Pacific.

The USA has beautiful and varied scenery. Mountain ranges include the Appalachians in the east and the Rockies and Sierra Nevada-Cascade ranges in the west. There are also vast grassy plains and barren deserts.

The first inhabitants of the country were the AMERICAN INDIANS, whose ancestors came from Asia about 20,000 years ago. VIKINGS, under Leif Ericsson (900s–1000s), were probably the first Europeans to land in North America. But serious exploration along the

UNITED ARAB EMIRATES: FACTS AND FIGURES
Official language: Arabic.
Currency: Dirham.
Religion: Sunni Moslem.
The largest of the Emirates are Abu Dhabi and Dubai; the others are Sharjah, Ajman, Umm al Quwain, Ras al Khaimah, and Fujeirah.

UNITED NATIONS
Specialized Agencies of the United Nations:
Food and Agriculture Organization (FAO). General Agreement on Tariffs and Trade (GATT). Inter-Governmental Maritime Consultative Organization (IMCO). International Atomic Energy Agency (IAEA). International Bank for Reconstruction and Development (World Bank; IBRD). International Civil Aviation Organization (ICAO). International Development Association (IDA). International Finance Corporation (IFC). International Fund for Agricultural Development (IFAD). International Labour Organization (ILO). International Monetary Fund (IMF). International Telecommunications Union (ITU). United Nations

▼An observer of the UN peace-keeping force, near the Suez canal in Egypt.

Educational, Scientific and Cultural Organization (UNESCO). Universal Postal Union (UPU). World Health Organization (WHO). World Intellectual Property Organization (WIPO). World Meteorological Organization (WMO).

UNITED STATES: FACTS AND FIGURES
Official language: English.
Currency. Dollar.
Area: 9,363,128 sq km (3,615,124 sq miles).
Population: 236,381,000 (1984 est.).
Capital: Washington DC.
Highest peak: Mount McKinley, 6194 m (20,320 ft), in Alaska.
Longest river: Missouri, 4368 km (2714 miles) long, a tributary of the Mississippi River.
Largest cities: New York City (pop. 17,807,000); Los Angeles (12,373,000), Chicago (8,035,000), Philadelphia (5,755,000), San Francisco (5,685,000), Detroit (4,577,000).
Religion: About two-thirds of the population is Protestant, one-fourth Roman Catholic, 3 per cent Jewish.
There are 50 states. Alaska is by far the largest, but California has most people. The 13 original states were Connecticut, Delaware, Georgia, Maryland, Massachusetts, New Hampshire, New Jersey, New York, North Carolina, Pennsylvania, Rhode Island, South Carolina and Virginia. The newest states are Alaska and Hawaii, which both became states in 1959.

URUGUAY: FACTS AND FIGURES
Official language: Spanish.
Currency: Peso.
Religion: Mainly Roman Catholic.
Chief rivers: Uruguay, Negro, Rio de la Plata.
Largest cities: Montevideo (pop. 1,376,000), Las Piedras (90,000).

Atlantic coast of what is now the USA began during the Age of Exploration in the early 1500s (see COLUMBUS).

The English were the first to settle in large numbers and, by 1760, there were 13 British colonies in the eastern USA, containing about 1,500,000 people. However, the colonies united and became independent after the REVOLUTIONARY WAR (also called the American War of Independence) of 1775–1783. The new nation soon expanded southwards and westwards. A dispute over slavery threatened the nation's unity in the mid-1800s, and a CIVIL WAR was fought from 1861–1865.

In the late 1800s, the USA began to play an increasingly important part in world affairs. After participating in World Wars I and II, the USA emerged as one of the two great super-powers, the other being RUSSIA.

The population is very diverse. About $87\frac{1}{2}$ per cent are descendants of people from all over Europe. Another 11 per cent are black Americans, the descendants of African slaves. Smaller groups include the American Indians (now 0.3 per cent) and Chinese, Japanese, Filipino, Puerto Rican and Mexican Americans.

The most important sector of the economy is manufacturing and the USA produces about half of the world's manufactured goods. The USA has tremendous mineral resources and is the world's leading producer of copper, oil and natural gas, phosphates, sulphur and uranium. It has large reserves of coal, iron ore and lead. Vast areas of the country are fertile farmland or lush pasture and the USA is a major food-producer. However, farming is highly mechanized and only about 3.5 per cent of the people work on the land. (See NEW YORK; WASHINGTON DC) ◁

UNIVERSE Our name for all the matter, energy and space in existence. Our most powerful telescopes have revealed that the universe contains at least 10,000 million star systems, or GALAXIES. Most scientists think that the universe was created in a gigantic explosion called the Big Bang. Others think that matter is being created all the time. All are agreed that the universe is expanding, as astronomical observations clearly indicate that the galaxies are getting farther apart all the time. It is possible that this expansion will be followed by a period of contraction, and that the whole process will then repeat. This is called the oscillation theory.

UNIVERSITY An institute of higher EDUCATION with the power to award degrees. The first European university was founded at Salerno, Italy in the 9th century AD, followed in the 12th century by those at Bologna, Paris and Oxford. Universities consist of teachers (lecturers), students trying to get a degree

(undergraduates) and students who have been given a degree and are doing further study (graduate or research students). In England a first degree is awarded by examination after three or four years' study.

UR An ancient city in MESOPOTAMIA. In the Bible it is called Ur of the Chaldees, and is named as the home of ABRAHAM. Its site was discovered in the 19th century. Excavations by Sir Leonard Woolley showed that it had been inhabited from about 3500 BC. At one time it seems to have experienced a great flood, and this may have given rise to the Bible legend.

URANIUM A hard, silvery metallic ELEMENT that is radioactive (see RADIOACTIVITY). It occurs as compounds in pitchblende and other minerals. Natural uranium contains two main ISOTOPES – uranium-238 (99.28 per cent) and uranium-235 (0.71 per cent). Uranium-238 can be converted into plutonium-239. This can be used as a fuel in nuclear fission reactions (see ATOMIC ENERGY). And uranium-235 is itself an important nuclear fuel.

URANUS One of the SOLAR SYSTEM's outer PLANETS, being located between the orbits of Saturn and Neptune. Uranus is a cold planet with an atmosphere of methane and HYDROGEN. It has five SATELLITES.

URINE An amber-coloured liquid excreted by MAMMALS. It is made in the KIDNEYS from water and waste products filtered out of the blood. Humans excrete about 1 litre (1.75 pt) a day.

URUGUAY A republic in south-eastern SOUTH AMERICA, bordering the Atlantic. Uruguay has 2,990,000 people (1984 est.) and an area of 177,508 sq km (68,536 sq miles). The capital is Montevideo. Farming is the chief occupation, especially cattle- and sheep-rearing, and meat, wool and textiles are exported. ◁

▼ The five satellites of Uranus are all shown on this photograph. The faintest, Miranda, appears just to the left of the planet. Uranus is very cold, about −170°C (−274°F) as it is very far from the Sun. It was discovered in 1781.

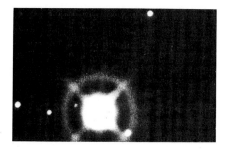

V

VACCINE A substance to make a person immune to a specific disease. Most are injected, but some are given by mouth. They work by stimulating the body's natural resistance (see ANTIBODY). Routine childhood vaccinations are given against a number of diseases, including POLIOMYELITIS, DIPHTHERIA and WHOOPING COUGH. (See JENNER, EDWARD; VIRUS)

VACUUM An absolutely empty space. In practice, it is impossible to remove every trace of matter from a space. So the term is generally used to mean a region of extremely low air pressure. Even outer space contains matter in the form of widely spaced atoms.

VALENCE Also called valency, the number of chemical BONDS with which an atom or a radical (group containing different atoms) can link with other atoms. Chlorine, for example, has a valence of one, while zinc has a valence of two. For this reason, each MOLECULE of the compound zinc chloride ($ZnCl_2$) contains one zinc atom linked by its bonds to two chlorine atoms, as its formula shows. Iron and some other elements have more than one valence – that is, atoms of these elements may join with different numbers of other elements.

VALLEY A depression in the Earth's surface. Most valleys are worn out by rivers, but some river valleys are deepened by GLACIERS. Rift valleys occur when a block of land sinks between roughly parallel faults.

VALVE An electronic device that passes current in one direction only. The *diode* valve consists of a glass vacuum tube containing

▶ *This boy is being vaccinated against tuberculosis. Mass vaccination campaigns have done much to wipe out diseases.*

two electrodes – an electrically heated cathode and an anode. A positive charge on the anode makes it attract negatively charged electrons (see ATOMS) 'boiled off' from the cathode. In the *triode* valve, an extra electrode, called the grid, is placed between the cathode and anode to control the electron flow.

The diode is used merely to rectify current – that is, allow it to flow in one direction only. Triode valves can also amplify (strengthen) signals. A small varying voltage applied to the grid causes large variations in the electron flow through the valve. Most valves have extra electrodes to improve performance or to enable them to perform more complicated tasks. Today, TRANSISTORS have largely replaced valves in electronic equipment.

VAMPIRE BAT Small BAT found in the forests of Central and South America. Despite the name, only one species of Vampire feeds entirely on the blood of other animals. It attacks its victims at night while they are asleep. With its sharp teeth, the bat cuts the

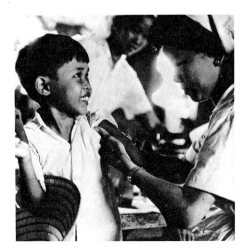

VANILLA The vanilla orchid is a vine which produces a fruit shaped like a cylindrical pod. This pod contains numerous tiny black seeds in an oily black pulp. Before the beans are ripe, they are cut from the vine. They are cured in large oven rooms, so that the beans shrink and turn brown in colour. The beans then have the true vanilla flavour. Vanilla extract is produced by chopping the beans and mixing them with alcohol which absorbs the flavour.

VATICAN CITY: FACTS AND FIGURES
Languages: Italian is the official language of the state; Latin is the official language of the Holy See.
Currency: Italian lira.

VENEZUELA: FACTS AND FIGURES
Official language: Spanish.
Currency: Bolivar.
Religion: Roman Catholic.
Largest cities: Caracas (pop. 2,944,000), Maracaibo (901,000).
Chief river: Orinoco.
About 70 per cent of the population is of mixed Indian and European ancestry.
Venezuela became independent from Spain in 1811.

skin and then laps up the blood. Other species live on insects and fruit.

VAN GOGH, VINCENT Dutch painter (1853–1890). He became a friend of GAUGUIN and was a leading Post-Impressionist artist (see IMPRESSIONISM). He painted very quickly using bold brush strokes and bright colours to create an immediate impact. He committed suicide after some years in a mental asylum.

VANILLA Climbing ORCHID grown in tropical countries – especially Madagascar – for its aromatic pod. The pod, about 10 cm (4 in) long, contains many tiny seeds. It is dried and the flavouring is extracted by a complicated process. Vanilla is used to flavour all kinds of foods. ◁

VARICOSE VEINS VEINS on the surface of the skin that are swollen and sore. They usually occur on the inside of the legs, and may need surgery. Varicose veins appear more often in people who are overweight and those whose work involves a lot of standing.

VARNISHES Transparent protective coatings made from chemicals called RESINS. Varnishes are used on wood, metal, fabrics, paper and other materials. Some varnishes are used for electrical insulation.

VATICAN CITY A state which houses the government of the ROMAN CATHOLIC CHURCH. Vatican City, in Rome, covers 44 hectares (108.7 acres) and has a population of 1000. It encloses St Peter's Basilica, the largest of all Christian churches. ◁

VEGETABLE PLANT grown for food. Usually only part of the plant is eaten, either the root, stem, leaf, seed or fruit. ONIONS and

CARROTS are root vegetables, but asparagus is a stem vegetable. Members of the CABBAGE family, such as sprouts and kale, are all leaf vegetables. PEAS and BEANS are seed vegetables while CUCUMBERS and TOMATOES are fruit vegetables. Some vegetables, such as LETTUCE, are eaten raw, while others, such as TURNIPS, are cooked. People who only eat vegetables and never have any animal food, such as meat and fish, are called vegetarians.

VEIN One of the BLOOD vessels that take blood back to the heart from the various parts of the body. Most veins carry blood that has no oxygen left in it, but the veins leading from the LUNGS to the heart carry blood that is again rich in oxygen. Veins have thin walls, and valves to help the blood beat the pull of gravity. The blood's flow back to the heart is helped by the squeezing action of muscles.

VELÁSQUEZ, DIEGO RODRÍGUEZ DE SILVA Y Spanish painter (1599–1660). In 1623 he became court painter to Philip IV of Spain, and completed many royal portraits. He is best known for *Las Meninas* (a court group study) and the *Rokeby Venus*. His style of painting was influenced by TITIAN, RUBENS and Tintoretto.

VELOCITY The speed of a body measured in a given direction. A vehicle travelling due north at a given speed would have the same velocity in that direction. But, while travelling at the same constant speed, it could be said to have a smaller velocity in the north-easterly direction, and zero velocity in the easterly direction.

VELVET A fabric with a thick soft pile of short, raised threads all over its surface. It is used largely for curtains and furnishings. True velvet is made from silk, but it is also made from RAYON.

VENEREAL DISEASES Certain contagious diseases that are usually only passed on by the act of sexual intercourse (see SEX). The major diseases in this group are gonorrhoea and syphilis.

VENEZUELA A republic in northern SOUTH AMERICA. Venezuela has 16,851,000 people (1984 est.) and an area of 912,050 sq km (352,144 sq miles). The capital is Caracas. This tropical country is the world's fifth largest oil producer, and revenue from oil is being used to develop the economy. ◁

VENICE A beautiful city built on mud islands in a lagoon in north-east ITALY. Venice

◀ *Venezuela's chief resource is oil. Much of it is produced from oil wells in Lake Maracaibo.*

has 341,000 people (1984). Founded in AD 452, Venice was a great sea power in the Middle Ages. It now attracts many tourists.

VENOM Poisonous fluid given out by certain SNAKES, JELLYFISH and other animals. It is usually injected into the victim by biting or stinging. Venomous creatures usually live in tropical regions.

VENTRILOQUISM The art of speaking so that the sound seems to come from somewhere or someone else. It takes great practice; usually the lips are held as still as possible.

VENUS (GODDESS) The Roman goddess of love and beauty – the counterpart of the Greek goddess Aphrodite. She was said to have been born full-grown from the sea foam. She was mother of Eros (Cupid) and of Aeneas (one of the legendary founders of Rome).

VENUS (PLANET) Of all the PLANETS in the SOLAR SYSTEM, Venus is our closest neighbour. It is covered with dense white cloud and can be seen clearly from the Earth. Venus looks like an extremely bright star, and is visible some time before and after the true stars can be seen. For this reason, Venus is sometimes called the Evening Star or Morning Star. ▷

▼ The Soviet landing probe Venera 12 visited the surface of Venus in 1975 and sent back the first photographs.

▲ Louis XIV's magnificent palace at Versailles. The facade is 415 metres (1361 ft) long. The king employed Europe's finest architects, craftsmen, painters, sculptors and landscape gardeners.

VENUS' FLY TRAP Insect-eating plant found on marshland in the southern US. Bog soil lacks nitrogen so the Venus' Fly Trap gets this vital element from digesting insects. Its leaves have two parts which are hinged together and which snap shut when an insect lands òn them. The plant attacks the victim with special juices, takes in its protein and so obtains the extra nitrogen.

VERB The part of speech that describes actions (*he eats*) and states (*he knows*). It may be one word or several (*has been eating*). Words change according to person (*I eat, he eats*), tense (*eat, ate*) and mood (*he has eaten, he has been eating*).

VERSAILLES A town just south of Paris best known for its palace, established by LOUIS XIV as the seat of the French monarchy. The palace is more than 800 metres ($\frac{1}{2}$ mile) long, and took over 100 years to complete. Its hundreds of rooms include the famous Hall of Mirrors. Versailles was the site of the Peace Conference that ended World War I.

VERTEBRATE An animal with a backbone (see SPINAL COLUMN). Vertebrates form just one of the 21 major groups – *phyla* – into which the animal kingdom is divided (see CLASSIFICATION OF LIVING THINGS). Yet they include the most developed and important

VENUS (PLANET): FACTS:
Orbital period: 224 days.
Rotation period: 243 days.
Length of day: 2760 days.
Surface temperature: 480°C.
Main atmospheric content: Carbon dioxide.
Moons: None.

Eight probes, all launched from the USSR, have landed on the planet Venus. The Soviet landing craft have all descended through the thick Venusian atmosphere by parachute. Veneras 9 and 10 sent back the first successful photographs taken on the surface of another planet. The USA has sent three successful probes to take photographs and measurements from close range. These have shown that Venus has no strong magnetic field like that of Earth, even though the planets seem to be made up in a similar way. Photographs taken by spacecraft show nothing but swirling clouds.

THE VERTEBRATES

Bird

Mammal

Amphibian

Fish

▲ The Leatherback Turtle is a reptile weighing more than half a tonne.

▲ Major types of animal vertebrates (excluding Man).

▼ Among the most common amphibians are the newt and frog.

Newt

Frog

▲ Apes can walk upright on two legs. They belong to the primate family tree, which includes Man.

▼ Ostriches belong to the flightless group of birds known as ratites.

▲ Most fish (left) have a swim bladder which helps them float, but not the shark (right). It would sink to the sea bottom if it did not keep moving.

animals in the world. The main classes of vertebrates are FISH, AMPHIBIANS, REPTILES, BIRDS and MAMMALS. All vertebrate animals have SKELETONS which are inside their bodies and which are made of bone. This type of skeleton is called an endo-skeleton. Vertebrates appeared on Earth about 450 million years ago. These first backboned creatures were fishes. Then came amphibians, reptiles, mammals and lastly, about 150 million years ago, birds.

VESUVIUS A VOLCANO overlooking the Bay of Naples in Italy. Vesuvius erupted in AD 79, destroying the towns of Herculaneum and POMPEII. It has erupted many times since then, the last eruption being in 1944.

VICTORIA A beautiful and prosperous Australian state, Victoria has a population of 4,076,000 (1984) and an area of 227,618 sq km (87,884 sq miles). The capital is MELBOURNE. The Murray River forms the state's northern boundary. About 75 per cent of the land is farmed. Various crops are grown and cattle and sheep are reared. Manufacturing is now the most important industry. Victoria became a separate British colony in 1851.

VICTORIA CROSS The highest British decoration for bravery, founded by Queen VICTORIA in 1856. The medal is bronze with a crimson ribbon. Originally all the crosses were made from the metal of Russian cannons captured at Sevastopol in the CRIMEAN WAR.

VICTORIA FALLS On the River ZAMBESI in southern Africa, the Victoria Falls is about 102 metres (335 ft) high. It was discovered by David LIVINGSTONE in 1855.

VICTORIA, QUEEN Queen of Great Britain (born 1819, reigned 1837–1901). She suc-

▲ The eruption of Vesuvius on August 24, AD 79, buried alive thousands of the citizens of Pompeii.

ceeded on the death of her uncle, William IV. In 1840 she married Prince Albert of Saxe-Coburg, and raised a large family before his death in 1861. She then spent many years in retirement, and became unpopular; but she recaptured public affection at her jubilees (1887 and 1897). She was made Empress of India in 1876, and ruled the BRITISH EMPIRE during the period of its greatest power. ▷

VIENNA Capital of AUSTRIA. Vienna has a population of 1,531,000. Built along the River DANUBE, the city is a great cultural centre, associated with such composers as BEETHOVEN, MOZART, Franz Schubert and Johann Strauss.

VIETNAM A communist republic in southeast ASIA with 56,567,000 people (1984 est.) and an area of 332,559 sq km (128,402 sq miles). The capital is Hanoi. Formerly French Indo-china, Vietnam was partitioned in 1954. War between the North and South ended in 1975, when North Vietnam occupied the South. (See CAMBODIA) ▷

▼ The French army at Dien Bien Phu, in Vietnam. In 1954 the country was split into the communist state of North Vietnam and the weak states of South Vietnam, Laos and Cambodia.

VICTORIA, QUEEN Queen Victoria was not only the longest reigning British monarch, she was also the longest-lived: 81 years, 243 days. She beat George III by four days.

VIETNAM: FACTS AND FIGURES
Official language: Vietnamese.
Currency: Dong.
Religion: The majority practice Buddhism and animism.
Largest cities: Ho Chi Minh City (pop. 3,420,000), Hanoi (2,571,000), Haiphong (1,279,000).

VIKINGS The Vikings were such a warlike race, they could not imagine a heaven in which there was no fighting, so they buried their dead with all their weapons for use in Valhalla.

▼ This picture was painted in the early years of Queen Victoria's reign. Her reign was very long and her happy marriage to Prince Albert produced nine children.

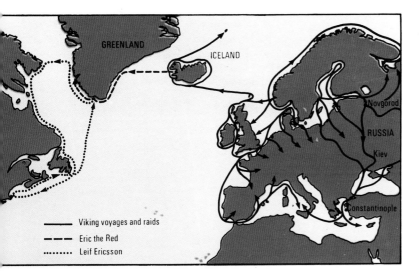

◄ *The Vikings discovered Iceland in about AD 870. Settlers soon followed and a farming community grew up there. In 982 Eric the Red discovered Greenland.*

preserving food by pickling (soaking in vinegar). It is traditionally made from wine (wine vinegar), beer (malt vinegar) or cider (cider vinegar). Some cheap modern vinegar is made chemically.

VIOLET Small flowering plant found in most parts of the world. Its leaf is heart-shaped and its flower is generally purple or white. Some varieties have a very strong scent.

VIOLIN A stringed musical instrument, played with a bow. It has a hollow resonant body and a long neck. The strings are held down at different points on the neck to give the various notes. The violin developed in the 17th century from the earlier viol, and is now the chief instrument of the ORCHESTRA. Famous violin makers include Stradivarius. ◁

VIRUS A minute organism – much smaller than BACTERIA – that can only be seen with an electron microscope. Viruses can only grow and reproduce inside living CELLS. Some use animal cells, others use plant cells. The virus

▼ *The Vikings were great sea voyagers, and even sailed as far as North America.*

VIOLIN Antonio Stradivari (1644-1737), the great Italian master of violin-making, signed his violins with the Latin spelling of his name 'Stradiuarius' or 'Stradivarius'. He made about 1000 instruments, but only about 600 remain. Stradivari was still making violins in his native Cremona until his death at the age of 93, and it is said that the instruments made in his last year were still among his finest. He also made violas and cellos. Some experts believe that the secret of Stradivari's success was in the rich amber-coloured varnish that he used, a secret which has been lost.

VIKINGS Scandinavian sea-warriors of the 8th-10th centuries AD. They raided and settled on the coasts of Britain and western Europe; sailed as far afield as Constantinople, Africa and Greenland; and were the first discoverers of America. Two main waves of Viking warriors invaded England. The first forced AL-FRED THE GREAT to give up a large part of his territory in 885. The second ended by establishing Canute and his sons as Kings of England (1016–1042). The NORMANS were also of Viking origin. ◁

VINE Woody-stemmed, climbing plant grown for its green or black berry fruits called GRAPES. Vineyards (fields of vines) are a common sight in Mediterranean countries and in other warm temperate lands. The word vine is also used to describe any climbing plant with a strong, woody stem.

VINEGAR A weak mixture of acetic acid and water, used for flavouring food and also for

► In explosive volcanoes like this one, gases in the molten rock are heated, expand and then explode. A cloud of steam, gas, dust, rock and lava bursts out.

makes the 'host' cell produce virus material instead of normal cell material. As a result, the host cell is damaged, perhaps fatally, and this eventually causes illness in the animal or plant. Many diseases that attack human beings are caused by viruses. They include smallpox, measles and the common cold. Doctors try to protect people from viral diseases by vaccination. The VACCINE itself is made from viruses.

VITAMINS Certain substances needed by the body in tiny quantities. They are not used to make any part of the body, but have to be there for many body processes to go on. For example, vitamin A is needed for growth. There are a few vitamins that the body can put together for itself, from other chemicals. But most have to be supplied by FOOD. Some people take vitamin pills, but a proper DIET should make this unnecessary.

VODKA A type of ALCOHOL made in Russia and Poland – a strong drink, with no colour and little flavour. Good vodka is made from RYE, cheap vodka from potatoes. It is famous as the Russian national drink.

VOICE The SOUND of the human voice is made by air passing over the vocal chords (which are two folds of mucous membrane in the LARYNX). Movements of the TONGUE and lips change the sound into words, and the resulting sounds are strengthened by resonating in the hollow sinuses of the skull (see SINUS). Use of the voice is controlled by the brain, so brain damage can cause loss of speech.

VOLCANO Either a hole in the ground from which MAGMA, gas and steam are erupted, or a mountain formed from hardened magma. There are about 455 active volcanoes on land, with another 80 or so beneath the oceans. There are many more that are now extinct. (See VESUVIUS) ▷

VOLGA RIVER Europe's longest river, the Volga flows 3690 km (2290 miles) through European RUSSIA to its large delta in the CASPIAN SEA, where there are over 200 outlets.

VOLT The SI UNIT for measuring electrical pressure, or electromotive force (e.m.f.). The

► Vultures and ravens scavenge on a carcase, removing the decaying flesh and leaving only skin and bone. Scavenging beetles then take over and destroy the remains completely.

volt is also used to measure the difference in pressure, known as potential difference (p.d.), between two points in an electrical circuit. The volt is defined as the potential difference between the ends of a conductor carrying a current of one AMPERE when one WATT of power is being dissipated.

VULTURE Large bird of prey with a bare neck and head, found in the warmer parts of Asia, Africa and Europe. Vultures do not kill their prey but feed on the carcases of dead animals. In hot countries, vultures are useful birds as they eat up carrion before it has time to rot in the heat and cause disease.

VOLCANO The greatest known volcanic explosion was Krakatoa, in 1883. Ash shot 80 km (50 miles) into the air, and the sound of the explosion was heard nearly 5000 km (3000 miles) away.

Most volcanoes occur in the 'ring of fire', a broad belt that lies around the Pacific Ocean. Other volcanic belts run down the centre of the Atlantic and across the Mediterranean.

W

▼ Walruses live in large herds along the Arctic shores. They use their tusks to help them move, to dig up molluscs from the sea-bed and as weapons. Walrus herds are now protected by law.

WALES Part of the United Kingdom of GREAT BRITAIN and Northern Ireland, Wales consists mostly of beautiful mountains and plateaus. River valleys and fertile coastal plains cover about one-third of the land. The most important regions are the coal-mining and metal-manufacturing areas in south-eastern Wales. Another small coalfield is in the north-east. Farming is also important.

England conquered Wales in 1282 and the two countries were united in 1536. But the Welsh people have retained their own individual culture. The Welsh language belongs to the GAELIC family. In 1981 almost 19 per cent of the people of Wales spoke Welsh, but most of them also spoke English. ◁

WALNUT Deciduous TREE belonging to the northern hemisphere. It is grown for its fine wood and its edible nut of the same name. The nuts are hard-shelled and grow inside a pulpy case. Walnut wood has an attractive grain (pattern) and is highly prized by furniture makers.

WALRUS Large, heavily-built sea MAMMAL related to the SEAL. Walruses have a grey wrinkled skin and are usually over 3 metres (10 ft) in length. They also have two long, powerful tusks. The tusks are used for scraping their chief food, shellfish, off rocks and for fighting. Walruses collect in great herds and live in shallow coastal waters within the Arctic Circle.

WAR OF 1812 A war between Great Britain and the United States, during the Napoleonic Wars. The British blockaded American ports

to prevent their trading with France and seized many American ships and sailors. At the same time, the Americans attempted an invasion of Canada. The British eventually won control at sea, and marched on Washington, burning the White House. But the war was inconclusive and peace was officially made in 1814. In a final battle, the British were beaten at New Orleans (1815).

WARSAW Capital of POLAND. Warsaw has 1,650,000 people (1984 est.). Situated on the River Vistula, it is a major manufacturing, trading and cultural centre. It was largely rebuilt after World War II. ▷

WARS OF THE ROSES The civil wars fought in England (1455–1485) between the House of Lancaster (whose badge was a red rose) and the House of York (whose badge was a white one). Lancaster had ruled since 1399, but under the reign of HENRY VI, their power was weakened and this gave the Yorkists a chance to claim the throne. The House of York ruled from 1461–1485 (except during 1470–1471), but this rule ended with the defeat of Richard III by Henry TUDOR, who belonged to a branch of Lancaster. The wars exhausted the power of the nobility.

WASHINGTON DC Capital of the USA. Washington DC (District of Columbia) covers 158 sq km (61 sq miles) and has a population, including suburbs, of 3,429,000 (1984). It was founded in 1791.

WASHINGTON, GEORGE First President of the United States. A Virginia plantation owner (1732–1799), he led the growth of opposition to British control, and was made Commander-in-Chief of the rebel forces at the start of the American REVOLUTIONARY WAR. After the Constitutional Convention (which drew up the basic laws [Constitution] of the US), he was elected President in 1789 and

▲ The wasp's black and yellow colouring warns off other creatures.

again in 1793. His politics emphasized stability and order. ▷

WASP INSECT, often black and yellow, found all over the world and related to the BEE. The female has a sharp sting. Some species live alone, others live in colonies grouping thousands of insects. These social wasps build intricate nests of wood pulp which they make themselves using wood fibres and saliva. Adult wasps eat sweet things such as nectar and ripe fruit, but the larvae need animal food and feed on other insects. ▷

WATER Just over 70 per cent of the Earth's surface is covered with water, on which all life depends. Most of this water is in the OCEANS, from which it evaporates to fall later as rain, snow or hail. Water that falls on land eventually evaporates or drains into the rivers and flows back into the seas and oceans. This continuing process is called the water cycle. Besides supporting life, water helps to shape

▼ The water cycle. The Sun heats the oceans and lakes, evaporating moisture. In rising, this condenses to form clouds. Moisture from clouds falls as precipitation (rain or snow). Some moisture is re-evaporated, some returns to the atmosphere through transpiration of plants, and some returns as water to the sea.

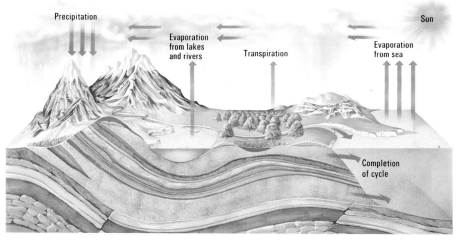

Precipitation
Sun
Evaporation from lakes and rivers
Transpiration
Evaporation from sea
Completion of cycle

WATER COLOUR A form of ART using paints that are mixed with water (rather than the usual oil colours). It was used for medieval ILLUMINATED MANUSCRIPTS, but not widely adopted by artists till the 18th century. The light, clear colours of water paint are ideal for impressions of landscape and weather. Important water-colour artists include TURNER, Constable and CÉZANNE.

WATERFALL Waterfalls are caused by water wearing away rock at different speeds. If a river flows over a join between hard rock and soft rock, it wears away the soft rock more quickly, and, after many years, makes a deep 'step'. The most famous waterfalls are Niagara, between the US and Canada, and Victoria Falls in Africa. ◁

WATERLOO, BATTLE OF The final battle of the Napoleonic Wars (June, 1815). Napoleon BONAPARTE had returned from exile, and had regained control of France. At Waterloo he met an army of British, Germans, Dutch and Belgians, under WELLINGTON. At the end of the day the arrival of the Prussians, under Blücher, ensured a decisive French defeat.

WATERMELON Tropical creeping plant grown for its very large fruit. Watermelons have a green skin and a red, juicy flesh full of seeds. As watermelons are 90 per cent water, they are cool and refreshing to eat.

WATER POLO A game played in a swimming pool with an inflated ball, and two teams

▼ Arthur Wellesley, Duke of Wellington, led the army at Waterloo. A brilliant leader, Wellington was under-estimated by Napoleon.

WATERFALL: FACTS AND FIGURES
Highest: Angel Falls, in Venezuela, 979 m (3212 ft).
Greatest single drop: Angel Falls, about 800 m (2625 ft).
Greatest flow: Sete Quedas in Brazil and Paraguay, averaging 13,300 cu m (460,000 cu ft) per second.
Broadest: Khône Falls in Laos, nearly 11 km (6.8 miles) across.

▲ The spectacular Iguassu Falls is some three kilometres long and 82 metres (270 ft) high (taller than Niagara Falls). Heavily forested islands break up the falls into many cascades. Wildlife around the fall is abundant, and some of it unique to this place. Sunlight on the continual spray causes almost constant rainbows to occur.

the land, wearing away valleys and depositing material elsewhere. Chemically, pure water is known as hydrogen oxide, formula H_2O. It is unusual in that, on cooling, it contracts to reach maximum density at 4°C (39°F), and then expands on freezing at 0°C (32°F). This expansion causes water pipes to burst in cold weather. (See WATER POWER; WATER SUPPLY). ◁

Wat

of seven swimmers with four reserves each side. The ball is thrown from one swimmer to another, and each team tries to score goals. It is an OLYMPIC sport.

WATER POWER Since Roman times, man has used the water wheel to obtain useful energy from the water flowing in rivers. At first, buckets were fitted to the rim of a vertically mounted wheel that dipped into the water. The wheel turned as the moving water pushed against the buckets. Later water wheels had wooden paddles instead of buckets. Water wheels were still commonly used in the 1800s. Many flour mills, saws, pumps and other machines were driven by water power. Today, HYDROELECTRIC POWER stations use the energy of flowing water to drive TURBINES. These are linked to GENERATORS that produce electricity. In some areas, electricity is generated using the energy of waves and tides.

WATER SKIING Skiing on water, in which the person is towed along by a motor boat. As a competition, water skiing includes slalom (steering round markers), distance jumping and figure skiing.

WATER SUPPLY Vast amounts of water are used daily in towns and cities. It is obtained from rivers, reservoirs and lakes. Because such water contains dirt and disease-causing bacteria, it undergoes special treatment before distribution. Chemicals are added to make suspended solids separate out. And bacteria are removed by filtration or killed by adding CHLORINE.

WATT The SI UNIT of POWER. One watt is used when work is done, or energy consumed, at the rate of one JOULE per second. The watt is also equal to the power used when an electric current of one AMPERE flows through a conductor across which a potential difference of one VOLT is maintained. One horsepower is equal to 745.7 watts.

WATT, JAMES Scottish engineer (1736–1819) who greatly improved the efficiency of the STEAM ENGINE. As a result of this work, steam engines were established as an alternative to water power in factories in the 1780s, during the booming Industrial Revolution. ▷

WATTLE A plant found in Australia belonging to the *acacia* family, and well adapted to drought conditions. It produces branches suitable for interwoven (wattle) roofs and fencing. Its golden flower is the Australian national emblem.

WAVES Most waves are caused by winds which blow across the open sea. The height of

▶ *Weather maps use symbols, as on the map opposite, to give a summary of weather conditions at a given place and time. The lines are isobars; they show places with the same air pressure.*

a wave increases as winds grow in strength. But waves do not move water particles along. A corked bottle in the open sea merely bobs up and down with the passing waves. Its position hardly changes unless it is moved by the wind or a current. ▷

WAX The name given to a number of different substances, from various animal, plant and mineral sources (e.g. beeswax, the wax in the ear, paraffin wax, sealing wax). All are solids, do not dissolve in water, and melt at low temperatures.

WEASEL World's smallest carnivore. Weasels, about 17cm (8in) long, have red-brown fur with white underparts. They are savage hunters and feed mostly on voles, mice and rats. Weasels are found all over the northern hemisphere. ▷

WEATHER FORECASTING Throughout the world, meteorologists at weather stations record information, such as atmospheric pressure, temperature, rainfall and wind speed (see METEOROLOGY). This information is transmitted to forecast centres, where it is used to compile weather charts. Lines called *isobars* are drawn on maps to show places of equal atmospheric pressure. From such maps, forecasters can predict how the weather will change. Television pictures transmitted from weather SATELLITES to ground stations enable meteorologists to observe cloud patterns in the region. ▷

▼ *The weasel attacks prey larger than itself, by biting the back of its victim's neck. It is only about 17 cm (8 in) long.*

WATT, JAMES Watt's inventions included a steam condenser to make a more effective steam engine, and a cranking system to convert the to-and-fro motion of a piston in a cylinder into the round-and-round motion of a wheel. He also invented a governor to regulate engine speed, a throttle valve, and a steam heating system.

WAVES The energy of breaking waves can hurl great loads about. On the Oregon coast in North America waves throw rocks weighing 45 kg (100 lb) so high that one lighthouse has steel bars to protect its light. Yet this light stands 42 m (139 ft) above the sea. When a fierce storm once hit the French coast at Cherbourg, waves moved a 65-tonne concrete block 18 m (60 ft).

WEASEL Some people say that the 'least weasel' of cold, far northern lands is the world's smallest carnivore. Others argue that 'least weasels' are no more than females of the ordinary weasel. A least weasel (if that is what it is) may measure only 15.8 cm (6 in) from nose to tail tip.

WEATHER FORECASTING Serious experiments in forecasting weather began in 1860. Modern methods date from studies by Norwegian scientists at the end of World War I. These showed that depressions form where cold polar air collides with warm air from the tropics. The weather symbols these scientists devised appear upon this weather map.

Terms used in weather forecasting:

Front A front is a narrow band of changing weather between two air masses.

Warm Front The boundary between a mass of cold air and a following mass of warm air.

Cold Front The reverse of a warm front – the boundary between a warm air mass and a following mass of cold air.

Depression A region of low pressure with spiralling winds which may stretch for hundreds of miles. Depressions bring periods of unsettled weather.

Occluded Front When a cold front catches up with a warm front, the warm air between is pushed up away from the ground.

Anticyclone A large area of high pressure. In the northern hemisphere, winds blow clockwise in an anticyclone.

Cyclone A large area of low pressure. Winds rotate anticlockwise in the northern hemisphere.

Humidity The amount of moisture, or water vapour, in the air.

Precipitation Drops of water or ice crystals that fall as rain, sleet or snow.

Isobars Lines connecting places that have the same air pressure.

Isotherms Lines connecting places that have the same temperature.

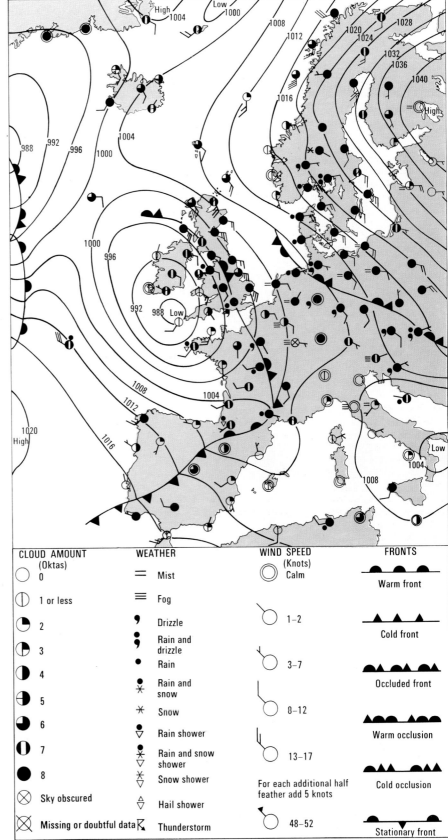

CLOUD AMOUNT (Oktas)	WEATHER	WIND SPEED (Knots)	FRONTS
0	Mist	Calm	Warm front
1 or less	Fog	1–2	Cold front
2	Drizzle	3–7	Occluded front
3	Rain and drizzle	8–12	Warm occlusion
4	Rain	13–17	Cold occlusion
5	Rain and snow	For each additional half feather add 5 knots	Stationary front
6	Snow		
7	Rain shower	48–52	
8	Rain and snow shower		
Sky obscured	Snow shower		
Missing or doubtful data	Hail shower		
	Thunderstorm		

Wea

WEAVING Making fabric by interlacing threads at right angles to each other. It is done on a LOOM. The vertical (lengthwise) threads (the *warp*) are fixed in place first. Then a crosswise thread (the *weft*) is laced through, back and forth from one side of the loom to the other. A shuttle is used to feed the weft more easily through the warp threads. Coloured threads can be used to give patterns. Machine looms were first invented in 1780, and now make woven TEXTILES at great speed.

WEEVIL Type of BEETLE distinguished by its long snout. Weevils, with over 60,000 species, form the largest family in the animal kingdom and are found all over the world. In general, each species feeds on a particular plant and many do great damage to crops.

WEIGHT LIFTING Lifting weights as an exercise or a sport. In the *snatch*, the weight is lifted from the floor to a locked overhead position in one movement. In the *clean and jerk*, the weight is lifted to rest on the chest, then to an overhead position. Contestants are divided into classes according to their body weights.   ▷

WELDING Joining two pieces of metal by heat and/or pressure. The junction becomes soft or liquid, and fuses together. Sometimes a filler metal is added to bridge the join. Common melting techniques use a gas flame or an electric arc, or feed electricity into the metal.

WELLINGTON Capital of NEW ZEALAND. Wellington is situated on the south coast of North Island. It has 343,000 people (1983) and is one of New Zealand's busiest ports. MAORIS once lived around the harbour. The first European settlement was set up in 1839

▲ *In weight lifting, the greatest overhead lifts from the ground now exceed 250 kg (550 lb).*

WEIGHT LIFTING: CLASSES
Flyweight 52 kg/114$\frac{1}{2}$ lb limit; bantam 56 kg/123$\frac{1}{4}$ lb; feather 60 kg/132$\frac{1}{4}$ lb; light 67.5 kg/148$\frac{3}{4}$ lb; middle 75 kg/165$\frac{1}{4}$ lb; light-heavy 82.5 kg/181$\frac{3}{4}$ lb; light-heavy 82.5 kg/181$\frac{3}{4}$ lb; middle-heavy 90 kg/198$\frac{1}{4}$ lb; heavy 110 kg/242$\frac{1}{2}$ lb; super-heavy, over 110 kg.

WHALE A big blue whale weighs more than 30 elephants. The tongue alone is as heavy as 10 men. A child could crawl through the largest arteries.

WHEAT In one recent year four nations produced over half the world's total output. Their shares were: USSR 23 per cent; United States 13.5 per cent; China 10 per cent; India 6 per cent.

▼ The blue whale is over 30 metres (100 ft) long — probably the biggest animal that has ever lived. It may weigh up to 150 tonnes. It lives in the Antarctic and feeds off tiny sea-creatures called krill.

WELLINGTON, DUKE OF British soldier and Tory statesman (1769–1852). After making his reputation in India, he fought the Peninsular War in Spain and Portugal against Napoleon's generals (1808–14), and then defeated Napoleon at WATERLOO. As Tory Prime Minister (1828–30) he was not a success, but he went on holding CABINET posts up to 1846.

WELLS, H. G. English writer (1866–1946). Trained as a scientist, he became famous for the first modern SCIENCE FICTION in English (*The Time Machine, The War of the Worlds*). He later turned to comic realism (*Kipps, The History of Mr Polly*) and theories of social progress (*The Outline of History*).

WESTERN AUSTRALIA The largest AUSTRALIAN state, Western Australia has a population of 1,363,000 (1984) and an area of

▼ A team of Australian harvesters cut a sea of wheat. People have grown wheat for thousands of years. Much of the world's wheat is grown in Canada, the USA, Australia and Russia.

2,527,621 sq km (975,920 sq miles). The capital is PERTH. Large areas are desert or semi-desert. But crop farming is important in the south-west and livestock are reared in parts of the interior and north. Mining is especially important, because Western Australia has huge reserves of iron ore and other minerals.

WEST INDIES An island chain separating the Caribbean Sea from the Atlantic Ocean. The largest islands are CUBA, Hispaniola (divided between the Dominican Republic and Haiti), JAMAICA and Puerto Rico (a self-governing Commonwealth of the USA). The tropical islands of the West Indies are mainly agricultural and sugar cane is the chief crop, together with fruits and tobacco. Tourism is increasing, especially during the warm winters. Most of the islands are volcanic.

In 1492 Christopher COLUMBUS thought that he had reached Asia and so the islands were, wrongly, named the Indies. Spain first controlled the area, but later France, the Netherlands and Britain established colonies and African slaves were imported to work on the European plantations. Today most people are of Negro, European or mixed ancestry. English, French and Spanish are the main languages.

WESTMINSTER ABBEY A famous church in London, originally a monastery, consecrated in 1065. It was gradually rebuilt (1245–1528) and later added to by Christopher WREN in 1740. All the English monarchs, except one, have been crowned there. It is also the traditional burial place of famous people, such as statesmen and writers.

WHALE Large sea MAMMAL found in all the world's oceans. Although whales look like fish and have two flippers, they are very different. Their skeleton is totally unlike a fish skeleton and they breathe with lungs – not with gills. This means they have to surface to get rid of used air and to take in fresh air. All whales eat animal food and most of them swim together in herds known as schools.

There are two groups of whales: toothed whales and whalebone whales. Toothed whales have teeth and feed on fish and other sea creatures. Whalebone whales live on PLANKTON. Instead of teeth, they have a row of whalebone plates inside the mouth which act as a sieve and strain the tiny animals from the water. The Earth's largest animal, the blue whale, is a whalebone whale, and has been known to reach a length of 34 metres (113 ft). ◁

WHEAT The world's most important food crop. Wheat is a cultivated GRASS and is the main CEREAL grown in temperate countries. Much of the world's wheat is produced in North America, the USSR, Argentina and

Whe

Australia. Wheat grain is ground into flour or coarser substances and used to make bread, pasta (macaroni, etc) and breakfast cereals. ◁

WHEEL The sledge was man's first land vehicle. To make it easier to haul over rough ground, round logs were sometimes placed beneath it. Later, discs cut from a log were pivoted to the sides of the vehicle. This is how the wheel came into being some 5500 years ago. ▷

WHISKY A type of alcoholic drink made chiefly in Scotland, Ireland and the United States. It is a strong amber spirit, made from barley or (in America) from maize or rye. Malted grain (that has sprouted and then been dried) is used to set off fermentation into alcohol.

WHOOPING COUGH An infectious fever, *pertussis*, caused by a bacterium. It mainly attacks children, causing catarrh and spasms of coughing that end in a distinctive wheezing breath. ANTIBIOTICS can help, but the main approach is prevention by vaccination.

WILLIAM THE CONQUEROR Duke of Normandy (1027–1087), he led the successful invasion of England by the NORMANS, defeating the Anglo-Saxons under Harold at the Battle of Hastings (1066). After being crowned King (as William I) he gradually conquered all England and parts of Wales and Ireland. His reign marks the triumph of the *feudal system* – a 'pyramid' system of allegiance and ownership leading from the lowest peasant, through the nobles, up to the king.

WILLIAM III King of Great Britain (born 1650, reigned 1688–1702), also known as William of Orange. He was a grandson of CHARLES I and son of William of Orange, the Dutch leader. He himself became the Dutch *stadholder* in 1672. In 1688 he was invited to England by the opponents of JAMES II, and accepted the throne jointly with his wife Mary, James' daughter (though a Bill of Rights gave real power to PARLIAMENT). In 1690 he defeated the ex-king James II in Ireland.

WILLOW Deciduous TREE found in many parts of the world, generally growing near water. Willow wood has many uses ranging from cricket bats to wicker baskets and high-quality drawing charcoal.

WINDMILL A mill powered by the action of the wind on wooden or metal 'sails'. Windmills appeared in western Europe in the 12th century, and were mainly used for grinding corn. Today lightweight metal windmills are

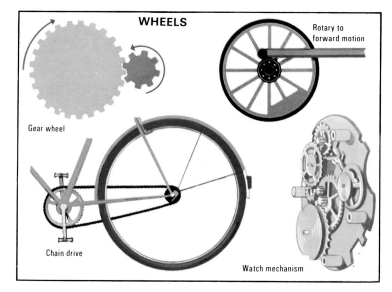

WHEELS

Gear wheel

Rotary to forward motion

Chain drive

Watch mechanism

used in some parts of the world to pump water and sometimes to generate electricity. ▷

WINDSOR, HOUSE OF The name of the present British royal family. After the accession of George I the family name was Hanover, but Queen Victoria's children took the surname of their father, Prince Albert, which was Saxe-Coburg-Gotha. This was used by Edward VII, but was changed to Windsor during World War I because of anti-German feeling. The monarchs using the name Windsor have been George V, Edward VIII, George VI and Elizabeth II.

WINE An alcoholic drink made from the juice of GRAPES. A YEAST organism found on the skin of grapes turns the fruit sugar into alcohol by a process known as fermentation. Wine can be white or red (depending on the grapes it is made from) and sweet or dry (depending on whether fermentation is allowed to continue until all the fruit sugar has gone). France is the country most famous for its wines, but Italy produces more wine than any other country.

WITCHCRAFT The supposed ability to work magical spells, with the help of evil spirits or the devil. Up to the Middle Ages there were many 'wise women', who had a wide knowledge of herbs and healing. But fear of these women or 'witches' became general in western Europe from the 15th to 17th centuries, and led people to believe that their knowledge was evil. Many harmless women were executed as a result.

WOMBAT Burrowing MARSUPIAL related to the KOALA and found only in Australia. Wombats are furry, short-legged creatures about 1.2 metres (4 ft) long. They spend the

WHEEL About 5500 years ago a Sumerian in what is now Iraq scratched an outline on a clay tablet. It showed a four-wheeled sledge with four solid wheels. This is the first known picture of the wheel. The first wheel may have been a solid disc, but the oldest actually found was shaped from three planks joined by two wooden cross-pieces. Ox-carts with such wheels are still made and used in India.

WINDMILL The world's largest windmill has three blades that sweep out a circle more than 50 m (164 ft) across. This Danish device produces enough electricity to heat 2000 one-bar electric fires. American engineers plan to build even larger windmills.

382

and fibres are compressed in the centre of the trunk. They form the heartwood. Heartwood is very hard and solid. The rest of the trunk, full of working tubes, forms the sapwood. Sapwood is softer and less durable than heartwood. There are two types of wood: softwood and hardwood. Softwood comes mostly from CONIFERS. Much of it is turned into pulp which is used for making paper, rayon, plastics and cellophane. Hardwood comes from broadleaved trees and is mainly used for furniture and construction work. ◁

WOODCUT A picture printed from a wooden block. The picture is drawn onto the block of wood and the background is then cut away, leaving the original lines of the drawing on a raised surface. This surface is covered with ink and then pressed onto paper. It is the oldest known form of PRINTING and was used by the Chinese in the 3rd century BC.

WOODPECKER Bird which spends most of its time pecking at tree trunks and branches. There are over 200 species of woodpecker, found in all continents except Australia. Most

▼A cross-section of a tree-trunk showing the darker heartwood and the lighter sapwood. The annual growth rings in the trunk can also be seen.

WOOD The heaviest wood is black ironwood from Africa. Bulk for bulk it weighs half as much again as water, in which it sinks like stone. The lightest wood comes from one kind of Cuban tree. Bulk for bulk it weighs less than one-twentieth as much as water.

▲ *A greater spotted woodpecker feeds its young.*

day asleep in their burrows, then come out at night to feed on grass and roots.

WOMEN'S RIGHTS There have been two main movements to establish legal rights for women in this century: the fight for the right to vote, and (more recently) the fight for economic and social equality with men, which is still going on.

WOOD Tough, inner part of TREES and shrubs. A tree trunk consists of tubes, carrying water and food, and strong fibres. As the tree gets older, it grows more tubes and fibres and the trunk becomes thicker and thicker. The older tubes (no longer carrying food or water)

Woo

▶ *Among certain breeds, the shearing of a single sheep can produce enough wool to make seven men's suits.*

of them are brightly coloured and all have strong, sharp bills. They use their bills to find insect food under the bark of trees and to drill holes in the trunk for their nests.

WOOL The natural covering found on sheep – a modified type of hair. It was probably the first fibre to be made into cloth by spinning and WEAVING. It can be turned into smooth (worsted) or 'hairy' (woollen) material, and is used for blankets, carpets, tweed and gaberdine clothes, and knitted articles. In the Middle Ages, Britain's wealth was based on trading wool.

WORK When a force causes an object to move, we say that work is done. The SI UNIT of work is the JOULE, equal to a force of one newton acting through a distance of one metre. Work is done when any form of energy is used. Units called WATTS are used to measure POWER – the rate at which work is done.

WORLD WAR I The 1914–1918 war, between the Allied Powers (led by Britain, France and Russia) and the Central European Powers (led by Germany, Austria-Hungary and Turkey). It was caused by several territorial rivalries. (The immediate trigger was the assassination in the Balkans of the heir to the Austrian throne.) The struggle in western Europe quickly bogged down in opposing lines of trenches. These scarcely moved for the rest of the war, despite appalling loss of life (about 10 million deaths). On other fronts: Russians losses were heavy and sparked off the Russian Revolution; the German fleet avoided battle, but her submarines sank many merchant ships and almost starved Britain into surrender; and Lawrence of Arabia led an Arab revolt against the Turks. After her allies had dropped out, and the US had joined the Allies, Germany was forced to capitulate by the growth of revolutionary movements in her own cities. The Treaty of Versailles, 1919, forced her to pay enormous war damages.

WORLD WAR II The 1939–1945 war, between the Allies (led by Britain, America and Russia) and the Axis Powers (HITLER's Germany, MUSSOLINI's Italy, and Japan). Before it began there were many invasions and annexations (seizures of land) by the Axis Powers, ending in Germany's invasion of Poland in September 1939. This was followed

▶ *Canadian troops repulse an attack at the second battle at Ypres, 1915. Conditions in the trenches were appalling in World War I.*

in 1940 by the rapid German conquest of Denmark, Norway, the Netherlands, Belgium and France, then the air battle for invasion of Britain. Here Germany failed, but in 1941 invaded the Balkans, North Africa and Russia. In 1942 came the turning-point; German armies were defeated in Russia (Stalingrad) and North Africa (by the British at Alamein). Also Japan's attack on the US navy at Pearl Harbor, though very successful, brought the might of the United States into the war. In

▲ *Top: The Spad was a favourite fighter aircraft of World War I. Nearly 15,000 were built and flown by the French, Americans, Italians and Belgians. With its 140 hp engine and twin Vickers machine guns, it was a fast and stable machine and a deadly weapon.*

WORLD WAR II This war killed more people than any other war in history. Probably 55 million soldiers and civilians died. Fewer than 10 million died in World War I, the next most devastating conflict.

1943 the Allies invaded Italy while the Russians drove the Germans back from the east. The Allied invasion of France (*D Day*) in 1944, led to the liberation of France, Belgium and the Netherlands. This and the Russian advance brought the invasion and surrender of Germany in 1945. Meanwhile in the Pacific the steady American advance had brought Japan within bombing range. The dropping of two atomic bombs (see HIROSHIMA) in 1945, rapidly brought an end to the war. ◁

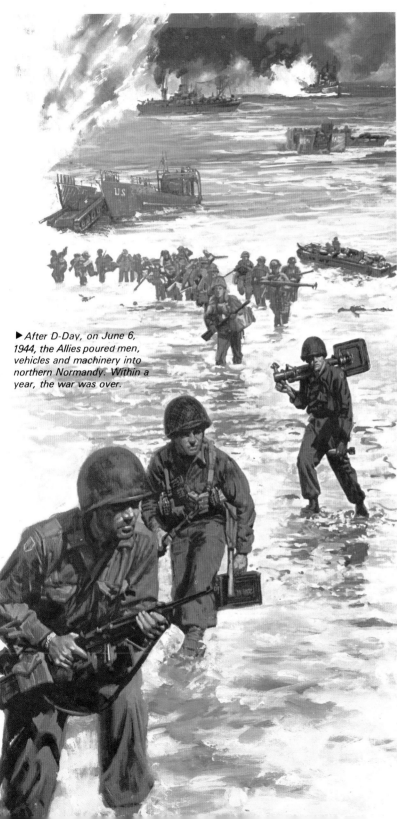

▶ After D-Day, on June 6, 1944, the Allies poured men, vehicles and machinery into northern Normandy. Within a year, the war was over.

WORM Common name for a large assortment of animals with long thin bodies. There are many different groups of worms. Some are very primitive, such as flatworms and roundworms; these mostly live as PARASITES inside other animals or plants. Others are more complex and have bodies built up of segments. Segmented worms are called *annelids*. The earthworm is an annelid.

WREN, CHRISTOPHER English architect (1632–1723). He began as a scientist, but the Great Fire of London (1666) gave him his opportunity as an architect. His plan for the complete rebuilding of the city was not used, but he did have the chance to design many new London churches – including St Paul's Cathedral, his masterpiece. His other buildings include the Royal Exchange, Royal Naval College and Marlborough House.

WRESTLING A fighting sport in which the two opponents try to throw each other to the ground. There are many styles of wrestling, such as Japanese, Turkish and British. The two OLYMPIC styles are Graeco-Roman and freestyle.

WRIGHT BROTHERS Orville (1871–1948) and Wilbur (1867–1912), the American pioneers of flying. While running a cycle repair business they made a wind tunnel for aeronautical research. They then built an aircraft that Orville successfully flew on December 17, 1903. This was man's first controlled flight in a heavier-than-air machine.

WRITING Written speech developed over many thousand years. Take the sentence 'Man kills tiger'. At first, a picture of a man killing a tiger was used. Then standard pictures were used: one for man, one meaning kill, and one for tiger. Later the pictures became associated with the sound of the words, which meant they could be used to make up other words (just as you might draw a picture of an eye to mean 'I'). This led on to ALPHABETS of sounds, but still without any vowels: 'Mn klls tgr'. Finally the Greeks added vowels, for a complete alphabet as used today.

WROUGHT IRON A form of iron made by a *puddling* process that removes almost all impurities. It was the main construction material used during the INDUSTRIAL REVOLUTION, before the development of cheap STEEL.

X

XEROGRAPHY A means of copying printed matter, widely used in offices. A metal plate is coated with selenium, a substance that conducts electricity when exposed to light. The copy is projected through a lens, and a positively charged hidden image is stored on the plate. The plate is dusted with negative black powder which clings to the image. Paper is rolled on the plate and given a positive charge which attracts the powder image to the paper. The paper is heated to melt the powder and form a permanent image on the paper.

X-RAYS A form of ELECTROMAGNETIC WAVES discovered in 1895 by Wilhelm Röntgen. He produced the rays by accident when passing electricity through a gas at extremely low pressure. Röntgen found that the waves passed through the human body and would record its bone patterns on a photographic plate. This technique is now widely used in hospitals for studying patients' bones and internal organs.

XYLOPHONE A musical instrument, made up of rows of wooden bars that are struck with hammers. The bars are of different lengths to give the different notes. Xylophones are often used for special effects.

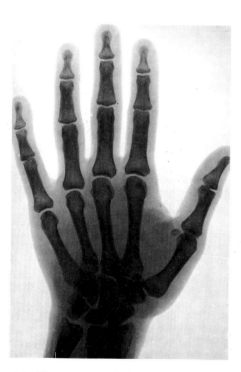

▲ An X-ray negative of a human hand, showing the bone structure. X-rays are very short wavelength electromagnetic waves, produced when a stream of high-energy electrons bombards matter. X-rays are absorbed to a greater degree by the bones than by the flesh, which is less dense. Rays cloud a photographic plate most when they have passed through flesh, and least when they have passed through bone. Breaks and cracks in the bone will thus show up clearly on the X-ray.

▶ An X-ray machine used to diagnose ailments inside your body – for example tooth decay or bone fractures.

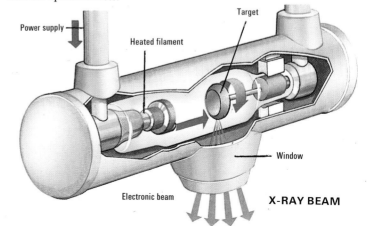

Power supply

Heated filament

Target

Window

Electronic beam

X-RAY BEAM

Y

YEMEN (SAN'A): FACTS AND FIGURES
Area: 195,000 sq km (75,290 sq miles).
Population: 6,660,000 (1984 est.).
Capital: San'a (pop. 278,000).

YEMEN (ADEN): FACTS AND FIGURES
Area: 287,683 sq km (111,075 sq miles).
Population: 2,225,000 (1984 est.)
Capital: Aden (pop. 264,000).

YAK Large ox-like animal about 2 metres (6 ft) high, with a shaggy black coat and long horns. Yaks live on the cold, high plateaus of central Asia and have long been domesticated. They are kept as beasts of burden and also for their milk, meat and hides.

YANGTZE, RIVER See Chang Jiang.

YEAST Certain kind of FUNGUS which consists of tiny oval cells instead of the usual threads. Yeasts have special digestive juices which turn sugar into alcohol and carbon dioxide. There are many different yeasts. The best-known ones are those used for making BREAD, BEER and WINE. In bread-making, carbon-dioxide bubbles given out by the yeast cause the dough to rise. In brewing and wine-making, the yeast converts sugar from malt and grapes into alcohol.

YEMEN Two poor Arab nations in Arabia. The People's Democratic Republic of Yemen (capital, Aden) occupies the southern part of the Arabian peninsula. Its population is 2,225,000 (1984 est.) and its area is 287,683 sq km (111,075 sq miles). The Yemen Arab

▼ Yaks are among the largest wild cattle, yet they climb nimbly in the mountains of central Asia. They can carry heavy loads.

Republic (capital San'a) has 6,660,000 people (1984 est.), and an area of 195,000 sq km (75,290 sq miles).

YIDDISH LANGUAGE The language still used by many JEWS for ordinary conversation. It developed in medieval times, based on German with added words from Hebrew, Russian and Polish. Yiddish literature grew from folk-songs and fables, to include poetry, novels, and more recently, newspapers.

YOGA A Hindu spiritual system, that aims to develop the soul and end the cycle of reincarnation (see HINDUISM). The yoga popular in the West is *Hatha* (physical) yoga, which uses special postures and breathing exercises to give control of mind and body.

YOGURT Yogurt is a Turkish word for fermented milk. It is a thick, sour curd-like food prepared by adding a special bacteria to milk. Yogurt is a popular diet food as it has few calories.

YUGOSLAVIA A communist republic on the Mediterranean Sea. Yugoslavia has a population of 22,963,000 (1984 est.) and an area of 255,804 sq km (98,766 sq miles). The capital is Belgrade. The coast is an attractive tourist area. Inland, there are barren mountains, but fertile plains cover the north-east. Yugoslavia was created in 1918. A communist government took over in 1945, but it has remained independent of Russia and China. About a third of the population belongs to the Orthodox Church; a quarter of the people are Roman Catholic. The chief river is the DANUBE, with its tributaries. In addition to Belgrade, with a population of 1,204,000, the largest cities are Zagreb (602,000), Skopje (440,000) and Sarajevo (400,000).

ZAIRE A republic in west-central AFRICA. Zaire (formerly Congo) has 29,671,000 people (1984 est.) and an area of 2,345,409 sq km (905,567 sq miles). The capital is Kinshasa. Much of the country is in the basin of the mighty Zaire (CONGO) River. The chief resources are copper, diamonds and other minerals.

ZAMBESI, RIVER This river, Africa's fourth longest, flows about 2575 km (1600 miles) across southern Africa before emptying into the INDIAN OCEAN. The Kariba Dam, Lake Kariba and the VICTORIA FALLS are on the Zambesi.

ZAMBIA A republic in south-central AFRICA. Zambia has 6,445,000 people (1984 est.) and an area of 752,614 sq km (290,586 sq miles). The capital is Lusaka. Formerly called Northern Rhodesia, Zambia's chief source of income comes from its copper exports, but farming is the occupation of most of the people. ▷

ZEBRA Black and white striped animal closely related to the HORSE. No two zebras have the same stripe pattern. Zebras live in Africa, south of the Sahara. Like horses, they are grazing animals and can run very fast.

ZEUS In Greek mythology, the ruler of the gods. He and his brothers killed their father Kronos, and divided his realm. Zeus took the upper world, Hades the underworld and Poseidon the sea. His chief wife was Hera, but he also had many children by mortal women.

ZIGGURAT A type of PYRAMID built in ancient Sumer, BABYLONIA and ASSYRIA. The sides were built in huge 'steps', each storey set in from the one below. Ziggurats were used as temples, and for observing stars.

▲ *The people of ancient Mesopotamia, in the Middle East, built brick ziggurats over 4000 to 2500 years ago.*

▼ *Zebras at a waterhole. They live in herds on the grassy African plains and can run swiftly. Lions are their worst enemy.*

388

◀ The ruins of ancient Zimbabwe – once a great empire, now renamed for the modern African republic that was formerly Rhodesia.

ZINC A hard, blue-white metallic ELEMENT that occurs as various compounds. The metal is used to make the cases of battery cells, and as a protective coating in GALVANIZING. Zinc is also used to make various alloys, notably brass.

ZODIAC A name given by ancient astrologers to the band of the sky through which the Sun and Moon, and the five planets then known, all appear to move. They divided it into 12 equal parts, each named after its own constellation of stars: Aries, Taurus, Gemini, Cancer, Leo, Virgo, Libra, Scorpio, Sagittarius, Capricorn, Aquarius and Pisces.

ZAMBIA: FACTS AND FIGURES
Official language: English.
Currency: Kwacha.
Largest cities: Lusaka (pop. 538,000), Kitwe (315,000).

ZIMBABWE-RHODESIA: FACTS AND FIGURES
Official language: English.
Currency: Dollar.
Religion: Christianity and animism.
Chief rivers: Zambesi, Limpopo.
Largest cities: Harare (pop. 681,000), Bulawayo (429,000).
The population is 95 per cent indigenous Bantu, 4 per cent European descent.

ZIMBABWE (RUINS) Ancient massive stone ruins in southern Zimbabwe, discovered in 1868. They include a fortress, a temple and a tower, and are thought to date from around 1500. They mark the site of the capital of two empires formed by members of the Shona tribe, and were a major trading centre.

ZIMBABWE A land-locked republic in southern Africa, formerly the British colony of Southern Rhodesia (later called Rhodesia). It has 7,980,000 people (1984 est.) and an area of 390,580 sq km (150,804 sq miles). The capital is Harare. In colonial times Europeans formed about $4\frac{1}{2}$ per cent of the population, but controlled the government. In 1965 they declared Rhodesia independent. Britain denounced this action as illegal. A long guerrilla war followed, until in 1979 the Europeans agreed to majority rule. In 1980 the country became a republic and took the name Zimbabwe, after the ancient ruins of Zimbabwe. Europeans now form only about 2 per cent of the population. ▷

ZOO A place where wild animals are kept in captivity (the name is short for 'zoological gardens'). The earliest known zoo was in ancient Egypt c. 1500 BC. The first in England was the royal menagerie started by Henry I. This eventually formed the basis of London's Regent's Park Zoo. Zoos are used for entertainment, education, scientific research and the preservation of rare species. Most have mammals, birds, reptiles and amphibians, and some have fish and insects. There are now also drive-through zoos and wildlife parks.

ZULU An African Negro people of the BANTU family, noted for their massive physique. Originally cattle-herders, they were formed into a warrior nation by their great king Shaka, c. 1820. With the help of a new short stabbing spear they conquered a wide area, but in the late 19th century were beaten by the Boers and British. About 3 million are left today, as labourers in South Africa.

▼ Zulu women wearing beaded headdresses at a festival. Zulus are the biggest single group of black Africans in South Africa.

Additional Countries: Facts and Figures

ANDORRA:
Area: 453 sq km (180 sq miles).
Population: 33,000 (1978 est.).
Capital: Andorra la Vella.
Government: Principality.
Official language: Catalan.
Currency: French franc, Spanish peseta.
The French president and the Spanish bishop of Urgel are supposed to rule Andorra. However, an elected council really does so. Andorra is in the Pyrenees between France and Spain.

BENIN:
Area: 112,622 sq km (70,000 sq miles).
Population: 3,825,000 (1984 est.).
Capital: Porto Novo.
Government: Republic.
Official language: French.
Currency: CFA franc.
Independence date: 1960.
Benin, in West Africa, was formerly called Dahomey. The people are divided into about 50 language groups.

BHUTAN:
Area: 47,000 sq km (18,000 sq miles).
Population: 1,389,000 (1984 est.).
Capital: Thimphu.
Government: Monarchy.
Official language: Dzongkha.
Currency: Ngultrum.
Bhutan is a small land-locked kingdom between north-eastern India and China (Tibet). India handles Bhutan's foreign affairs.

BURKINA FASO:
Area: 274,200 sq km (106,000 sq miles).
Population: 6,582,000 (1984).
Capital: Ougadougou.
Government: Republic.
Official language: French.
Currency: CFA franc.
Date of independence: 1960.
Burkina Faso, in West Africa, was formerly called Upper Volta. It changed its name in 1984. It is one of the world's poorest countries. Most of its soils are infertile.

BURUNDI:
Area: 27,834 sq km (10,750 sq miles).
Population: 4,537,000 (1984)
Capital: Bujumbura.
Government: Republic.
Official language: Kirundi, French.
Currency: Franc.
Independence date: 1962.
Burundi, in East Africa, is a small, densely populated nation. Most people are poor and coffee is the main product.

CAMEROON:
Area: 475,442 sq km (183,000 sq miles).
Population: 9,605,000 (1984).
Capital: Yaounde.
Government: Federal Republic.
Official language: French, English.
Currency: CFA franc.
Independence date: 1960.
Cameroon, in Central Africa, has over 200 groups of people, each with its own language and traditions.

CENTAL AFRICAN REPUBLIC:
Area: 622,984 sq km (241 sq miles).
Population: 2,516,000 (1984).
Government: Republic.
Official language: French.
Currency: CFA franc.
The central African Republic is a remote, landlocked country that was formerly a French colony.

COLOMBIA:
Area: 1,138,914 sq km (440,000 sq miles).
Population: 28,217,000 (1984).
Capital: Bogotá.
Government: Republic.
Official language: Spanish.
Currency: Peso.
Colombia, in South America, was ruled by Spain from 1536 until 1819. Today more than two-thirds of the people are mestizos (people of mixed Indian and European origin). The chief export is coffee.

COMORO ISLANDS:
Area: 2,171 sq km (800 sq miles).
Population: 431,000 (1984).
Capital: Dzaoudzi.
Currency: Franc.
Government: Republic.
Date of independence: 1975.
Official language: French.
The Comoro State is an island nation in the northern Mozambique Channel. Farming is the main activity in this former French territory.

DJIBOUTI:
Area: 22,000 sq km (15,862 sq miles).
Population: 364,000 (1984).
Capital: Djibouti. ˋ
Currency: Djibouti franc.
Government: Republic.
Official language: French.
Date of independence: 1977.
Djibouti, in north-eastern Africa, was ruled by France until 1977. It borders the Red Sea. About half the people live in the important port of Djibouti.

DOMINICAN REPUBLIC:
Area: 48,734 sq km (18,816 sq miles).
Population: 6,102,000 (1984).
Capital: Santo Domingo.
Government: Republic.
Official language: Spanish.
Currency: Peso.
The Dominican Republic occupies eastern Hispaniola, a West Indian island. Most people are of European and black African descent. Farming is the main activity.

EQUATORIAL GUINEA:
Area: 28,051 sq km (10,800 sq miles).
Population: 383,000 (1984).
Capital: Malabo.
Government: Republic.
Official language: Spanish.
Currency: Ekuele.
Date of independence: 1968.
Equatorial Guinea, in Central Africa, consists of a mainland area called Rio Muni, and a fertile island called Macias Nguema, named after the country's first president.

GABON:
Area: 267,667 sq km (103,000 sq miles).
Population: 1,131,000 (1984).
Capital: Libreville.
Government: Republic.
Official language: French.
Currency: CFA franc.
Date of independence: 1960.
Gabon, on the Equator in Central Africa, is a hot, wet country covered mostly by forests. It produces oil, manganese, uranium and timber, and is quite wealthy by African standards.

GAMBIA:
Area: 11,295 sq km (4,300 sq miles).
Population: 630,000 (1984).
Capital: Banjul.
Government: Republic.
Official language: English.
Currency: Dalasi.
Date of independence: 1965.
Gambia, in West Africa, is a small, poor country; peanuts account for nearly all its exports.

GRENADA:
Area: 344 sq km (133 sq miles).
Population: 111,000 (1984).
Capital: St. George's.
Currency: East Caribbean dollar.
Government: Eric Gairy overthrown by coup on March 13, 1979. JEWEL (Joint endeavour for welfare, education and liberation) is in control.
Official language: English.
Date of independence: 1974.
Grenada is the southernmost of the Windward Islands in the West Indies. The islands are mountainous and are volcanic in origin. Known as the Isle of Spice, Grenada is famous for its nutmeg, cocoa and cinnamon.

GUINEA-BISSAU:
Area: 36,125 sq km (14,000 sq miles).
Population: 875,000 (1984).
Capital: Bissau.
Government: Republic.
Official language: Portuguese.
Currency: Escudo.
Date of independence: 1974.
Guinea-Bissau, in West Africa, was formerly Portuguese Guinea. Most people are farmers.

HAITI:
Area: 27,750 sq km (10,714 sq miles).
Population: 5,185,000 (1984).
Capital: Port-au-Prince.
Government: Republic.
Official language: French.
Currency: Gourde.
Haiti occupies western Hispaniola in the West Indies. Most people are Negroes. The chief crop is coffee and bauxite (aluminium ore).

LIECHTENSTEIN:
Area: 157 sq km (62 sq miles).
Population: 28,000 (1984).
Capital: Vaduz.
Government: Principality.
Official language: German.
Currency: Swiss franc.
Liechtenstein, a small country ruled by a prince, is closely linked with Switzerland.

MALDIVE ISLANDS:
Area: 298 sq km (115 sq miles).
Population: 173,000 (1984).
Capital: Male.
Government: Republic.
Official language: Dihevi.
Currency: Rufiyaa.
Date of independence: 1965.
Fishing is the main industry of the Maldive Islands, south-west of India. Coconut products are also important.

MAURITANIA:
Area: 1,030,700 sq km (398,000 sq miles).
Population: 1,832,000 (1984).
Capital: Nouakchott.
Government: Republic.
Official language: Arabic, French.
Currency: Ouguiya.
Date of independence: 1960.
Mauritania is a dry, hot country in north-west Africa. Most people are Arab or Berber Moslems but the people in the far south are black Africans.

MAURITIUS:
Area: 2,045 sq km (720 sq miles).
Population: 1,011,000 (1984).
Capital: Port Louis.
Official language: English.
Government: Monarchy.
Currency: Rupee.
Date of independence: 1968.
Mauritius is an island nation in the Indian Ocean. The largest group of people are Indians. There are also some Africans, Chinese, Europeans and people of mixed origin. Hinduism, Christianity and Islam are the chief religions. The main product is sugar-cane.

NAURU:
Area: 21 sq km (8 sq miles).
Population: 8,000 (1984).
Capital: Nauru.
Government: Republic.
Official language: English.
Currency: Australian dollar.
Date of independence: 1968.
Nauru is a small Micronesian coral island. It exports phosphates to Australia, New Zealand and Japan, but it imports food.

NEPAL:
Area: 140,797 sq km (54,000 sq miles).
Population: 16,107,000 (1984).

Capital: Katmandu.
Government: Monarchy.
Official language: Nepali.
Currency: Rupee.
Nepal is a land-locked kingdom between India and China. Mt Everest is in the north. Nepal is the birthplace of Gautama Buddha.

NIGER:
Area: 1,267,000 sq km (458,000 sq miles).
Population: 5,940,000 (1984).
Capital: Niamey.
Government: Republic.
Official language: French.
Currency: CFA franc.
Date of independence: 1960.
Niger, in northern Africa, is a remote country with no coastline. Nomadic groups of Berbers, called Tuaregs, keep livestock in the north. Crop farming is confined to the far south, where the people are mostly black Africans. The main export crop is peanuts.

OMAN:
Area: 212,457 sq km (82,000 sq miles).
Population: 1,193,000 (1984).
Capital: Muscat.
Government: Monarchy.
Official language: Arabic.
Currency: Rial.
Oman, a Sultanate in the south-eastern part of the Arabian peninsula, borders the Gulf of Oman and the Indian Ocean. Much of the land is desert and oil is the main resource.

PAPUA NEW GUINEA:
Area: 475,300 sq km (183,513 sq miles).
Population: 3,425,000 (1984).
Capital: Port Moresby.
Government: Monarchy.
Official language: English.
Currency: Kina.
Date of independence: 1978.
Papua New Guinea includes the eastern part of New Guinea which was once ruled by Australia, islands of the Bismarck Archipelago, and Bougainville in the Solomon Islands. The major group of people are Melanesians.

QATAR:
Area: 11,000 sq km (4,250 sq miles).
Population: 295,000 (1984).
Capital: Doha.
Government: Monarchy.
Official language: Arabic.
Currency: Riyal.
Qatar is an Emirate which occupies a peninsula jutting out from Arabia into the Persian Gulf. The wealth of the country comes from oil.

RWANDA:
Area: 26,338 sq km (10,000 sq miles).
Population: 5,871,000 (1984).
Capital: Kigali.

Government: Republic.
Official language: Kinyarwanda, French.
Currency: Franc.
Date of independence: 1962.
Rwanda is a small but densely populated nation in East Africa. Like Burundi, it has three main groups of people: the Hutu, the tall Tutsi and a few pygmies.

SAN MARINO:
Area: 60.5 sq km (23.4 sq miles).
Population: 22,000 (1984).
Capital: San Marino.
Official language: Italian.
Currency: Italian lire.
San Marino, in Italy, was founded as a city state in AD 301, and has been in customs union with Italy since 1862. The Heads of the State are two Captains-Regent, appointed every six months.

SENEGAL:
Area: 196,192 sq km (76,000 sq miles).
Population: 6,397,000 (1984).
Capital: Dakar.
Government: Republic.
Official language: French.
Currency: CFA franc.
Date of independence: 1960.
Senegal, in West Africa, encloses Gambia; but attempts to unite the two nations have failed because Gambia has an English culture, while Senegal has a French one.

SEYCHELLES:
Area: 278 sq km (107 sq miles).
Population: 65,000 (1984).
Capital: Victoria.
Government: Republic.
Official language: English, French.
Currency: Rupee.
Date of independence: 1976.
The Seychelles, a nation in the Indian Ocean, contains about 90 islands. The largest is Mahe, on which the capital is situated. The chief products are copra and cinnamon.

SIERRA LEONE:
Area: 71,740 sq km (28,000 sq miles).
Population: 3,536,000 (1984).
Capital: Freetown.
Government: Republic.
Official language: English.
Currency: Leone.
Date of independence: 1961.
The capital of Sierra Leone, Freetown, was founded as a home for freed slaves. The British first took ex-slaves there in 1787. There are now about 42,000 Creoles, who are descendants of the slaves. The most valuable resources are minerals, especially diamonds and iron ore.

SOMALI REPUBLIC:
Area: 637,657 sq km (246,000 sq miles).
Population: 4,539,000 (1984).
Capital: Mogadishu.
Government: Republic.

Official language: Somali.
Currency: Somali shilling.
The Somali Republic occupies the 'Horn of Africa'. Somali-speaking people also live in neighbouring Djibouti, Ethiopia and Kenya. Many Somalis want to unite all Somali-speaking people in one nation.

SURINAM:
Area: 163,265 sq km (63,000 sq miles).
Population: 370,000 (1984).
Capital: Paramaribo.
Government: Republic.
Official language: Dutch.
Currency: Guilder.
Surinam became independent from the Netherlands in 1975. About half the people are of African descent. There are some American Indians and others of Indonesian, Indian, Chinese and European origin.

SWAZILAND:
Area: 17,363 sq km (6,700 sq miles).
Population: 626,000 (1984).
Capital: Mbabane.
Government: Monarchy.
Currency: Lilangeni.
Official language: English.
Date of independence: 1968.
Swaziland is enclosed by South Africa and Mozambique. This small country is developing quickly. Sugar, timber, livestock and minerals are the chief products.

TOGO:
Area: 56,000 sq km (21,600 sq miles).
Population: 2,872,000 (1984).
Capital: Lomé.
Government: Republic:
Official language: French.
Currency: CFA franc.
Date of independence: 1960.
Togo, in West Africa, is a poor country. Most people grow only enough food to feed their families. The major products are phosphates, cocoa and coffee. There are 30 main groups of people in Togo.

TONGA:
Area: 700 sq km (270 miles).
Population: 107,000 (1984).
Capital: Nuku'alofa.
Government: Monarchy.
Official language: Tongan, English.
Currency: Pa'anga.
Date of independence: 1970.
Tonga is a Polynesian island group in the Pacific. The islands are either made of volcanic rock or coral. The chief products are copra and bananas.

TRINIDAD AND TOBAGO:
Area: 5,128 sq km (1,979 sq miles).
Population: 1,166,000 (1984).
Capital: Port-of-Spain.
Government: Republic.
Official language: English.

Currency: Dollar.
Date of independence: 1962.
Trinidad and Tobago, in the West Indies, is the world's main producer of natural asphalt. However, oil products are more valuable. Tourism and farming are also important.

WESTERN SAMOA:
Area: 2,842 sq km (1,097 sq miles).
Population: 159,000 (1984).
Capital: Apia.
Government: Monarchy.
Official language: English.
Currency: Tala.
Date of independence: 1962.
Western Samoa is a Polynesian nation in the Pacific. It was ruled by New Zealand from 1920 to 1961. The islands are volcanic and mountainous with coral reefs bordering the coasts. The largest islands are Savai'i and Upola. The chief products are copra, cocoa and bananas.

Inventions

4000–3000 BC	Bricks—in Egypt and Assyria	
c.3000 BC	Wheel—in Asia	
c.3000 BC	Plough—in Egypt and Mesopotamia	
c.500 BC	Abacus—the Chinese	
c.300 BC	Geometry—Euclid (Gk.)	
200s BC	Screw (for raising water)—Archimedes (Gk.)	
AD 105	Paper (from pulp)—Ts'ai Lun (Chin.)	
AD 250	Algebra—Diophantus (Gk.)	
c.1000	Gunpowder—the Chinese	
c.1100	Magnetic compass—the Chinese	
c.1100	Rocket—the Chinese	
c.1440	Printing press (movable type)—Johannes Gutenberg (Ger.)	
1520	Rifle—Joseph Kotter (Ger.)	
1589	Knitting machine—William Lee (Eng.)	
c.1590	Compound microscope—Zacharias Janssen (Neth.)	
1593	Thermometer—Galileo (It.)	
1608	Telescope—Hans Lippershey (Neth.)	
1614	Logarithms—John Napier (Scot.)	
1636	Micrometer—William Gascoigne (Eng.)	
1637	Co-ordinate geometry—René Descartes (Fr.)	
1640	Theory of numbers—Pierre de Fermat (Fr.)	
1642	Calculating machine—Blaise Pascal (Fr.)	
1643	Barometer—Evangelista Torricelli (It.)	
1650	Air pump—Otto von Guericke (Ger.)	

1656	Pendulum clock—Christian Huygens (Neth.)	
1665–75	Calculus—Sir Isaac Newton (Eng.) & Gottfried Leibniz (Ger.) independently	
1675	Pressure cooker—Denis Papin (Fr.)	
1698	Steam pump—Thomas Savery (Eng.)	
1712	Steam engine—Thomas Newcomen (Eng.)	
1714	Mercury thermometer—Gabriel Fahrenheit (Ger.)	
1725	Stereotyping—William Ged (Scot.)	
1733	Flying shuttle—John Kay (Eng.)	
1735	Chronometer—John Harrison (Eng.)	
1752	Lightning conductor—Benjamin Franklin (US)	
1764	Spinning jenny—James Hargreaves (Eng.)	
1765	Condensing steam engine—James Watt (Scot.)	
1768	Hydrometer—Antoine Baumé (Fr.)	
1783	Parachute—Louis Lenormand (Fr.)	
1785	Power loom—Edmund Cartwright (Eng.)	
1790	Sewing machine—Thomas Saint (Eng.)	
1793	Cotton gin—Eli Whitney (US)	
1796	Lithography—Aloys Senefelder (Ger.)	
1800	Electric battery—Count Alessandro Volta (It.)	
1800	Lathe—Henry Maudslay (Eng.)	
1804	Steam locomotive—Richard Trevithick (Eng.)	

1815	Miner's safety lamp—Sir Humphry D (Eng.)	
1816	Metronome—Johann Mälzel (Ger.)	
1816	Bicycle—Karl von Sauerbronn (Ger.)	
1817	Kaleidoscope—David Brewster (Scot	
1822	Camera—Joseph Niepce (Fr.)	
1823	Digital calculating machine—Charles Babbage (Eng.)	
1824	Portland cement—Joseph Aspdin (En	
1825	Electromagnet—William Sturgeon (En	
1826	Photograph (permanent)—Joseph Niepce (Fr.)	
1827	Match—John Walker (Eng.)	
1828	Blast furnace—James Neilson (Scot.)	
1831	Dynamo—Michael Faraday (Eng.)	
1834	Reaping machine—Cyrus McCormick (US)	
1836	Revolver—Samuel Colt (US)	
1837	Telegraph—Samuel F. B. Morse (US)	
1839	Vulcanized rubber—Charles Goodyea (US)	
1844	Safety match—Gustave Pasch (Swed	
1846	Sewing machine—Elias Howe (US)	
1849	Safety pin—Walter Hunt (US)	
1852	Gyroscope—Léon Foucault (Fr.)	
1853	Passenger lift—Elisha Otis (US)	
1855	Celluloid—Alexander Parkes (Eng.)	
1855	Bessemer converter—Henry Bessemer (Eng.)	

855 Bunsen burner—Robert Bunsen (Ger.)
858 Refrigerator—Ferdinand Carré (Fr.)
858 Washing machine—Hamilton Smith (US)
859 Internal combustion engine—Etienne Lenoir (Fr.)
861 Linoleum—Frederick Walton (Eng.)
862 Rapid-fire gun—Richard Gatling (US)
865 Cylinder lock—Linus Yale, Jr. (US)
866 Dynamite—Alfred Nobel (Swed.)
867 Typewriter—Christopher Sholes (US)
868 Lawn mower—Amariah Hills (US)
870 Margarine—Hippolyte Mège-Mouriés (Fr.)
873 Barbed wire—Joseph Glidden (US)
876 Telephone—Alexander Graham Bell (Scot.)
876 Carpet sweeper—Melville Bissell (US)
877 Phonograph—Thomas Edison (US)
878 Microphone—David Edward Hughes (Eng./US)
879 Incandescent lamp—Thomas Edison (US)
879 Cash register—James Ritty (US)
884 Fountain pen—Lewis Waterman (US)
884 Linotype—Ottmar Mergenthaler (US)
885 Motorcycle—Edward Butler (Eng.)
885 Vacuum flask—James Dewar (Scot.)
885 Electric transformer—William Stanley (US)
886 Electric fan—Schuyler Wheeler (US)

1886 Halftone engraving—Frederick Ives (US)
1887 Gramophone—Emile Berliner (Ger./US)
1887 Monotype—Tolbert Lanston (US)
1887 Motor-car engine—Gottlieb Daimler & Karl Benz (Ger.), independently
1888 Pneumatic tyre—John Boyd Dunlop (Scot.)
1888 Kodak camera—George Eastman (US)
1890 Rotogravure—Karl Klic (Czech.)
1892 Zip fastener—Whitcomb Judson (US)
1895 Wireless—Guglielmo Marconi (It.)
1895 Photoelectric cell—Julius Elster & Hans Geitel (Ger.)
1895 Safety razor—King C. Gillette (US)
1897 Diesel engine—Rudolf Diesel (Ger.)
1898 Submarine—John P. Holland (Ire./US)
1899 Tape recorder—Valdemar Poulsen (Den.)
1901 Vacuum cleaner—Cecil Booth (Eng.)
1902 Radio-telephone—Reginald Fessenden (US)
1903 Aeroplane—Wilbur & Orville Wright (US)
1904 Diode—John Fleming (Eng.)
1906 Triode—Lee De Forest (US)
1908 Bakelite—Leo Baekeland (Belg./US)
1908 Cellophane—Jacques Brandenberger (Switz.)
1911 Combine harvester—Benjamin Holt (US)
1913 Geiger counter—Hans Geiger (Eng.)

1914 Tank—Ernest Swinton (Eng.)
1915 Tungsten filament lamp—Irving Langmuir (US)
1918 Automatic rifle—John Browning (US)
1925 Television (working system)—John Logie Baird (Scot.) & others
1925 Frozen food process—Clarence Birdseye (US)
1926 Rocket (liquid fuel)— Robert H. Goddard (US)
1930 Jet engine—Frank Whittle (Eng.)
1931 Cyclotron—Ernest Lawrence (US)
1935 Nylon—Wallace Carothers (US)
1939 Electron microscope—Vladimir Zworykin and others (US)
1944 Automatic digital computer—Howard Aiken (US)
1946 Electronic computer—J. Presper Eckert & John W. Mauchly (US)
1947 Polaroid camera—Edwin Land (US)
1948 Transistor—John Bardeen, Walter Brattain & William Shockley (US)
1948 Xerography—Chester Carlson (US)
1948 Long-playing record—Peter Goldmark (US)
1954 Maser—Charles H. Townes (US)
1960 Laser—Theodore Maiman (US)
c.1967 Quartz wristwatch—Seiko Co. (Jap.)
1969 Microprocessor—E. Hoff (US)
1982 Compact disc—Philips (NL), Sony (Jap.)

Discoveries

543 Sun as centre of solar system—Copernicus (Pol.)
590 Law of falling bodies—Galileo (It.)
609 Laws of planetary motion—Johannes Kepler (Ger.)
662 Relation between gas pressure and volume—Robert Boyle (Eng./Ire.)
669 Phosphorus—Hennig Brand (Ger.)
675 Measurement of speed of light—Olaus Römer (Dan.)
678 Wave theory of light—Christian Huygens (Dut.)
687 Laws of gravitation and motion—Isaac Newton (Eng.)
751 Nickel—Axel Cronstedt (Swe.)
755 Magnesium—Sir Humphry Davy (GB)
766 Hydrogen—Henry Cavendish (GB)
772 Nitrogen—Daniel Rutherford (GB)
774 Oxygen—Joseph Priestly (GB); Karl Scheele (Swe.)
774 Chlorine—Karl Scheele (Swe.)
781 Uranus (planet)—William Herschel (GB)
783 Tungsten—Fausto & Juan José de Elhuyar (Sp.)
1789 True nature of combustion—Antoine Lavoisier (Fr.)
1797 Chromium—Louis Vauquelin (Fr.)
1803 Atomic structure of matter—John Dalton (GB)
1811 Molecular hypothesis—Amadeo Avogadro (It.)
1817 Cadmium—Friedrich Stromeyer (Ger.)
1820 Electromagnetism—Hans Christian Oersted (Dan.)

1824 Silicon—Jöns Berzelius (Swe.)
1826 Bromine—Antoine Balard (Fr.)
1826 Laws of electromagnetism— André Ampère (Fr.)
1827 Law of electric conduction—Georg Ohm (Ger.)
1827 Aluminium—Hans Christian Oersted (Dan.)
1831 Electromagnetic induction—Michael Faraday (GB); discovered previously, but not published, by Joseph Henry (US)
1839 Ozone—Christian Schönbein (Ger.)
1841 Uranium—Martin Klaproth (Ger.)
1846 Neptune (Planet)—Johann Galle (Ger.), from predictions of others
1864 Electromagnetic theory of light—James Clerk Maxwell (GB)
1868 Helium—Sir William Ramsay (GB)
1869 Periodic arrangement of elements—Dmitri Mendeleev (Russ.)
1886 Electromagnetic waves—Heinrich Hertz (Ger.)
1886 Fluorine—Henri Moissan (Fr.)
1894 Argon—Sir William Ramsay & Baron Rayleigh (GB)
1895 X-rays—Wilhelm Roentgen (Ger.)
1896 Radioactivity—Antoine Becquerel (Fr.)
1897 Electron—Sir Joseph Thomson (GB)
1898 Radium—Pierre & Marie Curie (Fr.)
1900 Quantum theory—Max Planck (Ger.)
1905 Special theory of relativity—Albert Einstein (Swi.)
1910 Russell-Hertzsprung diagram (star pattern)—Henry Russell & Eijnar Hertzsprung (US)
1913 Atomic number—Henry Moseley (GB)
1915 General theory of relativity—Albert Einstein (Swi.)
1919 Proton—Ernest Rutherford (GB)
1924 Wave nature of electron—Louis de Broglie (Fr.)
1926 Wave mechanics—Erwin Schrödinger (Aus.)
1927 Uncertainty principle—Werner Heisenberg (Ger.)
1930 Pluto (planet)—Clyde Tombaugh (US), from prediction by Percival Lowell (US) in 1905
1931 Existence of neutrino (atomic particle)—Wolfgang Pauli (Ger.)
1931 Deuterium (heavy hydrogen)—Harold Urey (US)
1932 Neutron—James Chadwick (GB)
1932 Positron—Carl Anderson (US)
1935 Existence of meson (atomic particle)—Hideki Yukawa (Jap.)
1940 Plutonium—G.T. Seaborg et al. (US)
1950 Unified field theory—Albert Einstein (Swi./US)
1950 Theory of continuous creation of matter—Fred Hoyle (GB)
1955 Antiproton—Emilio Segré & Owen Chamberlain (US)
1958 Radiation belts surrounding earth—James Van Allen (US)
1963 Quasars—Thomas Matthews & Allan Sandage (US)

Weights and Measures

Length

Metric units
millimetre (mm)
10 mm = 1 centimetre (cm)
100 cm = 1 metre (m)
1,000 m = 1 kilometre (km)

1 micron (μ) = 10^{-6}m (i.e. 1 micrometre)
1 millimicron (mμ) = 10^{-9}m (i.e. 1 nanometre)
1 angstrom (Å) = 10^{-10}m (i.e. 100 picometres)

Imperial units
inch (in)
12 in = 1 foot (ft)
3 ft = 1 yard (yd)
1,760 yd = 1 mile = 5,280 ft

1 mil = $\frac{1}{1000}$ in
12 lines = 1 in
1 link = 7.92 in
100 links = 1 chain = 22 yd
1 rod, pole, or perch = $5\frac{1}{2}$ yd
4 rods = 1 chain
10 chains = 1 furlong = 220 yd
8 furlongs = 1 mile
3 miles = 1 league (statute)

Area

Metric units
square millimetre (mm²)
100 mm² = 1 square centimetre (cm²)
10,000 cm² = 1 square metre (m²)
100 m² = 1 are (a) = 1 square decametre
100 a = 1 hectare (ha) = 1 square hectometre
100 ha = 1 square kilometre (km²)

Imperial units
square inch (in²)
144 in² = 1 square foot (ft²)
9 ft² = 1 square yard (yd²)
4,840 yd² = 1 acre
640 acres = 1 square mile (mile²)

625 square links = 1 square rod
16 square rods = 1 square chain
10 square chains = 1 acre
36 square miles = 1 township (US)

Volume

Metric units
cubic millimetre (mm³)
1,000 mm³ = 1 cubic centimetre (cm³)*
1,000 cm³ = 1 cubic decimetre (dm³) = 1 litre
1,000 dm³ = 1 cubic metre (m³)
1,000,000,000 m³ = 1 cubic kilometre (km³)

Imperial units
cubic inch (in³)
1,728 in³ = 1 cubic foot (ft³)
27 ft³ = 1 cubic yard (yd³)
5,451,776,000 yd³ = 1 cubic mile (mile³)

Capacity

Metric units
millilitre (ml)
1,000 ml = 1 litre (l)
100 l = 1 hectolitre (hl)

Imperial units
gill
4 gills = 1 pint
2 pints = 1 quart
4 quarts = 1 gallon = 277.274 in³

(dry)
2 gallons = 1 peck
4 pecks = 1 bushel
8 bushels = 1 quarter
36 bushels = 1 chaldron

(Apothecaries' fluid)†
minim (min)
60 min = 1 fluid drachm (fl. dr.)
8 fl. dr. = 1 fluid ounce (fl. oz)
5 fl. oz = 1 gill
20 fl. oz = 1 pint

60 minims (US) = 1 fluid dram (US)
8 fluid drams (US) = 1 fluid ounce (US)

US units
1 US gallon (liquid) = 0.8327 gallon (imp.)
1 US gallon (dry) = 0.9689 gallon (imp.)
1 fluid oz (US) = 1.0408 fl. oz (apoth.)

Weight

Metric units
milligram (mg)
1,000 mg = 1 gram (g)
1,000 g = 1 kilogram (kg)
100 kg = 1 quintal (q)
1,000 kg = 1 metric ton, or tonne (t)

Imperial units (Avoirdupois)
grain (gr); dram (dr)
7,000 gr = 1 pound (lb)
16 dr = 1 ounce (oz)
16 oz = 1 lb
14 lb = 1 stone
28 lb = 1 quarter
112 lb = 1 hundredweight (cwt)
20 cwt = 1 (long) ton = 2,240 lb

2,000 lb = 1 short ton (US)

(Troy)
24 gr = 1 pennyweight (dwt)
20 dwt = 1 (Troy) ounce‡ = 480 gr
12 (Troy) oz = 1 (Troy) lb (US) = 5,760 gr

(Apothecaries')†
20 gr = 1 scruple
3 scruples = 1 drachm
8 drachms = 1 (apoth.) ounce = 480 gr
12 (apoth.) oz = 1 (apoth.) pound = 0.82 lb

*Used to be abbreviated c.c. †Apothecaries' measures no longer legal.
‡For gold and silver the ounce (divided decimally) is the sole unit of weight.

Angle

second (″)
60″ = 1 minute (′)
60′ = 1 degree (°)
90° = 1 quadrant, or right-angle
4 quadrants = 1 circle = 360°
1 radian = 57.2958° = 57°17′44.8″
2π radians = 1 circle = 360°
1° = 0.017453 radian

Miscellaneous measures §

Nautical
1 span = 9 in
8 spans = 1 fathom = 6 ft
1 cable's length = $\frac{1}{10}$ nautical mile
1 nautical mile (old) = 6,080 ft
1 nautical mile (international) = 6,076.1 ft
    = 1.151 statute miles (= 1.852 metres)
60 nautical miles = 1 degree
3 nautical miles = 1 league (nautical)
1 knot = 1 nautical mile per hour
1 ton (shipping, UK) = 42 cubic feet
1 ton (displacement) = 35 cubic feet
1 ton (register) = 100 cubic feet

Crude oil (petroleum)
1 barrel = 35 imperial gallons
    = 42 US gallons

Timber
1,000 millisteres = 1 stere = 1 m³
1 board foot = 144 in³ (12×12×1 in)
1 cord foot = 16 ft³
1 cord = 8 cord feet
1 hoppus foot = 4/π ft³ (round timber)
1 Petrograd standard = 165 ft³

Paper (writing)
24 sheets = 1 quire
20 quires = 1 ream = 480 sheets

Paper (printing)
516 sheets = 1 ream
2 reams = 1 bundle
5 bundles = 1 bale

Printing
1 point = $\frac{1}{72}$ in
1 pica = $\frac{1}{6}$ in = 12 points

Cloth
1 ell = 45 in
1 bolt = 120 ft = 32 ells

Brewing
9 gallons = 1 firkin
4 firkins = 1 barrel = 36 gallons
6 firkins = 1 hogshead = 54 gallons
4 hogsheads = 1 tun

Counting
1 dozen = 12
12 dozen = 1 gross = 144
12 gross = 1 great gross = 1,728

Others
1 nail = $2\frac{1}{4}$ inches
1 hand = 4 in (height of horses)
1 circular mil = 0.000000785 in² (electric wire)
1 slug = 32.174 lb (gravitational unit)
1 carat = 200 mg (gems)
1 hogshead = $52\frac{1}{2}$ imperial gallons
    or 63 gallons wine (old)
    or 46 gallons claret wine
    or 100 gallons molasses

§Mostly obsolescent.

Time

second (s, or sec)
60 s = 1 minute (min)
60 min = 1 hour (h, or hr)
24 h = 1 day (d)
7 days = 1 week
365$\frac{1}{4}$ days = 1 year
10 years = 1 decade
100 years = 1 century

1,000 years = 1 millennium
1 mean solar day = 24 h 3 min 56.555 s
1 sidereal day = 23 h 56 min 4.091 s
1 solar, tropical, or equinoctial year =
    365.2422 d (365 d 5 h 48 min 46 s)
1 siderial year = 365.2564 d
    (365 d 6 h 9 min 9.5 s)
1 synodic (lunar) month = 29.5306 d
1 siderial month = 27.3217 d
1 lunar year = 354 d = 12 synodic months

Cooking Measurements and Food Values

APPROXIMATE OVEN TEMPERATURES

description	electric °F	°C	gas no.*
very cool	225°	107°	¼ (240°)
	250°	121°	½ (265°)
cool	275°	135°	1 (290°)
	300°	149°	2 (310°)
warm	325°	163°	3 (335°)
moderate	350°	177°	4 (355°)
fairly hot	375°	191°	5 (375°)
	400°	204°	6 (400°)
hot	425°	218°	7 (425°)
very hot	450°	232°	8 (450°)
	475°	246°	9 (470°)

*Temperature equivalents of the gas numbers are given in °F in parentheses.

CALORIES NEEDED PER DAY

age	both sexes	
0–1	800	Calorie requirements depend on age, sex, and activity. At about 9 years old, boys start to need more than girls, who generally expend less energy, because they weigh less and have a layer of fat to keep in heat.
1–2	1,200	
2–3	1,400	
3–5	1,600	
5–7	1,800	
7–9	2,100	

age	male	female
9–12	2,500	2,300
12–15	2,800	2,300
15–18	3,000	2,300
18–35	2,700 (normal life)	2,200 (normal life)
	3,600 (very active)	2,500 (very active)
		2,400 (pregnant)
		2,700 (breast feeding)
35–65	2,600	2,200
65–75	2,300	2,100
75 on	2,100	1,900

VITAMINS

vitamin	chief source	needed for
Vitamin A	Carotene (which body can convert to Vit. A) in carrots, egg yolks, butter, yellow or orange fruits, vegetables	growth; prevention of dry skin; formation of visual purple, which aids vision in dim light; lack of Vit. A can lead to atrophy of white of eyeball
Vitamin B₁ (thiamine)	wheat germ, bread, pork, liver, potatoes, milk	prevention of beri-beri
Vitamin B₂ (riboflavine)	milk, eggs, liver	lack may result in skin disorders, inflammation of tongue, and cracked lips
Biotin	liver, yeast, milk, butter	probably concerned with healthy skin
Folic acid	many green vegetables, liver, yeast, mushrooms	prevention of one form of anaemia
Nicotinic acid (niacin)	yeast, liver, bread, wheat germ, kidney, milk	prevention of pellagra
Pantothenic acid	many foods, but abundant in liver, yeast, and eggs	lack may play part in skin disorders
Vitamin B₆ (pyridoxine)	meat, fish, milk, yeast	lack can lead to convulsions in babies or anaemia in adults
Vitamin B₁₂ (cyanocobalamin)	liver, kidney, eggs, fish	formation of red blood cells; healthy nerve tissue
Vitamin C	fresh fruit and vegetables	prevention of scurvy
Vitamin D	margarine, fish, oils, eggs, butter; also formed in skin exposed to sunlight	formation of bones; lack causes rickets in children
Vitamin E	most foods	little known
Vitamin K	green vegetables; also formed by bacteria in intestine	clotting of blood

CALORIFIC VALUE OF FOODS

average portion	calories
Apple (1) 5 oz (142 g)	70
Bacon (fried) 2 oz (57 g)	250–320
Banana (1) 5 oz (142 g)	110
Beans, green (boiled) 4 oz (113 g)	10
Beef (roast) 3 oz (85 g)	325
Beef steak (grilled) 6 oz (170 g)	520
Beer (bitter) 1 pint (0·6 l)	180
Bread (white, 1 slice) 1 oz (28 g)	73
Butter ½ oz (14 g)	110
Cabbage (boiled) 5 oz (142 g)	15
Carrots (boiled) 4 oz (113 g)	24
Celery (raw) 4 oz (113 g)	8
Cheese (cheddar) 1 oz (28 g)	112
Cheese (cottage) 1 oz (28 g)	29
Chicken (roast) 4 oz (113 g)	220
Chocolate (milk) 2 oz (57 g)	300
Cod (grilled) 4 oz (113 g)	170
Coffee (white, no sugar) 6 fl oz (170 ml)	25
Corn flakes 1 oz (28 g)	100
Cream (double) ½ oz (14 g)	64
Egg (boiled, 1) 2 oz (57 g)	90
Grapefruit (½) 7 oz (198 g)	42
Honey ½ oz (14 g)	41
Lamb (roast) 3 oz (85 g)	250
Lettuce 2 oz (57 g)	5
Magarine ½ oz (14 g)	110
Melon (1 slice) 5 oz (142 g)	30
Milk (cup) 6 fl oz (170 ml)	110
Orange (1) 6 oz (170 g)	60
Peanuts 2 oz (57 g)	330
Potatoes (fried) 4 oz (113 g)	270
(boiled, baked) 4 oz (113 g)	90
Rice (boiled) 6 oz (170 g)	600
Sardines (tinned) 3 oz (85 g)	240
Sausages (pork, 2) 4 oz (113 g)	400
Spinach (boiled) 1½ oz (43 g)	10
Spirits (measure) 1 fl oz (28 ml)	63
Strawberries 5 oz (142 g)	35
Sugar 2 oz (57 g)	215,
1 teaspoon	25
Tea (cup, no sugar) 6 fl oz (170 ml)	15
Tomato (1) 3 oz (85 g)	12
Wine, dry (glass) 4 fl oz (114 ml)	84
sweet (glass) 4 fl oz (114 ml)	128

USEFUL MEASURES

Imperial

2 teaspoons	=	1 dessertspoon
2 dessertspoons	=	1 tablespoon
16 tablespoons	=	1 cup
2 cups	=	1 pint
1 pint	=	20 fl. oz

American

1 Amer. pint	=	16 fl. oz
1 Amer. cup	=	8 fl. oz

Metric (working) equivalents

1 teaspoon	=	5 ml
1 Amer. teaspoon	=	4 ml
1 pint	=	½ litre (approx.)
1 litre	=	1¾ pints (approx.)
1 lb	=	½ kilo (approx.)

Level teaspoons per oz (approx.)

Breadcrumbs (dry)	3–4
Cheese (grated)	3–4
Flour	2
Gelatine	2
Raisins, etc.	2
Rice	2
Sugar (granulated)	1

Useful Information

ARCHITECTS

Adam, Robert (1728–92), Scottish
Alberti, Leone Battista (1404–72), Italian
Bernini, Lorenzo (1598–1680), Italian
Bramante, Donato (1444–1514), Italian
Brunelleschi, Filippo (1377–1446), Italian
Gaudí, Antoni (1852–1926), Spanish
Gropius, Walter (1883–1969), German
Jones, Inigo (1573–1652), English
Le Corbusier (1887–1965), French-Swiss
Michelangelo (1475–1546), Italian
Mies van der Rohe, Ludwig (1886–1969), Ger./US
Nash, John (1752–1835), English
Nervi, Pier Luigi (1891–   ), Italian
Niemeyer, Oscar (1907–   ), Brazilian
Palladio, Andrea (1518–80), Italian
Wren, Sir Christopher (1632–1723), English
Wright, Frank Lloyd (1869–1959), American

Tallest structures

The world's tallest building is the 110-storey 1,454 ft (443 m) Sears Tower in Chicago, USA. With TV antennae, it reaches 1,800 ft (548.6 m). The world's tallest structure is the 2,120 ft (646 m) mast of Warszawa Radio at Konstantynow, near Plock, in Poland. Made of galvanized steel, it was completed in May 1974.

The highest structures of ancient times were the pyramids of Egypt. The Great Pyramid of Cheops, at el-Gizeh, built in about 2580 BC, reached a height of 480.9 ft (146.6 m). It was another 4,000 years before this was surpassed — by the central tower of Lincoln Cathedral, England, which was completed in 1548 and stood 525 ft (160 m) before it toppled in a storm.

PERIODS OF ARCHITECTURE

Greek	600s – 100s BC
Roman	100s BC – AD 400s
Byzantine	AD 400s – 1453
Romanesque (N. Europe)	mid-900s – late 1100s
Norman (England)	late 1000s – 1100s
Gothic (France)	mid-1100s – 1400s
Renaissance (Italy)	1400s – 1500s
French Renaissance	1500s
Baroque (Italy)	1600–1750
Georgian (England)	1725–1800
Rococo (Italy)	mid-1700s
Regency (England)	1800–1825
Art Nouveau (Europe)	1890–1910
Expressionism (Germany)	1910–1930s
Functionalism	1920s–
International Style	1920s–
Brutalism	1950s–
Post-Modernism	1980

TWELVE LABOURS OF HERCULES

1 Killing Nemean lion
2 Killing Hydra (many-headed snake)
3 Capturing hind of Artemis
4 Capturing Erymanthian boar
5 Cleansing Augean stables in a day
6 Killing man-eating Stymphalian birds
7 Capturing Cretan wild bull
8 Capturing man-eating mares of Diomedes
9 Procuring girdle of Amazon Hippolyta
10 Killing the monster Geryon
11 Stealing apples from garden of Hesperides
12 Bringing Cerberus up from Hades

THE NINE MUSES

Name	Art	Symbol
Calliope	Epic poetry	Tablet & stylus
Clio	History	Scroll
Erato	Love poetry	Lyre
Euterpe	Lyric poetry	Flute
Melpomene	Tragedy	Tragic mask, sword
Polyhymnia	Sacred song	none
Terpsichore	Dancing	Lyre
Thalia	Comedy; pastoral poetry	Comic mask, shepherd's staff
Urania	Astronomy	Globe

DERIVATION OF DAYS AND MONTHS

day	named after
Sunday	the Sun
Monday	the Moon
Tuesday	Tiu, Norse god of war
Wednesday	Woden, Anglo-Saxon chief of gods
Thursday	Thor, Norse god of thunder
Friday	Frigg, Norse goddess
Saturday	Saturn, Roman god of harvests
January	Janus, Roman god of doors and gates
February	Februa, Roman period of purification
March	Mars, Roman god of war
April	aperire, Latin 'to open'
May*	Maia, Roman goddess of spring and growth
June*	Juno, Roman goddess of marriage
July	Julius Caesar
August	Augustus, first emperor of Rome
September	septem, Latin 'seven'
October	octo, Latin 'eight'
November	novem, Latin 'nine'
December	decem, Latin 'ten'

* According to some scholars, May comes from *majores* (older men), June from *juniores* (young men), to whom months were held to be sacred.

THE TWELVE APOSTLES

Peter (Simon)
Andrew
James the Less
John the Evangelist
Philip of Bethsaida
Bartholomew
Thomas (also known as Didymus)
Matthew (also known as Levi)
Simon the Canaanite (also known as Simon Zelotes)
Jude (also known as Judas, Thaddaeus, and Lebbaeus)
James the Greater
Judas Iscariot

Paul and Barnabas are also sometimes classed as apostles, although they were not among the original 12. Matthias took the place of Judas Iscariot.

ROMAN-GREEK EQUIVALENTS

Roman	Greek	Roman	Greek
Aesculapius	Asclepius	Luna	Selene
Apollo	Apollo	Mars	Ares
Aurora	Eos	Mercury	Hermes
Bacchus	Dionysus	Minerva	Athene
Ceres	Demeter	Mors	Thanatos
Cupid	Eros	Neptune	Poseidon
Cybele	Rhea	Ops	Rhea
Diana	Artemis	Pluto	Pluto
Dis	Hades	Proserpine	Persephone
Faunus	Pan	Saturn	Cronos
Hecate	Hecate	Sol	Helios
Hercules	Heracles	Somnus	Hypnos
Juno	Hera	Ulysses	Odysseus
Jupiter	Zeus	Venus	Aphrodite
Juventas	Hebe	Vesta	Hestia
Latona	Leto	Vulcan	Hephaestus

'ARCHIES & 'OCRACIES

anarchy	harmony, without law
aristocracy	a privileged order
autocracy	one man, absolutely
bureaucracy	officials
democracy	the people
despotocracy	a tyrant
diarchy	two rulers or authorities
ergatocracy	the workers
ethnocracy	race or ethnic group
gerontocracy	old men
gynocracy	women
hierocracy	priests
isocracy	all – with equal power
kakistocracy	the worst
matriarchy	a mother (or mothers)
meritocracy	those in power on ability
monarchy	hereditary head of state
monocracy	one person
ochlocracy	the mob
oligarchy	small exclusive class
patriarchy	male head of family
plutocracy	the wealthy
stratocracy	the military
technocracy	technical experts
theocracy	divine guidance

ALPHABETS

Greek

Letter	Name	Transliteration
Α α	alpha	a
Β β	beta	b
Γ γ	gamma	g
Δ δ	delta	d
Ε ε	epsilon	e
Ζ ζ	zeta	z
Η η	eta	ē
Θ θ	theta	th
Ι ι	iota	i
Κ κ	kappa	k
Λ λ	lambda	l
Μ μ	mu	m
Ν ν	nu	n
Ξ ξ	xi	x (ks)
Ο ο	omicron	o
Π π	pi	p
Ρ ρ	rho	r
Σ σ,ς*	sigma	s
Τ τ	tau	t
Υ υ	upsilon	u, y
Φ φ	phi	ph
Χ χ	chi	kh, ch
Ψ ψ	psi	ps
Ω ω	omega	o

Hebrew

Letter	Name	Transliteration
א	aleph†	'
ב	beth	b
ג	gimel	g
ד	daleth	d
ה	heh	h
ו	waw	w
ז	zayin	z
ח	heth	ḥ
ט	teth	ṭ
י	yod	y
ךכ*	kaph	k, kh
ל	lamed	l
םמ*	mem	m
ןנ*	nun	n
ס	samekh	s
ע	ayin	'
ףפ*	peh	p, ph
ץצ*	sadhe	ṣ
ק	qoph	q
ר	resh	r
ש	shin	sh
שׂ	sin	ś
ת	taw	t

Russian

Letter		Transliteration
А	а	a
Б	б	b
В	в	v
Г	г	g
Д	д	d
Е	е	e, ye
Ж	ж	zh
З	з	z
И	и	i
Й	й	i
К	к	k
Л	л	l
М	м	m
Н	н	n
О	о	o
П	п	p
Р	р	r
С	с	s
Т	т	t
У	у	u
Ф	ф	f
Х	х	kh
Ц	ц	ts
Ч	ч	ch
Ш	ш	sh
Щ	щ	shch
Ы	ы	i
Ь	ь	'
Э	э	e
Ю	ю	yu
Я	я	ya

*Form used at end of word.

†Not transliterated when initial.

THE PROPHETS

Traditional classification according to their writings:

Major Prophets – Isaiah, Jeremiah, Ezekiel, and (except in Hebrew scriptures) Daniel

Minor Prophets – Hosea, Joel, Amos, Obadiah, Jonah, Micah, Nahum, Habakkuk, Zephaniah, Haggai, Zechariah, and Malachi

---

FAMOUS 'FATHERS'

These are some of the people to whom the name 'father' is given because of their pioneer work in various fields

Father of Anatomy Andreas Vesalius (1514–1564), Belgian physician.

Father of Angling Isaak Walton (1593–1683), English writer.

Father of Chemistry Robert Boyle (1627–1691), Irish chemist and physicist.

Father of Comedy Aristophanes (c.445–c.385 BC), Greek playwright.

Father of Courtesy Richard de Beauchamp, Earl of Warwick (1382–1429), English soldier.

Father of Ecclesiastical History Eusebius of Caesarea (c.260–c.340), theologian and historian.

Father of Economics Adam Smith (1723–1790), Scottish philosopher.

Father of English History The Venerable Bede (673–735), English monk and scholar.

Father of English Poetry Geoffrey Chaucer (c.1340–1400), English merchant and diplomat, author of *The Canterbury Tales*.

Father of English Prose Alfred the Great, king of Wessex (848–899), who translated Latin texts into the Saxon tongue.

Father of English Song Caedmon (lived around 670), English herdsman and poet.

Father of Epic Poetry Homer, traditional Greek author of the *Iliad* and the *Odyssey*; lived sometime between 1200 and 850 BC.

Father of the Faithful The Patriarch Abraham (lived c.1900 BC).

Father of Geometry Euclid (lived c.300 BC), Greek mathematician.

Father of Greek Tragedy Aeschylus (525–426 BC), Greek soldier and dramatist.

Father of His Country Title given to several people in history, including Cicero, Julius Caesar, Augustus, Andronicus Palaeologus II, George Washington, Mahatma Gandhi.

Father of History Herodotus (c.484–424 BC), Greek traveller and writer.

Father of Letters Francis I of France (1494–1547) and Lorenzo de' Medici (1449–1492), Florentine statesman, share this title.

Father of Mathematics Thales of Miletus (c.640–546 BC), Greek philosopher.

Father of Medicine Hippocrates (460–c.370 BC), Greek physician.

Father of Moral Philosophy St Thomas Aquinas (1225–1274), Italian Dominican philosopher.

Father of Nuclear Physics Lord Rutherford (1871–1937), New Zealand/British physicist.

Father of Ridicule François Rabelais (c.1494–1553), French monk.

Father of Wireless Guglielmo Marconi (1874–1937), Italian inventor.

Founding Fathers American statesmen of the War of Independence, including Benjamin Franklin, Alexander Hamilton, and George Washington.

Pilgrim Fathers English settlers who landed at Plymouth, Massachusetts, in 1620 to seek religious freedom in America.

Geology

MOH'S HARDNESS SCALE*

mineral	simple hardness test	Moh's hardness
Talc	Crushed by finger nail	1.0
Gypsum	Scratched by finger nail	2.0
Calcite	Scratched by copper coin	3.0
Fluorspar	Scratched by glass	4.0
Apatite	Scratched by a penknife	5.0
Feldspar	Scratched by quartz	6.0
Quartz	Scratched by a steel file	7.0
Topaz	Scratched by corundum	8.0
Corundum	Scratched by diamond	9.0
Diamond		10.0

* Used for testing hardness of materials, by comparing them with the 10 standard minerals.

GEMSTONES

mineral	colour	Moh's hardness
Agate	brown, red, blue, green, yellow	7.0
Amethyst	violet	7.0
Aquamarine	sky blue, greenish blue	7.5
Beryl	green, blue, pink	7.5
Bloodstone	green with red spots	7.0
Chalcedony	all colours	7.0
Citrine	yellow	7.0
Diamond	colourless, tints of various colours	10.0
Emerald	green	7.5
Garnet	red and other colours	6.5–7.25
Jade	green, whitish, mauve, brown	7.0
Lapis lazuli	deep blue	5.5
Malachite	dark green banded	3.5
Moonstone	whitish with blue shimmer	6.0
Onyx	various colours with straight coloured bands	7.0
Opal	black, white, orange-red, rainbow coloured	6.0
Ruby	red	9.0
Sapphire	blue, and other colours	9.0
Serpentine	red and green	3.0
Soapstone	white, may be stained with impurities	2.0
Sunstone	whitish-red-brown flecked with golden particles	6.0
Topaz	blue, green, pink, yellow, colourless	8.0
Tourmaline	brown-black, blue, pink, red, violet-red, yellow, green	7.5
Turquoise	greenish-grey, sky blue	6.0
Zircon	All colours	7.5

METALS AND THEIR ORES

metal	ores	metal	ores
Aluminium	bauxite, AL_2O_3	Magnesium	magnesite, dolomite, both $MgCO_3$; kieserite, $MgSO_4.H_2O$; carnallite, $KCl.MgCl_2.6H_2O$
Antimony	stibnite, Sb_2S_3		
Beryllium	beryl, $3BeO.Al_2O_3.6SiO_2$; chrysoberyl, $BeAl_2O_4$		
Bismuth	bismuth glance (bismuthinite), Bi_2S_3; bismite, Bi_2O_3	Manganese	pyrolusite, MnO_2; hausmannite, Mn_3O_4
Calcium	limestone, marble, chalk, all $CaCO_3$; gypsum, alabaster, both $CaSO_4$; fluorspar, CaF_2; rock phosphate, $CaPO_4$	Mercury	cinnabar, HgS
		Nickel	millerite, NiS; pentlandite, $(Fe,Ni)S$; garnierite, $(Ni;Mg)SiO_3.xH_2O$
Chromium	chromite, $FeCr_2O_4$	Potassium	carnallite, $KCl.MgCl_2.6H_2O$; saltpetre, KNO_3
Cobalt	smaltite, $CoAs_2$; cobaltite, CoAsS	Silver	silver glance (argentite), AgS_2; horn silver, AgCl
Copper	copper pyrites (chalcopyrite), $CuFeS_2$; copper glance (chalcocyte), Cu_2S; cuprite, Cu_2O; bornite, Cu_5FeS_4	Sodium	rock salt, NaCl; Chile saltpetre, $NaNO_3$
		Strontium	strontianite, $SrCO_3$; celestine, $SrSO_4$
Iron	haematite, Fe_2O_3; magnetite, Fe_3O_4; siderite, $FeCO_3$; (iron pyrites, FeS_2)	Tin	tinstone (cassiterite), SnO_2
		Titanium	rutile, TiO_2; ilmenite, $FeO.TiO_2$
		Uranium	pitchblende (uraninite), UO_2
Lead	galena, PbS; cerussite, $PbCO_3$; massicot, PbO	Zinc	zinc blende (sphalerite), ZnS; calamine, $ZnCO_3$
Lithium	spodumene, $LiAl (SiO_3)_2$		

NB: Gold and platinum occur in the earth as elements. Cadmium compounds are found in zinc ores

GEOLOGICAL TIME SCALE

ERAS	PERIODS	EPOCHS	millions of years ago	life forms
Cenozoic	Quaternary	Holocene (recent)		(end of ice age) development of man
			2	
		Pleistocene		(ice ages) mammoths, woolly rhinoceroses
			7	
	Tertiary	Pliocene		mammals spread; earliest men
			26	
		Miocene		whales and apes
			38	
		Oligocene		modern types of mammals
			54	
		Eocene		first horses and elephants
			65	
		Palaeocene		early mammals
			136	
Mesozoic	Cretaceous			end of dinosaurs; flowering plants spread
			193	
	Jurassic			giant dinosaurs; first birds
			225	
	Triassic			small dinosaurs; first mammals
			280	
Palaeozoic	Permian			
			345	
	Carboniferous (Pennsylvanian and Mississippian)			forests formed coal; first reptiles
			398	
	Devonian			first forests and land animals, amphibians
			435	
	Silurian			first land plants
			500	
	Ordovician			first fishes
			570	
	Cambrian			
			1,850	
Precambrian	Proterozoic			sea animals without backbones; seaweeds
	Archaeozoic			first primitive plants and animals
	Azoic		4,000	(earliest known rocks)
			4,500	(earth formed)

Elements and Alloys

CHEMICAL ELEMENTS

name	symbol	at. no.	at. wt	name	symbol	at. no.	at. wt
Actinium	Ac	89	(227)	Mercury	Hg	80	200.59
Aluminium	Al	13	26.98154	Molybdenum	Mo	42	95.94
Americium	Am	95	(243)	Neodymium	Nd	60	144.24
Antimony	Sb	51	121.75	Neon	Ne	10	20.179
Argon	Ar	18	39.948	Neptunium	Np	93	237.0482
Arsenic	As	33	74.9216	Nickel	Ni	28	58.70
Astatine	At	85	(210)	Niobium	Nb	41	92.9064
Barium	Ba	56	137.34	Nitrogen	N	7	14.0067
Berkelium	Bk	97	(247)	Nobelium	No	102	(255)
Beryllium	Be	4	9.01218	Osmium	Os	76	190.2
Bismuth	Bi	83	208.9804	Oxygen	O	8	15.9994
Boron	B	5	10.81	Palladium	Pd	46	106.4
Bromine	Br	35	79.904	Phosphorus	P	15	30.97376
Cadmium	Cd	48	112.40	Platinum	Pt	78	195.09
Caesium	Cs	55	132.9054	Plutonium	Pu	94	(244)
Calcium	Ca	20	40.08	Polonium	Po	84	(209)
Californium	Cf	98	(251)	Potassium	K	19	39.098
Carbon	C	6	12.011	Praseodymium	Pr	59	140.9077
Cerium	Ce	58	140.12	Promethium	Pm	61	(145)
Chlorine	Cl	17	35.453	Protactinium	Pa	91	231.0359
Chromium	Cr	24	51.996	Radium	Ra	88	226.0254
Cobalt	Co	27	58.9332	Radon	Rn	86	(222)
Copper	Cu	29	63.546	Rhenium	Re	75	186.207
Curium	Cm	96	(247)	Rhodium	Rh	45	102.9055
Dysprosium	Dy	66	162.50	Rubidium	Rb	37	85.4678
Einsteinium	Es	99	(254)	Ruthenium	Ru	44	101.07
Erbium	Er	68	167.26	Samarium	Sm	62	150.4
Europium	Eu	63	151.96	Scandium	Sc	21	44.9559
Fermium	Fm	100	(257)	Selenium	Se	34	78.96
Fluorine	F	9	18.99840	Silicon	Si	14	28.086
Francium	Fr	87	(223)	Silver	Ag	47	107.868
Gadolinium	Gd	64	157.25	Sodium	Na	11	22.98977
Gallium	Ga	31	69.72	Strontium	Sr	38	87.62
Germanium	Ge	32	72.59	Sulfur	S	16	32.06
Gold	Au	79	196.9665	Tantalum	Ta	73	180.9479
Hafnium	Hf	72	178.49	Technetium	Tc	43	(97)
Helium	He	2	4.00260	Tellurium	Te	52	127.60
Holmium	Ho	67	164.9304	Terbium	Tb	65	158.9254
Hydrogen	H	1	1.0079	Thallium	Tl	81	204.37
Indium	In	49	114.82	Thorium	Th	90	232.0381
Iodine	I	53	126.9045	Thulium	Tm	69	168.9342
Iridium	Ir	77	192.22	Tin	Sn	50	118.69
Iron	Fe	26	55.847	Titanium	Ti	22	47.90
Krypton	Kr	36	83.80	Tungsten (Wolfram)	W	74	183.85
Lanthanum	La	57	138.9055	Uranium	U	92	238.029
Lawrencium	Lr	103	(260)	Vanadium	V	23	50.9414
Lead	Pb	82	207.2	Xenon	Xe	54	131.30
Lithium	Li	3	6.941	Ytterbium	Yb	70	173.04
Lutetium	Lu	71	174.97	Yttrium	Y	39	88.9059
Magnesium	Mg	12	24.305	Zinc	Zn	30	65.38
Manganese	Mn	25	54.9380	Zirconium	Zr	40	91.22
Mendelevium	Md	101	(258)				

Notes: The atomic weights (at. wt.) are based on the exact number 12 as assigned to the atomic mass of the principal isotope of carbon, carbon-12, and are provided through the courtesy of the International Union of Pure and Applied Chemistry (IUPAC) and Butterworths Scientific Publications.
Values in parentheses are for certain radioactive elements whose atomic weights cannot be quoted precisely without knowledge of origin; the value given in each case is the atomic mass no. of the isotope of longest known half-life.
Elements with atomic numbers 104 and 105 were discovered in 1969 and 1970 respectively, and have provisionally been named Rutherfordium (104) and Hahnium (105); neither name will become official until approved by IUPAC.

SELECTED SPECIFIC GRAVITIES

substance	S. G.
Alcohol	0.8
Aluminium	2.7
Asbestos	2.4
Benzene	0.7
Borax	1.7
Butter	0.9
Charcoal	0.4
Copper	8.9
Cork	0.25
Corundum	4.0
Diamond	3.5
Gold	19.3
Granite	2.7
Ice (at 0°C)	0.92
Iridium	22.42
Lead	11.3
Limestone	2.6
Marble	2.7
Milk	1.03
Nylon	1.14
Olive oil	0.9
Osmium*	22.57
Paraffin oil	0.8
Perspex	1.2
Petroleum	0.8
Pitch	1.1
Plaster of Paris	1.8
Platinum	21.9
Polystyrene	1.06
Polythene	0.93
PVC	1.4
Sand	1.6
Silver	10.5
Steel (stainless)	7.8
Talc	2.8
Tar	1.0
Tin	7.3
Tungsten	19.3
Turpentine	0.85
Uranium	19.0
Water	1.0
sea water	1.03
Wood:	
balsa	0.2
bamboo	0.4
beech	0.75
boxwood	1.0
cedar	0.55
mahogany	0.8
teak	0.9

*Densest of all measurable elements

ALLOYS

name	composition
copper	
Aluminium bronze	90% Cu, 10% Al
Manganese bronze	95% Cu, 5% Mn
Gun metal bronze	90% Cu, 10% Sn
Red brass	90% Cu, 10% Zn
Naval brass	70% Cu, 29% Zn, 1% Sn
Yellow brass	67% Cu, 33% Zn
Nickel silver	55% Cu, 18% Ni, 27% Zn

name	composition
gold	
18-carat gold	75% Au, 25% Ag & Cu
Palladium, or white, gold	90% Au, 10% Pd
iron	
Steel	99% Fe, 1% C
Stainless steel	Fe with 0.1–2.0% C, up to 27% Cr or 20% W or 15% Ni and lesser amounts of other elements

name	composition
silver	
Sterling silver	92.5% Ag, 7.5% Cu
US silver	90% Ag, 10% Cu
miscellaneous	
Britannia metal	90% Sn, 10% Sb
Dentist's amalgam	70% Hg, 30% Cu
Type metal	82% Pb, 15% Sb, 3% Sn

INDEX

Page numbers in *italics* refer to illustrations.

Hollywood, Calif., U.S.A. 175
Holmes, Sherlock 175
Holocene epoch 398
Holography 175
Holtermann nugget 159
Holy Grail 176
Holy Roman empire 84, 168, 176
Homer 176
Homo erectus pekinensis see Peking Man
Homo sapiens 248
Homosexuality 176
Honduras 176
Honey 176
Honey bee 55, *188*
Honeycomb *55*
Honeycreeper 59
Honeypot ant *28*
Hong Kong 176, *176*
Honolulu, Hawaii 169
Honshu (is., Jap.) 197
Hoof 176
Hop 177
Hopis Indians 26
Horizontal bar 167, *167*
Hormone 156, *157*, 177
Horn 177
 see also Nail
Horn, Cape 177
Horse 133, 177, *177*, *183*
Horse-racing 177, 178
 see also Derby; Steeplechase
Horshoe Falls see Niagara Falls
Horus 274
Hospital 178
 see also Surgery
Hot spring *see* Geyser
Hound 178
 see also Greyhound
Hour candle *96*
Hour glass *96*
House at Pooh Corner, The (Milne) 236
Houseboat *176*
House fly 178, *178*
House of Commons 178
House of Lords 178, *269*
House of the Faun *284*
House plant 178, *178*
Hovercraft 178
Howling monkey 238
Hua Kuo-feng 89
Hudson, Henry 179
Hudson Bay 179
Hugo, Victor 179
Humerus *325*
Humidity 179, 379
Hummingbird 59, 179, *179*
Hundred Years War 179, *179*, 199
Hungary 179
Huns 179
Hunting 180, *180*
Hurdling 180
Huron, lake 163
Hurricane 180
 see also Typhoon
Huygens, Christian 96
Hyades star cluster *352*
Hydrocarbons 180
Hydrochloric acid 9, 180
Hydroelectric power 180, *180*, 328
Hydrofoil 180, *180*

Hydrogen 180
Hydrogen bomb 44, 148, 181
Hyena 181
Hygeia 38
Hygiene 181
Hypnosis 181
Hypocaust *307*
Hypochondria 181
Hypothalamus *64*

I

Ibadan, Nig. *16*, 251
Iberian peninsula see Portugal; Spain
Ibex 182, *182*
Ibis 182
Ibiza 48
Ibo 251
Ice 182
Ice Age 182, *183*
Iceburg 182, *182*
Ice cream 182
Ice hockey 184
Iceland 184, *184*, *373*
Ice sheet 156, *183*
Ice skating 184
Ichthyosaur 184, *184*
Icon 184
Ignatius of Loyola, St. 198
Igneous rock 305
 see also Granite
Ignition *189*
Iguana 184
Ikeya-Seki comet 99
Iliad (Homer) 176, 360
Illiteracy 184
Illuminated manuscript 184, *184*
Illustration 184
Immunity *see* Antibody; Vaccine
Impala 185
Imperial measure 394, 395
Impressionism *35*, 185, *238*
Incas 185, *185*
Incense 185
Income tax 185
Incubation 185
Independence, American War of *see* Revolutionary War, American
India 186, *186*
Indian see American Indians
Indian cobra 97
Indian elephant 127
Indian Ocean 186, 258
Indochina 186
Indonesia 186, *186*
Industrial Revolution 129, 186, *186*
Inertia 187
Infantry 187
Inflation 187
Influenza 187
Infrared rays *126*, .187
Infra-red sensing 298
Ink 187, *187*
Inlaying 187
Inorganic chemistry 187
Inquisition 188
Insanity 188
Insect 188, *188*
Insecticide 188

Insomnia 188
Instinct 188, *188*
Insulator 188
Insulin 177
Insurance 188
 see also Lloyd's
Intaglio *see* Photogravure
Integrated circuits *100*, 126, 189, *189*
Intelligence 189
Interest 189
Interglacial period *183*
Interior decoration 189
Internal combustion engine 189, *189*, *190*
 see also Motor car; Motorcycle
Intestine *116*, 190
Inventions 190, *191*, *392*
Invertebrate 190
Iodine 190
Ion 53, 190
Ionic Order 75
Ionosphere *41*, 42, 190
Iran 190
 see also Persia
Iraq 190
Ireland 190, *190*
Iris 192
Iris (eye) *134*
Irish wolfhound 190
Iron 190
Iron curtain 91, 192
Iron lung 192, *192*
Ironwood *383*
Iroquois Indians 26
Irrigation *124*, *125*, 192, 328
Islam *118*, 192, *193*, *300*
Islamabad, Pak. 266
Island 193
Isobar *378*
Isotherm *379*
Isotope 43, 193, *193*, 296, 297, 342
Israel 193, *194*
Israelites 299
Istanbul, Turk. 69, 362
Isthmus 194
Italy 194, *195*
Ivan the Great 195
Ivan the Terrible (Ivan IV) 195
Ivory 195, *195*
Ivory Coast 195
Ivy 195

J

Jackal 196
Jackass 38
Jade 196, *196*
Jaguar 196
Jail see Prison
Jakarta 186, 193
Jamaica 196, *196*
James I (King of Eng., James VI of Scot.) 196
James II (King of Eng. and Scot.) 196, 382
James Baines (clipper ship) *96*
Jansky, Karl 41
Japan *10*, 197, *197*, *300*
Jasmine 197
Jason 159
Jaundice 197

Java 198
Java Man 29
Javelin throw 198
Jaw *351*
Jazz 198
Jefferson, Thomas 198
Jeffries, John 50
Jellyfish 198, *198*, see also Portuguese Man-of-war
Jenner, Edward 198, *198*
Jericho 198
Jerusalem, Israel 193, *194*, 198
Jesuits 198
Jesus Christ 198
Jet propulsion *15*, 22, *151*, 199, *199*
Jewellery *152*, 199, *199*
 see also Gem
Jews 199, 376, 387
 see also Judaism
Jidda, Saudi Arabia 315
Joan of Arc 199
Johannesburg, S. Afr. 199
John (King of Eng.) 223
Johnson, Samuel 199
Joliot, Jean-Frederic and Irene 110
Jordan 200
Jordan, river 200
Joule 200
Joule, James Prescott 200
Jove *see* Jupiter
Jubilee 65
Judaism 200, 300
 see also Passover; Synagogue
Judo 200
Jujitsu 200
Julian calendar 91
Jumbo-jet 22
Jupiter (god) 200, *200*
Jupiter (planet) 150, 200, *200*, *278*, *279*, *329*, 334
Jurassic period 32, 398
Jury 200, *208*
Justinian 69
Jutland peninsula 115

K

Ka'aba 193, 231
Kabul, Afg. 16
Kalgoorlie, Austral. 201
Kalimantan 62
Kampala, Uganda 365
Kampuchea 201
Kangaroo 201, *201*, 230
Kaohsiung, Taiwan 350
Kaolin 285
Kapital, Das (Marx) 231
Karachi, Pak. 266
Karate 201
Karun, river 190
Karyobionts 281
Kashmir 186
Kayak 201
Keats, John 201
Kelly, Ned 201
Kelp 320
Kemi, river 139
Kennedy, John F. 109, 202, *202*
Kenya *158*, 202

Nail 247
Nairobi, Kenya 202
Nanda Devi 186
Nantuka 182
Napoleon *see* Bonaparte, Napoleon
Napoleonic Wars 377, 380
Narcissus 247
Narwhal 247
Naseby 93
Nassau, Bah. 48
National Socialist German Workers' Party 175, *175*
NATO 247
Natterjack toad *173*
Natural gas 247, *247*
Nauru 391
Nautical measure 394
Nautilus 247
Navajo Indians 26
Navigation 68, 84, 91, 96, 248, 295, 322
Navy 248
Nazi party *see* National Socialist German Workers' Party
Ndjamena, Chad 82
Neanderthal Man 29, *183, 248, 248*
Neap tide 356, *356*
Nebuchadnezzar 46, 248
Nebula 248, 255
see also Galaxy
Nectarine 248
Needle 248
Needlework 248
see also Crocheting
Negroid race 37, 293, 294, *294,* 330, *389*
Nelson, Horatio 248
Neolithic period 18
Neon 248
Nepal 391
Neptune (god) 249
Neptune (planet) 249, 278, *279, 329*
Nero 249
Nervous system 249, 265, 283, 294
see also Brain
Nest 249
Netherlands 249
Nettle 9
Neurons 18
Neutron 42, *42*
New Brunswick, Can. 74
Newcastle (Austral.) 249
Newcastle upon Tyne, Eng. 250
New Delhi, India 186
Newfoundland, Can. 74
New Guinea 7, *250, 250,* 391
New Model Army 108
New Orleans, battle of 376
New South Wales 250
Newspaper 250, 288, 337
Newt *173,* 250
Newton, Isaac 125, 143, 161, 250, 316, *352,* 353
Newton, unit of force 143
New York City *128, 326*
New York City, U.S.A. 250
New Zealand 251, *251*
Niagara Falls 251
Nicaragua 251
Nickel 251
Nicosia, Cyprus 110

Nicotine 251
Niger 391
Nigeria *16,* 251
Nightingale, Florence *107,* 251
Nightingale 251
Nile *125,* 251
Nile, battle of the 248
Nimbostratus clouds 97, *97*
Nimbus (satellite) *313*
Nine-banded armadillo 34
Nipkow, Paul 353
Nirvana 67
Nitric acid 251
Nitrogen 252
Nobel prizes 252
Nobel, Alfred 252
Noctilucent cloud *41*
Noise 252
Nolan, Sydney 252
Nomads 206, 225, 238, 252
see also Bedouin; Gypsies
Non-vascular plant 281
Nö play 10
Nordenskjöld, Nils 254, *254*
Normans 252, 382
Norman architecture 252, *252*
Normandy landings *385*
Norsemen *see* Vikings
North America 252, *253*
see also the individual countries
North Atlantic Treaty Organization *see* NATO
Northeast passage 254
Northern Ireland *see* Ireland
Northern Rhodesia *see* Zambia
Northern Territory 252
North Island *see* New Zealand
North Korea *see* Korea
North Pole *see* Arctic
North Sea 254
Norway *138,* 254, *254*
Northwest Territory, Can. 74
Norwegian lobster *215*
Nose 254, *350*
see also Smell
Nostradamus 61
Note (music) 278
Notre Dame cath., Paris 269
Noun 254
Nova 255
Nova Scotia, Can. 255
Novel 255
Noverre, Jean Georges 48
Nuclear energy 255, *255, 256*
see also Atomic energy
Nuclear fusion *see* Fusion, nuclear
Nuclear power station 126, *256*
Nuclear reactor 255, *255, 256*
Nuclear submarine *343*
Nucleus (biol.) 80, *81*
Nucleus of the atom 42, *42,* 255
Nurek arch dam *111*
Nut 256
Nutmeg 256
Nutrition 256
Nyasaland *see* Malawi
Nylon 256

O

Oak *58,* 257
Oaks flat race 177

Oasis 257, *310*
Oats 257
Obelisk 257
Oboe 257
Observatory 257, *257*
see also Radio astronomy
Occipital lobe 64, *64*
Ocean liner *323*
Oceans 8, 258, *258,* 356
see also Atlantic Ocean; Indian Ocean; Pacific Ocean; Sea
Octane rating 258
October War *194*
Octopus 259, *259*
Odysseus *see* Ulysses
Odyssey 259
Oedipus 259, 336
Oersted, Hans 126
Oesophagus 116
Oestrogen *157*
Ohm 259
Ohm's law 259
Ohm, Georg 259
Oils 31, *247,* 259, 315, *315, 369;* measurement 394
Oil stove *191*
Oligocene epoch 398
Olive 260
Olympic games 261
Oman 391
Omar, mosque of, Jerusalem *118*
Onion 261
Ontario, Can. 74
Ontario, lake 163
Onyx 261
Opal 261, *261*
Opera 194, 261; house *348*
Operating theatre *346*
Opium 261
Oporto, Port. 286
Opossum 261
Optical scanner 100
Optics *see* Lenses; Microscope; Mirrors; Prism; Telescope
Orange *147,* 261
Orang-utan 261, *261, 371*
Orbit 262
Orchestra 262, *262*
Orchid 10, 262
Order of the Garter *see* Garter, Order of the
Ordovician period 398
Ore 262, *263*
Oregon, U.S.A. *366*
Organ (instrument) 262
Organelles 81
Origin of the Species, The (Darwin) 112
Oriola, Christian d' 137
Orrerey 278
Orthodox church *300*
Osaka, Jap. 197
Oscillation theory 367
Oscilloscope 262
Oslo, Norw. 254
Osmium 115
Osmosis 264
Osprey *123,* 264
Ostia, It. *307*
Ostrich 59, 264
Ostrogoths 160
Osztrics, I. *137*
Ottawa, Can. 73

Otter 264, *264*
Otter trawl *139*
Ottoman empire 362
Oulu, river 139
Ovary 62, 157
Owl *114,* 264, *264*
Ox *302*
Oxidation and reduction 264
Oxygen 86, 264
Oyster 264
Ozone 264

P

Pacific Ocean 258, 265
Paddlesteamer *323*
Pagoda *300*
Paille-maille see Croquet
Pain 265
Paint 265
Painting 78, 265, *265*
see also Fresco; Miniature painting; Mural; Water colour
Pakistan 266
Palaeocene epoch 398
Palaeozoic era 398
Paleolithic period 248, *248*
Palermo, Sicily 324
Palestine 199, 267
Pallas 38
Palma, Majorca 48
Palm tree 267
Palomar Observatory, Mount *352,* 353
Pan 246
Panama 267
Panama canal 267
Pan-American Highway 304
Pancreas 116, *157,* 267
Panda 267, *267*
Pantograph 216
Paper 267; measure 394
Paper money *see* Banknote
Papua New Guinea *see* New Guinea
Papyrus 57, 267
Parabola 267
Paraffin heater *191*
Paraffins 268
Paraguay 268
Parallel bar 167
Parasite 268, 376, 385
Parathyroid gland *157*
Parchment 268
Parietal lobes 64, *64*
Paris 268, *268*
Paris, prince of Troy 170
Parliament 92, 269, *269*
see also House of Commons; House of Lords
Parliament, French 269
Parliamentary forces *see* Roundheads
Parrot 269, *371*
see also Macaw
Parsley *172,* 270
Parthenon 31, *165,* 270
Partridge 270
Pascal, Blaise 100
Pasha (Drake's ship) 118
Passover 270
Pasteur, Louis 270, *270*
Pasteurization 270
Pastoral farming 136